bedfordstmartins.com/techcomm

Mike Markel

TechComm Web

Technical Communication   Seventh Edition

Quick Search

GO

Advanced Search

TechComm Web, the book companion site for *Technical Communication*, Seventh Edition, by Mike Markel, expands the book's resources by providing additional materials for every chapter and by directing students and instructors to the best Web resources available in technical communication.

Resources are organized below by chapter and by type of feature. To find a resource (and read a description), please select a chapter or category.

References to page numbers on this site refer to the seventh edition of the textbook.

View Content by Chapter

Chapter 1: Introduction to Technical Communication
Chapter 2: Understanding Ethical and Legal Considerations
Chapter 3: Understanding the Writing Process
Chapter 4: Writing Collaboratively
Chapter 5: Analyzing Your Audience and Purpose
Chapter 6: Communicating Persuasively

Student Resources

● Links Library

● Interactive Sample Documents

● Tutorials

● Self-Study Quizzes

● Flashcards

● Additional Exercises, Projects, and Cases

● Forms for Technical Communication

Other Resources at Bedford/St. Martin's

● Exercise Central

● Research Room

● Diana Hacker's Research and Documentation Online

● Model Documents Gallery

Login
E-mail Address:

Password:

GO

I am not registered.
Sign me up as a:
• Student
• Instructor

• About the Author

• About the Contributors

This site also contains materials for instructors. If you are an instructor and would like more information about what is available, please visit TechComm Web and click on "instructor preview page." We confirm all users' status as instructors before granting them access to these portions of the site.

Technical Communication

Seventh Edition

Technical Communication

Mike Markel
Boise State University

BEDFORD/ST. MARTIN'S
Boston • New York

For Bedford / St. Martin's

Developmental Editor: Sara Eaton
Associate Editor: Caroline Thompson
Editorial Assistant: Amy Hurd
Assistant Editor, Publishing Services: Maria Burwell
Production Supervisor: Jennifer Wetzel
Marketing Manager: Richard Cadman
Project Management: Books By Design, Inc.
Cover Design: Donna Dennison
Cover Art: © Digital Vision
Composition: Monotype Composition Co., Inc.
Printing and Binding: RR Donnelly & Sons Company

President: Joan E. Feinberg
Editorial Director: Denise B. Wydra
Editor in Chief: Karen S. Henry
Director of Marketing: Karen R. Melton
Director of Editing, Design, and Production: Marcia Cohen
Manager, Publishing Services: Emily Berleth

Library of Congress Control Number: 2002115974

Copyright © 2004 by Bedford/St. Martin's

Manufactured in the United States of America.

9 8 7 6 5 4
f e d c b a

For information, write: Bedford/St. Martin's, 75 Arlington Street, Boston, MA 02116 (617-399-4000)

ISBN: 0–312–40338–0

Acknowledgments

Figure, p. 9: Cover from Xerox Corporation brochure, "The Document Center at a Glance" (Xerox Corporation, 2000). Courtesy of Xerox Corporation.

Figure 1.1: March of Dimes WalkAmerica Web site home page, <www.modimes.org /WalkAmerica/default.htm>. Courtesy March of Dimes Birth Defects Foundation.

Figure, p. 13: Canon Mexicana Web page. Copyright © 2001 Canon, Inc.

Figure, p. 25: STC Ethical Guidelines for Technical Communicators. <www.stc.org /ethical.html>. Used by permission of the Society for Technical Communicators.

Acknowledgments and copyrights are continued at the back of the book on pages 681–682, which constitute an extension of the copyright page.

PREFACE FOR INSTRUCTORS

The principles of good technical communication do not change, and *Technical Communication* remains a thorough, accessible introduction to planning, drafting, and designing technical documents. The seventh edition of this text, however, reflects the many exciting developments that have occurred in technical communication—and in ways to teach it—in the last few years. Most prominent among these developments are the greatly expanded importance of the World Wide Web and electronic communication tools and the increased emphasis on intercultural communication.

Overview of the Seventh Edition

Technical Communication includes comprehensive coverage of the major types of technical documents, the most current coverage of technology, a wide variety of realistic examples and writing models, a focus on rhetorical concerns, and in-depth treatment of ethics in technical communication. The seventh edition retains the organization that instructors found so successful in the sixth edition. The text is organized into five parts, highlighting the importance of the writing process in technical communication and giving equal weight to the development of text and graphics in a document.

Part One, "The Technical-Communication Environment," provides students with a basic understanding of important topics in technical communication, including ethical and legal considerations, the role of the writing process in planning and developing technical documents, and the practice of collaborating on documents.

Part Two, "Planning the Document," focuses on rhetorical concerns, such as considering audience and purpose, and communicating persuasively, in addition to the process of gathering information through primary and secondary research, and planning the organization of documents.

Part Three, "Developing the Textual Elements," encompasses both drafting and revising text in a document. This part describes techniques for writing definitions and descriptions, improving the coherence of text, improving sentence style, and writing front and back matter.

Part Four, "Developing the Visual Elements," addresses the fundamentals of designing the whole document as well as the individual page. This part also includes advice on creating graphics for both print and online documents.

Part Five, "Applications," covers a wide range of types of technical communication: letters, memos, and e-mails; job-application materials, including print and electronic résumés; proposals; informal reports, such as progress and status reports, incident reports, and meeting minutes; formal reports, including informational, analytical, and recommendation reports; instructions and manuals; Web sites; and oral presentations.

New Features

The seventh edition introduces several new features that show the effect of new technologies on the way people produce technical communication and communicate with each other.

- *NEW Interactive Sample Documents*—featured in every chapter—provide "real world" samples as both models and active-learning tools. This innovative feature allows students to apply what they have just read as they analyze a real business document. Questions in the margin encourage students to consider the document rhetorically. The answers to these questions—as well as eight additional Interactive Sample Documents and their answers—are available on TechComm Web, making them valuable classroom and review activities.
- *NEW Reviewing the Process charts* at the end of each of the applications chapters summarize and reinforce the unique rhetorical considerations involved in creating each type of document.
- *NEW Strategies for Intercultural Communication features* in every chapter help familiarize students with the increasingly global workplace and offer practical approaches to communicating across cultures.

Expanded Coverage

While developing the seventh edition, I reexamined every chapter and relied on the input of fellow technical-communication instructors to inform my decisions about revising the text. Thus, in addition to new features, the book's coverage has been expanded in the following key areas to reflect a wider range of technical documents and new methods of developing them.

- *Understanding multicultural audiences.* Chapter 5, "Analyzing Your Audience and Purpose," contains a greatly expanded discussion of the challenges of addressing readers from other cultures.
- *Research methods.* Chapter 7, "Researching Your Subject," includes new guidelines for narrowing a research topic and planning a research strategy.
- *Preparing text for translation.* Chapter 11, "Drafting and Revising Effective Sentences," includes a new discussion of techniques writers can use to make it easier for translators to work with their text.

- *Understanding design principles.* Chapter 13, "Designing the Document," introduces new terms—*proximity, alignment, repetition,* and *contrast*—that help students understand the basic principles of design.

- *Citing graphics.* Chapter 14, "Creating Graphics," now includes advice for properly citing graphics as sources.

- *Electronic portfolios and job interviews.* Chapter 16, "Preparing Job-Application Materials," includes a discussion of electronic portfolios as used in the job search. In addition, the chapter now discusses how to prepare for job interviews.

- *Planning proposals.* Chapter 17, "Writing Proposals," includes a new discussion of using storyboards to plan proposals.

- *Incident reports.* Chapter 18, "Writing Informal Reports," now includes a discussion of incident reports, such as accident reports or safety reports.

- *Oral presentations.* Chapter 22, "Making Oral Presentations," devotes additional attention to presentation-graphics software, showing students how to use slides to help listeners understand the organization of a presentation. The chapter also includes an expanded presentation evaluation form.

- *Documentation models.* The appendix now has more models for documenting electronic sources using APA and MLA styles.

Expanded Ancillary Package

Technical Communication continues to provide the highest-quality supplements.

- *TechComm Web* <bedfordstmartins.com/techcomm>. Fully integrated through cross-references in the margins of the book, the companion Web site offers the best and most comprehensive resources for students and instructors. Interactive Sample Documents, links to additional resources, flashcards, and revised online quizzes reinforce students' understanding of the chapters. Instructors can find everything from additional exercises, projects, and cases to password-protected reading quizzes to download and distribute to students, sample syllabi, in-class activities, and PowerPoint® slides that can be adapted for classroom use. In addition to "Making the Transition from Composition to Technical Communication," TechComm Web now offers three new teaching topics: "Integrating Technology," "Using *Technical Communication* in Distance Courses," and "Addressing Plagiarism."

- *Online Tutorials.* Online tutorials on evaluating online sources, creating presentation graphics, using basic document design functions, and designing Web sites guide students through some of their most common communication challenges.

- *Instructor's Resource Manual.* The resource manual is fully revised to act as a guide for using the text and TechComm Web together and fully integrating the companion Web site into a course. The revised manual also includes sample syllabi for ten-week and upper-level courses and a greatly expanded chapter-by-chapter teaching guide.
- *Transparency Masters.* The graphics from the text are provided in a convenient form that can be easily adapted for classroom use. The electronic files of the transparencies may also be downloaded from TechComm Web.

Acknowledgments

All the examples in the book—from single sentences to complete documents—are real. Some were written by my students at Boise State University. Some were written by engineers, scientists, health-care providers, and businesspersons with whom I have worked as a consultant for almost 30 years. Because much of the information in these documents is proprietary, I have silently changed brand names and other identifying information. I thank the dozens of individuals—students and professionals alike—who have graciously allowed me to reprint their writing. They have been my best teachers.

The seventh edition of *Technical Communication* has benefited greatly from the perceptive observations and helpful suggestions of my fellow instructors throughout the country. Some completed extensive questionnaires about the previous edition; others reviewed the current edition in its draft form. I thank Suzann Welty Barr, University of Arkansas at Little Rock; Sandra Becker, University of Minnesota—Twin Cities; Anne Bliss, University of Colorado—Boulder; John Brocato, Mississippi State University; Diane Carr, Midlands Technical College; Laura Carroll, Abilene Christian University; Edward Cottrill, University of Massachusetts—Amherst; Bonnie Devet, College of Charleston; Patrick Ellingham, Broward Community College; Stephen F. Evans, University of Kansas; Jane Fife, University of Tennessee at Chattanooga; Anthony Flinn, Eastern Washington University; Betty Freeland, University of Arkansas at Little Rock; Alexander Friedlander, Drexel University; Laura Gabinger, Johnson & Wales University; India Rose Givan, Oklahoma State University; Angela M. Gulick, Parkland College; Lila Harper, Central Washington University; June Chase Haskins, Southwest Texas State University; Ruth Heflin, Kansas City Kansas Community College; Darold Leigh Henson, Southwest Missouri State University; Eric Hill, Oregon State University; Jonathan Himes, Texas A&M University; Linda Houts-Smith, University of North Dakota; Mitchell H. Jarosz, Delta College; Rebecca L. Juarez, California State University at Bakersfield; Karen M. Kuralt, University of Arkansas at Little Rock; Steve Lazenby, University of North Carolina, Charlotte; Robert Gerard Lester, Portland Community College; Annette Burke Lyttle, Pikes Peak Community College; Jacqueline S. Palmer, Texas A&M University; Richard C.

Raymond, University of Arkansas at Little Rock; Susan Rode-Perkins, Washington University; Natalie D. Segal, Ward College of Technology, University of Hartford; Tim Smith, Southwestern Michigan College; Rhonda Stanton, Southwest Missouri State University; Bill Stiffler, Hartford Community College; Tom Stuckert, University of Finlay; Elizabeth Thompson, Oklahoma Wesleyan University; Susan Tilka, Southwest Texas State University; David Tillyer, City College of New York; Janice Walker, Georgia Southern University; Julia M. Williams, Rose-Hulman Institute of Technology; Steven Youra, California Institute of Technology.

I also thank the following instructors who contributed their insights and suggestions for the *Instructor's Resource Manual:* John Brocato, Mississippi State University; Laura Carroll, Abilene Christian University; Betty Freeland, University of Arkansas at Little Rock; Lila M. Harper, Central Washington University; Jonathan Himes, Texas A&M University; Janice R. Walker, Georgia Southern University.

I want to thank, too, my colleagues at Boise State University—Jim Frost, Rick Leahy, Dennis Meier, Dawn Burns, Theresa Hollenbeck, and Ellen McKinney—whose ideas and suggestions have helped me improve the text.

I would like to acknowledge three other colleagues from Boise State University. Kevin Wilson wrote many of the questions used in the online quizzes, as well as many of the classroom activities. John Battalio critiqued the chapter on Web design and wrote many new questions for the online quizzes, as well as several of the teaching topics and tutorials. Roger Munger contributed online-quiz questions, teaching topics, and tutorials. In addition, Roger revised and expanded the *Instructor's Resource Manual.* These three colleagues have made the book and the companion Web site much stronger, and I greatly appreciate their expertise and hard work.

I have been fortunate, too, to work with a terrific team at Bedford/St. Martin's, led by Sara Eaton, an editor of remarkable intelligence and energy. Sara has helped me improve the text in many big and small ways. She is responsible for the book's much-improved treatment of intercultural communication, the expanded collection of samples, and the new "Interactive Sample Documents" feature.

I also want to express my appreciation to Joan Feinberg, Denise Wydra, Karen Henry, and Leasa Burton for assembling the first-class team that has worked so hard on this edition, including Emily Berleth, Caroline Thompson, Amy Hurd, Katie Schooling, Coleen O'Hanley, and Nancy Benjamin and Janis Owens of Books By Design. For me, Bedford/St. Martin's continues to exemplify the highest standards of professionalism in publishing. They have been endlessly encouraging and helpful. I hope they realize the value of their contributions to this book.

My greatest debt, however, is, as always, to my wife, Rita, who over the course of many months and, now, seven editions, has helped me say what I mean.

A Final Word

I am more aware than ever before of how much I learn from my students, my fellow instructors, and my colleagues in industry and academia. If you have comments or suggestions for making this a better book, please get in touch with me at the Department of English at Boise State University, Boise, ID 83725. My phone number is (208) 426-3088, or you can send me an e-mail from the companion Web site: <bedfordstmartins.com/techcomm>. I hope to hear from you.

Mike Markel

BRIEF CONTENTS

xi

CONTENTS

10. Drafting and Revising Coherent Documents   *218*

PART FOUR
DEVELOPING THE VISUAL ELEMENTS   *285*

APPENDIX
REFERENCE HANDBOOK *591*

PART ONE

THE TECHNICAL-COMMUNICATION ENVIRONMENT

Introduction to Technical Communication

1

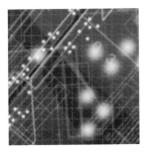

According to the Plain English Network (2002), writing and other communication skills are highly valued in the workplace:

- *Ninety-six percent of the nation's one thousand largest employers say employees must have good communication skills to get ahead.*

- *Almost 90 percent of over 800 business school graduates credited their writing skills with helping to accelerate their advancement.*

- *More than 80 percent of Fortune 400 companies identified writing skills as their organization's greatest weakness.*

- *Communication skills head the list of traits wanted in employees by eight recently surveyed companies, including Nike.*

WHAT IS TECHNICAL COMMUNICATION?

On TechComm Web

For additional samples, activities, and links related to this chapter, see <bedfordstmartins.com/techcomm>.

When you make technical documents, you are creating, designing, and transmitting technical information so that people can understand it easily and use it safely, effectively, and efficiently.

Much of what you read every day—textbooks, phone books, procedures manuals at the office, environmental impact statements, journal articles, Web sites, the owner's manual for your car—is technical communication. The words and the graphics in these documents are meant to help an audience understand a subject or carry out a task.

WHO PRODUCES TECHNICAL COMMUNICATION?

Most technical communication is produced by one of two different categories of people:

- *Technical professionals.* Technically trained individuals do a lot of writing, including e-mails, letters, proposals, and reports.

- *Technical communicators.* Technical communicators create documents such as manuals, proposals, reports, sales literature, Web sites, letters, journal articles, and speeches. Many technical communicators still call themselves technical writers (or tech writers) even though the term *technical communicator* more accurately reflects the increasing importance of graphics and the use of other media, such as online documentation.

On TechComm Web

For more on what technical communicators do, see Saul Carliner's *Information Designer's Toolkit.* Click on Links Library for Ch. 1 on <bedfordstmartins.com /techcomm>.

THE ROLE OF TECHNICAL COMMUNICATION IN BUSINESS AND INDUSTRY

The working world depends on written communication. Within most modern organizations, virtually every action is documented in writing, whether on paper or online. Here are a few examples:

a memo or an e-mail to request information or identify a problem

a set of instructions to introduce and explain a new process or procedure

a proposal to persuade management to authorize a project

a report to document a completed project

an oral presentation to explain a new policy to employees

Every organization also communicates with other organizations and often with the public, using materials such as these:

inquiry letters, sales letters, goodwill letters, and claim and adjustment letters to customers, clients, and suppliers

Web sites to describe products and solicit job applications

research reports for external organizations

articles for trade and professional journals

On TechComm Web

For more information about technical communicators, see the Society for Technical Communication site and the Institute of Scientific and Technical Communicators site. Click on Links Library for Ch. 1 on <bedfordstmartins.com /techcomm>.

TECHNICAL COMMUNICATION AND YOUR CAREER

The course you are taking now will help you meet the demands of the working world. In fact, your first step in obtaining a professional position is to write two technical documents—an application letter and a résumé—that help an organization decide whether to interview you.

Once you start work, you will write e-mails, memos, letters, marketing materials, and short reports, or contribute to larger projects, such as proposals and Web sites. Your supervisors will be looking at your communication skills as well as your technical abilities.

Job ads in newspapers and professional journals suggest that the working world values good communication skills. The following ad from an organization that manufactures medical instruments is typical:

Design Assurance Engineer. Duties include performing electronic/mechanical product, component, and material qualifications. Requires spreadsheet/word-processing abilities, and excellent written/oral communication skills. BSEE or biology degree preferred.

This job ad, and many others just like it, mentions not only computer skills but also communication skills.

According to *Training* magazine (Galvin, 2001), more than 60 percent of companies offer regularly scheduled training courses in communication skills; another 35 percent offer that training as needed. Only 4 percent of

In This Book

For more about job-application materials, see Ch. 16.

companies report that they do not offer any training in communication skills. The facts of corporate life today are simple: if you cannot communicate well, you are less valuable; if you can, you are more valuable.

CHARACTERISTICS OF TECHNICAL COMMUNICATION

Technical communication has seven major characteristics.

Addresses Particular Readers

Perhaps the most significant characteristic of technical communication is that it addresses particular readers. For instance, if you are planning to write a proposal for your supervisor, you will think about his or her job responsibilities, the level of detail he or she would be interested in reading, and personal factors such as history with the organization and attitudes toward your ideas. These factors can help you decide what kind of document to write, how to structure it, how much detail to include, and what sentence style and vocabulary to use. If you are writing to several people whose backgrounds and needs vary, you will want to structure the document so that they can easily locate and understand the information they seek.

If you do not know the reader, you can create an audience profile. For example, if readers of your brochure are police officers responsible for purchases, you don't know their gender or age or other personal characteristics, but you know that they share a police background and a common responsibility for approving expenditures.

Remember also that your writing might be read by people you never intended as your audience: managers and executives in your organization, the public, or the press. Avoid writing anything that will embarrass you or your organization if someone for whom it was not intended sees it.

Technical communication has seven major characteristics:

Addresses particular readers

Helps readers solve problems

Reflects an organization's goals and culture

Is produced collaboratively

Uses design to increase readability

Consists of words or graphics or both

Is produced using high-tech tools

In This Book

For more about addressing a particular audience, see Ch. 5, p. 75.

STRATEGIES FOR INTERCULTURAL COMMUNICATION

Communicating Across Cultures

Often, you will write for people from different cultures or whose native language is different from yours. These readers will react differently to the design, organization, and writing style of documents than people from your own culture. Therefore, you will need to consider these cultural differences as you write. A good first step is to read a full-length discussion of the topic, such as one or more of the following respected books:

• Hall, E. T., & Hall, M. R. (1990). *Understanding cultural differences.* Yarmouth, ME: Intercultural Press.

- Hofstede, G. H. (2001). *Culture's consequences: Comparing values, behaviors, institutions and organizations across nations.* Thousand Oaks, CA: Sage.
- Trompernaars, F., & Hampden-Turner, C. (1997). *Riding the waves of culture: Understanding diversity in global business* (2nd ed.). New York: McGraw-Hill.
- Victor, D. A. (1992). *International business communication.* New York: HarperCollins.

Helps Readers Solve Problems

Technical communication is not meant to express a writer's creativity or to entertain readers; it is intended to help readers learn or do something. For instance, you read your company's employee-benefits manual to help you decide which benefits package you should select. You read it, in other words, because you need information to help you analyze a situation and solve a problem.

Reflects an Organization's Goals and Culture

Technical communication furthers an organization's goals. For example, a state government department that oversees vocational-education programs submits an annual report to the state legislature, as well as a lot of technical information for the public: flyers, brochures, pamphlets, radio and television advertisements, and course materials, such as texts, workbooks, and Web pages. These documents help the department secure its funding and reach its audience.

Technical communication also reflects an organization's culture. Some organizations have a rigid hierarchy and expect employees to write only to their immediate supervisors and to others on their own level, for example, and to format their documents in a particular way. In other organizations, the culture permits or even encourages employees to make their own decisions on these questions.

Is Produced Collaboratively

Although you will often work alone in writing short documents, you will probably work as part of a team when producing more-complicated documents. Collaboration can range from having a colleague review your two-page memo to working with a team of a dozen technical professionals and technical communicators on a 200-page catalog.

In This Book

For more about collaboration, see Ch. 4.

Collaboration is common in technical communication because no one person has all the information, skills, or time to create a large document. Writers, editors, designers, and production specialists work with subject-matter experts—the various technical professionals—to create a better document than any one of them could have made working alone.

Successful collaboration requires interpersonal skills. You have to listen to people with other views and from other business and ethnic cultures, express yourself clearly and diplomatically, and compromise.

Uses Design to Increase Readability

Technical communicators use design features—typography, spacing, color, special paper, and so forth—to accomplish three basic purposes:

In This Book

For more about design, see Ch. 13.

- *To make the document look attractive and professional.* If the document attracts the reader and creates a positive impression, you are more likely to accomplish your goal.
- *To help the reader navigate the document.* Because a technical document can be long and complicated and most readers want to read only parts of it, design features, such as headings, color, or highlighting, help readers see where they are and get where they want to be.
- *To help the reader understand the document.* For instance, if all the safety warnings in a manual appear in a color and size different from the rest of the text, readers will be better able to recognize the importance of the information.

Consists of Words or Graphics or Both

Most technical documents include words and graphics. In technical communication, graphics help the writer perform five main functions:

In This Book

For more about graphics, see Ch. 14.

- make the document more interesting and appealing to readers
- communicate and reinforce difficult concepts
- communicate instructions and descriptions of objects and processes
- communicate large amounts of quantifiable data
- communicate with nonnative speakers

Is Produced Using High-Tech Tools

Virtually every technical document created these days, from e-mails to large manuals, was made using high-tech tools, such as the personal computer. Technical communicators rely on word-processing, graphics, and desktop-publishing software. As information technology becomes more powerful, easier to use, and less expensive, technical communicators and technical professionals alike continuously upgrade their skills.

Interactive Sample Document:
Studying How Technical Communication Combines
Words and Graphics
This is a cover from an eight-page quick-start brochure that accompanies a photo-copier. The questions in the margin ask you to consider how technical communica-tion combines words and graphics. The answers to these questions are available on TechComm Web.

Source: Xerox Corporation, 2000.

1. How have the writers used graphical elements in the sentence below the title to emphasize the message in that sentence?

2. In what other ways have the writers used words and graphics to make the document more interest-ing and appealing to readers?

3. How have the writers used text and graphics to present the tasks that people can accomplish with this machine?

On TechComm Web

To find the answers to these questions, click on Interactive Sample Documents for Ch. 1 on <bedfordstmartins.com /techcomm>.

A LOOK AT A SAMPLE DOCUMENT

The home page from the March of Dimes Walk America Web site (2002) in Figure 1.1 is an excellent example of technical communication. It illustrates a number of the characteristics of technical communication discussed in this chapter.

On TechComm Web

To view Fig. 1.1 in context on the Web, click on Links Library for Ch. 1 on <bedfordstmartins.com /techcomm>.

The Web page **reflects the organization's culture:** the phrase "Walk America, Saving babies, together" defines the organization's mission.

It **uses words and graphics:** the "Be a hero . . . " text next to the photograph of the mother and child conveys a message of being a hero to babies and children. The use of corporate logos draws attention to the companies' names more effectively than a textual list of the companies' names would.

It **uses design to increase readability:** the user can see that the main links are presented as buttons at the top and as phrases along the right.

It **helps readers solve problems:** the links enable readers to sign up for the walk, and the search function helps them get in touch with their local March of Dimes chapter.

■ **Figure 1.1   A Web Page That Shows the Characteristics of Technical Communication**

*An excellent example of technical communication, this Web page is **addressed to particular readers:** people interested in the March of Dimes Walk America. Like most technical documents, it was **produced collaboratively** (by technical communicators, graphic artists, Web authors, and others), **using high-tech tools,** including a word processor, a graphics program, and a Web editor.*
Source: March of Dimes, 2002 <www.modimes.org/WalkAmerica/Default.htm>.

Measures of excellence in technical communication:
Honesty
Clarity
Accuracy
Comprehensiveness
Accessibility
Conciseness
Professional appearance
Correctness

MEASURES OF EXCELLENCE IN TECHNICAL COMMUNICATION

Eight measures of excellence characterize all technical communication.

Honesty

The most important measure of excellence in technical communication is honesty. You have to tell the truth and not mislead the reader. There are three reasons to be honest as a communicator:

- *It is the right thing to do.* Technical communication is about helping people understand how to make wise choices as they use the information available in a high-tech culture.

- *If you are dishonest, readers can get hurt.* Misinforming your readers or deliberately omitting important information can have serious consequences—in some cases, injury or death.

- *If you are dishonest, you and your organization could face serious legal charges.* If a court finds that your document failed to provide honest, appropriate information and that this failure led to a substantial injury or loss, you and your organization are likely to have to pay millions of dollars.

In This Book

For more about the ethical and legal aspects of technical communication, see Ch. 2.

Clarity

Your goal is to produce a document that conveys a single meaning the reader can understand easily. The following directive, written by the British navy (*Technical Communication,* 1990), is an example of what to avoid:

> It is necessary for technical reasons that these warheads should be stored upside down, that is, with the top at the bottom and the bottom at the top. In order that there may be no doubt as to which is the top and which is the bottom, for storage purposes, it will be seen that the bottom of each warhead has been labeled with the word TOP.

Technical communication must be clear for two reasons:

- *Unclear technical communication can be dangerous.* A carelessly drafted building code, for example, could tempt contractors to save money by using inferior materials or techniques.

- *Unclear technical communication is expensive.* The average cost of a telephone call to a customer-support center is about $20–30 (Mead, 1998). Clear technical communication in the product's documentation—its instructions—can greatly reduce the number and length of such calls.

Accuracy

Accuracy seems a simple concept: you must record the facts carefully. A slight inaccuracy can confuse and annoy your readers. A major inaccuracy can be dangerous and expensive.

In another sense, however, accuracy is a question of ethics. Technical communication must be as objective and unbiased as you can make it. If readers suspect that you are slanting information—by overstating or omitting facts—they will doubt the validity of the entire document. Technical communication must be clear and organized, but it must also be reasonable, fair, and truthful.

Comprehensiveness

A good technical document provides all the information readers need. It describes the background so that readers unfamiliar with the subject can understand it. It contains sufficient detail so that readers can follow the discussion and carry out any required tasks. It refers to supporting materials clearly or includes them as attachments.

Comprehensiveness is crucial because readers need a complete, self-contained discussion in order to use the information safely, effectively, and efficiently. A document also often serves as the official company record of a project, from its inception to its completion.

Accessibility

In This Book

For more about making documents accessible, see Chs. 10 and 13.

Most technical documents—both in print and online—are made up of small, independent sections. Because few people will read a document from the beginning to the end, your job is to make its various parts accessible. That is, readers should not be forced to flip through the pages or click links unnecessarily to find the appropriate section. For example, a Web page should include a site map and a clear set of navigation links to help readers understand where they are.

Conciseness

In This Book

For more about writing concisely, see Ch. 11.

In a sense, conciseness works against clarity and comprehensiveness. For a technical explanation to be absolutely clear, it must describe every aspect of the subject in great detail. But a document also must be concise enough to be useful to a busy reader. To balance these conflicting demands, you must make the document just long enough to be clear—given the audience, purpose, and subject—but not a word longer. You can shorten most writing by 10 to 20 percent simply by eliminating unnecessary phrases, choosing short words rather than long ones, and using economical grammatical forms. Your job is to figure out how to convey a lot of information economically.

Professional Appearance

You start to communicate before anyone reads the first word of the document. If the document looks neat and professional, readers will form a positive impression of both the content and the authors.

Your documents should adhere to the format standards of your organization or your professional field. In addition, your documents should be well designed and neatly printed. For example, a letter should follow one of the traditional letter formats and have generous margins.

Correctness

Good technical communication observes the conventions of grammar, punctuation, spelling, and usage. Violating the rules of correctness can confuse readers or even make your writing inaccurate. If you mean to write "The three inspectors — Bill, Mary, and I — attended the session" but you use commas instead of dashes, your readers might think six people (not three) attended.

Most of the time, however, violating the rules of correctness hurts your writing because it makes you look unprofessional. If your writing is full of errors, readers will wonder if you were similarly careless in gathering, analyzing, and presenting the technical information. If readers become skeptical about your professionalism, they will be less likely to accept your conclusions or follow your recommendations.

Technical communication is meant to fulfill a mission: to convey information to a particular audience so that they understand something or carry out a task. To accomplish these goals, it must be honest, clear, accurate, comprehensive, accessible, concise, professional in appearance, and correct.

Exercise

On TechComm Web

For more exercises, click on Additional Exercises, Projects, and Cases for Ch. 1 on <bedfordstmartins.com/techcomm>.

1. **Internet Activity** Form small groups to study the following Web page from Canon Mexicana (2002). Meet to discuss which characteristics of technical communication you see in this excerpt. How effective is this excerpt? What changes would you make to improve it? Present your ideas in a brief memo to your instructor. (For more on memos, see Chapter 15, page 378.)

Source: Canon Inc., 2002 <canon.com/gateway/region/americas.html>.

Projects

2. Locate an owner's manual for a consumer product, such as a coffeemaker, bicycle, or hair dryer. In a memo to your instructor, describe and evaluate the manual. To what extent does it meet the measures of excellence discussed in this chapter? In what ways does it fall short of these measures? Submit a photocopy of the document (or a representative portion of it) with your memo. (For more on memos, see Chapter 15, page 378.)

3. **Internet Activity**   Locate a document on the Web that you believe to be an example of technical communication. Describe the aspects of the document that illustrate the characteristics of technical communication discussed in this chapter. Then evaluate the effectiveness of the document. Write your response in a memo to your instructor. Submit a printout of the document (or a representative portion of it) with your assignment. (For more on memos, see Chapter 15, page 378.)

CASE
Practicing What We Preach

You and the other members of your group are college interns working for your local chapter of the Society for Technical Communication, the world's largest professional organization for technical communicators. The president of your chapter would like you to analyze the chapter's Web site to see how well it conforms to principles of effective technical communication.
    Follow these steps to carry out this task.

1. Study Chapter 1 of your text, particularly the section called "Measures of Excellence in Technical Communication," beginning on page 10.

2. Study one of the following guides to Web style to familiarize yourself with principles of designing effective sites:
   • *W3Schools.com*
   • *Webmonkey*
   • *Web Style Guide*

3. From the Society for Technical Communication Web site, link to the site of your nearest local chapter, then begin analyzing it. Focus on the criteria of clarity (how easy it is to understand the information in the site), comprehensiveness (how much information is contained in the site), accessibility (how easy it is to navigate the site), and professional appearance (how well the site presents a professional image for the chapter).

4. Write a memo to the chapter president communicating your findings. (For more on memos, see Chapter 15, page 378.)

Understanding Ethical and Legal Considerations

2

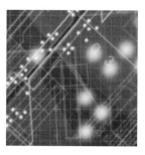

Brent Gardner, assistant general counsel for Hewlett-Packard Company in Boise, Idaho, credits the company's ethical standards with its performance in the marketplace:

The founders of HP set an expectation that employees act with the highest standards of ethics. They felt it was good business: if you act ethically with your customers there will be a bond of trust established and they will come back.

On TechComm Web

For additional samples, activities, and links related to this chapter, see <bedfordstmartins.com /techcomm>.

As a technical professional or technical communicator, you need a basic understanding of ethical principles, if only because you are likely to confront ethical dilemmas on the job. For instance, you might be asked to write a document in such a way that it could mislead the reader. Should you go along, out of loyalty to your company, or resist because misleading readers might cause harm? Technical communicators and technical professionals alike also need to understand several areas of the law related to communication.

Ethical and legal pitfalls can lurk within the words and graphics of many kinds of documents. Here are a few examples.

Proposals. You might be asked to exaggerate or lie about your organization's past accomplishments, pad the résumés of the project personnel, list as project personnel some workers who in fact will not be contributing to the project, or present an unrealistically short work schedule.

Progress reports. You might be asked to describe the project as proceeding smoothly, even though it isn't.

Completion reports. You might be asked to change or leave out data that are inconsistent with the report's findings.

Product information. You might be asked to exaggerate the quality of products shown in catalogs or manuals or to downplay the hazards of using these products.

Web sites. You might be asked to copy the source code of a competitor's site and then make minor changes so that you are not technically violating the competitor's copyright.

Graphics. You might be asked to hide an item's weaknesses in a photograph by manipulating the photo electronically. Or you might be tempted to leave out some data in a graph, or even make up data.

A BRIEF INTRODUCTION TO ETHICS

Some people think that if an act is legal, it is ethical. Most people, however, believe that ethical standards are more demanding than legal standards. It is legal, for example, to try to sell an expensive life-insurance policy to an impoverished elderly person who has no dependents and therefore no need for such a policy. Yet many people would consider such an attempt unethical.

For many people, ethics is a matter of intuition, what their gut feelings tell them about the rightness or wrongness of an act. Others see ethics in terms of their own religion or the Golden Rule: treat others as you would like them to treat you. Although philosophers cannot agree on what constitutes ethical conduct, most would agree to the following definition: *Ethics is the study of the principles of conduct that apply to an individual or a group.*

The ethicist Manuel G. Velasquez (1998) outlines four moral standards he considers useful in thinking about ethical dilemmas:

- *Rights.* This standard concerns individuals' basic needs and welfare. Everyone agrees, for example, that people have a right to a reasonably safe workplace.

- *Justice.* This standard concerns how the costs and benefits of an action or a policy can be distributed fairly among a group. For example, the cost of maintaining a highway should be borne, in part, by people who use that highway. However, because everyone benefits from the highway, it is just that general funds also be used.

- *Utility.* This standard concerns the positive and negative effects that an action or a policy has on the public. For example, if a company is considering closing a plant, utility requires that the company's leaders consider not only the money they would save but also the financial hardship of laid-off workers and the economic effect of the closing on the rest of the community.

- *Care.* This standard concerns the relationships we have with other individuals. We owe care and consideration to all people, but we have greater responsibilities to people in our family, our workplace, and our community.

These standards often conflict. For instance, according to the care standard, you might wish to promote a friend of yours in the company, even though he is not the most deserving candidate. According to the justice standard, promoting the friend would be unfair to other candidates. In terms of utility, the promotion would probably not be in the best interests of the organization, although it might be in the best interests of your friend.

When there is a conflict, the rights standard is usually considered the most important; justice, the second most important; utility, the third most important; and care, the fourth. However, simply ranking the four standards cannot solve all ethical problems. In an individual case, a "less important" standard could outweigh a "more important" one. For instance, if the power company has to cross your property to repair a transformer, utility (the need to restore power to all the people affected by the problem) outweighs rights (your right to private property). The power company is, of course, obligated to respect your rights as much as possible by explaining what it wants to do, trying to accommodate your schedule, and repairing any damage done to your property.

Ethical problems are difficult to resolve because no rules exist to determine when one standard outweighs another. In the example of the transformer, how many customers have to go without power before the power company is ethically justified in violating the property owner's right of ownership? Is it a thousand? A hundred? Ten? Only one? There is no "correct" answer.

Bodies of law relevant to technical communication:

Copyright law

Trademark law

Contract law

Liability law

On TechComm Web

For more about copyright law, see the U.S. Copyright Office site. Click on Links Library for Ch. 2 on <bedfordstmartins.com/techcomm>.

YOUR LEGAL OBLIGATIONS

Although most people believe that ethical obligations are more comprehensive and more important than legal obligations, the two sets of obligations are closely related in the United States. Our ethical values have shaped many of our laws. For this reason, professionals should know the basics of four different bodies of law.

Copyright Law

The Copyright Act of 1976 protects the author of any published or unpublished work—such as printed material, software, and photographs—whether the author is an individual or a corporation. The author is entitled to profit from the sale and distribution of the work in exchange for making the work accessible.

The concept by which work is made accessible is called *fair use*. Under fair-use guidelines, you have the right to use material, without getting permission, for purposes such as criticism, commentary, news reporting, teaching, scholarship, or research. Unfortunately, *fair use* is not a specific legal term but a convention that is interpreted differently in various situations.

Writers often treat fair use in different ways depending on whether they are creating an internal document (one that will be published and used only within the organization) or an external document (one that will be published and used by people outside the organization).

For internal documents, such as employee manuals, writers are likely to use material from the existing manual, even if the original author cannot be identi-

Determining "Fair Use"

Courts consider four factors in disputes over fair use:

▶ *The purpose and character of the use, especially whether the use is for profit.* Profit-making organizations are scrutinized more carefully than non-profits.

▶ *The nature and purpose of the copyrighted work.* When the information is essential to the public—for example, medical information—fair use is applied more liberally.

▶ *The amount and substantiality of the portion of the work used.* A 200-word passage would be a small portion of a book but a large portion of a 500-word brochure. Although you will see guidelines stating that fair use covers up to 400 words, the courts have not always adhered to that number.

▶ *The effect of the use on the potential market for the copyrighted work.* Any use of the work that is likely to hurt the author's potential to profit from the original work will probably not be considered fair use.

Fair use does not apply to graphics: you must obtain written permission to use any graphics.

fied or no longer works for the organization. This practice is legal under the concept known as *work made for hire.* Anything written—or revised—on the job by an employee being paid by the organization is the organization's property.

However, for external documents, such as user's guides, writers are much more careful about fair use. They will acknowledge the earlier authors and illustrators and refrain from reprinting material unless they are certain that the material meets work-made-for-hire guidelines.

On TechComm Web

The U.S. Copyright Office site also describes *work made for hire.* Click on Links Library for Ch. 2 on <bedfordstmartins.com/techcomm>.

Dealing with Copyright Questions

Consider the following advice when using material from another source:

▶ *Abide by the fair-use concept.* Do not rely on excessive amounts of another source's work.

▶ *Seek permission.* Write to the source, stating what portion of the work you wish to use and the publication you wish to use it in. The source is likely to charge you for permission.

In This Book

For more about documenting your sources, see Appendix A. For more about copyright issues and the Web, see Ch. 21, p. 562.

▶ *Cite your sources accurately.* Citing sources fulfills your ethical obligation and strengthens your writing by showing the reader the range of your research. It also protects you in case some of the facts or interpretations in your work turn out to be inaccurate: you have not claimed that you were solely responsible for them.

▶ *Discuss authorship questions openly.* Talk candidly with everyone who contributed to the document. Some contributors might deserve to be listed as authors; others should only be credited in an acknowledgment section.

▶ *Consult legal counsel if you have questions.* Exactly who created a document, or whether the document has been altered without the author's knowledge or permission, is sometimes difficult to determine. In the case of multimedia products, which can require dozens of permissions for each minute of running time, you will have many questions related to permissions. Consult your organization's legal counsel. Doing so shows good faith, an important factor if the copyright question goes to court.

Trademark Law

On TechComm Web

For more on trademarks, see the U.S. Patent and Trademark Office Web site. Click on Links Library for Ch. 2 on <bedfordstmartins.com /techcomm>.

Companies use *trademarks* and *registered trademarks* to ensure that the public recognizes the name or logo of their products.

• A *trademark* is a word, phrase, name, or symbol that is identified with a company. The company uses the ™ symbol after the product name to claim the design or device as a trademark. For instance, Adobe Systems Incorporated claims PageMaker™ as a trademark. Claiming a trademark permits a company to go to state court to try to prevent other companies from using the trademarked item for their own products.

• A *registered trademark* is a word, phrase, name, or symbol that the company has registered with the U.S. Patent and Trademark Office. The company can then use the ® symbol after the product name. Registering a trademark, a process that can take years, ensures much more legal protection in the United States, as well as in other nations.

As a communicator, you are responsible for using the trademark and registered trademark symbols accurately when you refer to a company's products.

Protecting Trademark

Use the following strategies to protect your client's or employer's trademark:

▶ *Distinguish trademarks from other material.* Use boldface, italics, a different typeface or size, or a different color to distinguish the trademarked item.

▶ *Use the trademark symbol.* At least once in each document—preferably, the first time—use the appropriate symbol after the name or logo, followed by an asterisk. At the bottom of the page, include a statement such as the following: "*COKE is a registered trademark of the Coca-Cola Company."

▶ *Use the trademarked item as an adjective, not as a noun or a verb.* Trademarks can become confused with the generic term they refer to. Use the trademarked item along with the generic term, as in Xerox® photocopier or LaserJet® printer.

▶ *Do not use the plural form or the possessive form of the term.* Doing so reduces the uniqueness of the item and encourages the public to think of the term as generic.

DOES NOT PROTECT TRADEMARK	take some Kodacolors®
PROTECTS TRADEMARK	take some photographs using Kodacolor® film
DOES NOT PROTECT TRADEMARK	Kodacolor's® fine quality
PROTECTS TRADEMARK	the fine quality of Kodacolor® film

Contract Law

Contract law deals with agreements between two parties. In most cases, disputes concern whether a product lives up to the manufacturer's claims. These claims are communicated as express warranties or implied warranties.

An *express warranty* is a written or oral statement that the product has a particular feature or can perform a particular function. For example, a statement in a printer manual that the printer produces 17 pages per minute is an express warranty. An *implied warranty* is a warranty that is not written or spoken explicitly but rather inferred by the purchaser. For example, if a user's manual for a printer shows sample pages printed in color, the company is making an implied warranty that the printer can print in color. Implied warranties also occur in more-casual communications, such as letters to customers or conversations between salespeople and customers.

Liability Law

A product-liability action is "a lawsuit for personal injury, death, property damage, or financial loss caused by a defective product" (Helyar, 1992, p. 126). Liability is an important concern for communicators because courts frequently rule that manufacturers are responsible for providing adequate operating instructions and warning consumers about the risks of using their products.

GUIDELINES

Abiding by Liability Laws

Helyar (1992) summarizes the communicator's obligations and offers 10 guidelines for abiding by liability laws.

▶ *Understand the product and its likely users.* Learn everything you can about the product and its users.

▶ *Describe the product's functions and limitations.* Help people determine whether it is the right product to buy. In one case, the manufacturer was found liable for not stating that its electric smoke alarm does not work during a power outage.

▶ *Instruct users on all aspects of ownership.* Include assembly, installation, use and storage, testing, maintenance, first aid and emergencies, and disposal.

▶ *Use appropriate words and graphics.* Use common terms, simple sentences, and brief paragraphs. Structure the document logically and include specific directions. Make graphics clear and easy to understand; where necessary, show people performing tasks. Make the words and graphics appropriate to the education, mechanical ability, manual dexterity, and intelligence of intended users. For products that will be used by children or nonnative speakers of your language, include graphics illustrating important information.

▶ *Warn users about the risks of using or misusing the product.* Warn users about the dangers of using the product, such as electrical shock or chemical poisoning. Describe the cause, extent, and seriousness of the danger. A car manufacturer was found liable for not having warned consumers that parking a car on grass, leaves, or other combustible material could cause a fire. For particularly dangerous products, explain the danger and how to avoid it, then describe how to use the product safely. Use *mandatory language,* such as *must* and *shall,* rather than *might, could,* or *should.* Use the words *warning* and *caution* appropriately.

▶ *Include warnings along with assertions of safety.* When product information says that a product is safe, readers tend to pay less attention to warnings. Therefore, include detailed warnings to balance the safety claims.

In This Book

For a discussion of safety terms, see Ch. 20, p. 523.

⬇

▶ *Make directions and warnings conspicuous.* Safety information must be in large type and easily visible, appear in an appropriate location, and be durable enough to withstand ordinary use of the product.

▶ *Make sure that the instructions comply with applicable company standards and local, state, or federal statutes.*

▶ *Perform usability testing on the product (to make sure it is safe and easy to use) and on the instructions (to make sure they are accurate and easy to understand).*

▶ *Make sure users receive the information.* If you discover a problem after the product has been shipped to the retailer, get in touch with the users by direct mail or e-mail if possible or newspaper advertising if not. Automobile-recall notices are one example of how manufacturers contact their users.

> **In This Book**
>
> For a discussion of usability testing, see Ch. 3, p. 46.

CODES OF CONDUCT AND WHISTLEBLOWING

Between 70 and 90 percent of large corporations have codes of conduct (Murphy, 1995), as do almost all professional societies. Codes of conduct vary greatly from organization to organization. Many are a few paragraphs long; some are several volumes.

An effective code has three major characteristics:

• *It protects the interest of the public rather than the interests of the members of the organization or profession.* For instance, it should condemn unsafe building practices but not advertising, because advertising increases competition and thus lowers prices.

• *It is specific and comprehensive.* A code is ineffective if it merely states that people must not steal, or if it does not address ethical offenses typical in the company or profession, such as bribery in companies that do business in other countries.

• *It is enforceable.* A code is ineffective if it does not stipulate penalties, up to and including dismissal from the company or expulsion from the profession.

Do codes of conduct really encourage ethical behavior? Sometimes, yes. James Burke, chairman and CEO of Johnson & Johnson, was praised for taking all Tylenol products off store shelves in 1982 after product tampering killed seven people. However, nobody knows whether codes encourage ethical behavior, because it is impossible to tell how many unethical acts were prevented because people were inspired or frightened by a code.

> **On TechComm Web**
>
> For a detailed code, from the Institute of Technical and Scientific Communicators, click on Links Library for Ch. 2 on <bedfordstmartins.com/techcomm>.

> **On TechComm Web**
>
> For links to codes of conduct from around the world, see Codes of Conduct/Practice/Ethics from Around the World. Click on Links Library for Ch. 2 on <bedfordstmartins.com/techcomm>.

> **On TechComm Web**
>
> To read Johnson & Johnson's well-known Credo, click on Links Library for Ch. 2 on <bedfordstmartins.com/techcomm>.

Although many codes are too vague to be useful in determining whether a person has violated one of their principles, writing and implementing a code can be valuable because it forces an organization to clarify its own values and can foster an increased awareness of ethical issues. Texas Instruments, like many organizations, encourages employees to report ethical problems to a committee or a person—sometimes called an *ethics officer* or an *ombudsperson*—who investigates and reaches an impartial decision. Figure 2.1 shows Texas Instruments' "TI Ethics Quick Test" and the links to the company's other ethics resources and policies. If you think there is a serious ethical problem in your organization, find out what resources your organization has to deal with it. If there are no resources, work with your supervisor to resolve the problem.

What do you do if you have exhausted all the resources at your organization and, if appropriate, the professional organization in your field? The next step will likely involve *whistleblowing,* which is the practice of going public with information about serious unethical conduct within an organization. For example, an engineer is blowing the whistle in telling a regulatory agency or a newspaper that quality-control tests on a company product were faked.

Ethicists such as Manuel Velasquez (1998, pp. 456–457) argue that whistleblowing is justified if you have tried to resolve the problem through internal channels, if you have strong evidence that the problem is hurting or will hurt other parties, and if the whistleblowing is reasonably certain to prevent or stop the wrongdoing. But Velasquez also points out that whistleblowing is likely to hurt the employee, his or her family, and any other parties. Whistleblowers can be penalized through negative performance appraisals, transfers to undesirable locations, or isolation within the company. As many ethicists say, doing the ethical thing does not always advance a person's career.

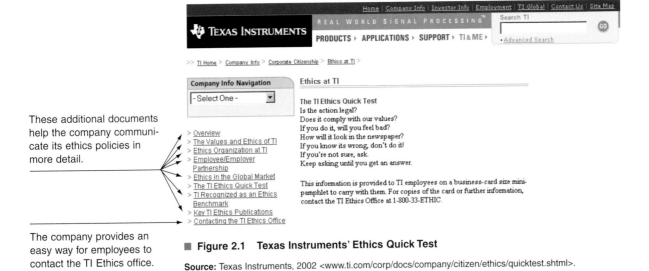

These additional documents help the company communicate its ethics policies in more detail.

The company provides an easy way for employees to contact the TI Ethics office.

■ **Figure 2.1   Texas Instruments' Ethics Quick Test**

Source: Texas Instruments, 2002 <www.ti.com/corp/docs/company/citizen/ethics/quicktest.shtml>.

Interactive Sample Document:
Analyzing a Code of Conduct

The following code of conduct, presented here in its entirety, is published by the Society for Technical Communication (STC). The questions in the margin ask you to think about the characteristics of an effective code (as outlined on page 23). The answers to these questions are available on TechComm Web.

STC ETHICAL GUIDELINES FOR TECHNICAL COMMUNICATORS

As technical communicators, we observe the following guidelines in our professional activities. Their purpose is to help us maintain ethical practices.

Legality
We observe the laws and regulations governing our professional activities in the workplace. We meet the terms and obligations of contracts that we undertake. We ensure that all terms of our contractual agreements are consistent with the *STC Ethical Guidelines*.

Honesty
We seek to promote the public good in our activities. To the best of our ability, we provide truthful and accurate communications. We dedicate ourselves to conciseness, clarity, coherence, and creativity, striving to address the needs of those who use our products. We alert our clients and employers when we believe material is ambiguous. Before using another person's work, we obtain permission. In cases where individuals are credited, we attribute authorship only to those who have made an original, substantive contribution. We do not perform work outside our job scope during hours compensated by clients or employers, except with their permission; nor do we use their facilities, equipment, or supplies without their approval. When we advertise our services, we do so truthfully.

Confidentiality
Respecting the confidentiality of our clients, employers, and professional organizations, we disclose business-sensitive information only with their consent or when legally required. We acquire releases from clients and employers before including their business-sensitive information in our portfolios or before using such material for a different client or employer or for demo purposes.

Quality
With the goal of producing high-quality work, we negotiate realistic, candid agreement on the schedule, budget, and deliverables with clients and employers in the initial project planning stage. When working on the project, we fulfill our negotiated roles in a timely, responsible manner and meet the stated expectations.

Fairness
We respect cultural variety and other aspects of diversity in our clients, employers, development teams, and audiences. We serve the business interests of our clients and employers, as long as such loyalty does not require us to violate the public good. We avoid conflicts of interest in the fulfillment of our professional responsibilities and activities. If we are aware of a conflict of interest, we disclose it to those concerned and obtain their approval before proceeding.

Professionalism
We seek candid evaluations of our professional performance from clients and employers. We also provide candid evaluations of communication products and services. We advance the technical communication profession through our integrity, standards, and performance.

---

1. How effectively does this code protect the interests of the public rather than those of STC members? What specific words or phrases demonstrate this?

2. How specific and comprehensive is this code?

3. How enforceable is this code? How could it be made more enforceable?

On TechComm Web

To find the answers to these questions, click on Interactive Sample Documents for Ch. 2 on <bedfordstmartins.com/techcomm>.

Source: Society for Technical Communication <www.stc.org/ethical.html>. Used by permission of the Society for Technical Communication, Arlington, Virginia.

PRINCIPLES FOR ETHICAL COMMUNICATION

As an employee, you are obligated to further your employer's legitimate aims and to refrain from any activities that run counter to them. You need to be honest, to present information accurately, and to avoid conflicts of interest that pit your own personal goals against those of the organization. In addition, you are obligated to help your organization treat its customers fairly by providing safe and effective products or services. The seven principles for ethical communication can help you fulfill these obligations.

Abide by Relevant Laws

You must adhere to the laws governing intellectual property. Here are some examples:

- *Do not plagiarize.* When you want to publish copyrighted material, such as graphics you find on the Web, get written permission from the copyright owner.
- *Honor the laws regarding trademarks.* For instance, use the trademark symbol (™) and the registered trademark symbol (®) properly.
- *Live up to the express and implied warranties on your company's products.*
- *Abide by all laws governing product liability.* Helyar's (1992) guidelines presented in this chapter on pages 22–23 are a good introduction.

Abide by the Appropriate Corporate or Professional Code of Conduct

Codes often go beyond legal issues to express ethical principles, such as telling the truth, reporting information accurately, respecting the privacy of others, and avoiding conflicts of interest.

Tell the Truth

The simplest, strongest guideline is to present information honestly and accurately. The Golden Rule in the Christian tradition and similar statements in virtually every other religious tradition provide a powerful rationale for telling the truth.

Sometimes, employees are asked to lie about their own company's products or about those of their competitors. Obviously, lying—knowingly providing inaccurate information—is unethical. Your responsibility is to resist this pressure, by going over the supervisor's head, if necessary. Telling the truth also means not covering up negative information. If the package for a portable compact-disc player suggests that it can be used by joggers but does not mention that the bouncing will probably make it skip, that statement is misleading.

Don't Mislead Your Readers

A misleading statement, one that invites or even encourages the reader to reach a false conclusion, is ethically no better than lying. Avoid these four common kinds of misleading technical communication:

- *False implications.* If you work for SuperBright and write "Use only SuperBright batteries in your new flashlight," you imply that only that brand will work. If that is untrue, the statement is misleading. Communicators sometimes use clichés such as *user-friendly, ergonomic,* and *state of the art* to make the product sound better than it is. Use specific, accurate information to back up your claims about a product.

- *Exaggerations.* If you say "Our new Operating System 2500 makes system crashes a thing of the past," but the product only makes them less likely, you are exaggerating. Provide the specific technical information on the reduction of crashes. Do not write "We carried out extensive market research" if all you did was make a few phone calls.

- *Legalistic constructions.* It is unethical to write "The 3000X was designed to operate in extreme temperatures, from −40 degrees to 120 degrees Fahrenheit" if the product cannot operate reliably in those temperatures. Although the statement might technically be accurate—the product was *designed* to operate in those temperatures—it is misleading.

- *Euphemisms.* If you refer to someone's being fired, say *fired* or *released,* not *granted permanent leave* or *offered an alternative career opportunity.*

In This Book

For a more detailed discussion of misleading writing, see Ch. 11. For a discussion of avoiding misleading graphics, see Ch. 14.

Be Clear

Clear writing helps your readers understand your message easily. Your responsibility is to write as clearly as you can to help your audience understand what you are saying.

For instance, if you are writing a product warranty, make it as simple and straightforward as you can. Don't hide behind big words and complicated sentences. Design your documents so that readers can easily find the information they seek. Use tables of contents, indexes, and other accessing devices to help your readers find what they need.

In This Book

For techniques for writing clearly, including avoiding discriminatory language, see Ch. 11.

Avoid Discriminatory Language

Don't use language that discriminates against people because of their sex, religion, ethnicity, race, sexual orientation, or physical or mental abilities.

Acknowledge Assistance from Others

Don't suggest that you did all the work yourself if you didn't. Cite your sources and your collaborators accurately and graciously.

In This Book

For more about citing sources, see Ch. 7, p. 139, and Appendix, Part A, p. 592.

STRATEGIES FOR INTERCULTURAL COMMUNICATION

Communicating Ethically Across Cultures

Companies face special challenges when they market their products and services to people in other countries and to people in their home countries who come from other cultures:

- *Companies have to make their communications understandable and clear to their target audiences.* The company that does not modify its information risks offending its audience and losing the opportunity to do business.

- *Companies are ethically obligated not to reinforce patterns of discrimination in product information.* It would be wrong, for example, to include a photograph of a workplace setting that excludes women. This principle is what Donaldson (1989) calls the moral minimum.

- *Companies are not obligated to challenge the prevailing prejudice directly.* A company is not obligated to include a photograph that shows women performing roles they do not normally perform within that culture; nor is it obligated to portray women wearing clothing or makeup or jewelry that is likely to offend local standards. But there is nothing to prevent organizations from adopting a more activist stance. Organizations that actively oppose discrimination are acting admirably.

In This Book

For a discussion of sexist writing, see Ch. 11, p. 257.

Revision Checklist

- ❏ Did you abide by relevant laws? (p. 26)
- ❏ Did you abide by the appropriate corporate or professional code of conduct? (p. 26)
- ❏ Did you tell the truth? (p. 26)

Did you avoid using
- ❏ false implications? (p. 27)
- ❏ exaggerations? (p. 27)

- ❏ legalistic constructions? (p. 27)
- ❏ euphemisms? (p. 27)
- ❏ clichés? (p. 27)

- ❏ Did you avoid discriminatory language? (p. 27)
- ❏ Did you acknowledge any assistance you received from others? (p. 27)

Exercise

On TechComm Web

For more exercises, click on Additional Exercises, Projects, and Cases for Ch. 2 on <bedfordstmartins.com/techcomm>.

1. It is late April and you need a summer job. In a local newspaper you see an ad for a potential job. The only problem is that the ad specifically mentions that it is "a continuing, full-time position." You know that you will be returning to college in the fall. Is it ethical for you to apply for the job without mentioning this fact? Why or why not? If you feel it is unethical to withhold the information that you plan to return to college in the fall, is there any way you can ethically apply? Be prepared to share your ideas with the class.

Projects

On TechComm Web

For more projects, click on Additional Exercises, Projects, and Cases for Ch. 2 on <bedfordstmartins.com/techcomm>.

2. **Internet Activity** Find an article or advertisement in a newspaper or magazine or on the Web that you feel contains untrue or misleading information. Write a memo to your instructor describing the ad and analyzing the unethical techniques. How might the information have been presented more honestly? Include a photocopy or a printout of the ad with your memo. (For more on memos, see Chapter 15, page 378.)

3. **Internet Activity** Study your college or university's code of conduct for students on the Web. Then write a memo to your instructor describing and evaluating it. Consider such questions as the following: How long is the code? How comprehensive is it? Does it provide detailed guidelines or merely make general statements? Where does the code appear? From your experience, does it appear to be widely publicized, enforced, and adhered to? Are there sources of information on campus that could provide information on how the code is applied? (For more on memos, see Chapter 15, page 378.)

4. **Group Activity** Form small groups. Study the code of conduct of a company or organization in your community. (Many companies and other organizations post their codes on their Web sites.)

- One group member could study the code to analyze how effectively it states the ideals of the organization, describes proper and improper behavior and practices for employees, and spells out penalties.

- Another group member could interview the officer who oversees the use of the code in the organization. Who wrote the code? What were the circumstances that led the organization to write it? Is it based on another organization's code? Does this officer of the organization believe the code is effective? Why or why not?

- A third group member could secure the code of one of the professional groups in the organization's field (search for the code on the Web). For example, if the local organization produces electronic equipment, a professional group would be the Institute for Electrical and Electronics Engineers, Inc. To what extent does the code of the local organization reflect the principles and ideals of the professional group's code?

- As a team, write a memo to your instructor presenting your findings. Attach the local organization's code to your memo. (For more on memos, see Chapter 15, page 378.)

On TechComm Web

For more cases, click on Additional Exercises, Projects, and Cases for Ch. 2 on <bedfordstmartins.com /techcomm>.

C A S E
The Name Game

Crescent Petroleum, an oil refining corporation based in Riyadh, Saudi Arabia, has issued a request for proposals for constructing an intranet that will link its headquarters with its three facilities in the United States and Europe. McNeil Informatics, a networking consulting company, is considering responding with a proposal. Most of the work will be performed at the company headquarters in Riyadh.

Crescent Petroleum was established 40 years ago by family members who are related by marriage to the Saudi royal family. At the company headquarters, the support staff and clerical staff include women, most of whom are related to the owners of the company. The professional, managerial, and executive staff is all male, which is traditional in Saudi corporations. Crescent is a large company, with revenues in the billions of dollars.

McNeil is a small firm—12 employees—established two years ago by Denise McNeil, a 29-year-old computer scientist with a master's degree in computer engineering. She is working on her MBA while getting her company off the ground. Her employees include both males and females at all levels. The chief financial officer is female, as are several of the professional staff, and the technical writer is male.

Denise McNeil traveled to New York from her headquarters in Pittsburgh to attend a briefing by Crescent. All the representatives from Crescent were middle-aged Saudi men; Denise was the only female among the representatives of the seven companies that attended the briefing. When Denise shook hands with Mr. Fayed, the team leader, he smiled slightly as he mentioned that he did not realize that McNeil Informatics was run by a woman. Denise did not know what to make of his comment, but she got a strong impression that the Crescent representatives felt uncomfortable in her presence. During the break, they drifted off to speak with the men from the other six vendors, leaving Denise to stand awkwardly by herself.

On her flight back to Pittsburgh, Denise McNeil thought about the possibility of gender discrimination but decided to bid for the project anyway, because she believed her company could write a persuasive proposal. McNeil Informatics had done several projects of this type successfully in the last year.

Back at the office, she met with Josh Lipton, the technical writer, to fill him in.

"When you put in the boilerplate about the company, I'd like you to delete the stuff about me founding the company. Don't say that a woman is the president, okay? And when you assemble the résumés of the project team, I'd like you to just use the first initials, not the first names."

"I don't understand, Denise. What's going on?" Josh asked.

"Well, Crescent looks like an all-male club, very traditional. I'm not sure they would want to hire us if they knew we've got a lot of women at the top," Denise replied.

"You know, Denise, there's another problem."

"Which is?"

"I'm thinking of the lead engineer we used in the other networking projects this year . . . "

"Mark Feldman," she said, sighing. "What do you think we ought to do?"

"I don't know," Josh said. "I guess we could use another person. Or kind of change his name on the résumé."

"Let me think about this a little bit. I'll get back to you later."

What should Denise do about the fact that the person she wishes to designate as the lead engineer has an ethnic last name that might elicit a prejudiced reaction from Crescent officials? Is Denise's decision to disguise the sex of her employees—and to cover up her own role in founding her company—justified by common sense, or is it giving in to what she perceives as prejudice? Should she assign someone other than Mark Feldman to run the project? Should she tailor his name to disguise his ethnicity? Present your response in a memo to your instructor. (For more on memos, see Chapter 15, page 378.)

This case first appeared in *Ethics in Technical Communication: A Critique and Synthesis* (Westport, CT: Greenwood, 2001), by Mike Markel.

3

Understanding the Writing Process

Stephanie Rosenbaum, a consultant, on the importance of usability testing to the process of writing large documents:

You're never done with usability testing, just as you're never done with development or support.

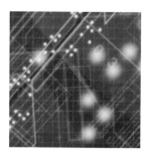

Everybody's approach to the writing process—planning, drafting, and revising—is somewhat different. And every document you write poses special challenges. Therefore, you should consider the information in this chapter as a collection of suggestions or guidelines, not as a rigid set of instructions.

On TechComm Web

For additional samples, activities, and links related to this chapter, see <bedfordstmartins.com/techcomm>.

PLANNING

The planning phase can take more than a third of the total time spent on a writing project. Planning is critically important for every document, from an e-mail to a book-length manual.

Planning involves:

Analyzing your audience

Analyzing your purpose

Generating ideas about your topic

Researching additional information

Organizing and outlining your document

Devising a schedule and a budget

Analyzing Your Audience

Because technical communication addresses a particular audience, the first step in writing a document is to analyze your audience. Sometimes you can talk with your audience before and during your work on the document. These conversations can help you learn what your readers already know, what they want to know, and how they would like the information presented. You can test out drafts, making changes as you go.

Even if you cannot work with your audience while writing the document, you still need to learn everything you can about your audience in advance. Start by determining whether your most important readers are experts, technicians, managers, or general readers. Knowing this information helps you determine the best scope, organization, and style for your document. Then, for each of your most important readers, try to answer the following three questions:

In This Book

For more about analyzing your audience, see Ch. 5, p. 74.

On TechComm Web

For more about analyzing an audience, see Writing Guidelines for Engineering and Science Students. Click on Links Library for Ch. 3 on <bedfordstmartins .com/techcomm>.

- *Who is your reader?* Consider such factors as education, job experience and responsibilities, skill in reading English, cultural characteristics, and personal preferences.
- *What are your reader's attitudes and expectations?* Consider the reader's attitudes toward the topic and your message, as well as the reader's expectations about the kind of document you will be presenting.
- *Why and how will the reader use your document?* Think about the physical environment in which the document will be used, the way the reader will read the document, and the reader's skill in reading.

Analyzing Your Purpose

In This Book

For more about analyzing your purpose, see Ch. 5, p. 96.

You cannot start to write until you can state the purpose (or purposes) of the document. Ask yourself these questions:

- After your readers have read your document, what do you want them to know or to do?
- What beliefs or attitudes do you want them to hold?

A statement of purpose might be as simple as this: "The purpose of this report is to recommend whether the company should adopt a health-promotion program." Although the statement of purpose might not appear in this form in the final document, you need to state it clearly during the planning stage. A clear understanding of your purpose helps you stay on track as you gather and organize your information and draft your document.

Generating Ideas about Your Topic

Generating ideas is a way to start mapping out what information you will need to include in the document, where to put it, and what additional information may be required.

First, find out what you already know about the topic using any of the following techniques:

On TechComm Web

For an excellent discussion of journalistic questions and other techniques for generating ideas, see Paradigm Online Writing Assistant. Click on Links Library for Ch. 3 on <bedfordstmartins.com/techcomm>.

- *Asking journalistic questions:* who, what, when, where, why, *and* how. In a few minutes, you will know how much more research you need to do.
- *Brainstorming.* When you brainstorm, you spend 10 or 15 minutes listing ideas about your subject. List them quickly, using short phrases. Brainstorming frees your mind, allowing you to think of as many ideas as possible that relate to your subject. Later, when you construct an outline, you will find that some of these items probably do not belong in the document. Just toss them out.
- *Freewriting.* When you freewrite, you write without plans or restrictions. You don't prepare an outline, stop to think about sentence construction, or consult a reference book. You just make the pen or the cursor move. Although the text you create rarely becomes a part of the final document,

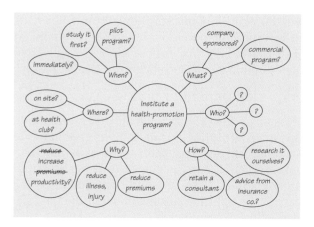

The writer has started with the journalistic questions. Notice that she doesn't yet know how to answer the question "Who?" She has to go back to her sources to find out who actually administers these kinds of programs.

■ **Figure 3.1   Clustering**

freewriting can help you determine what you do and do not understand. And one phrase or sentence might spark an important idea.

- *Talking with someone.* Discussing your topic with someone is an excellent way to find out what you already know about it and to generate new ideas. Have the person ask you questions as you speak. You will quickly get a sense of how clearly you understand your topic, what additional information you will need, and what questions your readers will want answered. You will also find yourself making new connections from one idea to another.

- *Clustering.* Write your main idea or main question in the middle of the page. Then draw a circle around it. Write second-level ideas around the main idea. Then add third-level ideas around the second-level ideas. Figure 3.1 is a cluster for a report on health-promotion programs.

- *Branching.* There is one major difference between clustering and branching: in the cluster format, the movement from larger to smaller ideas is from the center to the perimeter; in the branching format, it is from top to bottom. Figure 3.2 is a branching diagram.

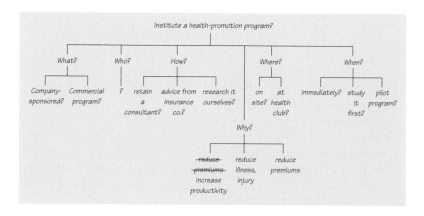

■ **Figure 3.2   Branching**

As you think more about your topic, you will revise your sketch. For example, you might subdivide a branch that contains many more sub-branches than the others. A short branch might signal that you need more research, or it might just be a smaller idea that is fine as it is.

Researching Additional Information

In This Book

For more about conducting research, see Ch. 7.

Once you have a good idea of what you already know about your topic, you need to obtain the rest of the information you will need. You can find and evaluate what other people have already written by reading reference books, scholarly books, and articles in the library. And you will find useful information on the Internet. In addition, you might compile new information by interviewing experts, distributing surveys and questionnaires, making observations, and conducting experiments.

Organizing and Outlining Your Document

On TechComm Web

For more about outlining, see Paradigm Online Writing Assistant. Click on Links Library for Ch. 3 on <bedfordstmartins.com/techcomm>.

Although each document will have its own structure, you can use or adapt existing organizational patterns to your own situation so that you don't need to start from scratch. For instance, the comparison-and-contrast pattern might be an effective way to organize a discussion of different health-promotion programs. The cause-and-effect pattern might work well for a discussion of the effects that implementing a program might produce.

At this point, your organization is only tentative. When you start to draft, you might find that the pattern you have chosen isn't working well, or that you need further information that doesn't fit into the pattern you have chosen. Don't let these problems discourage you. They happen to all writers.

Once you have a tentative plan, write an outline to help you stay on track as you draft. To keep your purpose clearly in mind as you work, you may want to write it at the top of your page before you begin your outline.

Making an outline involves five main tasks:

- *Grouping similar items.* If you used brainstorming to generate ideas, you have not yet grouped similar items. Start by looking at the first item on your list and determining what major category it belongs to. For instance, if it belongs in the background section, scan the list for other items that belong there, too. Then determine the logical category of the next item, and link it to other items that belong in the same category. Repeat this process until all the items have been either grouped into logical categories or discarded.

  Even though the outline is incomplete, some writers like to start drafting at this point. They want to see what they have to say, and the only sure way to do that is to start to write. Once they have started drafting, they sequence paragraphs instead of outline items. Other writers feel more comfortable working from a more refined outline. For them, the next step is to sequence the items in each group.

- *Ordering the items in the groups.* In some cases, ordering items in each group is simple. For instance, if an item precedes another in time or is more important, it should come first.

- *Organizing the groups.* Often your readers expect a particular structure. For instance, the body of a formal report usually begins with an introduction followed by a detailed discussion and the major findings. If your material does not lend itself to a traditional pattern, you'll need to devise one that your readers will find clear and easy to follow.

- *Avoiding common logical problems.* As you refine your outline, avoid *faulty coordination* and *faulty subordination.* Faulty coordination occurs when a writer equates items that are not of equal value or not at the same level of generality, as this portion of an outline illustrates.

Faulty coordination	*Proper coordination*
Common household tools	Common household tools
• screwdrivers	• screwdrivers
• drills	• drills
• claw hammers	• hammers
• ball peen hammers	—claw hammers
	—ball peen hammers

Faulty subordination occurs when an item is made a subunit of a unit to which it does not belong.

Faulty subordination	*Proper subordination*
Power sources for lawnmowers	Power sources for lawnmowers
• manual	• manual
• gasoline	• gasoline
• electric	• electric
• riding mowers	

"Riding mowers" is out of place because it is not a power source; it is a type of lawnmower. Whether it belongs in the outline at all is another question, but it doesn't belong here.

Faulty subordination also occurs when only one subunit is listed. The solution is to incorporate the single subunit into the unit. In the following example, item 1.1 has been deleted and restated as item 1.

Single subunit	*Proper subordination*
Three types of sound-reproduction systems:	Three types of sound-reproduction systems:
1. records	1. phonograph records
1.1 phonograph records	2. tapes
2. tapes	2.1 cassette
2.1 cassette	2.2 open reel
2.2 open reel	3. compact discs
3. compact discs	

- *Choosing an outline format.* If you are creating an outline purely for your own use, don't worry about its format. However, if someone else is going to read your outline, use one of the two standard outline formats: the traditional alphanumeric format or the decimal format.

Traditional outline	Decimal outline
I.	1.
A.	1.1
1.	1.1.1
2.	1.1.2
B.	1.2
1.	1.2.1
a.	1.2.2
b.	2.
(1)	2.1 etc
(2)	
(a)	
(b)	
2. etc.	

Use whichever system helps you stay organized. As you draft your outline, consider using the *outline view* on your word processor. Figure 3.3 shows the main features of the outline view.

In this pull-down menu, select the number of levels you wish to display on the outline.

The arrow buttons promote or demote an item in the hierarchy.

The headings, with each level indented, show the hierarchy of the document.

Note that the writer has chosen to display the body text for two of the four subheadings.

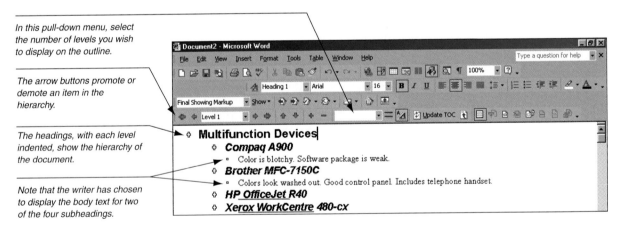

■ **Figure 3.3   The Outline View**

Devising a Schedule and a Budget

During the planning stage, you also need to decide when you will provide various portions of the document to your readers and how much you can spend on the project.

For instance, for the project on health-promotion programs, your readers might need a report to help decide what to do before the new fiscal year begins in two months. In addition, your readers might want a progress report submitted halfway through the project. Making a schedule is often a collaborative process: you meet with your main readers, who tell you when they need the information, and you estimate how long the different tasks will take.

You also need to set up a budget. In addition to the time you will need to do the project, you might incur additional expenses. For example, you might need to travel to visit companies with different kinds of health-promotion programs. You might need to conduct specialized database searches, create and distribute questionnaires to employees, or conduct interviews at remote locations. Some projects call for *usability testing*—evaluating potential users as they try out a system or a document. This testing needs to be included in your budget.

In This Book

For more on progress reports, see Ch. 18, p. 466.

In This Book

For more on usability testing, see p. 46.

DRAFTING

When you have at least a preliminary outline, it is time to start drafting. Some writers like to draft right on the outline on their screens. Others prefer to place a paper copy of their outline on the desk next to their keyboard.

On TechComm Web

Purdue University's OWL has many instructional handouts covering all aspects of the writing process. Click on Links Library for Ch. 3 on <bedfordstmartins.com /techcomm>.

GUIDELINES

Drafting Effectively

Try the following techniques when you begin to draft or when you get stuck in the middle of drafting.

▶ *Get comfortable.* Choose a good chair set at the right height for the keyboard and adjust the light so that it doesn't reflect off the screen.

▶ *Start with the easiest topics.* Instead of starting at the beginning of the document, begin with the section you most want to write.

▶ *Draft quickly.* Try to make your fingers keep up with your brain. Turn the phrases from your outline into paragraphs. You'll revise later.

▶ *Don't stop to get more information or to revise.* Set a timer and draft for an hour or two without stopping. When you come to an item that requires more research, skip to the next item. Don't worry about sentence structure or spelling.

▶ *Try invisible writing.* Darken the screen so that you can look only at your hardcopy outline or the keyboard. You won't be tempted to stop typing so often to revise what you have just written.

▶ *Stop in the middle of a section.* When you stop, do so in the middle of a paragraph or even in the middle of a sentence. This way you will find it easy to conclude the idea you were working on when you begin writing again. This technique will help you avoid writer's block, the mental paralysis that can set in when you stare at a blank page.

On TechComm Web

For more help with designing documents with a word processor, click on Tutorials on <bedfordstmartins .com/techcomm>.

Three of the more-advanced word-processing tools—templates, styles, and automated hypertext linking and Web-conversion tools—can make your work drafting the document easier.

Using Templates

Templates are preformatted designs for different types of documents, such as letters, memos, newsletters, and reports. Templates incorporate the design specifications for the document, including typeface, type size, margins, and spacing. Once you select a template, you just type in the information; the document is already designed. Using templates, however, can lead to three problems:

In This Book

See Ch. 13 for more about design and Ch. 14 for more about graphics.

- *Templates do not always reflect the best design principles.* For instance, most letter and memo templates default to 10-point rather than 12-point type, which is easier on the eyes of most readers.

- *Readers get tired of seeing the same designs.* If you choose a memo template from Microsoft Word, for instance, your memos will look like those of many other writers. Modifying the templates, or creating your own designs, can give your documents a fresher look.

- *Templates cannot help you answer the important questions about your document.* Although memo templates can help you format information, they cannot help you figure out how to organize and write a document. Sometimes templates can even send you the wrong message. For example, résumé templates in word processors present a set of headings that might work better for some job applicants than for others.

The more you rely on templates, the less likely you are to learn how to use the software to make your documents look professional.

Using Styles

In This Book

For an explanation of using styles to set up a table of contents, see Ch. 12, p. 274.

Styles are like small templates in that they apply to the design of smaller elements, such as headings and body text, but they are much more valuable than templates.

Like templates, styles save you time. As you draft your document, you don't need to add all the formatting each time, for example, you want to designate an item as a first-level heading (the most emphatic heading level in your document). When you finish drafting, you simply put your cursor in the text you want to be a first-level heading and use a pull-down menu to select that style. The text automatically incorporates all the specifications of a first-level heading.

Styles also help ensure consistency, because you don't have to change four or five technical specifications every time you want to change an item's style. And if you decide to modify a style—by adding italics to a heading, for

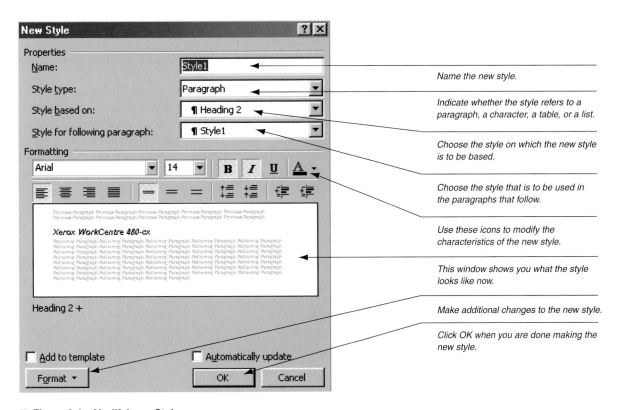

■ **Figure 3.4   Modifying a Style**

This window appears when you modify a style.

instance—you change it only once; the software automatically changes every instance of that style in the document. As you create collaborative documents, styles make it easier for the different collaborators to achieve a consistent look.

Figure 3.4 shows the window you use to change the specifications of the styles used in Microsoft® Word 2002.

Using Automated Hypertext Linking and Web-Conversion Tools

Word-processing software today is designed to make it easier to print documents in the traditional way or to display them on the Web. Automated hypertext linking and Web conversion tools help you cut down on the time needed to produce documents for the two media.

Automated hypertext linking is a function that recognizes Web addresses and formats them as active links. This way, readers see the Web address

In This Book

For more about Web-conversion tools and browsers, see Ch. 21, p. 550.

underlined as a link and can click it to launch a Web browser and go to that site—provided, of course, that they are reading the document online. If your document isn't meant to be read online, you should disable automated hypertext linking.

A *Web-conversion tool* or a *Web editor* is a software program used to add code to a document so that it can be viewed using a Web browser. Although a Web editor can save you *much* of the work involved in changing word-processed files into HTML files, it adds a lot of unnecessary code and it still cannot handle every kind of design or effect you wish to create. If you want to create a complex Web page—and make sure people using any Web browser can view it—you still have to learn coding.

REVISING

Revising is the process of making sure that the document says what you want it to say and says it professionally. You cannot hope to simply read your draft, waiting for the problems to leap off the page. Some of them might, but most won't. Instead, develop your own technique for revising.

Studying the Document by Yourself

The first step in revision is to read and reread the document. Many writers go through their documents several times: once for overall meaning and clarity, once for organization and logical development, and once for correctness. Experiment to learn what technique works best for you.

Revise a document by:
Studying the document by yourself
Using revision software
Seeking help from someone else
Testing readers as they use the document

On TechComm Web

See Robin A. Cormier's excellent essay (1997) on revising. Click on Links Library for Ch. 3 on <bedfordstmartins.com/techcomm>.

On TechComm Web

For examples of checklists, see the *Writer's Handbook* in the Grammar and Style section of the University of Wisconsin Writing Center. Click on Links Library for Ch. 3 on <bedfordstmartins.com/techcomm>.

GUIDELINES

Revising by Yourself

Try the following strategies for revising your draft before you show it to your instructor, other students, or co-workers.

▶ *Let it sit.* Set the document aside for a while, overnight if possible, to gain some distance and see it as your readers will.

▶ *Read it aloud.* Listen for awkward phrases, poorly developed ideas, illogical reasoning, or missing evidence.

▶ *Use checklists.* Modify checklists, such as those in this book, to include the points your instructors have made about your writing.

▶ *Review a printout of your draft.* You can revise effectively right on the screen, but be sure to print a copy of your draft, too. Because a printer provides a much sharper image than a screen, you'll see the draft—and its problems—as your readers will.

Using Revision Software

Word processors include three major revising tools: spell checkers, grammar checkers, and thesauri. Although these tools can be valuable, they have limitations.

Spell Checkers   A *spell checker* alerts you when it sees a word that isn't in its dictionary. Although that word might be misspelled, it might be correctly spelled but not in the spell checker's dictionary. You can add the word to your dictionary so that the spell checker will recognize it in the future. If your spell checker is set to alert you as soon as you have typed a word that is not in the dictionary—by highlighting the word or making a beeping sound—consider turning off this function so that you can concentrate on drafting. Fix the spelling later, as you revise.

You probably already know that a spell checker cannot tell whether you have used the correct word. If you have typed "We need too dozen test tubes," the spell checker won't see a problem.

Grammar Checkers   A *grammar checker* can help you identify and fix potential grammatical and stylistic problems, such as wordiness, subject/verb disagreement, and double negatives. Many grammar checkers identify abstract words and suggest more-specific ones or point out sexist terms and provide nonsexist alternatives.

Figure 3.5 shows a screen illustrating how grammar checkers work. As you can see, they can have serious drawbacks. For this reason, many writing

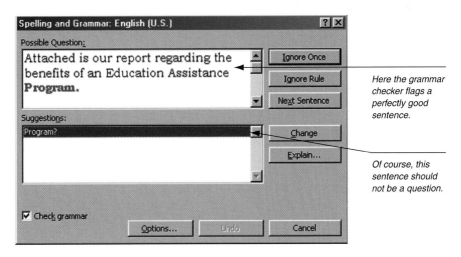

■ **Figure 3.5   Grammar Checker**

teachers advise that, unless you are a capable and experienced writer who knows when to ignore bad advice, you shouldn't use a grammar checker at all.

Thesauri   A *thesaurus* (plural *thesauri*) lists synonyms or related words. An electronic thesaurus has the same strengths and weaknesses as a printed one: if you can't quite think of the word you are looking for, it can help you remember it. But the listed terms might not be related to the key term closely enough to function as synonyms. Unless you know the shades of difference, you might substitute an inappropriate word. For example, one electronic thesaurus includes *infamous* and *notorious* as synonyms for *famous.* If you use either, you could embarrass yourself badly.

The revision tools discussed in this section cannot replace a careful reading by you and by other people. These tools don't understand your subject, your audience, and your purpose. They cannot identify unclear explanations, contradictions, inaccurate data, inappropriate tone, and so forth. Use the tools, but don't rely on them. Revise your document yourself, then get help from someone you trust.

Seeking Help from Someone Else

In This Book

For more on reviewing another person's draft, see Ch. 4, p. 61.

For technical documents, it is best to turn to two kinds of people for help:

- *Subject-matter experts.* If, for instance, you have written about alternative technologies for automobiles, you could ask an automotive expert to review it. Important documents are routinely reviewed by technical experts before being released to the public.
- *People who are like those in the targeted audience.* People who fit the profile of the eventual readers can help you see problems you or other knowledgeable readers don't notice. Knowledgeable readers might not be sufficiently critical because they will understand the document even if it isn't clear.

STRATEGIES FOR INTERCULTURAL COMMUNICATION

Having Your Draft Reviewed by a Person from the Target Culture

If your readers come from another culture, try to have your draft reviewed by someone from that culture. Sometimes people in the United States incorrectly assume that their own cultural values are shared by everyone. A reader from another culture can help you answer questions such as the following:

- *Have you made correct assumptions about how readers will react to your ideas?* As discussed in Chapter 5, people from some cultures would likely consider a company-sponsored health-promotion program perfectly appropriate and would feel obligated to participate; people from other cultures would likely consider it to be an unreasonable intrusion into employees' private lives.

- *Have you chosen appropriate kinds of evidence?* As discussed in Chapter 6, some cultures favor hard evidence: test results, statistical data, and so forth. Other cultures favor traditional ideas and testimonials from authorities.

- *Have you organized the draft effectively?* As discussed in Chapter 8, in most Western cultures, documents move from general information to specific information. In many other cultures, the sequence is reversed.

- *Have you designed the document and crafted the sentences appropriately?* As discussed in Chapters 12 and 13, people from other cultures might be surprised by some design elements used in reports, such as marginal comments. And most nonnative speakers benefit from the use of short sentences and simple vocabulary.

When you ask someone for help, provide specific instructions. Tell the person as much as you can about your audience and purpose and about the tasks you still need to complete. Then tell the person what kinds of problems you want him or her to look for; better yet, write them down. Here's an example:

Juan —

Thanks a lot for agreeing to look at this draft. I'm particularly interested in the following points:

- Is the background clear? Do you understand the relationship between the insurance company's decision and our study?
- Does the description of each of the three major programs seem proportional, or do I seem to go into more detail on one or more of them?
- Does the draft of the questionnaire on p. 17 work? See any problems? I'm particularly concerned about leading questions or questions that could logically have more than one valid response.

Don't worry about copy editing: I'm going to go over it carefully later. Please get back to me with questions.

As I mentioned on the phone, I'd love to get your response by Thursday, March 14.

Regards,
Ann

Writing a note such as this increases the chances that your colleagues will be able to point out your document's strengths and sections that need to be expanded, deleted, or revised. The note also reduces the chance that your reader will waste time working on something you don't need.

Testing Readers as They Use the Document

Although analyzing a document can provide valuable information, it cannot tell you how well the document will work in the hands of the people who will use it. To find that out, you must test readers as they use the document. *Usability testing* is the process of performing experiments with people who represent real users to see how well they understand a document and how easily they can use it. Instructions and manuals are the types of documents that most often undergo usability testing. This section covers five topics:

- the goals of usability testing
- the basic concepts of usability testing
- preparing for a usability test
- conducting a usability test
- interpreting and reporting the data from a usability test

The information in this section is based on Rubin (1994) and Dumas and Redish (1993).

On TechComm Web

For an article describing OCLC's usability testing program, click on Links Library for Ch. 3 on <bedfordstmartins.com/techcomm>.

The Goals of Usability Testing   The two main goals of usability testing are to improve product safety and to save money. An effective document reduces the risk that a customer will be injured in assembling or using the product. As discussed in Chapter 2, courts are now finding companies guilty of publishing "defective" instructions and manuals. Usability testing can also save money by helping the company understand and exploit the product's competitive advantages and by reducing the number of service calls and customer-support staff. In addition, usability testing can reduce the need to update the product, improve related products, and increase customer satisfaction.

The Basic Concepts of Usability Testing   There are three basic principles of usability testing:

- *Usability testing permeates product development.* Usability testing involves testing the document rigorously and often to make sure it works and is easy to use.
- *Usability testing involves studying real users as they use the product.* A company learns important information from real users that it would not have learned from people in the organization.

- *Usability testing involves setting measurable goals and determining whether the product meets them.* Usability testing involves determining in advance what the user is supposed to be able to do. For instance, in testing a help system for a word-processing program, the testers might decide that the user should be able to find the section on saving a file and perform that task successfully in less than two minutes.

Preparing for a Usability Test   Usability testing requires careful planning. According to Kantner (1994), planning accounts for one-half to three-quarters of the time devoted to testing. Eight main tasks must be accomplished in planning a usability test:

- *Understand your users' needs.* Companies frequently conduct *focus groups,* bringing people together for a few hours to discuss a product or an issue. Companies also test existing products, have experts review the product, and conduct on-site interviews and observations of real users in the workplace.
- *Determine the purpose of the test.* You can test an idea before the product is even designed, to see if people understand it and like it. Or you can test a prototype to see if it is easy to use, or a finished product to see if it needs any last-minute improvements.
- *Staff the test team.* Extensive programs in usability testing involve many specialists, each doing one job. Smaller programs involve only a handful of people, each of whom does many tasks.
- *Set up the test environment.* A basic environment includes a room for the test participant, equipped with VCRs to record the test, and another room for the test observers.
- *Develop a test plan.* A *test plan* is a proposal requesting resources; it describes and justifies what the testers plan to do.

In This Book

For information on proposals, see Ch. 17.

- *Select participants.* Testers recruit participants who match the profile of the intended users. Generally, it is best not to use company employees, who might know more about the product than a real user will.
- *Prepare the test materials.* Most tests require legal forms, an orientation script to help the participant understand the purpose of the test, background questionnaires, instructions for the participant to follow, and a log for the testers to record data during the test.
- *Conduct a pilot test.* A pilot test is a usability test for the usability test. A pilot test can uncover problems with the equipment, the document being tested, the test materials, and the test design.

Conducting a Usability Test   There are three important aspects of conducting the usability test:

- *Staying organized.* Make a checklist and a schedule for the test day, including every task that every person, including the test participant, is to carry out.

- *Interacting with the participant.* Testers use different techniques for eliciting information from the test participant. Among the most popular is the *think-aloud protocol,* in which the participant says aloud what he or she is thinking: "I guess I'm supposed to press ENTER here, but I'm not sure because the manual didn't say to do it."

- *Debriefing the participant.* After the test, those administering it usually have questions about the participant's actions. For this reason, they debrief—that is, interview—the participant.

Interpreting and Reporting the Data from a Usability Test   After a usability test, testers have a great deal of data, including notes, questionnaires, and videotapes. There are three steps in turning that data into useful information:

- *Tabulate the information.* Testers gather all the information from the test, including *performance* measures, such as how long it took a participant to complete a task, and *attitude* measures, such as how easy the participant found it to perform the task.

- *Analyze the information.* Testers analyze the information, concentrating on the most important problems revealed in the test and trying to determine the severity and the frequency of each one.

- *Report the information.* Writing a clear, comprehensive report often leads the testers to insights they might not have achieved otherwise.

Although usability testing might seem extremely expensive and difficult, testers who are methodical, open-minded, and curious about how people use the document find that it is the least expensive and most effective way to improve its quality.

Interactive Sample Document:
Learning from Usability Testing

The following passage (National Cancer Institute, 2002) is an excerpt from results of usability tests on a new instant messaging service on a government health-care Web site. The questions in the margin ask you to think about usability testing (as discussed on pages 46–48). The answers to these questions are available on TechComm Web.

Initial Testing of the Name, Logo and Graphics

When designing a new feature such as an instant messaging service on a Web site, the right name and graphic can help communicate the purpose, goals, and establish a brand identity. Obtaining input from your users early on in the design process helps ensure the name and logo are consistent with their expectations.

Initial branding names and designs were usability tested to determine user preferences and performance. Users were given a description of the instant messaging service, then shown the names and logos and asked to choose those that best reflected the service.

Users were then placed on a Web page and given a scenario that was impossible to complete. We asked what they would do to try to complete the task, and wanted to see if users saw the icon and clicked on it for help.

Lessons Learned

1. Users should choose the graphics, not the developers. Most users chose the Question Mark icon (the simplest and most familiar of the designs), while developers favored the Faces icon (a more subtle and artistic approach). See Figure 1.

Figure 1 — Initial Logos Developed and Tested

1. Which of the basic concepts of usability testing are most apparent in this opening section?

2. The testers **did not** say to the participants, "Can you find the help icon?" Why not?

3. How does point 1 show the value of choosing test participants carefully?

On TechComm Web

To find the answers to these questions, click on Interactive Sample Documents for Ch. 3 on <bedfordstmartins.com /techcomm>.

Source: National Cancer Institute, 2002 <www.usability.gov/lessons/IM_learned.html>.

Revision Checklist

In planning the document, did you
- ❏ analyze your audience? (p. 33)
- ❏ analyze your purpose? (p. 34)

In generating ideas about your topic, did you consider
- ❏ asking journalistic questions? (p. 34)
- ❏ brainstorming? (p. 34)
- ❏ freewriting? (p. 34)
- ❏ talking with someone? (p. 35)
- ❏ clustering? (p. 35)
- ❏ branching? (p. 35)

In organizing and creating an outline, did you
- ❏ consider generic patterns, such as comparison and contrast? (p. 36)
- ❏ group similar items? (p. 36)
- ❏ order the items within the groups? (p. 36)
- ❏ organize the groups? (p. 37)
- ❏ avoid common logical problems such as faulty coordination and faulty subordination? (p. 37)
- ❏ choose an appropriate outline format? (p. 38)
- ❏ use the outline view in your word processor? (p. 38)

In drafting, did you
- ❏ first make yourself comfortable? (p. 39)

- ❏ start with the easiest topics? (p. 39)
- ❏ draft quickly? (p. 39)
- ❏ keep going when you needed more information? (p. 39)
- ❏ stop in the middle of a section? (p. 39)
- ❏ use the styles on your word processor? (p. 40)

In revising your document by yourself, did you
- ❏ let it sit? (p. 42)
- ❏ read it aloud? (p. 42)
- ❏ use checklists? (p. 42)

In revising the document, did you
- ❏ use the spell checker and proofread for spelling errors? (p. 43)
- ❏ use the grammar checker carefully? (p. 43)
- ❏ use the thesaurus carefully? (p. 43)

Did you revise the document by obtaining help from
- ❏ appropriate subject-matter experts? (p. 44)
- ❏ people similar to the eventual readers? (p. 44)

In revising the document, did you
- ❏ test readers as they used the document if possible? (p. 46)

Exercises

On TechComm Web

For more exercises, click on Additional Exercises, Projects, and Cases for Ch. 3 on <bedfordstmartins.com/techcomm>.

1. Read the online help about using the outline view in your word processor. Make a file with five headings, each of which has a sentence of body text. Practice using the outline feature to do the following tasks:
   a. change a level-one heading to a level-two heading
   b. move the first heading on your outline to the end of the document
   c. hide the body text that goes with one of the headings

2. Create a brief brainstorming list for a report on one of the following topics:
   - the need for a technical-communication course tailored to students in your major
   - the need for computer-skills training for students in your major
   - how to use the Internet to look for a job
   - a problem on campus, such as a shortage of parking or inexpensive off-campus housing

   Do a 10-minute freewrite on this same topic and then create a cluster sketch or a branching sketch on it.

3. In each of the following excerpts from outlines, identify the logical problem. Then, revise each excerpt to fix the problem.

  a. Arguments for requiring that all students take a computer-skills course
  - Students would be better prepared for their course work.
  - Students would be better prepared for professional employment.
  - Students come to college with different levels of computer skills.

  b. Problems with inexpensive PCs
  - insufficient multimedia capabilities
    - poor audio quality
    - poor graphics
  - insufficient memory
    - not enough RAM
  - skimpy documentation
  - skimpy software
    - no antivirus software
    - cheap office suites
    - no entertainment software

  c. Types of computer printers
  - dot-matrix printers
  - laser printers
  - ink-jet printers
  - color laser printers

4. Internet Activity Read a current article about science or technology from an online newspaper, such as the *New York Times* <www.nytimes.com> or *USA Today* <www.usatoday.com>. Were the six journalistic questions (see p. 34) answered in the article? Make a list of the answers.

Project

On TechComm Web

For more projects, click on Additional Exercises, Projects, and Cases for Ch. 3 on <bedfordstmartins.com/techcomm>.

5. Your word processor probably contains a number of templates for such documents as letters, memos, faxes, and résumés. Evaluate one of these templates. Is it clear and professional looking? Does it present an effective design for all users or only for some? What changes would you make to the template to improve it? Write a memo to your instructor presenting your findings. (For more on memos, see Chapter 15, page 378.)

C A S E
The Writing Process Online

This case is best for groups of three or four. Assume that your technical-communication instructor, who also teaches first-year writing courses, has asked your group to make a document to help first-year college students learn the writing process. Specifically, your instructor would like a one-page handout to give to first-year students that describes the top 10 Internet sites explaining the writing process: planning, drafting, and revising. Your instructor suggests that you start your search at Purdue University's Online Writing Laboratory <http://owl.english.purdue.edu>. Following the links from the Purdue site, study a number of sites, noting their strengths. Then create the one-page handout for your instructor.

On TechComm Web

For more cases, click on Additional Exercises, Projects, and Cases for Ch. 3 on <bedfordstmartins.com/techcomm>.

4

Writing Collaboratively

ON THE IMPORTANCE OF COMMUNICATION IN COLLABORATION . . . .

| Eric Verzuh, project-management consultant, on the role of communication (1999, p. 244): | *Good communication is . . . a factor common to all successful projects. When people work together to accomplish a unique goal, they need to coordinate their activities, agree on responsibilities, and reevaluate the cost-schedule-quality equilibrium.* |

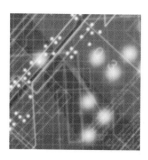

Collaborative writing—people working together to create a document—is common in organizations. One survey found that 87 percent of 520 professionals collaborate at least some of the time (Ede & Lunsford, 1990, p. 20). Another study of more than 400 professionals found that they often write collaboratively (Couture & Rymer, 1989, p. 78).

People collaborate in writing everything from memos to books. Longer, more complex, or more important documents—such as proposals, reports, manuals, corporate annual reports, and Web sites—are most likely to be written collaboratively.

Figure 4.1 shows three basic patterns of collaboration.

On TechComm Web

For additional samples, activities, and links related to this chapter, see <bedfordstmartins.com/techcomm>.

ADVANTAGES AND DISADVANTAGES OF COLLABORATION

Ede and Lunsford's study (1990, p. 50) found that 58 percent of writers considered collaborative writing to be very productive or productive, whereas 42 percent found it not very productive or not at all productive. Collaborative writing has both advantages and disadvantages.

Advantages of Collaboration

Writers who collaborate can create a better document and improve the way an organization functions:

- *Collaboration draws on a greater knowledge base.* A collaborative document can be more comprehensive and more accurate than a single-author document.

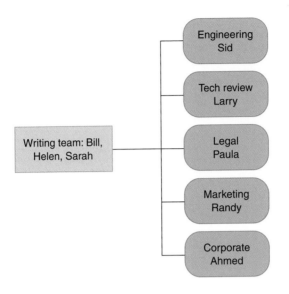

Collaboration based on job specialty. *On this team, an engineer is the subject-matter expert, the person in charge of contributing all the technical information; other professionals are in charge of their own specialties. The writing team writes, edits, and designs the document.*

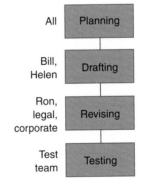

Collaboration based on the stages of the writing process. *Group members collaborate during the planning stage by sharing ideas about the document's content, organization, and style, then establish a production schedule and an evaluation program. They collaborate less during the drafting stage, because drafting collaboratively is much more time consuming than drafting individually. During the revising phase, they return to collaboration.*

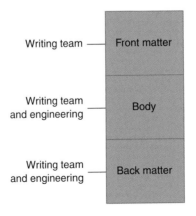

Collaboration based on the section of the document. *One person takes responsibility for one section of the document, another person does another section, and so forth. This pattern is common for large projects with separate sections, such as proposals.*

■ **Figure 4.1**
Patterns of Collaboration

- *Collaboration draws on a greater skills base.* No one person can be an expert manager, writer, editor, graphic artist, and production person.
- *Collaboration provides a better idea of how the audience will read the document.* Each group member acts as an audience, offering more questions and suggestions than one person could while writing alone.
- *Collaboration improves communication among employees.* Because group members share a goal, they learn about each other's jobs, responsibilities, and frustrations.
- *Collaboration helps acclimate new employees to an organization.* New employees learn how things work in the organization—which people to see, what forms to fill out, and so forth—as well as what the organization values, such as the importance of ethical conduct and the willingness to work hard and sacrifice for an important initiative.

Disadvantages of Collaboration

Collaboration can also have important disadvantages:

- *Collaboration takes more time than individual writing.* It takes longer to collaborate because of the time needed for the collaborators to communicate.
- *Collaboration can lead to groupthink.* When group members value getting along more than thinking critically about the project, they are prone to *groupthink*. Groupthink, which promotes conformity, can result in an inferior document, because no one wants to cause a scene by asking tough questions.
- *Collaboration can yield a disjointed document.* Sections written by different people can contradict or repeat each other or be written in different styles. To prevent these problems, writers need to plan and edit the document carefully.
- *Collaboration can lead to inequitable workloads.* Despite the project leader's best efforts, some people will end up doing more work than others.
- *Collaboration can reduce collaborators' motivation to work hard on the document.* The smaller the role a person plays in the project, the less motivated he or she is to make the extra effort.
- *Collaboration can lead to interpersonal conflict.* People can disagree about the best way to create the document or about the document itself. Such disagreements can hurt the working relationship during the project and long after.

CONDUCTING MEETINGS

Collaboration involves conducting meetings. The following discussion covers four aspects of meetings.

Conducting meetings involves:

Setting your group's agenda

Conducting efficient face-to-face meetings

Communicating diplomatically

Critiquing a group member's draft

Setting Your Group's Agenda

It's important to get your group off to a smooth start. In the first meeting, start to define your group's agenda.

GUIDELINES

Setting Your Agenda

▶ *Define the group's task.* What document, or "deliverable," will your group submit? Every group member has to agree, for example, that your task is to revise the employee manual by April 10 and that the revision must be no longer than 200 pages. You also need to agree on aspects of the task that are more conceptual, including clearly defining the audience, purpose, and scope of the document.

▶ *Choose a group leader.* This person serves as the link between the group and management. (In a school setting, the group leader represents the group in communicating with the instructor.) The group leader also keeps the group on track, leads the meetings, and coordinates communication among group members.

▶ *Define tasks for each group member.* As Figure 4.1 shows, the division of labor can follow different patterns. All group members will participate in each phase of the project, and each group member will review the document at every stage. However, each member will have chief responsibility for a task to which he or she is best suited.

▶ *Establish working procedures.* Before starting to work, members need answers—in writing, if possible—to the following questions:

  –When and where will we meet?

  –What procedures will we follow in the meetings?

  –How—and how often—are we to communicate with other group members, including the leader?

▶ *Establish a procedure for resolving conflict.* Disagreements about the project can be very valuable. Give every member a chance to express ideas fully, find areas of agreement, and try to resolve the conflict by vote.

▶ *Create a style sheet.* If all group members draft using a similar style, the document will need less revision. Discuss as many style questions as you can: use of headings and lists, paragraph style and length, level of formality, and so forth. You will probably need to continue this discussion in a follow-up meeting.

▶ *Establish a work schedule.* Starting with the date the document is due, work backward to create a schedule for the entire project. For example, to submit a proposal on February 10, you must complete an outline by January 25, a draft by February 1, and a revision by February 8. These dates are called *milestones*.

In This Book

For discussions of style, see Chs. 10 and 11.

In This Book

Fig. 4.2 shows a work schedule form.

▶ *Create evaluation materials.* Group members have a right to know how their work will be evaluated. In schools, students often evaluate themselves and other group members. But in the working world, managers are more likely to do the evaluations.

In This Book

Fig. 4.3 on p. 58 shows a form that group members can use to evaluate other group members. Fig. 4.4 on p. 59 shows a self-evaluation form.

WORK-SCHEDULE FORM

Name of Project:

Principal Reader:

Other Readers:

Group Members:

Milestones	Responsible Member	Status	Date
Deliver Document			
Proofread Document			
Send Document to Print Shop			
Complete Revision			
Review Draft Elements			
Assemble Draft			
Establish Tasks			

Progress Reports	Responsible Member	Status	Date
Progress Report 3			
Progress Report 2			
Progress Report 1			

Meetings	Agenda	Location	Date	Time
Meeting 3				
Meeting 2				
Meeting 1				

Notes

Notice that milestones sometimes are presented in reverse chronological order; the delivery-date milestone, for instance, comes first. On other forms, items are presented in normal chronological order.

The form includes spaces for listing the person responsible for each milestone and progress report and for stating the progress toward each milestone and progress report.

On TechComm Web

For printable versions of Figs. 4.2, 4.3, and 4.4, click on Forms for Technical Communication on <bedfordstmartins.com/techcomm>.

▪ **Figure 4.2   Work-Schedule Form**

GROUP-MEMBERS EVALUATION FORM

Your name: _____

Title of the project: _____

Date: _____

Instructions

Use this form to evaluate the other members of your group. Write the name of each group member other than yourself in one of the columns, then assign a score of 0 to 10 (0 being the lowest grade, 10 the highest) to each group member for each criterion. Then total the scores for each member. Because each group member has different strengths and weaknesses, the scores you assign will differ. On the back of this sheet, write any comments you wish to make.

	Group Members			
Criteria				
1. Regularly attends meetings	1._____	1._____	1._____	1._____
2. Is prepared at the meetings	2._____	2._____	2._____	2._____
3. Meets deadlines	3._____	3._____	3._____	3._____
4. Contributes good ideas in meetings	4._____	4._____	4._____	4._____
5. Contributes ideas diplomatically	5._____	5._____	5._____	5._____
6. Submits high-quality work	6._____	6._____	6._____	6._____
7. Listens to other members	7._____	7._____	7._____	7._____
8. Shows respect for other members	8._____	8._____	8._____	8._____
9. Helps to reduce conflict	9._____	9._____	9._____	9._____
10. Your overall assessment of this person's contribution	10._____	10._____	10._____	10._____
Total Points	_____	_____	_____	_____

■ **Figure 4.3**
Group-Members
Evaluation Form

SELF-EVALUATION FORM

Your name: _____   Date: _____

Title of the project: _____

Instructions

On this form, record and evaluate your own involvement in this project. In the Log section, record the activities you performed as an individual and those you performed as part of the group. For all activities, record the date and the number of hours you spent. In the Evaluation section, write two brief statements, one about aspects of your contribution you think were successful and one about the aspects you want to improve.

Log Individual Activities	Date	Number of Hours
Activities as Part of Group	Date	Number of Hours

Evaluation
Aspects of My Participation That Were Successful

Aspects of My Participation That I Want to Improve in the Future

■ **Figure 4.4**
Self-Evaluation Form

Conducting Efficient Face-to-Face Meetings

Human communication is largely nonverbal. That is, people communicate through words but also through the tone, rate, and volume of their speech. They communicate, too, through body language. For this reason, face-to-face discussions provide the most information about what a person is thinking and feeling —and the best opportunity for group members to understand one another.

On TechComm Web

For an excellent discussion of how to conduct meetings, see Matson (1996). Click on Links Library for Ch. 4 on <bedfordstmartins.com /techcomm>.

In This Book

For a discussion of meeting minutes, see Ch. 18, p. 476.

GUIDELINES

Conducting Efficient Meetings

▶ *Arrive on time.* If you know you will have to miss a meeting, notify the group leader as soon as possible.

▶ *Stick to an agenda.* Create the agenda beforehand so that everyone can come prepared. Don't stray too far from the agenda. If you need to discuss a point that isn't on the agenda, schedule another meeting.

▶ *Record the important decisions made at the meeting.* One group member should serve as secretary by making a record of the meeting focusing on decisions the group makes and tasks to be carried out next.

▶ *Summarize your accomplishments and make sure every member understands his or her assignment.* The group leader should formally close the meeting by summarizing the progress the group has made and stating the tasks each group member is to perform before the next meeting. If possible, the secretary should give each group member this informal set of meeting minutes.

Communicating Diplomatically

Because collaborating on an important project is stressful, it can lead to interpersonal conflict. People can become frustrated and angry with each other because of personality clashes or because of disputes about the project. If the project is to succeed, however, group members have to work together productively. When you speak in a group meeting, you want to appear helpful, not critical or overbearing.

GUIDELINES

Communicating Diplomatically

▶ *Listen carefully.* Set aside preconceptions based on the speaker's age, race, cultural background, appearance, or sex. Maintain eye contact with the speaker, paying attention to the ideas—the evidence and

⬇

logic—not to the words. Compare the speaker's message with what you already know about the subject. Think of questions to ask later. If you don't understand what the speaker said, ask for clarification.

▶ *Let the speaker finish.* Don't interrupt.

▶ *Give everyone a chance to speak.*

▶ *Avoid personal remarks and insults.* Be tolerant and respectful of other people's views and working methods. Doing so is right—and smart. It is ethical to treat people respectfully, as you want them to treat you. And it is practical: if you anger people, they will go out of their way to oppose you.

▶ *Don't overstate your position.* A modest qualifier such as "I think" or "it seems to me" is an effective signal to your listeners that you realize that everyone may not share your views.

OVERBEARING My plan is a sure thing; there's no way we're not going to kill Allied next quarter.

DIPLOMATIC I think this plan has a good chance of success: we're playing off our strengths and Allied's weaknesses.

In the diplomatic version, the speaker calls it "this plan," not "my plan."

▶ *Don't get emotionally attached to your own ideas.* When people oppose you, try to understand why. Digging in is usually unwise—unless it's a matter of principle—because, although you may be right and everyone else wrong, it's not likely.

▶ *Ask pertinent questions.* Bright people ask questions to understand what they hear and to connect it to other ideas. Asking pertinent questions also encourages other group members to examine what they hear.

▶ *Pay attention to nonverbal communication.* Bob might *say*, for example, that he understands a point, but his facial expression might show that he doesn't. If a group member looks confused, ask him or her about it. A direct question is likely to elicit a statement that will help the group clarify its discussion.

Critiquing a Group Member's Draft

In collaborating, group members often critique drafts written by other group members. Knowing how to do it without offending the writer is a valuable skill.

GUIDELINES

Critiquing a Draft

▶ *Start with a positive comment.* Even if the draft is weak, begin with a positive statement: "You've obviously put a lot of work into this, Joanne. Thanks." Or, "This is a really good start. Thanks, Joanne."

▶ *Discuss the larger issues first.* Begin with the big issues: organization, development, logic, evidence, design, and graphics. Then work on paragraph development, and then on sentence-level matters and word choice. Leave editing and proofreading until the end of the process.

▶ *Talk about the writing, not the writer.*

| RUDE | You don't explain clearly why this criterion is relevant. |
| BETTER | I'm having trouble understanding how this criterion relates to the topic. |

▶ *Focus on the group's document, not on the group member's draft.* Your goal is to improve the quality of the document you will submit, not to evaluate the writer or the draft. Offer constructive suggestions.

| RUDE | Why didn't you include the price comparisons here, like you said you would? |
| BETTER | I wonder if the report would be stronger if we include the price comparisons here. |

In the better version, the speaker focuses on the goal—to create an effective report—rather than on the writer's failure to include something. Also, the speaker qualifies his recommendation by saying, "I wonder if. . . ." This approach sounds constructive rather than boastful or annoyed.

USING GROUPWARE AND OTHER COMMUNICATION MEDIA

Communicating electronically may require:

Using the comment, revision, and highlighting features on a word processor

Using e-mail to send files

Using groupware

Electronic media are useful collaborative tools for two reasons:

• *Face-to-face meetings are not always possible or convenient.* Electronic media enable people to communicate *asynchronously.* That is, a person can read an e-mail when it is convenient, not when the writer sent it.

• *Electronic communication is digital.* Group members can store and revise comments and drafts, incorporating them as the document develops.

Communicating electronically often involves three important skills.

Using the Comment, Revision, and Highlighting Features on a Word Processor

Word processors offer three powerful features you will find useful in collaborative work.

- The *comment feature* lets a reader add electronic comments to a writer's file. The text that has been commented on appears as highlighted material or in a cartoon bubble in the margin. These comments can also be printed out. Figure 4.5 shows the comment feature.

- The *revision feature* lets readers mark up a text by deleting, revising, and adding words while allowing the writer of the text to keep track of who made which suggested changes.

  This problem could have been averted if the technical writer and the engineer had developed a style guide together and discussed their differences. Both needed to ~~give a little~~ compromise on their standards in order to reach an agreement.

  In this passage, the reader recommends that the writer substitute the word "compromise" for the phrase "give a little." (The vertical rule, called a *change bar,* indicates that a change has been made on that line.) The writer can accept or reject any of the reader's suggestions.

- The *highlighting feature* lets a reader use one of about a dozen "highlighting pens" to call the writer's attention to a particular passage.

  This problem could have been averted if the technical writer and the engineer had developed a style guide together and discussed their differences. Both needed to compromise on their standards in order to reach an agreement.

  Each reader can use a different color, or a single reader can use one color to signal one kind of comment and another color to signal another kind. The writer can easily remove the highlighting.

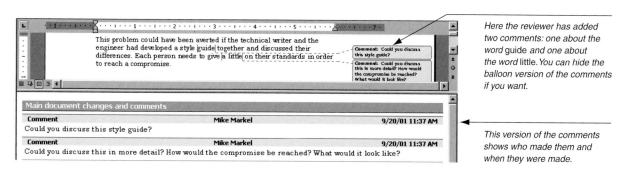

■ **Figure 4.5   The Comment Feature on a Word Processor**

Using E-mail to Send Files

Most e-mail software lets you attach a file to an e-mail message. This means that you can easily send a file, such as a document written in WordPerfect or a spreadsheet in Excel. A recipient who has the software in which the document was saved can open it.

Using Groupware

On TechComm Web

For a tutorial on NetMeeting's collaborative tools, see Microsoft's site. Click on Links Library for Ch. 4 on <bedfordstmartins.com /techcomm>.

Groupware is software that lets people at the same or different locations plan, draft, revise, and track a document. You may already be familiar with groupware programs such as Lotus Notes™ or Microsoft NetMeeting™. Manufacturers of office suites such as Microsoft and Corel are putting more and more collaboration features in their products.

Team members at different locations can perform five important collaborative activities:

- *Sharing files.* Team members can post files to a document library, enabling other team members to view them or download them.

- *Carrying out asynchronous discussions.* Team members can carry out discussions by posting comments to a discussion list. All team members can read and download the posts at their convenience.

- *Commenting on documents.* Team members can attach comments to files, without actually changing the files.

- *Distributing announcements.* Team members can post announcements, such as reminders about deadlines or schedule revisions.

- *Creating automated change notifications.* Team members can sign up to be notified by e-mail when a document has been changed.

Many groupware programs also offer two additional tools:

- *Whiteboards.* Whiteboard software lets people at different locations draw on the screen as if they were all in a room with a whiteboard. Anything drawn on one screen is displayed immediately on every screen. The image can be printed or saved as a file. Figure 4.6 shows the whiteboard screen from Microsoft's NetMeeting.

- *Videoconferencing.* Standard video cameras can be connected to computers, enabling people to see each other as they talk. Figure 4.7 shows a videoconference.

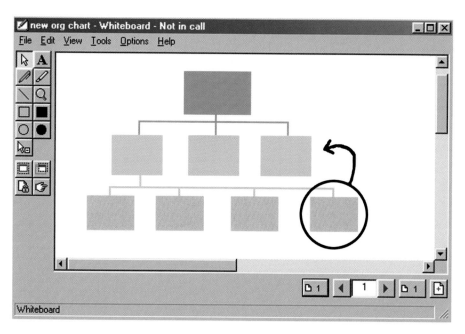

■ **Figure 4.6 A Whiteboard Screen**

*All the people participating in the whiteboard session see the same screen. Whenever anyone
changes anything on his or her screen, all participants see the change on their screens.*

*The camera mounted on top of
the monitor sends a video image
to the other group of participants.
More sophisticated video-
conferencing systems use
room-mounted cameras that can
capture the image of everyone in
a room.*

*Most videoconferencing systems
let participants display additional
"windows" on the screen, such as
computer files or desktops.*

■ **Figure 4.7 A Videoconference**

Source: Aethra, 2003 <www.aethra.com/prod_img/41_foto_2_g.jpg>.

Interactive Sample Document:
Critiquing a Draft Clearly and Diplomatically

This is an excerpt from the methods section of a report about computer servers. In this section, the writer is explaining the tasks he performed in analyzing different servers. In a later section, he explains what he learned from the analysis. The comments in the balloons were inserted into the document by the author's colleague.

The questions in the margin ask you to think about techniques for critiquing (as outlined on page 62). The answers to these questions are available on TechComm Web.

1. What is the tone of the comments? How can they be improved?

2. How well does the collaborator address the larger issues?

3. How well does the collaborator address the writing, not the writer?

4. How do the collaborator's comments focus on the goal of the document, rather than judge the quality of the writing?

On TechComm Web

To find the answers to these questions, click on Interactive Sample Documents for Ch. 4 on <bedfordstmartins.com/techcomm>.

> The first task of the on-site evaluations was to set up and configure each server. We noted the relative complexity of setting up each system to our network.
>
> **Comment:** Huh? What exactly does this mean?
>
> After we had the system configured, we performed a set of routine maintenance tasks: Add a new memory module, swap a hard-drive, swap a power supply and perform system diagnostics.
>
> **Comment:** Okay, good. Maybe we should explain why we chose these tests.
>
> We recorded the time and relative difficulty of each task, and the relative difficulty. Also, we tried to gather a qualitative feeling for how much effort would be involved in the day-to-day maintenance of the systems.
>
> **Comment:** What kind of scale are you using? If we don't explain it, it's basically useless.
>
> **Comment:** Same question as above.
>
> After each system was set up, we completed the maintenance evaluations and began the benchmark testing. We ran the complete WinBench and NetBench test suites on each system. We chose several of the key factors from these tests for comparison.
>
> **Comment:** Will readers know these are the right tests? Should we explain?

GENDER AND COLLABORATION

Effective collaboration involves two related challenges: maintaining the group as a productive, friendly working unit and accomplishing the task. Scholars of gender and collaboration see these two challenges as representing the feminine and the masculine perspectives.

Any discussion of gender studies must begin with a qualifier: in discussing gender, we are generalizing; we are not talking about particular people. In other words, the differences in behavior between two men or between two women are likely to be greater than the difference between men and women in general.

The differences in how the sexes communicate and work in groups have been traced to every culture's traditional family structure. As the primary caregivers, women have learned to value nurturing, connection, growth, and cooperation; as the primary breadwinners, men have learned to value separateness, competition, debate, and even conflict (Chodorow, 1978).

For decades, scholars have studied the speech differences between women and men. Women tend to use more qualifiers and "tag" questions, such as "Don't you think?" (Tannen, 1990). Some scholars, however, suggest that women might be using these patterns because it is expected of them, and that they use them mainly in groups that include men (McMillan, Clifton, McGrath, & Gale, 1977). Many experts caution against using qualifiers and tag questions, which can suggest subservience and powerlessness.

In collaborative groups, women appear to value consensus and relationships, to show more empathy, and to demonstrate superior listening skills (Borisoff & Merrill, 1987). Women talk more about topics unrelated to the task (Duin, Jorn, & DeBower, 1991), but this talk is central to maintaining group coherence. Men appear to be more competitive and more likely to assume leadership roles. Scholars of gender recommend that all professionals strive to achieve an androgynous mix of the skills and aptitudes commonly associated with both women and men.

STRATEGIES FOR INTERCULTURAL COMMUNICATION

Collaborating Across Cultures

Most collaborative groups in industry and in the classroom include people from other cultures. The challenge for all group members is to understand the ways in which cultural differences can affect group behavior. People from other cultures

- might find it difficult to assert themselves in collaborative groups
- might be unwilling to respond with a definite "no"
- might be reluctant to admit when they are confused or to ask for clarification
- might avoid criticizing others
- might avoid initiating new tasks or performing creatively

Even the most benign gesture of friendship on the part of a U.S. student can cause confusion. If a U.S. student casually asks a Japanese student about her major and the courses she is taking, the Japanese student might find the question too personal but consider it perfectly appropriate to talk about her family and her religious beliefs (Lustig & Koester, 1993, p. 234). Therefore, you should remain open to encounters with people from other cultures without jumping to conclusions about what their actions might or might not mean.

In This Book

For more about multicultural issues, see Ch. 5, p. 87.

Collaborator's Checklist

In your first group meeting, did you
- ❏ define the group's task? (p. 56)
- ❏ choose a group leader? (p. 56)
- ❏ define tasks for each group member? (p. 56)
- ❏ establish working procedures? (p. 56)
- ❏ establish a procedure for resolving conflict? (p. 56)
- ❏ create a style sheet? (p. 56)
- ❏ establish a work schedule? (p. 56)
- ❏ create evaluation materials? (p. 57)

To conduct efficient face-to-face meetings, do you
- ❏ arrive on time? (p. 60)
- ❏ stick to an agenda? (p. 60)
- ❏ make sure that a group member records important decisions made at the meeting? (p. 60)
- ❏ make sure that a group member summarizes your accomplishments and that every member understands what his or her assignment is? (p. 60)

To communicate diplomatically, do you
- ❏ listen carefully? (p. 60)

- ❏ let the speaker finish? (p. 60)
- ❏ let others talk? (p. 61)
- ❏ avoid personal remarks and insults? (p. 61)
- ❏ avoid overstating your position? (p. 61)
- ❏ avoid getting emotionally attached to your own ideas? (p. 61)
- ❏ ask pertinent questions? (p. 61)
- ❏ pay attention to body language? (p. 61)

In critiquing a group member's draft, do you
- ❏ start with a positive comment? (p. 62)
- ❏ discuss the larger issues first? (p. 62)
- ❏ talk about the writing, not the writer? (p. 62)
- ❏ focus on the group's document, not on the group member's draft? (p. 62)

If appropriate, do you
- ❏ use the comment, revision, and highlighting features on a word processor? (p. 63)
- ❏ use e-mail to send files? (p. 64)
- ❏ use groupware? (p. 64)

Exercises

On TechComm Web

For more exercises, click on Additional Exercises, Projects, and Cases for Ch. 4 on <bedfordstmartins.com/techcomm>.

1. Experiment with the comment, revision, and highlighting features on your word processor. Using online help if necessary, learn how to make, revise, and delete comments; make, undo, and accept revisions; and add and delete highlights.

2. **Internet Activity** Using a search engine, find e-mail shareware or freeware on the Internet. Download the software and install it on your computer at home. Learn how to use the feature that lets you send attached files.

3. **Group Activity** You have probably had a lot of experience working in collaborative teams in previous courses or on the job. Brainstorm for five minutes, listing some of your best and worst experiences participating in collaborative teams. Choose one positive experience and one negative experience. Think about why the positive experience went well. Was there a technique that a team member used that accounted for the positive experience? Think about why the negative experience went wrong. Was there a technique or action that accounted for the negative experience? How might the negative experience have been prevented—or fixed? Be prepared to share your responses with the rest of the class.

Project

On TechComm Web

For more projects, click on Additional Exercises, Projects, and Cases for
Ch. 4 on <bedfordstmartins.com/techcomm>.

4. **Group Activity**   Your college or university wishes to update
its Web site to include a section called "For Prospective
International Students." Along with members of your
group, first determine whether your school already has
information of particular interest to prospective international students. If it does, write a memo to your instructor
describing and evaluating the information. Is it accurate?
Comprehensive? Clear? Useful? What kinds of information should be added to the site to make it more effective?

   If the school's site does not have this information,
perform the following tasks:

- *Plan.* What kind of information should it include? Does
  some of this information already exist, or does it all
  have to be created from scratch? For example, can you
  create a link to information on how to obtain a student
  visa, or does this information not exist on the Web?
  Write an outline of the main topics that should be
  covered.

- *Draft.* Write the following sections: "Where to Live on or
  Near Campus," "Social Activities on or Near Campus,"
  and "If English Is Not Your Native Language." What
  graphics could you include? Are they already available?
  What other sites should you link to for these three
  sections?

In a memo, present your suggestions to your instructor.
(For more on memos, see Chapter 15, page 378.)

CASE
The Reluctant Collaborator

Some of the projects in your technical-communication course are to be
completed collaboratively. The instructor has assigned you to a group; the
other members of the group are Allison and Ken. Allison is a senior in mechanical engineering; Ken is a junior in computer science. You are a senior
in accounting. Along with your collaborative assignments, each member of
the group is to submit the two forms presented in this chapter (Figures 4.3
and 4.4): the evaluation form for the other members of the group and the
self-evaluation form. In addition, each member is invited to submit any
notes, drafts, or other documents to show the instructor the work he or she
contributed to the project.

   At your first group meeting, you choose a leader: Allison. As a senior in
mechanical engineering, she has had a lot of experience working collaboratively and is happy to take on the task of supervising your group's work. The
first meeting, to discuss topics for a research proposal, is scheduled for
7 P.M. the next night in Conference Room 3 in the library.

On TechComm Web

For more cases, click on Additional
Exercises, Projects, and Cases for
Ch. 4 on <bedfordstmartins.com
/techcomm>.

It is 7:15, the night of the meeting, and Ken has not arrived. Neither Allison nor you had heard from Ken before the meeting with word that he would be late. At 7:30, you and Allison decide to phone Ken. There is no answer.

You and Allison are angry that Ken hasn't arrived or sent a friend to tell the group that he will be late or will have to cancel. The two of you are unwilling to start work on the project without Ken there. You decide to cancel the meeting. Allison tells you she will call him from home later that evening.

At about 9:00 P.M. you get a call from Allison. She reached Ken a few minutes before. He said he had car trouble that night and apologized. Allison asks you if the group could meet the next afternoon at 3:00 in the library. Allison tells you that Ken agreed to her request that each group member bring a list of three possible topics to the meeting. You agree and write the time in your appointment book.

The next day, at 3:15, Ken rushes into the room. "Sorry I'm late," he says with a smile. You and Allison give him a cold look. Allison begins the discussion.

"Okay, we each agreed to bring three topics to the meeting today. Ken, what have you got?"

"That was for today? I'm really sorry. I just blew that off."

Allison turns to you, and you read off your three topics. Then she reads hers. The three of you agree to select one of Allison's topics: a feasibility study of software used in creating engineering drawings. You set a time for the next meeting and decide on an agenda.

As you conclude the meeting, Allison asks you if you could stay a minute. Ken leaves.

"I'm not happy with what I see developing with Ken," she says. "We're going to be slowed down if he doesn't come to the meetings or prepare. What do you think we should do?"

In a memo to your instructor, respond to the following questions: How should you respond to Allison? Should you merely hope that Ken starts to participate more responsibly? Is there some way to delegate tasks that will motivate Ken to participate more actively? Should you and Allison go ahead with the project, letting Ken participate when he chooses to? Should Allison talk with him? Should both of you talk with him together? Should you go to your instructor? (For more on memos, see Chapter 15, page 378.)

PART TWO

PLANNING THE DOCUMENT

Analyzing Your Audience and Purpose

5

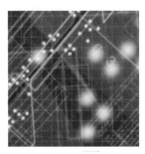

George Rimolower, a translator, comments on the need to consider the cultural background of your audience as you plan your communication:

McDonald's printed take-out bags decorated with flags from around the world. On the bag was additional text translated into the different languages of the countries the flags depicted. Had McDonald's taken the time to consult with a cultural expert, they would have avoided committing the major mistake of printing bags that contained a Saudi flag with scripture from the Koran. This was extremely offensive to the Saudis. To print the Saudi flag, which contains holy scripture, on a disposable bag that would wind up in a garbage heap was sacrilegious. (G. Rimolower, personal communication, August 14, 1996)

On TechComm Web

For additional samples, activities, and links related to this chapter, see <bedfordstmartins.com/techcomm>.

The content and form of every technical document you write are determined by the writing situation: your audience and your purpose. Understanding the writing situation helps you devise a strategy to meet your readers' needs — and your own. Audience and purpose are not unique to technical communication. When a classified advertisement describes a job, for example, the writing situation is clear:

AUDIENCE   prospective applicants

PURPOSE   to describe the job opening and motivate qualified persons to apply

Once you have identified the two basic elements of your writing situation, you must analyze each of them before deciding what to say and how to say it.

ANALYZING AN AUDIENCE

In her book *Dynamics in Document Design,* Karen Schriver (1997) describes three techniques for analyzing an audience:

- *Thinking.* If you are writing an employee-benefit manual, you think about the strengths and weaknesses of similar manuals you have used. You study samples of these manuals, noting what works and what doesn't. You brainstorm with your collaborators on the project, trying to think of good ideas.

- *Listening.* You go to people who already have the current manual and ask for their opinions. Do they know they have the manual? Do they use it? What do they like or dislike about it? You distribute questionnaires or per-

In This Book

For more on questionnaires, see Ch. 7, p. 152. For more on usability testing, see Ch. 3, p. 46.

form usability testing. As you start to create the new manual, you show potential readers drafts and ask for critiques.

- *Classifying.* By classifying readers, you can decide what kind of information to include, how to organize it, what kind of writing style to use, and so forth. You classify your readers into categories on the basis of their knowledge of your subject.

As Schriver points out, it is best to use all three approaches. The following discussion describes in more detail how to classify your audience and use the information you gain to help you plan the document.

IDENTIFYING PRIMARY AND SECONDARY AUDIENCES

Start by classifying your readers into two categories:

- A *primary audience* of people who have a direct role in responding to your document. They might be readers who use your document in doing their jobs. They might evaluate and revise it, or they might act on your recommendations. An executive who decides whether to authorize building a new facility is a primary reader. So is the treasurer who has to determine whether the organization can pay for it.
- A *secondary audience* of people who need to stay aware of developments in the organization, such as salespeople who want to know where a new facility will be located, what products it will produce, and when it will be open. A secondary audience will not directly act on or respond to your document.

The needs of your primary audience are more central than those of your secondary audience. For example, if several members of your primary audience need to know a project's financial details, you should provide that information prominently. But if only members of a secondary audience will need that information, you should probably put it in a less prominent part of the document.

The next step in classifying your audience is to determine what basic categories they might belong to.

On TechComm Web

For more about audience analysis, see Writing Guidelines for Engineering and Science Students. Click on Links Library for Ch. 5 on <bedfordstmartins .com/techcomm>.

BASIC CATEGORIES OF READERS

Although each person is unique, try to classify your readers according to their knowledge of your subject. In general, every reader can be classified into one of four categories: the expert, the technician, the manager, or the general reader. These categories are only generalizations, but most people fit into one or perhaps two of them. Ellen DeSalvo, for example, a Ph.D. in materials engineering, would be an expert in that particular field; she might also be the manager of the materials group at her company.

Categories of readers:

The expert

The technician

The manager

The general reader

The Expert

The expert is a highly trained individual with an extensive theoretical and practical understanding of the subject. Often an expert carries out basic or applied research and communicates these research findings. Here are some examples of experts:

> a *physician* trying to understand the AIDS virus who delivers papers at professional conferences and writes research articles for scholarly journals

> an *engineer* trying to devise a simpler, less expensive test for structural flaws in composite materials

> a *forester* trying to plan a strategy for dealing with the threat of forest fires during droughts

In short, almost everyone with a postgraduate degree — and many people with an undergraduate degree in a technical field — is an expert in one area.

Because experts are curious about their subject and understand its theory, they usually have no trouble with technical concepts, formulas, graphics, and vocabulary. Therefore, when you write for experts, you can get right to the details of the technical subject without spending time on the basics. In addition, most experts are comfortable with long sentences, if the sentences are well constructed and no longer than necessary.

Figure 5.1, an excerpt from the patent granted to Dean Kamen and associates for his Segway personal-transportation device, illustrates the needs and interests of the expert reader. The passage describes the microcomputer that controls the device.

The Technician

The technician takes the expert's ideas and turns them into real products and procedures. The technician builds, operates, maintains, and repairs mechanisms, and sometimes teaches other people how to operate them. An engineer having a problem with an industrial laser will talk with a technician. After they agree on a possible cause of the problem and a way to fix it, the technician will go to work.

Like experts, technicians are very interested in their subject, but they know less about theory. Technicians do not want complex theoretical discussions; they want to finish a task safely, effectively, and quickly. Therefore, they need schematic diagrams, parts lists, and step-by-step instructions. Most technicians prefer short or medium-length sentences and common vocabulary, especially in documents such as step-by-step instructions.

Figure 5.2, an excerpt from the patent grant for Segway, illustrates the needs and interests of the technician. The passage describes the microcomputer that controls the device.

A simplified control algorithm for achieving balance in the embodiment of the invention according to FIG. 1 when the wheels are active for locomotion is shown in the block diagram of FIG. 6. The plant 61 is equivalent to the equations of motion of a system with a ground contacting module driven by a single motor, before the control loop is applied. T identifies the wheel torque. The character theta identifies the fore-aft inclination (the pitch angle of the vehicle with respect to gravity, i.e., the vertical), X identifies the fore-aft displacement along the surface relative to the reference point, and the dot over a character denotes a variable differentiated with respect to time. The remaining portion of the figure is the control used to achieve balance. The boxes 62 and 63 indicate differentiation. To achieve dynamic control to insure stability of the system, and to keep the system in the neighborhood of a reference point on the surface, the wheel torque T in this embodiment is set to satisfy the following equation:

$$T = K.sub.1\ .theta. + K.sub.2\ .theta. + K.sub.3\ x + K.sub.4\ x$$

The gains K.sub.1, K.sub.2, K.sub.3, and K.sub.4 are dependent upon the physical parameters of the system and other effects such as gravity. The simplified control algorithm of FIG. 6 maintains balance and also proximity to the reference point on the surface in the presence of disturbances such as changes to the system's center of mass with respect to the reference point on the surface due to body motion of the subject or contact with other persons or objects.

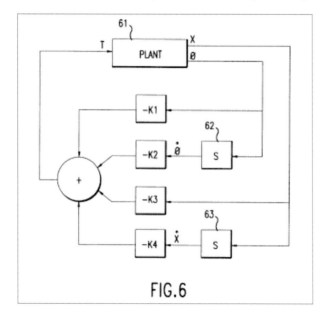

FIG.6

The two-digit numbers (such as 61) refer to components shown in the block diagram below.

Writing addressed to experts often includes high-level theoretical discussions. Here the writers are describing the mathematical algorithm used to balance the Segway.

Notice, too, that the passage uses technical vocabulary and relatively long sentences. Expert readers generally are comfortable with this style.

■ **Figure 5.1**
Writing Addressed to an Expert Audience

This passage, from the patent application for the Segway personal-transportation device, discusses advanced concepts of interest to engineers and physicists.
Source: Kamen et al., 1999 <www.uspto.gov>.

The three-digit numbers (such as 273) refer to components shown in the block diagram below.

The writers assume that technicians are comfortable with the concepts and vocabulary related to the microprocessor and that they can interpret the block diagram without assistance.

FIG. 29 is a block diagram providing detail of the driver interface assembly 273 of FIG. 27. A peripheral microcomputer board 291 receives an input from joystick 292 as well as from inclinometer 293. The inclinometer provides information signals as to pitch and pitch rate. (The term "inclinometer" as used in this context throughout this description and in the accompanying claims means any device providing an output indicative of pitch or pitch rate, regardless of the arrangement used to achieve the output; if only one of the pitch and pitch rate variables is provided as an output, the other variable can be obtained by suitable differentiation or integration with respect to time.) To permit controlled banking into turns by the vehicle (thereby to increase stability while turning) it is also feasible to utilize a second inclinometer to provide information as to roll and roll rate or, alternatively, the resultant of system weight and centrifugal force. Other inputs 294 may also be desirably provided as an input to the peripheral micro controller board 291. Such other inputs may include signals gated by switches (knobs and buttons) for chair adjustment and for determining the mode of operation (such as lean mode or balance mode described below). The peripheral micro controller board 291 also has inputs for receiving signals from the battery stack 271 as to battery voltage, battery current, and battery temperature. The peripheral micro controller board 291 is in communication over bus 279 with the central micro controller board 272.

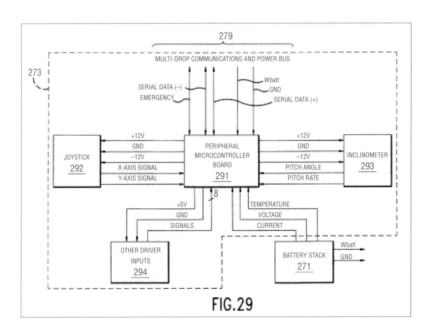

FIG.29

■ **Figure 5.2**
Writing Addressed to Technicians

The Manager

The manager is harder to define than the technician, because *manager* describes what a person does rather than what a person knows. A manager makes sure an organization operates smoothly and efficiently. For instance, the manager of the procurement department at a manufacturing plant sees that raw materials are purchased and delivered on time so that production continues.

Upper-level managers, known as executives, address longer-range concerns. They foresee problems years ahead by considering questions such as the following:

- Is current technology at the company becoming obsolete?

- How expensive are the newest technologies?

- How much would they disrupt operations if they were adopted?

- What other plans would have to be postponed or dropped altogether?

- When would the new technologies start to pay for themselves?

- What has been the experience of other companies that have adopted these new technologies?

Executives are concerned with these and dozens of other broad questions that go beyond day-to-day managerial concerns.

Managers want to know the bottom line. They have to get a job done on schedule; they don't have time to consider theory in the way an expert does. Rather, managers must juggle constraints—financial, personnel, time, and informational—and make logical and reasonable decisions quickly. And they have to communicate with their own supervisors.

In writing to a manager, try to determine his or her technical background and then choose an appropriate vocabulary and sentence length. Focus on practical information. For example, if you are a police officer describing a new product to the police chief, you might begin with some theoretical background but then concentrate on the product's capabilities and its advantages over competing products.

If you know that your reader will take your information and use it in a document addressed to executives, make your reader's job easier. Include an executive summary (see Chapter 12, page 274) and use frequent headings (Chapter 10, page 220) to highlight your major points. Ask your reader if there is an organizational pattern, a format, or a strategy for writing the document that will help him or her use your document as source material.

Figure 5.3, an excerpt from a press release from Segway, illustrates the interests and needs of the manager.

Segway's business plan calls for selling the device first to large corporate customers, such as the U.S. Postal Service and police departments. After the public becomes accustomed to seeing the device, the company will sell it to individuals.

This passage explains how this business plan will work. Rather than focusing on technical information about the device, the passage concentrates on issues that a manager needs to understand: efficiency and safety.

Tampa Postmaster Rich Rome today announced that the Tampa Post Office is the first United States Postal Service site to test feasibility of the Segway™ Human Transporter (HT), a self-balancing, electric-powered transportation device, for use in mail delivery.

"The United States Postal Service has a long history of testing innovative modes of transportation," said Postmaster Rome. "As an organization dedicated to deploying technology that drives efficiency, we are proud to be selected as a test site and look forward to giving the Segway HT a thorough evaluation."

The Segway HT will be used on five "park and loop" residential delivery routes where a portion of deliveries are made by a letter carrier on foot. Each route has approximately 500 delivery addresses.

The Postal Service will be evaluating whether use of the Segway HT results in greater delivery efficiency. "To determine the potential for cost savings and increased efficiency, we'll be evaluating delivery time using the Segway HT compared to straight walking time, as well as safety and ergonomics," said Rome. With the Segway HT, up to 35 pounds of mail normally carried by the letter carrier can be transferred to satchels mounted on the human transporter.

"We believe the Segway HT will provide the U.S. Postal Service with a meaningful solution that enables letter carriers to do their job more efficiently and with less physical demand," said Dean Kamen, Segway LLC's chairman and CEO.

■ **Figure 5.3   Writing Addressed to a Manager**

Source: Norton, 2002 <www.segway.com/consumer/team/press_releases/pr_011402.html>.

The General Reader

Often your writing will address the general reader, sometimes called the *layperson*. A nuclear scientist reading about economics is a general reader, as is a historian reading about astronomy.

The layperson reads out of curiosity or self-interest. An article in the magazine supplement of the Sunday paper—on ways to increase the populations of endangered species in zoos, for example—will attract the general reader's attention if it seems interesting and well written. The general reader may also seek specific information that will bring direct benefits: someone interested in buying a house might read articles on new alternative-financing methods.

In writing to a general audience, use simple vocabulary and relatively short sentences. Translate jargon into standard English and use analogies and examples to clarify your discussion. Include the human angle: how the situation affects people. Present any special background—historical or ethical, for example—so that your reader can follow the discussion easily. Concentrate on the implications of this information for the general reader. For example, in discussing a new substance that removes graffiti from buildings, focus on its effectiveness and cost, not on its chemistry.

Figure 5.4 on page 82, an excerpt from a newspaper article about the Segway, illustrates the interests and needs of the general reader.

GUIDELINES

Writing for the Basic Categories of Readers

These guidelines summarize the discussion of how to write for the basic categories of readers.

Audience	Reasons for Reading	Guidelines for Writing
Expert	To gain an understanding of the theory and its implications.	Include theory, technical vocabulary, formulas, and sophisticated graphics.
Technician	To gain a hands-on understanding of how something works or how to carry out a task.	Include graphics. Use common words, short sentences, and short paragraphs. Avoid excessive theory.
Manager	To learn the bottom-line facts to aid in making decisions.	Focus on managerial implications, not technical details. Use short sentences and simple vocabulary. Put details in appendices.
General reader	To satisfy curiosity and for self-interest.	Use short sentences and paragraphs, human appeal, and an informal tone.

INDIVIDUAL CHARACTERISTICS OF READERS

Knowing that a reader is, for example, a manager can tell you something about what that person might want to see in a communication. But it doesn't tell you whether that person is a native speaker of English, whether she is receptive or hostile to your message, or whether she needs to use information from your document in a document she is writing. In other words, placing a reader into a category doesn't tell you anything about that reader as an individual. Try to find out as much as you can about your reader's individual characteristics.

Determine individual characteristics by asking:

Who is your reader?

What are your reader's attitudes and expectations?

Why and how will your reader use your document?

Who Is Your Reader?

In thinking about who your reader is, consider six specific factors:

- *The reader's education.* Think not only about the person's degree but also about when the person earned the degree. A civil engineer who earned a B.S. in 1983 has a much different background from the person who earned the same degree in 2003. Also consider formal and informal course work the person has completed while on the job.

   Knowing your readers' educational backgrounds helps you determine how much supporting material to provide, what level of vocabulary to use, what kind of sentence structure and length to use, what types

Writing addressed to the general reader must be interesting. This passage begins with the writer's report of his test drive on the Segway. Notice that the writer uses details to characterize Dean Kamen, the Segway inventor. The purpose of this passage is to give the reader a sense of what it was like to ride the Segway, not to explain how it works or whether it will succeed in the marketplace.

"Come to me!"

On a quiet Sunday morning in Silicon Valley, I am standing atop a machine code-named Ginger—a machine that may be the most eagerly awaited and wildly, if inadvertently, hyped high-tech product since the Apple Macintosh. Fifty feet away, Ginger's diminutive inventor, Dean Kamen, is offering instruction on how to use it, which in this case means waving his hands and barking out orders.

"Just lean forward," Kamen commands, so I do, and instantly I start rolling across the concrete right at him.

"Now, stop," Kamen says. How? This thing has no brakes. "Just think about stopping." Staring into the middle distance, I conjure an image of a red stop sign—and just like that, Ginger and I come to a halt.

"Now think about backing up." Once again, I follow instructions, and soon I glide in reverse to where I started. With a twist of the wrist, I pirouette in place, and no matter which way I lean or how hard, Ginger refuses to let me fall over. What's going on here is all perfectly explicable—the machine is sensing and reacting to subtle shifts in my balance—but for the moment I am slack-jawed, baffled. It was Arthur C. Clarke who famously observed that "any sufficiently advanced technology is indistinguishable from magic." By that standard, Ginger is advanced indeed.

This photograph shows a person on a Segway, surrounded by pedestrians and a bicyclist on a crowded sidewalk. This photograph shows the general reader what the Segway looks like and reinforces the theme of the article: that the Segway is intended to be a personal-transportation device. As such, the Segway will be competing with pedestrians and bicyclists, not automobiles.

Gregory Heisler for *Time*

■ **Figure 5.4**
Writing Addressed to the General Reader

Source: Heilemann, 2001
<www.time.com/time/business
/article/0,8599,186660,00.html>.

of graphics to include, and whether to provide such formal elements as a glossary or an executive summary.

Discovering your readers' educational backgrounds can be difficult. You cannot ask people to send you their current résumés. But you can try to learn as much as possible in conversation with your colleagues.

- *The reader's professional experience.* A nurse with a decade of experience might have represented her hospital on a community committee to encourage citizens to give blood and might have contributed to the planning for the hospital's new delivery room. In short, her range of experience might have provided several areas of competence or expertise that you need to consider as you plan the document's content and style.

- *The reader's job responsibility.* Consider the major job responsibility of your primary reader and how your document will help that person accomplish it. For example, if you are writing a feasibility study on ways to cool the air for a new office building and you know that your reader—an upper-level manager—has to worry about utility costs, you need to explain how you are estimating future utility costs.

- *The reader's personal characteristics.* The reader's age might suggest how he or she will read and interpret your document. A senior manager at age 60 is probably less interested in tomorrow's technology than a 30-year-old manager is. Does your reader have any other personal characteristics you should consider, such as impaired vision, that would affect the way you write and design your document?

- *The reader's personal preferences.* One person might hate to see the first-person pronoun *I* in technical documents. Another might find the word *interface* distracting when the writer isn't discussing computers. A good way to learn a person's preferences is to read that person's own documents. You should try to accommodate as many of your reader's preferences as you can.

- *The reader's cultural characteristics.* What you know about your reader's cultural characteristics can help you appeal to his or her interests and avoid being confusing or offensive. As discussed later in this chapter (page 87), cultural characteristics can affect virtually every aspect of a reader's comprehension of a document and perception of the writer.

What Are Your Reader's Attitudes and Expectations?

In thinking about your reader's attitudes and expectations, consider these three factors:

- *Your reader's attitude toward you.* Most people will like you because you are hardworking, intelligent, and cooperative. Some won't. If a reader's animosity toward you is irrational or unrelated to the current project, try to earn that person's respect and trust by meeting him or her on some neutral ground, perhaps by discussing other, less volatile projects or some shared interest, such as gardening, skiing, or science-fiction novels.

- *Your reader's attitude toward the subject.* If possible, discuss the subject thoroughly with your primary readers to determine whether they are positive, neutral, or negative toward it. Here are some basic strategies for responding to different attitudes.

If . . .	Try this . . .
Your reader is neutral or positively inclined toward your subject	Write the document so that it responds to the reader's needs; make sure that vocabulary, level of detail, organization, and style are appropriate.
Your reader is hostile to the subject or your approach to it	• Try to find out what the objections are, then answer them directly. Explain why the objections are not valid or are less important than the benefits. • Organize the document so that your recommendation follows your explanation of the benefits. This strategy encourages the hostile reader to understand your argument rather than to reject it out of hand. • Avoid describing the subject as a dispute. Seek areas of agreement and concede points. Avoid trying to persuade readers overtly; people don't like to be persuaded, because it threatens their ego. Instead, suggest that there are new facts that need to be considered. People are less reluctant to change their minds when they realize that there are additional facts to be considered.
Your reader was instrumental in creating the policy or procedure that you are arguing is ineffective	In discussing the present system's shortcomings, be especially careful if you risk offending one of your readers. When you address such an audience, don't write, "The present system for logging customer orders is completely ineffective." Instead, write, "While the present system has worked well for many years, new developments in electronic processing of orders might enable us to improve logging speed and reduce errors substantially."

- *Your reader's expectations about the document.* Think about how your readers expect to see the information treated in terms of scope, organizational pattern, and amount of detail. Consider, too, the type of document; if your reader expects to see the information presented as a memo, use a memo unless some other format would clearly work better.

Why and How Will Your Reader Use Your Document?

In thinking about how your reader will use your document, consider the following four factors:

- *Your reader's reasons for reading your document.* Does the reader need to use the document to carry out a task? To learn the answer to a specific question? To understand the broad outlines of the subject? The more specifically you can answer such questions, the more likely your document will meet your reader's needs.

- *The way your reader will read your document.* Will he or she
  - file it?
  - skim it?
  - read only a portion of it?
  - study it carefully?
  - modify it and submit it to another reader?
  - try to implement recommendations?
  - use it to perform a test or carry out a procedure?
  - use it as a source document for another document?

    If only 1 of your 15 readers will study the document for detailed information, you don't want the other 14 people to have to wade through it. Therefore, put this information in an appendix. If you know that your reader wants to use your status report as raw material for a report to a higher-level reader, try to write a report that requires little rewriting. You might use the reader's own writing style and send the reader the file so that your report can be merged with the new document without requiring retyping.

- *Your reader's reading skills.* Your assessment of your reader's reading skills should influence every aspect of your thinking. First, consider whether you should be writing at all, or whether it would be better to use videotapes, for example, or an oral presentation or computer-based training. If you decide to write, consider whether your reader can understand how to use the type of document you have selected, handle the level of detail you will present, and understand your graphics, sentence structure, and vocabulary.

- *The physical environment in which your reader will read your document.* Technical documents are often formatted in a special way or constructed of special materials to improve their effectiveness in particular physical settings. Documents used in poorly lit places might be printed in larger-than-normal type. Some documents might be used on ships or on aircraft or in garages, where they might be exposed to wind, salt water, and grease. You might have to use special waterproof bindings, oil-resistant or laminated paper, coded colors, and unusual-sized paper.

In This Book

For more about designing a document for use in different environments, see Ch. 13, p. 293.

GUIDELINES

Identifying Individual Characteristics of Readers

Use the specific questions in the following table to identify your reader's individual characteristics.

General Questions	Specific Questions
Who is your reader?	• What is the reader's education? • What is the reader's professional experience? • What is the reader's job responsibility? • What are the reader's personal characteristics? • What are the reader's personal preferences? • What are the reader's cultural characteristics?
What are your reader's attitudes and expectations?	• What is the reader's attitude toward you? • What is the reader's attitude toward the subject? • What are the reader's expectations about the document?
Why and how will your reader use your document?	• Why is the reader reading your document? • How will the reader read your document? • What is the reader's reading skill? • What is the physical environment in which the reader will read your document?

WRITING FOR MULTIPLE AUDIENCES

Many documents of more than a few pages are addressed to more than one reader. Often, multiple audiences consist of people with widely different backgrounds. Some might be experts or technicians, others might be managers, and still others might be general readers.

If you think your document will have a number of readers, consider making it *modular:* break it up into components addressed to different kinds of readers. A modular report might contain an executive summary for the managers who don't have the time, knowledge, or desire to read the whole report. It might also contain a full technical discussion for expert readers, an implementation schedule for technicians, and a financial plan in an appendix for budget officers.

Figure 5.5 illustrates the concept of a modular report.

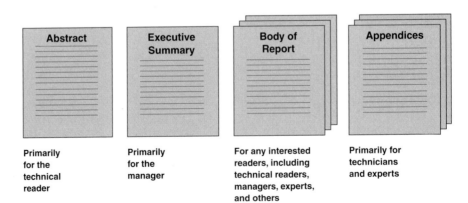

Abstract	**Executive Summary**	**Body of Report**	**Appendices**
Primarily for the technical reader	Primarily for the manager	For any interested readers, including technical readers, managers, experts, and others	Primarily for technicians and experts

■ **Figure 5.5**
A Modular Report

THE AUDIENCE PROFILE SHEET

To help you analyze your audience, you might fill out an audience profile sheet for each primary and secondary reader (assuming, of course, that there are just a few).

Assume that you work in the drafting department of an architectural engineering firm. You know that the company's computer-assisted design (CAD) software is out of date and that recent CAD technology would make it easier and faster for the draftspeople to do their work. You want to persuade your company to authorize buying a CAD workstation that costs about $4,000. Your primary reader is Harry Becker, manager of the Drafting and Design Department. Figure 5.6 is an audience profile sheet for Harry Becker.

COMMUNICATING ACROSS CULTURES

Our society and our workforce are becoming increasingly diverse, both culturally and linguistically, and businesses are exporting more and more goods and services. As a result, technical communicators and technical professionals often communicate with nonnative speakers of English in the United States and abroad and with speakers of other languages who read texts translated from English into their own languages.

The economy of the United States depends on international trade. In 2000, the United States exported over $1 trillion worth of goods and services (U.S. Bureau, 2002, p. 787). In 1999, direct investment abroad by U.S. companies totaled more than $1 trillion (U.S. Bureau, 2002, p. 794). Exports are responsible for four of five new jobs created in the United States (Lustig & Koester, 1999). In addition, the population of the United States itself is truly multicultural. Each year, the United States admits more than half a million immigrants (U.S. Bureau, 2002, p. 10). In 2002, one in ten United States residents was foreign born (U.S. Bureau, 2002, p. 45).

Effective communication requires an understanding of culture: the beliefs, attitudes, and values that motivate people's behavior.

Understanding the Cultural Variables "On the Surface"

Communicating effectively with people from another culture requires understanding a set of cultural variables that lie on the surface. You need to know, first, what language or languages you should use. You also need to be aware of political, social, religious, and economic factors that can affect how readers will interpret your documents. Understanding these factors is not an exact science, but it does require that you learn as much as you can about the culture of those you are addressing.

On TechComm Web

For a version of this form that you can print out or save as a word-processing file, click on Forms for Technical Communication on <bedfordstmartins.com/techcomm>.

AUDIENCE PROFILE SHEET

Reader's Name: Harry Becker

Reader's Job Title: Manager, Drafting and Design Department

Kind of Reader: Primary __X__ Secondary ____

Education: B.S., Architectural Engineering, Northwestern, 1989. CAD/CAM Short Course, 1989; Motivating Your Employees Seminar, 1991; Writing on the Job Short Course, 1994

Professional Experience: Worked for two years in a small architecture firm. Started here 12 years ago as a draftsperson. Worked his way up to Assistant Manager, then Manager. Instrumental in the Wilson project, particularly in coordinating personnel and equipment.

Job Responsibilities: Supervises a staff of 12 draftspersons. Approves or denies all requests for capital expenditures over $2,000 coming from his department. Works with employees to help them make the best case for the purchase. After approving or denying the request, forwards it to Tina Buterbaugh, Manager, Finance Dept., who maintains all capital expenditure records.

Personal Characteristics: N/A

Personal Preferences: Likes straightforward documents, lots of evidence, clear structure. Dislikes complicated documents full of jargon.

Cultural Characteristics: Nothing of note.

Attitude Toward the Writer: No problems.

Attitude Toward the Subject: He understands and approves of my argument.

Expectations about the Subject: Expects to see a clear argument with financial data and detailed comparisons of available systems.

Expectations about the Document: Expects to see a report, with an executive summary, of about 10 pages.

Reasons for Reading the Document: To offer suggestions and eventually approve or deny the request.

Way of Reading the Document:
Skim it ____   Study it __X__ Read a portion of it ____   Which portion? ____
Modify it and submit it to another reader ____
Attempt to implement recommendations ____
Use it to perform a task or carry out a procedure ____
Use it to create another document ____
Other ____   Explain.

Reading Skill: Excellent

Reader's Physical Environment: N/A

■ **Figure 5.6**
An Audience Profile Sheet

You should modify this form to meet your own needs and those of your organization.

A brief example: an American manufacturer of deodorant launched an advertising campaign in Japan in which a cute octopus applied the firm's product under each of its eight arms. But the campaign failed. In Japan, an octopus has eight legs, not eight arms (Bathon, 1999).

In *International Technical Communication,* Nancy L. Hoft (1995) describes seven major cultural variables that lie on the surface:

- *Political.* This category includes trade issues and legal issues (for example, some countries forbid imports of certain foods or chemicals) and laws about intellectual property, product safety, and liability.

- *Economic.* In many developing countries, most people cannot afford personal computers. You need to know the economic status of the people with whom you communicate.

- *Social.* This category covers many issues, including gender and business customs. In most Western cultures, women play a much greater role in the workplace than they do in many Middle Eastern and Asian cultures. And business customs—including forms of greeting, business dress, and gift giving—vary from culture to culture.

- *Religious.* Religious differences can affect diet, attitudes toward individual colors, styles of dress, holidays, and hours of business.

- *Educational.* In the United States, some 40 million people are only marginally literate. In other cultures, that rate can be much higher or much lower. In some cultures, classroom learning with a teacher is considered the most acceptable way to study; in others, people are encouraged to study on their own.

- *Technological.* If you sell high-tech products, you need to know whether your readers have the hardware, the software, and the technological infrastructure to use them.

- *Linguistic.* In some countries, English is taught to all children starting in grade school; in other countries, English is discouraged because it is seen as a threat to the national language. In many cultures, the orientation of text on a page and in a book is not from left to right.

In addition to these basic differences, there are dozens of other factors you need to understand. For instance, the United States is the only major country that has not adopted the metric system. Americans also use periods to separate whole numbers from decimals, and commas to separate thousands from hundreds. Much of the rest of the world reverses this usage.

United States: 3,425.6
Europe: 3.425,6

In the United States, the format for writing out and abbreviating dates is different from that of most other cultures:

United States: March 2, 2003   3/2/03

Europe: 2 March 2003   2/3/03

Japan: 2 March 2003   03/3/2

These cultural variables on the surface are important in an obvious way. You can't send a fax to a person who doesn't have access to a fax machine. However, there is another set of cultural characteristics — those beneath the surface — that you also need to understand.

Understanding the Cultural Variables "Beneath the Surface"

Scholars of multicultural communication have identified a set of cultural variables that, while less obvious than those discussed in the previous section, are just as important. Table 5.1, which is based on an excellent article by Tebeaux and Driskill (1999), explains six key variables and how they are reflected in technical communication.

As you consider this set of cultural variables, keep four points in mind:

- *Each variable represents a spectrum of attitudes.* Terms such as *high context* and *low context*, for instance, represent the two end points on a scale. Many cultures occupy a middle ground between high context and low context.

- *The six variables do not line up in a clear pattern.* Although Table 5.1 suggests in several places that there are clear relationships between several of the variables — for example, individualistic cultures tend to see a great distance between business and personal lives — in any one culture, the six variables do not form a consistent pattern. For example, the dominant culture in the United States is highly individualistic rather than group oriented but only about midway along the scale of attitudes toward accepting uncertainty.

- *Different organizations within the same culture can vary greatly.* For example, one software company in Germany might have a management style that does not tolerate uncertainty, whereas another software company in Germany might have a management style that tolerates a lot of uncertainty.

- *An organization's cultural attitudes are fluid, not static.* How organizations operate is determined not only by the dominant culture but also by their own people. As new people join an organization, its culture changes. The IBM of 1983 is not the IBM of 2003.

For you as a communicator, this set of variables therefore offers no answers. Instead, it offers a set of questions that you need to consider. You cannot know in advance the attitudes of the people in an organization. You have to interact with them for a long time before you can reach even tentative conclusions.

■ **Table 5.1   Cultural Variables "Beneath the Surface"**

Variable	Explanation	How This Variable Is Reflected in Technical Communication
Focus on individuals or groups	Some cultures, especially in the West, value individuals more than groups. The typical employee doesn't see his or her identity as being defined by the organization. Other cultures, particularly in Asia, value groups more than individuals. The typical employee sees himself or herself first as a member of the organization rather than an individual who works there.	Communication addressed to people from individualistic cultures focuses on the writer's and readers' needs rather than on those of the two organizations. Writers use the pronoun *I* rather than *we*. Letters are addressed to the principal reader and signed by the writer. Communication addressed to people from group-oriented cultures focuses on the organization's needs rather than on those of the writer and readers. Documents emphasize the benefits to be gained by the two organizations through a cooperative relationship. Writers emphasize the relationship between the writer and reader rather than the specific technical details of the message. Writers use *we* rather than *I*. They might address letters to "Dear Sir," and use the organization's name, not their own, in the complimentary close.
Distance between business life and private life	In some cultures, especially in the West, people separate their business lives from their private lives. When the workday ends, they are free to go home and spend their time as they wish. In other cultures, particularly in Asia, people see a much smaller distance between their business lives and their private lives. Even after the day ends, they still see themselves as employees of the organization. Cultures that value individualism tend to see a great distance between business and personal lives. Cultures that are group oriented tend to see a smaller distance between business life and private life.	Communication addressed to people from cultures that see a great distance between business lives and private lives focuses on the technical details of the communication, with relatively little reference to personal information about the writer or the reader. Communication addressed to people from cultures that see a smaller distance between business lives and personal lives contains much more personal information—about the reader's family and health—and more information about, for example, the weather and the seasons. The goal is to build a formal relationship between the two organizations. Both the writer and the reader are, in effect, on call after business hours and are likely to transact business during long social activities such as elaborate dinners or golf games.
Distance between ranks	In some cultures, the distance in power and authority between workers within an organization is small. This small distance is reflected in a close working relationship between supervisors and their subordinates. In other cultures, the distance in power and authority between workers within an organization is great. Supervisors do not consult with their subordinates. Subordinates use formal names and titles—"Mr. Smith," "Dr. Jones"—when addressing higher-ranking people.	In cultures with a small distance between ranks, communication is generally less formal. Informal documents (e-mails and memos) are appropriate, and writers often sign their documents with their first names only. Keep in mind, however, that many people in these cultures resent inappropriate informality, such as receiving letters or e-mails addressed "Dear Jim" if they have never met the writer. In cultures with a great distance between ranks, communication is generally formal. Writers tend to use their full professional titles and to prefer formal

⬇

Table 5.1 *(Continued)*

Variable	Explanation	How This Variable Is Reflected in Technical Communication
Distance between ranks *(continued)*	Cultures that focus on individualism and that separate business and private lives tend to have a smaller distance between ranks.	documents (such as letters) to informal ones (such as memos and e-mails). Writers make sure their documents are addressed to the appropriate person and contain the formal design elements (such as title pages and letters of transmittal) that signal their respect for their readers.
Nature of truth	Some cultures feel that truth is a universal concept. An action is either wrong or right. There are no exceptions. If facts are presented clearly and comprehensively, all reasonable readers will understand them in the same way. Other cultures think that truth is a more complex and relative concept, and that reasonable people can have different perspectives on complex ethical issues.	In cultures that take a universal approach to truth, such as the United States, documents tend to be comprehensive and detailed. They spell out the details of the communication, leaving nothing to interpretation. In cultures that take a relative view of truth, documents tend to be less detailed and less conclusive. Discussions might seem vague, as if the writer is unwilling to reach a clear conclusion.
Need to spell out details	Some cultures value full, complete communication. The written text must be comprehensive, containing all the information a reader needs to understand it. These cultures are called *low context.* Other cultures value documents in which some of the details are merely implied. This implicit information is communicated through other forms of communication that draw upon the personal relationship between the reader and the writer, as well as social and business norms that prevail in the culture. These cultures are called *high context.* Low-context cultures tend to be individualistic; high-context cultures tend to be group oriented.	In low-context cultures, writers spell out all the details. Documents are like contracts in that they provide the specific information that indicates the rights and responsibilities of both the writer and the readers and explain procedures in great detail. In high-context cultures, writers tend to omit information that they consider obvious because they don't want to insult the reader. For example, a manual written for people in a high-context culture might not mention that a remote control for a television set requires batteries, because everyone knows that a remote control needs a power source.
Attitudes toward uncertainty	In some cultures, people are comfortable with uncertainty. They communicate less formally and rely less on written policies. In many cases, they rely more on a clear set of guiding principles, as communicated in a code of conduct or a mission statement. In other cultures, people are uncomfortable with uncertainty. Businesses are structured formally, and they use written procedures for communicating.	In cultures that tolerate uncertainty, written communication tends to be less detailed. Oral communication is used to convey more of the information that is vital to the relationship between the writer and the readers. In cultures that value certainty, communication tends to be detailed. Policies are lengthy and specific, and forms are used extensively. Everyone knows what he or she is supposed to do, and there is a wide distance between ranks.

The value of being aware of the variables is that they can help you study the communications from people in that organization and become more aware of underlying values that affect how they will interpret your documents.

Considering Cultural Variables as You Write

The challenge of communicating effectively with a person from another culture is that you are communicating with a person, not a culture. You cannot be sure which cultures have influenced that person (Lovitt, 1999). For example, a 50-year-old Japanese-born manager for the computer-manufacturer Fujitsu in Japan has been shaped by the Japanese culture, but he also has been influenced by the culture of his company and of the Japanese computer industry in general. It is also likely that he has worked outside of Japan for several years and has absorbed influences from another culture.

A further complication is that when you communicate with a person from another culture, to that person *you* are from another culture, and you cannot know how much that person is trying to accommodate your cultural patterns. As Bell (1992) points out, the communication between the two of you is carried out in—and creates—a third, hybrid culture. When you write to a large audience, the complications increase. A group of managers for Fujitsu represents a far more complex mix of cultural influences than one manager for Fujitsu.

No brief discussion of cultural variables can answer questions about how to write for a particular multicultural audience. You need to do your homework on the culture of your readers. Read everything you can about the society. As you plan the document, seek assistance from someone native to the culture who can help you prevent blunders that might confuse or offend your readers.

Start by reading some of the basic guides to communicating with people from other cultures, and study guides to the particular culture you are investigating. In addition, numerous sites on the Internet provide useful guidelines that can help you write to people from another culture. Here, for instance, is an excerpt from a guide to writing letters to the Japanese (Anderson School, 2002):

> A Japanese letter is the reverse of one in the West, in the sense that you proceed first from the general to the specific. You need to begin with the social niceties, with small talk about the weather, the holidays, or some seasonal reference. Include at least a paragraph of such material before getting to the heart of the correspondence. You may begin the business section with a phrase such as: "We are so happy that your business is becoming even more prosperous," and then state your business in a "soft" manner. Even then, do not be overly direct or assertive. Use phrases like: "I am not sure . . . "; "I wonder if . . . "; "I hope this is not too bold a request but. . . . " Also include some sort of reference to the personal, trusting relationship you have both put so much effort into, and how you desire its continuance. Your letter should end with a closing general phrase at the bottom, followed by the date. The date is given in the reverse order of dates in the West: the year, the month, and then the day.

On TechComm Web

For a discussion of communication practices in China, see Coggin, Coggin, and Li's "Living and Working in China: Understanding Communication Requirements." Click on Links Library for Ch. 5 on <bedfordstmartins.com/techcomm>.

If possible, study the documents written by people to whom you will be writing. If you don't have access to documents written by your readers, try to locate documents written in English by people from that culture. Figure 5.7 shows several excerpts from documents on the Internet that provide useful glimpses into cultural variables.

Crafting Graphics and Design for Multicultural Readers

One of the challenges in writing to people from another culture is that they are likely to be nonnative speakers of English. One way to overcome the language barrier is to use effective graphics and design the document effectively.

In This Book

For a discussion of Simplified English, see Ch. 11, p. 259.

In This Book

For more on voice, see Ch. 11, p. 250.

In This Book

For more on graphics, see Ch. 14.

STRATEGIES FOR INTERCULTURAL COMMUNICATION

Writing for Readers from Other Cultures

The following eight guidelines will help you communicate more effectively with multicultural audiences:

- *Limit your vocabulary.* Every word should have only one meaning, as called for in Simplified English and in other basic-English languages.
- *Keep sentences short.* There is no magic number, but try for an average length of no more than 20 words.
- *Define abbreviations and acronyms in a glossary.* Don't assume that your readers know what a GFI (ground fault interrupter) is, because the abbreviation is derived from English vocabulary and word order.
- *Avoid jargon unless you know your readers are familiar with it.* For instance, your readers might not know what a *graphical user interface* is.
- *Avoid idioms and slang.* Because these terms are culture specific, it is wise to avoid them. If you tell your Japanese readers that your company plans to put on a "full court press," most likely they will be confused.
- *Use the active voice whenever possible.* The active voice is easier for nonnative speakers of English to understand than the passive voice.
- *Be careful with graphics.* The garbage-can icon on the Macintosh computer has often been cited as a graphic that does not translate well, because garbage cans have different shapes and can be made of different materials in other countries.
- *Be sure someone from the target culture reviews your document.* Even if you have had help in planning the document, have it reviewed before you publish and distribute it.

Excerpt	Commentary
From a Japanese electronics company (Suzuki, 2002)	
At FDK, we take pride in being a manufacturer who puts great importance on the quality of materials. We make sure that our electronic components satisfy customers, taking full advantage of the advanced material technologies that we have developed over many years.	Notice the direct statement about the importance of satisfying the customer's needs. The Japanese culture stresses building a strong business relationship for the benefit of both parties.
To supply the most suitable products for each customer in the fastest, most economical and efficient way, we utilize CAE (computer-aided engineering) systems for optimal design, purchase parts and command the synergy of production and sales facilities around the world.	Again, the writer stresses satisfying the customer's needs.
Many more innovations are needed in digitization, networking and other fields of electronics if an advanced information society is to become reality in the 21st century. Also, technologies friendly to the global environment are increasingly sought. FDK strives to answer these needs by applying its material technologies and by serving as the customer's best partner in building a safer and more enriching society.	Although this document provides some information about the company, the focus is on how the company will satisfy the customer's needs and, in so doing, build "a safer and more enriching society."
From an administrator for India's railway network (Jain, 2002)	
Indian Railways, the single largest infrastructural organisation under a single management, have evolved highly responsive and effective systems of disaster management of various kinds particularly attributable to a sacred continuing mission of ensuring safety and continuity of rail traffic under all circumstances. Over 150 years of its existence, the Railways have nurtured and perfected an organisational temperament in which every threat to the continuity of the traffic is dealt with in the same manner as if an accident has occurred. Such perceptions are deeply ingrained into the temperament of the Railway personnel cutting across the hierarchical positions and, therefore, each impending disaster is preceded by meticulous planning, mobilization and strategy formulation even before the disaster actually occurs.	The cultural value of service to other people is communicated as early as the first sentence, with its reference to "a sacred continuing mission of ensuring safety and continuity of rail traffic under all circumstances." The writer refers to the railway's long history of excellent service to the people of India. To someone from the United States, references to the employees' "deeply ingrained" attitudes and "meticulous planning" might sound insincere and self-serving. To an Indian audience, these phrases sound perfectly appropriate.
From the head of the Patent Office in Finland (Enäjärvi, 2002)	
Year 2000 has been a good year as concerns the results of the National Board of Patents and Registration of Finland (NBPR) and the further improvement of our client service. As for the productivity of work, however, we simply could not match the result for 1999 which was 12.2%. In 2000, the productivity of work grew by 4.1% and cost per unit dropped by 2.4% (as compared to 1.9% in 1999). Considering that there has been a rise of almost 100% in the productivity of work over the past ten years, it will not be humanly possible to achieve such high figures in the future. Thus the result for 2000 should be considered excellent. For these results and the work being done, I extend my warm thanks to the whole staff of the office.	Although this Finnish manager's use of English does not sound exactly like a native speaker's, his strategy sounds very much like that used in the United States. In reporting that his organization's progress in 2000 was good, he appears to be saying that he is disappointed, but of course he is merely creating an opportunity to remind readers of the extraordinary productivity gains made in 1999. Then he puts the data into perspective and acknowledges the contributions of his colleagues.

■ **Figure 5.7 Passages Reflecting Cultural Variables**

However, the use of graphics and design can differ from culture to culture. A business letter written in Australia uses a different size paper and a different format than a similar letter in the United States. An icon for a file folder in a software program made in the United States could confuse European readers, who use a different size and shape for file folders in offices (Bosley, 1999). A series of graphics arranged left to right could confuse readers from the Middle East, who read from right to left. For this reason, you need to study samples of documents written by people from the culture you are addressing to learn the important differences.

In This Book

For more on design for multicultural readers, see Ch. 13, p. 293. For more on graphics for international readers, see Ch. 14, p. 354.

In recent years, however, documents from different cultures have started to look more like each other in their design and use of graphics. There are three main reasons for this:

- *International business is increasing each year.* Many documents from around the world are crossing people's desks, leading to a homogenization of graphic and design styles.
- *The use of the Web is increasing dramatically.* Documents written by people around the world are routinely distributed on the Web in the form of PDF (portable document format) files, increasing readers' exposure to graphic and design styles.
- *Most communicators around the world are using the same word-processing software.* The templates in the versions of the software sold in different countries are very similar or even identical.

In This Book

For more on templates, see Ch. 3, p. 40.

DETERMINING YOUR PURPOSE

Once you have identified and analyzed your audience, it is time to examine your purpose in writing. Ask yourself this: "What do I want this document to accomplish?" When your readers have finished reading what you have written, what do you want them to *know* or *believe?* What do you want them to *do?* Your writing should help your readers carry out a task, understand a concept, or hold a particular belief.

In defining your purpose, think of a verb that represents it. (Sometimes, of course, you have several purposes.) The following list of examples has been classified into two categories: verbs used to communicate information to your readers and verbs used to convince them to accept a particular point of view.

Communicating Verbs		*Convincing Verbs*
to describe	to outline	to assess
to explain	to authorize	to request
to inform	to define	to propose
to illustrate	to summarize	to recommend
to review		to forecast
		to evaluate

This classification is not absolute. For example, *to review* could in some cases be a *convincing verb* rather than a *communicating verb:* one writer's review of a complicated situation might be very different from another's.

Here are a few examples of how you can use these verbs to clarify the purpose of your document (the verbs are italicized).

> This report *describes* the research project intended to determine the effectiveness of the new waste-treatment filter.

> This letter *authorizes* the purchase of six new PCs for the Jenkintown facility.

> This memo *recommends* that we revise the Web site as soon as possible.

Sometimes your real purpose differs from your expressed purpose. For instance, if your real purpose is to persuade your reader to lease a new computer system rather than purchase it, you might phrase the purpose this way: *to explain the advantages of leasing over purchasing.* As mentioned earlier in the chapter, many readers don't want to be *persuaded* but are willing to learn new facts or ideas.

GAINING MANAGEMENT'S APPROVAL

After you have analyzed your audience and purpose, consider gaining the approval of management before you proceed. The larger and more complex the project and the document, the more sense it makes to be sure that you are on the right track before you invest too much time and effort.

For example, imagine that you are planning the CAD equipment project. You already have a good understanding of your audience and purpose, and you are forming a general outline in your mind. But before you actually start to write an outline or gather the information you will need, spend another 10 or 15 minutes making sure your primary reader agrees with your thinking. You don't want to waste days or even weeks working on a document that won't fulfill its purpose. If you have misunderstood what your supervisor wants, it is far easier to fix the problem at this early stage.

Your statement can also serve another purpose: if you want your reader's views on which of two strategies to pursue, you can describe each one and ask your reader to state a preference.

What should this statement look like? It doesn't matter. You can write an e-mail or a memo, as long as you clearly and briefly state what you are trying to do. Here is an example of the statement you might submit to your boss about the CAD equipment.

Harry:

　　Please tell me if you think this is a good approach for the proposal on CAD equipment. *The purpose of the memo*

　　Outright purchase of the complete system will cost more than $1,000, so you would have to approve it and send it on for Tina's approval. (I'll provide leasing costs *A statement of the audience for the proposal*

Interactive Sample Document:
Examining Cultural Variables in a Business Letter

These two versions of the same business letter were written by a sales manager for an American computer company. The first letter was addressed to a potential customer in the United States; the second version was addressed to a potential customer in Japan. The questions in the margin ask you to think about how the cultural variables affect the nature of evidence, the structure of the letters, and their tone (see pages 93–94). The answers to these questions are available on TechComm Web.

Server Solutions
Cincinnati, OH 46539
Nadine Meyer
Director of Marketing

July 3, 2003

Mr. Philip Henryson
Director of Purchasing
Allied Manufacturing
1321 Industrial Boulevard
Boise, ID 83756

Dear Mr. Henryson:

Thank you for your inquiry about our PowerServer line of servers. I'm happy to answer your questions.

The most popular configuration is our PowerServer 3000. This model is based on the Intel® Xeon processor, ServerSure High-End UltraLite chipset with quad-peer PCI architecture, and embedded RAID. The system comes with our InstallIt system-management CD, which lets you install the server and monitor and manage your network with a simple graphical interface. With six PCI slots, the PowerServer 3000 is equipped with redundant cooling as well as redundant power, and storage expandability to 950 GB. I'm taking the liberty of enclosing the brochure for this system to fill you in on the technical details.

The PowerServer 3000 has performed extremely well on a number of industry benchmark tests. I'm including with this letter copies of feature articles on the system from *PC World, InternetWeek,* and *Windows 2000 Magazine.*

It would be a pleasure for me to arrange for an on-site demo at your convenience. I'll give you a call on Monday to see what dates would be best for you. In the meantime, please do not hesitate to get in touch with me directly if you have any questions about the PowerServer line.

I look forward to talking with you next week.

Sincerely,

Nadine Meyer

Nadine Meyer
Director of Marketing

Attachments:
   "PowerServer 3000 Facts at a Glance"
   "Another Winner from ServerSolutions"
   "Mid-Range Servers for 2003"
   "Four New Dual-Processor Workhorses"

Server Solutions
Cincinnati, OH 46539
Nadine Meyer
Director of Marketing

Mr. Kato Kirisawa
Director of Purchasing
Allied Manufacturing
3-7-32 Kita Urawa
Saitama City
Saitama Pref. 336-0002
Japan

Dear Sir:

It is my sincere hope that you and your loved ones are healthy and enjoying the pleasures of summer. Here in the American Midwest, the warm rays of the summer sun are accompanied by the sounds of happy children playing in the neighborhood swimming pools. I trust that the same pleasant sounds greet you in Saitama City.

Your inquiry about our PowerServer 3000 suggests that your company is growing. Allied Manufacturing has earned a reputation in Japan and all of Asia for a wide range of products manufactured to the most demanding standards of quality. We are not surprised that your company requires new servers that can be expanded to provide fast service for more and more clients.

For more than 15 years, Server Solutions has had the great honor of manufacturing the finest computer servers to meet the needs of our valued customers all over the world. We use only the finest materials and most innovative techniques to ensure that our customers receive the highest quality, uninterrupted service that they have come to expect from us.

One of my great pleasures is to talk with esteemed representatives such as yourself about how Server Solutions can help them meet their needs for the most advanced servers. I would be most gratified if our two companies could enter into an agreement that would be of mutual benefit.

Sincerely,

Nadine Meyer

Nadine Meyer
Director of Marketing

Attachments:
    "PowerServer 3000 Facts at a Glance"
    "Another Winner from ServerSolutions"
    "Mid-Range Servers for 2003"
    "Four New Dual-Processor Workhorses"

2003 July 3

1. How does the difference in the salutation (the "Dear Mr. Smith" part of the letter) reflect a cultural difference?

2. Does the first paragraph have any function beyond delaying the discussion of business?

3. What is the function of telling Mr. Kirisawa about his own company? How does this paragraph help the writer introduce her own company's products?

4. To a reader from the United States, the third paragraph would probably seem thin. What aspect of Japanese culture makes it effective in the context of this letter?

5. Why doesn't the writer make a more explicit sales pitch at the end of the letter?

On TechComm Web

To find the answers to these questions, click on Interactive Sample Documents for Ch. 5 on <bedfordstmartins.com/techcomm>.

A statement of the purpose, followed by early statements of the scope of the document.

as well.) I want to show that our CAD hardware and software are badly out of date and need to be replaced. I'll be thorough in recommending new equipment, with independent evaluations in the literature, as well as product demonstrations. The proposal should specify what the current equipment is costing us and show how much we can save by buying the recommended system.

I'll call you later today to get your reaction before I begin researching what's available.

Renu

In composing this statement, the writer drew on her audience profile sheets of the two principal readers. She describes a logical, rational plan for proposing the equipment purchase.

Once you have received your primary reader's approval, you can feel confident about starting to gather information.

Revision Checklist

Following is a checklist for analyzing your audience and purpose. Remember that your document might be read by one person, several people, a large group, or several groups with various needs.

In analyzing your audience, did you consider the following questions about your most important readers?
- ❏ What is your reader's educational background? (p. 81)
- ❏ What is your reader's professional experience? (p. 83)
- ❏ What is your reader's job responsibility? (p. 83)
- ❏ What are your reader's personal characteristics? (p. 83)
- ❏ What are your reader's personal preferences? (p. 83)
- ❏ What are your reader's cultural characteristics? (p. 83)
- ❏ What is your reader's attitude toward you? (p. 83)

- ❏ What is your reader's attitude toward the subject? (p. 84)
- ❏ What are your reader's expectations about the subject? (p. 84)
- ❏ What are your reader's expectations about the document? (p. 84)
- ❏ Why is your reader reading your document? (p. 84)
- ❏ How will your reader read your document? (p. 85)
- ❏ What is your reader's reading skill? (p. 85)
- ❏ What is the physical environment in which your reader will read your document? (p. 85)

Did you fill out an audience profile sheet for your primary and secondary audiences that considers
- ❏ education? (p. 81)
- ❏ professional experience? (p. 83)
- ❏ cultural characteristics? (p. 83)
- ❏ personal preferences? (p. 83)
- ❏ attitudes toward you and your subject? (p. 84)
- ❏ use of the document? (p. 85)
- ❏ physical environment? (p. 85)

In planning to write for an audience from another culture, did you consider the following cultural variables:

❏ political? (p. 89)
❏ economic? (p. 89)
❏ social? (p. 89)
❏ religious? (p. 89)
❏ educational? (p. 89)
❏ technological? (p. 89)
❏ linguistic? (p. 89)

In planning to write for an audience from another culture, did you consider the other set of cultural variables:

❏ focus on individuals or groups? (p. 91)
❏ distance between business life and private life? (p. 91)
❏ distance between ranks? (p. 91)
❏ nature of truth? (p. 92)
❏ need to spell out details? (p. 92)
❏ attitudes toward uncertainty? (p. 92)

In writing for a multicultural audience, did you

❏ limit your vocabulary? (p. 94)
❏ keep sentences short? (p. 94)
❏ define abbreviations and acronyms in a glossary? (p. 94)
❏ avoid jargon unless you know that your readers are familiar with it? (p. 94)
❏ avoid idioms? (p. 94)
❏ use the active voice whenever possible? (p. 94)
❏ use graphics carefully? (p. 94)
❏ have the document reviewed by someone from the target culture? (p. 94)

❏ Did you consider your purpose in writing and express it in the form of a verb or verbs? (p. 96)

Exercises

On TechComm Web

For more exercises, click on Additional Exercises, Projects, and Cases for Ch. 5 on <bedfordstmartins.com/techcomm>.

1. **Internet Activity** Choose a 200-word passage from a technical article addressed to an expert audience, one related to your major course of study. (You can find a technical article on the Web by using a directory search engine, such as Yahoo!, selecting a subject area such as "science," then selecting "journals." In addition, many federal government agencies publish technical articles and reports on the Web.) Rewrite the passage so that it is clear and interesting to the general reader. Submit the original passage along with your revision.

2. The following passage is an advertisement from a translation service. Revise the passage to make it more appropriate for a multicultural audience.

> If your technical documents have to meet the needs of a global market but you find that most translation houses are swamped by the huge volume, fail to accommodate the various languages you require, or make your deadlines, where do you turn?
>
> Well, your search is over. Translations, Inc. provides comprehensive translations in addition to full-service documentation publishing.
>
> We utilize ultrasophisticated translation programs that can translate a page in a blink of an eye. Then our crack linguists comb each document to give it that personalized touch.
>
> No job too large! No schedule too tight! Give us a call today!

Projects

On TechComm Web

For more projects, click on Additional Exercises, Projects, and Cases for
Ch. 5 on <bedfordstmartins.com/techcomm>.

3. Internet Activity Audience is your primary consideration
in many types of nontechnical writing. Choose a one- or
two-page magazine advertisement or Web site for an
economy car, such as a Geo, and one for a luxury car, such
as a Mercedes. In a memo to your instructor, contrast the
audiences for the two ads according to age, sex, economic
means, hobbies, interests, and leisure activities. In contrasting the two audiences, consider the explicit information in the ads—the writing—as well as the implicit
information—hidden persuaders such as background
scenery, color, lighting, angles, and the situation por-
trayed by any people photographed. Keep in mind that
your purpose is to contrast the two audiences, not merely
to describe the content of the ad or its design. Submit
color photocopies or the original ads from the magazines
or sites along with your memo. (For more on memos, see
Chapter 15, page 378.)

4. Group/Internet Activity Form small groups and study two
Web sites that advertise competing products. For instance,
you might choose the Web sites of two car manufacturers,
two television shows, or two music publishers. Have each
person in the group, working *alone,* compare and contrast
the two sites according to these three criteria:

a. the kind of information they provide: hard, technical
information or more emotional information

b. the use of multimedia such as animation, sound, or
video

c. the amount of interactivity they invite, that is, the extent to which you can participate in activities while
you visit the site

After each person has separately studied the sites and
taken notes about the three points, come together as a
group. Each person should share his or her findings and
then discuss the differences as a group. Which aspects of
these sites cause the most difference in group members'
reactions? Which aspects seemed to elicit the most consistent reactions? In a brief memo to your instructor, describe
and analyze how the two sites were perceived by the different members of the group. (For more on memos, see
Chapter 15, page 378.)

On TechComm Web

For more cases, click on Additional
Exercises, Projects, and Cases for
Ch. 5 on <bedfordstmartins.com
/techcomm>.

C A S E
**Planning an Apology to a Customer from the People's
Republic of China**

You work in the Marketing Department at Zander Instruments, a manufacturer of scientific measurement instruments used in the pharmaceutical,
chemical, and semiconductor industries. Your latest product is an x-ray
scanner used by airlines to inspect cargo pallets to be sure they contain
the cargo that is listed on the cargo manifest and do not contain narcotics
or contraband.

After a negotiation that lasted more than four months, your company
signed a contract to supply 15 of these devices, at a total cost of over $2
million, to China Air, on July 1. In the contract, you agreed to provide complete product documentation, including operating and routine-maintenance
instructions, in Modern Chinese, the written language used in the People's
Republic of China.

It is July 14. Today you received a letter from Haiwang Guo, Director of Operations for China Air, who is unhappy that, although the shipment of scanners arrived on July 1, the Chinese documentation was missing. In its place was a set of documentation in English. The company had planned for a ceremony, to be held July 3 in its Beijing headquarters, to celebrate the purchase and installation of the new scanners at the five major airports the airline serves. Because of the lack of Chinese documentation, the airline was unable to install the equipment by July 3. The ceremony, which had been publicized throughout June, was cancelled on July 2, embarrassing Haiwang Guo and the other China Air managers.

You have learned that the Chinese documentation was delayed because of translation problems. It will be available next week, and you have already arranged to have it hand delivered to Haiwang Guo, complete with a letter of apology. Your company president has asked you to draft that letter. You decide that the first step is to interview a knowledgeable person from the People's Republic to learn what you can about how formal apologies are handled there. One of your former professors is from the People's Republic; you think she might be willing to sit down with you for 10 or 15 minutes. Write a set of questions you would like to ask the professor before drafting the letter. For each question, write a brief paragraph explaining how the answer to the question might help you complete an appropriate letter of apology to China Air. For example, you might want to know whether the letter should be highly formal in its vocabulary. (For more information on letters of complaint and adjustment, see Chapter 15, page 372. For information on interviews, see Chapter 7, page 150.)

6

Communicating
Persuasively

According to Katherine J. Mayberry (2002, p. 166) from the Rochester Institute of Technology, image and reality coincide in persuasive writing:

In successful arguments, writers project an image of intelligence . . . and trustworthiness. There is nothing false or superficial about this kind of image: these qualities cannot be created out of thin air; they must be true reflections of the writer and thus are developed over time and through experience.

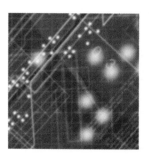

As discussed in Chapter 5, any communication has at least one and perhaps two main purposes: to communicate information and to convince readers to accept a particular viewpoint. Both tasks involve persuasion.

In technical communication, your job is often to convince a reader of a viewpoint—about what factors caused a situation, for example, or what a company ought to do to solve a problem. If you are lucky, you will be reinforcing a viewpoint the reader already has. Sometimes, however, you want to change the reader's mind.

Communicating information also involves persuasion, although in a less obvious way. To increase the chances that your reader will trust that your facts are accurate and appropriate, make sure your document is clear, comprehensive, accessible, correct, and professional in appearance.

Whether you are presenting a viewpoint or communicating information, you are presenting an *argument*: an arrangement of facts and judgments about some aspect of the world.

On TechComm Web

For additional samples, activities, and links related to this chapter, see <bedfordstmartins.com/techcomm>.

CONSIDERING THE CONTEXT OF YOUR ARGUMENT

An argument can be as short as a sentence or as long as a multivolume report. It can take many forms, including oral communication. And it can discuss almost any kind of issue. Here are some examples:

from a description of a construction site:

Features A, B, and C characterize the site.

from a study of why a competitor is outselling your company:

Company X's dominance can be attributed to four major factors: A, B, C, and D.

from a feasibility study considering four courses of action:

Alternative A is better than alternatives B, C, and D.

from a set of instructions for performing a task:

The best and safest way to perform the task is to complete task A, then task B, and so on.

To develop an effective argument, you must understand your audience's broader goals and work within constraints.

Understanding Your Audience's Broader Goals

On TechComm Web

For an excellent discussion of persuasion, see Business Communication: Managing Information and Relationships. Click on Links Library for Ch. 6 on <bedfordstmartins.com/techcomm>.

When you analyze your audience, think about their broader goals. Certainly, most people want their company to prosper, yet most people are also concerned about their own welfare and interests within the company. Your argument is more likely to be effective if it responds to three goals that most people share: security, recognition, and personal and professional growth.

Security   People resist controversial actions that might hurt their own interests. Those who stand to lose their jobs will likely oppose an argument that their division be eliminated, even if there are many valid reasons to support the argument. Another aspect of security is workload; most people resist an argument that calls for them to work more. This resistance is not necessarily a sign of laziness; additional work may be unreasonable because people want to spend time with their families and pursue other interests.

Recognition   People like to be praised for their hard work and their successes. Where appropriate in technical documents, be generous in your praise. Similarly, people hate being humiliated in public. Therefore, allow people to save face. Avoid criticizing their actions or positions and speculating about their motivations. Instead, present your argument as a response to the company's present and future needs. Look ahead, not back, and be diplomatic.

Personal and Professional Growth   People want to develop and grow on the job and in their personal lives. In an obvious way, this means that they want to learn new skills and assume new duties. This desire is also reflected in efforts to improve how the organization treats its employees and customers, relates to the community, and coexists with the environment. Your argument will be more persuasive if you can show how the recommended action will help your organization become an industry leader, for example, or help needy people in your city or reduce environmental pollution. We want to be associated with—and contribute to—organizations that are good at what they do and that help us become better people.

On TechComm Web

To view Fig. 6.1 in context on the Web, click on Links Library for Ch. 6 on <bedfordstmartins.com /techcomm>.

Figure 6.1, from the employment section on the Microsoft Web site, profiles an employee the company believes reflects the personality and character of those who work at Microsoft.

"My personal experience exemplifies the range of opportunities at Microsoft. I've worked on numerous internal information systems, 6 different products that have shipped, and multiple internal testing tools. I've been a Developer, Tester, Lead, and Manager—all in 5 years."

Today, as Test Manager, Patrick loves "pounding on the products to find bugs before the customer sees them. It's technically challenging and often includes complete development cycles of its own. The real bonus is that you have more freedom to choose how you want to solve any particular problem. It's your responsibility to come up with what tools are needed, design them, code them, and run them. Many of these testing tools turn into products of their own which get shipped in resource kits or the retail product itself." But what he finds even more rewarding is seeing the people on his team succeed. "I expect the people working for me to challenge my thoughts and assumptions constantly. I also don't expect people to treat me as a hoop to jump through to get to my manager or others. They are encouraged to go directly to whoever can make the decisions."

Personal and professional growth is the theme of the first paragraph: Patrick Blackburn has had numerous opportunities to grow with the company.

In paragraph two, Blackburn continues the theme of opportunities for personal and professional growth. In addition, he refers to the recognition that he derives from doing an important job that lets him solve problems creatively and act independently.

■ **Figure 6.1   Appealing to an Audience's Broader Goals**

By profiling employee Patrick Blackburn in the employment section of the Microsoft Web site, the company hopes to encourage like-minded people to apply for positions.
Source: Microsoft, 2002 <www.microsoft.com/jobs/people/patrick.htm>.

Working Within Constraints

In planning a persuasive document, you need to work within the constraints that shape your working environment. As a student writer, you routinely work within constraints: the amount of information you can gather for a paper, the required length and format, the due date, and so forth. In business, industry, and government, similar constraints play a role.

Ethical Constraints   Your greatest responsibility is always to your own sense of what constitutes ethical behavior. Being asked to lie or mislead can directly challenge your ethical standards, but in most cases, you have options. Some organizations and professional communities have a published code of conduct. In addition, many large companies have ombudspersons, who help employees resolve ethical conflicts. If you conclude that you are being asked to act unethically, take advantage of the resources available to you.

In This Book

For more on ethical and legal constraints, see Ch. 2.

Legal Constraints   Abide by all applicable laws on labor practices, environmental issues, fair trade, consumer rights, and so forth. If you think the action recommended by your supervisor might be illegal, meet with your organization's legal counsel and, if necessary, attorneys outside the organization.

Political Constraints   Don't spend all your energy and credibility on a losing cause. If you know that your proposal would help the company but that management disagrees with you or that the company can't afford to approve it, try to figure out what you might achieve through some other means, or scale back the idea. Two big exceptions to this rule are matters of ethics and matters of safety. As discussed in Chapter 2, ethical and legal constraints may mean compromise is unacceptable.

Informational Constraints   The most common informational constraint you might face is that the information you need is not available. You might want your organization to buy a piece of equipment, for example, but you can't find reports on the kinds of controlled tests that would convince a skeptical reader.

What do you do? You tell the truth. Explain the situation, weighing the available evidence and carefully noting what is missing. You will lose your most important credential—your credibility—if you unintentionally suggest that your evidence is better than it really is. In the same way, you don't want your readers to think that you don't realize your information is incomplete. They will doubt your technical knowledge.

In This Book

For more on collaboration, see Ch. 4.

Personnel Constraints   The most typical personnel constraint you might face is a lack of access to as many collaborators as you need. In such cases, present a clear and persuasive proposal to hire the personnel you need. However, don't be surprised if you have to make do with fewer people than you want.

Financial Constraints   Financial restraints are related to personnel constraints: if you had unlimited funds, you could hire all the personnel you need. But financial constraints can also affect other kinds of resources: you might not be able to print as many copies of the document as you want, or you might need to settle for black-and-white instead of full color.

In This Book

For more on scheduling, see Ch. 3, p. 38.

Time Constraints   Start by determining the document's deadline. (Sometimes a document will have several intermediate deadlines.) Then create a schedule. Keep in mind that tasks almost always take longer than estimated. And when you collaborate, the number of potential problems increases, because when one person is delayed, others may lack the necessary information to proceed, causing a logjam.

Format and Tone Constraints   You will be expected to work within one additional set of constraints:

- *Format.* Format constraints are limitations on the size, shape, or style of a document. For example, all tables and figures must be presented at the end of the report, or the recipients of a memo must be listed in alphabetical order. If you are writing to someone in your own organization, follow the format constraints described in the company style guide, if there is one, or check similar documents to see what other writers have done. Also ask more-experienced co-workers for their advice. If you are writing to someone outside your organization, learn what you can about that organization's preferences.

- *Tone.* The tone of your writing will be dictated by your relationship to your audience. When addressing superiors, use a formal, polite tone. When addressing peers or subordinates, use a less formal tone but be equally polite.

CRAFTING A PERSUASIVE ARGUMENT

Persuasion is important, whether you wish to affect a reader's attitude or merely present information clearly.

Identifying the Elements of Your Argument

A persuasive argument has three main elements:

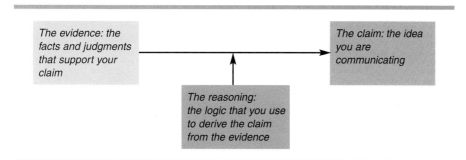

To craft a persuasive argument:

Identify the elements of a persuasive argument.

Use the right kinds of evidence.

Consider opposing viewpoints.

Decide where to present the claim.

The *claim* is the conclusion you want your readers to accept. For example, your claim might be that your company should institute flextime, a scheduling approach that gives employees some flexibility in when they begin and end their workdays. You want your readers to agree with this idea and to take the next steps toward instituting flextime.

The *evidence* is the information you want your readers to consider. For the argument about flextime, the evidence might include the following:

- The turnover rate of our female employees is double that of our male employees.

- At exit interviews, 40 percent of our female employees under the age of 38 state that they quit because they cannot be home for their school-age children.
- Replacing a staff-level employee costs us about one-half the employee's annual salary; replacing a professional-level employee, a whole year's salary.
- Other companies have found that flextime significantly decreases turnover among female employees under the age of 38.
- Other companies have found that flextime has additional benefits and introduces no significant problems.

The *reasoning* is the logic you use to connect the evidence to your claim. In the discussion of flextime, the reasoning involves three links:

- Flextime appears to have reduced the turnover problem among younger female employees at other companies.
- Our company is similar to these other companies.
- Flextime therefore is likely to prove helpful at our company.

Using the Right Kinds of Evidence

People most often react favorably to four kinds of evidence:

- *"Commonsense" arguments.* Here, *commonsense* means, "most people would think that. . . ." The following sentence presents a commonsense argument that flextime is a good idea:

    Flextime makes sense because it gives people more control over how they plan their schedules.

    A commonsense argument appeals to a person's understanding of the world. It says, "I don't have hard evidence to support my conclusion, but it stands to reason that. . . ." In this case, the argument is that people like to have as much control over their time as possible. If your audience's commonsense arguments match yours, your argument is likely to be persuasive.

- *Numerical data.* Numerical data—statistics—are generally more persuasive than commonsense arguments.

    Statistics drawn from the personnel literature (McClellan, 2002) show that, among Fortune 500 companies, flextime decreases turnover by 25–35 percent among female employees younger than 38.

    Notice that the writer states that the study covered many companies, not just one or a handful. If the sample size were small, the claim would be much less persuasive. (The discussion of logical fallacies later in this chapter explains such *hasty generalizations*.)

- *Examples.* An example makes an abstract point more concrete and therefore more vivid and memorable.

  > Mary Saunders tried for weeks to arrange for child care for her two preschoolers that would enable her to start work at 7 A.M., as required at her workplace. The best she could manage was having her children stay with a non-licensed provider. When conditions at that provider led to ear infections in both her children, Mary decided that she could no longer continue working.

  Examples are often used in conjunction with numerical data. The example gives the problem a human dimension, but the argument also requires numerical data to show that the problem is part of a pattern, not a fluke or a coincidence.

- *Expert testimony.* A message from an expert is more persuasive than the same message from someone without credentials. A well-researched article on flextime written by a respected business scholar in a reputable business journal is likely to be persuasive. When you make arguments, you will often cite expert testimony from published sources or interviews you have conducted.

In This Book

For advice on evaluating information from the Internet, see Ch. 7, p. 145.

Considering Opposing Viewpoints

When you present an argument, you need to address opposing points of view. If you are proposing that your company study whether to institute flextime and you know that several of your important readers oppose flextime, you need to consider their objections. If you don't, your opponents will simply conclude that your proposal is flawed because it doesn't address problems associated with flextime.

In meeting the skeptical or hostile reader's possible objections to your case, you can use one of several tactics:

- *The opposing argument is based on illogical reasoning or on inaccurate or incomplete facts.* For instance, you can counter the argument that flextime increases utility bills by citing unbiased research studies showing that it does not.

- *The opposing argument is valid but less powerful than your own.* If you can show that the opposing argument makes sense but is outweighed by your own argument, you appear to be a fair-minded person who understands that reality is complicated. You can counter the argument that flextime reduces carpooling opportunities by showing that only 3 percent of your employees use carpooling, and that three-quarters of these employees favor flextime anyway because of its other advantages.

- *There might be a way to reconcile the two arguments.* If an opposition argument is not invalid or clearly inferior to your own, you can offer to study the situation thoroughly to find a solution that incorporates the best from

Interactive Sample Document:
Confronting Opposing Views

The following passage, excerpted from a statement from the University of Michigan (2001), defends the university's use of race and ethnic background in admitting students. The university's policy is intended to increase the racial and ethnic diversity of its student population, helping prepare students to live in a multicultural world. Opponents claim that the policy is illegal because it is discriminatory: the university admits some less-qualified applicants and denies admission to others who are more-qualified.

The questions in the margin ask you to consider the tactics and tone for responding to a reader's possible objections (as discussed on page 111). The answers to these questions are available on TechComm Web.

1. In this first answer, what strategy is the writer using in addressing an opposing viewpoint?

2. In this second answer, what strategy is the writer using in addressing an opposing viewpoint?

3. Study the writer's tone in this answer. What words and passages undermine the counterargument?

On TechComm Web

To find the answers to these questions, click on Interactive Sample Documents for Ch. 6 on <bedfordstmartins.com/techcomm>.

Q&A re University of Michigan Admissions Policies
Following are answers to some common questions about our admissions processes and the lawsuits we are facing.

Q. Is it lawful for the University to consider race in admissions?
A. Yes, under current law, universities are permitted to take an applicant's race into account. The Supreme Court in its 1978 Bakke ruling said that the educational benefit of diversity is a compelling government interest justifying the use of race as a factor in admissions, as long as all students admitted are fully qualified and their admissions are not based on quotas.

Justice Powell, who wrote the Court's decision in the Bakke case, said race could be used as a "plus factor" in an admissions process. When race is used as a plus factor, it necessarily influences admissions decisions. At its simplest, whenever an adjustment is made for any characteristic, that adjustment may prove to have made a difference in the ultimate admissions decision.

Our consideration of race is legal according to Bakke, because race is only one of many factors that admissions counselors use in selecting students for admission to the University. Our admissions processes do not use quotas, targets or other numeric goals, and only qualified students with a high probability of succeeding at Michigan are offered admission.

Q. Does the University's consideration of race hurt a white student's chances of getting into the University?
A. No. The numbers of minority applicants are extremely small compared to the numbers of white students who apply to the University. The Law School, for example, this past year offered admission to 38 percent of its white applicants and 35 percent of black applicants. Out of a fall 2000 entering class of 367, only 37 students were African American. Similarly, of the approximately 15,000 applications received each year for admissions to the College of Literature, Science & the Arts, only about 1,600 come from underrepresented minorities. It is not mathematically possible that the small numbers of minority students who apply and are admitted are "displacing" a significant number of white students under any scenario.

William Bowen and Derek Bok, in their book "The Shape of the River," look at the nationwide statistics concerning admissions to selective universities. They determined that even if all selective universities used a race-blind admissions system, the probability of being admitted for a white student would go only from 25 percent to 26.2 percent.

Q. Isn't the fact that you're being sued evidence that you're doing something wrong?
A. The Center for Individual Rights (CIR), which brought these two lawsuits, is a special-interest legal organization funded by private sources. It has mounted a campaign of lawsuits and legislative initiatives in an attempt to dismantle affirmative action programs nationwide. CIR doesn't really care how the University considers race in its admissions policies, nor whether 20 points is the right amount to "count" race in our undergraduate admissions system. They find just as much fault with the Law School admissions process, which does not use a point system at all. For CIR, any consideration of race in an attempt to build a diverse educational environment is wrong. We hold a profoundly different view. We believe our system is the best one available to enroll academically qualified students of all races, and furthermore, that it is legal and fair.

Source: University of Michigan, 2001 <www.umich.edu/%7Eurel/admissions/faqs/q&a.html>.

each argument. For example, if flextime might cause serious problems for your company's many carpoolers, you could propose a trial period during which you would study several ways to help employees find other carpooling opportunities. If the company cannot solve the problem, or if most of the employees prefer the old system, you will switch back to it. This proposal can remove much of the threat posed by your ideas. If your argument turns out to be ill advised, you will admit it, and no permanent harm will result.

When you address an opposing argument, be gracious and understated. Focus on the argument. If you embarrass or humiliate your opposition, you undermine your own credibility and motivate your opponents to continue opposing you.

There is no one best place to address opposing arguments. In general, however, if you know that important readers hold opposing views, address those views relatively early in your argument. Your goal is to show *all* your readers that you are a fair-minded person who has thought carefully about the subject and that your argument is stronger than the opposing arguments.

Deciding Where to Present the Claim

In most cases, the best place to state your claim is at the start of the argument. Then provide the evidence and, if appropriate, the reasoning. Sometimes, however, it is more effective to place the claim *after* the evidence and the reasoning. This indirect structure works best if a large number of readers oppose your claim. If you present your claim right away, these readers might become alienated and stop paying attention. You want a chance to present your evidence and your reasoning without causing this kind of undesirable reaction.

AVOIDING LOGICAL FALLACIES

Logical fallacies can undercut the persuasiveness of your writing. Table 6.1 explains some of the most common logical fallacies.

■ **Table 6.1   Common Logical Fallacies**

Fallacy	Explanation	Example and Comment
Ad hominem, also called *argument against the speaker*	Argument against the writer, not the writer's argument.	"Of course Matthew favors buying more computers—he's crazy about computers."
		The fact that Matthew loves computers doesn't necessarily mean that his argument for buying more computers is unwise.

⬇

Table 6.1 *(Continued)*

Fallacy	Explanation	Example and Comment
Argument from ignorance	A claim is true because it has never been proven false, or false because it has never been proven true.	"Nobody has ever proven that global warming is occurring. Therefore, global warming is a myth." The fact that a concept has not yet been proven does not necessarily mean that it is false. Perhaps the measurement techniques are insufficiently precise or not yet available.
Appeal to pity	An argument based on emotion, not reasons.	"We shouldn't sell the Ridgeway division. It's been part of the company for over forty years." The fact that the division has long been a part of the company is not in itself a good reason to retain it.
Argument from authority	An argument that a claim is valid because the person making the claim is an authority.	"According to Dr. Smith, global warming is definitely a fact." Even if Dr. Smith is a recognized authority in this field, saying that global warming is a fact is not valid unless you present a valid argument to support it.
Circular argument, also called *begging the question*	An argument that assumes what it is attempting to prove.	"Compaq is more successful than its competitors because of its consistently high sales." Because "more successful" means roughly the same thing as achieving "consistently high sales," this statement says only that Compaq outsells its competitors. The writer needs to explain *why* Compaq outsells its competitors and is therefore more successful.
Either-or argument	An argument that poses only two alternatives when in fact there might be more.	"If we don't start selling our products online, we're going to be out of business within a year." This statement does not explain why these are the only two alternatives. The company might improve its sales by taking measures other than selling online.
Ad populum argument, also called the *bandwagon argument*	An argument that a claim is valid because many people think it is or act as if it is.	"Our four major competitors have started selling online. We should too." The fact that our competitors are selling online is not in itself an argument that we should.

Fallacy	Explanation	Example and Comment
Hasty generalization, sometimes called *inadequate sampling*	An argument that draws conclusions on the basis of an insufficient number of cases.	"The new Gull is an unreliable car. Two of my friends own Gulls, and both have had reliability problems." Before reaching any valid conclusions, you would have to study a much larger sample and compare your findings with those for other cars in the Gull's class.
Post-hoc reasoning (the complete phrase is *post hoc, ergo propter hoc*)	An argument that claims that, because A precedes B, A caused B.	"There must be something wrong with the new circuit breaker in the office. Ever since we had it installed, the air conditioners haven't worked right." Maybe the air conditioners are malfunctioning because of the circuit breaker, but the malfunctioning might have other causes.
Oversimplifying	An argument that omits important information in establishing a causal link.	"The way to solve the balance-of-trade problem is to improve the quality of the products we produce." Although improving quality is important, international trade balances are determined by many factors, including tariffs and currency rates, and therefore cannot be explained by simple cause-and-effect reasoning.

PRESENTING YOURSELF EFFECTIVELY

A big part of presenting yourself effectively is showing that you know the appropriate facts and theories about your subject. However, you also need to come across as a professional.

The following paragraph shows how a writer can demonstrate the qualities of cooperativeness, moderation, fair-mindedness, and modesty:

This plan is certainly not perfect. For one thing, it calls for a greater up-front investment than we had anticipated. And the return-on-investment through the first three quarters is likely to fall short of our initial goals. However, I think this plan is the best of the three alternatives for the following reasons. . . . Therefore, I recommend that we begin planning immediately to implement the plan. I am confident that this plan will enable us to enter the flat-screen market successfully, building on our fine reputation for high-quality advanced electronics.

In the first three sentences, the writer acknowledges the problems with his recommendation.

The use of "I think" adds an attractive modesty; the recommendation might be unwise.

The recommendation itself is moderate; the writer does not claim that the plan will save the world.

In the last two sentences, the writer shows a spirit of cooperativeness by focusing on the company's goals.

GUIDELINES

Creating a Professional Persona

Your *persona* is how you appear to your readers. Demonstrating the following characteristics will help you establish an attractive professional persona.

▶ *Cooperativeness.* Make clear that your goal is to solve a problem, not advance your own interests.

▶ *Moderation.* Be moderate in your judgments. The problem you are describing will not likely spell doom for your organization, and the solution you propose will not solve all the company's problems.

▶ *Fair-mindedness.* Acknowledge the strengths of opposing points of view, even as you offer counterarguments.

▶ *Modesty.* If you fail to acknowledge that you don't know everything, someone else will be sure to volunteer that insight.

STRATEGIES FOR INTERCULTURAL COMMUNICATION

Persuading Multicultural Audiences

As discussed in Chapter 5, cultures differ significantly in matters such as business customs and also in their most fundamental values. These differences also affect persuasive writing. Culture determines two factors:

• *What makes an argument persuasive.* Statistics and experimental data are fundamental kinds of evidence in the West, but testimony from respected authority figures is much more persuasive in the East.

• *How to structure an argument.* In a Western culture, the claim is usually presented up front. In an Eastern culture, it is likely to be delayed or to remain unstated but implied.

When you write for an audience from another culture, use two techniques:

• Study that culture and adjust the content, structure, and style of your arguments.

• Include in your budget the cost of having your important documents reviewed and edited by a person from the target culture. Few people are experts on cultures other than their own.

USING GRAPHICS AND DESIGN AS PERSUASIVE ELEMENTS

Graphics and design elements are fundamentally important in communicating persuasively because they help you convey both technical data and nontechnical information. Figure 6.2, for example, shows a typical combination of verbal and visual techniques used to make a persuasive argument on a corporate Web page.

Graphics and design can also be used to present evidence in a less technical way. Figure 6.3 on page 118 shows a portion of the main page from a cruise line's Web site.

product information

→ summary

→ specifications

  product benefits

→ warranty

→ what they're saying

The claim in this screen is that the computer is easy to use. The first piece of evidence is the photo of the happy user.

easy to deploy

With 9 to 12 month product lifecycles, stable software images, and tools and services to centrally build and deploy your notebooks, the HP Professional line helps you reduce the workload and cost of deployment.

→ view the easy to deploy demonstration   more information

The claim is elaborated in the blue boxes. The first box elaborates the claim that the computer is "easy to deploy."

easy to manage

Every professional line PC, Notebook, or e-pc from HP comes with HP Toptools to let you manage HP and non-HP PCs as well as servers, printers and more. Combining the built-in manageability of HP professional line with HP Toptools enables fewer IT resources to manage more PCs. It complements, and integrates with, other network and software management solutions such as HP OpenView, and Microsoft SMS.

→ view the easy to manage demonstration   more information

After a paragraph presenting the evidence for this claim, the designer presents two links — one to see a demonstration and one to find more evidence — that are intended to further support the claim.

■ **Figure 6.2   Verbal and Visual Techniques in Persuasion**

This screen shows the product-benefits page for a notebook computer.
Source: Hewlett Packard Corporation, 2002 <www.hp.com/notebooks/us/eng/products/omnibook_6100/omnibook_6100_benefits.htm>.

The Bridge Cams—live video from the ships—give a sense of the cruise experience.

The three snapshots suggest the range of experiences to be enjoyed on a Princess cruise.

The photograph behind the three snapshots evokes the feeling of standing on the deck, looking out at the limitless sea.

■ **Figure 6.3   Graphics and Design Used to Create a Persuasive Message**

In this sample, the words do some of the persuasive work, but the graphics and design do much more of it. The photographs and the live videos are the main persuasive elements.
Source: Princess Cruises, 2001 <www.princess.com/home.jsp>.

LINKING PERSUASION AND ETHICS

The young actor asks the old actor, "What's the key to great acting?" The old actor replies, "Sincerity. Once you learn how to fake sincerity, . . ." Any discussion of image and persuasion has to address the question at the heart of this old joke. Does a writer have to be cooperative to appear cooperative?

Well, not really. There are tricks for appearing cooperative, and they can work for a while. But the easiest way to appear honest and cooperative is to *be* honest and cooperative. As suggested in Chapter 2, you need to tell the truth and not mislead your readers. As suggested in Chapter 4, you need to be cooperative, diplomatic, and constructive. And as suggested in this chapter, you need to remember people's broader goals: to protect their own security, to achieve recognition, and to learn and grow in their professional lives.

A LOOK AT SEVERAL PERSUASIVE ARGUMENTS

The following examples of technical communication show how the persuasive elements of an argument differ depending on a writer's purpose. Figure 6.4 presents two paragraphs from a student's job-application letter.

Figure 6.5, a statement about the AT&T Foundation's disaster-relief program, illustrates an effective use of tone and evidence.

At Western State University, I have earned 87 credits toward a degree in Technical Communication. I have been a full-time student (no fewer than 12 credit hours per semester) while working full time for the Northwest Watershed Research Center. The four upper-division courses I am taking this semester, including Advanced Technical Communication and Technical Editing, are required for the B.A. in Technical Communication.

In addition to my formal education, I have completed 34 training courses on the job. These courses have included diverse topics such as financial management, the Fair Labor Standards Act, the Americans with Disabilities Act, career-development opportunities in public affairs, and software applications such as MS Office, Quark Xpress, and RoboHelp.

Without making her claim explicit, the writer presents evidence that she is hardworking and lets the prospective employer draw his or her own conclusions.

In listing some of the training courses she has taken, the writer supports an earlier claim that her broad background might be of use to her next employer.

■ **Figure 6.4   Persuading a Prospective Employer**

A student writer uses specific examples in an effort to persuade a prospective employer.

Lending a Helping Hand

At no time does AT&T's largesse shine more brightly than in the aftermath of natural disasters. When natural disasters strike not only are our employees ready to respond rapidly, the company has established funding criteria that facilitate immediate action. In the last two years, AT&T and its employees responded to disasters that included floods, tornadoes, hurricanes, and earthquakes in Texas, Florida, Puerto Rico, Central America, and China. AT&T also has a long-standing relationship with the <u>American Red Cross</u> to support relief efforts with donations, volunteers and services.

Local community health and human services needs are primarily addressed through annual grants to local United Ways. In 2000, the AT&T Foundation contributed $4 million and employee contributions totaled $7.9 million. AT&T is among the top contributors to <u>United Way</u> with total contributions since 1984 exceeding $110 million.

The statement begins with a general comment about AT&T's commitment to disaster relief.

Notice how the photograph of two people in front of a damaged building gives AT&T a human "face."

Then the statement gives evidence of this commitment in the form of a list of disasters to which the company responded.

The statement concludes with impressive numerical data to support the claim that the company is a good corporate citizen.

■ **Figure 6.5   Persuading Employees and Customers**

Published on AT&T's Web site, this statement aims to persuade readers that AT&T is a socially responsible company.
Source: AT&T Foundation, 2002 <www.att.com/foundation/programs/community.html>.

Revision Checklist

In analyzing your audience, did you consider their broader goals of
❏ maintaining security? (p. 106)
❏ achieving recognition? (p. 106)
❏ growing personally and professionally? (p. 106)

In planning, did you consider the following constraints:
❏ ethical? (p. 107)
❏ legal? (p. 107)
❏ political? (p. 108)
❏ informational? (p. 108)
❏ personnel? (p. 108)
❏ financial? (p. 108)
❏ time? (p. 108)
❏ format and tone? (p. 108)

In crafting a persuasive argument, did you
❏ use the three-part structure of claim, evidence, and reasoning? (p. 109)
❏ choose the appropriate kinds of evidence? (p. 110)
❏ consider opposing viewpoints? (p. 111)
❏ decide where to present the claim? (p. 113)

In writing the argument, did you avoid the following logical fallacies:
❏ *ad hominem* argument? (p. 113)
❏ argument from ignorance? (p. 114)
❏ appeal to pity? (p. 114)
❏ argument from authority? (p. 114)
❏ circular argument? (p. 114)
❏ either-or argument? (p. 114)
❏ *ad populum* argument? (p. 114)
❏ hasty generalization? (p. 115)
❏ *post-hoc* reasoning? (p. 115)
❏ oversimplifying? (p. 115)

In drafting your argument, did you create a persona that is
❏ cooperative? (p. 116)
❏ moderate? (p. 116)
❏ fair-minded? (p. 116)
❏ modest? (p. 116)

In addressing a multicultural audience, did you consider
❏ what types of evidence and what argument structures would be most effective? (p. 116)

Exercises

On TechComm Web

For more exercises, click on Additional Exercises, Projects, and Cases for Ch. 6 on <bedfordstmartins.com/techcomm>.

1. **Internet Activity**   Visit the Web site of a car manufacturer, such as Ford <www.ford.com> or Mercedes Benz <www.mbusa.com>. Identify the major techniques of persuasion used in the words and graphics on the site. For example, what claims are made? What types of evidence are used? Is the reasoning sound?

2. For each of the following items, write one paragraph identifying the logical flaw:

   a. The election couldn't have been fair—I don't know anyone who voted for the winner.

   b. It would be wrong to prosecute Allied for age discrimination; Allied has always been a great corporate neighbor.

   c. Increased restrictions on smoking in public are responsible for the decrease in smoking.

   d. Bill Jensen's proposal to create an on-site day-care center is just the latest of his hare-brained ideas.

   e. Since the introduction of cola drinks at the start of this century, cancer has become the second greatest killer in the United States. Cola drinks should be outlawed.

   f. If mutual-fund guru Peter Lynch recommends this investment, I think we ought to buy it.

   g. We should not go into the DRAM market; we have always been a leading manufacturer of integrated processors.

   h. The other two hospitals in the city have implemented computerized patient recordkeeping; I think we need to do so, too.

   i. Our Model X500 didn't succeed because we failed to sell a sufficient number of units.

   j. No research has ever established that Internet businesses can earn money; they will never succeed.

Project

On TechComm Web

For more projects, click on Additional Exercises, Projects, and Cases for Ch. 6 on <bedfordstmartins.com/techcomm>.

3. **Group Activity**   Form groups of two for this research project on multicultural communication styles. Follow these steps:

   a. Each person in the group will secure a document written in English by a person working in a company or government agency outside the United States. Using a search engine, enter the name of a country and the word *business*. For example, enter *Nicaragua business*. Find the Web site of a business, then print out the About the Company page or some similar page, such as Mission or Projects. Or enter the name of a country and the word *government*, such as *Nicaragua government*. Find a government agency that has published a report that is available on the Internet. Print several pages of the report.

   b. On your copy of the pages you have printed, disguise the country of origin by blacking out the name of the company or government agency and any other information that would indicate the country of origin of the document.

   c. Exchange pages with the other person from your group. Study your partner's pages. Do the pages show a different strategy of persuasion than you would expect from a writer in the United States? For instance, does the writer support his or her claims with the kind of evidence you would expect to see in the United States? Is the organization of the information as you would expect it to be in the United States? Does the writer create a persona as you would expect to see in the United States?

   d. Meet with your partner and explain to him or her what you see in the pages that is similar or different from what you would expect if the document came from the United States. Ask your partner whether he or she saw the same things. Present your findings in a memo to your instructor. (For more on memos, see Chapter 15, page 378.)

CASE
Being Persuasive about Privacy

You and the other members of your group are in the Corporate Communications department at Lucent, which posts on its Web site the following privacy statement (Lucent, 2002). Your new supervisor, Andrew Dugan, has asked you to take a look at it. "I'm not wild about this statement," he tells you. "Right from the first paragraph, where it says we want to balance the benefits of e-commerce and our customers' right to privacy, something seems off. Would you mind studying the statement and getting back to me on whether it's got some problems and how we could fix it?" Identify those elements of persuasion that are used effectively—and those that are used ineffectively—and write a memo responding to Mr. Dugan's request. (For more on memos, see Chapter 15, page 378.)

Lucent Technologies Privacy Statement

Lucent Technologies Inc. has long recognized that individuals with whom we conduct business value their privacy. However, in order to conduct global business in this increasingly electronic economy, the collection of personal

On TechComm Web

For more cases, click on Additional Exercises, Projects, and Cases for Ch. 6 on <bedfordstmartins.com/techcomm>.

information is often necessary and desirable. It is Lucent's goal to balance the benefits of e-commerce with the right of individuals to prevent the misuse of their personal information.

The Collection of Personal Information

In some circumstances, Lucent may request personal information from you, like your name, e-mail address, company name, or telephone number. Your response to these inquiries is strictly voluntary. Lucent uses this information to customize your experience on our Web site. In addition, Lucent may use this information for other business purposes, such as to alerting you to products and services that can assist you in your business, promoting site registration, and assisting in order processing.

In general, you can visit our site without divulging any personal information. However, there are areas of this site that require this information to complete their customization functions, and may not be available to those choosing not to reveal the information requested.

Collecting Domain Information

Lucent also collects domain information as part of its analysis of the use of this site. This data enables us to become more familiar with which customers visit our site, how often they visit, and what parts of the site they visit most often. Lucent uses this information to improve its Web-based offerings. This information is collected automatically and requires no action on your part.

Disclosure to Third Parties

In cases where we believe your business interests will be served, Lucent may share your information (with the exception of account, credit card, and ordering information) with Lucent BusinessPartners, who can alert you about new products and services to improve your competitive edge. If you receive unwanted marketing materials from any of our BusinessPartners, please let them know that you wish to be removed from their contact list.

Use of Cookies

Some pages on this site use "cookies," which are small files that the site places on your hard drive for identification purposes. These files are used for site registration and customization the next time you visit us. You should note that cookies cannot read data off of your hard drive. Your Web browser may allow you to be notified when you are receiving a cookie, giving you the choice to accept it or not. By not accepting cookies, some pages may not fully function and you may not be able to access certain information on this site.

Researching Your Subject

7

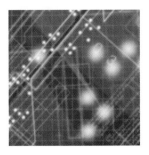

University at Albany librarian Laura Cohen (2002) on the hit-or-miss nature of Internet research:

The Internet is a self-publishing medium. This means that anyone with a small amount of technical skill and access to a host computer can publish on the Internet. It is important to remember this when you locate sites in the course of your research. Internet sites change over time according to the commitment and inclination of the creator. Some sites demonstrate an expert's knowledge, while others are amateur efforts. Some may be updated daily, while others may be outdated.

On TechComm Web

For additional samples, activities, and links related to this chapter, see <bedfordstmartins.com/techcomm>.

One of the main points in Chapter 6 was that persuasive arguments require clear and compelling evidence. This chapter focuses on conducting *primary research* and *secondary research* to find information to use as evidence. Primary research involves creating technical information yourself. Secondary research involves collecting information that other people have discovered or created. The most common ways to perform secondary research are to read books and journals and search the Internet, but researchers also talk with colleagues, consult databases, and attend conferences.

This chapter presents secondary research first. Only rarely would you conduct primary research before doing secondary research. To design the experiments or the field research that goes into primary research, you need a thorough understanding of the information that already exists about your subject.

NARROWING A TOPIC

Before you begin researching a topic, be sure the topic is sufficiently focused so that you can find useful information that will meet your audience's needs.

GUIDELINES

Narrowing a Topic

Use these techniques to narrow a broad topic.

▶ *Examine your own interest in the subject.* You will do a better job researching a topic that interests you. For example, a recent assault on campus may have piqued your interest in studying student awareness of the nature and extent of campus crime.

⬇

▶ *Perform secondary research to learn more about the issues.* Your next step is to learn as much as you can about your topic—in this case, campus crime—by reading books, articles, and Web sites. This research will help you learn about the many issues involved in campus crime. You will find that a tremendous amount of information is available on this topic, including studies that describe what campus crime is, what causes it, and how to reduce it.

▶ *Narrow the topic by subject, time, place, or event.* In your research, you might find several articles about the 1998 Amendment to the Family Education Rights and Privacy Act (FERPA). The amendment allows colleges and universities to withhold student disciplinary records— including criminal records—from law-enforcement agencies. This aspect of your topic gives you a way to focus your discussion of campus crime. You can also narrow the topic by time (campus crime over the last two years), by place (crime on your campus), or by event (a burglary of computer equipment from a lab on your campus last month).

▶ *Formulate a research question.* You can see whether your topic is sufficiently narrow by trying to formulate a research question.

TOO BROAD	"What is the 1998 Amendment to the Family Education Rights and Privacy Act (FERPA)?"
SUFFICIENTLY NARROW	"Would modifying the 1998 Amendment to the Family Education Rights and Privacy Act (FERPA) reduce campus crime?"

PLANNING A RESEARCH STRATEGY

How do you determine what kind of information you need for your document? Think about three factors:

- *Your audience.* Are your most important readers experts, technicians, managers, or general readers? What are their personal characteristics, their attitudes toward your subject, their motivations for reading? If you are writing to an expert audience that might be skeptical about your message, you need to do a lot of research to gather the evidence for a convincing argument.

- *Your purpose.* Why are you writing? Understanding your purpose often helps you understand the types of information readers will expect. For example, if you are proposing that your company investigate buying new equipment, you need to gather the kinds of information usually presented in proposals: expert opinions on your subject, management plans for carrying out the project, budget information, and so forth.

In This Book

For more on audience and purpose, see Ch. 5.

In This Book

For more about ways to generate ideas about your topic, see Ch. 3, p. 34.

- *Your subject.* What do you already know about your subject? What do you still need to find out? Using techniques such as freewriting and brainstorming, you can determine those aspects of the subject you need to investigate.

Your ideas about your audience, purpose, and subject will develop and change as you get further into the project. Students often think that, once they do their research, they're done with that phase of the project. In fact, the process of researching a subject and writing a document is anything but linear. During the drafting stage or even the revision stage, you might realize that you need to do more research. Experienced writers know that they're done researching only when they see the final draft of the document slide out of the printer.

GUIDELINES

Understanding How to Plan a Research Strategy

If you plan your research strategy carefully, the whole project will flow smoothly. Follow these nine steps:

1. *Work out a schedule and a budget for the project that requires the research.* When is the deliverable—the document or the presentation—due? Do you have a budget for phone calls, database searches, or travel to libraries or other sites?

2. *Visualize the deliverable.* What kind of document will you need to deliver: a proposal, a report, a Web site? What kind of oral presentation will you need to deliver?

3. *Determine what information will need to be part of that deliverable.* Draft an outline of the contents, focusing on the kinds of information that readers will expect to see in each part. For instance, if you are going to make a presentation to your supervisors about the use of e-mail in your company, your audience will expect specific information about the number of e-mails written and received by company employees, as well as the amount of time employees spend reading and writing it.

4. *Determine what information you still need to acquire.* Make a list of the pieces of information you don't have. For instance, for the e-mail presentation, you might realize that you have anecdotal information about employee use of e-mail (everyone seems to use it a lot), but you don't have any specifics.

5. *Create questions you need to answer.* Make a list of questions, such as the following:

   - How many e-mails are written each day in our company?
   - How many people receive each e-mail?

- How much server space is devoted to e-mails?

- How much time do people in each department spend writing and reading e-mail?

Writing the questions in a list forces you to think carefully about your topic. One question suggests another, and soon you have a lengthy list that you need to answer.

6. *Conduct secondary research.* For the e-mail presentation, you want to find out about e-mail usage in organizations similar to yours and what policies these organizations are implementing. You can find this information in journal articles and from Web-based sources, such as online journals, discussion groups, and bulletin boards.

7. *Conduct primary research.* You can answer some of your questions by consulting company records, by interviewing experts (such as the people in the Information Technology department in your company), and by conducting surveys and interviews of representative employees.

8. *Evaluate your information.* As discussed later in this chapter, once you have your information, you need to evaluate its quality: is it accurate, comprehensive, unbiased, and current?

9. *Do more research.* If the information you have acquired doesn't sufficiently answer your questions, do more research. And, if you have thought of additional questions that need to be answered, do more research. When do you stop doing research? You will stop only when you think you have enough high-quality information to create the deliverable. For this reason, you will need to establish and stick to a schedule that will allow for multiple phases of research.

STRATEGIES FOR INTERCULTURAL COMMUNICATION

Planning a Research Strategy for Multicultural Audiences

As discussed in Chapters 5 and 6, readers bring their cultural values to the documents they read. For readers from some cultures, persuasion depends more on authority and tradition than on statistical evidence. When you plan a research strategy, think about what kinds of evidence your readers will consider appropriate. If you are writing to European readers about telemedicine, for instance, try to find information from European authorities and about European telemedicine. This information will interest your readers and will likely reflect their cultural values and expectations.

CONDUCTING SECONDARY RESEARCH

On TechComm Web

Finding reliable sources is easier if you start searching from a reputable list of links, such as that of the WWW Virtual Library, sponsored by the World Wide Web Consortium. Click on Links Library for Ch. 7 on <bedfordstmartins .com/techcomm>.

For students, the best place to find information is a college or university library. Most college libraries have substantial reference collections and receive the major professional journals. Large universities have more-comprehensive collections. Many large universities have specialized libraries that complement selected graduate programs, such as those in zoology or architecture. Large cities often have special scientific or business libraries that are open to the public.

In addition, libraries often have their own Web sites. These sites typically offer access to the library's holdings as well as to reliable databases and other online sources. Because librarians have selected these sources for their quality, library Web sites are one of the most reliable starting points on the Internet.

For professionals, the best place to begin a search might be the organization's information center. An *information center* is the organization's library, a resource that collects different kinds of information critical to the organization's operations.

At both public and private libraries, the most important information sources are the reference librarians. They are always willing to suggest resources—specialized directories, bibliographies, or collections that you didn't know existed. They can also assist you in using online databases. And they will tell you if the library doesn't have the information you need and suggest other libraries to try.

Understanding the Research Media

Media used to publish information:

Print

Online databases

Digital disks, such as CD-ROM

Web sites

Online discussion groups

Today, most technical information is being distributed not only in print but also through one or several digital media. For instance, the federal government is likely to publish census information in printed reports and books, on CDs, and on Web sites.

You will probably use information published in five major media.

Print   Books, journals, reports, and other documents will continue to be produced in print because printed information is portable, and you can write on it. For documents that do not need to be updated periodically, print remains a useful and popular medium. And to find it you will continue to use online catalogs, as you do now.

Online Databases   Most libraries—even many public libraries—have facilities for online searching. The largest database service is DIALOG Information Services, which offers electronic access to more than 6 billion pages of articles, conference proceedings, news, and statistics in scientific, technical, and medical literature, as well as business, trade, and academic studies. DIALOG also provides access to more than 100 full-text newspapers and thousands of magazines and journals in more than 900 databases. The big disadvantage of commercial online databases is their expense; a simple search can cost more than $50.

For information on database services, see the journal *Online*. For information on how to use databases, see the *Gale Directory of Databases and Information Companies* (Detroit: Gale, 2002). Or search the Web using the "reference" category of a directory search engine.

Digital Disks   Digital disks, including DVD and CD-ROM, are likely to become the dominant form of information storage in all research libraries because of their low cost and small size. Currently, digital disks are used primarily to store research tools such as indexes, abstract services, and reference texts. However, full-text disks—holding the full texts of journal articles and books—are fast coming on the market. *Fulltext Sources Online* (Medford, NJ: Information Today), a semiannual directory, lists 15,000 journals, newspapers, newsletters, and television and radio transcripts available in full text online.

Web Sites   Because there are so many Web sites—some 36 million in 2002 (Zakon, 2002)—searching for information on the Web can be a challenge. As one anonymous writer put it, the Web "is an enormous library in which someone has turned out the lights and tipped the index cards all over the floor." It takes practice to learn to use the Web effectively.

There are three basic ways to locate Web sites: enter the URL of the site you wish to visit; enter a keyword or phrase in a search engine; or use a directory search engine to do a subject search. Figures 7.1 through 7.6 show how to use Web pages to conduct research.

Online Discussion Groups   There are two major forums for online discussions: Usenet newsgroups and electronic mailing lists.

Usenet newsgroups, sometimes called *bulletin boards,* publish e-mail messages sent by members of the group. Newsgroups give participants an opportunity to discuss issues, ask questions, and get answers. Usenet consists of thousands of newsgroups organized according to 10 basic categories, including computer science, science, recreation, and business. In a Usenet newsgroup, mail is not sent to individual computers but stored on databases, which you then access.

Electronic mailing lists are like newsgroups in that they publish e-mail messages sent by members. The basic difference is that mailing lists send e-mail messages to every person who subscribes. The mail comes to you; you don't go to it, as you do with a newsgroup.

Discussions on newsgroups and electronic mailing lists vary greatly in quality. Discussions on topics such as astronomy tend to contain high-level talk by experts from universities, research institutes, and the government. Discussions on topics such as UFOs or *Star Trek* tend not to.

On TechComm Web

To find the Gale Directory, click on Links Library for Ch. 7 on <bedfordstmartins.com/techcomm>.

On TechComm Web

To link to Fulltext Sources Online, click on Links Library for Ch. 7 on <bedfordstmartins.com/techcomm>.

On TechComm Web

For more information on search engines, click on Links Library for Ch. 7 on <bedfordstmartins.com/techcomm>.

On TechComm Web

For sites that list online discussion groups, click on Links Library for Ch. 7 on <bedfordstmartins.com/techcomm>.

Google, one of the most popular search engines, lets you search the entire Web for any kind of information, or only for images, or only for newsgroups. It includes a directory, which is a list of subjects that you can browse.

Type your keywords here.

Using an advanced search can save you time and frustration. (See Figure 7.2.)

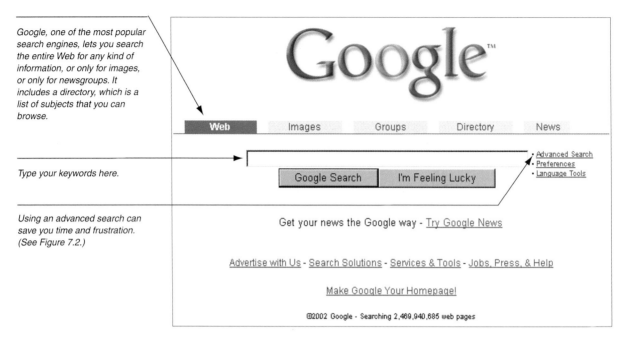

■ **Figure 7.1   The First Screen of a Search Engine**

Source: Google, 2002 <www.google.com>.

Advanced searches let you customize the search in a number of ways.

The search engine automates the Boolean operators: the "and," "or," and "not" parameters that let you specify the keyword search.

The pull-down menus let you customize the search according to a number of parameters, including language, date, and kind of information contained in the site.

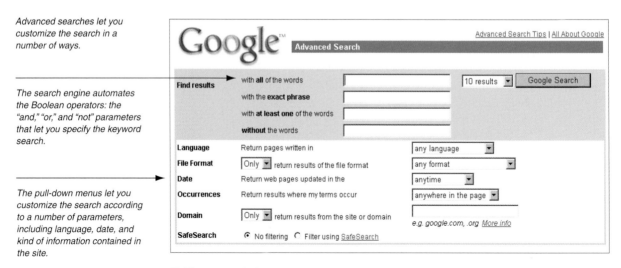

■ **Figure 7.2   Using the Advanced Search Function of a Search Engine**

Source: Google, 2002 <www.google.com/advanced_search?hl=en>.

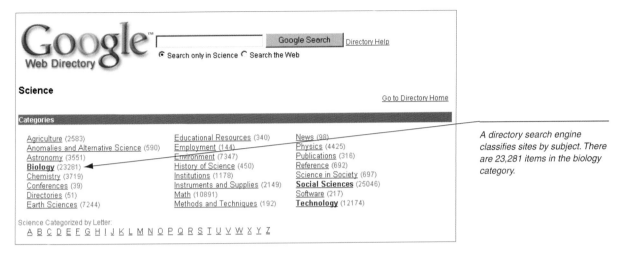

A directory search engine classifies sites by subject. There are 23,281 items in the biology category.

■ **Figure 7.3   Directory Listings**

Use the listings to drill down deeper into the Web. This screen shows Google's listings for its science category.
Source: Google, 2002 <http://directory.google.com/Top/Science/>.

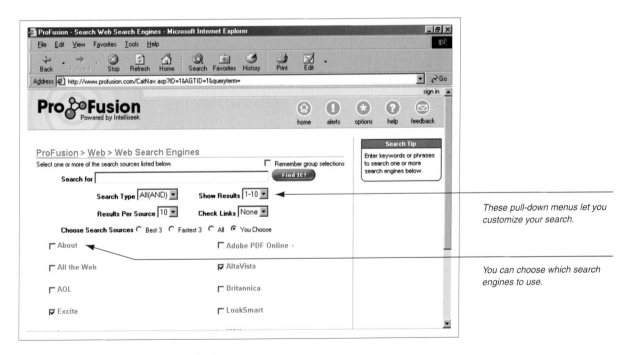

These pull-down menus let you customize your search.

You can choose which search engines to use.

■ **Figure 7.4   Using a Metasearch Engine**

Metasearch engines, such as ProFusion.com, submit your keywords to a number of different search engines at once.
Source: ProFusion.com, 2002 <www.profusion.com/CatNav.asp?ID=1&AGTID=1&queryterm=>.

If you get a message indicating that the site you want is not at the address where you think it should be, first check your spelling of the URL. Also try checking back later: the server could be overloaded or down for maintenance.

Then try pruning the URL by removing "ezeditor.htm" and trying again. If that doesn't work, remove "products" too. Eventually, you may end up at the organization's home page, where you might be able to use a site map or index to find the pages you want.

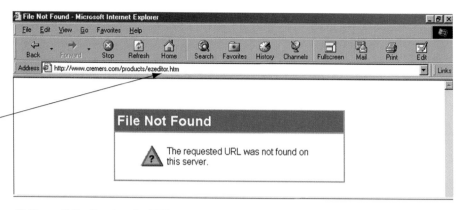

■ **Figure 7.5   Pruning the URL**

If you think you might want to visit the site again, bookmark it.

You can save a file (with or without the HTML codes) to your computer using the "save as" command in the "file" pull-down menu.

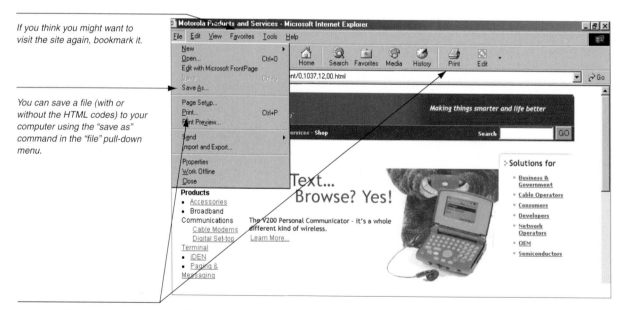

You can print the page by using the print command or the print icon.

■ **Figure 7.6   Saving and Printing a Web Page**

Information on the Web is covered by copyright, just like printed information. When you save material from the Web to your computer, be sure to record the source's bibliographic information.

Source: Motorola, 2002 <www.motorola.com/content/0,1037,12,00.html>.

Using Basic Research Tools

There is a tremendous amount of information in the different media. The trick is to learn how to find what you want. This section discusses five basic research tools.

Online Catalogs   An online catalog is a database of books, microforms, films, compact discs and phonograph records, tapes, and other materials. In most cases, an online catalog lists and describes the holdings at one particular library or a group of libraries.

Figures 7.7 through 7.9 show how to search one online catalog.

Basic research tools:

Online catalogs

Reference works

Periodical indexes

Newspaper indexes

Abstract services

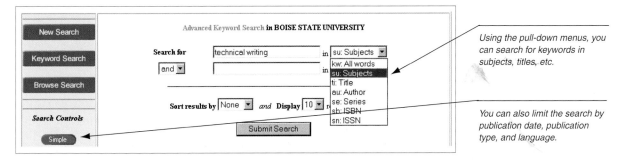

■ Figure 7.7   Searching for an Item on a Web-based Online Catalog

Source: Boise State University, 2002 <http://catalyst.boisestate.edu/CHOOSE:next=html/!DBNAME!_>.

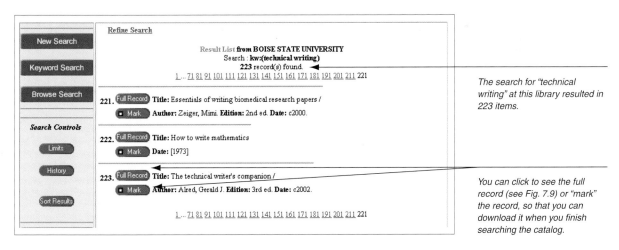

■ Figure 7.8   List of Items Resulting from a Keyword Search on an Online Catalog

This screen shows the brief records of the last three items in the list.
Source: Boise State University, 2002 <http://catalyst.boisestate.edu/CHOOSE:next=html/!DBNAME!_>.

The record is hyperlinked to related information. This link will take you to other titles about software documentation.

The record also indicates whether the item is checked out of the library. This title is in processing; it is not yet on the shelves.

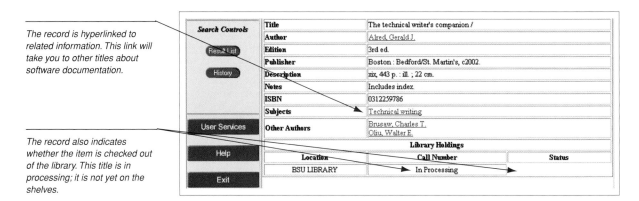

Search Controls	Title	The technical writer's companion /
	Author	Alred, Gerald J.
Result List	Edition	3rd ed.
	Publisher	Boston : Bedford/St. Martin's, c2002.
History	Description	xix, 443 p. : ill. ; 22 cm.
	Notes	Includes index.
	ISBN	0312259786
	Subjects	Technical writing
User Services	Other Authors	Brusaw, Charles T.
		Oliu, Walter E.

Library Holdings

Location	Call Number	Status
BSU LIBRARY	In Processing	

■ **Figure 7.9   Detailed Record of a Title from the Keyword Search**

The detailed record provides all the bibliographic information you will need to document your source.
Source: Boise State University, 2002 <http://catalyst.boisestate.edu/CHOOSE:next=html/!DBNAME!_>.

Reference Works   Reference works include general dictionaries and encyclopedias, biographical dictionaries, almanacs, atlases, and dozens of other general research tools. These print and online works are especially useful when you begin a research project because they provide an overview of the subject and often list the major works in the field.

How do you know if there is a dictionary of the terms used in a given field? The following reference books — the guides-to-the-guides — list the many resources available:

- Harris, S. (Ed.). (1994). *The New York Public Library book of how and where to look it up.* New York: Macmillan.

- Kieft, R. (Ed.). (forthcoming). *Guide to reference sources* (12th ed.). Chicago: American Library Association.

- Mullay, M., & Schlicke, P. (Eds.). (1998–2000). *Walford's guide to reference material* (8th ed.). 3 vols. London: Library Association.

To find information on the Web, use a library Web site or search engine and go to its "reference" section. There you will find numerous sites that contain links to excellent collections of reference works online. A few examples:

- The Best Information on the Net

- CyberStacks(sm)

- The Internet Public Library

On TechComm Web

For links to these and other reference sources, click on Links Library for Ch. 7 on <bedfordstmartins.com/techcomm>.

Periodical Indexes   Periodicals are an excellent source of information for most research projects because they offer recent, authoritative discussions of limited subjects. The biggest challenge in using periodicals is identifying and locating the dozens of relevant articles that are published each month. Although only half a dozen major journals may concentrate on your field, a useful article might appear in one of hundreds of other publications. A periodical index, which is simply a list of articles classified according to title, subject, and author, can help you determine which journals you want to locate.

There are periodical indexes in all fields. The following brief list gives you a sense of the diversity of titles:

- *Applied Science & Technology Index*
- *Business Periodicals Index*
- *Readers' Guide to Periodical Literature*
- *Engineering Index*

You can also use a directory search engine. Many directory categories include a subcategory called "journals" or "periodicals" listing online and printed sources.

Once you have created a bibliography of printed articles you want to study, you have to find them. Check your library's online catalog or *serials holding catalog,* the book that lists all the journals your library receives. If your library does not have an article you want, you can use one of two techniques for securing it:

- *Interlibrary loan.* Your library uses an online directory to learn which nearby library has the article. That library makes a photocopy of the article and sends it to your library. The advantage of an interlibrary loan is that it is a free (or very inexpensive) service to you. The disadvantage is that it can take up to two weeks or longer for the article to arrive at your library.

- *Document-delivery services.* If you are in a hurry, you can log on to a document-delivery service, such as Ingenta, which searches a database of 13 million articles in 27,000 periodicals. If the service has the article, it faxes it to you or makes an electronic copy available.

Newspaper Indexes   Many major newspapers around the world are indexed by subject. The three most important indexed U.S. newspapers are the following:

- *The New York Times.* Perhaps the most reputable U.S. newspaper for national and international news.

- *The Christian Science Monitor.* Another highly regarded general newspaper.

On TechComm Web

For links to online newspapers, click on Links Library for Ch. 7 on <bedfordstmartins.com/techcomm>.

- *The Wall Street Journal.* The most authoritative news source on business, finance, and the economy.

Many newspapers are now available free on the Web and can be searched electronically. Keep in mind, however, that the print version and the electronic version of a newspaper can vary greatly. If you wish to cite a quotation from an article in a newspaper, the print version is the preferred one.

In This Book

For more about abstracts, see Ch. 12, p. 269.

Abstract Services   Abstract services are like indexes but also provide abstracts: brief summaries of the article. In most cases, reading the abstract will enable you to decide whether to seek out the full article. The title of an article, alone, is often a misleading indicator of its contents.

Some abstract services, such as *Chemical Abstracts,* cover a broad field, but many are specialized rather than general. *Adverse Reaction Titles,* for instance, covers research on the subject of adverse reactions to drugs. Figure 7.10, a screen from the *Chemical Abstracts* CD-ROM, shows the basic components of an abstract.

Researching Government Information

The U.S. government is the world's biggest publisher. In researching any field of science, engineering, or business, you are likely to find that a government agency or department has produced a relevant brochure, report, or book.

Government publications are not usually listed in the indexes and abstract journals. The *Monthly Catalog of United States Government Publications,* available on paper, on CD, and on the Web, provides extensive access to these materials.

On TechComm Web

For links to the Monthly Catalog, to FirstGov, and to other government information, click on Links Library for Ch. 7 on <bedfordstmartins .com/techcomm>.

Printed government publications are usually cataloged and shelved separately from other kinds of materials. They are classified according to the Superintendent of Documents system, not the Library of Congress system. The reference librarian or the government documents specialist can help you use government publications.

You can also access many government sites and databases on the Internet. The major entry point for federal government sites is FirstGov, which links to more than 51 million pages of government information and services. It also features a topical index, online transactions, and links to state and local government.

For additional information on government publications, consult these two printed guides:

On TechComm Web

For an excellent guide to using government information, see Patricia Cruse and Sherry DeDecker's "How to Effectively Locate Federal Government Information on the Web." Click on Links Library for Ch. 7 on <bedfordstmartins.com/techcomm>.

- Hoffman, F. W. (1998). *Guide to popular U.S. government publications* (5th ed.). Englewood, CO: Libraries Unlimited. (A CD-ROM version of the book was published in 2000 by Infosential Press.)
- Morehead, J. (1999). *Introduction to United States government information sources* (6th ed.). Englewood, CO: Libraries Unlimited.

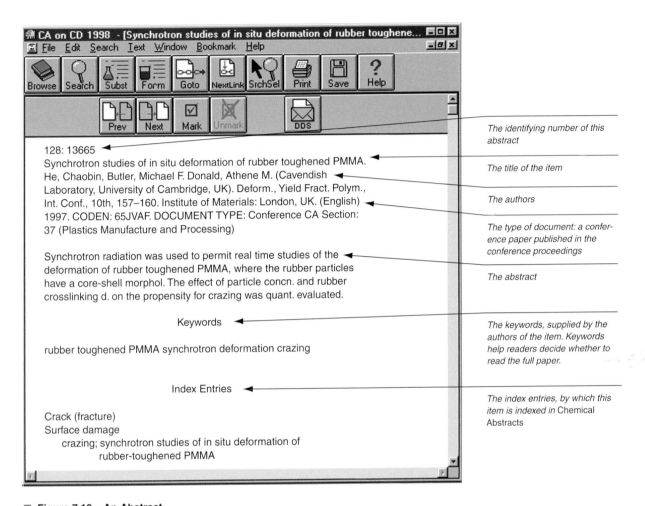

Figure 7.10   An Abstract

Source: Chemical Abstracts Service, 2002 <www.cas.org/ONLINE/CD/CACD/QUICKSTART/author.html>.

Skimming Your Sources and Taking Notes

To record the information that will eventually go into your document, you need to skim your potential sources and take notes. Don't try to read every potential source. A careful reading of a work that looks promising might prove disappointing. You might also get halfway through a book and realize that you must start writing immediately to submit your document on time.

Skimming Books and Articles

To skim effectively, read the following parts of books and articles.

In a book, skim:	*In an article, skim:*
• *the preface and introduction:* to understand the writer's approach and methods	• *the abstract:* to get an overview of the article's content
• *the acknowledgments section:* to learn about help the author received from other experts in the field, or about the author's use of primary research or other resources	• *the introduction:* to understand the article's purpose, main ideas, and organization
• *the table of contents:* to understand the book's scope and organization	• *the notes and references:* to understand the nature and extent of the author's research
• *the notes at the ends of chapters or at the end of the book:* to understand the nature and extent of the author's research	• *the headings and several of the paragraphs:* to understand the article's organization and the quality and relevance of the information
• *the index:* to determine the extent of the coverage of the information you need	
• *a few paragraphs from different portions of the text:* to gauge the quality and relevance of the information	

Skimming will not always tell you whether a book or article is going to be useful, but it can tell you if a work is *not* going to be useful: because it doesn't cover your subject, for example, or because it is too superficial or too advanced. Eliminating the sources you don't need will give you more time to spend on the ones you do.

Note taking is often the first step in writing the document. The best way to take notes is electronically. If you can download files from the Internet, download bibliographic references from a CD-ROM database, and take notes on a laptop computer, you will save a lot of time and prevent many errors. If you do not have access to these electronic tools, get a pack of note cards.

Most note taking involves three kinds of activities: paraphrasing, quoting, and summarizing. Knowing how to paraphrase, quote, and summarize is important for two reasons:

In This Book

For a discussion of plagiarism, see Appendix, Part A, p. 592.

- To a large extent, the work you do at this point will determine the quality of your finished product. You want to record the information accurately and clearly. Mistakes made at this point can be hard to catch later, and they can ruin your document.

- You want to use your sources responsibly. You don't want to plagiarize unintentionally.

GUIDELINES

Recording Bibliographic Information

Record the bibliographic information for each source from which you take notes.

Information to Record for a Book	Information to Record for an Article
• author	• author
• title	• title of the article
• publisher	• title of the periodical
• place of publication	• volume
• year of publication	• number
• call number	• date of publication
	• pages on which the article appears
	• call number of the periodical

Paraphrasing   A paraphrase is a restatement, in your own words, of someone else's words. If you simply copy someone else's words—even a mere two or three in a row—you must use quotation marks.

In taking notes, what kind of material should you paraphrase? Any information that you think might be useful: background data, descriptions of mechanisms or processes, test results, and so forth.

Figure 7.11 shows a paraphrased passage based on the following discussion. The author is explaining the concept of performance-centered design.

Original Passage

In performance-centered design, the emphasis is on providing support for the structure of the work as well as the information needed to accomplish it. One of the best examples is TurboTax®, which meets all the three main criteria of effective performance-centered design:

- *People can do their work with no training on how to use the system.* People trying to do their income tax have no interest in taking any kind of training. They want to get their taxes filled out correctly and quickly, getting all the deductions they are entitled to. These packages, over the years, have moved the interface from a forms-based one, where the user had to know what forms were needed, to an interview-based one that fills out the forms automatically as you answer questions. The design of the interface assumes no particular computer expertise.
- *The system provides the right information at the right time to accomplish the work.* At each step in the process, the system asks only those questions that are rele-

vant based on previous answers. The taxpayer is free to ask for more detail or may proceed through a dialog that asks more-detailed questions if the taxpayer doesn't know the answer to the higher-level question. If a taxpayer is married filing jointly, the system presents only those questions for that filing status.

- *Both tasks and systems change as the user understands the system.* When I first used TurboTax 6 years ago I found myself going to the forms themselves. Doing my taxes generally took about 2 days. Each year I found my need to go to the forms to be less and less. Last year, it took me about 2 hours to do my taxes, and I looked at the forms only when I printed out the final copy.

This paraphrase is inappropriate because the three bullet points are taken word for word from the original. The fact that the student omitted the explanations from the original is irrelevant. These are direct quotes, not paraphrases.

Lovgren, "Achieving Performance-centered Design"
<www.reisman-consulting.com/pages/a-Perform.html>

example of performance-centered design:
TurboTax® meets three main criteria:

- People can do their work with no training on how to use the system.
- The system provides the right information at the right time to accomplish the work.
- Both tasks and systems change as the user understands the system.

a. Inappropriate paraphrase

This paraphrase is appropriate because the words are different from those used in the original.

When you turn your notes into a document, you are likely to reword your paraphrases. Be sure you don't accidentally use wording from the original source. As you revise your document, check a copy of the original source document to be sure you haven't unintentionally reverted to the wording from the source.

Lovgren, "Achieving Performance-centered Design"
<www.reisman-consulting.com/pages/a-Perform.html>

example of performance-centered design:
TurboTax® meets three main criteria:

- You don't have to learn how to use the system.
- The system knows how to respond at the appropriate time to what the user is doing.
- As the user gets smarter about using the system, the system gets smarter, making it faster to complete the task.

b. Appropriate paraphrase

■ **Figure 7.11   Inappropriate and Appropriate Paraphrased Notes**

Source: Adapted from Lovgren, 2000 <www.reisman-consulting.com/pages/a-Perform.html>.

Paraphrasing Accurately

▶ *Study the original until you understand it thoroughly.*

▶ *Rewrite the relevant portions of the original.* Use complete sentences, fragments, or lists, but don't compress the material so much that you'll have trouble understanding it later.

▶ *Title the information so that you'll be able to identify its subject at a glance.* The title should include the general subject and the author's attitude or approach to it, such as "Criticism of open-sea pollution-control devices."

▶ *Include the author's last name, a short title of the article or book, and the page number of the original.* You will need this information later in citing your source.

Quoting   Sometimes you will want to quote a source, either to preserve the author's particularly well-expressed or emphatic phrasing or to lend authority to your discussion. Avoid quoting passages of more than two or three sentences, or else your document will look like a mere compilation. Your job is to integrate an author's words and ideas into your own thinking, not merely to introduce a series of quotations.

Although you probably won't be quoting long passages in your document, recording a complete quotation in your notes will help you recall its meaning and context more accurately when you are ready to integrate it into your own work.

The simplest form of quotation is an author's exact statement:

As Jones states, "Solar energy won't make much of a difference for at least a decade."

To add an explanatory word or phrase to a quotation, use brackets:

As Nelson states, "It [the oil glut] will disappear before we understand it."

Use ellipses (three spaced dots) to show that you are omitting part of an author's statement:

ORIGINAL STATEMENT	"The generator, which we purchased in May, has turned out to be one of our wisest investments."
ELLIPTICAL QUOTATION	"The generator . . . has turned out to be one of our wisest investments."

According to the documentation style recommended by the Modern Language Association (MLA), if the author's original statement has ellipses, you should add brackets around the ellipses that you introduce:

ORIGINAL STATEMENT	"I think reuse adoption offers . . . the promise to improve business in a number of ways."
ELLIPTICAL QUOTATION	"I think reuse adoption offers . . . the promise to improve business [. . .]."

In This Book

For more on formatting quotations, see "Quotation Marks," "Ellipses," and "Brackets" in Appendix, Part A. For a discussion of how to document quotations, see Appendix, Part A, p. 592.

Summarizing   Summarizing is the process of rewriting a passage in your own words to make it shorter while still retaining its essential message. Writers summarize to help them learn a body of information or create a draft of one or more of the summaries that will go into the document.

Most long technical documents contain several kinds of summaries:

- a letter of transmittal (see page 269) that provides an overview of the document
- an abstract (see page 269), a brief technical summary
- an executive summary (see page 274), a brief nontechnical summary directed to the manager
- a conclusion (see page 182) that draws together a complicated discussion

The guidelines and examples in this chapter explain how to summarize the printed information you uncover in your research.

GUIDELINES

Summarizing

The following advice focuses on extracting the essence of a passage by summarizing it.

1. *Read the passage carefully several times.*
2. *Underline key ideas.* Look for them in the titles, headings, topic sentences, transitional paragraphs, and concluding paragraphs.
3. *Combine key ideas.* Study what you have underlined. Paraphrase the underlined ideas. Don't worry about your grammar, punctuation, or style at this point.
4. *Check your draft against the original for accuracy and emphasis.* Check that you record statistics and names correctly and that your version of a complicated concept faithfully represents the original. Check that you get the proportions right; if the original devotes 20 percent of its space to a particular point, your draft should not devote 5 percent or 50 percent to that point.
5. *Record the bibliographic information carefully.* Even though a summary might contain all your own words, you still must cite it, because the main ideas are someone else's. If you don't have the bibliographic information in an electronic form, put it on note cards.

Figure 7.12 is a narrative history of television technology addressed to the general reader. Figure 7.13 is a summary that includes the key terms. This summary is 10 percent of the length of the original.

A BRIEF HISTORY OF TELEVISION

Although it seems as if television has been around for a long time, it's a relatively new science, younger than rocketry, internal medicine, and nuclear physics. In fact, some of the people that helped develop the first commercial TV sets and erect the first TV broadcast antennas are still living today.

The Early Years

The first electronic transmission of a picture was believed to have been made by a Scotsman, John Logie Baird, in the cold month of February 1924. His subject was a Maltese Cross, transmitted through the air by the magic of television (also called "Televisor" or "Radiovision" in those days) the entire distance of ten feet.

To say that Baird's contraption was crude is an understatement. His Televisor was made from a cardboard scanning disk, some darning needles, a few discarded electric motors, piano wire, glue, and other assorted odds and ends. The picture reproduced by the original Baird Televisor was extremely difficult to see—a shadow, at best.

Until about 1928, other amateur radiovision enthusiasts toyed around with Baird's basic design, whiling away long hours in the basement transmitting Maltese Crosses, model airplanes, flags, and anything else that would stay still long enough under the intense light required to produce an image. (As an interesting aside, the lighting for Baird's 1924 Maltese Cross transmission required 2,000 volts of power, produced by a roomful of batteries. So much heat was generated by the lighting equipment that Baird eventually burned his laboratory down.)

Baird's electromechanical approach to television led the way to future developments in transmitting and receiving pictures. The nature of the Baird Televisor, however, limited the clarity and stability of images. Most of the sets made and sold in those days required the viewer to peer through a glass lens to watch the screen, which was seldom over seven by ten inches in size. What's more, the majority of screens had an annoying orange glow that often marred reception and irritated the eyes.

Modern Television Technology

In the early 1930s, Vladimir Zworykin developed a device known as the iconoscope camera. About the same time, Philo T. Farnsworth was putting the finishing touches on the image dissector tube, a gizmo that proved to be the forerunner of the modern cathode ray tube or CRT—the everyday picture tube. These two devices paved the way for the TV sets we know and cherish today.

The first commercially available modern-day cathode ray tube televisions were available in about 1936. Tens of thousands of these sets were sold throughout the United States and Great Britain, even though there were no regular television broadcasts until 1939, when RCA started what was to become the first American television network, NBC. Incidentally, the first true network transmission was in early 1940, between NBC's sister stations WNBT in New York City (now WNBC-TV) and WRGB in Schenectady.

■ **Figure 7.12**
Original Passage

Source: Based on McComb, 1991.

Postwar Growth

World War II greatly hampered the development of television, and during 1941–1945, no television sets were commercially produced (engineers were too busy perfecting radar, which, interestingly enough, contributed significantly to the development of conventional TV). But after the war, the television industry boomed. Television sets were selling like hot-cakes, even though they cost an average of $650 (based on average wage earnings, that's equivalent to about $4,000 today).

Progress took a giant step in 1948 and 1949 when the four American networks, NBC, CBS, ABC, and Dumont, introduced quality, "class-act" programming, which at the time included *Kraft Television Theatre, Howdy Doody*, and *The Texaco Star Theatre* with Milton Berle. These famous stars of the stage and radio made people want to own a television set.

Color and Beyond

Since the late 1940s, television technology has continued to improve and mature. Color came on December 17, 1953, when the FCC approved RCA's all-electronic system, thus ending a bitter, four-year bout between CBS and RCA over color transmission standards. Television images beamed via space satellite caught the public's fancy in July of 1962, when Telstar 1 relayed images of AT&T chairman Frederick R. Kappell from the U.S. to Great Britain. Pay-TV came and went several times in the 1950s, 1960s, and 1970s; modern-day professional commercial videotape machines were demonstrated in 1956 by Ampex; and home video recorders had appeared on retail shelves by early 1976.

■ **Figure 7.12**   *(Continued)*

Summary: A Brief History of Television

In 1924, Baird made the first electronic transmission of a picture. The primitive equipment produced only a shadow. Although Baird's design was modified by others in the 1920s, the viewer had to look through a glass lens at a small screen that gave off an orange glow.

Zworykin's iconoscopic camera and Farnsworth's image dissector tube—similar to the modern CRT—led in 1936 to the development of modern TV. Regular broadcasts began in 1939 on the first network, NBC. Research stopped during WWII, but after that, sales grew, even though sets cost approximately $650, the equivalent of $4,000 today.

Color broadcasts began in 1953; satellite broadcasting began in 1962; and home VCRs were introduced in 1976.

Key terms: television, history of television, NBC, color television, satellite broadcasting, video cassette recorders, Baird, Zworykin, Farnsworth.

■ **Figure 7.13   Summary of the Original Passage**

Evaluating the Information

With more information than you can possibly use, you try to figure out what it all means. You realize that you still have some questions, that some of the information is incomplete, some contradictory, and some just unclear. There is no shortage of information; the challenge is to find good information. Look for information that is

- *Accurate.* If you are researching whether your company should consider flextime scheduling, you start by determining the number of employees who might be interested in flextime. If you estimate that number to be 500 but it is in fact closer to 50, you might end up wasting a lot of time doing an unnecessary study.

- *Unbiased.* You want sources that have no financial stake in the project. A private company that transports workers in vans might be a biased source of information on flextime because of an interest in contracting with your company.

- *Comprehensive.* You want to hear from different kinds of people—in terms of gender, cultural characteristics, and age—and from people representing all views of the topic.

- *Appropriately technical.* Good information is sufficiently detailed to respond to the needs of your readers but not so detailed that they cannot understand it. For the study of flextime, you need to find out whether opening your building an hour early and closing it an hour late will significantly affect your utility costs. You can get this information by interviewing people in operations and in security; you will not need to do a detailed analysis of all the utility records of the company.

- *Current.* If your information is 10 years old, it might not accurately reflect today's situation.

- *Clear.* You want information that is easy to understand; otherwise, you'll waste time figuring it out, and you might misinterpret it.

The most difficult kind of material to evaluate is information from the Internet, because it appears on the Internet without passing through the formal review procedure used for books and professional journals. Therefore, you have to be particularly careful in evaluating Internet information.

On TechComm Web

For links to sources on finding and evaluating Internet information, click on Links Library for Ch. 7 on <bedfordstmartins.com/techcomm>.

CONDUCTING PRIMARY RESEARCH

Although the library and the Internet offer a wealth of secondary sources, you will often need to conduct primary research to acquire new information. There are six major categories of primary research.

Evaluating Print and Online Sources

Criteria	For Printed Sources	For Online Sources
Authorship	Do you recognize the name of the author? Can you learn about the author's credentials and current position from a biographical note? If this information is not included in the document itself, can you find it in a who's who or by searching for other books or other journal articles by the author?	If you do not recognize the author's name, did you find the site by linking from another reputable site? Does the site contain links to other reputable sites? Does the site contain biographical information—the author's current position and credentials? Can you use a search engine to find other references to the author's credentials or other documents by the author?
Publishing body	What is the publisher's reputation? To be reliable, a book should be published by a reputable trade, academic, or scholarly publisher; a journal should be sponsored by a professional association or university. Are the editorial board members well-known names in the field? Trade publications—magazines about a particular industry or group —often promote the interests of that industry or group. For example, don't automatically assume the accuracy of information in trade publications for loggers or environmentalists. If you doubt the authority of a book or journal, ask the reference librarian or a professor.	Can you determine the publishing body's identity from headers or footers? Is the publishing body reputable in the field? If the site comes from a personal account on an Internet service provider, the author might be writing outside his or her field of expertise. Many Internet sites exist largely for public relations or advertising. For instance, the home page for the White House is not going to provide information critical of the administration. Likewise, the Web sites of corporations and other organizations are unlikely to contain information critical of those corporations or organizations.
Knowledge of the literature	Does the author appear to be knowledgeable about the major literature in the field? Is there a bibliography? Are there notes throughout the document?	Analyze the Internet source as you would any other source. Often, references to other sources will take the form of links.
Accuracy and verifiability of the information	Is the information based on reasonable assumptions? Does the author clearly describe the methods and theories used in producing the information, and are they appropriate to the subject? Has the author used sound reasoning? Has the author explained the limitations of the information?	Is the site well constructed? Is the information well written? Is the information based on reasonable assumptions? Are the claims supported by appropriate evidence? Has the author used sound reasoning? Has the author explained the limitations of the information? Are sources cited?

On TechComm Web

For more help with evaluating online sources, click on Tutorials on <bedfordstmartins.com /techcomm>.

Criteria	For Printed Sources	For Online Sources
Timeliness	Does the document rely on recent data? Was the document published recently?	Was the document created recently? Was it updated recently? If a site is not yet complete, be wary.

Inspections

Types of primary research:

Inspections

Experiments

Field research

Interviews

Letters of inquiry

Questionnaires

Regardless of your field, you are likely to encounter many sentences that begin "An inspection was conducted to determine. . . ." A civil engineer can often determine what caused the crack in a foundation by inspecting the site; an accountant can often determine the financial health of an organization by inspecting its financial records.

These professionals are looking at a site, an object, or a document (for example, the financial records) and applying their knowledge and professional judgment to what they see. Sometimes the inspection techniques are more complicated. A civil engineer inspecting foundation cracking might want to test hunches by studying a soil sample.

When you carry out an inspection, take good notes. Try to answer the appropriate journalistic questions—*who, what, when, where, why,* and *how*—as soon as you can. Where appropriate, photograph or sketch the site or print the output from computer-assisted inspections. You will probably need the data later for your document.

Experiments

Learning to conduct the many kinds of experiments used in a particular field can take months or even years. This discussion is a brief introduction.

In many cases, conducting an experiment involves four phases.

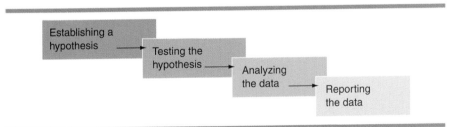

- *Establishing a hypothesis.* A hypothesis is an informed guess about the relationship between two factors. In a study relating gasoline octane and miles per gallon, a hypothesis might be the following: "A car will get 10 percent better mileage with 89 octane gas than with 87 octane."

Interactive Sample Document:
Evaluating Information from Internet Sources

This image is an excerpt from a Web page about teenage deaths in motor vehicles. The questions in the margin ask you to consider the guidelines for evaluating Internet sources (on pages 146–147). The answers to these questions are available on TechComm Web.

1. What is the publishing body for this site? Is it reputable? Is the information within the realm of the publishing body's expertise?

2. How can the information be verified?

3. How timely is the information?

On TechComm Web

To find the answers to these questions, click on Interactive Sample Documents for Ch. 7 on <bedfordstmartins.com/techcomm>.

Male drivers (age 16-20) with blood alcohol concentrations in the 0.05-0.08 percent range are 17 times more likely than sober teenagers to be killed in single-vehicle crashes. The corresponding comparison for females is 7 times more likely. At BACs of 0.08-0.10, risks are even higher, 52 times for males, 15 times for females.[1]

WHEN THEY DIED

Fifty-four percent of teenage motor vehicle deaths in 2000 occurred on Friday, Saturday, and Sunday.

Forty-one percent of teenage motor vehicle deaths in 2000 occurred between 9 pm and 6 am.

REFERENCES

[1] Zador, P.L.; Krawchuck, S.; and Voas, R.B. 2000. Alcohol-related relative risk of driver fatalities and driver involvement in fatal crashes in relation to driver age and gender: an update using 1996 data. *Journal of Studies on Alcohol* 61:387-95.

OTHER FATALITY FACTS TOPICS: General | Alcohol | Bicycles | Children | Elderly | Gender | Large Trucks | Motorcycles | Passenger Vehicles | Pedestrians | Roadside Hazards | State by State

©1996-2002, Insurance Institute for Highway Safety, Highway Loss Data Institute | Copyright and Use of Images Notice
Last modified: 27-Mar-2002

Source: Insurance Institute for Highway Safety, 2002 <www.highwaysafety.org/safety_facts/fatality_facts/teens.htm>.

In This Book

For more about reports, see Chs. 18 and 19.

- *Testing the hypothesis.* Usually, you need an experimental group and a control group. These two groups are identical except for the condition you are studying: in the above example, the gasoline. The control group would be a car running on 87 octane. The experimental group would be an identical car running on 89 octane. The experiment would consist of driving the two cars over an identical course at the same speed—preferably in some sort of controlled environment, such as a laboratory—over a given distance, such as 1,000 miles. At the end of the 1,000 miles, you would calculate the miles per gallon. The results would either support or refute your original hypothesis.

- *Analyzing the data.* You must try to understand whether your data show merely a correlation—one factor changing along with another—or a causal relationship. For example, we know that sports cars are involved in more fatal accidents than sedans, but we don't know whether the car has much to do with that fact, or whether driving habits are the important factor.

- *Reporting the data.* When researchers report their findings, they try to explain as clearly as they can what they did, why they did it, what they saw, what it means, and what ought to be done next.

Field Research

Whereas an experiment is quantitative (it yields statistical data that can be measured), field research is usually qualitative. It yields data that cannot be measured or, at least, cannot be measured as precisely as experimental data. Often in field research you seek to understand the quality of an experience. For instance, you might want to understand how a new seating arrangement would affect group dynamics in a classroom. You could design a study in which you observed and recorded the classes and perhaps interviewed the students and the instructor about their reactions. Then you could do the same in a traditional classroom and compare the results.

Some kinds of studies have both quantitative and qualitative elements. In the case of the classroom seating arrangements, you could include some quantitative measures, such as the number of times students talked with each other. You could also distribute questionnaires to elicit the opinions of the students and the instructor. If you used these same quantitative measures on enough classrooms, you could gather valid quantitative information.

When you are doing quantitative or qualitative studies on the behavior of animals—from rats to monkeys to people—try to minimize two common problems:

- *The effect of the experiment on the behavior you are studying.* In studying the effects of the classroom seating arrangement, try to minimize the effects of your own presence. For instance, make sure that the camera is placed unobtrusively and that it is set up before the students arrive, so they don't see the process. Still, any time you bring in a camera, you can never be sure that what you witness is typical. Even an outsider who sits quietly can disrupt typical behavior.
- *Bias in the recording and analysis of the data.* Bias can occur because researchers want to confirm their hypotheses. In an experiment to determine whether word processors help students write better, the researcher is likely to see improvement where other people don't. For this reason, the experiment should be designed so that it is *double blind.* That is, the students doing the writing shouldn't know what the experiment is about so they won't change their behavior to support or negate the hypothesis. And the data being analyzed should be disguised so that researchers don't know whether they are examining the results from the control group or the experimental group. If the control group wrote in ink and the experimental group used word processors, for example, the control group's papers should be formatted on a word processor, so that all the papers look identical.

Conducting an experiment or field research is relatively simple; the hard part is designing your study so that it accurately measures what you want it to measure.

Interviews

Interviews are extremely useful when you need information on subjects that are too new to have been discussed in the professional literature or inappropriate for widespread publication (such as local political questions).

In choosing a respondent—a person to interview—determine three things:

- *What you want to find out.* Only then can you begin to search for a person who can provide the information.

- *Who could provide this information.* The ideal respondent is an expert willing to talk. Unless the respondent is an obvious choice, such as the professor carrying out the research you are studying, use directories, such as local industrial guides, to locate potential respondents.

- *Whether the person is willing to be interviewed.* On the phone or in writing, state what you want to ask about. The person might not be able to help you but might be willing to refer you to someone who can. Explain why you have decided to ask him or her. (A compliment works better than admitting that the person you really wanted to interview is out of town.) Explain what you plan to do with the information, such as write a report or give a talk. Then, if the person is willing to be interviewed, set up an appointment at his or her convenience.

GUIDELINES

Conducting an Interview

Preparing for the interview

- *Do your homework.* Don't conduct an interview to avoid doing other kinds of research. If you ask questions that are already answered in the professional literature, the respondent might become annoyed and uncooperative.

- *Prepare good questions.* Good questions are clear, focused, and open.

  - Be clear. The respondent should be able to understand what you are asking.

UNCLEAR	Why do you sell Trane products?
CLEAR	What are the characteristics of Trane products that led you to include them in your product line?

    The unclear question can be answered in a number of unhelpful ways: "Because they're too expensive to give away" or "Because I'm a Trane dealer."

  - Be focused. The question must be narrow enough to be answered briefly. If you want more information, you can ask a follow-up question.

On TechComm Web

For an excellent discussion of interview questions, see Joel Bowman's *Business Communication: Managing Information and Relationships.* Click on Links Library for Ch. 7 on <bedfordstmartins.com/techcomm>.

| | UNFOCUSED | What is the future of the computer industry? |
| | FOCUSED | What will the American chip industry look like in 10 years? |

–Ask open questions. Your purpose is to get the respondent to talk. Don't ask a lot of questions that have yes or no answers.

| | CLOSED | Do you think the federal government should create industrial partnerships? |
| | OPEN | What are the advantages and disadvantages of the federal government's creating industrial partnerships? |

- *Check your equipment.* If you will be taping the interview, test your tape recorder or video camera to make sure it is operating properly.

Beginning the interview	• *Arrive on time.*
	• *Thank the respondent for taking the time to talk with you.*
	• *State the subject and purpose of the interview and what you plan to do with the information.*
	• *If you wish to tape the interview, ask permission.*
Conducting the interview	• *Take notes.* Write down important concepts, facts, and numbers, but don't take such copious notes that you are still writing when the respondent finishes an answer.
	• *Start with prepared questions.* Because you are likely to be nervous at the start, you might forget important questions. It is wise to begin with prepared questions.
	• *Be prepared to ask follow-up questions.* Listen carefully to the respondent's answer and be ready to ask a follow-up question or request a clarification. Have your other prepared questions ready, but be willing to deviate from them. The respondent probably will lead you in unexpected directions.
	• *Be prepared to get the interview back on track.* Gently return to the point if the respondent begins straying unproductively, but don't interrupt rudely or show annoyance.
Concluding the interview	• *Thank the respondent.*
	• *Ask for a follow-up interview.* If a second meeting would be useful, ask to arrange a second meeting.
	• *Ask for permission to quote the respondent.* If you think you might want to quote the respondent by name, ask permission now.
After the interview	• *Write down the important information while the interview is fresh in your mind.* (This step is unnecessary, of course, if you have recorded the interview.) If you will be printing a transcript of the interview, make the transcript now.
	• *Send a brief thank-you note.* Within a day or two, send a note that shows you appreciate the courtesy and that you value what you have learned. In the letter, confirm any previous offers you have made, such as sending the respondent a copy of your final document.

Figure 7.14 is from a transcript of an interview with an attorney specializing in information technology. The interviewer is a student who is writing about legal aspects of software ownership.

Letters of Inquiry

In This Book

For more about inquiry letters, see Ch. 15, p. 367.

A letter of inquiry can be a useful alternative to a personal interview. If you are lucky, your respondent will provide detailed and helpful answers. However, the respondent might not clearly understand what it is you want to know or might choose not to help you. Although the strategy of the inquiry letter is essentially that of a personal interview, inquiry letters can be less successful, because the recipient has not already agreed to provide information and might not respond. Also, an inquiry letter, unlike an interview, gives you little opportunity to follow up by asking for a clarification.

Questionnaires

Questionnaires enable you to solicit information from a large group of people. However, questionnaires rarely yield completely satisfactory results, for three reasons:

- *Some of the questions will misfire.* No matter how carefully you draft your questions, respondents will misinterpret some of them or supply useless answers.

- *You won't obtain as many responses as you want.* The response rate will almost never exceed 50 percent. In most cases, it will be closer to 10–20 percent.

- *You cannot be sure the respondents are representative.* People who feel strongly about an issue are much more likely to respond than are those who do not. For this reason, you need to be careful in drawing conclusions based on a small number of responses to a questionnaire.

When you send a questionnaire, you are asking the recipient to do you a favor. Your goal should be to construct questions that will elicit the information you need as simply and efficiently as possible.

Asking Effective Questions   To ask effective questions, keep two points in mind:

- *Use unbiased language.* Don't ask "Should U.S. clothing manufacturers protect themselves from unfair foreign competition?" Instead, ask "Are you in favor of imposing tariffs on men's clothing?"

- *Be specific.* If you ask "Do you favor improving the safety of automobiles?" only an eccentric would answer no. Instead, ask "Do you favor requiring automobile manufacturers to equip new cars with side-impact air bags, which would raise the price by an average of $300 per car?"

Interview Transcript, Page 1

Q. Why is copyright ownership important in marketing software?

A. If you own the copyright, you can license and market the product and keep other people from doing so. It could be a matter of millions of dollars if the software is popular.

Q. Shouldn't the programmer automatically own the copyright?

A. If the programmer wrote the program on personal time, he or she should and does own the copyright.

Q. So "personal time" is the critical concept?

A. That's right. We're talking about the "work-made-for-hire" doctrine of copyright law. If I am working for you, anything I make under the terms of my employment is owned by you.

Q. What is the complication, then? If I make the software on my machine at home, I own it; if I'm working for someone, my employer owns it.

A. Well, the devil is in the details. Often the terms of employment are casual, or there is no written job description or contract for the particular piece of software.

Q. Can you give me an example of that?

A. Sure. There was a 1992 case, *Aymes* v. *Bonelli*. Bonelli owned a swimming pool and hired Aymes to write software to handle recordkeeping on the pool. This was not part of Bonelli's regular business; he just wanted a piece of software written. The terms of the employment were casual. Bonelli paid no health benefits, Aymes worked irregular hours, usually unsupervised—Bonelli wasn't a programmer. When the case was heard, the court ruled that even though Bonelli was paying Aymes, Aymes owned the copyright because of the lack of involvement and participation by Bonelli. The court found that the degree of skill required by Aymes to do the job was so great that, in effect, he was creating the software by himself, even though he was receiving compensation for it.

Q. How can such disagreements be prevented? By working out the details ahead of time?

A. Exactly. The employer should have the employee sign a statement that the project is being carried out as work-made-for-hire, and should register the copyright with the U.S. Copyright Office in Washington. Conversely, employees should try to have the employer sign a statement that the project is not work-made-for-hire, and should try to register the copyright themselves.

Q. And if agreement can't be reached ahead of time?

A. Then stop right there. Don't do any work.

Notice how the student prompts the attorney to expand her answers.

Notice how the student responds to the attorney's answers, making the interview more of a discussion.

■ **Figure 7.14**
Excerpt from an Interview

Table 7.1 explains common types of questions used in questionnaires.
Include a letter or memo with the questionnaire. For someone outside
your organization, this document is an inquiry letter (sometimes with the
questions themselves on a separate sheet). Therefore, it must clearly indicate
who you are, why you are writing, what you plan to do with the information,
and when you will need it. For people within your organization, provide the
same information in a memo or an e-mail accompanying a questionnaire.

Figure 7.15 shows a sample questionnaire.

■ **Table 7.1   Common Types of Questions Used in Questionnaires**

Type of Question	Example	Comments
Multiple choice	Would you consider joining a company-sponsored sports team? Yes_____ No_____	The respondent selects one of the alternatives.
Likert scale	The flextime program has been a success in its first year. strongly disagree __ __ __ __ __ __ strongly agree	The respondent ranks the degree to which he or she agrees or disagrees with the statement. Using an even number of possible responses (six, in this case) increases your chances of obtaining useful data; with an odd number, too many respondents choose the middle response.
Semantic differentials	simple __ __ __ __ __ __ difficult interesting __ __ __ __ __ __ boring	The respondent registers a response along a continuum between a pair of opposing adjectives. Usually, these questions measure a person's feelings about a task, an experience, or an object. As with Likert scales, using an even number of possible responses increases the chances of obtaining useful data.
Ranking	Please rank the following work schedules in order of preference. Put a 1 next to the schedule you would most like to have, a 2 next to your second choice, and so on. 8:00–4:30 _____ 9:00–5:30 _____ 8:30–5:00 _____ flexible _____	The respondent indicates a priority among a number of alternatives.
Short answer	What do you feel are the major advantages of the new parts-requisitioning policy? 1._____ 2._____ 3._____	The respondent writes a brief answer using phrases or sentences.
Short essay	The new parts-requisitioning policy has been in effect for a year. How well do you think it is working? _____ _____ _____	Although an essay question can yield information you never would have found using closed-end questions, you will receive fewer responses, simply because they require more effort from the respondent. Also, essays cannot be quantified precisely, as the data from the other types of questions can.

September 5, 2003

To: All employees
From: William Bonoff, Vice President of Operations
Subject: Evaluation of the Lunches Unlimited food service

As you may know, every two years we evaluate the quality and cost of the food service that caters our lunchroom. We would like you to help in our evaluation by sharing your opinions about the food service. Please note that your responses will remain anonymous. Please drop the completed questionnaires in the marked boxes near the main entrance to the lunchroom.

1. Approximately how many days per week do you eat lunch in the lunchroom?
   0 _____ 1 _____ 2 _____ 3 _____ 4 _____ 5 _____

2. At approximately what time do you eat in the lunchroom?
   11:30–12:30 _____ 12:00–1:00 _____ 12:30–1:30 _____ varies _____

3. A clean table is usually available.
   Strongly Disagree _____ _____ _____ _____ _____ _____ Strongly Agree

4. The Lunches Unlimited personnel are polite and helpful.
   Strongly Disagree _____ _____ _____ _____ _____ _____ Strongly Agree

5. Please comment on the quality of the different kinds of food you have eaten in the lunchroom.
   a. Daily specials
      excellent _____ good _____ satisfactory _____ poor _____
   b. Hot dogs and hamburgers
      excellent _____ good _____ satisfactory _____ poor _____
   c. etc.

6. What *foods* would you like to see served that are not served now?
   _____

7. What *beverages* would you like to see served that are not served now?
   _____

8. Please comment on the prices of the foods and beverages served.
   a. Hot meals (daily specials)
      too high _____ fair _____ a bargain _____
   b. Hot dogs and hamburgers
      too high _____ fair _____ a bargain _____
   c. etc.

9. Would you be willing to spend more money for a better-quality lunch if you thought the price was reasonable?
   yes, often _____ sometimes _____ not likely _____

10. On the other side of this sheet, please provide whatever comments you think will help us evaluate the catering service.

Thank you for your assistance.

Likert-scale questions 3 and 4 make it easy for the writer to quantify data about subjective impressions.

Short-answer questions 6 and 7 are best for soliciting ideas from respondents.

■ **Figure 7.15**
Questionnaire

In This Book

For more on testing documents, see Ch. 3, p. 46.

Testing the Questionnaire   Before you send out *any* questionnaire, show it and the accompanying letter or memo to a few people who can help you identify any problems. After you have revised the materials, test them on people whose backgrounds are similar to those of your real respondents. Revise the materials a second time, and, if possible, test them again. Once you have sent the questionnaire, you cannot revise it and re-send it to the same people.

Administering the Questionnaire   Determining who should receive the questionnaire can be simple or difficult. If you want to know what the residents of a particular street think about a proposed construction project, your job is easy. But if you want to know what mechanical-engineering students in colleges across the country think about their curricula, you will need background in sampling techniques to isolate a representative sample.

Include a self-addressed, stamped envelope with the questionnaires sent to people outside your organization. Send a memo or an e-mail to people within your organization.

Revision Checklist

Did you
- [ ] choose a topic? (p. 124)
- [ ] analyze your audience and purpose? (p. 125)
- [ ] determine how to carry out the research? (p. 125)
- [ ] determine what you know — and don't know — about the topic? (p. 126)
- [ ] plan a research strategy, covering both secondary and primary research? (p. 126)
- [ ] consult the appropriate reference books, including periodical indexes, newspaper indexes, abstract services, government publications, guides to business and industry, online databases, CD-ROM, and the Web? (p. 133)
- [ ] study the information by skimming, taking notes, and summarizing? (p. 137)

Did you, in evaluating information, carefully assess
- [ ] the author's credentials? (p. 146)
- [ ] the publishing body? (p. 146)
- [ ] the author's knowledge of literature in the field? (p. 146)
- [ ] the accuracy and verifiability of the information? (p. 146)
- [ ] the timeliness of the information? (p. 147)

Did you, if appropriate,
- [ ] conduct inspections? (p. 147)
- [ ] conduct experiments? (p. 147)
- [ ] perform field research? (p. 149)
- [ ] conduct interviews? (p. 150)
- [ ] send letters of inquiry? (p. 152)
- [ ] administer questionnaires? (p. 152)

Exercises

On TechComm Web

For more exercises, click on Additional Exercises, Projects, and Cases for Ch. 7 on <bedfordstmartins.com/techcomm>.

1. **Internet Activity**   Use a search engine to find at least 10 sites about some key term or concept in your field, such as "ge-netic engineering," "hospice care," or "fuzzy logic." For each site, write a brief paragraph explaining why it would or would not be a credible source of information for a research report.

2. **Internet Activity**   Using a search engine, answer the following questions. Provide the URL of each site you mention.

If your instructor requests it, submit your answers as an e-mail to him or her.

a. What are the three largest or most important professional organizations in your field (for example, if you are a construction management major, your field is construction management or civil engineering or industrial engineering)?

b. What are three important journals read by people in your field?

c. What are the three most important online discussion lists or bulletin boards read by people in your field?

d. What are the date and location of an upcoming national or international professional meeting for people in your field?

e. Name and describe, in one paragraph for each, three major issues being discussed by practitioners or academics in your field. For instance, nurses might be discussing the effect of managed care on the quality of medical care delivered to patients.

3. Revise the following interview questions to make them more effective. In a brief paragraph for each, explain why you have revised it as you have.

a. What is the role of communication in your daily job?

b. Do you think it is better to relocate your warehouse or go to just-in-time manufacturing?

c. Isn't it true that it's almost impossible to train an engineer to write well?

d. Where are your company's headquarters?

e. Is there anything else you think I should know?

4. Revise the following questions from questionnaires to make them more effective. In a brief paragraph for each, explain why you have revised it as you have.

a. Does your company provide tuition reimbursement for its employees? Yes_____ No_____

b. What do you see as the future of bioengineering?

c. How satisfied are you with the computer support you receive?

d. How many employees work at your company? 5–10_____ 10–15_____ 15 or more_____

e. What kinds of documents do you write most often? memos_____ letters_____ reports_____

Projects

On TechComm Web

For more projects, click on Additional Exercises, Projects, and Cases for Ch. 7 on <bedfordstmartins.com/techcomm>.

5. **Group Activity** Form small groups and describe and evaluate your college or university's Web site. A different member of the group might carry out each of the following tasks:

• In an e-mail to the site's Webmaster, ask questions about the process of creating the site. For example, how involved with the content and design of the site was the Webmaster? What is the Webmaster's role in maintaining the site?

• Analyze the kinds of information the site contains and determine whether the site is intended primarily for faculty, students, alumni, legislators, or prospective students.

• Determine the overlap between information on the site and information in printed documents published by the school. In those cases in which they overlap, is the information on the site merely a duplication of the printed information, or has it been revised to take advantage of the unique capabilities of the Web?

In a memo to your instructor, present your findings and recommend how the site might be improved. (For more on memos, see Chapter 15, page 378.)

6. Your major department has remodeled its offices to include a small coffee room and lounge. They have asked their student organization to recommend which journals and books they should buy to stock the bookshelf in the new coffee room. Make a list of five print journals and ten reference books that you think would be useful to advanced undergraduates in your major. For each item, include a brief paragraph explaining why you think it is an appropriate choice.

On TechComm Web

For more cases, click on Additional Exercises, Projects, and Cases for Ch. 7 on <bedfordstmartins.com /techcomm>.

CASE
Projecting a Credible Image for Your Organization

You and the other members of your group are interns working for the International Society for Microbial Ecology (ISME). Founded in 1998, the ISME wishes to establish its reputation as a serious and credible organization of scientists. Your supervisor, Alan Winston, who serves as the Webmaster for ISME, has asked you to study the organization's Web site <http://microbes.org> and report to him on which aspects of the site help the organization project a professional image and which don't. "Our credibility," he tells you, "has to come across on our site. If we are to increase membership, journal subscriptions, and conference attendance, we have to make sure people know who we are and what we're up to." Write a memo to Winston, presenting your findings. (For more on memos, see Chapter 15, page 378.)

Organizing Your Information

8

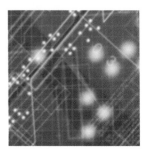

The technical communicators and scholars Charles T. Brusaw, Gerald J. Alred, and Walter E. Oliu (2000, pp. 383–384) on the role of organization in technical communication:

An appropriate method of development makes it easy for readers to understand your topic and moves the topic smoothly and logically from an introduction (or opening) to a conclusion.

On TechComm Web

For additional samples, activities, and links related to this chapter, see <bedfordstmartins.com/techcomm>.

At this point, you should know for whom you are writing, and why, and you have done most of your research. Now it is time to start organizing the information that will make up the body of your document.

BASIC PRINCIPLES OF ORGANIZING TECHNICAL INFORMATION

You should keep three principles in mind as you organize your information:

- analyze your audience and purpose
- use conventional patterns of organization
- display your organizational pattern prominently in the document

Analyzing Your Audience and Purpose

In This Book

For more about audience and purpose, see Ch. 5.

Although you have thought about your audience and purpose as you planned and researched your subject, your initial analyses of audience and purpose are likely to change as you continue. Therefore, it is useful to review your assessment of audience and purpose before you proceed.

Will your audience like the message you will present? If they will, you can announce your main point early in the document. If they won't, you need to consider an organizational pattern that presents your important evidence before your main message. Is your audience used to seeing a particular organizational pattern in the kind of document you will be writing? If they are, you will probably want to use that pattern, unless you have a very good reason to use a different one.

What is your purpose in writing the document? Do you want your audience to understand a body of information or to accept a point of view and perhaps act on it? One purpose might call for a brief report without any appendices; the other might require a detailed report, complete with appendices that enable some of your readers to carry out tasks.

STRATEGIES FOR INTERCULTURAL COMMUNICATION

Organizing Documents for Readers from Other Cultures

Organization patterns can vary from culture to culture. If you can, study documents written by people from the culture you are addressing to see whether they favor an organizational pattern different from the one you are considering.

- *Does the text follow expected organizational patterns?* For example, this chapter discusses the general-to-specific organization. Does the text you are studying reverse the pattern, presenting the specific information first?

- *Do the introductions and conclusions present the kind of information you would expect?* For instance, in the United States, introductions often present the main findings; in other cultures, the main findings are not presented until late in the document.

- *Is the text organized into paragraphs?*

- *Does the text appear to be organized linearly?* Is the main idea presented first in a topic sentence or thesis statement? Does supporting information follow?

- *Does the text use headings?* If so, does it use more than one level?

If you find that documents from the culture you plan to address are organized very differently from what you're used to, you should take extra steps to ensure that your message is not obscured by an organizational pattern that is unfamiliar to your readers.

Using Conventional Patterns of Arrangement

This chapter presents a number of conventional patterns of arrangement, such as the chronological pattern and the spatial pattern. You should begin by asking yourself whether a conventional pattern for presenting your information already exists. Using a conventional pattern makes things easier for you as a writer and for your audience.

For you, a conventional pattern serves as a template or checklist, helping you remember which information to include and where to put it. In a proposal, for example, you include a budget, which you put near the end or in an appendix. For your audience, a conventional pattern makes your document easier to read and understand. Readers who are familiar with proposals can find the information they want because you have put it where others have put similar information.

Does this mean that technical communication is merely the process of filling in the blanks? No. You need to assess the writing situation continuously as you work. If you think you could communicate your ideas better by modifying a conventional pattern or by devising a new pattern, do so. However, you gain nothing if an existing pattern would work just as well.

Displaying Your Arrangement Prominently

Make it easy for your readers to understand the overall arrangement of your information. Displaying your arrangement prominently involves three main steps:

In This Book

For more on tables of contents, see Ch. 12, p. 273. For more on headings and topic sentences, see Ch. 10, pp. 220 and 224.

- *Creating a detailed table of contents.* If your document has a table of contents, including at least two levels of headings helps readers find the information they seek.
- *Using headings liberally.* Headings break up the text, making your page more interesting visually, and communicate the subject of the section, improving the readers' understanding.
- *Using topic sentences at the beginnings of your paragraphs.* The topic sentence announces the main point of a paragraph and helps the reader understand the details that follow.

Patterns typically used in organizing information:

Chronological

Spatial

General to specific

More important to less important

Comparison and contrast

Classification and partition

Problem-methods-solution

Cause and effect

BASIC PATTERNS OF ORGANIZING INFORMATION

Every argument calls for its own organizational pattern. Long, complex arguments often require several organizational patterns. For instance, one part of a document might be a causal analysis of the problem you are writing about, whereas another might be a comparison and contrast of two options for solving that problem.

This section discusses eight organizational patterns.

Chronological

The chronological—or time-line—pattern commonly describes events. Here are some examples of chronology as an organizing pattern:

In an *accident report,* you describe the events in the order in which they occurred.

In the background section of a *report,* you describe the events that led to the present situation.

In a *reference manual,* you explain how to carry out a task by describing the steps in sequence.

On TechComm Web

For a discussion of organizing information, see Paradigm Online Writing Assistant. Click on Links Library for Ch. 8 on <bedfordstmartins.com/techcomm>.

GUIDELINES

Organizing Information Chronologically

▶ *Provide signposts.* If the passage is more than a few hundred words long, use headings. Choose words such as *step, phase, stage,* and *part,* and consider numbering them. Add descriptive phrases to focus readers' attention on the topic of the section:

Phase One: Determining Our Objectives

Step 3: Installing the Lateral Supports

At the paragraph and sentence levels, transitional words such as *then, next, first,* and *finally* help readers follow your discussion.

▶ *Consider using graphics to complement the text.* Graphics can clarify and emphasize chronological passages. Flowcharts, in particular, help you emphasize chronological passages for all kinds of readers, from the most expert to the general reader.

▶ *Analyze events where appropriate.* Although chronology is an easy pattern to use, it doesn't explain why or how an event happened, or what it means. For instance, the largest section of an accident report is usually devoted to the chronological discussion, but the report is of little value unless it explains what caused the accident, who bears responsibility, and how such accidents can be prevented.

In This Book

For more on graphics, see Ch. 14.

In This Book

For more on transitions, see Ch. 10, p. 228.

Figure 8.1, an excerpt from an online encyclopedia, uses the chronological pattern to present the early history of computing.

On TechComm Web

To view Fig. 8.1 in context on the Web, click on Links Library for Ch. 8 on <bedfordstmartins.com /techcomm>.

Spatial

The spatial pattern is commonly used to describe objects and physical sites. Here are some examples of the use of spatial organization:

In an *accident report,* you describe the physical scene of the accident.

In a *feasibility study* about building a facility, you describe the property on which it would be built.

In a *proposal* to design a new microchip, you describe the layout of the new chip.

The writer uses chronology—the time pattern—to organize the discussion.

When the writer wants to present detailed information, he shifts away from chronology to technical description, as in this explanation of the Pascaline.

The writer returns to chronology as the organizing principle in presenting the next major developments.

The abacus, which emerged about 5,000 years ago in Asia Minor and is still in use today, may be considered the first computer. This device allows users to make computations using a system of sliding beads arranged on a rack. Early merchants used the abacus to keep trading transactions. But as the use of paper and pencil spread, particularly in Europe, the abacus lost its importance. It took nearly 12 centuries, however, for the next significant advance in computing devices to emerge. In 1642, Blaise Pascal (1623–1662), the 18-year-old son of a French tax collector, invented what he called a numerical wheel calculator to help his father with his duties. This brass rectangular box, also called a Pascaline, used eight movable dials to add sums up to eight figures long. Pascal's device used a base of ten to accomplish this. For example, as one dial moved ten notches, or one complete revolution, it moved the next dial—which represented the ten's column—one place. When the ten's dial moved one revolution, the dial representing the hundred's place moved one notch and so on. The drawback to the Pascaline, of course, was its limitation to addition.

In 1694, a German mathematician and philosopher, Gottfried Wilhem von Leibniz (1646–1716), improved the Pascaline by creating a machine that could also multiply. Like its predecessor, Leibniz's mechanical multiplier worked by a system of gears and dials. Partly by studying Pascal's original notes and drawings, Leibniz was able to refine his machine. The centerpiece of the machine was its stepped-drum gear design, which offered an elongated version of the simple flat gear. It wasn't until 1820, however, that mechanical calculators gained widespread use. Charles Xavier Thomas de Colmar, a Frenchman, invented a machine that could perform the four basic arithmetic functions. Colmar's mechanical calculator, the arithometer, presented a more practical approach to computing because it could add, subtract, multiply and divide. With its enhanced versatility, the arithometer was widely used up until the First World War. Although later inventors refined Colmar's calculator, together with fellow inventors Pascal and Leibniz, he helped define the age of mechanical computation.

■ **Figure 8.1   Information Organized According to the Chronological Pattern**

Source: Jones Telecommunications & Multimedia Encyclopedia, 1999 <www.digitalcentury.com/encyclo/update/comp_hd.html>.

GUIDELINES

Organizing Information Spatially

▶ *Provide signposts.* Help your readers follow the argument by using words and phrases that indicate location (*to the left, above, in the center*) in headings, topic sentences, and support sentences.

▶ *Consider using graphics to complement the text.* Diagrams, drawings, photographs, and maps help readers understand the spatial relationships.

▶ *Analyze events where appropriate.* A spatial arrangement doesn't explain itself; you still have to do the analysis: a diagram of a floor plan cannot explain why the floor plan is effective or ineffective.

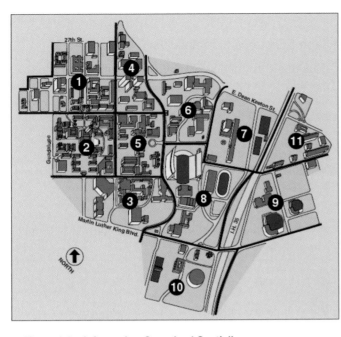

University of Texas at Austin
Main Campus

1 Communication

2 Tower

3 Perry-Castañeda Library

4 Engineering

5 East Mall

6 Law School

7 LBJ School & Museum

8 Stadium

9 Disch-Falk

10 Erwin Center

11 Physical Plant

This map is divided into 11 regions, each marked with a numeral. The user clicks on a numbered region next to the map for a detailed map of that region.

■ **Figure 8.2   Information Organized Spatially**

The spatial pattern helps the reader by breaking a very large area into smaller portions, making the campus easier to navigate.
Source: University of Texas at Austin, 2000 <www.utexas.edu/maps/main/overview>.

Figure 8.2, a Web-based map of the University of Texas campus, illustrates a spatial arrangement of information. A spatial arrangement could also be used in the text. For instance, each of the eleven regions of the campus could be discussed in accompanying paragraphs.

General to Specific

The general-to-specific pattern is used when readers need a general understanding of a subject before they can understand and remember the details. The general-to-specific pattern is used in many kinds of technical documents:

In a *report,* you include an executive summary—an overview for managers—before the body of the report.

In a set of *instructions,* you provide general information about the necessary tools and materials and about safety measures before providing the step-by-step instructions.

In a *memo,* you present the background information before going into the details.

On TechComm Web

To view Fig. 8.2 in context on the Web, click on Links Library for Ch. 8 on <bedfordstmartins.com /techcomm>.

Organizing Information from General to Specific

▶ *Provide signposts.* In the introduction, explain that you will address general issues first and then move on to specific concerns. If appropriate, incorporate the words *general* and *specific* or other relevant terms in the major headings or at the start of the text for each item you are describing.

▶ *Consider using graphics to complement the text.* Diagrams, drawings, photographs, and maps of varying detail help your reader understand the general or fine points of the information.

Figure 8.3 is an example of how to organize information from general to specific.

This paragraph, which begins Chapter 1 of a lengthy report about the government's efforts to control the toxic effects of carbon monoxide, is an advance organizer: it presents the main points that will be discussed in more detail in the discussion that follows. Because they present general information, advance organizers help readers understand the more specific information that comes next.

This paragraph presents a general description of carbon monoxide, explaining why the federal government monitors and regulates it.

This paragraph is an advance organizer for this chapter of the report.

Here the writers begin their specific discussion of the legislative requirements that were mentioned briefly in the previous paragraph.

This document is an update of *Air Quality Criteria for Carbon Monoxide,* published by the U.S. Environmental Protection Agency (EPA) in 1991, and will serve as the basis for reevaluating the current National Ambient Air Quality Standards (NAAQS) for carbon monoxide (CO) set in 1994. Carbon monoxide is one of six ubiquitous ambient air pollutants covered by the Federal Clean Air Act (CAA) requiring an assessment of the latest scientific knowledge as a requisite step in the development of standards to protect public health and welfare. . . .

Carbon monoxide, a trace constituent of the troposphere, is produced both by natural processes and human activities. Because plants can both metabolize and produce CO, trace levels are considered a normal constituent of the natural environment. Although ambient concentrations of CO in the vicinity of urban and industrial areas can exceed global background levels, there are no reports of these currently measured levels of CO producing any adverse effects on plants or microorganisms. Ambient concentrations of CO, however, may be detrimental to human health and welfare, depending on the levels that occur in areas where humans live and work and on the susceptibility of exposed individuals to potentially adverse effects.

This chapter presents a brief summary of the legislative and regulatory history of the CO NAAQS and the rationale for the existing standards, and it gives an overview of the issues, methods, and procedures utilized in the preparation of the present document.

1.1 Legislative Requirements

Two sections of the CAA govern the establishment, review, and revision of the NAAQS. Section 108 (U.S. Code, 1991) directs the Administrator of EPA to identify and issue air quality criteria for pollutants that reasonably may be anticipated to endanger public health or welfare. These air quality criteria are to reflect the latest scientific information useful in indicating the kind and extent of all identifiable effects on public health or welfare that may be expected from the presence of the pollutant in ambient air.

Section 109(a) of the CAA (U.S. Code, 1991) directs the Administrator of EPA to propose and promulgate primary and secondary NAAQS for pollutants identified under Section 108. Section 109(b)(1) defines a primary standard as one that the attainment and maintenance of which, in the judgment of the Administrator, based on the criteria and allowing for an adequate margin of safety, is requisite to protect the public health. . . .

■ **Figure 8.3   Information Organized from General to Specific**

Source: U.S. Environmental Protection Agency, 2000 <www.epa.gov/ncea/pdfs/coaqcd.pdf>.

More Important to Less Important

The more-important-to-less-important pattern recognizes that readers often want the bottom line—the most important information—first.

Here are examples of the use of the more-important-to-less-important pattern:

In an *accident report,* you describe the three most important factors that led to the accident before describing the less-important factors.

In a *feasibility study* about building a facility, you present the major reasons that the site is appropriate, then the minor reasons.

In a *proposal* to design a new microchip, you describe the major applications for the new chip, then the minor applications.

GUIDELINES

Organizing Information from More Important to Less Important

▶ *Provide signposts.* Tell your readers how you are organizing the passage. For instance, in the introduction of a proposal to design a new microchip, you might write, "The three applications for the new chip, each of which is discussed below, are arranged from most important to least important."

Be straightforward. If you have two very important points and three less important points, present them that way: group the two important points and label them, as in "Major Reasons to Retain Our Current Management Structure." Then present the less-important factors as "Other Reasons to Retain Our Current Management Structure." Being straightforward makes the material easier to follow and enhances your credibility.

▶ *Explain why one point is more important than another.* Don't just say that you will be arranging the items from more important to less important. Explain why the more important point is more important.

▶ *Consider using graphics to complement the text.* Diagrams and numbered lists often help to suggest levels of importance.

Figure 8.4, from a memo written by an executive at a company that sells equipment for manufacturing semiconductors, shows the more-important-to-less-important organizational structure.

Comparison and Contrast

Typically, the comparison-and-contrast pattern is used to describe and evaluate two or more options. This pattern lies at the heart of the feasibility study,

In This Book

For more on feasibility reports, see Ch. 19, p. 490.

A THREE-POINT PROGRAM TO IMPROVE SERVICE

As you know, our most significant goal for this year has been to improve our customer service. Over the past six weeks, we have attempted to learn what our customers expect—and demand—in the service they receive. Toward that end, we have attended numerous conferences and conducted many focus groups.

What we have learned from recent conferences of semiconductor purchasers and from the focus groups is that customers expect and demand better service than the industry currently provides. By better service I don't mean merely returning phone calls. I mean something much more ambitious and difficult to attain: helping our customers do their jobs by anticipating and addressing their total needs. For this reason, I have formed a Customer Satisfaction Panel, chaired by Maureen Bedrich, whose job will be to develop policies that will enable us to improve the quality of the service we offer our customers.

I have asked the panel, under Maureen Bedrich's direction, to consider three major areas:

- improving the ease of use of our equipment
- improving preventive and corrective maintenance
- improving our compatibility with other vendors' products

Improving the Ease of Use of Our Equipment

User friendliness is the most important area we need to improve, because it affects our customers during the entire lifetime of the product. When we deliver a new product, we have to sit down with customers and explain how to integrate it into their manufacturing processes. This session is time-consuming and costly for us and for them. Therefore, we must explore the option of automating it....

Improving Preventive and Corrective Maintenance

The second most important area for study is improving preventive and corrective maintenance. Our customers will no longer tolerate down times approaching 10 percent; they will accept no more than 2 percent to 3 percent. Preventive maintenance is critical in our industry because gases used in vapor-deposition systems periodically have to be removed from the inside of the equipment. Customers want to be able to plan for these stoppages to reduce costs. Currently, we have no means of helping them do so....

Improving Our Compatibility with Other Vendors' Products

Finally, we have to accept the fact that because no one in our industry is likely to control the market, we have to make our products more compatible with those of other manufacturers. This means that we must be willing to put our people on-site to see what the customers' setup is and help them determine how to modify our product to fit in efficiently. We can no longer offer a "take-it-or-leave-it" product.

I hope you will extend every effort to work constructively with Maureen and her committee over the coming months to ensure that we improve the overall service we offer our customers.

This bulleted list serves as an advance organizer for the document.

The writer states his organizational pattern in the topic sentence and explains why this first area is the most important one he will discuss.

The writer again indicates his organizational pattern.

■ **Figure 8.4**
Information Organized from More Important to Less Important

a document that compares two or more options under consideration. Here are examples of the use of the comparison-and-contrast pattern:

> In a *memo,* you compare and contrast the credentials of three finalists for a job.
>
> In a *proposal* to design a new microchip, you compare and contrast two different strategies for designing the chip.
>
> In a *report* describing a legal challenge that your company faces, you compare and contrast several options for responding.

The first step in comparing and contrasting two or more items is to determine the *criteria*: the standards or needs you will use in studying the items. For example, a comparison and contrast between two music keyboards might use the number of keys as one criterion. One keyboard might have 48 keys, whereas the other might have 64. Another criterion might be weight. One might weigh 25 pounds; the other, 46 pounds.

Often you compare and contrast several items as part of a decision-making process. That is, you need to decide which item best suits your needs. For instance, if you need to choose an elective to take next semester, your only criterion might be the time it is offered: it must meet at 10 o'clock on Mondays, Wednesdays, and Fridays. For this criterion, MWF 10 is a *required characteristic,* sometimes called a *minimum specification.* However, you probably have other criteria: you would like the course to be interesting, to look good on your transcript, and so on. These other criteria are examples of *desired characteristics,* sometimes called *evaluative criteria.*

Almost always, you will need to consider several criteria in writing a document using comparison and contrast as an organizational scheme. For a recommendation report on which computer to buy, for example, you would probably include a required characteristic—that the computer be compatible with your company's network—and some desired characteristics—such as ease of operation, reliability, and expandability. You will evaluate each option—each computer—first by eliminating those that fail to meet the required characteristic and then by comparing and contrasting the remaining options according to the desired characteristics.

Two typical patterns for organizing a comparison-and-contrast discussion are *whole by whole* and *part by part.* The following table illustrates the difference between them. In this table, two printers—Model 5L and Model 6L—are being compared and contrasted according to three criteria: price, resolution, and print speed.

You can have it both ways. If you want to use a part-by-part pattern to emphasize particular aspects, you can begin the discussion with a general description of the various items. Once you have chosen the overall pattern—whole-by-whole or part-by-part—you can decide how to organize the second-level items. That is, in a whole-by-whole passage, you have to sequence the "aspects"; in a part-by-part passage, you have to sequence the "options."

For most documents, a more-important-to-less-important pattern will work well because readers want to get to the bottom line as soon as possible.

The whole-by-whole pattern provides a coherent picture of each option: the 5L and the 6L. This pattern works best if your readers need an overall assessment of each option, or if each option is roughly equivalent according to the criteria.

Whole by Whole	Part by Part
Model 5L	Price
• price	• Model 5L
• resolution	• Model 6L
• print speed	
	Resolution
Model 6L	• Model 5L
• price	• Model 6L
• resolution	
• print speed	Print Speed
	• Model 5L
	• Model 6L

The part-by-part pattern lets you focus your attention on the criteria. If, for instance, Model 5L produces much better resolution than Model 6L, the part-by-part pattern reveals this difference more effectively than the whole-by-whole pattern does. The part-by-part pattern is best for detailed comparisons and contrasts.

For some documents, however, other patterns might work better. People who write for readers outside their own company often reverse the more-important-to-less-important pattern because they want to make sure their audience reads the whole discussion. This pattern is also popular with writers who are delivering bad news. If, for instance, you want to justify recommending that your organization not go ahead with a popular plan, the reverse sequence lets you explain the problems with the popular plan before you present the plan you recommend. Otherwise, readers might start to formulate objections before you have had a chance to explain your position.

Figure 8.5, an excerpt from a technical article about two computer operating systems, shows a comparison-and-contrast passage organized according to the part-by-part pattern.

GUIDELINES

Organizing Information by Comparison and Contrast

▶ *Establish criteria for the comparison and contrast.* Choose criteria that are consistent with the needs of your audience.

▶ *If appropriate, determine whether each criterion calls for a required characteristic or a desired characteristic.* This step applies only if you will be using the comparison and contrast pattern as part of a decision-making process.

▶ *Evaluate each item according to the criteria you have established.* Draw your conclusions.

▶ *Organize the discussion.* Choose either the *whole-by-whole* or *part-by-part* pattern or some combination of the two. Then organize the second-level items.

▶ *Consider using graphics to complement the text.* Graphics can clarify and emphasize comparison-and-contrast passages. Diagrams, drawings, and tables are common ways to provide such clarification and emphasis.

LINUX V. WINDOWS

To fairly judge the Linux versus Windows 2000 competition, you need to look at all the costs associated with administrating a network server, not just the actual cost of software. You need to look at the learning curve associated with each OS, as well as the ease of installation. You also must be aware of the cost of technical support, and the cost of not being able to get any when you need it. Let's have a look at each of these elements in a head-to-head comparison.

The Learning Curve
When it comes to administering a Linux server, Linux is UNIX. A good UNIX, maybe even a great UNIX, but it *is* UNIX. This means you will have to learn *vi* and *emacs*. You'll need to edit an endless number of oddly named text files and run an endless number of oddly named command-line utilities. If you were annoyed by the DOS prompt, you don't want to fool around with Linux. There are, however, a number of people who have spent much of their adult lives working in text windows, editing files with vi. These UNIX gurus are out there, and, for a price, they'll administer your Linux servers.

With Windows 2000, the learning curve, while not minimal, is less steep. Administration is done through an endless number of utilities, each containing a myriad of check boxes, OK buttons, and dropdown lists. Yet, on most dialog boxes, there's a Help button.

Winner: Slight edge to Windows 2000

Ease of Installation
Linux has gained a lot of ground in this area over the last few years. Professional installation programs are now available from places like Red Hat, though these do come at a small cost.

The installation program for Windows 2000 will also represent an improvement from the NT 4.0 installation process. Additions, such as Plug-and-Play compatibility and extended hardware support, will make installing the server software quick and painless, especially with the newer systems.

Winner: Tie

Technical Support
For Linux, there's very little in the way of conventional customer support. There are no "800" numbers or Help lines. If you have a problem, you can send a message to comp.os.linux, or post a message on one of the numerous Linux Web-based message boards, and hope that someone can help you. The truth is, most likely someone can, but there are no guarantees.

Microsoft provides a toll-free customer service number. You may have to wait, you may have to keep asking different people the same question (or different questions to the same person), but eventually you'll get some kind of answer.

Winner: Windows 2000

The author introduces the passage by naming the criteria according to which he will compare and contrast the two computer operating systems.

Each section is organized the same way: a paragraph about Linux, a paragraph about Windows 2000, and the author's conclusion.

■ **Figure 8.5**
Information Organized by Comparison and Contrast

Source: Andrews, 2000
<www.zdnet.com/devhead/stories /articles/0,4413,2163578,00.html>.

Classification and Partition

Classification is the process of assigning items to categories. For instance, all the students at a university could be classified by sex, age, major, and any number of other characteristics. You can also create subcategories within categories. For instance, within the category of students majoring in business at your college, you can create subcategories: males and females.

Here are examples of the use of classification as an organizing pattern:

In a *feasibility study* about building a facility, you classify sites into two categories: domestic and foreign.

In a *journal article* about ways to treat a medical condition, you classify the treatments as surgical and nonsurgical.

In a description of a major in a *college catalog,* you classify courses as required or elective.

Partition is the process of breaking a unit into its components. For example, a stereo system could be partitioned into the following components: CD player, tuner, amplifier, and speakers. Each component is separate, but together they form a whole stereo system. Each component can, of course, be partitioned further.

Partition is used in descriptions of objects, mechanisms, and processes (see Chapter 9). Here are examples of the use of partition:

In an *equipment catalog,* you use partition to describe the major components of one of your products.

In a *proposal,* you use partition to present a detailed description of an instrument being proposed for development.

In a *brochure,* you describe how to operate a product by describing each of its features.

GUIDELINES

Organizing Information by Classification or Partition

▸ *Choose a basis of classification or partition that fits your audience and purpose.* If you are writing a warning about snakes for hikers in a particular state park, your basis of classification will probably be whether the snakes are poisonous. You will describe all the poisonous snakes, then all the nonpoisonous ones.

▸ *Use only one basis of classification or partition at a time.* If you are classifying graphics programs according to their technology—paint programs and draw programs—do not include another basis of classification, such as cost.

⬇

▶ *Avoid overlap.* In classifying, make sure that no single item could logically be placed in more than one category. In partitioning, make sure that no listed component includes another listed component. Overlapping generally occurs when you change the basis of classification or the level at which you are partitioning a unit. In the following classification of bicycles, for instance, the writer introduces a new basis of classification that results in overlapping categories:

– mountain bikes

– racing bikes

– comfort bikes

– 10-speed bikes

The first three items share a basis of classification: the type of bicycle. The fourth item has a different basis of classification: number of speeds. Adding the fourth item is illogical because a particular 10-speed bike could be a mountain bike, a touring bike, or a racing bike.

▶ *Be inclusive.* Include all the categories necessary to complete your basis of classification. For example, a partition of an automobile by major systems would be incomplete if it included the electrical, fuel, and drive systems but not the cooling system. If your purpose or audience requires that you omit a category, tell your readers that you are doing so.

▶ *Arrange the categories in a logical sequence.* Use a reasonable plan: chronology (first to last), spatial development (top to bottom), importance (most important to least important), and so on.

▶ *Consider using graphics to complement the text.* Block diagrams are commonly used in classification passages; drawings and diagrams are often used in partition passages.

In Figure 8.6, a discussion of nondestructive testing techniques, the writer uses classification effectively in introducing nondestructive testing to a technical audience. Notice that the writer could have used another basis for classification: sensitivity. The four techniques range from very sensitive to less sensitive.

Figure 8.7 on page 175 is an example of partition. For more examples of partition, see Chapter 9, which includes descriptions of objects, mechanisms, and processes (page 204).

Notice that the writer clearly explains the sequence of the document's organization.

This simple block diagram helps the readers get an overview of the subject.

TYPES OF NONDESTRUCTIVE TESTING

Nondestructive testing of structures permits early detection of stresses that can cause fatigue and ultimately structural damage. The least sensitive tests isolate macrocracks. More sensitive tests identify microcracks. The most sensitive tests identify slight stresses. All sensitivities of testing are useful because some structures can tolerate large amounts of stress—or even cracks—before their structural integrity is threatened.

Currently there are four techniques for nondestructive testing, as shown in Figure 1. These techniques are presented from least sensitive to most sensitive.

Figure 1. Types of Nondestructive Testing

Body-Wave Reflection
In this technique, a transducer sends an ultrasonic pulse through the test material. When the pulse strikes a crack, part of the pulse's energy is reflected back to the transducer. Body-wave reflection cannot isolate stresses: the pulse is sensitive only to relatively large cracks.

Surface-Wave Reflection
The transducer generates an ultrasonic pulse that travels along the surface of the test material. Cracks reflect a portion of the pulse's energy back to the transducer. Like body-wave reflection, surface-wave reflection picks up only macrocracks. Because cracks often begin on interior surfaces of materials, surface-wave reflection is a poor predictor of serious failures.

Ultrasonic Attenuation
The transducer generates an ultrasonic pulse either through or along the surface of the test material. When the pulse strikes cracks or the slight plastic deformations associated with stress, part of the pulse's energy is scattered. Thus, the amount of the pulse's energy decreases. Ultrasonic attenuation is a highly sensitive method of nondestructive acoustic testing.

Here the writer introduces a second level of classification.

There are two methods of ultrasonic attenuation. One technique reflects the pulse back to the transducer. The other uses a second transducer to receive the pulses sent through or along the surface of the material.

Acoustic Emission
When a test specimen is subjected to a great amount of stress, it begins to emit waves; some are in the ultrasonic range. A transducer attached to the surface of the test specimen records these waves. Current technologies make it possible to interpret these waves accurately for impending fatigue and cracks.

■ **Figure 8.6**
Information Organized by Classification and Subclassification

The writer classifies nondestructive testing into four categories.

This "kit contents" page from a user manual for a camera partitions the kit into its components. The manual then discusses each of the components.

■ **Figure 8.7   Information Organized by Partition**

Source: Canon, 2002 <www.powershot.com/powershot2/s330/kit.html>.

Problem-Methods-Solution

The problem-methods-solution pattern reflects the logic used in carrying out a project. The three components of this pattern are simple to identify:

- *Problem.* A description of what was not working (or not working as effectively as it should), or what opportunity exists for improving current processes.
- *Method.* The procedure performed to confirm the analysis of the problem, solve the problem, or exploit the opportunity.
- *Solution.* The statement of whether the analysis of the problem was correct, or of what was discovered or devised to solve the problem or capitalize on the opportunity.

In most cases, you will present these three components in the order you see here. Sometimes, however, you might vary the sequence. For example, you might want to present the problem first and then go directly to the solution, leaving the methods for last. This sequence deemphasizes the methods, a strategy appropriate for readers who already know them well or don't need to understand them. When readers want to focus on the solution, you might begin with the solution and then discuss the problem and methods.

Here are some examples of the use of the problem-methods-solution pattern:

In a *proposal,* you describe a problem in your business, how you plan to carry out your research, and how your deliverable (an item or a report) can help solve the problem.

In a *completion report* about a project to improve a manufacturing process, you describe the problem that motivated the project, the methods you used to carry out the project, and the findings: the results, conclusions, and recommendations.

GUIDELINES

Organizing Information by Problem-Methods-Solution

▶ *In describing the problem, be clear and specific.* Don't write, "our energy expenditures are getting out of hand." Instead, write that "the energy usage has increased 7 percent in the last year" and that "the utility costs have risen 11 percent." Then calculate the total increase in energy costs.

▶ *In describing your methods, help your readers understand what you did and why you did it that way.* Because most technical problems can be approached using several methods, you might need to justify your choices. Why, for example, did you use a *t*-test in calculating the statistics in an experiment? If you can't defend your choice, you might lose credibility.

▶ *In describing the solution, don't overstate.* Avoid claims such as "this project will increase our market share from 7 percent to 10 percent within 12 months." Instead, be cautious: "This project promises to increase our market share from 7 percent to 10 percent or even 11 percent." This way, you won't be embarrassed if things don't turn out as well as you had hoped.

▶ *Choose a logical sequence.* The most common sequence is to start with the problem and conclude with the solution. However, different sequences work equally well as long as you provide a preliminary summary to give readers an overview and provide headings or some other design elements (see Chapter 10) to help readers find the information they want.

▶ *Consider using graphics to complement the text.* Graphics, such as flowcharts, diagrams, and drawings, can clarify and emphasize problem-methods-solution passages.

The example of the problem-methods-solution argument in Figure 8.8 is based on a discussion about improving child safety in automobiles.

CHILD RESTRAINT LAWS

The Problem

A 1996 Safety Board child-passenger safety study involving more than 180 restrained children showed that the children tended to be restrained in systems too advanced for their physical development. For example, the report showed that 52 children used vehicle seat belts when they should have been placed in child restraint systems or booster seats.

The results can be tragic. In the summer of 1996 in Washington State, a 4-year-old, 45-pound boy was buckled into a lap/shoulder belt by his mother in accordance with State law. When their sport utility vehicle rolled over in a violent crash, the boy's lap/shoulder belt remained buckled, but the young boy was ejected from the restraint and the car, and killed.

The Centers for Disease Control and Prevention (CDC) issued a report in February 1999 indicating that 4- through 8-year-olds are not being protected because of gaps in the State laws that govern child safety seats. As a result, the CDC estimates that almost 500 children die on our highways every year because they are not properly secured in restraint systems—booster seats—that are appropriate for their age, height, and weight.

Twenty-eight States and the District of Columbia require children of all ages (infants through teenagers) to be buckled up, although most permit seat belts to be substituted for child safety seats or booster seats. Only eight States require all children age 4 and under to be in child safety seats.

In addition, 6 out of 10 children killed in traffic crashes are not buckled up at all. The number of children killed each year could be reduced by 50 percent if every child were buckled up. There should be no tolerance for unbuckled children. State child restraint laws should be enforced and supported to reduce the number of children killed and injured in traffic crashes.

What We Are Doing

Although all 50 States and the District of Columbia have child passenger protection laws, in 1996, the Safety Board called on the States to strengthen their child restraint laws to do the following:

* Require all children under 4 years old to be in child safety seats.
* Require that 4- to 8-year-old children use auto safety booster seats.
* Eliminate provisions that permit children under 8 years old to be buckled up in a seat belt.
* Require all children under age 13 to ride in the back seat, if a seat is available.

Safety Improvements

We are starting to see States take positive steps to improve child safety in automobiles. As a result of the Safety Board's urging, the following actions were taken:

* Washington State and California enacted laws in 2000 to require children under 6 years of age or 60 pounds to ride in a booster seat.
* Delaware, North Carolina, and Rhode Island now require children to ride in the back seat of air bag–equipped cars. In Louisiana, all children less than 13 years of age must ride in the rear seat when one is available.

The Safety Board recently began an education campaign "Boost 'em before you Buckle 'em" to ensure that 4- to 8-year-olds get buckled up in age-appropriate restraint systems.

Our efforts at educating state legislatures and executives continue, but we are beginning to see real progress in protecting America's most vulnerable automobile passengers.

The writer uses statistics and examples to define the problem of child safety in automobiles.

The writer describes the actions taken by the Safety Board—the methods—to combat the problems described earlier in the discussion.

The writer describes the "solution": the results of the efforts made by the Safety Board. Naturally, the solutions do not completely fix the problem, but they represent progress.

■ **Figure 8.8
Information Organized by
the Problem-Methods-
Solution Pattern**

Source: National Transportation Safety Board, 2000 <www.ntsb .gov/Publictn/2000/SR0002.pdf>.

Cause and Effect

Technical communication often involves cause-and-effect discussions. Sometimes you will reason forward, from cause to effect. If we raise the price of a particular product we manufacture (cause), what will happen to our sales (effect)? Sometimes you will reason backward, from effect to cause. Productivity went down by 6 percent in the last quarter (effect); what factors led to this decrease (causes)? Cause-and-effect reasoning, therefore, provides a way to answer the following two questions:

- What will be the effect(s) of X?
- What caused X?

Here are examples of the use of cause and effect as an organizing pattern:

In an *environmental impact statement*, you argue that a proposed construction project would have three important effects on the ecosystem.

In the recommendation section of a *report*, you argue that a recommended solution would improve operations in two major ways.

In a *memo*, you describe a new policy, then explain the effects you anticipate the policy will have.

Cause-effect relationships are difficult to describe because there is no scientific way to determine causes or effects. You draw on your common sense and your knowledge of your subject. When you try to determine, for example, why the product you introduced last year failed to sell, you start with the obvious possibilities: the market was saturated, the product was of low quality, the product was poorly marketed, and so forth. The more you know about your subject, the more precise and more insightful your analysis will be.

A causal discussion can never be certain. You cannot prove why a product failed in the marketplace. But you can explain why you think the causes or effects you are identifying are the most plausible ones. For instance, to make a plausible case that the main reason your product failed is that it was poorly marketed, you can show that, in the past, your company's other unsuccessful products were marketed in similar ways. This argument does not confirm that poor marketing was the problem, but it makes the claim plausible. Similarly, if you can show that your best-selling products have been marketed very differently from the unsuccessful one, that reasoning helps make the claim plausible.

GUIDELINES

Organizing Information by Cause and Effect

▶ *Explain your reasoning.* If your point is that the product was marketed poorly, use specific facts and figures—the low marketing budget, delays in beginning the marketing campaign, and so forth—that support your claim.

- *Avoid overstating your argument.* For instance, if you write that Steve Jobs, the founder of Apple, "created the computer revolution," you are claiming too much. It is better to write that Steve Jobs "was one of the central players in creating the computer revolution."
- *Avoid logical fallacies.* Logical fallacies, such as hasty generalizations or *post-hoc* reasoning, can also undermine your discussion.
- *Consider using graphics to complement the text.* Graphics, such as flowcharts, organization charts, diagrams, and drawings, can clarify and emphasize cause-and-effect passages.

In This Book

For more on logical fallacies, see Ch. 6, p. 113.

Figure 8.9, a discussion of the increased use of color in documents, illustrates an effective cause-and-effect argument.

INTRODUCTIONS AND CONCLUSIONS

Drafting the passages in the body of a document involves using and modifying the basic organizational patterns described in this chapter. Two more elements of the body — the introduction and the conclusion — are also fundamental to the success of your document.

Introductions

An introduction helps readers understand your discussion by explaining *what* information you are going to present, *how* you are going to present it, and *why* you choose to present it that way. If you communicate these points clearly, your readers will be more willing to read the document and better able to understand and remember it.

Your document can have one introduction (at the beginning) or several introductions (one at the beginning and one at the start of each major section).

Every document calls for a different kind of introduction. A brochure on swimming pool safety obviously needs little introduction — perhaps only a brief review of the statistics on injuries and deaths. But the introduction to a scholarly article, which needs to conform to the practices in a particular academic field, might require many elements. To draft the introduction to the body of your document, use your common sense and study similar documents to note the conventions in your field and the expectations of your readers.

Readers rely on an introduction to answer seven questions.

An introduction should answer these seven questions:

What is the subject?

What are the key terms that will be used in the argument?

What is the purpose of the argument?

What is the background of the subject?

What is the relevant literature, and what are its limitations?

What is the scope of the argument?

What is the organization of the argument?

The first four paragraphs present factors related to the way people respond to color in documents.

Here the writer presents the main effect.

Here the writer presents additional causes: the popularity of color on the Internet . . .

the decreased cost of using color in print documents . . .

and the high quality of color copiers and printers.

IT'S A COLORFUL WORLD

Color grabs your attention, improves understanding, emphasizes key data, highlights comparisons, and adds prestige to a document. It's one of the most important elements for effective communication.

Until recently, most hard-copy documents have existed as black marks on white paper. Creating visually powerful color documents used to be the province of skilled graphic artists using special equipment and expensive, slow processes.

However, there's no doubt that color is the first element people notice when they glance at a document. The majority of respondents to a Xerox-sponsored study (89%) believe that color increases the effectiveness of business communications. The respondents also feel that color enhances a company's image (88%).

Color adds a new spectrum of understanding by focusing attention on specific material. And studies show that a customer's payment rate jumps by as much as 30% when color is used in an invoice.

Based on these facts, financial institutions, law firms, universities, and businesses in other industries are becoming more aware of the value of color.

The Internet and the World Wide Web are also fueling this migration. The increasing use of the web as a medium for publishing digital documents is certain to expand the demand for, and the use of, color documents in businesses. Virtually all web pages are in color. It's only a matter of time before customers will demand the same color in their daily documents as on their screens.

Until now, cost was a major barrier. Color machines were limited to environments such as graphic design agencies, in-plant printers or quick printers where their use was economically justified. To produce top-quality color, office workers often sent work out to a copy shop, a service bureau, or an in-plant print department.

Today, a wide array of color copiers and printers offer near-offset image quality, excellent running speeds, and finishing accessories for multiple sets. Most significantly, these new machines are networkable, allowing them to be shared by large teams for high productivity and lower cost.

By bringing individuals and color closer together, the world of business documents will eventually be as colorful as the world at large.

■ **Figure 8.9**
A Discussion Organized by the Cause-and-Effect Pattern

In this passage from the Xerox Corporation Web site, the author is explaining the factors (the causes) that have led to the new popularity of color in documents (the effect).
Source: Xerox, 2001 <www.xerox.com/go/xrx/template/009.jsp?view=Feature&Xcntry=USA&Xlang=en_US&Xseg=home&ed_name=Colorful_World_2>.

- *What is the subject?* Answer this question explicitly, even though your readers might already know the answer.

  This report describes the relationship between the courts and the scientific community on the subject of phantom risk. In an age of tremendous technological advances, some new products and practices might pose health risks. The conflict explored in this report is that, whereas the courts require certainty (they need to know whether a plaintiff was or was not injured by a technology), the scientific community often cannot supply a definitive answer.

- *What are the key terms that will be used in the argument?*

  Phantom risk refers to alleged but uncertain risks associated with a scientific or technological practice. For instance, weak magnetic fields represent a phantom risk in that the scientific community is uncertain whether they represent any health risk at all, or, if they do, what the threshold for such risks might be.

  In This Book

  For more about definitions, see Ch. 9, p. 194.

- *What is the purpose of the argument?* Explain what you hope to achieve in the discussion.

  This report has two main purposes: to summarize the conflict between the legal and scientific communities and to propose three principles to guide the future debate on the legal ramifications of phantom risk.

- *What is the background of the subject?* Present the information that readers will need to understand the discussion.

  It is inevitable that some people will be injured by high-tech devices and procedures, and one of the foundations of our legal system is that victims be able to seek redress of their injuries through the legal system. However, science does not offer the kind of certainty the legal system requires. Are breast implants dangerous? Cautious scientists would have to admit that they don't know, but different constituencies answer yes and no with self-assurance and conviction. When courts render false-positive judgments—by ruling that harmless products and services have caused injuries—they put companies out of business and deprive people of their products and services. When courts render false negatives—by finding that harmful products and services have not injured anyone—they endanger the public. Currently, there is no way to reconcile the different cultures and practices of the legal and scientific communities.

- *What is the relevant literature, and what are its limitations?* Show your readers that you have done the necessary research on your topic.

  Although a number of researchers have studied the topic of phantom risk, most of the studies have examined individual cases from either the legal or scientific perspective. For instance, the asbestos issue has been discussed from the scientific perspective by Wilkins (2002), Thomas (2000), and Rivera (2002), and the legal perspective by Halloran (2001), Bradford (1999), and De Moss (2002). The edited collection by Foster et al. (1999), the first to attempt a detailed look at the conflict, offers only piecemeal opinions about the different phantom-risk issues, without providing a theoretical framework for reconciling the two cultures.

- *What is the scope of the argument?* Explain what you are including or excluding.

> This report focuses on four phantom-risk issues: electrical and magnetic field risks, spermicide cancer risks, asbestos risks, and secondhand-smoke risks. It reviews the scientific evidence and the legal opinions for each issue. Where appropriate, it discusses the social policy resulting from the legal actions.

- *What is the organization of the argument?*

> In the sections that follow, I treat each phantom-risk issue separately, as a case study. After a background discussion, I fill in the scientific consensus, followed by the legal precedents and, where appropriate, the resultant social policy. I conclude the article with a recommendation that we discuss three principles for reconciling the legal and scientific approaches to phantom-risk issues.

Figure 8.10 is an excerpt from the introduction to a report about small, modular nuclear reactors.

Conclusions

A conclusion should answer these four questions:

What are the main ideas communicated in the argument?

What should be done next?

How can the reader find more information?

How can we help you in the future?

In discussions of writing, the word *conclusion* has two meanings. One meaning refers to the inferences drawn from technical data. For instance, after investigating whether your company should switch from paper-based to online documentation, you might conclude that the change would be unwise at this time; that conclusion, along with others, would appear in the "Conclusions" section of your feasibility report. This kind of conclusion is discussed in Chapter 19.

Conclusion also refers to the final part of a document or a section of a document. The following discussion concerns this second sense of the word. Although some kinds of documents, such as parts catalogs, do not usually have a conclusion, most do.

- *What are the main ideas communicated in the argument?* Readers can forget material, especially material from the beginning of a long document. Therefore, it is a good idea to summarize the important ideas. The following examples are from a report on reuse-adoption programs: companywide programs to increase the reuse of systems and software.

> Our analysis yielded two main conclusions. First, reuse adoption is good engineering and good business; it can reduce expenses and increase productivity and quality. Second, reuse adoption is a complex procedure that requires a substantial amount of planning and supervision. If the program is carried out casually or thoughtlessly, it can backfire and cause more problems than it solves.

- *What should be done next?* Offer recommendations.

> I recommend that we convene a committee to study the feasibility of converting to a reuse-adoption plan. Specifically, we should carry out a Phase I analysis to determine the answers to the following four questions:

INTRODUCTION

Recent trends in nuclear reactor power plant designs have led to the development of numerous designs and proposed concepts for small modular nuclear reactors with a wide variety of safety and engineering features. These new power plants may prove attractive for remote communities where the current ability to generate electric power depends on costly shipments of fuels, resulting in relatively expensive and possibly uncertain electricity supplies. In fiscal year 2001, Congress provided funding and direction to perform a study on this issue, according the following language contained in the Senate Report (S. Rept.) 106-395:

> The Committee is aware that recent improvements in reactor design might make feasible small modular reactors with attractive characteristics for remote communities that otherwise must rely on shipments of relatively expensive and sometimes environmentally undesirable fuels for their electric power. To be acceptable, such a reactor would have to be inherently safe, be relatively cost effective, have intrinsic design features which would deter sabotage or efforts to divert nuclear materials, have infrequent refueling, and be largely factory constructed and deliverable to remote sites. . . .

This report describes the results of the study performed in response to this direction. The study specifically addresses the characteristics mentioned in S. Rept. 106-395, dividing the discussion into three critical aspects: technical, regulatory, and economic issues. Information on numerous designs and concepts was gathered from submissions received in response to the announcement of this study in *Commerce Business Daily*, February 26, 2001, and the *Federal Register*, February 27, 2001, as well as from literature and Internet searches. The depth of information received, however, varied. For instance, more detailed information on the Remote-Site Modular Helium Reactor was received in response to the announcement for information on small modular reactors (SMR) and is reflected in the length of its review in Chapter 3. For most of the other SMR designs and concepts reviewed, the basic layout of the facility has been established, perhaps even to some of the smallest details, but design trade-offs and optimization have not been performed, and the detailed engineering to build the plant has not been completed. As a result, this report contains no illustrations of any plant designs or concepts.

For the technical assessment, emphasis has been placed on evaluating the viability and maturity of each SMR, including identification of any recent or innovative developments, and the time that would be required for further development and potential deployment. The effect of current licensing requirements has been explored, and possible beneficial modifications have been identified. Estimates of the expected costs of generic SMRs and comparisons with current electricity rates in typical remote locations have been provided.

*The authors begin with a **background** statement that briefly describes the subject and the occasion for the report: Congress's directive to carry out the study.*

*The quotation from Congress's directive helps the writers describe their **subject**: small modular nuclear reactors.*

*The writers describe the **purpose** of the report.*

*Next, the writers describe their **methods.***

*The writers point out a **limitation** of their report: their source material varied in quantity and quality.*

*Although the writers have done a good job in describing the **scope** of the report, they did not explain the **organization** of the report.*

On TechComm Web

To see Fig. 8.10 in context on the Web, click on Links Library for Ch. 8 on <bedfordstmartins.com/techcomm>.

■ **Figure 8.10**
A Sample Introduction

Source: U.S. Department of Energy, 2001 <http://nuclear.gov/reports/Cong-Rpt-may01.pdf>.

1. Is demand in our market sufficient for the kinds of products that are appropriate for reuse adoption?
2. What effect will reuse adoption have on . . .

- *How can the reader find more information?* Sometimes this portion of the conclusion is a sales message; sometimes it is not.

   I have asked Corporate Information to get the six articles listed in the references section. These articles will be gathered and routed next week. Please read them and be prepared to offer any questions or concerns at our meeting on August 15, at which time we will discuss the recommendations.

- *How can we help you in the future?* If you can, offer to provide services.

   I think reuse adoption offers the promise to improve our business in a number of ways. Please feel free to get in touch with me, either before or after you read the articles, to discuss this initiative.

Figure 8.11 is an excerpt from the conclusion of the report on small modular nuclear reactors.

*The authors begin by summarizing their **major finding:** small modular nuclear reactors seem promising technically and economically.*

*The writers describe **what should be done next.** A number of technical and regulatory issues need to be resolved.*

CONCLUSION

Overall, it appears that there are SMR designs and concepts that meet the criteria set forth in Senate Report 106-395. These new small reactors have no insurmountable technical issues to hinder development and deployment, and the projected range of costs for SMRs are comparable with current rates charged in some remote communities. Moreover, U.S. experience with small reactors has shown that these facilities can be safely constructed and operated. One issue requiring further study is the lack of supporting infrastructures for supplying fuel for each of the SMRs. Depending on the fuel type, suitable fuel fabrication facilities may not currently exist, and would need to be constructed and qualified. Currently, this may be of particular concern for gas-cooled reactors using graphite fuel, although potential pebble-bed reactor development might alter this situation. Further, some of the new SMRs are cooled by gas or liquid metals, and some of the more viable designs and concepts face licensing questions which are outside the traditional NRC light water reactor experience. As a result, the current regulatory guidelines may not be fully applicable. Additionally, it is not clear to what extent the elimination of a conventional containment would be acceptable to the NRC. This would need to be explored. Also, it would be beneficial to further refine the SMR cost estimates after determining the full extent of potential regulatory issues in order to make fully informed decisions regarding development and deployment in remote communities.

■ **Figure 8.11   A Sample Conclusion**

*The Web site on which this report is presented **invites readers to inquire for more information** on how the organization can provide further assistance. The writers do not **offer to help readers in the future** because their job is to carry out research, not to provide assistance to industry or the public.*
Source: U.S. Department of Energy, 2001 <http://nuclear.gov/reports/Cong-Rpt-may01.pdf>.

On TechComm Web

To see Fig. 8.11 in context on the Web, click on Links Library for Ch. 8 on <bedfordstmartins.com /techcomm>.

Interactive Sample Document:
Identifying the Elements of a Conclusion

This excerpt is from the conclusion of a research report on musculoskeletal disorders (MSD) (based on Bernard, 1997). The purpose of the report is to present the best available information about causes and extent of MSDs. The questions in the margin ask you to think about conclusions (as discussed on pages 182–184). The answers to these questions are available on TechComm Web.

CONCLUSION

A substantial body of credible epidemiologic research provides strong evidence of an association between MSDs and certain work-related physical factors when there are high levels of exposure and especially in combination with exposure to more than one physical factor (e.g., repetitive lifting of heavy objects in extreme or awkward postures) [Table 1].

The consistently positive findings from a large number of cross-sectional studies, strengthened by the limited number of prospective studies, provides *strong evidence* for increased risk of work-related MSDs for some body parts. This evidence can be seen from the strength of the associations, lack of ambiguity in temporal relationships from the prospective studies, the consistency of the results in these studies, and adequate control or adjustment for likely confounders. . . .

In general, there is limited detailed quantitative information about exposure-disorder relationships between risk factors and MSDs. The risk of each exposure depends on a variety of factors such as the frequency, duration, and intensity of physical workplace exposures. Most of the specific exposures associated with the *strong evidence* involved daily whole shift exposure to the factors under investigation.

The number of jobs in which workers routinely lift heavy objects, are exposed on a daily basis to whole body vibration, routinely perform overhead work, work with their necks in chronic flexion position, or perform repetitive forceful tasks is unknown. While these exposures do not occur in most jobs, a large number of workers may indeed work under these conditions. The BLS data indicate that the total employment is over three million in the industries with the highest incidence rates of cases involving days away from work from overexertion in lifting and repetitive motion. . . .

This critical review of the epidemiologic literature identified a number of specific physical exposures strongly associated with specific MSDs when exposures are intense, prolonged, and particularly when workers are exposed to several risk factors simultaneously. This scientific knowledge is being applied in preventive programs in a number of diverse work settings. While this review has summarized an impressive body of epidemiologic research, we recognize that additional research would be quite valuable. The MSD components of the National Occupational Research Agenda efforts are principally directed toward stimulation of greater research on MSDs and occupational factors, both physical and psychosocial. Research efforts can be guided by the existing literature, reviewed here, as well as by data on the magnitude of various MSDs among U.S. workers.

For additional information about occupational safety and health problems, call 1-800-35-NIOSH (1-800-356-4674), or visit the NIOSH Home Page on the World Wide Web at http://www.cdc.gov/niosh/homepage.html.

Copies of this and other NIOSH documents are available from the National Institute for Occupational Safety and Health, Publications Dissemination, 4676 Columbia Parkway, Cincinnati, OH 45226-1998.

Telephone: 1-800-35-NIOSH (1-800-356-4674); Fax: (513) 533-8573; E-mail: pubstaff@cdc.gov.

For each of these four questions, determine if the question is answered in this conclusion. If it is, in which paragraph (or paragraphs) is it answered?

1. What are the main ideas communicated in the argument?

2. What should be done next?

3. How can the reader find more information?

4. How can we help you in the future?

On TechComm Web

To find the answers to these questions, click on Interactive Sample Documents for Ch. 8 on <bedfordstmartins.com/techcomm>.

Revision Checklist

Did you
- [ ] analyze your audience and purpose? (p. 160)
- [ ] consider using a conventional pattern of arrangement? (p. 161)
- [ ] display your organization prominently by
  - [ ] creating a detailed table of contents? (p. 162)
  - [ ] using headings liberally? (p. 162)
  - [ ] using topic sentences at the beginnings of your paragraphs? (p. 162)

The following checklists cover the eight organizational patterns discussed in this chapter, as well as introductions and conclusions.

Chronological and Spatial

Did you
- [ ] provide signposts, such as headings or transitional words or phrases? (p. 163)
- [ ] consider using graphics to complement the text? (p. 163)
- [ ] analyze events where appropriate? (p. 163)

General to Specific

Did you
- [ ] provide signposts, such as headings or transitional words or phrases? (p. 166)
- [ ] consider using graphics to complement the text? (p. 166)

More Important to Less Important

Did you
- [ ] provide signposts, explaining clearly that you are using this organizational pattern? (p. 167)
- [ ] make clear why the first point is the most important, the second is the second most important, and so forth? (p. 167)
- [ ] consider using graphics to complement the text? (p. 167)

Comparison and Contrast

Did you
- [ ] establish criteria for the comparison and contrast? (p. 169)
- [ ] choose a structure — whole-by-whole or part-by-part — that is most appropriate for your audience and purpose? (p. 169)

- [ ] choose appropriate organizational patterns for your second-level items? (p. 169)
- [ ] consider using graphics to complement the text? (p. 170)

Classification and Partition

Did you
- [ ] choose a basis consistent with the audience and purpose of the document? (p. 172)
- [ ] use only one basis at a time? (p. 172)
- [ ] avoid overlap? (p. 173)
- [ ] include all the appropriate categories? (p. 173)
- [ ] arrange the categories in a logical sequence? (p. 173)
- [ ] consider using graphics to complement the text? (p. 173)

Problem-Methods-Solution

Did you
- [ ] describe the problem clearly and specifically? (p. 176)
- [ ] if appropriate, justify your methods? (p. 176)
- [ ] avoid overstating your solution? (p. 176)
- [ ] arrange the discussion in a sequence consistent with the audience and purpose of the document? (p. 176)
- [ ] consider using graphics to complement the text? (p. 176)

Cause and Effect

Did you
- [ ] explain your reasoning? (p. 178)
- [ ] avoid overstating your argument? (p. 179)
- [ ] avoid logical fallacies? (p. 179)
- [ ] consider using graphics to complement the text? (p. 179)

The following questions cover introductions and conclusions.

Introductions

Did you
- [ ] explain the subject of the document? (p. 181)
- [ ] define all key terms that will be used in the discussion? (p. 181)
- [ ] explain the purpose of the discussion? (p. 181)

❑ explain the background of the subject? (p. 181)
❑ review the relevant literature, explaining its limitations? (p. 181)
❑ explain the scope of the discussion? (p. 182)
❑ explain the organization of the discussion? (p. 182)

Conclusions

Did you
❑ summarize the main ideas in the document? (p. 182)
❑ recommend what should be done next? (p. 182)
❑ explain how the reader can find more information? (p. 184)
❑ describe how you can help? (p. 184)

Exercises

On TechComm Web

For more exercises, click on Additional Exercises, Projects, and Cases for Ch. 8 on <bedfordstmartins.com/techcomm>.

1. **Internet Activity**   Using a search engine, find the Web site of a company that makes a product used by professionals in your field (personal computers are a safe choice). Locate three discussions on the site. For example, you will probably find the following: a passage devoted to ordering a product from the site (using a chronological pattern), a description of a product (using a partition argument), a passage describing why the company's products are superior to those of the competitors (using a cause-and-effect argument). Print a copy of the passages you've identified.

2. For each of the lettered topics that follow, identify the best organizational pattern for a discussion of the subject. For example, a discussion of distance education and on-campus courses could be organized using the comparison-and-contrast pattern. Write a brief explanation about why this would be the best organizational pattern to use. (Use each of the organizational patterns discussed in this chapter at least once.)

   a. how to register for courses at your college or university

   b. how you would propose reducing the time required to register for classes or to change your schedule

   c. your car's dashboard

   d. the current price of gasoline

   e. advances in manufacturing technology

   f. the reasons you chose your college or major

   g. a student organization on your campus

   h. the tutorials that come with two different software programs

   i. personal computers

   j. how you would propose increasing the ties between your college or university and local business and industry

   k. college courses

   l. increased security in airports

   m. the room in which you are sitting

   n. the three most important changes you would like to see at your school

   o. a guitar

   p. cooperative education and internships for college students

   q. digital and analog photography

   r. how to prepare for a job interview

3. Write a 500-word discussion of one of the lettered topics in Exercise 2. If appropriate, include graphics. Preface your discussion with a sentence explaining the audience and purpose of the discussion.

Project

4. **Group Activity** Form small groups for this project about organizing information. Review the background section in the government regulation (U.S. Department of Labor, 1997) presented in the case that follows. Write a memo to your instructor describing and analyzing the organization of this passage. Which techniques discussed in this chapter do the authors of this excerpt use? How effectively do they use them? What would you do differently? To see the full document, go to <www.osha-slc.gov/Publications /Osha3144.pdf>. (For more on memos, see Chapter 15, page 378.)

C A S E
Introducing a Document

You are an intern at the U.S. Department of Labor. Your supervisor, Allen Young, has asked you to study the document on methylene chloride that is excerpted below. The full document, which can be found at <www.osha-slc .gov/Publications/Osha3144.pdf>, is intended for a managerial and general audience. "It's got a disclaimer statement at the front of the document, and a background statement," Allen tells you, "but I think it needs an introduction. Would you mind taking a look at it and drafting an introduction?" Write an introduction for this document.

Background

When established under the authority of the *Occupational Safety and Health Act of 1970*, the Occupational Safety and Health Administration (OSHA) had 2 years to adopt existing federal standards or national consensus standards[1] so it would have standards in place to enforce. OSHA chose to adopt existing federal standards issued under the *Walsh-Healey Public Contracts Act*, which were derived from threshold limit values of the American Conference of Governmental Industrial Hygienists and consensus standards from standards-developing organizations such as the American National Standards Institute (ANSI).

For methylene chloride, OSHA adopted an ANSI standard under Subpart Z of *Title 29 Code of Federal Regulations* (CFR), Part 1910.1000 to ensure that employee exposure did not exceed 500 parts per million parts of air (500 ppm) as an 8-hour time-weighted average (TWA) — i.e., the average exposure during an 8-hour period.

Since 1971, however, industrial experience, new developments in technology, and emerging scientific data clearly indicate that this limit did not adequately protect worker health. The agency realized the need to better control worker exposure to methylene chloride due to its harmful health effects.

Methylene chloride, also called dichloromethane, is a volatile, colorless liquid with a chloroformlike odor. Inhalation and skin exposure are the predominant means of exposure to methylene chloride. Inhaling the vapor causes mental confusion, lightheadedness, nausea, vomiting, and headache. With acute, or short-term exposure, methylene chloride acts as an anesthetic; continued exposure may cause staggering, unconsciousness, and even death. High concentrations of the vapors may cause irritation of the eyes and respiratory tract and aggravate the symptoms of angina. Skin contact with liquid methylene chloride causes irritation and burns. Splashing methylene chloride into the eyes causes irritation. Studies on laboratory animals indicate that long-term (chronic) exposure causes cancer.

Methylene chloride is used in various industrial processes in many different industries: paint stripping, pharmaceutical manufacturing, paint remover manufacturing, metal cleaning and degreasing, adhesives manufacturing and use, polyurethane foam production, film base manufacturing, polycarbonate resin production, and distribution and formulation of solvents.

The agency adopted the methylene chloride final rule on January 10, 1997, as published in the *Federal Register*. The rule became effective on April 10, 1997.

---

[1] Consensus standards are developed by private, standards-developing organizations and are discussed and substantially agreed upon through consensus by industry, labor, and other representatives.

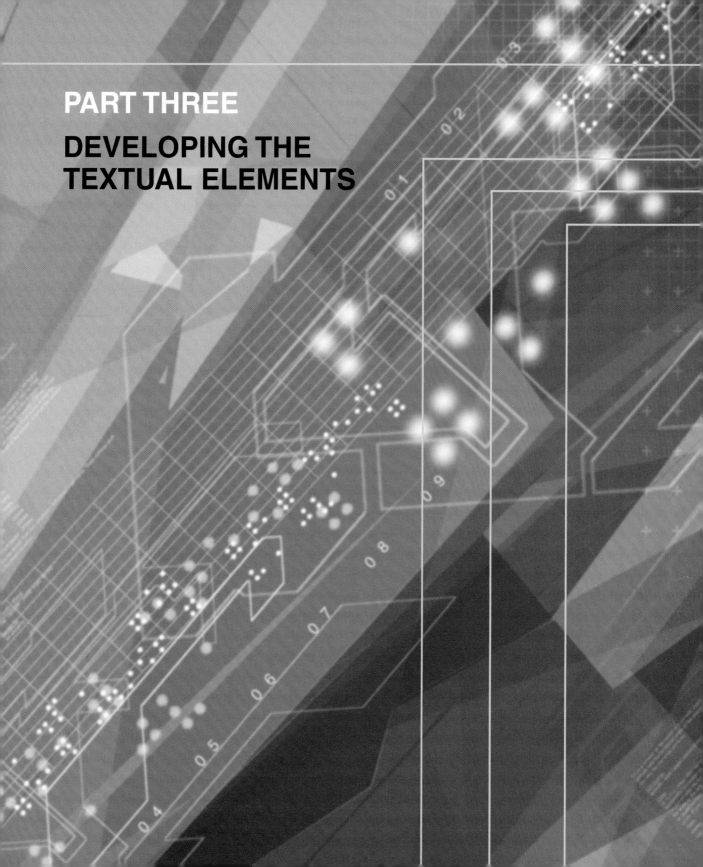

PART THREE

**DEVELOPING THE
TEXTUAL ELEMENTS**

Drafting and Revising Definitions and Descriptions

9

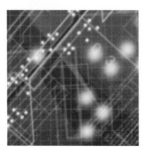

The technical-communication scholar Anne Eisenberg (1992, p. 159) on the role of definitions in technical communication:

Usually your reader knows less about the subject than you. This is true whether you write for administrators outside your particular area, for marketing people, or for people following a set of instructions. Only rarely will you have peers for an audience. This means you'll need to explain. Definitions are crucial for these explanations, for they are the kernels out of which the reader's understanding will grow.

On TechComm Web

For additional samples, activities, and links related to this chapter, see <bedfordstmartins.com/techcomm>.

Definitions and descriptions use words and, in most cases, graphics to help readers understand concepts, and they are fundamental to technical communication. Definitions help readers understand what you mean by a word or phrase. Descriptions usually provide a fuller picture of an object, a mechanism, or a process, often going into detail about the components of the object or the stages of the process.

UNDERSTANDING THE ROLE OF DEFINITIONS

The world of business and industry depends on clear definitions. Suppose you are told at a job interview that the employer pays tuition and expenses for employees' job-related education. You'll need to study the employee-benefits manual to understand just what the company will pay for. Who, for instance, is an *employee*? Is it anyone who works for and is paid by the company? Maybe. But perhaps the company defines an employee as someone who has worked for the company full time (40 hours per week) for at least six uninterrupted months. What is *tuition*? Does the definition include incidental laboratory or student fees? What is *job-related education*? Does a course about time management qualify under the company's definition? What, in fact, constitutes *education*?

Definitions are common in communicating policies and standards "for the record." Definitions also have many uses outside legal or contractual contexts. Two such uses occur frequently.

- *Definitions clarify a description of a new development or a new technology in a technical field.* For instance, a zoologist who has discovered a new animal species names and defines it.

- *Definitions help specialists communicate with less knowledgeable readers.* A manual explaining how to tune up a car includes definitions of parts and tools.

Definitions, then, are crucial in many kinds of technical communication, from brief letters and memos to technical reports, manuals, and journal articles. All readers, from the general reader to the expert, need effective definitions to carry out their jobs.

Writing effective definitions requires thought and planning. Before you can do so, you should analyze the writing situation, determine the kind of definition needed, and decide where to place the definition.

ANALYZING THE WRITING SITUATION FOR DEFINITIONS

The first step in writing effective definitions is to analyze the writing situation: the audience and the purpose of your document.

Unless you know who your readers will be and how much they know about the subject, you cannot determine which terms to define or what kind of definition to write. Physicists wouldn't need a definition of *entropy,* but lawyers might. Builders know what a Molly bolt is, but many insurance agents don't.

Think, too, about your purpose. For readers who need only a basic understanding of a concept—say, time-sharing vacation resorts—a brief, informal definition is usually sufficient. However, readers who need to understand an object, process, or concept thoroughly and be able to carry out tasks associated with it need a more formal and elaborate definition. For example, the definition of a "Class 2 Alert" written for operators at a nuclear power plant must be comprehensive, specific, and precise.

> **Steps in preparing to write a definition:**
>
> Analyze the writing situation.
>
> Determine the kind of definition needed.
>
> Decide where to place the definition.

> **In This Book**
>
> For more on audience and purpose, see Ch. 5.

STRATEGIES FOR INTERCULTURAL COMMUNICATION

Defining Terms for Readers from Another Culture

If you are writing to people whose first language is not English, consider the following:

- *Add a glossary: a list of definitions.* For more on glossaries, see Chapter 12, page 279.

- *Use Simplified English and easily recognizable terms in definitions.* For more on Simplified English, see Chapter 11, page 259.

- *Pay close attention to key terms.* Be sure to carefully define terms that are essential to a reader's understanding of the document. If, for instance, your document is about angioplasty, you will want to be especially careful when defining it.
- *Use visuals to help readers understand a term or concept.* Graphics are particularly helpful to readers of different languages, and graphics reduce the cost of translating text from one language to another.

Types of definitions:

Parenthetical

Sentence

Extended

DETERMINING THE KIND OF DEFINITION TO WRITE

Definitions can be short or long, informal or formal; it depends on your audience and your purpose. There are three basic types.

Writing Parenthetical Definitions

A *parenthetical definition* is a brief clarification placed in an existing sentence. Sometimes a parenthetical definition is simply a word or phrase, enclosed in parentheses or commas, or introduced by a colon or a dash. In the following examples, the term being defined is shown in italics, and the definition is underscored:

> The crane is located on the *starboard* (<u>right</u>) side of the ship.

> Summit Books announced its intention to create a new *colophon* (<u>emblem or trademark</u>).

A parenthetical definition can also take the form of a longer explanatory phrase or clause:

> Motorboating is permitted in the *Jamesport Estuary*, <u>the portion of the bay that meets the mouth of the Jamesport River.</u>

> Before the metal is plated, it is immersed in the *pickle*: <u>an acid bath that removes scales and oxides from the surface.</u>

Parenthetical definitions are not meant to be comprehensive; they serve mainly as quick and convenient ways of introducing terms. When addressing general readers, especially, make sure that the definition itself is clear. You have gained nothing if readers don't understand it:

> Next, check for blight on the epicotyl, the stem portion above the cotyledons.

This parenthetical definition would be clear if your readers were botanists, but unnecessary because they wouldn't need a definition of *epicotyl*. General readers, on the other hand, would need a definition of *epicotyl* that is free of other specialized terms, such as *cotyledons*.

Writing Sentence Definitions

A sentence definition—a one-sentence clarification—is more formal than a parenthetical definition. A sentence definition usually follows a standard pattern: the item to be defined is placed in a category of similar items and then distinguished from them.

Item	= Category	+ Distinguishing Characteristics
A flip flop	is a circuit	containing active elements that can assume either one of two stable states at any given time.
An electrophorous	is a laboratory instrument	used to generate static electricity.
Hypnoanalysis	is a psychoanalytical technique	in which hypnosis is used to elicit information from a patient's unconscious mind.
An electron microsocope	is a microscope	that uses electrons rather than visible light to produce magnified images.

In many cases, a sentence definition also includes a graphic. For example, the definitions of electrophorus and electron microscope would probably include photographs, diagrams, or drawings.

Sentence definitions are useful when your readers require a more formal or more informative clarification than brief parenthetical definitions can provide. Writers often use sentence definitions to present a working definition for a particular document: "In this report, *electron microscope* refers to any microscope that uses electrons rather than visible light to produce magnified images." Such definitions are sometimes called *stipulative definitions* because the writer is stipulating how the term will be used in the document.

GUIDELINES

Writing Effective Sentence Definitions

The following four suggestions can help you write effective sentence definitions:

▶ *Be specific in stating the category and the distinguishing characteristics.* If you write, "A Bunsen burner is a burner that consists of a vertical metal tube connected to a gas source," the imprecise category—"a burner"—defeats the purpose of your definition: many types of large-scale burners use vertical metal tubes connected to gas sources.

▶ *Don't describe a specific item if you are defining a general class of items.* If you wish to define *catamaran,* don't describe a particular catamaran. The catamaran you see on the beach in front of you might be made by Hobie and have a white hull and blue sails, but those characteristics are not essential to catamarans in general.

▶ *Avoid writing circular definitions, that is, definitions that merely repeat the key words or the distinguishing characteristics of the item being defined in the category.* The definition "A required course is a course that is required" is useless: required of whom, by whom? However, in defining electron microscope, you can repeat *microscope* because *microscope* is not the difficult part of the item. The purpose of defining *electron microscope* is to clarify the word *electron* as it applies to a particular type of microscope.

▶ *Be sure the category contains a noun or a noun phrase rather than a phrase beginning with* when, what, *or* where.

INCORRECT	A brazier is what is used to . . .
CORRECT	A brazier is a metal pan used to . . .
INCORRECT	Hypnoanalysis is when hypnosis is used to . . .
CORRECT	Hypnoanalysis is a psychoanalytical technique in which . . .

Writing Extended Definitions

Techniques used in extended definitions:

Graphics

Examples

Partition

Principle of operation

Comparison and contrast

Analogy

Negation

Etymology

History of the term

An *extended definition* is a detailed clarification—usually consisting of one or more paragraphs—of an object, a process, or an idea. Often an extended definition begins with a sentence definition, which is then elaborated. For instance, the sentence definition "An electrophorus is a laboratory instrument used to generate static electricity" tells you the basic function of the device, but it doesn't explain how it works, what it is used for, and its strengths and limitations. An extended definition would address these and other topics.

There is no one way to "extend" a definition. Your analysis of the audience and purpose of your communication will help you decide which method to use. In fact, an extended definition sometimes employs several of the following nine techniques.

Graphics Perhaps the most common way to present an extended definition in technical communication is to use a graphic, then explain it. Obviously, graphics are useful in defining physical objects, but they are also an effective way to present concepts and ideas. A definition of *temperature inversion,* for instance, might include a diagram showing the forces that create temperature inversion.

The following excerpt from an extended definition of *parallelogram* shows an effective combination of words and illustrations.

A *parallelogram* is a four-sided plane whose opposite sides are parallel with each other and equal in length. In a parallelogram, the opposite angles are the same, as shown in the sketch below.

Examples   Examples are particularly useful in making an abstract term easier to understand. The following paragraph is an extended definition of *hazing activities* (Fraternity, 1997).

No chapter, colony, student or alumnus shall conduct nor condone hazing activities. Hazing activities are defined as: "Any action taken or situation created, intentionally, whether on or off fraternity premises, to produce mental or physical discomfort, embarrassment, harassment, or ridicule. Such activities may include but are not limited to the following: use of alcohol; paddling in any form; creation of excessive fatigue; physical and psychological shocks; quests, treasure hunts, scavenger hunts, road trips or any other such activities carried on outside or inside of the confines of the chapter house; wearing of public apparel which is conspicuous and not normally in good taste; engaging in public stunts and buffoonery; morally degrading or humiliating games and activities; and any other activities which are not consistent with academic achievement, fraternal law, ritual or policy or the regulations and policies of the educational institution or applicable state law."

This extended definition is effective because the writer has presented a clear sentence definition followed by numerous examples.

Partition   Partitioning is the process of dividing a thing or an idea into smaller parts so that the reader can understand it more easily. The following example, from a study of technology in nursing (U.S. Congress, 1995a, p. 133), uses partition to define *clinical decision support system*.

In This Book

For more about partitioning, see Ch. 8, p. 172.

A knowledge-based system designed for clinical use, sometimes called a *clinical decision support system* (CDSS), usually involves three components:

1. *Data on the patient* being diagnosed or treated are either entered into the system manually, captured automatically from diagnostic or monitoring equipment, or drawn from an electronic patient record.
2. A *knowledge base* contains rules and decision algorithms that incorporate knowledge and judgment about the health problem at hand and alternative tests and treatments for it, mainly in the form of "if-then" statements, such as "if the patient's potassium is less than 3.0 mEq/dl and the patient is on digoxin, then warn the clinician to consider potassium supplementation."
3. An *inference engine* combines information from both the patient data and the knowledge base to perform specified tasks, outlined in appendix C.

Principle of Operation   Describing the principle of operation—the way something works—is an effective way to develop an extended definition, especially for an object or a process. The following excerpt from an extended definition of a parabolic dish solar-energy system (U.S. Department of Energy, 2001) is based on the mechanism's principle of operation.

This paragraph describes the principle of operation of the device. This principle is illustrated in the diagram.

A Solar Dish-Engine System is an electric generator that "burns" sunlight instead of gas or coal to produce electricity. The figure shows the two major parts of a system—the solar concentrator (or dish) and the power conversion unit (PCU). The dish tracks the sun over the course of a day and reflects concentrated sunlight to a single point, its focus, where it is converted in the PCU into heat to power an engine/generator to produce electricity. These systems are modular, allowing their assembly into plants ranging in size from a few kilowatts to tens of megawatts. They are made from readily available materials (steel, aluminum, and glass) using conventional manufacturing techniques common to the automotive industry.

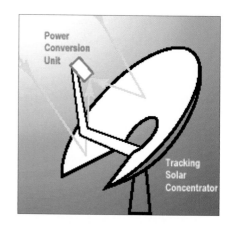

In This Book

For more on comparison and contrast, see Ch. 8, p. 167.

Comparison and Contrast   Using comparison and contrast, a writer discusses the similarities or differences between the item being defined and an item with which readers are more familiar. The following definition of 3G wireless (National Telecommunications, 2000) contrasts today's technology with tomorrow's.

In this excerpt from a discussion of 3G technology, today's technology . . .

. . . is contrasted with tomorrow's.

The latest advance in mobile communications technology, "third-generation" (3G) wireless, will be capable of combining the powerful technologies of wireless communications and the Internet. Today's wireless service, used for analog and digital cellular phones and pagers, was designed to transmit voice and brief text messages. These devices transfer data at relatively slow speeds, around 9.6 kilobits per second (kbps)—significantly slower than conventional 56 kbps dial-up modems. 3G devices, by contrast, will transmit data at speeds between 144 kbps and 2 megabits per second, about as fast as a cable modem or digital subscriber line. Increasing the data-transfer rate allows mobile phones, hand-held computers, and other products to become multimedia access devices. Further, the international standards that have been developed for 3G allow global roaming with a single device.

Analogy   An *analogy* is a specialized kind of comparison. In a traditional comparison, the writer compares one item to another similar item: an electron microscope to a common microscope, for example. In an analogy, however, the item being defined is compared to an item that is in some ways completely different but that shares some essential characteristic. For instance, the central processing unit of a computer is often compared to a brain. Obviously, these two items are very different, except that the relationship of the central processing unit to the computer is similar to that of the brain to the body.

The following example (Sweetman, 2002), from an explanation of a radar system on a JointSTAR, a U.S. reconnaissance airplane, shows the effective use of an analogy.

> This radar system acts much like a VCR in the hands of one of 18 operators onboard the plane, who can fast-forward through images recorded during the previous 6 hours or run them backward to show, for example, where a column of vehicles originated. If the targets stop moving, the radar operator can take a high-resolution picture of the area and store it until motion is spied again. Data can be relayed to commanders on the ground, fighters and other planes in the air, and to the Pentagon for analysis and action.

The writer of this passage uses the VCR analogy to explain how the operator uses the radar system. But, obviously, the radar system differs from a VCR in most ways.

Negation   A special kind of contrast is sometimes called *negation* or *negative statement*. Negation clarifies a term by distinguishing it from a different term with which the reader might confuse it. The following example uses negation to distinguish the term *ambulatory* from *ambulance*.

> An ambulatory patient is not a patient who must be moved by ambulance. On the contrary, an ambulatory patient is one who can walk without assistance from another person.

Negation is rarely the only technique used in an extended definition; in fact, it is used most often in a sentence or two at the start. Once you have stated what the item is not, you still have to state what it is.

Etymology   *Etymology,* the derivation of a word, is often a useful and interesting way to develop a definition. The following example uses the etymology of *spam* — unsolicited junk e-mail — to define it.

> For many decades, Hormel Foods has manufactured a luncheon meat called Spam, which stands for "Shoulder Pork and hAM"/"SPiced hAM." Then, in the 1970s, the English comedy team Monty Python's Flying Circus broadcast a skit about a restaurant that served Spam with every dish. In describing each dish, the waitress repeats the word *Spam* over and over, and several Vikings standing in the corner chant the word repeatedly. In the mid 1990s, two businessmen hired a programmer to write a program that would send unsolicited ads to thousands of electronic newsgroups. Just as Monty Python's chanting Vikings drowned out other conversation in the restaurant, the ads began drowning out regular communication online. As a result, people started calling unsolicited junk e-mail *spam*.

Etymology is a popular way to begin definitions of *acronyms*, which are abbreviations pronounced as words, as illustrated in the following examples.

SCUBA stands for self-contained underwater breathing apparatus.

RAID, which stands for Redundant Arrays of Independent Disk Drives, refers to a computer storage system that can withstand a single (or, in some cases, even double) disk failure.

Etymology, like negation, is rarely used alone in technical communication, but it is an effective way to introduce an extended definition.

History of the Term   A common way to define a term is to explain its history. Often an extended definition explains the original use of the term and then describes how the meaning has changed in response to historical events or technological advances. The following example (Roblee & McKechnie, 1981, pp. 15–16) uses the history of the term *arson* to define it:

In general, the common-law definition of *arson* was traditionally the willful burning of the house of another, including all outhouses or outbuildings adjoining thereto. The emphasis was on another's habitation, and his life and safety at the place where he or she resided. Then, many legal issues began to arise. Was a school a dwelling? a jail? a church? The common-law courts began to view the crime of arson as being against the habitation or possessions of another.

Gradually, laws were enacted to plug the loopholes of the common-law definition of *arson.* The first laws brought all buildings or structures into the scope of arson, provided they had human occupancy of any kind on a regular basis. Later, the occupancy requirements were dropped. Today, *arson* is a term applied to the willful and intentional burning of all types of structures, vehicles, forests, fields, and so on.

A Sample Extended Definition   Figure 9.1 is an example of an extended definition addressed to a general audience.

DECIDING WHERE TO PLACE THE DEFINITION

If you are writing a parenthetical definition, you do not need to worry about where to put it; it goes in the sentence in which the term first appears. For sentence definitions and extended definitions, however, you need to decide where to put them.

Definitions are typically placed in one or more of these six locations:

- *In the text.* The text is an appropriate place for parenthetical and sentence definitions that many or most of your readers will need, and for extended definitions of important terms.

- *In a marginal gloss.* Parenthetical and sentence definitions can be placed in the margin of the document.

THE GREENHOUSE EFFECT

Energy from the sun drives the earth's weather and climate, and heats the earth's surface; in turn, the earth radiates energy back into space. Atmospheric greenhouse gases (water vapor, carbon dioxide, and other gases) trap some of the outgoing energy, retaining heat somewhat like the glass panels of a greenhouse.

Without this natural "greenhouse effect," temperatures would be much lower than they are now, and life as known today would not be possible. Instead, thanks to greenhouse gases, the earth's average temperature is a more hospitable 60°F. However, problems may arise when the atmospheric concentration of greenhouse gases increases.

Since the beginning of the industrial revolution, atmospheric concentrations of carbon dioxide have increased nearly 30%, methane concentrations have more than doubled, and nitrous oxide concentrations have risen by about 15%. These increases have enhanced the heat-trapping capability of the earth's atmosphere. Sulfate aerosols, a common air pollutant, cool the atmosphere by reflecting light back into space; however, sulfates are short-lived in the atmosphere and vary regionally.

Why are greenhouse gas concentrations increasing? Scientists generally believe that the combustion of fossil fuels and other human activities are the primary reason for the increased concentration of carbon dioxide. Plant respiration and the decomposition of organic matter release more than 10 times the CO_2 released by human activities; but these releases have generally been in balance during the centuries leading up to the industrial revolution with carbon dioxide absorbed by terrestrial vegetation and the oceans.

What has changed in the last few hundred years is the additional release of carbon dioxide by human activities. Fossil fuels burned to run cars and trucks, heat homes and businesses, and power factories are responsible for about 98% of U.S. carbon dioxide emissions, 24% of methane emissions, and 18% of nitrous oxide emissions. Increased agriculture, deforestation, landfills, industrial production, and mining also contribute a significant share of emissions. In 1997, the United States emitted about one-fifth of total global greenhouse gases.

The Greenhouse Effect

Some solar radiation is reflected by the earth and the atmosphere.

Solar radiation passes through the clear atmosphere

Most radiation is absorbed by the earth's surface and warms it

Some of the infrared radiation passes through the atmosphere, and some is absorbed and re-emitted in all directions by greenhouse gas molecules. The effect of this is to warm the earth's surface and the lower atmosphere.

Infrared radiation is emitted from the earth's surface

Estimating future emissions is difficult, because it depends on demographic, economic, technological, policy, and institutional developments. Several emissions scenarios have been developed based on differing projections of these underlying factors. For example, by 2100, in the absence of emissions control policies, carbon dioxide concentrations are projected to be 30–150% higher than today's levels.

The first paragraph of this extended definition of greenhouse effect begins with a general description and ends with a sentence that explains the etymology of the term.

The body of this extended definition is a discussion of the factors that have increased the greenhouse effect.

Questions are effective in topic sentences, particularly in discussions aimed at general readers.

This diagram aids the reader by visually summarizing the principle of operation of the greenhouse effect.

On TechComm Web

To view Fig. 9.1 in context on the Web, click on Links Library for Ch. 9 on <bedfordstmartins.com /techcomm>.

■ **Figure 9.1**
An Extended Definition

Source: U.S. Environmental Protection Agency, 2001 <www.epa.gov/globalwarming /climate/index.html>.

- *In a hyperlink.* In a hypertext document such as a Web page, definitions can be put in a separate file, enabling the reader to click on highlighted or underlined words to view the definitions.

- *In footnotes.* Footnotes are a logical place for an occasional sentence definition or extended definition. The reader who doesn't need it will ignore it. However, footnotes can slow readers down by interrupting the flow of the discussion. If you think you will need more than one footnote for a definition on every two to three pages, consider including a glossary.

In This Book

For more about glossaries and appendices, see Ch. 12, pp. 279 and 281.

- *In a glossary.* A glossary—an alphabetized list of definitions—can accommodate sentence definitions and extended definitions of fewer than three or four paragraphs in one convenient location. A glossary can be placed at the beginning of a document (for example, after the executive summary in a report) or at the end, preceding the appendices.

- *In an appendix.* An appendix is an appropriate place for an extended definition of one page or longer, which would be cumbersome in a glossary or in a footnote and, unless it explains a crucial term, too distracting in the text.

UNDERSTANDING THE ROLE OF DESCRIPTIONS

Technical communication often requires descriptions: verbal and visual representations of objects, mechanisms, and processes.

- *Objects.* An object is anything ranging from a physical site such as a volcano or some other kind of natural phenomenon, to a synthetic artifact, such as a hammer. A tomato plant is an object, as is an automobile tire or a book.

- *Mechanisms.* A mechanism is a synthetic object consisting of a number of identifiable parts that work together. A DVD player is a mechanism, as is a voltmeter, a lawnmower, or a submarine.

In This Book

For more about instructions, see Ch. 20, p. 522.

- *Processes.* A process is an activity that takes place over time: the earth was formed; steel is made; plants perform photosynthesis. *Descriptions of processes*, which explain how something happens, differ from *instructions*, which explain how to do something. Readers of a process description want to *understand* the process; readers of instructions want a step-by-step guide to help them *perform* it. A process description answers the question "How is wine made?" A set of instructions answers the question "How do I make wine?"

Descriptions of objects, mechanisms, and processes appear in virtually every kind of technical communication. Here are a few examples:

An employee who wants to persuade management to buy some equipment includes a mechanism description of the equipment in the proposal to buy it.

A company manufacturing a consumer product provides a description and a graphic on its Web site to attract buyers.

A developer who wants to build a housing project includes in his environmental impact statement descriptions of the geographical area and of the process he will use in developing that area.

Notice that a description is usually part of a larger document. For example, a maintenance manual for an air-conditioning system might begin with a mechanism description of the system to help the reader understand first how it operates, and then how to fix or maintain it.

ANALYZING THE WRITING SITUATION FOR DESCRIPTIONS

Before you begin to write a description, consider carefully how the audience and the purpose of the document will affect what you write.

What does the audience already know about the general subject? For example, if you want to describe how the next generation of industrial robots will affect car manufacturing, you first have to know whether your readers understand the current process and whether they understand robotics.

Your sense of your audience will determine not only whether you use technical vocabulary but also your sentence and paragraph structure and length. Another audience-related factor is your use of graphics. Less knowledgeable readers need simple graphics; they might have trouble understanding sophisticated schematics or decision charts. As you consider your audience, think about whether any of your readers are from other cultures and might therefore expect different topics, organization, or writing style in the description.

Consider, too, your purpose. What are you trying to accomplish with this description? If you want your readers to understand how a personal computer works, write a *general description* that applies to several varieties of computers. If you want your readers to understand how a specific computer works, write a *particular description*. A general description of personal computers might classify them by size, then go on to describe palmtops, laptops, and desktops in general terms. A particular description, however, will describe only one model of personal computer, such as a Millennia 200. Your purpose will determine every aspect of the description, including its length, the amount of detail, and the number and type of graphics.

WRITING THE DESCRIPTION

There is no single structure or format to use in writing descriptions. Because they are written for different audiences and different purposes, they can take many shapes and forms. However, the following four suggestions will guide you in most situations.

> **In This Book**
>
> For more on audience and purpose, see Ch. 5.

> **Principles for writing descriptions:**
>
> Clearly indicate the nature and scope of the description.
>
> Introduce the description clearly.
>
> Provide appropriate detail.
>
> Conclude the description.

Clearly Indicate the Nature and Scope of the Description

In This Book

For more about titles, see Ch. 10, p. 219, and Ch. 12, p. 269. For more about headings, see Ch. 10, p. 220.

If the description is to be a separate document, give it a title. If the description is to be part of a longer document, give it a section heading. In either case, clearly state the subject and indicate whether the description is general or particular. For instance, a general description of an object might be entitled "Description of a Minivan," and a particular description, "Description of the 2003 Honda Odyssey." A general description of a process might be called "Description of the Process of Designing a New Production Car," and a particular description, "Description of the Process of Designing the Saturn L-Series."

Introduce the Description Clearly

Provide the information that readers need to understand the detailed information that follows. Introductions to descriptions are usually general: you want to give readers a broad understanding of the object, mechanism, or process. You might also provide a graphic that introduces your readers to the overall concept. For example, in describing a process, you might include a flowchart summarizing the steps in the body of the description; in describing an object, such as a bicycle, you might include a photograph or a drawing showing the major components you will describe in detail in the body.

Table 9.1 shows some of the basic kinds of questions you might want to answer in introducing object, mechanism, and process descriptions. If the answer is obvious, simply move on to the next question.

Figure 9.2 shows the introductory graphic accompanying a description of a remote-control unit and the enlarged graphic for one of the parts.

■ **Table 9.1 Questions to Answer in Introducing a Description**

For Object and Mechanism Description	*For Process Descriptions*
• *What is the item?* You might start with a sentence definition.	• *What is the process?* You might start with a sentence definition.
• *What is the function of the item?* If the function is not implicit in the sentence definition, state it clearly: "Electron microscopes magnify objects that are smaller than the wavelengths of visible light."	• *What is the function of the process?* Unless the function is obvious, state it: "The central purpose of performing a census is to obtain current population figures, which government agencies use to revise legislative districts and determine revenue-sharing."
• *What does the item look like?* Include a photograph or drawing if possible (see Ch. 14 for more about incorporating graphics with text). If not, use an analogy or comparison: "The	• *Where and when does the process take place?* "Each year the stream is stocked with hatchery fish in the first week of March." Omit these facts only if you are certain your readers already know them.

For Object and Mechanism Description	For Process Descriptions

cassette that encloses the tape is a plastic shell, about the size of a deck of cards." Mention the material, texture, color, and the like, if relevant. Sometimes an object is best pictured with both graphics and words.

- *How does the item work?* In a few sentences, define the operating principle. Sometimes objects do not "work"; they merely exist. For instance, a ship model has no operating principle.

- *What are the principal parts of the item?* Limit your description to the principal parts. A description of a bicycle, for instance, would not mention the dozens of nuts and bolts that hold the mechanism together; it would focus on the chain, gears, pedals, wheels, and frame.

- *Who or what performs the process?* If there is any doubt about who or what performs the process, state it.

- *How does the process work?* "The four-treatment lawn-spray plan is based on the theory that the most effective way to promote a healthy lawn is to apply different treatments at crucial times during the growing season. The first two treatments—in spring and early summer—consist of . . ."

- *What are the principal steps of the process?* Name the steps in the order in which you will describe them. The principal steps in changing an automobile tire, for instance, include jacking up the car, replacing the old tire with the new one, and lowering the car back to the ground. Changing a tire also includes secondary steps, such as placing chocks against the tires to prevent the car from moving once it is jacked up. Explain or refer to these secondary steps at the appropriate points in the description.

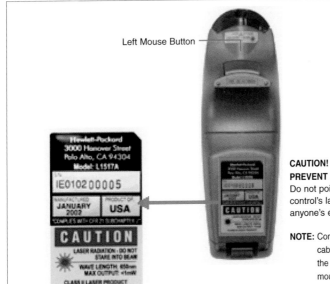

■ **Figure 9.2   Graphic with Enlarged Detailed Graphic**

Source: Hewlett Packard, 2002 <http://h200004.www2.hp.com/bc/docs/support/SupportManual/bpia6001/bpia6001.pdf>.

Interactive Sample Document:
Introducing a Description

The following introduction to a description of food irradiation is addressed to the general reader. The questions in the margin ask you to think about the discussion of introducing process descriptions in Table 9.1 (on pages 206–207). The answers to these questions are available on TechComm Web.

Table 9.1 presents six questions that should be answered in an introduction to a process description:

1. What is the process?

2. What is the function of the process?

3. Where and when does the process take place?

4. Who or what performs the process?

5. How does the process work?

6. What are the principal steps of the process?

Determine whether each of these questions is answered and, if so, where.

On TechComm Web

To find the answers to these questions, click on Interactive Sample Documents for Ch. 9 on <bedfordstmartins.com/techcomm>.

What Is Food Irradiation?
Food irradiation is a process in which products are exposed to radiant energy including gamma rays, electron beams, and x-rays in amounts approved by the Food and Drug Administration (FDA). . . .

Why Is Food Irradiated? What Are the Benefits?
Food is irradiated to make it safer. It can reduce the risk of foodborne illness by destroying harmful bacteria, parasites, insects, and fungi.

Irradiation does not destroy all pathogens (very tiny disease-causing organisms) in amounts approved by the FDA for refrigerated or frozen raw meat and poultry sold to consumers, but it does reduce their number. To sterilize food (destroy all pathogens), a higher amount of radiation must be used. Hospitals have used irradiation for many years to sterilize food for cancer patients and others with weakened immune systems. Some perishable food taken into space by astronauts is irradiated because the food must be guaranteed free of disease-causing organisms.

It also reduces spoilage. Like freezing, canning, and drying, irradiation can also extend the shelf life of perishable food products. For example, irradiated strawberries stay unspoiled in the refrigerator up to 3 weeks versus only 3 to 5 days for untreated berries.

How Is Food Irradiated?
At a food irradiation plant that uses gamma radiation, food is irradiated in an area that is surrounded by concrete walls at least 6-feet thick, which keep any rays from escaping. The radiation source, usually Cobalt 60, is held in a resting position in a pool of water. A conveyor system transports the meat or poultry product to the area. The radiation source is then raised out of the water and the food is exposed for a defined period of time. When the source is raised, lights and alarms are sounded to make people aware that the product is being irradiated. Once the food is irradiated, the source automatically returns to the resting position, and the food leaves the area for further processing.

Source: U.S. Department of Agriculture, 2000.

Provide Appropriate Detail

The body of a description—the part-by-part or step-by-step section—treats each major part or step as a separate item. In describing an object or a mechanism, you define each part and then, if applicable, describe its function, operating principle, and appearance. Your discussion of the appearance should include shape, dimensions, material, and physical details such as texture and color (if essential). Some descriptions might call for other qualities, such as weight or hardness. If a part has important subparts, describe them in the same way.

In describing a process, treat each major step as if it were a separate process. Do not repeat your answer to the question about who or what performs the action unless a new agent performs a particular step, but do answer the other important questions: what the step is, what its function is, and when, where, and how it occurs. If the step has important substeps, explain them clearly.

A description resembles a map with a series of detailed insets. A description of a computer system would include a keyboard as one of its parts. The description of the keyboard, in turn, would include the numeric keypad as one of its parts. And the description of the numeric keypad would include the arrow keys as one of its parts. The level of detail depends on the complexity of the item and the readers' needs. The same principle applies in describing processes: a step might have substeps. For each substep, you would probably need to describe who or what performs it (if it is not obvious), and you would need to describe what the substep is, what its function is, and when, where, and how it occurs.

GUIDELINES

Providing Appropriate Detail in Descriptions

Use the following techniques to flesh out your descriptions.

For Object and Mechanism Descriptions	For Process Descriptions
• *Choose an appropriate organizing principle.* Two organizational principles are common: –Functional: how the item works or is used. In a radio, for instance, the sound begins at the receiver, travels into the amplifier, and then flows out through the speakers. –Spatial: based on the physical structure of the item: from top to bottom, east to west, outside to inside, and so forth. Descriptions can be organized in various ways. For instance, the description of a house could be organized functionally (the different electrical and mechanical systems) or spatially (top to bottom, inside to outside, east to west, and so on). A complex description can	• *Structure the step-by-step description chronologically.* If the process is a closed system—such as the cycle of evaporation and condensation—and thus has no first step, begin with any principal step. • *Explain causal relationships among steps.* Don't present the steps as if they have nothing to do with one another. In many cases, one step causes another. In the operation of a four-stroke gasoline engine, for instance, each step creates the conditions for the next step. • *Use the present tense.* Discuss steps in the present tense unless you are writing about a process that occurred in the historical past. For example, use the past tense in describing how the Snake River aquifer was formed: "The molten

↓

For Object and Mechanism Descriptions	For Process Descriptions
use a combination of patterns at different levels in the description. • *Use graphics.* Present a graphic for each major part. Use photographs to show external surfaces, drawings to emphasize particular items on the surface, and cutaways and exploded diagrams to show details beneath the surface. Other kinds of graphics, such as graphs and charts, are often useful supplements (see Chapter 14).	material condensed. . . ." However, use the present tense in describing how steel is made: "The molten material is then poured into. . . ." The present tense helps readers understand that, in general, steel is made this way. • *Use graphics.* Whenever possible, use graphics to clarify each step. Consider additional flowcharts or other kinds of graphics, such as photographs, drawings, and graphs. For example, in a description of how a four-stroke gasoline engine operates, you could use diagrams to illustrate the position of the valves and the activity occurring during each step.

Conclude the Description

A description typically has a brief conclusion that summarizes it and prevents readers from overemphasizing the part or step discussed last.

A common technique for concluding descriptions of mechanisms and of some objects is to state briefly how the parts function together. At the end of a description of a telephone, for example, the conclusion might include the following paragraph:

> When you make a phone call, everything that happens depends on the flow of current through the phone lines, and on what your phone and the other person's phone do with that current. When the phone is taken off the hook, a current flows through the carbon granules. The intensity of the speaker's voice causes a greater or lesser movement of the phone's diaphragm and thus a greater or lesser intensity in the current flowing through the carbon granules. The phone receiving the call converts the electrical waves back into sound waves by means of an electromagnet and a diaphragm. The varying intensity of the current transmitted by the phone line alters the strength of the current in the electromagnet, which in turn changes the position of the diaphragm. The movement of the diaphragm reproduces the speaker's sound waves.

Like an object or mechanism description, a process description usually has a brief conclusion: a short paragraph summarizing the principal steps. Here, for example, is the concluding section of a description of how a four-stroke gasoline engine operates:

> In the intake stroke, the piston moves down, drawing the air-fuel mixture into the cylinder from the carburetor. As the piston moves up, it compresses this mixture in the com-

pression stroke, creating the conditions necessary for combustion. In the power stroke, a spark from the spark plug ignites the mixture, which burns rapidly, forcing the piston down. In the exhaust stroke, the piston moves up, expelling the burned gases.

For descriptions of more than a few pages, a discussion of the implications of the process might be appropriate. For instance, a description of the Big Bang might conclude with a discussion of how the theory has been supported and challenged by recent astronomical discoveries and theories.

ANALYZING SOME DESCRIPTIONS

A look at some sample descriptions will give you an idea of how different writers adapt basic approaches for a particular audience and purpose.

Figure 9.3 shows the extent to which a process description can be based on graphics. The topic is drivetrain efficiencies for vehicles powered by internal-combustion engines and for vehicles powered by electricity. The audience is the general reader.

Figure 9.4 shows two screens from a Web site about the use of biometrics in security systems. The audience is the general reader.

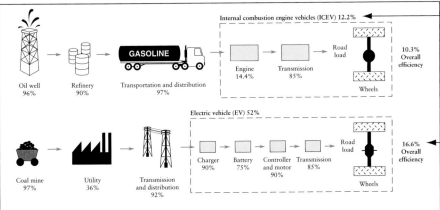

At each step in the process of turning raw materials into energy to power the vehicles, the efficiency is noted in percentage.

Finally, at the right side, the overall efficiencies of the two technologies are compared.

NOTE: An electric drivetrain can be three to four times as efficient as a mechanical ICE drivetrain (e.g., 52 percent for electric vehicles (EVs) versus 12 percent for ICEVs). This efficiency differential drops substantially when the overall fuel chain efficiency for ICEVs and EVs is taken into consideration (16.6 percent for coal-powered EVs versus 10.3 percent for gasoline-powered ICEVs). The fuel chain efficiency for EVs could be much higher if new power generation technologies are deployed. Advanced coal plants might achieve efficiencies close to 50 percent, while efficiencies of 60 percent are possible for advanced natural gas plants. With an advanced natural gas plant the overall fuel chain efficiency for EVs could rise to 27 percent.

SOURCE: John Brogan and S. Venkateswaran, "Diverse Choices for Hybrid and Electric Motor Vehicles," in *Proceedings of the International Conference on Urban EVs* (Stockholm, Sweden: Organization for Economic Cooperation and Development, May 1992).

■ **Figure 9.3   A Process Description Based on a Graphic**

Notice how effectively graphics show the relative efficiencies of an internal combustion engine vehicle (top row) and an electric vehicle (bottom row). The graphics clarify the process and make it interesting.
Source: U.S. Congress, Office of Technology Assessment, 1995b.

This graphic, part of an article about the use of biometrics in security systems, uses the Web to create an interesting, informative description.

The screen shown here is the introduction to biometrics. It presents the principle of operation underlying all biometric systems.

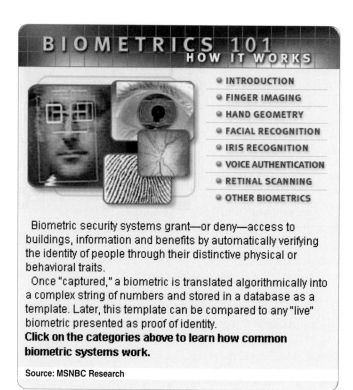

This screen shows the graphic and text that appear when the user clicks on "Retinal Scanning." A new graphic and explanation appear, describing this principle.

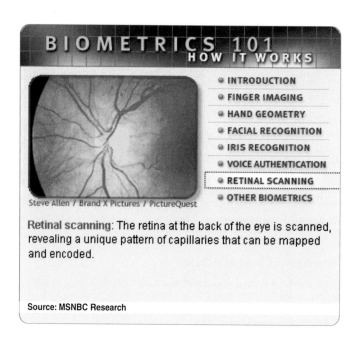

■ **Figure 9.4
Excerpts from a Web-based Description**

Source: Masterson, 2001 <www
.msnbc.com/news/654788
.asp?cp1=1>.

Figures 9.5 and 9.6 are excerpts from a description of a piece of atmospheric-testing hardware used by the Naval Research Laboratory in its Defense Meteorological Satellite Program. The excerpt here, taken from the Web site, is the main page for the description.

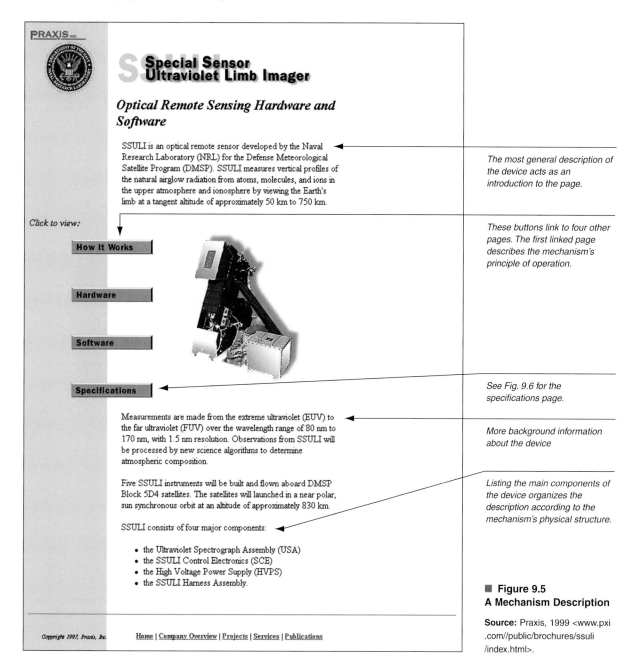

The most general description of the device acts as an introduction to the page.

These buttons link to four other pages. The first linked page describes the mechanism's principle of operation.

See Fig. 9.6 for the specifications page.

More background information about the device

Listing the main components of the device organizes the description according to the mechanism's physical structure.

■ **Figure 9.5**
A Mechanism Description

Source: Praxis, 1999 <www.pxi
.com//public/brochures/ssuli
/index.html>.

Special Sensor Ultraviolet Limb Imager

SSULI Specifications

SSULI Specifications

Field of View:	0.1 degrees vertical and 2.4 degrees horizontal
Field of Regard:	30 degrees by 2.4 degrees
Scanning Range:	10 to 40 degrees below the host spacecraft y-direction
Sensitivity:	0.5 count per second per Rayleigh at 83.4 nm
Spectral Range:	80 to 170 nm with a resolution of 1.5 nm or less
Scanning Rate:	Up to 6 degrees per second

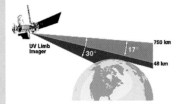

Geometry of SSULI Limb Scans

SSULI Observables

Parameter	Species	Wavelength
Dayside Ionosphere	O+	834 Å
Dayside Ionosphere	O	911 Å, 1304 Å, 1356 Å
Dayside Neutral Density	O	989 Å, 1304 Å, 1356 Å, 1641 Å
Dayside Neutral Density	N_2	1085 Å (N+), N2 LBH Bands
Dayside Neutral Density	O_2	Schumann-Runge, Absorption of N2 LBH
Nightside Neutral Density	O	1356 Å
Temperatures	---	Emission Scale Heights

Return to Introduction | Hardware | Software | How It Works

■ **Figure 9.6   Specifications**

An important kind of description is called a specification. *A typical specification consists of a graphic and a set of statistics about the device and its performance characteristics. You will see specifications on devices as small as transistors and as large as aircraft carriers.*
Source: Praxis, 1999 <www.pxi.com//public/brochures/ssuli/index.html>.

Revision Checklist

This checklist covers **parenthetical, sentence, and extended definitions:**

❏ Are all necessary terms defined? (p. 194)

Are the parenthetical definitions
❏ appropriate for the audience? (p. 196)
❏ clear? (p. 196)
❏ smoothly integrated into the sentences? (p. 196)

Does each sentence definition
❏ contain a sufficiently specific category and distinguishing characteristics? (p. 197)
❏ avoid describing one particular item when a general class of items is intended? (p. 198)
❏ avoid circular definition? (p. 198)
❏ contain a noun or a noun phrase in the category? (p. 198)
❏ Are the extended definitions developed logically and clearly? (p. 198)
❏ Are the definitions placed in the location most useful to the readers? (p. 202)

The following questions cover **descriptions of objects and mechanisms:**

❏ Did you clearly indicate the nature and scope of the description? (p. 206)

In introducing the description, did you answer, if appropriate, the following questions:
❏ What is the item? (p. 206)
❏ What does it do? (p. 206)
❏ What is its function? (p. 206)
❏ What does it look like? (p. 206)
❏ What is its principle of operation? (p. 207)
❏ What are its principal parts? (p. 207)

❏ Did you include a graphic identifying all the principal parts? (p. 210)

In providing detailed information, did you
❏ answer, for each of the major components, the questions for introducing the description, in this checklist? (p. 208)
❏ choose an appropriate organizing principle? (p. 209)
❏ include graphics for each of the components? (p. 210)

In concluding the description, did you
❏ summarize the major points in the part-by-part description? (p. 210)
❏ include (where appropriate) a description of the item performing its function? (p. 210)

The following questions cover **process descriptions:**

❏ Did you clearly indicate the nature and scope of the description? (p. 206)

In introducing the description, did you answer, if appropriate, the following questions:
❏ What is the process? (p. 206)
❏ What is its function? (p. 206)
❏ Where and when does the process take place? (p. 206)
❏ Who or what performs it? (p. 207)
❏ How does the process work? (p. 207)
❏ What are its principal steps? (p. 207)
❏ Did you include a graphic identifying all the principal steps? (p. 210)

In providing detailed information, did you
❏ discuss the steps in chronological order or other logical sequence? (p. 209)
❏ make clear the causal relationships among the steps? (p. 209)
❏ include graphics for each of the principal steps? (p. 210)

Exercises

On TechComm Web

For more exercises, click on Additional Exercises, Projects, and Cases for Ch. 9 on <bedfordstmartins.com/techcomm>.

1. Add a parenthetical definition for each italicized term in the following sentences:

   a. Reluctantly, he decided to *drop* the physics course.

   b. Last week the computer was *down*.

   c. The department is using *shareware* in its drafting course.

   d. The tire plant's managers hope they do not have to *lay off* any more employees.

   e. Please submit your assignments *electronically*.

2. Write a sentence definition for each of the following terms:

   a. catalyst

   b. DVD player

   c. job interview

   d. Web site

   e. automatic teller machine

   f. fax machine

   g. intranet

3. Revise any of the following sentence definitions that need revision:

   a. A thermometer measures temperature.

   b. The spark plugs are the things that ignite the air-gas mixture in a cylinder.

   c. Parallel parking is where you park next to the curb.

   d. A strike is when the employees stop working.

   e. Multitasking is when you do two things at once while you're on the computer.

4. Identify the techniques used in writing the following extended definition intended for the general reader:

   > Holography, from the Greek *holos* (entire) and *gram* (message), is a method of photography that produces images that appear to be three-dimensional. A holographic image seems to change as the viewer moves in relation to it. For example, as the viewer moves, one object on the image appears to move in front of another object. In addition, the distances between objects in the image seem to change.
   >
   > Holographs are produced by coherent light, that is, light of the same wavelength, with the waves in phase and of the same amplitude. This light is produced by laser. Stereoscopic images are created by incoherent light—random wavelengths and amplitudes, out of phase. The incoherent light, which is natural light, is focused by a lens and records the pattern of brightness and color differences of the object being imaged.
   >
   > How are holographic images created? The laser-produced light is divided as it passes through a beam splitter. One portion of the light, called the *reference beam,* is directed to the emulsion—the "film." The other portion, the object beam, is directed to the subject and then reflected back to the emulsion. The reference beam is coherent light, whereas the object beam becomes incoherent because it is reflected off the irregular surface of the subject. The resulting dissonance between the reference beam and the object beam is encoded; the beam splitter records not only the brightness of the different parts of the subject but also the different distances from the laser. This encoding creates the three-dimensional effect of holography.

Projects

On TechComm Web

For more projects, click on Additional Exercises, Projects, and Cases for Ch. 9 on <bedfordstmartins.com/techcomm>.

5. Write a 500–1,000-word extended definition of one of the following terms, or of a term used in your field of study. If you do secondary research, cite your sources clearly and accurately. In addition, check that any graphics you use are appropriate for your audience and purpose. In a brief note at the start, indicate the audience and purpose for your definition.

   a. flextime

   b. binding arbitration

   c. robotics

d. an academic major (don't focus on any particular major; instead, define what a major is)

e. bioengineering

f. fetal-tissue research

6. **Internet Activity** Locate an extended definition in one of your textbooks, in a journal article, or on a Web site. In a memo to your instructor, describe the techniques the author uses to define the term. Then evaluate the effectiveness of these techniques. Submit a photocopy of the definition along with your assignment. (For more on memos, see Chapter 15, p. 378.)

7. Write a 500–1,000-word description of one of the following items or of a piece of equipment used in your field. Include appropriate graphics. In a note preceding the description, specify your audience and indicate the type of description (general or particular) you are writing.

   a. locking bicycle rack

   b. deadbolt lock

   c. photocopy machine

d. cooling tower at a nuclear power plant

e. jet engine

f. ammeter

g. MP3 player

h. automobile jack

i. PDA

8. Write a 500–1,000-word description of one of the following processes or a similar process with which you are familiar. Include appropriate graphics. In a note preceding the description, specify your audience and indicate the type of description (general or particular) you are writing. If you use secondary sources, cite them properly (see Appendix, Part A, p. 592, for documentation systems).

   a. how a nuclear power plant works

   b. how a food co-op works

   c. how a suspension bridge is constructed

   d. how we see

   e. how a baseball player becomes a free agent

CASE
Describing a New Fighter Jet

You are a student intern working for the Seattle, Washington, Chamber of Commerce. To publicize the business environment in Seattle, the chamber is assembling a directory of leading high-technology manufacturers in the Seattle area. One of the major corporations to be featured in this directory is Boeing. You have been asked to write a brief description—no more than three or four double-spaced pages—of one of Boeing's newest military jets: the F-22 Raptor. When you phone the public-affairs office at Boeing, you are told that all the information you will need about the F-22 is on their Web site <www.boeing.com> and that you are free to refer to the text and graphics in doing your project, as long as you cite Boeing in quoting any text or reproducing any graphics. Write the description of the F-22 for a general audience.

On TechComm Web

For more cases, click on Additional Exercises, Projects, and Cases for Ch. 9 on <bedfordstmartins.com /techcomm>.

10 Drafting and Revising Coherent Documents

The scholar and former corporate affairs officer Charles Darling (2002) on coherence:

The most convincing ideas in the world, expressed in the most beautiful sentences, will move no one unless those ideas are properly connected. Unless readers can move easily from one thought to another, they will surely turn to something else or turn on the television.

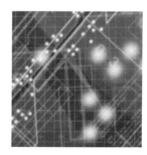

A coherent document hangs together. It flows smoothly from one part to the next, allowing the reader to concentrate on understanding its technical information. An incoherent document is harder to read; the reader can easily misunderstand the information or become confused, unable to determine how a particular point relates to one that preceded it.

Although a document might begin to take shape as you develop an outline, that shape will probably change, or become more refined, as you draft and revise. Titles, headings, lists, and paragraphs help to produce coherence in a document.

On TechComm Web

For additional samples, activities, and links related to this chapter, see <bedfordstmartins.com/techcomm>.

In This Book

For more about planning, drafting, and revising a document, see Ch. 3.

WRITING COHERENT TITLES

The title is a crucial element because it is your first opportunity to define the subject and purpose of the document for your readers. Everything else that follows has to relate clearly to the title.

You might want to put off giving a final title to your document. Until you have completed the document, you cannot be sure that the subject and purpose you established during the planning stages will not change. However, you should jot down a working title before you start drafting to give you a sense of direction, then come back to revise it at the end.

Precision is the key to a good title. For example, if you are writing a feasibility study on the subject of offering free cholesterol screening at your company, the title should contain the key terms *cholesterol screening* and *feasibility*. The following title would be effective:

Offering Free Cholesterol Screening at Thrall Associates: A Feasibility Study

If your document is an internal report discussing company business, you might not need to identify the organization. In that case, the following would be clear:

Offering Free Cholesterol Screening: A Feasibility Study

Or you could present the purpose before the subject:

A Feasibility Study of Offering Free Cholesterol Screening

Avoid substituting general terms, such as *health screening,* for *cholesterol screening*; the more precise your terms, the more useful your readers will find the title. Your readers should be able to paraphrase it in a clear, meaningful sentence. For instance, "A Feasibility Study of Offering Free Cholesterol Screening" could be paraphrased as: "This document reports on whether it is feasible to offer free cholesterol screening for our employees." But notice what happens when the title is incomplete: "Free Cholesterol Screening." The reader knows that the document has something to do with free cholesterol screening, but is the writer recommending that screening be instituted—or discontinued? Or is the writer reporting on how well an existing program is working?

WRITING COHERENT HEADINGS

A heading is a lower-level title inside a document. A clear, informative heading is vital because it announces the subject and purpose of the discussion that follows it. This information helps readers understand what they will be reading or, in some cases, whether they need to read it. For the writer, a heading eliminates the need for a sentence such as "Let us now turn to the advantages of the mandatory enrollment process."

Because headings are used to introduce text, you should avoid back-to-back headings. In other words, avoid following one heading directly with another heading:

3. Approaches to Neighborhood Policing

3.1 Community Policing

Instead, separate the headings with text, as in this example:

3. Approaches to Neighborhood Policing

Over the past decade, the scholarly community has reached a consensus that community policing offers significant advantages over the traditional patrol car–based approach. However, the traditional approach has some distinct strengths. In the following discussion, we define each approach and then explain its advantages and disadvantages. Finally, we profile three departments that have successfully made the transition to community policing while preserving the major strengths of the traditional approach.

3.1 Community Policing

The text after the heading "3. Approaches to Neighborhood Policing," called an *advance organizer,* introduces the material in section 3. It indicates the background, purpose, scope, and organization of the discussion that follows it. Advance organizers improve coherence by giving readers an overview of the discussion before they encounter the details.

GUIDELINES

Writing Effective Headings

▶ *Avoid long noun strings.* The following example is hard to understand:

> Production Enhancement Proposal Analysis Techniques

Instead, add prepositions to make the title clearer:

> Techniques for Analyzing the Proposal for Enhancing Production

This version says more clearly that the writer is going to describe the techniques.

▶ *Be informative.* In the preceding example, you could add information about how many techniques will be described:

> Three Techniques for Analyzing the Proposal for Enhancing Production

And you can go one step further by indicating what you wish to say about the three techniques:

> Advantages and Disadvantages of the Three Techniques for Analyzing the Proposal for Enhancing Production

Don't worry if the heading seems too long; clarity is more important than conciseness.

▶ *Use a grammatical form appropriate to your audience.* The question form works well for less-knowledgeable readers (Benson, 1985) or for native speakers of other languages:

> What Are the Three Techniques for Analyzing the Proposal for Enhancing Production?

The "how to" form is best for instructional material, such as manuals:

> How to Analyze the Proposal for Enhancing Production

The gerund form (*-ing*) works well for processes:

> Analyzing the Proposal for Enhancing Production

▶ *Avoid back-to-back headings.* Use advance organizers to separate the headings.

In This Book
For more about noun strings, see Ch. 11, p. 253.

In This Book
For more about how to format headings, see Ch. 13, p. 309.

WRITING COHERENT LISTS

Lists add a visual dimension to the text, making it easier for readers to understand the discussion. Lists work especially well for any kind of information that can be itemized or expressed in a sequence.

For readers, the chief advantage of a list is that it makes the information easier to read and remember: the logic of the discussion is evident in the design. The key terms in the list are set off with bullets or numbers, which help readers see them easily. This arrangement enhances coherence: readers see the overall structure before they read the detailed discussion.

The following discussion covers paragraphs that can be turned into lists. (For a discussion of using lists in individual sentences, see Chapter 11, pages 238–239.)

For you as a writer, turning paragraphs into lists has four advantages:

- *It forces you to look at the big picture.* As you start to draft your document, it is easy to lose sight of the information outside the paragraph you are working on. By looking for opportunities to create lists as you revise, you focus on the key idea in each paragraph. This practice increases your chances of noticing that an important item is missing or that an item needs to be clarified.

- *It forces you to examine the sequence.* As you turn some of your paragraphs into lists, you get a clearer look at the sequence of the information.

- *It forces you to create a clear lead-in.* In the lead-in, you can add a number designation that further forecasts the content and organization of the material that follows:

  > Auto imports declined last year because of four major factors:

  You can add the same kind of number signal in a traditional paragraph, but you are less likely to be thinking in these terms if you are not focusing on the bulleted list of items.

- *It forces you to tighten and clarify your prose.* When you make a list, look for a word, phrase, or sentence that identifies each item. Your focus shifts from weaving sentences together in a paragraph to highlighting key ideas. And once you have formatted the list, you can look at it critically and revise it until it is clear and concise.

Figure 10.1 shows a passage displayed in a paragraph form and in a list form. The authors are discussing the idea that engineers have a special social responsibility.

STRATEGIES FOR INTERCULTURAL COMMUNICATION

Using Headings and Lists Appropriately for Multicultural Audiences

In the United States and other Western countries, technical writers use headings and lists frequently. In many other cultures, however, headings and lists are considered informal and therefore inappropriate in some documents.

Try to find samples written by people from the culture you are addressing to examine their use of headings and lists. Consider the following questions in studying documents from other cultures:

• How does the writer make the information accessible?

• How does the writer show the relationship among units? Are items grouped, highlighted, listed, set off by headings, or set in a different typeface?

• How does the writer communicate to readers the organization of the document?

• How does the writer make transitions from one subject to another?

Paragraph Format	*List Format*	

Currently, there are three conceptions of the relation between engineering as a profession and society as a whole.

    The first conception is that there is no relation. Engineering's proper regard is properly instrumental, with no constraints at all. Its task is to provide purely technical solutions to problems.

    The second conception is that engineering's role is to protect. It must be concerned, as a profession, with minimizing the risk to the public. The profession is to operate on projects as presented to it, as an instrument; but the profession is to operate in accordance with important safety constraints, which are integral to its performing as a profession.

    The third conception is that engineering has a positive social responsibility to try to promote the public good, not merely to perform the tasks that are set for it, and not merely to perform those tasks such that risk is minimized or avoided in performing them. Rather, engineering's purpose as a profession is to promote the social good.

Currently, there are three conceptions of the relation between engineering as a profession and society as a whole.

• *There is no relation.* Engineering's proper regard is properly instrumental, with no constraints at all. Its task is to provide purely technical solutions to problems.

• *The engineer's role is to protect society.* Engineering is concerned, as a profession, with minimizing the risk to the public. The profession is to operate on projects as presented to it, as an instrument; but the profession is to operate in accordance with important safety constraints, which are integral to its performing as a profession.

• *The engineer's role is to promote social responsibility.* Engineering has a positive social responsibility to try to promote the public good, not merely to perform the tasks that are set for it, and not merely to perform those tasks such that risk is minimized or avoided in performing them. Rather, engineering's purpose as a profession is to promote the social good.

Turning the paragraph into a list forces the writer to create headings that sharply focus each bulleted entry.

By deleting the wordy topic sentences from the paragraph version, the writer saves space. The list version of the passage is almost the same length as the paragraph version, despite the indentations and extra white space.

■ **Figure 10.1 Paragraph Format and List Format**

Source: Based on Cohen & Grace, 1994.

WRITING COHERENT PARAGRAPHS

On TechComm Web

For more about paragraphing, see the Guide to Grammar and Writing. Click on Links Library for Ch. 10 on <bedfordstmartins.com/techcomm>.

There are two kinds of paragraphs: body paragraphs and transitional paragraphs.

A *body paragraph,* the basic structural unit for communicating technical information, is a group of sentences (or sometimes a single sentence) that is complete and self-sufficient and that contributes to a larger discussion. In an effective paragraph, all the sentences clearly and directly support one main point. In addition, the whole paragraph follows logically from the material that precedes it.

A *transitional paragraph* helps readers move from one major point to another. Usually it summarizes the previous point, introduces the next point, and helps readers understand how the two are related.

The following example of a transitional paragraph is taken from a manual explaining how to write television scripts. The writer has already described six principles of writing for an episodic program, including introducing characters, pursuing the plot, and resolving the action at the end of the episode.

The first sentence contains the word "then" to signal that it is introducing a summary.

The six basic principles of writing for episodic television, then, are the following:

- Reintroduce the characters.
- Make the extra characters episode-specific.
- Present that week's plot swiftly.
- Make the characters react according to their personalities.
- Resolve the plot neatly.
- Provide a denouement that hints at further developments.

The final sentence clearly indicates the relationship between what precedes it and what follows it.

But how do you put these six principles into action? The following section provides specific how-to instructions.

Structure Paragraphs Clearly

Most paragraphs consist of a topic sentence and the support.

The Topic Sentence Put the point—the topic sentence—up front. The topic sentence summarizes or forecasts the main point of the paragraph. Technical communication should be clear and easy to read, not full of suspense. If a paragraph describes a test you performed, include the result in your first sentence:

The point-to-point continuity test on Cabinet 3 revealed no problems.

Then go on to explain the details. If the paragraph describes a complicated idea, start with an overview. In other words, put the "bottom line" on top:

Mitosis occurs in four stages: (1) prophase, (2) metaphase, (3) anaphase, and (4) telophase.

Notice how difficult the following paragraph is to read. The writer has structured the discussion in the same order in which she performed her calculations:

DRAFT   Our estimates are based on our generating power during eight months of the year and purchasing it the other four. Based on the 2002 purchased power rate of $0.034/KW (January through April cost data) inflating at 8 percent annually, and a constant coal cost of $45–50, the projected 2003 savings resulting from a conversion to coal would be $225,000.

Putting the bottom line on top makes the paragraph much easier to read. In the revision, notice that the writer has added a numbered list after the topic sentence:

REVISION   The projected 2003 savings resulting from a conversion to coal are $225,000. This estimate is based on three assumptions: (1) that we will be generating power during eight months of the year and purchasing it the other four, (2) that power rates inflate at 8 percent from the 2002 figure of $0.034/KW (January through April cost data), and (3) that coal costs remain constant at $45–50.

Make sure each of your topic sentences relates clearly to the organizational pattern you are using. In a discussion of why water consumption in the United States is declining even though the population is increasing, for example, you might be using a more-important-to-less-important format and start a paragraph with the following topic sentence:

The most important reason for the decline in water usage is the increasing use of water-saving devices such as low-flow showerheads and toilets.

Your next paragraph should begin with a topic sentence that continues the more-important-to-less-important organization:

Also important in the decline of water usage is the role of increasing utility rates.

The phrase "also important" suggests that increasing utility rates are important, but less important than the water-saving devices discussed in the previous paragraph. Similarly, if your first topic sentence is "First, we need to . . . ," your next topic sentence should explicitly refer to the chronological pattern: "Second, we should. . . ."

The Support   The supporting information makes the topic sentence clear and convincing. Sometimes a few explanatory details provide all the support needed. At other times, however, this part of the paragraph must clarify a difficult thought or defend a controversial one.

The supporting information usually fulfills one of these five roles:

- It defines a key term or idea included in the topic sentence.
- It provides examples or illustrations of the situation described in the topic sentence.
- It identifies causes: factors that led to the situation.
- It defines effects: implications of the situation.
- It defends the assertion made in the topic sentence.

In This Book

For more about organizing information, see Ch. 8.

Supporting information is most often developed using the basic patterns of organization discussed in Chapter 8.

Paragraph Length   How long should a paragraph be? In general, 75 to 125 words are enough for a topic sentence and four or five supporting sentences. Long paragraphs are more difficult to read than short paragraphs because they require more focused concentration. And they can intimidate some readers, who then skip over them.

But don't let arbitrary guidelines about length take precedence over your own analysis of the audience and purpose. You might need only one or two sentences to introduce a graphic, for example. Transitional paragraphs are also likely to be quite short. If a brief paragraph fulfills its function, let it be. Do not combine two ideas in one paragraph simply to achieve a minimum word count.

You may need to break up your discussion of one idea into two or more paragraphs. An idea that requires 200 or 300 words to develop should probably not be squeezed into one paragraph.

GUIDELINES

Dividing Long Paragraphs

Here are three techniques for dividing long paragraphs.

Technique	Example
Break the discussion at a logical place. The most logical place to divide this paragraph is at the introduction of the second factor. Because the paragraphs are still relatively long, this strategy works best for skilled readers.	High-tech companies have been moving their operations to the suburbs for two main reasons: cheaper, more modern space and a better labor pool. A new office complex in the suburbs will charge from half to two-thirds of the rent charged for the same square footage in the city. And that money goes a lot further, too. The new office complexes are bright and airy. New office space is already wired for computers; and exercise clubs, shopping centers, and even libraries are often on-site. The second major factor attracting high-tech companies to the suburbs is the availability of experienced labor. Office workers and middle managers are abundant. In addition, the engineers and executives, who tend

⬇

Technique	Example
	to live in the suburbs anyway, are happy to forego the commuting, the city wage taxes, and the noise and stress of city life.

Make the topic sentence a separate paragraph and break up the support.
 	
This revision is easier for all readers to understand because the brief paragraph at the start clearly introduces the information. In addition, each of the two main paragraphs now has a clear topic sentence.
	High-tech companies have been moving their operations to the suburbs for two main reasons: cheaper, more modern space and a better labor pool.
	    First, office space is a bargain in the suburbs. A new office complex will charge from half to two-thirds of the rent charged for the same square footage in the city. And that money goes a lot further, too. The new office complexes are bright and airy. New office space is already wired for computers; and exercise clubs, shopping centers, and even libraries are often on-site.
	    Second, experienced labor is plentiful. Office workers and middle managers are abundant. In addition, the engineers and executives, who tend to live in the suburbs anyway, are happy to forego the commuting, the city wage taxes, and the noise and stress of city life.

Use a list. This is the easiest of the three versions for all readers because of the extra visual cues provided by the list format.	High-tech companies have been moving their operations to the suburbs for two main reasons: • *Cheaper, more modern space.* Office space is a bargain in the suburbs. A new office complex will charge anywhere from half to two-thirds of the rent charged for the same square footage in the city. And that money goes a lot further, too. The new office complexes are bright and airy. New office space is already wired for computers; and exercise clubs, shopping centers, and even libraries are often on-site. • *A better labor pool.* Office workers and middle managers are abundant. In addition, the engineers and executives, who tend to live in the suburbs anyway, are happy to forego the commuting, the city wage taxes, and the noise and stress of city life.

Use Coherence Devices Within and Between Paragraphs

In a coherent paragraph, the thoughts are linked together clearly and logically. Parallel ideas are expressed in parallel grammatical constructions. Even if the paragraph already moves smoothly from sentence to sentence, however, you can emphasize the coherence by adding transitional words and phrases, repeating key words, and using demonstrative pronouns followed by nouns.

Emphasizing coherence:

Add transitional words and phrases.

Repeat key words.

Use demonstrative pronouns followed by nouns.

Add Transitional Words and Phrases   Transitional words and phrases help the reader understand a discussion by explicitly signaling the logical relationship between two ideas. Table 10.1 lists the most common logical relationships between two ideas and some of the common transitions that express those relationships.

In the following examples, the first version contains no transitional words or phrases. Notice how much clearer the second version is.

WEAK	Neurons are not the only kind of cell in the brain. Blood cells supply the brain with oxygen and nutrients.
IMPROVED	Neurons are not the only kind of cell in the brain. *For instance,* blood cells supply the brain with oxygen and nutrients.
WEAK	The project was originally expected to cost $300,000. The final cost was $450,000.
IMPROVED	The project was originally expected to cost $300,000. *However,* the final cost was $450,000.
WEAK	The manatee population of Florida has been stricken by an unknown disease. Marine biologists from across the nation have come to Florida to assist in manatee-disease research.
IMPROVED	The manatee population of Florida has been stricken by an unknown disease. *As a result,* marine biologists from across the nation have come to Florida to assist in manatee-disease research.

Place transitions as close as possible to the beginning of the second idea. As shown in the examples above, the link between two sentences should be near the start of the second sentence.

You should also use transitional words to maintain coherence *between* paragraphs, just as you use them to maintain coherence *within* paragraphs.

◼ **Table 10.1 Transitional Words and Phrases**

Relationship	*Transition*
addition	also, and, finally, first (second, etc.), furthermore, in addition, likewise, moreover, similarly
comparison	in the same way, likewise, similarly
contrast	although, but, however, in contrast, nevertheless, on the other hand, yet
illustration	for example, for instance, in other words, to illustrate
cause-effect	as a result, because, consequently, hence, so, therefore, thus
time or space	above, around, earlier, later, next, to the right (left, west, etc.), soon, then
summary or conclusion	at last, finally, in conclusion, to conclude, to summarize

The link between two paragraphs should be near the start of the second paragraph.

Repeat Key Words   Repeating key words—usually nouns—helps readers follow the discussion. In the following example, the first version could be confusing:

UNCLEAR   For months the project leaders carefully planned their research. The cost of the work was estimated to be over $200,000.

   What is the work: the planning or the research?

CLEAR   For months the project leaders carefully planned their research. The cost of the research was estimated to be over $200,000.

From a misguided desire to be interesting, some writers keep changing their important terms. *Plankton* becomes *miniature seaweed,* then *the ocean's fast food.* Avoid this kind of word game; technical communication must be clear and precise.

Of course, too much repetition can be boring. You can vary nonessential terms, as long as you don't sacrifice clarity.

SLUGGISH   The purpose of the new plan is to reduce the problems we are seeing in our accounting operations. We hope to see a reduction in the problems by early next quarter.

BETTER   The purpose of the new plan is to reduce the problems we are seeing in our accounting operations. We hope to see an improvement by early next quarter.

Use Demonstrative Pronouns Followed by Nouns   Demonstrative pronouns—*this, that, these,* and *those*—can help you maintain the coherence of a discussion by linking ideas securely. In almost all cases, demonstrative pronouns should be followed by nouns. In the following examples, notice that a demonstrative pronoun by itself can be vague and confusing.

UNCLEAR   New screening techniques are being developed to combat viral infections. *These* are the subject of a new research effort in California.

   What is being studied in California: new screening techniques or viral infections?

CLEAR   New screening techniques are being developed to combat viral infections. *These techniques* are the subject of a new research effort in California.

UNCLEAR   The task force could not complete its study of the mine accident. *This* was the subject of a scathing editorial in the union newsletter.

   What was the subject of the editorial: the mine accident or the task force's inability to complete its study of the accident?

CLEAR   The task force failed to complete its study of the mine accident. *This fail-ure* was the subject of a scathing editorial in the union newsletter.

Even when the context is clear, a demonstrative pronoun used without a noun might interrupt the readers' progress by referring them back to an earlier idea.

INTERRUPTIVE   The law firm advised that the company initiate proceedings. This caused the company to search for a second legal opinion.

FLUID   The law firm advised that the company initiate proceedings. *This advice* caused the company to search for a second legal opinion.

Interactive Sample Document:
Identifying the Elements of a Coherent Paragraph

The following paragraph is taken from a report published by a water company. In this paragraph, the writer is describing how he decided on a method for increasing the company's business within his particular branch. (The sentences are numbered.)

The questions in the margin ask you to think about the qualities of coherent paragraphs (as outlined on pages 224–230). The answers to these questions are available on TechComm Web.

1. In what ways does the topic sentence function as it should?

2. Identify the transitional words or phrases. How are they used effectively?

3. Identify the repeated key words. How effectively does the writer use key words?

4. Identify the demonstrative pronouns followed by nouns. How effectively does the writer use them?

(1) We found that the best way to improve the Montana branch would be to add a storage facility to our existing supply sources. (2) Currently, we can handle the average demand on a maximum day; the storage facility will enable us to meet peaking requirements and fire-protection needs. (3) In conducting our investigation, we considered developing new supply sources with sufficient capacity to meet current and future needs. (4) This alternative was rejected, however, when our consultants (Smith and Jones) did ground-water studies that revealed that insufficient groundwater is available and that the new wells would have to be located too far apart if they were not to interfere with each other.

On TechComm Web

To find the answers to these questions, click on Interactive Sample Documents for Ch. 10 on <bedfordstmartins.com/techcomm>.

REVISING THE WHOLE DOCUMENT FOR COHERENCE

In looking for problems that need fixing, most writers look for the largest and most important problems first, then proceed to the smaller, less important ones. This way, they don't waste time on awkward paragraphs they might eventually decide to throw out. They begin revising by considering the document as a whole—for organization, content, and coherence—saving the editing of sentence-level concerns—such as grammar, punctuation, and spelling—for later.

GUIDELINES

Revising the Whole Document

In revising your document for coherence, answer the following seven questions:

▶ *Have you left out anything in turning your outline into a draft?* Check the outline to see that all the topics are presented in the document itself.

▶ *Have you included all the elements your readers expect to see?* If, for instance, the readers of a report expect a transmittal letter, they might be distracted if it is missing.

▶ *Is the organization logical?* Readers should be able to understand the logical progression from one topic to the next. Check the opening passages of each section to be sure they clearly and logically connect that section to the one that preceded it.

▶ *Is the content strong?* Have you presented your claims clearly and emphatically? Have you provided sufficient—and appropriate—evidence to support them? Is your reasoning valid and persuasive?

▶ *Do you come across as reliable, honest, and helpful?* Check to see that your persona is fully professional.

▶ *Are all the elements presented consistently?* Check to see that parallel items are presented consistently. For example, are all your headings on the same level structured the same way: as noun phrases or as *-ing* gerunds? And check for grammatical parallelism, particularly in lists.

▶ *Is the emphasis appropriate throughout the document?* If a major point is treated only briefly, mark it for possible expansion. If a minor topic is treated at great length, mark it for possible condensing.

On TechComm Web

For more advice on revising the whole document, see Purdue University's Online Writing Lab handouts on revising. Click on Links Library for Ch. 10 on <bedfordstmartins.com/techcomm>.

In This Book

For more on evidence and persona, see Ch. 6, p. 110.

Revision Checklist

Did you check the whole document to make sure that
- ❏ you didn't leave out anything in turning your outline into a draft? (p. 231)
- ❏ you include all the elements your readers expect to see? (p. 231)
- ❏ the organization is logical? (p. 231)
- ❏ the content is strong? (p. 231)
- ❏ you come across as reliable, honest, and helpful? (p. 231)
- ❏ all the elements are presented consistently? (p. 231)
- ❏ the emphasis is appropriate throughout the document? (p. 231)

Did you revise the title so that it
- ❏ clearly refers to your audience and the purpose of your document? (p. 219)
- ❏ is sufficiently precise and informative? (p. 219)

Did you revise the headings to
- ❏ avoid long noun strings? (p. 221)
- ❏ be informative? (p. 221)
- ❏ use the question form for less knowledgeable readers? (p. 221)
- ❏ use the "how to" form in instructional materials, such as manuals? (p. 221)
- ❏ use the gerund form (-*ing*) to suggest a process? (p. 221)
- ❏ avoid back-to-back headings by including an advance organizer? (p. 221)

- ❏ Did you look for opportunities to turn traditional paragraphs into lists? (p. 222)

Did you revise your paragraphs so that each one
- ❏ begins with a clear topic sentence? (p. 224)
- ❏ has adequate and appropriate support? (p. 225)
- ❏ is not too long for readers? (p. 226)
- ❏ uses coherence devices such as transitional words and phrases, repetition of key words, and demonstratives followed by nouns? (p. 227)

Exercises

On TechComm Web

For more exercises, click on Additional Exercises, Projects, and Cases for Ch. 10 on <bedfordstmartins.com/techcomm>.

1. Write a one-paragraph evaluation of each of the following titles. How clearly does the title indicate the subject and purpose of the document? On the basis of your analysis, rewrite each title.

   a. Recommended Forecasting Techniques for Haldane Company

   b. A Study of Digital Cameras

   c. Agriculture in the West: A 10-Year View

2. Write a one-paragraph evaluation of each of the following headings. How clearly does the heading indicate the subject of the text that will follow it? On the basis of your analysis, rewrite each heading to make it clearer and more informative. Invent any necessary details.

   a. Multigroup Processing Technique Review Board Report Findings

   b. The Great Depression of 1929

   c. Intensive-care Nursing

3. Revise the following passage (based on Snyder, 1993) using a list format. The subject is bioremediation: the process of using microorganisms to restore natural environmental conditions.

Scientists are now working on several new research areas. One area involves using microorganisms to make some compounds less dangerous to the environment. Although coal may be our most plentiful fossil fuel, most of the nation's vast Eastern reserve cannot meet air-pollution standards because it emits too much sulfur when it is burned. The problem is that the aromatic compound dibenzothiothene (DBT) attaches itself to hydrocarbon molecules, producing sulfur dioxide. But the Chicago-based Institute of Gas Technology last year patented a bacterial strain that consumes the DBT (at least 90 percent, in recent lab trials) while leaving the hydrocarbon molecules intact.

A second research area is the genetic engineering of microbes in an attempt to reduce the need for toxic chemicals. In 1991, the EPA approved the first genetically engineered pesticide. Called Cellcap, it incorporates a gene from one microbe that produces a toxin deadly to potato beetles and corn borers into a thick-skinned microbe that is hardier. Even then, the engineered bacteria are dead when applied to the crops.

A third research area is the use of microorganisms to attack stubborn metals and radioactive waste. Microbes have been used for decades to concentrate copper and nickel in low-grade ores. Now researchers are exploiting the fact that if certain bacteria are given special foods, they excrete enzymes that break down metals and minerals. For example, researchers at the U.S. Geological Survey found that two types of bacteria turn uranium from its usual form — one that easily dissolves in water — into another one that turns to a solid that can be easily removed from water. They are now working on doing the same for other radioactive waste.

4. Provide a topic sentence for each of the following paragraphs:

   a. _____. The goal of the Web Privacy Project is to make it simple for users to learn the privacy practices of a Web site and thereby decide whether to visit the site. Site owners will electronically "define" their privacy practices according to a set of specifications. Users will enter their own preferences through settings on their browsers. When a user attempts to visit a site, the browser will read the site's practices. If those practices match the user's preferences, the user will seamlessly enter the site. However, if the site's practices do not match the user's preferences, the user will be asked whether he or she wishes to visit the site.

   b. _____. The reason for this difference is that a larger percentage of engineers working in small firms may be expected to hold high-level positions. In firms with fewer than 20 engineers, for example, the median income was $62,200. In firms of 20 to 200 engineers, the median income was $60,345. For the largest firms, the median was $58,600.

5. The following paragraph was written by the contractor for a nuclear power plant. The audience is a regulator at the Nuclear Regulatory Commission (NRC), and the purpose of the paragraph is to convince the regulator to waive one of the regulations. In this paragraph, transitional words and phrases have been removed. Add an appropriate transition in each blank space. Where necessary, add punctuation.

   As you know, the current regulation requires the use of conduit for all cable extending more than 18 inches from the cable tray to the piece of equipment. _____ conduit is becoming increasingly expensive: up 17 percent in the last year alone. _____ we would like to determine whether the NRC would grant us any flexibility in its conduit regulations. Could we _____ run cable without conduit for lengths up to 3 feet in low-risk situations such as wall-mounted cable or low-traffic areas? We realize _____ that conduit will always remain necessary in high-risk situations. The cable specifications for the Unit Two report to the NRC are due in less than two months; _____ we would appreciate a quick reply to our request, because this matter will seriously affect our materials budget.

6. In each of the following exercises, the second sentence begins with a demonstrative pronoun. Add a noun after the demonstrative to enhance coherence.

   a. The Zoning Commission has scheduled an open hearing for March 14. This _____ will enable concerned citizens to voice their opinions on the proposed construction.

   b. The university has increased the number of parking spaces, instituted a shuttle system, and increased parking fees. These _____ are expected to ease the parking problems.

   c. Congress's decision to withdraw support for the supercollider in 1994 was a shock to the U.S. particle-physics community. This _____ is seen as instrumental in the revival of the European research community.

Project

On TechComm Web

For more projects, click on Additional Exercises, Projects, and Cases for Ch. 10 on <bedfordstmartins.com/techcomm>.

7. **Group Activity** Form small groups. Have each person in the group contribute a multipage document he or she has written recently, either in this class or in another. Make copies of this document for each group member. Have each member annotate the document according to the principles of coherence discussed in this chapter, and then write a summary statement at the end of the document highlighting those techniques that are done well and those that could be improved. Meet as a group to study these annotated documents. Write a memo to your instructor describing those aspects of the annotations on your document cited by more than one group member and those aspects cited by only one group member. Overall, what basic differences do you see among group members between the annotations and the summary statement? Do you think that, as a general practice, it would be worthwhile to have a draft reviewed and annotated by more than one person? What have you learned about the usefulness of peer review? (For more on memos, see Chapter 15, page 378.)

On TechComm Web

For more cases, click on Additional Exercises, Projects, and Cases for Ch. 10 on <bedfordstmartins.com /techcomm>.

C A S E
Writing Guidelines about Coherence

You are a public-information officer recently hired by the Agency for Health Care Policy and Research. One of your responsibilities is to make sure that your agency's public information on the Web is clear and accurate. Your supervisor, José Martinez, has asked you to write a set of guidelines for physicians and other researchers who write the articles you put on your site. You ask him why he thinks they need the guidelines. "Their writing is factually correct," José replies, "but because they are taking excerpts from longer, more scientific studies, their documents can be choppy. They need to be smoothed out." You ask your supervisor to point you in the right direction by identifying a sample that shows the qualities he wants you to describe. He directs you to the following brief report (U.S. Department of Health and Human Services, 1998) about a study of HIV patients. "This is a good sample of how to write to the general reader," José tells you. Study this report, noting the different techniques the writer has used to achieve coherence. Focus on the title, the headings, and the paragraphs. Write a brief set of guidelines using excerpts from this sample to illustrate your advice.

HCSUS Fact Sheet:
HIV Cost and Services Utilization Study

As HIV/AIDS spreads into different communities and as new therapies become available, policymakers require reliable information about the type and costs of the health care services that persons with HIV disease are receiving, so that informed resource-allocation decisions can be made. The HIV Cost and Services Utilization Study (HCSUS) is the first major research effort to collect information on a nationally representative sample of people in care for HIV infection.

HCSUS is examining costs of care, utilization of a wide array of services, access to care, quality of care, quality of life, unmet needs for medical and nonmedical services, social support, satisfaction with medical care, and knowledge of HIV therapies.

Who Is Conducting HCSUS?

HCSUS is funded through a cooperative agreement between the Agency for Health Care Policy Research (AHCPR) and RAND—a private nonprofit research institution in Santa Monica, CA. Supplemental funding has been provided by the Health Resources and Services Administration (HRSA), the National Institute of Mental Health (NIMH), the National Institute of Aging (NIA), the National Institute of Drug Abuse (NIDA), the National Institute of Dental and Craniofacial Research (NIDCR) (NIDR), and the Office of Minority Health Research (OMR).

HCSUS is being conducted by a consortium of private and Government institutions, centered at RAND. Local and national advisory groups have been established to facilitate communication between the HIV community and the research consortium.

What Is the Scope of HCSUS?

HCSUS is composed of a core study and several supplemental studies. The core study has enrolled a national probability sample of 2,864 HIV-infected adults who were receiving ongoing or regular medical care in the first 2 months of 1996. Respondents were sampled from 28 urban areas and 24 clusters of rural counties in the continental United States. Patients receiving services in hospitals, clinics, and private practice settings were enrolled. HCSUS oversampled women and members of staff model health maintenance organizations, to obtain more precise information on these specific populations.

Supplemental studies are examining HIV care delivery in rural areas, prevalence of mental and substance abuse disorders, oral health of HIV-positive individuals, and issues related to HIV-infected persons over 50 years of age. A supplemental sample of persons receiving care in rural areas was obtained to augment the core rural sample and to provide a basis for studies focused on the rural population with HIV infection. Another supplemental project is collecting data from the providers of care to HCSUS respondents.

The HCSUS design includes a baseline in-person interview with sampled patients, two follow-up interviews scheduled for 6 months and 12 months after the baseline interview, and abstractions of data from patients' medical, pharmaceutical, and billing records. All baseline and follow-up interviews were completed as of January, 1998. Abstraction of record data is currently in progress. In addition, a supplemental interview containing a standardized instrument to diagnose psychiatric disorders was administered to a subsample of approximately 1500 HCSUS respondents in conjunction with the first follow-up interview. Further, blood samples have been collected from a majority of HCSUS respondents and virological analyses are being initiated.

What Will HCSUS Examine?

The HCSUS will address a broad array of issues relevant to public policy formulation and to health services research:

- Cost, use, and quality of care.
- Access to care.
- Unmet needs for care.
- Quality of life.
- Social support.
- Knowledge of HIV.
- Clinical outcomes.
- Mental health.
- The relationship of these variables to provider type and patient characteristics.

Public use tapes containing data from the baseline interviews will be available in the summer of 1999. Data from subsequent interviews and from records abstraction will become available for public use subsequently.

Drafting and Revising Effective Sentences

11

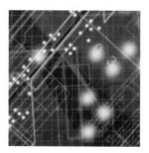

Writing teacher William Strunk (1918) on conciseness:

Vigorous writing is concise. A sentence should contain no unnecessary words . . . for the same reason that a drawing should have no unnecessary lines and a machine no unnecessary parts.

On TechComm Web

For additional samples, activities, and links related to this chapter, see <bedfordstmartins.com/techcomm>.

Technical communication is meant to get a job done. Therefore, make your sentences and words clear, concise, and easy to understand. People read technical communication to learn how to carry out a task, to keep abreast of developments, or to gather information. Your effective sentences will help them get their jobs done.

To structure effective sentences:

Use lists.

Put new and important information at the end of the sentence.

Choose an appropriate sentence length.

Focus on the "real" subject.

Focus on the "real" verb.

Express parallel elements in parallel structures.

Use modifiers effectively.

STRUCTURING EFFECTIVE SENTENCES

Good technical communication consists of clear, correct, and graceful sentences that convey information without calling attention to themselves. This section consists of seven principles for structuring effective sentences.

Use Lists

Many sentences in technical communication are long and complicated:

> We recommend that more work on heat-exchanger performance be done with a larger variety of different fuels at the same temperature, with similar fuels at different temperatures, and with special fuels such as diesel fuel and shale-oil-derived fuels.

Here readers cannot concentrate fully on the information because they are trying to remember all the "with" phrases following "done." If they could "see" how many phrases they had to remember, their job would be easier:

We recommend that more work on heat-exchanger performance be done

- with a larger variety of different fuels at the same temperature
- with similar fuels at different temperatures
- with special fuels such as diesel fuels and shale-oil-derived fuels

In this version, the arrangement of the words on the page reinforces the meaning. The bullets direct the reader's eyes to three items in a series, and the fact that each item begins at the same left margin helps, too.

If you don't have enough space to list the items vertically, or if you are not permitted to do so, number the items within the sentence:

We recommend that more work on heat-exchanger performance be done (1) with a larger variety of different fuels at the same temperature, (2) with similar fuels at different temperatures, and (3) with special fuels such as diesel fuels and shale-oil-derived fuels.

GUIDELINES

Creating Effective Lists

▶ *Set off each listed item with a number, a letter, or a symbol (usually a bullet).*

– Use numbered lists to suggest sequence (as in the numbered steps in a set of instructions) or priority (the first item is the most important). Using numbers helps readers see the total number of items in a list (as in the "Seven Warning Signals of Cancer" from the American Cancer Society). For sublists, use lowercase letters:

1. Item
   a. subitem
   b. subitem

2. Item
   a. subitem
   b. subitem

– Use bullets to avoid sequence or priority, such as for lists of people; everyone except number 1 gets offended. For sublists, use hyphens:

- Item
  – subitem
  – subitem

– Use an open (unshaded) box (❑) for checklists.

In This Book

For more on designing checklists, see Ch. 14, p. 346.

▶ *Break up long lists.* Most people can remember only 5 to 9 items easily; break up lists of 10 or more items.

Original List	Revised List
Tool kit:	*Tool kit:*
• hand saw	• Saws
• coping saw	– hand saw
• hacksaw	– coping saw
• compass saw	– hacksaw
• adjustable wrench	– compass saw
• box wrench	• Wrenches
• Stillson wrench	– adjustable wrench
• socket wrench	– box wrench
• open-end wrench	– Stillson wrench
• Allen wrench	– socket wrench
	– open-end wrench
	– Allen wrench

▶ *Present the items in a parallel structure.*

The nonparallel list is sloppy, a mixture of noun phrases (items 1, 3, 4, and 5), a verb phrase (item 2), and a participial phrase preceded by a dependent clause (item 6). The parallel list uses parallel verb phrases and deemphasizes the dependent clause in item 6 by placing it after the verb phrase. For more on parallelism, see p. 245.

Nonparallel	Parallel
Here is the sequence we plan to follow:	Here is the sequence we plan to follow:
1. construction of the preliminary proposal	1. write the preliminary proposal
2. do library research	2. do library research
3. interview with the Bemco vice president	3. interview the Bemco vice president
4. first draft	4. write the first draft
5. revision of the first draft	5. revise the first draft
6. after we get your approval, preparing the final draft	6. prepare the final draft, after we get your approval

▶ *Structure and punctuate the lead-in correctly.* Although standards vary from organization to organization, the most common lead-in consists of a grammatically complete clause followed by a colon, as shown in the following examples:

Following are the three main assets:

The three main assets are as follows:

The three main assets are the following:

If you cannot use a grammatically complete lead-in, use a dash or no punctuation at all:

The committee found that the employee

- did not cause the accident
- acted properly immediately after the accident
- reported the accident properly

▶ *Punctuate the list correctly.* Because rules for punctuating lists vary, you should find out whether people in your organization have a preference. If not, you can generally punctuate lists as follows:

– If the items are phrases, use a lowercase letter at the start. Do not use a period or a comma at the end. The white space to the right of the last item and between the list and the following line clearly indicates the end of the list.

The new facility will offer three advantages:

- lower leasing costs
- easier commuting distance
- a larger pool of potential workers

– If the items are complete sentences, use an uppercase letter at the start and a period at the end.

The new facility will offer three advantages:

- The leasing costs will be lower.
- The commuting distance for most employees will be shorter.
- The pool of potential workers will be larger.

– If the items are phrases followed by complete sentences, use an initial uppercase letter and a final period. Begin the complete sentences with uppercase letters and end them with periods. You can use italics to emphasize the main idea in each bullet point.

The new facility will offer three advantages:

- *Lower leasing costs.* The lease will cost $1,800 per month; currently we pay $2,300.
- *Easier commuting distance.* Our worker's average commute of 18 minutes would drop to 14 minutes.
- *A larger pool of potential workers.* In the last decade, the population has shifted westward to the area near the new facility. We would increase our potential workforce in both the semiskilled and managerial categories.

– If the list consists of two kinds of items — phrases and complete sentences — punctuate both with uppercase letters and periods.

The new facility will offer three advantages:

- Lower leasing costs.

- Easier commuting distance. Our workers' average commute of 18 minutes would drop to 14 minutes.
- A greater pool of potential workers. In the last decade, the population has shifted westward to the area near the new facility. We would increase our potential workforce in both the semiskilled and managerial categories.

In most lists, the second and subsequent lines, called *turnovers*, align under the first letter of the first line, highlighting the bullet or number to the left of the text. The *hanging indentation* helps the reader see and understand the organization of the passage.

Put New and Important Information at the End of the Sentence

Sentences are often easier to understand and more emphatic if new information appears at the end. For instance, if your company has labor problems, and you want to describe the possible results, you might structure the sentence like this:

> Because of the labor problems, we anticipate a three-week delay.

In this case, the *three-week delay* is the new information.

If your readers already expect a three-week delay but don't know why, reverse the structure:

> We anticipate the three-week delay in production because of labor problems.

Here, *labor problems* is the new and important information.

Try not to end the sentence with qualifying information that blunts the impact of the new information.

WEAK   The joint could fail under special circumstances.

IMPROVED   Under special circumstances, the joint could fail.

Put new or difficult terms at the end of the sentence.

WEAK   You use a wired glove to point to objects.

IMPROVED   To point to objects, you use a wired glove.

Choose an Appropriate Sentence Length

On TechComm Web

For more about varying sentence length, search for "sentence variety" in Guide to Grammar & Writing. Click on Links Library for Ch. 11 on <bedfordstmartins.com /techcomm>.

Sometimes sentence length affects the quality of the writing. In general, an average of 15 to 20 words is effective for most technical communication. A series of 10-word sentences would be choppy. A series of 35-word sentences would probably be too demanding. And a succession of sentences of approximately the same length would be monotonous.

In revising a draft, use your software to compute the average sentence length of a representative passage.

Avoid Overly Long Sentences   How long is too long? There is no simple answer, because ease of reading depends on the vocabulary, sentence structure, and sentence length; the reader's knowledge of the topic; and the purpose of the communication.

Often a draft will include sentences such as the following:

> The construction of the new facility is scheduled to begin in March, but it might be delayed by one or even two months by winter weather conditions, which can make it impossible or nearly impossible to begin excavating the foundation.

To make this confusing 40-word sentence easier to read, divide it into two sentences:

> The construction of the new facility is scheduled to begin in March. However, construction might be delayed until April or even May by winter weather conditions, which can make it impossible or nearly impossible to begin excavating the foundation.

As discussed in the Guidelines box on page 239, sometimes an overly long sentence can be fixed by creating a list.

Avoid Overly Short Sentences   Just as sentences can be too long, they can also be too short and choppy, as in the following example:

> Customarily, environmental cleanups are conducted on a "time-and-materials" (T&M) basis. Using the T&M basis, the contractor performs the work. Then, the contractor bills for the hours worked and the cost of equipment and materials used during the work. With the T&M approach, spending for environmental cleanups by private and government entities has been difficult to contain. Also, actual contamination reduction has been slow.

The problem here is that the sentences are choppy and contain too little information. In cases like this, the best way to revise is to combine sentences:

> Customarily, environmental cleanups are conducted on a "time-and-materials" (T&M) basis: the contractor performs the work, then bills for the hours worked and the cost of equipment and materials. With the T&M approach, spending for environmental cleanups by private and government entities has been difficult to contain, and contamination reduction has been slow.

Another problem with excessively short sentences is that they needlessly repeat key terms. Again, consider combining sentences:

SLUGGISH   I have experience working with various microprocessor-based systems. Some of these systems include the T90, RCA 9600, and AIM 7600.

BETTER   I have experience working with various microprocessor-based systems, including the T90, RCA 9600, and AIM 7600.

On TechComm Web

For more about using "real" subjects, see the e-handout on revising prose from the Writing Center @ Rensselaer. Click on Links Library for Ch. 11 on <bedfordstmartins.com/techcomm>.

Focus on the "Real" Subject

The conceptual or "real" subject of the sentence should also be the grammatical subject. Don't disguise or bury the real subject in a prepositional phrase following a weak grammatical subject. In the following examples, the weak subjects disguise the real subjects (the grammatical subjects are italicized).

WEAK   The *use* of this method would eliminate the problem of motor damage.

STRONG   This *method* would eliminate the problem of motor damage.

WEAK   The *presence* of a six-membered lactone ring was detected.

STRONG   A six-membered lactone *ring* was detected.

Another way to make the subject of the sentence prominent is to reduce the number of grammatical expletives: *it is, there is,* and *there are,* and related phrases.

WEAK   There is no alternative for us except to withdraw the product.

STRONG   We have no alternative except to withdraw the product.

WEAK   It is hoped that testing the evaluation copies of the software will help us make this decision.

STRONG   I hope that testing the evaluation copies of the software will help us make this decision.

In This Book

For more about using the passive voice, see p. 250.

This second example uses the expletive *it is* with the passive voice.

Expletives are not errors. Rather, they are conversational expressions that can clarify meaning by emphasizing the information that follows them.

EXPLETIVE   It is hard to say whether the recession will last more than a few months.

NO EXPLETIVE   Whether the recession will last more than a few months is hard to say.

The second version is harder to understand because the reader has to remember a long subject — "Whether the recession will last more than a few months" — before getting to the verb — "is." However, the sentence could also be rewritten in other ways to make it easier to understand and to eliminate the expletive.

I don't know whether the recession will last for more than a few months.

Nobody really knows whether the recession will last more than a few months.

Use the search function of your word processor to locate both weak subjects (usually they precede the word *of*) and expletives.

Focus on the "Real" Verb

A "real" verb, like a "real" subject, should stand out in every sentence. A common problem in technical communication is the inappropriate use of a *nominalized* verb—a verb that has been changed into a noun, then coupled with a weaker verb. *To install* becomes *to effect an installation*; *to analyze* becomes *to conduct an analysis.* Notice how nominalizing the verbs make the following sentences both awkward and unnecessarily long (the nominalized verbs are italicized).

WEAK   Each *preparation* of the solution is done twice.

STRONG   Each solution is prepared twice.

WEAK   *Consideration* should be given to an acquisition of the properties.

STRONG   We should consider acquiring the properties.

Like expletives, nominalizations are not errors. In fact, many common nouns are nominalizations: *maintenance, requirement,* and *analysis,* for example. In addition, nominalizations often effectively summarize an idea from a previous sentence (in italics below).

> The new *legislation* could delay our *entry* into the HDTV market. This *delay* could cost us millions.

Some software programs search for common nominalizations. With any word processor, however, you can identify most of them by searching for character strings such as *tion, ment, sis, ence, ing,* and *ance,* as well as the word *of.*

Express Parallel Elements in Parallel Structures

A sentence is parallel if its coordinate elements follow the same grammatical form. For example, the clauses are either passive or active, the verbs are either infinitives or participles, and so on. A recognizable pattern makes a sentence easier for the reader to follow.

For example, the verbs in the following sentence are unparallel because they do not use the same verb form.

UNPARALLEL   Our present system is costing us profits and reduces our productivity.

PARALLEL   Our present system is costing us profits and reducing our productivity.

In the following sentence, the first clause is subjunctive; the second, imperative.

UNPARALLEL   The compositor should follow the printed directions; do not change the originator's work.

PARALLEL   The compositor should follow the printed directions and should not change the originator's work.

On TechComm Web

For interactive exercises on parallelism and other topics discussed in this chapter, click on the link to Exercise Central on <bedfordstmartins.com/techcomm>.

When using parallel constructions, make sure that parallel items in a series do not overlap, causing confusion or even changing the meaning of the sentence:

CONFUSING   The speakers will include partners of law firms, businesspeople, and civic leaders.

"Partners" appears to apply to "businesspeople" and "civic leaders," as well as to law firms. The revision solves the problem by rearranging the items so that "partners" can apply only to "law firms."

CLEAR   The speakers will include businesspeople, civic leaders, and partners of law firms.

CONFUSING   We need to buy more lumber, hardware, tools, and hire the subcontractors.

The writer has linked two ideas inappropriately. The first idea is that we need to buy three things: lumber, hardware, and tools. The second is that we need to hire the subcontractors. Hiring is not in the same category as the items to buy.

CLEAR   We need to buy more lumber, hardware, and tools, and we need to hire the subcontractors.

Use Modifiers Effectively

Modifiers are words, phrases, and clauses that describe other elements in the sentence. To make your meaning clear, you must indicate whether a modifier provides necessary information about the word or phrase it refers to (its *referent*) or whether it simply provides additional information. You must also clearly identify the referent.

Distinguish Between Restrictive and Nonrestrictive Modifiers   As the term implies, a *restrictive modifier* restricts the meaning of its referent; it provides information that the reader needs to identify the referent and is, therefore, crucial to understanding the sentence. Notice that restrictive modifiers—italicized in the following examples—are not set off by commas:

The aircraft *used in the exhibitions* are slightly modified.

The phrase "used in the exhibitions" identifies which aircraft.

Please disregard the notice *you recently received from us.*

The phrase "you recently received from us" identifies which notice.

In most cases, the restrictive modifier doesn't require a relative pronoun, such as *that* or *which*. If you choose to use a pronoun, however, use *that* or *who* (for people):

The aircraft *that* are used in the exhibits are slightly modified.

A *nonrestrictive modifier* does not restrict the meaning of its referent: the reader does not need the information to identify the referent. If you omit the nonrestrictive modifier, the sentence retains its primary meaning.

> The Hubble telescope, *intended to answer fundamental questions about the origin of the universe*, was last repaired in 2002.
>
> When you arrive, go to the Registration Area, *which is located on the second floor.*

If you use a relative pronoun, choose *which* (*who* or *whom* when referring to a person). Be sure to use commas to separate a restrictive modifier from the rest of the sentence.

Avoid Misplaced Modifiers   The placement of the modifier often determines the meaning of the sentence, as the placement of *only* illustrates in the following sentences.

> *Only* Turner received a cost-of-living increase last year.
>
> *Meaning: Nobody else received one.*

> Turner received *only* a cost-of-living increase last year.
>
> *Meaning: He didn't receive a merit increase.*

> Turner received a cost-of-living increase *only* last year.
>
> *Meaning: He received a cost-of-living increase as recently as last year.*

> Turner received a cost-of-living increase last year *only*.
>
> *Meaning: He received a cost-of-living increase in no other year.*

Misplaced modifiers—those that appear to modify the wrong referent—are a common problem. Usually, the best solution is to place the modifier as close as possible to its intended referent.

MISPLACED   The subject of the meeting is the future of geothermal energy *in the downtown Webster Hotel.*

CORRECT   The subject of the meeting *in the downtown Webster Hotel* is the future of geothermal energy.

A *squinting modifier* falls ambiguously between two possible referents, so the reader cannot tell which one is being modified:

UNCLEAR   We decided *immediately* to purchase the new system.

> *Did we decide immediately, or did we decide to make the purchase immediately?*

CLEAR   We *immediately* decided to purchase the new system.

CLEAR   We decided to purchase the new system *immediately*.

A subtle form of misplaced modification can also occur with correlative constructions, such as *either . . . or, neither . . . nor,* and *not only . . . but also*:

UNPARALLEL   The new refrigerant not only decreases energy costs but also spoilage losses.

PARALLEL   The new refrigerant decreases not only energy costs but also spoilage losses.

Here, "decreases" applies to both "energy costs" and "spoilage losses." Therefore, the first half of the correlative construction should follow "decreases." Note that if the sentence contains two different verbs, the first half of the correlative construction should precede the verb:

The new refrigerant not only decreases energy costs but also reduces spoilage losses.

Avoid Dangling Modifiers   A dangling modifier has no referent in the sentence and can therefore be unclear:

DANGLING   Trying to solve the problem, the instructions seemed unclear.

This sentence appears to say that the instructions are trying to solve the problem. To correct the problem, rewrite the sentence, adding the clarifying information either within the modifier or next to it:

CORRECT   As I was trying to solve the problem, the instructions seemed unclear.

CORRECT   Trying to solve the problem, I thought the instructions seemed unclear.

Sometimes you can correct a dangling modifier by switching from the *indicative mood* (a statement of fact) to the *imperative mood* (a request or command):

DANGLING   To initiate the procedure, the BEGIN button should be pushed.

CORRECT   To initiate the procedure, push the BEGIN button.

CHOOSING THE RIGHT WORDS AND PHRASES

Choosing the right words and phrases:

Select an appropriate level of formality.

Be clear and specific.

Be concise.

Use inoffensive language.

The following section discusses four basic principles that will help you use the right words and phrases in the right places.

Select an Appropriate Level of Formality

Although no standard definition of levels of formality exists, most experts would agree on three levels:

INFORMAL   The Acorn 560 is a real screamer. With 3.2GHz of pure computing power, it slashes through even the thickest spreadsheets before you can say 2 + 2 = 4.

MODERATE   With its 3.2GHz microprocessor, the Acorn 560 can handle even the most complicated spreadsheets quickly.

FORMAL   With a 3.2GHz microprocessor, the Acorn 560 is a high-speed personal computer designed for computation-intensive applications such as large spreadsheets.

Technical communication usually requires a moderately or highly formal style.

To achieve the appropriate level and tone, think about your audience, your subject, and your purpose:

- *Audience.* You would write more formally to a group of retired executives than to a group of college students. You would likewise write more formally to the company vice president than to your subordinates, or in writing to people from most other cultures.

In This Book

For more on writing to a multicultural audience, see Ch. 5, p. 94.

- *Subject.* You would write more formally about a serious subject—safety regulations or important projects—than about plans for an office party.

- *Purpose.* You would write more formally in a report to shareholders than in a company newsletter. Instructions, however, tend to be relatively informal, often using the second person, contractions, and the imperative mood (see Chapter 20).

In general, it is better to err on the side of formality. Avoid an informal style in any writing you do at the office, for two reasons:

- *Informal writing tends to be imprecise.* In the example "The Acorn 560 is a real screamer," what exactly is a *screamer*?

- *Informal writing can be embarrassing.* If your boss spots your e-mail to a colleague, you might wish it didn't begin, "How ya doing, loser?"

Be Clear and Specific

Follow these seven guidelines to make your writing clear and specific:

- Use the active voice and the passive voice appropriately.
- Be specific.
- Avoid unnecessary jargon.
- Use positive constructions.
- Avoid long noun strings.
- Avoid clichés.
- Avoid euphemisms.

On TechComm Web

For more on choosing an appropriate voice, see "The Passive Engineer" by Helen Moody. Click on Links Library for Ch. 11 on <bedfordstmartins.com/techcomm>.

Use Active and Passive Voice Appropriately In a sentence using the active voice, the subject performs the action expressed by the verb: the "doer" of the action is the grammatical subject. In a sentence using the passive voice, by contrast, the subject receives the action. Compare the following examples (the subjects are italicized):

ACTIVE   *Dave Brushaw* drove the launch vehicle.

PASSIVE   The launch *vehicle* was driven by Dave Brushaw.

In most cases, the active voice works better than the passive voice because it emphasizes the agent. An active-voice sentence also is shorter because it does not require a form of the *to be* verb and the past participle, as a passive-voice sentence does. In the active version of the example sentence, for instance, the verb is "drove" rather than "was driven," and "by" is unnecessary.

The passive voice, however, is generally better in these four cases:

- When the agent is clear from the context:

  Students are required to take both writing courses.

  Here, the context makes it clear that the college sets the requirements.

- When the agent is unknown:

  The comet was first referred to in an ancient Egyptian text.

  We don't know who wrote this text.

- When the agent is less important than the action:

  The documents were hand-delivered this morning.

  It doesn't matter who the messenger was.

- When a reference to the agent is embarrassing, dangerous, or in some other way inappropriate:

  Incorrect data were recorded for the flow rate.

In This Book

For more on ethics, see Ch. 2.

Here, it might be unwise or tactless to specify who recorded the incorrect data. However, it is unethical to use the passive voice to avoid responsibility for an action.

The passive voice can also help you maintain the focus of your paragraph.

LANs have three major advantages. First, they are inexpensive to run. Second, they can be expanded easily. . . .

Some people believe that the active voice is inappropriate because it emphasizes the person who does the work rather than the work itself, making the writing less objective. In many cases, this objection is valid. Why write "I analyzed the sample for traces of iodine" if there would be no ambiguity about who did the analysis or no need to identify who did it? The passive focuses on the action, not the actor: "The samples were analyzed for traces of iodine." But if in doubt, use the active voice.

Other people argue that the passive voice produces a double ambiguity. In the sentence "The sample was analyzed for traces of iodine," the reader is not quite sure who did the analysis (you or someone else) or when it was done (during the project or some time previously). Although a passive-voice sentence can indicate the actor, the writer often fails to mention it.

The best approach is to recognize that the two voices differ and to use each of them where it is most effective.

Many grammar checkers can help you locate the passive voice. Some will advise you that the passive is undesirable, almost an error, but this advice is misleading. Use the passive voice when it works better than the active voice for your purposes.

Any word processor allows you to search for the forms of *to be* used most commonly in passive-voice expressions: *is, are, was,* and *were*. You can also search for *ed* to isolate past participles, which appear in most passive-voice constructions.

Be Specific   Being specific involves using precise words, providing adequate detail, and avoiding ambiguity.

- *Use precise words.* A Ford Taurus is an automobile, but it is also a vehicle, a machine, and a thing. In describing the Taurus, *automobile* is better than the less-specific *vehicle,* because *vehicle* can also refer to pickup trucks, trains, hot-air balloons, and other means of transport. As words become more abstract—from *machine* to *thing,* for instance—chances for misunderstanding increase.

- *Provide adequate detail.* Readers probably know less about your subject than you do. What might be perfectly clear to you might be too vague for them.

VAGUE	An engine on the plane experienced some difficulties.
	Which engine? What plane? What kinds of difficulties?
CLEAR	The left engine on the Martin 411 lost power during flight.

- *Avoid ambiguity.* Don't let readers wonder which of two meanings you are trying to convey.

AMBIGUOUS	After stirring by hand for 10 seconds, add three drops of the iodine mixture to the solution.
	After stirring the iodine mixture or the solution?
CLEAR	Stir the iodine mixture by hand for 10 seconds. Then add three drops to the solution.
CLEAR	Stir the solution by hand for 10 seconds. Then add three drops of the iodine mixture.

If you don't have the specific data, you should approximate—and clearly tell readers you are doing so—or explain why the specific data are unavailable and indicate when they will be available: "The fuel leakage is much greater than we had anticipated; we estimate it to be at least 5 gallons per minute, not 2." Or "The fuel leakage is much greater than we had anticipated; we expect to have specific data by 4 P.M. today."

Avoid Unnecessary Jargon   Jargon is shoptalk. To the general reader, *ATM* means automated teller machine; to an electrical engineer, it means asynchronous transfer mode. Although jargon is often ridiculed, it is useful in its proper sphere. However, using unnecessary jargon is inadvisable for four reasons:

- *It can be imprecise.* If you ask a co-worker to review a document and provide *feedback*, are you asking for a facial expression, body language, a phone call, or a written evaluation?
- *It can be confusing.* If we ask a computer novice to *boot* the system, he or she might have no idea what we're talking about.
- *It is often seen as condescending.* Many readers react as if the writer is showing off—displaying a level of expertise that excludes them. If readers are feeling alienated, they will likely miss the message.
- *It is often intimidating.* People might feel inadequate or stupid because they do not know what the writer is talking about. Obviously, this reaction undermines communication.

If you are addressing a technically knowledgeable audience, use jargon recognized in that field.

Use Positive Constructions   The term *positive construction* has nothing to do with a cheerful outlook on life. It indicates that the writer is describing what something is instead of what it is not. In the sentence "I was sad to see this project completed," "sad" is a positive construction. The negative construction would be "not happy."

Here are a few more examples of positive and negative constructions:

Positive Construction	Negative Construction	Positive Construction	Negative Construction
most	not all	inefficient	not efficient
few	not many	reject	cannot accept
on time	not late, not delayed	impossible	not possible
positive	not negative		

Readers understand positive constructions more quickly and more easily than negative constructions. Consider the following examples:

DIFFICULT   Because the team did not have sufficient time to complete the project, it was not surprising that it was unable to prepare a satisfactory report.

On TechComm Web

For advice on positive constructions, see the Security and Exchange Commission's *A Plain English Handbook.* Click on Links Library for Ch. 11 on <bedfordstmartins.com/techcomm>.

SIMPLER   Because the team had too little time to complete the project, it produced
               an unsatisfactory report.

Avoid Long Noun Strings

A noun string is a phrase with a series of nouns (or nouns, adjectives, and adverbs), all of which modify the last noun. For example, in the phrase *parking-garage regulations,* the first two words modify *regulations.* Noun strings save time, and if your readers understand them, they are fine. It is easier to write *passive-restraint system* than *restraint system that is passive.*

Hyphens can clarify noun strings by linking words that go together. For example, in the phrase *flat-panel monitor,* the hyphen links *flat* and *panel.* Together they modify *monitor.* In other words, it is not a *flat panel*, or a *panel monitor*, but a *flat-panel monitor.* However, noun strings are sometimes so long or so complex that hyphens can't ensure clarity. Consider untangling the phrases and restoring prepositions, as in the following example:

In This Book

For more on hyphens, see Appendix, Part C, p. 643.

UNCLEAR   preregistration procedures instruction sheet update

CLEAR   an update of the instruction sheet for preregistration procedures

An additional danger is that noun strings can sometimes sound pompous. If you are writing about a simple smoke detector, there is no reason to call it a *smoke-detection device*—or worse, a *smoke-detection system.*

Avoid Clichés

Good writing is original and fresh. Rather than use a cliché, say what you want to say in plain English. Instead of "thinking outside the box," write "thinking creatively." Other clichés include *pushing the envelope; mission critical; paradigm shift;* and *been there, done that.* The best advice is to avoid clichés: if you are used to hearing or reading a phrase, don't use it.

Compare the following cliché-filled sentence and its plain-English translation:

TRITE   Afraid that we were between a rock and a hard place, we decided to throw
               caution to the winds with a grandstand play that would catch our competi-
               tion with its pants down.

PLAIN   Afraid that we were in a difficult position, we decided on a risky, aggres-
               sive move that would surprise our competition.

Avoid Euphemisms

A euphemism is a polite way of saying something that makes people uncomfortable. The more uncomfortable the subject, the more often people resort to euphemisms. Dozens of euphemisms deal with drinking, bathrooms, sex, and death. David Lord (as quoted in Fuchsberg, 1990) lists 48 euphemisms for firing someone, including:

personnel surplus reduction	dehiring
workforce imbalance correction	decruiting
degrowing	redundancy elimination
indefinite idling	career-change-opportunity creation
corporate downsizing	

Don't use language to cloud reality. It's an ethical issue.

Be Concise

The following five principles promote concise technical communication:

- Avoid obvious statements.
- Avoid filler.
- Avoid unnecessary prepositional phrases.
- Avoid wordy phrases.
- Avoid pompous words.

Avoid Obvious Statements Writing can become sluggish if it overexplains. The italicized words in the following example are sluggish:

SLUGGISH   The market for *the sale of* flash memory chips is dominated by *two chip manufacturers*: Intel and Advanced Micro Systems. These two *chip manufacturers* are responsible for 76 percent of the $1.3 billion market *in flash memory chips* last year.

IMPROVED   The market for flash memory chips is dominated by Intel and Advanced Micro Systems, two companies that claimed 76 percent of the $1.3 billion industry last year.

Avoid Filler In our writing we sometimes use filler that is more suited to speech. Consider the following examples:

basically	kind of
certain	sort of
essentially	various

Such words are useful when you have to think on your feet but are meaningless in writing.

BLOATED   *I think that, basically,* the board felt *sort of* betrayed, *in a sense,* by the *kind of* behavior the president displayed.

BETTER   The board felt betrayed by the president's behavior.

Modifiers are not always meaningless. For instance, it might be wise to use *I think* or *it seems to me* to suggest your awareness of other views.

BLUNT   Next year we will face unprecedented challenges to our market dominance.

LESS BLUNT   In my view, next year we will face unprecedented challenges to our market dominance.

Of course, a sentence that sounds blunt to one reader can sound self-confident to another. As you write, keep your audience's preferences in mind.

Other fillers include redundant expressions, such as *collaborate together, past history, end result, any and all, each and every, still remain, completely eliminate,* and *very unique.* Say it once.

REDUNDANT   We initially began our investigative analysis with a sample that was spherical in shape and heavy in weight.

BETTER   We began our analysis with a sample that was heavy and spherical.

Avoid Unnecessary Prepositional Phrases   A prepositional phrase consists of a preposition followed by a noun or a noun equivalent, such as *in the summary, on the engine,* and *under the heading.* Unnecessary prepositional phrases, often used along with abstract nouns and nominalizations, can make your writing long and boring.

LONG   The increase *in* the number *of* students enrolled *in* the materials-engineering program *at* Lehigh University is a testament *to* the regard *in* which that program is held *by* the university's new students.

SHORTER   The growth of Lehigh University's materials-engineering program suggests that the university's new students consider it a good program.

Avoid Wordy Phrases   Wordy phrases also make writing long and boring. For example, some people write *on a weekly basis* rather than *weekly.* The long phrase appears to carry the weight of scientific truth, but *weekly* says the same thing more concisely.

Table 11.1 lists common wordy phrases and their more concise equivalents.

Compare the following wordy sentence and its concise translation:

WORDY   I am of the opinion that, in regard to profit achievement, the statistics pertaining to this month will appear to indicate an upward tendency.

CONCISE   I think this month's statistics will show an increase in profits.

Avoid Pompous Words   Writers sometimes think they will impress their readers by using pompous words—*initiate* for *begin, perform* for *do,* and

On TechComm Web

For a list of fancy words and redundant expressions, see Pacific Northwest National Laboratory. Click on Links Library for Ch. 11 on <bedfordstmartins.com/techcomm>.

■ **Table 11.1 Wordy Phrases and Their Concise Equivalents**

Wordy Phrase	Concise Phrase	Wordy Phrase	Concise Phrase
a majority of	most	in view of the fact that	because
a number of	some, many	it is often the case that	often
at an early date	soon	it is our opinion that	we think that
at the conclusion of	after, following	it is our recommendation that	we recommend that
at the present time	now	it is our understanding that	we understand that
at this point in time	now	make reference to	refer to
based on the fact that	because	of the opinion that	think that
despite the fact that	although	on a daily basis	daily
due to the fact that	because	on the grounds that	because
during the course of	during	prior to	before
during the time that	during, while	relative to	regarding, about
have the capability to	can	so as to	to
in connection with	about, concerning	subsequent to	after
in order to	to	take into consideration	consider
in regard to	regarding, about	until such time as	until
in the event that	if		

■ **Table 11.2 Fancy Words and Their Plain-Word Equivalents**

Fancy Word	Plain Word	Fancy Word	Plain Word
advise	tell	impact (verb)	affect
ascertain	learn, find out	initiate	begin
attempt (verb)	try	manifest (verb)	show
commence	start, begin	parameters	variables, conditions
demonstrate	show	perform	do
employ (verb)	use	prioritize	rank
endeavor (verb)	try	procure	get, buy
eventuate (verb)	happen	quantify	measure
evidence (verb)	show	terminate	end, stop
finalize	end, settle, agree, finish	utilize	use
furnish	provide, give		

prioritize for *rank*. In technical communication, plain talk is best. Compare the following pompous sentence with its plain English version:

POMPOUS   The purchase of a database program will enhance our record-maintenance capabilities.

PLAIN   Buying a database program will help us maintain our records.

Table 11.2 lists commonly used fancy words and their plain equivalents.

Interactive Sample Document:
Revising for Conciseness

The following passage is from a request for proposals published by the National Science Foundation. (Sentence numbers have been added for convenience.) The questions in the margin ask you to think about conciseness (as discussed on page 254). The answers to these questions are available on TechComm Web.

(1) Proposals that miss the target date will be handled as time permits. (2) Significant delays in submissions will prohibit inclusion of the proposal within the group reviews for the program as a whole, and this may necessitate postponement of the review process until the following fiscal year. (3) We also ask that you not submit proposals any earlier than one month before the appropriate target date, unless approved by the cognizant Program Director.

(4) The above date does not apply to proposals sent to the Physics Division in response to Foundation-wide solicitations, such as the Faculty Early Career Development (CAREER) or Research Experiences for Undergraduates (REU) programs. (5) These programs have specified target or deadline dates contained in their program announcements. (6) Demonstrably multidisciplinary proposals sent to the Physics Division, which are likely to be jointly reviewed with other programs within the Foundation, may be impacted by different target dates for the different programs involved. (7) If you are contemplating submitting such a proposal, you should contact the relevant Program Director in the Physics Division before submission.

Source: National Science Foundation, 2002 <www.nsf.gov/pubs/2002/nsf02139/nsf02139.txt>.

1. These two paragraphs contain many prepositional phrases. Identify two of them. For each one, is its use justified, or would the sentence be easier to understand if the sentence were revised to eliminate it?

2. These two paragraphs contain a number of examples of wordy phrases. Identify two of them. How can they be made into simpler, clearer expressions?

3. These two paragraphs contain a number of examples of pompous words. Identify two of them. How can they be translated into plain English?

On TechComm Web

To find the answers to these questions, click on Interactive Sample Documents for Ch. 11 on <bedfordstmartins.com/techcomm>.

Use Inoffensive Language

Writing to avoid offense is not merely a matter of politeness, it is a matter of perception. Language reflects attitudes, but it also helps to form attitudes. Writing inoffensively is one way to break down stereotypes.

Use Nonsexist Language   Sexist language favors one sex at the expense of the other. Although sexist language can shortchange men—as some writing

On TechComm Web

See Jenny R. Redfern's essay on sexist writing. Click on Links Library for Ch. 11 on <bedfordstmartins.com/techcomm>.

about nursing and similar female-dominated professions does—in most cases it shortchanges women. Common examples are nouns such as *workman* and *chairman*. In addition, when writers use male pronouns to represent both males and females—"Each worker is responsible for his work area"—they are using sexist language.

GUIDELINES

Avoiding Sexist Language

▶ *Replace the male-gender words with non–gender-specific words. Chairman,* for instance, can become *chairperson* or *chair. Firemen* are *firefighters, policemen* are *police officers.*

▶ *Switch to a different form of the verb.*

SEXIST	The operator must pass rigorous tests before he is promoted.
NONSEXIST	The operator must pass rigorous tests before being promoted.

▶ *Switch to the plural.*

NONSEXIST	Operators must pass rigorous tests before they are promoted.

Some organizations accept the use of plural pronouns with singular nouns, particularly in memos and other informal documents:

> If an employee wishes to apply for tuition reimbursement, they should consult Section 14.5 of the Employee Manual.

Careful writers and editors, however, still consider this construction a grammar error because it switches from singular to plural.

Sometimes, switching to the plural makes the sentence unclear:

UNCLEAR	Operators are responsible for their operating manuals.
	Does each operator have one operating manual or more than one?
CLEAR	Each operator is responsible for his or her operating manual.

▶ *Switch to* he or she, he/she, s/he, *or* his or her. *He or she, his or her,* and related constructions are awkward, especially if overused, but at least they are clear and inoffensive.

▶ *Address the reader directly.* Use *you* and *your,* or the understood *you.*

▶ *Alternate* he *and* she. The language scholar Joseph Williams (1997) and many other language authorities recommend alternating *he* and *she* from one paragraph or section to the next.

You can use your word processor to search for *he, man,* and *men,* the words and parts of words most often associated with sexist writing. Some grammar checkers search out common sexist terms and suggest alternatives. But use your common sense. You don't want to produce a sentence like this one from a benefits manual: "Every employee is responsible for the cost of his or her gynecological examination."

In This Book

For books about nonsexist writing, see the Selected Bibliography on p. 676.

Use Inoffensive Language When Referring to People with Disabilities

One in five Americans—more than 53 million people—has a physical, sensory, emotional, or mental impairment that interferes with daily life (Fujiura, 2001). In writing about people with disabilities, use the "people first" approach: treat the person as someone with a disability, not as someone defined by that disability. The disability is a condition the person has, not what the person is.

GUIDELINES

Using the People-First Approach

When writing about people with disabilities, follow these guidelines, which are based on Snow (2001).

▶ *Refer to the person first, the disability second.* Write "people with mental retardation," not "the mentally retarded."

▶ *Don't confuse* handicap *with* disability. *Disability* refers to the impairment or condition; *handicap* refers to the interaction between the person and his or her environment. A person can have a disability without being handicapped.

▶ *Don't refer to victimization.* Write "a person with AIDS," not "an AIDS victim" or "an AIDS sufferer."

▶ *Don't refer to a person as "wheelchair bound" or "confined to a wheelchair."* People who use wheelchairs to get around are not confined.

▶ *Don't refer to people with disabilities as abnormal.* They are atypical, not abnormal.

UNDERSTANDING SIMPLIFIED ENGLISH FOR NONNATIVE SPEAKERS

Because English is the language of more than half of the world's scientific and technical communication, millions of nonnative speakers of English read technical communication in English (Peterson, 1990).

Many companies and professional associations have created versions of Simplified English. Each version consists of a basic set of grammar rules and

On TechComm Web

For more about Simplified English, see Userlab's manual on Simplified English. Click on Links Library for Ch. 11 on <bedfordstmartins.com /techcomm>.

a vocabulary of about 1,000 words, each of which has only one meaning: *right* is the opposite of *left;* it does not mean *correct.* Each version of Simplified English is made for a specific discipline. For example, "AECMA Simplified English" is intended for aerospace workers.

Here is a sample of text and its Simplified English version.

ORIGINAL   Before filling the gas tank, it is necessary to turn off the propane line to the refrigerator. Failure to do so significantly increases the risk of explosion.

SIMPLIFIED ENGLISH   Before you pump gasoline into the gas tank, turn off the propane line to the refrigerator. If you do not turn off the propane tank, it could explode.

For more on Simplified English, see Peterson (1990).

PREPARING TEXT FOR TRANSLATION

As discussed in Chapter 5, more and more organizations prepare their documents and Web sites not only in English but also in other languages. Although you won't have to do the translating yourself, you should be aware of some simple steps you can take to make it easier for someone else to translate your writing. Luckily, most of these steps are the same ones you use to make your writing clear and easy to read in English.

On TechComm Web

For more on preparing text for translation, see George Rimalower's essay, "Crossing Borders — Tips for Preparing Your Writing for Subsequent Translation." Click on Links Library for Ch. 11 on <bedfordstmartins .com/techcomm>.

In This Book

For more on glossaries, see Ch. 12, p. 279.

STRATEGIES FOR INTERCULTURAL COMMUNICATION

Making Text Easy to Translate

Use these seven techniques to make it easy to translate your writing into other languages.

- *Use short sentences.* Try for an average of no more than 20 words.
- *Use the active voice.* The active voice ("You should do this procedure after the engine has run for 100 hours") is easier to translate than the passive voice ("This procedure should be done after the engine has run for 100 hours").
- *Use simple words.* Translators will find it easier to translate "do" than "perform."
- *Include a glossary.* If you need to use technical terms, define them in a glossary.
- *Use words that have only one meaning.* Write "This is the correct valve," not "This is the right valve," because *right* could also mean *the one on the right side.*

- *Use pronouns carefully.* Don't write "Matthews phoned Hawkins to learn whether he was scheduled to speak at the meeting." The translator might not know which person *he* refers to. Instead, write "Matthews phoned Hawkins to learn whether Hawkins was scheduled to speak at the meeting."

- *Avoid jokes, puns, and culture-bound references.* Humor doesn't translate well. If you refer to a box of computer pointing devices as "a box of mice," the translator might translate the words literally because the device is not known by that name everywhere. Also avoid other culture-bound references, such as sports metaphors ("hat trick") or references to national heroes or holidays.

Revision Checklist

Lists

❏ Is each list of the appropriate kind: numbered, lettered, bulleted, or checklist? (p. 239)
❏ Does each list contain an appropriate number of items? (p. 240)
❏ Are all the items in each list grammatically parallel? (p. 240)
❏ Is the lead-in to each list structured and punctuated properly? (p. 240)
❏ Are the items in each list punctuated properly? (p. 241)

Sentences

❏ Are the sentences structured with the new or important information near the end? (p. 242)
❏ Are the sentences the appropriate length: neither long and difficult to understand nor short and choppy? (p. 242)
❏ Does each sentence focus on the "real" subject? (p. 244)
❏ Have you reduced the number of expletives used as sentence openers? (p. 244)
❏ Does each sentence focus on the "real" verb, without weak nominalizations? (p. 245)
❏ Have you eliminated nonparallelism from your sentences? (p. 245)
❏ Have you used restrictive and nonrestrictive modifiers appropriately? (p. 246)

❏ Have you eliminated misplaced modifiers, squinting modifiers, and dangling modifiers? (p. 247)

Words and Phrases

Did you
❏ use active and passive voice appropriately? (p. 250)
❏ use precise words? (p. 251)
❏ provide adequate detail? (p. 251)
❏ avoid ambiguity? (p. 251)
❏ avoid unnecessary jargon? (p. 252)
❏ use positive rather than negative constructions? (p. 252)
❏ avoid long noun strings? (p. 253)
❏ avoid clichés? (p. 253)
❏ avoid euphemisms? (p. 253)
❏ avoid stating the obvious? (p. 254)
❏ avoid filler? (p. 254)
❏ avoid unnecessary prepositional phrases? (p. 255)
❏ use the most concise phrases? (p. 255)
❏ avoid redundancy? (p. 255)
❏ avoid pompous words? (p. 255)
❏ use nonsexist language? (p. 258)
❏ use the people-first approach in referring to people with disabilities? (p. 259)
❏ write in such a way that it will be easy to translate? (p. 260)

Exercises

On TechComm Web

For more exercises, click on Additional Exercises, Projects, and Cases for Ch. 11 and the link to Exercise Central on <bedfordstmartins.com/techcomm>.

1. Refer to the advice on pages 238–242 and rewrite each of the following sentences in the form of a list.

   a. The causes of burnout can be studied from three perspectives: physiological—the roles of sleep, diet, and physical fatigue; psychological—the roles of guilt, fear, jealousy, and frustration; environmental—the role of the physical surroundings at home and at work.

   b. There are several problems with the online registration system used at Dickerson University. First, lists of closed sections cannot be updated as often as necessary. Second, students who want to register in a closed section must be assigned to a special terminal. Third, the computer staff is not trained to handle student problems. Fourth, the Computer Center's own terminals cannot be used on the system; therefore, the university has to rent 15 extra terminals to handle registration.

2. The following sentences might be too long for some readers. Refer to the advice on pages 242–243 and break each sentence into two or more sentences.

   a. If we get the contract, we must be ready by June 1 with the necessary personnel and equipment to get the job done, so with this in mind a staff meeting, which all group managers are expected to attend, is scheduled for February 12.

   b. Once we get the results of the stress tests on the 125-Z fiberglass mix, we will have a better idea of where we stand in terms of our time constraints, because if the mix isn't suitable we will really have to hurry to find and test a replacement by the Phase 1 deadline.

   c. Although we had a frank discussion with Backer's legal staff, we were unable to get them to discuss specifics on what they would be looking for in an out-of-court settlement, but they gave us a strong impression that they would rather settle out of court.

3. The following examples contain choppy, abrupt sentences. Refer to the advice on page 243 and combine sentences to create a smoother style.

   a. I need a figure on the surrender value of a policy. The number of the policy is A4399827. Can you get me this figure by tomorrow?

   b. The program obviously contains an error. We didn't get the results we anticipated. Please ask Paul Davis to test the program.

   c. The supervisor is responsible for processing the outgoing mail. He is also responsible for maintaining and operating the equipment.

4. In the following sentences, the real subjects are buried in prepositional phrases or obscured by expletives. Refer to the advice on page 244 and revise the sentences so that the real subjects appear prominently.

   a. There has been a decrease in the number of students enrolled in our training sessions.

   b. It is on the basis of recent research that I recommend the new CAD system.

   c. The use of in-store demonstrations has resulted in a dramatic increase in business.

5. In the following sentences, unnecessary nominalization obscures the real verb. Refer to the advice on page 245 and revise the sentences to focus on the real verb.

   a. Pollution constitutes a threat to the Wilson Wildlife Preserve.

   b. Evaluation of the gumming tendency of the four tire types will be accomplished by comparing the amount of rubber that can be scraped from the tires.

   c. Reduction of the size of the tear-gas generator has already been completed.

6. Refer to the advice on pages 245–246 and revise the following sentences to eliminate nonparallelism.

   a. The next two sections of the manual discuss how to analyze the data, the conclusions that can be drawn from your analysis, and how to decide what further steps are needed before establishing a journal list.

   b. With our new product line, you would not only expand your tax practice, but your other accounting areas as well.

   c. Sections 1 and 2 will introduce the entire system, while Sections 3 and 4 describe the automatic application and step-by-step instructions.

7. Refer to the advice on pages 246–247 and revise the following sentences to correct punctuation or pronoun errors related to modifiers.

a. You press the Greeting-Record Button to record the Greeting which is stored on a microchip inside the machine.

b. This problem that has been traced to manufacturing delays, has resulted in our losing four major contracts.

c. Please get in touch with Tom Harvey who is updating the instructions.

8. Refer to the advice on pages 247–248 and revise the following sentences to eliminate the misplaced modifiers.

a. Over the past three years we have estimated that an average of eight hours per week are spent on this problem.

b. Information provided by this program is displayed at the close of the business day on the information board.

c. The computer provides a printout for the Director that shows the likely effects of the action.

9. Refer to the advice on page 248 and revise the following sentences to eliminate the dangling modifiers.

a. By following these instructions, your computer should provide good service for many years.

b. To examine the chemical homogeneity of the plaque sample, one plaque was cut into nine sections.

c. The boats in production could be modified in time for the February debut by choosing this method.

10. Refer to the advice on pages 248–249 and revise the following informal sentences to make them moderately formal.

a. The learning modules were put together by a couple of profs in the department.

b. The biggest problem faced by multimedia designers is that users freak if they don't see a button—or, heaven forbid, if they have to make up their own buttons!

c. If the University of Arizona can't figure out where to dump its low-level radioactive waste, Uncle Sam could pull the plug on millions of dollars of research grants.

11. Refer to the advice on pages 250–251 and rewrite the following sentences to remove inappropriate use of the passive voice.

a. Most of the information you need will be gathered as you document the history of the journals.

b. When choosing multiple programs to record, be sure that the proper tape speed has been chosen.

c. During this time I also co-wrote a manual on the Roadway Management System. Frequent trips were also made to the field.

d. Mistakes were made.

e. Come to the reception desk when you arrive. A packet with your name on it can be picked up there.

12. Refer to the advice on pages 254–255 and revise the following sentences to remove the filler.

a. In grateful appreciation of your patronage, we are pleased to offer you this free gift as a token gesture of our gratitude.

b. An anticipated major breakthrough in storage technology will allow us to proceed ahead in the continuing evolution of our products.

c. During the course of the next two hours, you will see a demonstration of our improved speech-recognition software, which will be introduced for the first time in November.

13. Refer to the advice on pages 251–252 and revise the following sentences by replacing the vague elements with specific information. Make up any reasonable details.

a. The results won't be available for a while.

b. The fire in the lab caused extensive damage.

c. A soil analysis of the land beneath the new stadium revealed an interesting fact.

14. Refer to the advice on page 252 and revise the following sentences to remove unnecessary jargon.

a. Please submit your research assignment in hard-copy mode.

b. The perpetrator was apprehended and placed under arrest directly adjacent to the scene of the incident.

c. The new computer lab supports both major platforms.

15. Refer to the advice on pages 252–253 and revise the following sentences to convert the negative constructions to positive constructions.

a. Williams was accused by management of filing trip reports that were not accurate.

b. We must make sure that all our representatives do not act unprofessionally toward potential clients.

c. The shipment will not be delayed if Quality Control does not disapprove any of the latest revisions.

16. Refer to the advice on page 253 and rewrite the following sentences to eliminate the long noun strings, which general readers might find awkward or difficult to understand.

    a. The corporate-relations committee meeting has been scheduled for next Thursday.

    b. The research team discovered a glycerin-initiated, alkylene-oxide-based, long-chain polyether.

    c. We are considering purchasing a digital-imaging capable, diffusion-pump equipped, tungsten-gun SEM.

17. Refer to the advice on page 253 and revise the following sentences to eliminate clichés.

    a. We hope the new program will positively impact all our branches.

    b. If we are to survive this difficult period, we are going to have to keep our ears to the ground and our noses to the grindstone.

    c. DataRight will be especially useful for those personnel tasked with maintaining the new system.

18. Refer to the advice on pages 253–254 and revise the following to eliminate euphemisms.

    a. Downsizing our workforce will enable our division to achieve a more favorable cash-flow profile.

    b. Of course, accident statistics can be expected to show a moderate increase in response to a streamlining of the training schedule.

    c. Unfortunately, the patient failed to fulfill his wellness potential.

19. Refer to the advice on page 254 and revise the following sentences to eliminate the obvious material.

    a. To register to take a course offered by the university, you must first determine whether the university will be offering that course that semester.

    b. The starting date of the project had to be postponed for a certain period of time due to a delay in obtaining the necessary authorization from the Project Oversight Committee.

    c. After you have installed DataQuick, please spend a few minutes responding to the questions about the process, then take the card to a post office and mail it to us.

20. Refer to the advice on pages 254–255 and revise the following sentences to remove meaningless filler.

    a. It would seem to me that the indications are that the project has been essentially unsuccessful.

    b. For all intents and purposes, our company's long-term success depends to a certain degree on various factors that are in general difficult to foresee.

    c. The presentation was quite well received overall, despite the fact that we received a rather small number of comment cards.

21. Refer to the advice on page 255 and revise the following sentences to eliminate unnecessary prepositional phrases.

    a. The complexity of the module will hamper the ability of the operator in the diagnosis of problems in equipment configuration.

    b. The purpose of this test of your aptitudes is to help you with the question of the decision of which major to enroll in.

    c. Another advantage of the approach used by the Alpha team is that interfaces of different kinds can be combined.

22. Refer to the advice on pages 255–256 and revise the following sentences to make them more concise.

    a. The instruction manual for the new copier is lacking in clarity and completeness.

    b. The software packages enable the user to create graphic displays with a minimum of effort.

    c. We remain in communication with our sales staff on a daily basis.

23. Refer to the advice on pages 255–256 and revise the following sentences to eliminate the pomposity.

    a. This state-of-the-art soda-dispensing module is to be utilized by the personnel associated with the Marketing Department.

    b. It is indeed a not insupportable inference that we have been unsuccessful in our attempt to forward the proposal to the proper agency in advance of the mandated date by which such proposals must be in receipt.

    c. Deposit your newspapers and other debris in the trash receptacles located on the station platform.

24. Refer to the advice on pages 257–259 and revise the following sentences to eliminate the sexism.

    a. Each doctor is asked to make sure he follows the standard procedure for handling Medicare forms.

b. Policemen are required to live in the city in which they work.

c. Professor Harry Larson and Ms. Anita Sebastian—two of the university's distinguished professors—have been elected to the editorial board of *Modern Chemistry*.

25. Refer to the advice on page 259 and revise the following sentences to eliminate the offensive language.

a. This year, the number of female lung-cancer victims is expected to rise because of increased smoking.

b. Mentally retarded people are finding greater opportunities in the service sector of the economy.

c. This bus is specially equipped to accommodate the wheelchair-bound.

Project

On TechComm Web

For more projects, click on Additional Exercises, Projects, and Cases for Ch. 11 on <bedfordstmartins.com/techcomm>.

26. **Group Activity** Form small groups. Have one person in the group distribute a multipage document he or she has written recently, either in this class or in another. Have each member annotate a copy of this document according to the principles of sentence effectiveness discussed in this chapter. Then write a summary statement about the document, highlighting its effective techniques of sentence construction and possible improvements. Meet as a group, study these annotated documents, and write a memo to your instructor describing the sentence features cited by more than one group member, as well as those aspects cited by only one group member. Overall, what are the basic differences between the annotations and the summary statement from one group member and those from another? Do you think that, as a general practice, it would be worthwhile to have a draft reviewed and annotated by more than one person? What have you learned about the usefulness of peer review? (For more on memos, see Chapter 15, page 378.)

On TechComm Web

For this case and additional cases, click on Additional Exercises, Projects, and Cases for Ch. 11 on <bedfordstmartins.com/techcomm>.

C A S E
Revising a Draft for Sentence Effectiveness

For three years you have been employed as a work-study student in your university's advising office. The office wishes to distribute a new pamphlet to incoming students describing the services it provides. A new work-study student, Kim Vavrick, has written the following brief introduction to advising. You have been asked to help her with it. Write her a memo evaluating the writing in her draft according to the material presented in this chapter. (For more on memos, see Chapter 15, page 378.)

Academic advising is counseling by a university representative, usually a faculty member, to assist the student achieve their goals for their education. The counseling's character, and the relationship that exists between the adviser and the student, change as the student's career in the academic setting progresses.

In the student's freshman and sophomore years, academic advising assists the student to identify, comprehend, and finalizing the sequence of university core requirements; that is, common classes such as English composition and basic science courses. It is also the case that academic advising may also serve to help the student clarify his academic strengths and interests in order to establish a major.

During these first two years, the interpersonal relationship between the student and the adviser are usually general and impersonal. The academic advisor may very well be someone with whom the student has little or no contact beyond obtaining a signature as a formality on paperwork. Similarly, the student may well never be enrolled in a course taught by the adviser, or otherwise become involved in the adviser's activities or academic interests.

This rarely succeeds in giving the student the optimal possible guidance for progressing in their academic career, however it is very economical and usually suitable. Faculty time and resources are expensive, limited commodities. Except in small, private institutions, there is rarely a large enough faculty to provide close and individual attention to each student who needs it. Student attrition rates are high in these first two years, many students flunk out of school before they have an opportunity to benefit from detailed, personal advice. Even among those who stay there is a high percentage of changes in academic majors. The emphasis on ensuring students understand and complete the core requirements ultimately ensures that those who do remain as students are able to progress along their degree path in a relatively smooth fashion.

In the student's junior and senior years, there is a shift in the emphasis. The goal of academic advising now is more to assist the student finish fulfilling their individual educational needs, and less to help the student meet the needs of the university. Academic advising helps the student make the best choices of the remaining options and requirements.

The relationship between the student and the adviser is closer in the last two years as well. The adviser is more personally acquainted with the student; he (or she) has seen the student periodically over a substantial period of time, and may even have instructed the student in one or more classes. The adviser is also more familiar with the major department, the courses it offers, and the colleagues who teach them, and can offer the student personal recommendations regarding many important and critical issues. Owing to the fact that the student is pursuing academic interests related to the adviser's, there is likely to be more interaction between them in academic projects and programs.

Academic advising also helps the student look beyond their undergraduate years. As the student comes close to concluding a degree program, they may be considering the possibility of entering a professional career, for example, or at extending their education in a graduate program. Academic advising serves to assist students again in making the educational choices, which will be most productive in meeting those goals.

Drafting and Revising Front and Back Matter

12

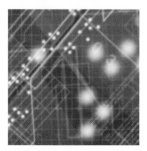

The indexer Richard Vacca (as cited in Rubens, 1992, p. 283) on the role of accessibility tools:

Technical literature collects and organizes facts, but these facts are worthless without reference points to guide the reader to them.

On TechComm Web

For additional samples, activities, and links related to this chapter, see <bedfordstmartins.com/techcomm>.

Front matter refers to elements that precede the body of a substantial document, such as title pages and tables of contents. *Back matter* refers to elements that follow the body, such as glossaries and lists of works cited. Front and back matter are common in proposals, reports, and manuals. Some elements, such as glossaries, are also found in other kinds of documents, such as brochures and flyers.

Front and back matter elements play various roles:

- *They help readers find the information they seek.* The table of contents and the index guide readers to the information they want.

- *They help readers decide whether to read the document.* The abstract, one kind of summary, helps readers decide whether they want to take the time to read the whole document.

- *They substitute for the whole document.* The executive summary is directed to managers, who often do not read anything else in the document.

- *They help readers understand the document.* The glossary, a list of definitions, clarifies terms for readers who don't know the subject thoroughly.

On TechComm Web

For more on creating front and back matter, see Saul Carliner's Designer's Toolkit. Click on Links Library for Ch. 12 on <bedfordstmartins.com/techcomm>.

- *They protect the document.* The cover might not contain any information but serve to enclose the document.

Most organizations have established formats for front and back matter. Study the style guide used in your company or—if there isn't one—examples from the files to see how other writers have assembled their documents.

WRITING THE FRONT MATTER

The front matter consists of seven elements.

The elements of the front matter are:

Letter of transmittal

Cover

Title page

Abstract

Table of contents

List of illustrations

Executive summary

Letter of Transmittal

The letter of transmittal introduces the primary reader to the purpose and content of the document. It is attached to the document, bound in with it, or simply placed on top of it. Even though the letter likely contains no information that is not included elsewhere in the document, it is important because it is the first thing the reader sees. It establishes a courteous and professional tone. Letters of transmittal are customary even when the writer and the reader both work for the same organization.

In addition to its overview of the main points in the document, a transmittal letter might state the methods used, acknowledge any assistance the writers have received, and refer to any errors or omissions in the document. But the transmittal letter is *not* a place to apologize to the reader or ask for the reader's patience or compassion.

Figure 12.1 illustrates a typical transmittal letter.

In This Book

For more about formatting a letter, see Ch. 15, p. 367.

Cover

The cover protects the document from normal wear and tear and from harsher environmental conditions such as water or grease. The cover usually contains the title of the document, the name and position of the writer, the date of submission, and the name or logo of the writer's company. Sometimes the cover also includes a security notice or a statement of proprietary information.

In This Book

For information about the materials used in covers and types of bindings, see Ch. 13, p. 295.

Title Page

Figure 12.2 on page 271 shows a typical title page. A more complex title page might also include a project number, a list of additional personnel who contributed to the document, and a distribution list.

Abstract

An abstract is a brief technical summary of the document, usually no more than 200 words. It addresses readers who are familiar with the technical subject and who need to decide whether they want to read the full document. In an abstract, you can use technical terminology and refer to advanced concepts in the field. Abstracts are sometimes published by abstract services, which are useful resources for researchers.

There are two types of abstracts: the *descriptive abstract* and the *informative abstract*. A descriptive abstract is most often used when space is at a premium.

In This Book

For more about abstract services, see Ch. 7, p. 136.

ALTERNATIVE ENERGY, INC.
1399 Soundview Drive
Bar Harbor, ME 00314
555-3267
www.altengy.com

April 3, 2003

Rivers Power Company
15740 Green Tree Road
Gaithersburg, MD 20760

Attention: Mr. J. R. Hanson, Project Engineering Manager

Subject: Project #619-103-823

We are pleased to submit "A Proposal for the Riverfront Energy Project" in response to your request of February 6, 2003.

The windmill described in the attached proposal uses the most advanced design and materials. Of particular note is the state-of-the-art storage facility described on pp. 14–17. As you know, storage limitations are a crucial factor in the performance of a generator such as this.

If you have any questions, please do not hesitate to call us.

Yours very truly,

Ruth Jeffries

Ruth Jeffries
Project Manager

Enclosures 2

The title and purpose of the document

Who authorized or commissioned the project

Principal findings

A polite conclusion

■ **Figure 12.1**
Letter of Transmittal

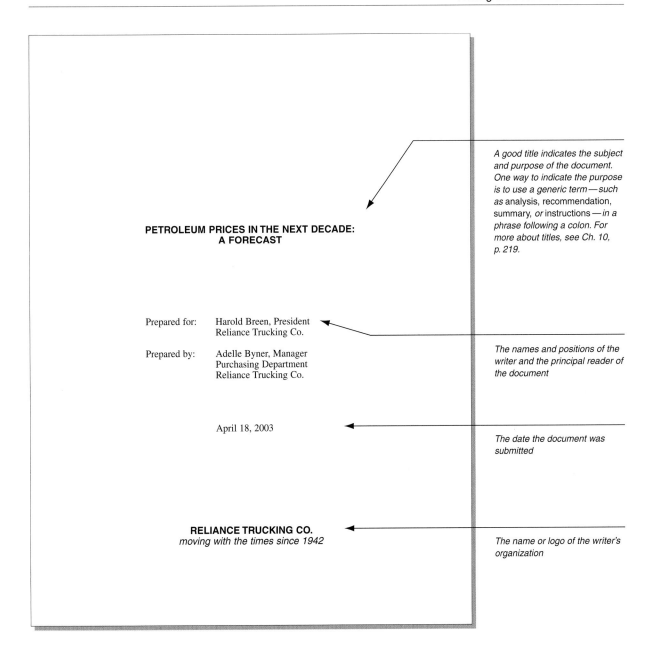

**PETROLEUM PRICES IN THE NEXT DECADE:
A FORECAST**

Prepared for: Harold Breen, President
                  Reliance Trucking Co.

Prepared by: Adelle Byner, Manager
                  Purchasing Department
                  Reliance Trucking Co.

April 18, 2003

RELIANCE TRUCKING CO.
moving with the times since 1942

A good title indicates the subject and purpose of the document. One way to indicate the purpose is to use a generic term — such as analysis, recommendation, summary, *or* instructions — *in a phrase following a colon. For more about titles, see Ch. 10, p. 219.*

The names and positions of the writer and the principal reader of the document

The date the document was submitted

The name or logo of the writer's organization

■ **Figure 12.2
Title Page**

Some government proposals, for example, call for a descriptive abstract to be placed at the bottom of the title page. The descriptive abstract—sometimes called the *topical* or *indicative* or *table-of-contents abstract*—describes the kinds of information contained in the document. It does not provide the major findings: the important results, conclusions, or recommendations. It simply lists the topics covered, giving equal emphasis to each. An informative abstract, by contrast, presents the major findings. If you don't know which kind the reader wants, write an informative one.

Abstracts often contain a list of a half-dozen or so keywords, which are entered into electronic databases. As the writer, one of your tasks is to think of the various keywords that will lead people to the information in your document.

Figure 12.3 illustrates the descriptive abstract, Figure 12.4 the informative abstract.

The distinction between descriptive and informative abstracts is not absolute. Sometimes you might have to combine elements of both in a single abstract. For instance, if there are 15 recommendations—far too many to list—you might simply note that the report includes numerous recommendations.

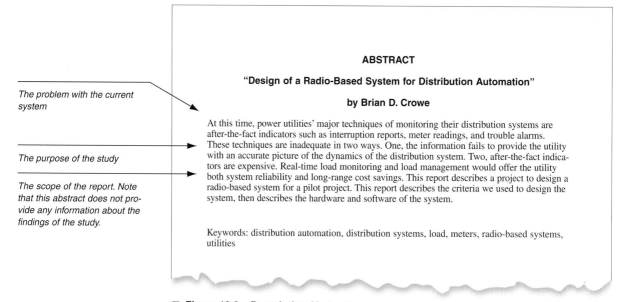

The problem with the current system

The purpose of the study

The scope of the report. Note that this abstract does not provide any information about the findings of the study.

ABSTRACT

"Design of a Radio-Based System for Distribution Automation"

by Brian D. Crowe

At this time, power utilities' major techniques of monitoring their distribution systems are after-the-fact indicators such as interruption reports, meter readings, and trouble alarms. These techniques are inadequate in two ways. One, the information fails to provide the utility with an accurate picture of the dynamics of the distribution system. Two, after-the-fact indicators are expensive. Real-time load monitoring and load management would offer the utility both system reliability and long-range cost savings. This report describes a project to design a radio-based system for a pilot project. This report describes the criteria we used to design the system, then describes the hardware and software of the system.

Keywords: distribution automation, distribution systems, load, meters, radio-based systems, utilities

■ **Figure 12.3   Descriptive Abstract**

The descriptive abstract essentially duplicates the major headings in the table of contents.
Source: Crowe, 1985.

ABSTRACT

"Design of a Radio-Based System for Distribution Automation"

by Brian D. Crowe

At this time, power utilities' major techniques of monitoring their distribution systems are after-the-fact indicators such as interruption reports, meter readings, and trouble alarms. This system is inadequate in that it fails to provide the utility with an accurate picture of the dynamics of the distribution system, and it is expensive. This report describes a project to design a radio-based system for a pilot project. The basic system, which uses packet-switching technology, consists of a base unit (built around a personal computer), a radio link, and a remote unit. The radio-based distribution monitoring system described in this report is more accurate than the after-the-fact indicators currently used, it is small enough to replace the existing meters, and it is simple to use. We recommend installing the basic system on a trial basis.

Keywords: distribution automation, distribution systems, load, meters, radio-based systems, utilities

An informative abstract, like a descriptive one, begins with the problem and the purpose of the study.

This type of abstract, however, describes some of the technical details of the study, culminating in the major findings: results, conclusions, and recommendations. The writer indicates the system's advantages and recommends that the system be installed on a trial basis.

■ **Figure 12.4   Informative Abstract**

The informative abstract describes the major findings of the study.
Source: Crowe, 1985.

Table of Contents

The table of contents, the most important guide to navigating the document, has two main functions: to help readers find the information they want and to help them understand the scope and organization of the document.

A table of contents uses the same headings as the document itself. Therefore, to create an effective table of contents, you must first make sure that the headings are clearly written and that you have provided enough of them. If the table of contents shows no entry for five or six pages, you probably need to divide the document into additional subsections. In fact, some tables of contents have one entry, or even several, for every document page.

The following table of contents, which relies exclusively on generic headings (those that describe an entire class of items), is too general to be useful.

Table of Contents

This methods section, which goes from page 4 to page 18, should have subentries to break up the text and to help readers find the information they seek.

For more-informative headings, combine the generic and the specific:

Recommendations: Five Ways to Improve Information-Retrieval Materials Used in the Calcification Study

Results of the Commuting-Time Analysis

Then build more subheadings into the report itself. For instance, in the "Recommendations" example above, you could create a subheading for each of the five recommendations. Once you have established a clear system of headings within the document, repeat them on the contents page. Use the same text attributes—capitalization, boldface, italics, and outline style (traditional or decimal)—you have used in the body. If you use styles in your word processor (see Chapter 3), you can make a table of contents automatically, but you may still have to modify the text attributes of the table-of-contents levels to match the text attributes in the document.

Figure 12.5 illustrates how to combine generic and specific headings. The report is entitled "Methods of Computing the Effects of Inflation in Corporate Financial Statements: A Recommendation."

When adding page numbers to your document, remember two points:

- The table of contents page does not list itself as an entry.
- Front matter is numbered using lowercase roman numerals (*i, ii,* and so forth), often centered at the bottom of the page. The title page of a document is not numbered, although it represents page *i*. The abstract is usually numbered page *ii*. The table of contents is usually not numbered, although it represents page *iii*. The body of the document is numbered with arabic numerals (1, 2, and so on), typically in the upper outside corner of the page.

In This Book

For more about text attributes, see Ch. 13, p. 303.

In This Book

For more on pagination, see Ch. 13, p. 298.

List of Illustrations

A *list of illustrations* is a table of contents for the figures and tables. List the figures first, then the tables. (If the document contains only figures, call it a *list of figures*. If it contains only tables, call it a *list of tables*.) You may begin the list of illustrations on the same page as the table of contents, or you may begin the list on a separate page and list it in the table of contents.

Figure 12.6 on page 276 shows a list of illustrations.

Executive Summary

The executive summary (sometimes called the *epitome, executive overview, management summary,* or *management overview*) is a brief condensation of the document addressed to managers, who rely on it to cope with the tremendous amount of paperwork they must read every day. Generally, managers need only a broad understanding of the projects the organization undertakes and how they fit together into a coherent whole.

CONTENTS

Managers can find the executive summary quickly and easily.

Other readers can find the information they need because Part 2 of the report contains many headings.

Using a decimal numbering system to identify the headings helps readers understand the organization of the document. For more information on numbering systems, see Ch. 3, pp. 37–38.

■ **Figure 12.5
Effective Table of
Contents**

LIST OF ILLUSTRATIONS

Figures

Tables

Figure 12.6 List of Illustrations

An executive summary for a document under 20 pages is typically one page (double-spaced). For a longer document, the maximum length is often calculated as a percentage of the document, such as 5 percent.

The executive summary presents information to managers in two parts:

- *Background.* This section explains the background of the project: the specific problem or opportunity—what was not working, or not working effectively or efficiently; or what potential modification of a procedure or product had to be analyzed.

- *Major findings and implications.* The methods are covered in only one or two sentences. The conclusions and recommendations, however, receive a full paragraph.

An executive summary differs from an informative abstract. An abstract focuses on the technical subject (such as whether the new radio-based system effectively monitors the energy usage); an executive summary concentrates on whether the system can improve operations *at a particular company.*

Figure 12.7 on page 278 shows the executive summary for the report mentioned in Figure 12.4.

GUIDELINES

Writing an Executive Summary

Follow these six suggestions in writing executive summaries:

▶ *Use specific evidence in describing the background.* For most managers, the best evidence includes costs and savings. Instead of writing that the equipment you are now using to cut metal foil is ineffective, write that the equipment jams once every 72 hours on average, costing $400 in materials and $2,000 in productivity. Then add up these figures for a monthly or an annual total.

▶ *Be specific in describing the research.* For instance, research suggests that if your company had a computerized energy-management system you could cut your energy costs by 20 to 25 percent. If your energy costs last year were $300,000, you could save $60,000 to $75,000.

▶ *Describe the methods briefly.* In most cases, an executive does not care how you did what you did. However, if you think your reader is interested, include a brief description—no more than a sentence or two.

▶ *Describe the findings in accordance with your readers' needs.* If your readers want to know your results, provide them. If your readers are unable to understand the technical data or are uninterested, go directly to the conclusions and recommendations.

▶ *Ask an outside reader to review your draft.* Give it to someone who has had no connection to the project. That person should be able to read your summary and understand what the project means to the organization.

▶ *Decide how to integrate the executive summary within the body of the document.* Many writers treat the executive summary as a major part of the document in the table of contents (see Figure 12.5 on page 275).

Executive Summary

Currently, we monitor our distribution system using after-the-fact indicators such as interruption reports, meter readings, and trouble alarms. This system is inadequate in two respects:

The executive summary describes the symptoms of the problem in financial terms. Notice the use of specific dollar figures.

- It fails to give us an accurate picture of the dynamics of the distribution system. To ensure enough energy for our customers, we must overproduce. Last year we overproduced by 7 percent, for a loss of $273,000.

- It is expensive. Escalating labor costs for meter readers and the increased number of difficult-to-access residences have led to higher costs. Last year we spent $960,000 reading the meters of 12,000 such residences.

This report describes a project to design a radio-based system for a pilot project on these 12,000 homes.

Notice how brief the discussion of the technology is.

The basic system, which uses packet-switching technology, consists of a base unit (built around a personal computer), a radio link, and a remote unit.

The radio-based distribution monitoring system described in this report is feasible because it is small enough to replace the existing meters and because it is simple to use. It would provide a more accurate picture of our distribution system, and it would pay for itself in 3.9 years. We recommend installing the system on a trial basis. If the trial program proves successful, radio-based distribution-monitoring techniques will provide the best long-term solution to the current problems of inaccurate and expensive data collection.

The writer describes the findings in a final paragraph. Notice that this last paragraph clarifies how the pilot program relates to the overall problem described in the first paragraph.

■ **Figure 12.7**
Executive Summary

Source: Crowe, 1985.

Interactive Sample Document:
Analyzing an Executive Summary

The following executive summary comes from a corporate report on purchasing PDAs for employees. The questions in the margin ask you to think about the discussion of executive summaries (beginning on page 274). The answers to these questions are available on TechComm Web.

Executive Summary

On May 11, we received approval to study whether PDAs could help our 20 engineers monitor their schedules, take notes, and store files they need in the field. In our study, we addressed these problems experienced by many of our engineers:

- They have missed deadlines and meetings and lost client information.
- They have been unable to access important files from the field.
- They have complained about the weight of the binders and other materials—sometimes weighing more than 40 pounds—that they have to carry.
- They have to spend time keyboarding notes that they took in the field.

In 2002, missed meetings and other schedule problems cost the company over $400,000 in lost business. And our insurance carrier settled a claim for $50,000 from an engineer who experienced back and shoulder problems due to the weight of his pack.

We researched the capabilities of PDAs, then established these criteria for our analysis:

- The PDA must weigh less than 10 ounces.
- It must be compatible with Windows 98, ME, NT, 2000, and XP.
- It must be graphics capable.
- The PDA must have wireless Internet access.
- The PDA must have at least 32 MB main memory and be expandable to 128 MB.
- The PDA must cost $500 or less.

On the basis of our analysis, we recommend that the company purchase five HP Jornada 547 PDAs, for a total cost of $1,050. These PDAs best meet all our technical and cost criteria. We further recommend that, after a 6-month trial period, the company decide whether to purchase an additional 15 Jornadas for the other engineers.

---

1. How clearly does the writer explain the background? Identify the problem or opportunity described in this executive summary.

2. Does the writer discuss the methods covered? If so, identify the discussion.

3. Identify the findings: the results, conclusions, and recommendations. How clearly has the writer explained the benefits to the company?

On TechComm Web

To find the answers to these questions, click on Interactive Sample Documents for Ch. 12 on <bedfordstmartins.com/techcomm>.

WRITING THE BACK MATTER

The back matter can include any or all of the following items: a glossary, list of symbols, references, and appendices.

Glossary and List of Symbols

A *glossary,* an alphabetical list of definitions, is particularly useful if some of your readers are unfamiliar with the technical vocabulary in your document. Instead of slowing down your discussion by defining technical terms as they appear, you can use boldface, or some similar method of highlighting words, to inform your readers that the term is defined in the glossary. The first time a

The elements of the back matter:

Glossary and list of symbols

References

Appendices

Glossary

Applicant: A state agency, local government, or eligible private nonprofit organization that submits a request to the Grantee for disaster assistance under the state's grant.

Case Management: A systems approach to providing equitable and fast service to applicants for disaster assistance. Organized around the needs of the applicant, the system consists of a single point of coordination, a team of on-site specialists, and a centralized, automated filing system.

Cost Estimating Format (CEF): A method for estimating the total cost of repair for large, permanent projects by use of construction industry standards. The format uses a base cost estimate and design and construction contingency factors, applied as a percentage of the base cost.

Declaration: The President's decision that a major disaster qualifies for federal assistance under the Stafford Act.

Hazard Mitigation: Any cost-effective measure that will reduce the potential for damage to a facility from a disaster event.

■ **Figure 12.8   Glossary**

Source: Based on Federal Emergency Management Agency, 2002 <www.fema.gov/r-n-r/pa/glossary.htm>.

boldfaced term appears, you explain this system in a footnote. For example, the body of the document might say, "Thus the **positron*** acts as the . . ." while a note at the bottom of the page explains:

*This and all subsequent terms in boldface are defined in the Glossary, page 26.

Although the glossary is usually placed near the end of the document, before the appendices, it can also be placed immediately after the table of contents if the glossary is brief (less than a page) and if it defines essential terms.

A list of symbols is formatted like a glossary, but it defines symbols and abbreviations rather than terms. It too may be placed before the appendices or after the table of contents.

Figure 12.8 shows an excerpt from a glossary. Figure 12.9 shows a list of symbols.

References

Many documents contain a list of references (sometimes called a *bibliography* or *works cited*) as part of the back matter. References, and the accompanying textual citations throughout the document, are called *documentation*. Documentation acknowledges your debt to your sources, establishes your credibility as a writer, and helps readers locate and review your sources. Appendix, Part A, page 592, describes documentation in detail.

List of Symbols

β	beta
CRT	cathode-ray tube
γ	gamma
Hz	hertz
rcvr	receiver
SNR	signal-to-noise ratio
uhf	ultra high frequency
vhf	very high frequency

■ **Figure 12.9**
List of Symbols

Appendices

An *appendix* is any section that follows the body of the document (and the list of references or bibliography, glossary, or list of symbols). Appendices (or *appendixes*) convey information that is too bulky for the body or that will interest only a few readers. Appendices might include maps, large technical diagrams or charts, computations, computer printouts, test data, and texts of supporting documents.

Appendices, usually labeled with letters rather than numbers (Appendix A, Appendix B, and so on), are listed in the table of contents and are referred to at the appropriate points in the body of the document. Therefore, they are accessible to any reader who wants to consult them.

STRATEGIES FOR INTERCULTURAL COMMUNICATION

Drafting Front and Back Matter for Different Cultures

All the elements discussed in this chapter are rooted in culture. For instance, in some cultures—or in some organizations—writers do not create executive summaries, or their executive summaries differ in length or organization from those discussed here. According to Honold (1999), German users of high-tech products rely on the table of contents in a manual because they like to understand the scope and organization of the manual. Therefore, the writers of manuals for German readers should include comprehensive, detailed tables of contents.

Study a sample of writing produced by people from the culture you are addressing to see their use of front and back matter.

Revision Checklist

Does the transmittal letter
- ❏ briefly state the methods you used? (p. 269)
- ❏ acknowledge any assistance you received? (p. 269)
- ❏ clearly state the title and, if necessary, the subject and purpose of the document? (p. 270)
- ❏ clearly state who authorized or commissioned the document? (p. 270)
- ❏ summarize your findings? (p. 270)
- ❏ courteously offer further assistance? (p. 270)

Does the cover include
- ❏ the title of the document? (p. 269)
- ❏ your name and position? (p. 269)
- ❏ the date of submission? (p. 269)
- ❏ the company name or logo? (p. 269)

Does the title page
- ❏ include a title that clearly states the subject and purpose of the document? (p. 271)
- ❏ list the names and positions of both you and your principal reader? (p. 271)
- ❏ include the date of submission of the document and any other identifying information? (p. 271)

Does the abstract
- ❏ list the document title, your name, and any other identifying information? (p. 272)
- ❏ clearly define the problem or opportunity that led to the project? (p. 272)
- ❏ briefly describe (if appropriate) the research methods? (p. 272)
- ❏ summarize the major results, conclusions, and recommendations? (p. 273)

Does the table of contents
- ❏ contain a sufficiently detailed breakdown of the major sections of the body of the document? (p. 273)
- ❏ reproduce the headings as they appear in your document? (p. 273)
- ❏ include page numbers? (p. 274)
- ❏ Does the list of illustrations (or list of tables or list of figures) include all the graphics found in the body of the document? (p. 274)
- ❏ clearly identify the executive summary? (p. 275)

Does the executive summary
- ❏ clearly state the problem or opportunity that led to the project? (p. 276)
- ❏ explain the major results, conclusions, recommendations, and managerial implications of your document? (p. 277)
- ❏ avoid technical vocabulary and concepts that a managerial audience is not likely to know? (p. 277)

- ❏ Does the glossary include definitions of all the technical terms your readers might not know? (p. 279)

- ❏ Does the list of symbols include all the symbols and abbreviations your readers might not know? (p. 279)

- ❏ Do the appendices include the supporting materials that are too bulky to present in the document body or are of interest to only a small number of your readers? (p. 281)

Exercises

On TechComm Web

For more exercises, click on Additional Exercises, Projects, and Cases for Ch. 12 on <bedfordstmartins.com/techcomm>.

1. The following letter of transmittal is from a report written by an industrial engineer to his company president. Write a one-paragraph evaluation that focuses on the clarity, comprehensiveness, and tone of the letter.

Dear Mr. Smith:

The enclosed report, "Robot and Machine Tools," discusses the relationship between robots and machine tools.

Although loading and unloading machine tools was one of the first uses for industrial robots, this task has only recently become commonly feasible. Discussed in this report are concepts that are crucial to remember in using robots.

Please excuse inconsistencies in the graphics cited since

they are from different sources. If at any time you need help understanding this report, let me know.

Sincerely yours,

2. The following executive summary is from a report titled "Analysis of Large-Scale Municipal Sludge Composting as an Alternative to Ocean Sludge-Dumping." Write a one-paragraph evaluation. How well does the executive summary present concise and useful information to the managerial audience?

Coastal municipalities currently involved with ocean sludge-dumping face a complex and growing sludge management problem. Estimates suggest that treatment plants will have to handle 65 percent more sludge in 2008 than in 1998, or approximately seven thousand additional tons of sludge per day. As the volume of sludge is increasing, traditional disposal methods are encountering severe economic and environmental restrictions. The EPA has banned all ocean sludge-dumping as of next January 1. For these reasons, we are considering sludge composting as a cost-effective sludge management alternative.

Sludge composting is a 21-day biological process in which waste-water sludge is converted into organic fertilizer that is aesthetically acceptable, essentially pathogen-free, and easy to handle. Composted sludge can be used to improve soil structure, increase water retention, and provide nutrients for plant growth. At $150 per dry ton, composting is currently almost three times as expensive as ocean dumping, but effective marketing of the resulting fertilizer could dramatically reduce the difference.

Project

On TechComm Web

For more projects, click on Additional Exercises, Projects, and Cases for Ch. 12 on <bedfordstmartins.com/techcomm>.

3. **Internet Activity** Scholars and librarians are trying to help the Modern Language Association and the American Psychological Association keep up with advances in electronic communication tools. In *Online!* <bedfordstmartins.com/online/index.html>, find the section called "Citation Styles." Download the sections that explain how the two associations cite Web sites, e-mail messages, and FTP documents. Compare and contrast the guidelines on these three types of citations. What are the basic differences between the two documentation styles? Overall, which do you find easier to understand? Which would be more effective in helping the reader find the source? Present your findings in a memo to your instructor. (For more on memos, see Chapter 15, page 378.)

On TechComm Web

For more cases, click on Additional Exercises, Projects, and Cases for Ch. 12 <bedfordstmartins.com/techcomm>.

CASE
Planning for Better Front and Back Matter

You and the other members of your group work as interns for Sam Perdue, a communications specialist in The National Institute of Allergy and Infectious Diseases, a division of the National Institutes of Health. Perdue calls your group in to discuss a problem.

"We've got a situation," he tells you. "Each year we publish dozens of reports. Our congressional funding—and our reputation within the scientific community—depend on the quality of these reports. I'm getting some heat from people I respect. They're telling me that they're having trouble using the reports because they can't find the information they need easily enough." Perdue singles out one of the reports as typical of the kind of communication they need to improve: "NIAID Counter-Bioterrorism Research Agenda for CDC Category A Agents." "Would you take a look at that report, figure out what we're doing wrong, and write me a memo recommending how to write these things so that they're easier to use?"

Study the document <www.niaid.nih.gov/dmid/pdf/biotresearchagenda .pdf>. Which elements of front and back matter in the report are effective? Which are ineffective? Which elements are missing and should be presented? Write a memo or report to your supervisor presenting your findings. Where appropriate, excerpt portions of the report to support your claims. (For more on memos, see Chapter 15, page 378.)

PART FOUR

**DEVELOPING THE
VISUAL ELEMENTS**

Designing the Document   13

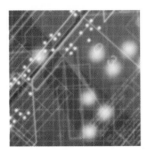

Professors of visual communication Charles Kostelnick and David D. Roberts (1998, p. 4) refute the idea that designing a document is a mysterious and subjective practice:

Practical design is fairly rational—in the sense that each step of the way you can understand why you're making design decisions, which will enable you to assert control over the process.

On TechComm Web

For additional samples, activities, and links related to this chapter, see <bedfordstmartins.com/techcomm>.

In This Book

To learn about special considerations in designing Web pages, see Ch. 21.

The effectiveness of a document largely depends on how well it is designed, because readers see the document before they actually read it. In less than a second, the document has made an impression on them, one that might determine how well they read it—or *whether* they read it. If you understand basic design principles, you can make a document that your readers will want to read—and that will help them understand and remember what you say.

GOALS OF DOCUMENT DESIGN AND PAGE DESIGN

In designing a document and its pages, you have five major goals:

Goals of document design:

To make a good impression on readers

To help readers understand the structure and hierarchy of the information

To help readers find the information they need

To help readers understand the information

To help readers remember the information

- *To make a good impression on readers.* Your documents should reflect your own professional standards and those of your organization.
- *To help readers understand the structure and hierarchy of the information.* As they navigate a document, readers should know where they are and where they are headed. They should also be able to see the hierarchical relationship between one piece of information and another.
- *To help readers find the information they need.* Usually, people don't read technical documents from cover to cover. Design elements (such as tabs, icons, and color), page design, and typography help readers find the information they need—quickly and easily.
- *To help readers understand the information.* Effective document and page design can clarify information. For instance, if you design a set of instructions so that text describing a step is next to its accompanying graphic, you have made it easier to understand.

- *To help readers remember the information.* An effective design helps readers create a visual image of the information, making it easier to remember. Text boxes, pull quotes, and similar design elements help readers remember important explanations and passages.

UNDERSTANDING DESIGN PRINCIPLES

To design effective documents and pages, you need to understand a few basic design principles. The following discussion is based on Robin Williams's *The Non-designer's Design Book* (Berkeley, CA: Peachpit Press, 1994).

You can create effective technical documents if you understand four principles of design:

- proximity
- alignment
- repetition
- contrast

Proximity

The principle of proximity is simple: group related items together. If two items appear close to each other, the reader will interpret them as related to each other. If they are far apart, the reader will interpret them as unrelated. Text describing a graphic should be positioned close to the graphic.

Figure 13.1 shows the proximity principle.

On TechComm Web

Also see Roger C. Parker's design site. Click on Links Library for Ch. 13 on <bedfordstmartins.com /techcomm>.

On TechComm Web

See John Magnik's essay, "Typography & Page Layout." Click on Links Library for Ch. 13 on <bedfordstmartins.com/techcomm>.

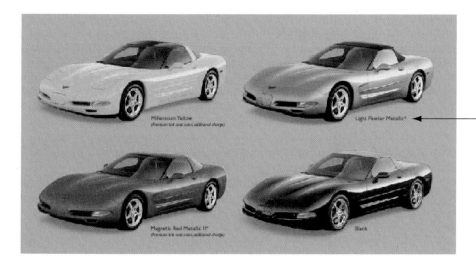

Text and graphics are clearly related by the principle of proximity. Each label is placed near the car to which it refers.

■ **Figure 13.1**
Effective Use of Proximity

Source: General Motors Corp., 2002 <www.chevrolet.com/gmnav /brochure/pdf/cor_catalog.pdf>.

Alignment

The principle of alignment is that you should consciously place text and graphics on the page so that they line up to create a unified whole. Alignment creates a visual focus that ties the different elements together.

Figure 13.2 shows how alignment works to help organize elements on a screen.

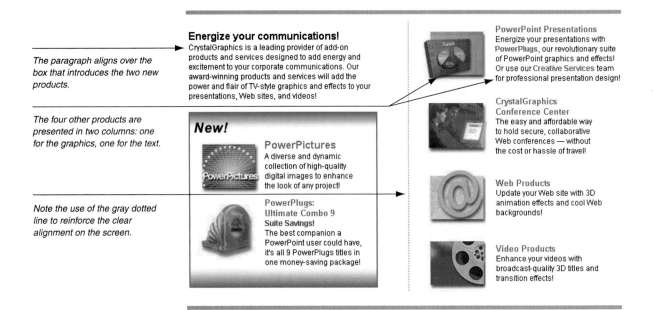

■ **Figure 13.2   Effective Use of Alignment**

The information on this screen falls into two main categories: the left column, consisting of the paragraph and the new-product box, and the right column, with the four other products. Alignment organizes the information on the screen.
Source: CrystalGraphics, Inc., 2002 <www.crystalgraphics.com>.

Repetition

The principle of repetition is that you should treat the same kind of information in the same way to create consistent patterns. For example, all first-level headings should have the same typeface, size, spacing above and below, and so forth. This repetition signals a connection between headings, making the content easier to understand. Other elements that are used to create consistent visual patterns are colors, icons, rules, and screens.

For instance, Figure 13.3 shows two pages from a manual that uses repetition effectively to help readers understand the information.

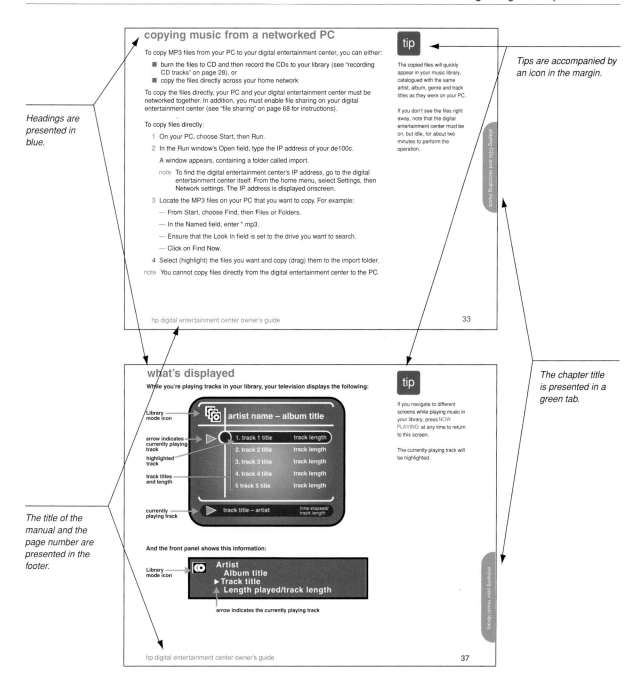

Headings are presented in blue.

The title of the manual and the page number are presented in the footer.

Tips are accompanied by an icon in the margin.

The chapter title is presented in a green tab.

■ **Figure 13.3   Effective Use of Repetition**

These pages from a user's manual show how the writer uses repetition to help the reader understand the meaning and location of different kinds of information in the manual.
Source: Hewlett Packard Company, 2002 <www.hp.com/cposupport/manual_set/lpg40530.pdf>.

Contrast

The principle of contrast works in several different ways in technical documents. For example, black print is easiest to see against a white background; larger letters stand out among smaller ones; information printed in a color, such as red, grabs attention more than information printed in black.

Figure 13.4 shows effective use of contrast.

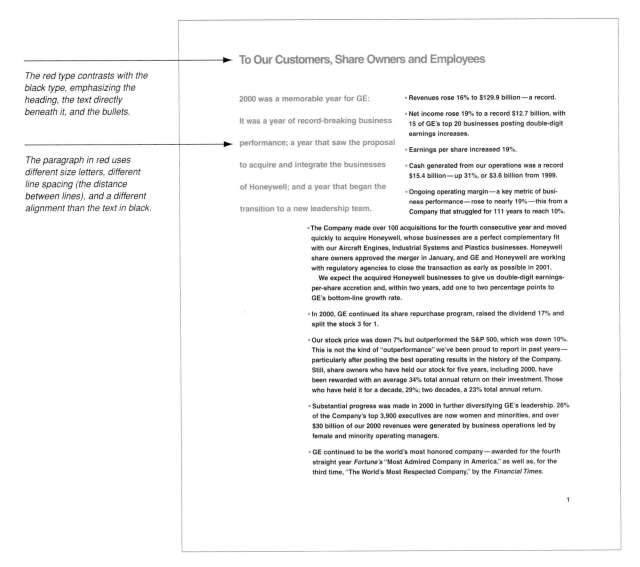

The red type contrasts with the black type, emphasizing the heading, the text directly beneath it, and the bullets.

The paragraph in red uses different size letters, different line spacing (the distance between lines), and a different alignment than the text in black.

■ **Figure 13.4   Effective Use of Contrast**

Source: General Electric Company, 2001 <www.ge.com/annual00/download/images/GEannual00.pdf>.

PLANNING THE DESIGN OF THE DOCUMENT AND THE PAGE

The first step in designing any kind of technical document is planning. Analyze your audience's needs and expectations, and consider your resources.

Analyzing Your Audience's Needs and Expectations

Consider such factors as the audience's knowledge of the subject, their attitudes, their reasons for reading, the way they will be using the document, and the kinds of tasks they will perform. For instance, if the document is a benefits manual for employees, you know that few people will read it like a novel, from start to finish, but many people will refer to it often. Therefore, you will want to build in as many accessing tools as you can: a table of contents and index, of course, but perhaps tabs or different colors of paper to identify each section.

Think too about your audience's expectations. Readers expect to see certain kinds of information presented in certain ways. Unless you have a good reason to present information in other ways, you should fulfill their expectations. For instance, tutorial information for complicated software programs is often presented in a small-format book, bound so that it lies flat on the table next to the keyboard.

In This Book

For more about analyzing your audience, see Ch. 5. For more about tables of contents, see Ch. 12, p. 273.

STRATEGIES FOR INTERCULTURAL COMMUNICATION

Designing Documents to Suit Cultural Preferences

Many aspects of design vary from one culture to another. In memos, letters, reports, and manuals, you may see significant differences in design practice. The best advice, therefore, is to study documents from the culture that you are addressing. Here are just a few design elements to look for:

- *Paper sizes.* Paper size will dictate some aspects of your page design. Therefore, if your document will be printed in another country, it makes sense to find out about standard paper sizes used there.

- *Typeface preferences.* A survey by Ichimura (2001) found that readers in Pacific Rim countries prefer sans-serif typefaces in body text, whereas Western readers prefer serifs. (Typography is discussed later in this chapter.)

- *Color preferences.* In China, for example, red suggests happiness, whereas in Japan it suggests danger.

- *Text direction.* If some people in your target audience read right to left but others read left to right, you might want to arrange your graphics vertically, from top to bottom, on the page; everybody reads from top to bottom. Or you might want to use arabic numerals to indicate the order in which items are to be read (Horton, 1993).

On TechComm Web

To view Ichimura's essay online, click on Links Library for Ch. 13 on <bedfordstmartins.com/techcomm>.

Determining Your Resources

Think about your resources of time, money, and equipment. Short, informal documents are generally produced in-house; for more-ambitious projects, you might need to subcontract some of the job to professionals. If your organization has a technical-publications department, consult the professionals there for information on scheduling and budgeting.

- *Time.* What is your schedule? A sophisticated design might require the expertise of professionals at service bureaus and print shops, and their services can require weeks. Creating even a relatively simple design for a newsletter can require many hours.

- *Money.* What is your budget? Can you afford professional designers and print shops? An in-house newsletter should look professional and attractive, but most managers would not authorize thousands of dollars for a sophisticated design. They would, however, authorize many thousands to design an annual report.

- *Equipment.* Although a word processor is fine for many routine design needs, you need graphics software and desktop-publishing programs for more complicated designs. A basic laser printer can produce attractive documents in black and white. For high-resolution color, however, you need a more expensive printer.

DESIGNING THE WHOLE DOCUMENT

On TechComm Web

For more help with designing documents using a word processor, click on Tutorials on <bedfordstmartins.com/techcomm>.

Before you begin to design individual pages, think through the design of the whole document—how you want the different elements to work together to accomplish your objectives.

There are four major elements to consider in designing the whole document: size, paper, bindings, and accessing tools.

Size

Size refers to two aspects of document design: page size and page count.

- *Page size.* Think about the best page size for your information and about how the document will be used. For a procedures manual that will sit on a shelf most of the time, standard 8.5 × 11-inch paper, punched to fit in a three-ring binder, is an obvious choice. For a software tutorial, you will probably want narrow columns in a document that fits easily on a desk while the reader works at the keyboard. Therefore, you might choose a 5.5 × 8.5-inch size. The physical dimensions of the document can be important if it is to be used in a cramped area or has to fit in a standard-size compartment, such as one in an airplane cockpit.

Paper comes precut in a number of standard sizes in addition to 8.5 × 11 inches, such as 4.5 × 6 inches and 6 × 9 inches. Although paper can be cut to whatever size you want, nonstandard sizes are more expensive. Check with your technical-publications department or a print shop for current prices and availability of paper sizes.

- *Page count.* The number of pages in a document is a cost factor and a psychological factor. Because paper is expensive and heavy, you want to reduce the number of pages as much as you can, especially if you are printing many copies and mailing them. The psychological factor is that people want to spend as little time as possible reading technical communication. Therefore, if you can figure out a way to design the document so that it is 15 pages long rather than 30—but still easy to read—your readers will appreciate it.

Paper

Paper is made not only in different standard sizes but also in different weights and with different coatings.

The lowest-quality paper is newsprint. Because it is extremely porous, it allows inks to bleed through to the other side and picks up smudges and oil. It can also turn yellow in as little as a few weeks. For these reasons, newsprint is generally used only for newspapers, informal newsletters, and similar quick, inexpensive bulk publications.

The most widely used paper is the relatively inexpensive stock used in photocopy machines and laser printers. Others include bond (for letters and memos), book paper (a higher grade that permits better print resolution), and text paper (an even higher grade used for more-formal documents such as announcements and brochures).

Most paper can be ordered coated or uncoated. The coating increases strength and durability, and it provides the best print resolution. However, some glossy coated papers produce an annoying glare. To deal with this problem, designers recommend paper with a slight tint. A bone white, for instance, produces less glare than a bright white.

Work closely with printing professionals. They know, for example, about UV-coated paper, which greatly reduces fading. And they know about recycled paper, which is constantly improving in quality and becoming less expensive.

Bindings

Technical documents of a few pages can be held together with a paper clip or a staple. But longer documents require more-sophisticated binding techniques. Table 13.1 illustrates and describes the four types of bindings commonly used in technical communication.

On TechComm Web

For more on bindings, see Jacci Howard Bear's "Binding Decisions." Click on Links Library for Ch. 13 on <bedfordstmartins.com/techcomm>.

■ **Table 13.1   Common Types of Bindings**

Loose-leaf binders. Loose-leaf binders are convenient when pages must be added and removed frequently. But a high-quality binder can cost as much as several dollars.

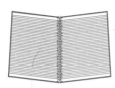

Ring or spiral binders. The wire or plastic coils or combs that hold the pages together let you open the document on a desk or even fold it over, so that it takes up the space of only one page. Print shops can bind documents of almost any size in plastic coils or combs for about a dollar each.

Saddle binding. The document is opened to its middle pages, and a set of large staples is inserted from the outside. Saddle binding is impractical for large documents.

Perfect binding. Pages are glued together along the spine edge, and a cover is attached. Perfect binding, which is used in book publishing, produces the most formal appearance, but it is relatively fragile, and the open document usually does not lie flat.

Accessing Tools

In a well-designed document, readers can easily find the information they seek. Most accessing tools use the design principles of repetition and contrast to help readers navigate the document. Table 13.2 explains six common kinds of accessing aids.

■ **Table 13.2   Typical Accessing Aids**

Radioactivity

Danger

Help

Keyboard

Icons. Icons are pictures that symbolize actions or ideas. A garbage can on your computer screen represents the task of deleting a file. An hourglass or a clock tells you to wait while the computer performs a task. Perhaps the most important icon is the stop sign, which alerts you to a warning. Icons depend on repetition: every time you see the warning icon, you know what kind of information the writer is presenting.

Beware of being too clever in thinking up icons. One computer manual uses a cocktail glass about to fall over to symbolize "tip." This is a bad idea, because the pun is not functional: when you think of a cocktail glass, you don't think of a tip for using computers. Don't use too many different icons either, or your readers will forget what each one represents.

■ **Table 13.2**   *(Continued)*

Color. Perhaps the strongest visual attribute is color (Keyes, 1993). Use color to draw attention to important features of the document, such as warnings, hints, major headings, and section tabs; but use it sparingly, or it will overpower everything else in the document.

Color exploits the principles of repetition (every item in a particular color is logically linked) and contrast (items in one color contrast with items in another color).

Use colors logically. Third-level headings should not be in color, for example, if first- and second-level headings are black.

Using a different color of paper for each section of a document is another way to simplify access.

In This Book

For more about using color, see Ch. 14, p. 327.

On TechComm Web

Color Vision Simulator, from Vischeck, lets you see what graphics look like to people with different color disabilities. Click on Links Library for Ch. 13 on <bedfordstmartins.com/techcomm>.

Dividers and tabs. You are already familiar with dividers and tabs — the heavy-paper sheets with the paper or plastic extensions — from loose-leaf notebooks. Tabs provide a place for a label, which enables readers to identify and flip to a particular section. Sometimes dividers and tabs are color-coded. Tabs work according to the design principle of contrast: the tabs literally stick out.

Read . . .   **To learn to . . .**
Ch. 1   connect to the net
Ch. 2   use e-mail

Cross-reference tables. These tables refer readers to related discussion. Cross-reference tables exploit the design principle of alignment.

Headers and footers. Headers and footers help readers see where they are in the text. In a book, for example, the headers on the left-hand pages might repeat the chapter number and title; those on the right-hand pages, the most recent first-level heading. Sometimes writers build other identifying information into the headers. For example, your instructor might ask you to identify your assignments with a header like the following: "Smith, Progress Report, English 302, page 6." Headers and footers work according to the principle of repetition; readers learn where to look on the page to see where they are.

On TechComm Web

For more help with headers and footers, click on Tutorials on <bedfordstmartins.com/techcomm>.

Page numbering. For one-sided documents, use arabic numerals in the upper right corner. (The first page of most documents is unnumbered.) For two-sided documents, put the page numbers near the outside margins.

Complex documents often use two number sequences: lowercase roman numerals (*i*, *ii*, and so on) for front matter, and arabic numerals for the body. The title page is unnumbered; the page following it is *ii*.

Appendices are often paginated with a number and letter combination: Appendix A begins with page A-1, followed by A-2, and so on; Appendix B starts with page B-1, and so on.

Sometimes documents list the total number of pages in the document (so recipients can be sure they have all of them). The second page is "2 of 17," and the third page is "3 of 17."

Documents that will be updated are sometimes numbered within each section: Section 3 begins with page 3-1, followed by 3-2; Section 4 begins with 4-1. This way, a complete revision of one section does not affect the pagination of subsequent sections.

On TechComm Web

For information on design principles and software, see the discussion about desktop publishing at About.com. Click on Links Library for Ch. 13 on <bedfordstmartins .com/techcomm>.

DESIGNING THE PAGE

A page of technical communication is effectively designed if the reader can recognize a pattern—such as where to look for certain kinds of information.

GUIDELINES

Understanding Learning Theory and Page Design

In designing the page, you want to create visual patterns that help readers find, understand, and remember information. Three principles, the result of research into how people learn, can help you design effective pages: chunking, queuing, and filtering.

▶ *Chunking.* People understand information best if it is delivered to them in chunks—small units—rather than all at once. In a business letter, which is typed single spaced, chunking involves double spacing between paragraphs, as shown in Figure 13.5.

Chunking, on the right, emphasizes units of related information.

a. Without chunking   b. With chunking

■ **Figure 13.5   Chunking**

▶ *Queuing.* Queuing refers to creating visual distinctions to indicate levels of importance. In a traditional outline, the roman numeral "I" heading is more important than the arabic numeral "1" heading. In designing a page, using more-emphatic elements—such as bigger type or boldface type—suggests importance.

   Another visual element of queuing is alignment. Designers start more-important information closer to the left margin and indent less important information. (An exception is titles, which are often centered in reports in the United States.) Figure 13.6 shows queuing by size and alignment.

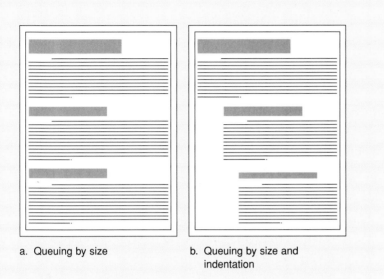

In figure a, the first-level head at the top is bigger than the second-level heads.

In figure b, each of the three headings is a different size, and the headings and accompanying text are aligned on different left margins.

a. Queuing by size

b. Queuing by size and indentation

■ **Figure 13.6   Queuing**

▶ *Filtering.* Filtering is the use of visual patterns to distinguish various types of information. In a set of instructions, a stop sign, for example, often signals safety information. Designers also use typography to produce the same effect. Introductory material might be displayed in larger type, and notes might appear in italics or another typeface. Figure 13.7 shows filtering.

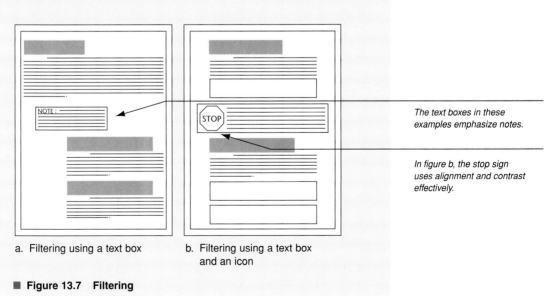

The text boxes in these examples emphasize notes.

In figure b, the stop sign uses alignment and contrast effectively.

a. Filtering using a text box

b. Filtering using a text box and an icon

■ **Figure 13.7   Filtering**

Page Layout

On TechComm Web

For more help with page layout, click on Tutorials on <bedfordstmartins.com/techcomm>.

Every page has two kinds of space: white space and space for text and graphics. The best way to design a page is to make a grid—a drawing of what the page will look like. In making a grid, you decide how to use white space and determine how many columns to have on the page.

Page Grids   As the phrase suggests, a *page grid* is like a map on which you chart where the text, the graphics, and the white space should go. To devise an effective grid, consider your audience, their purpose in reading, and their reading behavior.

Many writers like to begin with a *thumbnail sketch*, a rough drawing that shows how the different elements—text and graphics—will look on the page. Figure 13.8 shows several thumbnail sketches for a page from the body of a manual. Keep experimenting by sketching the different kinds of pages your document will have: body pages, front matter, and so on. When you are satisfied, make page grids. You can use either a computer or a pencil and paper, or you can combine the two techniques.

■ **Figure 13.8
Thumbnail Sketches**

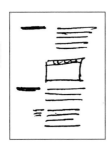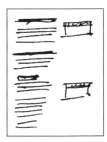

Figure 13.9 shows two simple grids: one using picas (the unit that printing professionals use; one pica equals one-sixth of an inch) and one using inches.

Experiment with different grids until you think you have a page design that is attractive, able to meet the needs of your readers, and appropriate for the information you are conveying. Figure 13.10 on page 302 shows some possibilities.

White Space   Sometimes called *negative space*, white space is the area of the paper with no writing or graphics: the space between two lines of text, the space between text and graphics, and, most obviously, the margins. White space directs readers' eyes to a particular element, emphasizing it. White space also helps readers see relationships among elements on the page.

Up to half the area on a typical page is given over to margins. Why so much? Margins serve four main purposes:

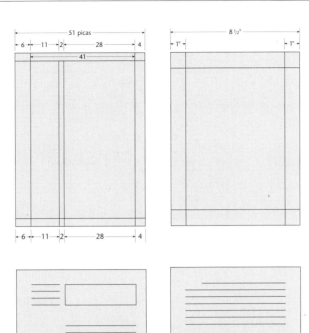

a. Grids using picas (left)
   and inches (right)

b. Pages based on the grids

■ **Figure 13.9**
**Sample Grids Using Picas
and Inches**

- They limit the amount of information on the page, making it easier to read and use.
- They provide space for binding and allow readers to hold the page without covering up the text.
- They provide a neat frame around the type.
- They provide space for marginal glosses. (Marginal glosses are discussed later in this chapter.)

Figure 13.11 on page 303 shows common margin widths for left-hand and right-hand pages.

White space can also set off and emphasize an element on the page. For instance, white space around a graphic separates it from the text and draws the reader's eye to it. White space between columns helps the reader to read the text easily. And white space between sections of text helps the reader see that one section is ending and another is beginning.

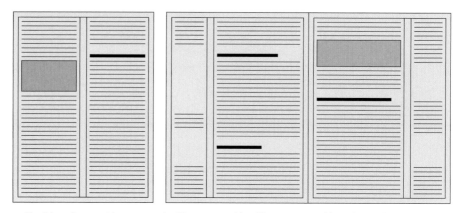

a. Double-column grid   b. Two-page grid, with narrow outside columns for notes

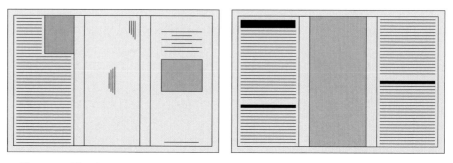

c. Three-panel brochure

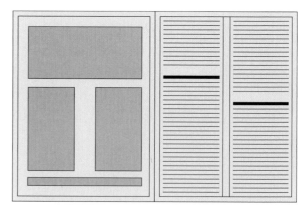

d. Two-page grid, with graphics on the left page and
double-column text on the right page

■ **Figure 13.10**
Common Grids

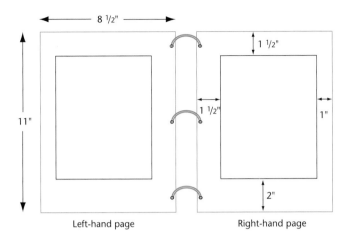

■ **Figure 13.11   Typical Margins for a Document That Is Bound Like a Book**

Increase the size of the margins when the subject becomes more difficult or when your readers become less knowledgeable about it.

Columns

Unlike the one-column documents you have written as a student, many of the documents you write on the job will have multiple columns. A multicolumn design offers three major advantages:

- Text is easier to read because the lines are shorter.
- Columns allow you to fit more information on the page, because many graphics can fit in one column or extend across two or more columns. In addition, a multicolumn design can accommodate more words on a page than a single-column design.
- Columns let you use the principle of repetition to create a visual pattern, such as text in one column, accompanying graphic in an adjacent column.

Typography

Typography is the study of type and the way people read it. When designers and technical communicators study typography, they learn about typefaces, families, case, and sizes. They also consider the white space of typography: line spacing, line length, and justification.

Typefaces   A typeface is a set of letters, numbers, punctuation marks, and other symbols, all bearing a characteristic design. There are thousands of typefaces, and more are designed every year. Figure 13.12 shows three contrasting typefaces.

On TechComm Web

See Design Sphere Online's set of links on typography and fonts. Click on Links Library for Ch. 13 on <bedfordstmartins.com/techcomm>.

This paragraph is typed in French Script typeface. You are unlikely to see this style of font in a technical document because it is too ornate and too hard to read. It is better suited to wedding invitations and other formal announcements.

This paragraph is Times Roman. It looks like the kind of type used by the *New York Times* and other newspapers in the nineteenth century. It is an effective typeface for text in the body of technical documents.

This paragraph is Univers, which has a modern, high-tech look. It is best suited for headings and titles in technical documents.

■ **Figure 13.12 Typefaces**

As Figure 13.13 illustrates, typefaces are generally classified into two categories: *serif* and *sans serif.*

Most of the time you will use standard typefaces such as Times Roman and Arial, which are included in your software and which your printer can reproduce. Remember, however, that different typefaces convey different impressions and that some cause more eye fatigue than others.

Type Families   Each typeface belongs to a family of typefaces, which consist of variations on the basic style, such as italic and boldface. Figure 13.14, for example, shows Helvetica.

As with typefaces, be careful not to overload your text with too many different members of the same family. Used sparingly and consistently, how-

Serif typefaces are often considered easier to read because the serifs — the short extensions on the letters — encourage the movement of the reader's eyes along the line.

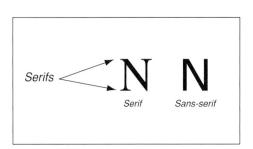

Sans-serif typefaces are harder on our eyes because the letters are less distinct from one another than they are in a serif typeface. However, sans-serif typefaces are easier to read on the screen and when printed on dot-matrix printers, because the letters are simpler.

The effect of serifs on readability might differ from culture to culture because if you see one kind of type often, you become used to it and read it quickly and easily.

■ **Figure 13.13   Serif and Sans-Serif Typefaces**

Sans-serif typefaces are used mostly for short documents and for headings.

Helvetica Light	***Helvetica Bold Italic***
Helvetica Light Italic	**Helvetica Heavy**
Helvetica Regular	***Helvetica Heavy Italic***
Helvetica Regular Italic	Helvetica Regular Condensed
Helvetica Bold	*Helvetica Regular Condensed Italic*

■ **Figure 13.14   Helvetica Family of Type**

ever, members of the same family can help you with filtering: calling attention to various kinds of text, such as warnings and notes, or even characters that readers are to type on the computer keyboard (Felker, Pickering, Charrow, Holland, & Redish, 1981). You will use italics for book titles and other elements, and you might use bold type for emphasis and headings, but you can go a long time without needing condensed and expanded versions of typefaces. And you can live a full, rewarding life without ever using outlined or shadowed versions.

Case   To ensure that your document is easy to read, use uppercase and lowercase letters as you would in any other kind of writing (see Figure 13.15).

The average person requires 10 to 25 percent more time to read text using all uppercase letters than to read text using both uppercase and lowercase. In addition, uppercase letters take up as much as 35 percent more space than lowercase letters (Haley, 1991). And if the text includes both uppercase and lowercase, readers will find it easier to see where new sentences begin (Poulton, 1968).

On TechComm Web

For more help with typography, click on Tutorials on <bedfordstmartins .com/techcomm>.

Lowercase letters are easier to read than uppercase because the individual variations from one letter to another are greater.

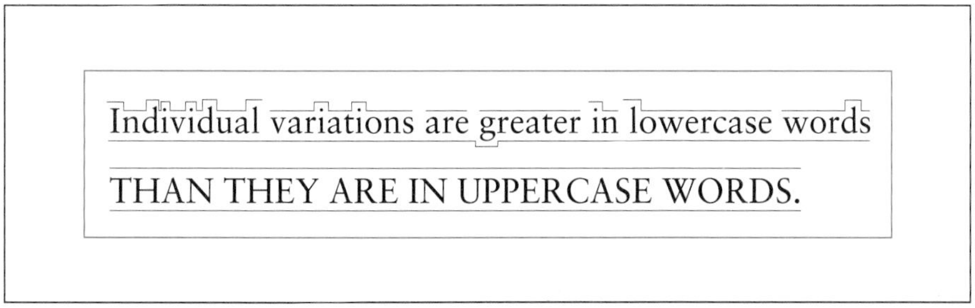

Individual variations are greater in lowercase words

THAN THEY ARE IN UPPERCASE WORDS.

■ **Figure 13.15   Individual Variations in Lowercase and Uppercase Type**

Type Sizes   Type size is measured according to a basic unit called a *point*. There are 12 points in a *pica* and 72 points in an inch.

In most technical documents 10-, 11-, or 12-point type is used for the body of the text:

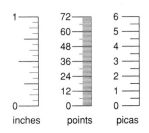

inches   points   picas

> This paragraph is printed in 10-point type. This size is easy to read, provided it is reproduced on a high-quality inkjet printer or laser printer.

> This paragraph is printed in 12-point type. If the document will be read by people over age 40, 12-point type is a good size because it is more legible than a smaller size.

> This paragraph is printed in 14-point size. This size is appropriate for titles or headings.

Type sizes used in other parts of the document include the following:

footnotes	8- or 9-point type
indexes	2 points smaller than body text
slides or transparencies	24- to 36-point type

In general, you should aim for at least a 2- to 4-point difference between the headings and the body. Too many size variations, however, might suggest a sweepstakes advertisement rather than a serious text.

Line Length   Ironically, the line length most often used on an 8.5 × 11-inch page—about 80 characters—is somewhat difficult to read. A shorter line of perhaps 50 to 60 characters is less demanding, especially in a long document (Biggs, 1980).

Line Spacing   Sometimes called *leading* (pronounced *ledding*), *line spacing* refers to the white space between lines or between a line of text and a graphic. If lines are too far apart, the page looks diffuse, the text loses coherence, and the reader tires quickly. If lines are too close together, the page looks crowded and becomes difficult to read. Some research suggests that smaller type, longer lines, and sans-serif typefaces all benefit from a little more line spacing. Figure 13.16 shows three variations in line spacing.

Line spacing is usually determined by the kind of document you are writing. Memos and letters are single-spaced; reports, proposals, and similar documents are often double-spaced or one-and-a-half spaced.

Line spacing can also be used to separate one section of text from another. Breaks between single-spaced paragraphs usually consist of one extra line. (Double-spaced and one-and-a-half-spaced text has no extra line spacing between paragraphs, but the first line of each paragraph is indented, as in handwritten documents.)

Figure 13.17 shows how line spacing can be used to distinguish one section of text from another and to separate text from graphics.

a.   **Excessive line spacing**

Aronomink Systems has been contracted by Cecil Electric Cooperative, Inc.

(CECI) to design a solid waste management system for the Cecil County

plant, Units 1 and 2, to be built in Cranston, Maryland. The system will consist

of two 600 MW pulverized coal-burning units fitted with high-efficiency elec-

trostatic precipitators and limestone reagent FGD systems.

b.   **Appropriate line spacing**

Aronomink Systems has been contracted by Cecil Electric Cooperative, Inc.
(CECI) to design a solid waste management system for the Cecil County
plant, Units 1 and 2, to be built in Cranston, Maryland. The system will
consist of two 600 MW pulverized coal-burning units fitted with high-
efficiency electrostatic precipitators and limestone reagent FGD systems.

c.   **Inadequate line spacing**

Aronomink Systems has been contracted by Cecil Electric Cooperative,
Inc. (CECI) to design a solid waste management system for the Cecil
County plant, Units 1 and 2, to be built in Cranston, Maryland. The system
will consist of two 600 MW pulverized coal-burning units fitted with high-
efficiency electrostatic precipitators and limestone reagent FGD systems.

■ **Figure 13.16**
Line Spacing

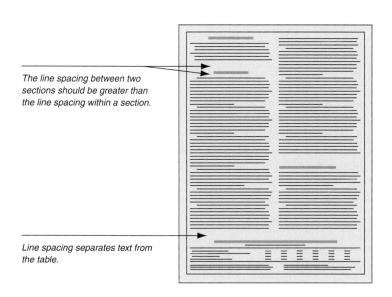

*The line spacing between two
sections should be greater than
the line spacing within a section.*

*Line spacing separates text from
the table.*

■ **Figure 13.17**
**Line Spacing Used to
Distinguish One Section
from Another**

Justification   Justification refers to the alignment of words along the left and right margins of the text. In technical communication, text is often *left-justified*; that is, except for paragraph indentations, the lines begin along a uniform left margin but end on an irregular right border, often called *ragged right.* Ragged right is most common in word-processed text (even though word processors can justify the right margin).

In justified text, also called *full-justified text,* both the left and right margins are justified. Justified text is seen most often in typeset, formal documents, such as books.

The following passage (United States Department of Agriculture, 2002) is presented first in left-justified form and then in justified form:

Notice that the space between words is uniform in left-justified text.

We recruited participants to reflect the racial diversity of the area in which the focus groups were conducted. Participants had to meet the following eligibility criteria: have primary responsibility or share responsibility for cooking in their household; prepare food and cook in the home at least three times a week; eat meat and/or poultry; prepare meat and/or poultry in the home at least twice a week; and not regularly use a digital food thermometer when cooking at home.

In justified text, the spacing between words is irregular, slowing down the reader. Because a big space suggests a break between sentences, not a break between words, the reader can become confused, frustrated, and fatigued.

We recruited participants to reflect the racial diversity of the area in which the focus groups were conducted. Participants had to meet the following eligibility criteria: have primary responsibility or share responsibility for cooking in their household; prepare food and cook in the home at least three times a week; eat meat and/or poultry; prepare meat and/or poultry in the home at least twice a week; and not regularly use a digital food thermometer when cooking at home.

Notice that the irregular spacing not only slows down reading but also creates "rivers" of white space. Readers are tempted to concentrate on the rivers running south rather than on the information itself.

Justification can make the text harder to read in one more way. Some word processors and typesetting systems automatically hyphenate words—sometimes incorrectly—that do not fit on the line. Hyphenation slows down and distracts the reader. Left-justified text does not require as much hyphenation as justified text does.

Designing Titles and Headings

Titles and headings should stand out visually on the page because they announce the introduction of a new idea.

Designing Titles   Because a title is the most important heading in a document, it should be displayed clearly and prominently. If it is on a cover page or a title page, you might present it in boldface in a large type size, such as 18 or 24 points. If it also appears at the top of the first page, you might make it slightly larger than the rest of the text—perhaps 16 or 18 points for a document printed in 12 point—but smaller than it is on the cover or title page. Titles are often centered horizontally on the page.

In This Book

For more on titling your document, see Ch. 10, p. 219.

Designing Headings   Readers should be able to tell when you are beginning a new topic. The most effective way to distinguish one level of headings from another is to use size variations (Williams & Spyridakis, 1992). Most readers will notice a 20-percent size difference between two levels. Boldface also sets off headings effectively. The least effective way to set off headings is underlining, because in many word processors the underline obscures the *descenders*, the portions of letters that extend below the body of the letters, such as in *p* and *y*.

In This Book

For more about using headings, see Ch. 10, p. 220.

In general, the more important the heading level, the closer it is to the left margin: first-level headings usually begin at the left margin, second-level headings are often indented a half inch, and third-level headings are often indented an inch. Indented third-level headings can also be run into the text.

In designing headings, use line spacing carefully. A perceivable distance between a heading and the text increases the impact of the heading. Consider these three examples:

On TechComm Web

For more help with designing headings, click on Tutorials on <bedfordstmartins.com/techcomm>.

Summary

In this example, the writer has skipped a line between the heading and the text that follows it. The heading stands out clearly.

Summary
In this example, the writer has not skipped a line between the heading and the text that follows it. The heading stands out, but not as emphatically.

Summary. In this example, the writer has begun the text on the same line as the heading. This run-in style makes the heading stand out the least.

Other Design Features

Table 13.3 shows five other design features that are used frequently in technical communication: rules, boxes, screens, marginal glosses, and pull quotes.

■ **Table 13.3   Rules, Boxes, Screens, Marginal Glosses, and Pull Quotes**

rules 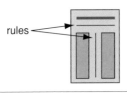	*Rules.* A rule is a design term for a straight line. Using a word processor, you can easily add horizontal or vertical rules to a document. Horizontal rules can separate headers and footers from the body of the page or divide two sections of text. Vertical rules can separate columns on a multicolumn page or identify revised text in a manual. Rules exploit the principles of alignment and proximity.
boxes 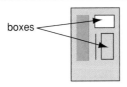	*Boxes.* Adding rules on all four sides of an item creates a box. Boxes can enclose graphics or special sections of text, or form a border for the whole page. Boxed text is often positioned to extend into the margin, giving it further emphasis. Boxes exploit the principles of contrast and repetition.
screen 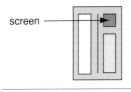	*Screens.* The background shading behind text or graphics for emphasis is known as a screen. The density can range from 1 percent to 100 percent; 5–10 percent is usually enough to provide emphasis without making the text illegible. You can use screens with or without boxes. Screens exploit the principles of contrast and repetition.
marginal gloss 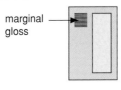	*Marginal glosses.* A marginal gloss is a brief comment on the main discussion, such as a summary statement, in the margin of the document. Marginal glosses are usually set in a different typeface—and sometimes in a different color—from the main discussion. Although marginal glosses can be helpful in providing a quick overview of the main discussion, they can also compete with the text for the reader's attention. Marginal glosses exploit the principles of contrast and repetition.
pull quote 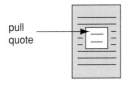	*Pull quotes.* A pull quote is a brief quotation, usually just a sentence or two, that is pulled from the text and displayed in a larger type size, and generally in a different typeface, often in a box. Newspapers and magazines use pull quotes to attract readers' attention and make them want to read the article. Pull quotes are inappropriate for reports and similar documents because they look too informal. They are increasingly popular, however, in newsletters. Pull quotes exploit the principles of contrast and repetition.

On TechComm Web

To view Figs. 13.18–13.20 in context on the Web, click on Links Library for Ch. 13 on <bedfordstmartins.com/techcomm>.

ANALYZING SOME PAGE DESIGNS

Figures 13.18–13.20 showing typical page designs used in technical documents, illustrate the concepts discussed in this chapter.

178 Federal Reserve Bulletin □ March 2002

proportions incorporated in the IP index from 1994 forward.

Beginning with this revision, the methods and data used to obtain estimates of value added in the electric utility industry have been improved. A change was necessary for several reasons. First, many of the data that had been used to compute value added were contained in an EIA publication that has been discontinued. Second, the EIA data on "utilities" include regulated entities only, and data covering all producers of electric power (that is, including the unregulated power generators) are required to avoid a severe understatement of the value added by the entire industry in 2000. Finally, a review of the earlier methods suggested value added was understated for the period preceding the deregulation of the industry.

The Federal Reserve's new estimates of value added for the electric utility industry were constructed according to the Census definition of value added, that is, industry revenue minus the cost of purchased material inputs. Data on industry revenue (including all establishments that distribute power to final users) were obtained from Statistical Yearbooks issued by the Edison Electric Institute; these data were combined with EIA measures of fuel costs to obtain an estimate of Census value added. The new figures were applied on a best-change basis for the period from 1992 forward; the 2002 revision will introduce refined results as well as revised figures for earlier years.

Changes to Individual Series

With this revision, the capacity series for natural gas extraction (part of SIC 13) incorporates new estimates developed by the EIA; the new estimates are substantially lower than the agency's previous figures that were used to derive the capacity for natural gas extraction. The new figures are designed to better reflect the ability of producing wells to deliver gas into the gathering and pipeline system, whereas previous EIA figures measured capacity at the wellhead only.

The source data for one other capacity series has changed. The index for silver capacity is now based on data from the USGS; previously it was derived using a trend-through-peak method.

The monthly production indicators for construction machinery and original equipment motor vehicle parts were refined. The weights used to combine the available product data for construction machinery were updated. The indicator for motor vehicle parts is now developed from monthly product data (engines, brakes, axles, and transmissions), production-worker hours, and motor vehicle assemblies; previously, the series was derived from the product only.

The annual estimates of motor vehicle repair parts were also improved; their derivation now includes information on the average age of the motor vehicle fleet.

LAN Equipment

The 2000 revision introduced a new IP series for the production of local area network (LAN) equipment (routers, switches, and hubs). The new series is not published in the monthly statistical release, but it is included in the broader IP aggregate for communications equipment and updated on an ongoing basis (see the March 2001 *Bulletin* article). Table 2 shows updates of the results for LAN equipment originally issued a year ago.   □

2. U.S. LAN equipment, 1992–2001

Period	Production index	Price index	Value of production (millions of dollars)
Annual estimates (1992 = 100)			
1992	100.000	100.000	1,648.8
1993	190.691	83.556	2,684.4
1994	298.728	74.243	3,736.6
1995	604.349	62.153	6,328.3
1996	953.621	57.123	9,177.7
1997	1,610.035	47.548	12,897.7
1998	2,480.329	34.327	14,344.5
1999	3,191.443	28.130	15,124.9
2000	4,163.164	24.406	17,118.2
Quarterly estimates (1996:Q1 = 100)			
1996:Q1	100.000	100.000	7,923.2
Q2	113.744	98.967	8,919.0
Q3	128.626	93.735	9,552.8
Q4	150.302	86.623	10,315.7
1997:Q1	161.797	84.029	10,772.1
Q2	183.502	79.683	11,585.3
Q3	224.022	77.535	13,762.2
Q4	262.123	74.493	15,471.1
1998:Q1	290.487	62.795	14,452.9
Q2	326.083	59.075	15,262.7
Q3	328.499	53.487	13,921.3
Q4	329.790	52.587	13,741.0
1999:Q1	417.721	48.619	16,091.2
Q2	419.060	47.117	15,644.2
Q3	394.817	46.808	14,642.6
Q4	402.795	44.249	14,121.6
2000:Q1	449.375	43.459	15,473.4
Q2	493.979	41.718	16,327.9
Q3	599.868	39.456	18,752.6
Q4	604.171	37.433	17,919.0
2001:Q1	538.767	34.889	14,893.0
Q2	465.929	34.232	12,651.6
Q3	471.295	31.602	11,814.1

The two-column format is economical because a lot of words fit on a page and because it lets the designer use narrow or wide graphics without wasting space.

The designer uses white space effectively to separate text from graphics and to set off headings.

The use of the second color—green—is effective in the graphic, but it doesn't provide much emphasis for the heading. The designer might use a darker green or increase the size of the heading.

■ **Figure 13.18   A Page from a Report**

This page from a report is designed to use space efficiently.

Source: United States Federal Reserve Board, 2002 <www.federalreserve.gov/pubs/bulletin/2002/0302_2nd.pdf>.

This is the header.

This combination of two rules signals a new heading.

In a numbered list, the turnovers (the second and subsequent lines) align under the text in the first line.

The figure number in the margin is emphatic, but some designers would object that the figure is not clearly part of step 2 in the text. There is no reason that the figure number could not align under the text in the numbered list.

This is the footer, containing the chapter number and page number.

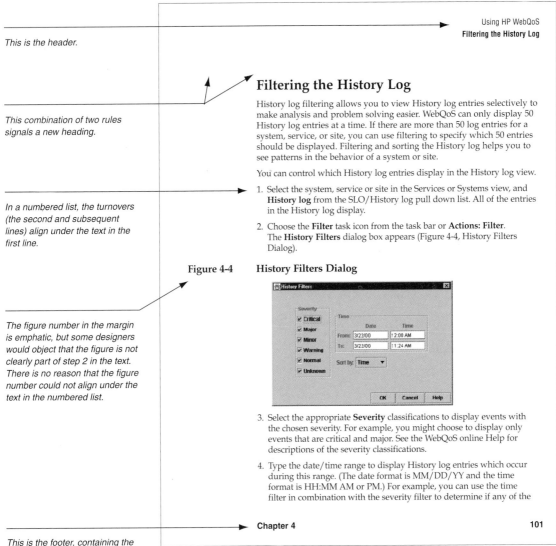

Using HP WebQoS
Filtering the History Log

Filtering the History Log

History log filtering allows you to view History log entries selectively to make analysis and problem solving easier. WebQoS can only display 50 History log entries at a time. If there are more than 50 log entries for a system, service, or site, you can use filtering to specify which 50 entries should be displayed. Filtering and sorting the History log helps you to see patterns in the behavior of a system or site.

You can control which History log entries display in the History log view.

1. Select the system, service or site in the Services or Systems view, and **History log** from the SLO/History log pull down list. All of the entries in the History log display.

2. Choose the **Filter** task icon from the task bar or **Actions: Filter**. The **History Filters** dialog box appears (Figure 4-4, History Filters Dialog).

Figure 4-4   **History Filters Dialog**

3. Select the appropriate **Severity** classifications to display events with the chosen severity. For example, you might choose to display only events that are critical and major. See the WebQoS online Help for descriptions of the severity classifications.

4. Type the date/time range to display History log entries which occur during this range. (The date format is MM/DD/YY and the time format is HH:MM AM or PM.) For example, you can use the time filter in combination with the severity filter to determine if any of the

Chapter 4   101

■ **Figure 13.19   A Clear Design**

This page from a user's manual shows a simple one-column design.
Source: Hewlett Packard Company, 2000 <http://ovweb.external.hp.com/lpe/doc_serv/>.

The involvement of undergraduate students is an important feature of RUI, which provides them with research-rich learning environments. However, the primary purpose of RUI is to support faculty research, thereby maintaining the intellectual vibrancy of faculty members in the classroom and research community.

RUI provides the following types of support:

- **Single-Investigator and Collaborative Faculty Research Projects**—Provides support through NSF research programs in response to proposals submitted by individual faculty members or by groups of collaborating investigators. RUI proposals differ from standard NSF proposals in that they include an RUI Impact Statement describing the expected effects of the proposed research on the research and education environment of the institution.

- **Shared Research Instrumentation and Tools**—Provides support for (1) the purchase or upgrade of instrumentation or equipment necessary to support research that will be conducted by several faculty members and (2) the development of new instrumentation.

- **Research Opportunity Awards (ROA's)**—Enable faculty members at predominantly undergraduate institutions to pursue research as visiting scientists with NSF-supported investigators at other institutions. ROA's are usually funded as supplements to ongoing NSF research grants. ROA's are intended to increase the visitors' research capability and effectiveness; improve research and teaching at their home institution; and enhance the NSF-funded research of the host principal investigator.

For More Information

For further information about the RUI activity, including guidelines for the preparation and submission of proposals, see program announcement NSF 00-144.

Prospective applicants for RUI grants and principal investigators interested in hosting an ROA visiting researcher are urged to contact a program officer in the appropriate discipline.

4. **Minority Research Planning Grants and Career Advancement Awards**—These awards are part of NSF's overall effort to give members of minority groups that are underrepresented in science and engineering greater access to scientific research support.

- **Minority Research Planning Grants (MRPG's)**—Enable eligible minorities who have not had prior independent Federal research support to develop competitive research projects by supporting preliminary studies and similar activities. These are one-time awards of up to $18K for a maximum of 18 months.

- **Minority Career Advancement Awards (MCAA's)**—Support activities that can expand the research career potential of promising applicants. These awards are

This page has no header or footer with page numbers or section headings.

Chunking is poor. The reader cannot easily see where one section begins and ends. There should be greater leading between sections than within sections.

The same typeface and size are used in the two different headings and at the start of the bullet items, violating the principle of repetition.

The effect of the bullets is diminished because the turnovers are not indented.

■ **Figure 13.20   A Poorly Designed Page**

Source: National Science Foundation, 2001 <www.nsf.gov/pubs/2001/nsf013/nsf013.pdf>.

Interactive Sample Document:
Analyzing a Page Design

The following page is from a company magazine. The questions in the margin ask you to think about page design (as discussed on pages 298–310). The answers to these questions are available on TechComm Web.

1. Describe the use of columns. In what ways do they work well?

2. Describe the text justification. In what ways, if any, would you revise the justification?

3. Describe the size and placement of the graphic. In what ways, if any, would you change its size and placement?

4. Describe the design characteristics of the text box. In what ways, if any, would you change its design?

5. Describe the use of white space. Is it insufficient? Sufficient? Excessive?

On TechComm Web

To find the answers to these questions, click on Interactive Sample Documents for Ch. 13 on <bedfordstmartins.com/techcomm>.

at Telecom Italia Mobile, Europe's largest cellular service provider. Similar collaborations and commercial trials are taking place among other vendors throughout the industry.

Reliability and quality of service
Before telecommunication service providers move to SS7oIP, they will need to know that an IP network's reliability and quality of service (QoS) can match the PSTN's. IP network developers have defined procedures to achieve this.

For example, Cisco's conception of an ITP-enabled network incorporates fault tolerance that ensures infrastructure reliability through multiple physical connections to the IP backbone. Maximizing the diversity of IP paths provides greater tolerance if a single path becomes unreachable due to a physical link failure. The fully meshed connectivity of an ITP network will allow any site to directly route message signaling units (MSUs) to any other site and reroute around a failed site. ITPs will be deployed in mated pairs, and each device will have two Ethernet interfaces to the IP backbone. This architecture provides the hardware redundancy required to handle failure in an element or interface.

Technology vendors have developed robust QoS policies to enhance the IP backbone's efficiency and reliability and to reduce packet drops and retransmission. The Cisco ITP gateway, for example, will support IP Precedence and differential services with eight QoS classes, thus ensuring predictable SS7 service delivery. Enhanced QoS enables operators to classify various types of SS7 traffic and provide specified classes with preferential treatment over the IP backbone. This capability requires no additional hardware.

Network management
Over the years, operators have benefited immeasurably from systems that manage signaling networks and network services. These tools provide

Agilent acceSS7 captures and displays the signaling messages exchanged across the SS7oIP core.

technical staff with a wealth of knowledge, and service providers have standardized operational practices around them. Indeed, the systems are so valuable that service providers will not likely adopt SS7oIP unless they're confident that the same management capabilities are available in IP networks. Fortunately, many vendors have adapted their management tools to SS7oIP.

Perhaps the most important example of this evolution is Agilent's successful effort to seamlessly extend acceSS7 to SS7oIP. Agilent acceSS7 is the world's most widely deployed link monitoring and management system, and it provides a network-wide visibility that enables comprehensive network and service assurance. The system includes tools for network surveillance, troubleshooting, business intelligence, fraud detection, interconnect management, and billing. Operators use acceSS7 in their legacy networks to maximize service quality, minimize customer churn, enhance revenue generation, and deploy new services quickly. Now they can extend the same solution to IP environments.

Agilent acceSS7 adds additional value in IP networks when deployed in con-

junction with element management systems such as the Cisco Signaling Gateway Manager (SGM). For example, if a misconfigured ITP routes traffice to the wrong destination, acceSS7 will enable operators to locate the device, which they can then reconfigure with Cisco SGM.

The future is now
SS7oIP is ready for commercial production. It has been standardized and tested for multivendor interoperability; it can be reliably delivered, in accord with comprehensive standards of service quality; and it can be monitored and managed as effectively as legacy SS7 networks. The benefits are significant: reduced infrastructure costs, enhanced efficiency, and new opportunities to deploy revenue-generating applications and services. Service providers can be confident that SS7oIP is a mature and profitable technology–It is the signaling network technology of the future, and the future is now.

IETF Sigtran protocols

- SCTP (Stream Control Transmission Protocol, RFC2960)–transport layer that provide reliable data transfer.

- M2PA (MTP2-User Peer-to-Peer Adaptation)–provides MTP3 with equivalent transport layer services as MTP2.

- M3UA (MTP3-User Adaptation)–client/server protocol providing a gateway to legacy SS7 network for IP-based applications that interface at the MTP3 layer.

- SUA (SCCP-User Adaptation)–client/server protocol providing a gateway to legacy SS7 network for IP-based applications that interface at the SCCP layer.

Source: Agilent, 2002.

Revision Checklist

Did you

❏ analyze your audience: their knowledge of the subject, attitudes, reasons for reading, and the kinds of tasks they will be carrying out? (p. 293)

❏ think about what your readers will expect to see when they pick up the document? (p. 293)

❏ design the document to suit readers' cultural preferences? (p. 293)

❏ determine your resources in time, money, and equipment? (p. 294)

❏ consider the best size for the document? (p. 294)

❏ consider the best paper for the document? (p. 295)

❏ consider the best binding for the document? (p. 295)

❏ think about which accessing tools would be most appropriate, such as icons, color, dividers, tabs, and cross-reference tables? (p. 296)

❏ devise a style for headers and footers? (p. 297)

❏ devise a style for page numbers? (p. 297)

❏ use color, if you have access to it, to highlight certain items, such as warnings? (p. 297)

❏ draw thumbnail sketches and page grids that define columns and white space? (p. 300)

❏ choose typefaces that are appropriate to your subject? (p. 303)

❏ use appropriate styles from the type families? (p. 304)

❏ use type sizes that are appropriate for your subject and audience? (p. 306)

❏ choose a line length that is suitable for your subject and audience? (p. 306)

❏ choose line spacing that is suitable for your line length, subject, and audience? (p. 306)

❏ decide on whether to use left-justified text or full-justified text? (p. 308)

❏ design your title for clarity and emphasis? (p. 309)

❏ work out a logical, consistent style for each heading level? (p. 309)

❏ use rules, boxes, screens, marginal glosses, and pull quotes where appropriate? (p. 310)

Exercises

On TechComm Web

For more exercises, click on Additional Exercises, Projects, and Cases for Ch. 13 on <bedfordstmartins.com/techcomm>.

1. Your word processor contains a number of templates for such documents as reports, letters, and memos. Study two templates for the same kind of document, for example, memos. What are the main differences between them? For what writing situations—audience, purpose, and subject—is each one most suited?

2. Study the first and second pages of an article in a journal in your field. Describe 10 design features you identify on these two pages. Which design features are most effective for the audience and purpose? Which are least effective?

Project

On TechComm Web

For more projects, click on Additional Exercises, Projects, and Cases for Ch. 13 on <bedfordstmartins.com/techcomm>.

3. **Group Activity**   Form groups of three for this collaborative exercise in analyzing design. Photocopy a page from a book or a magazine. Choose a page that does not contain advertisements. Each person works separately for the first part of this project:

- One person describes the design elements.

- One person evaluates the design. Which aspects of the design are effective, and which could be improved?

- One person creates a new design using thumbnail sketches.

Then, the group members meet and compare notes. Do all members of the group agree with the first member's description of the design? With the second member's analysis of the design? Do all members like the third member's redesign? What have your discussions taught you about design? Write a memo to your instructor presenting your findings. Include the photocopied page with your memo. (For more on memos, see Chapter 15, page 378.)

On TechComm Web

For more cases, click on Additional Exercises, Projects, and Cases for Ch. 13 on <bedfordstmartins.com /techcomm>.

CASE
The Underdesigned Data Sheet

You work in the publications department at Texas Instruments, which produces digital signal processing and analog technology products. Your boss, Louise Willis, approaches you one day. "We've got a problem. The manager would like us to redesign our data sheets so that they are more attractive and easier to read. Would you mind taking a look at this page and suggesting any improvements that we can build into our template?"

Study the following page from a TI data sheet (Texas Instruments, 2001). Describe its major design characteristics: its typography and its use of margins and white space. What are the strengths of its design? What are its weaknesses? What design features do you recommend changing or adding to make it more attractive and easier to read? If appropriate, devise headings that can be added to the page. Present your analysis and recommendations in a memo to Louise Willis. (For more on memos, see Chapter 15, page 378.)

SM320C6201B, SMJ320C6201B
DIGITAL SIGNAL PROCESSOR

SGUS031B – APRIL 2000 – REVISED AUGUST 2001

CPU description

The CPU fetches VelociTI advanced very-long instruction words (VLIW) (256 bits wide) to supply up to eight 32-bit instructions to the eight functional units during every clock cycle. The VelociTI VLIW architecture features controls by which all eight units do not have to be supplied with instructions if they are not ready to execute. The first bit of every 32-bit instruction determines if the next instruction belongs to the same execute packet as the previous instruction, or whether it should be executed in the following clock as a part of the next execute packet. Fetch packets are always 256 bits wide; however, the execute packets can vary in size. The variable-length execute packets are a key memory-saving feature, distinguishing the C62x CPU from other VLIW architectures.

The CPU features two sets of functional units. Each set contains four units and a register file. One set contains functional units .L1, .S1, .M1, and .D1; the other set contains units .D2, .M2, .S2, and .L2. The two register files each contain 16 32-bit registers for a total of 32 general-purpose registers. The two sets of functional units, along with two register files, compose sides A and B of the CPU (see Figure 1 and Figure 2). The four functional units on each side of the CPU can freely share the 16 registers belonging to that side. Additionally, each side features a single data bus connected to all the registers on the other side, by which the two sets of functional units can access data from the register files on the opposite side. While register access by functional units on the same side of the CPU as the register file can service all the units in a single clock cycle, register access using the register file across the CPU supports one read and one write per cycle.

Another key feature of the C62x CPU is the load/store architecture, where all instructions operate on registers (as opposed to data in memory). Two sets of data-addressing units (.D1 and .D2) are responsible for all data transfers between the register files and the memory. The data address driven by the .D units allows data addresses generated from one register file to be used to load or store data to or from the other register file. The C62x CPU supports a variety of indirect addressing modes using either linear- or circular-addressing modes with 5- or 15-bit offsets. All instructions are conditional, and most can access any one of the 32 registers. Some registers, however, are singled out to support specific addressing or to hold the condition for conditional instructions (if the condition is not automatically "true"). The two .M functional units are dedicated for multiplies. The two .S and .L functional units perform a general set of arithmetic, logical, and branch functions with results available every clock cycle.

The processing flow begins when a 256-bit-wide instruction fetch packet is fetched from a program memory. The 32-bit instructions destined for the individual functional units are "linked" together by "1" bits in the least significant bit (LSB) position of the instructions. The instructions that are "chained" together for simultaneous execution (up to eight in total) compose an execute packet. A "0" in the LSB of an instruction breaks the chain, effectively placing the instructions that follow it in the next execute packet. If an execute packet crosses the fetch packet boundary (256 bits wide), the assembler places it in the next fetch packet, while the remainder of the current fetch packet is padded with NOP instructions. The number of execute packets within a fetch packet can vary from one to eight. Execute packets are dispatched to their respective functional units at the rate of one per clock cycle and the next 256-bit fetch packet is not fetched until all the execute packets from the current fetch packet have been dispatched. After decoding, the instructions simultaneously drive all active functional units for a maximum execution rate of eight instructions every clock cycle. While most results are stored in 32-bit registers, they can be subsequently moved to memory as bytes or half-words as well. All load and store instructions are byte-, half-word-, or word-addressable.

TEXAS INSTRUMENTS

POST OFFICE BOX 1443 ● HOUSTON, TEXAS 77251–1443

14

Creating Graphics

An expert on the visual display of information, Edward R. Tufte (1999) defines an excellent graphic:

[The] greatest number of ideas in the shortest time with the least ink in the smallest space.

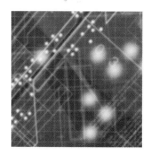

Graphics are the "pictures" in technical communication: drawings, maps, photographs, diagrams, charts, graphs, and tables. Graphics range in appearance from realistic (such as photographs) to highly abstract (such as organization charts). In terms of function, graphics range from the decorative, such as clip art that shows a group of people seated at a conference table, to highly informative, such as a table or a schematic diagram of an electronic device.

Graphics are important in technical communication because they can

- help you communicate information that is difficult to communicate with words
- help you clarify and emphasize information
- catch the reader's attention and interest
- help nonnative speakers of English understand the information
- help communicate information to multiple audiences with different interests, aptitudes, and reading habits

On TechComm Web

For additional samples, activities, and links related to this chapter, see <bedfordstmartins.com/techcomm>.

THE FUNCTIONS OF GRAPHICS

The most obvious reason to use graphics in a document is that they motivate people to study the document more closely. Research shows that 83 percent of what we learn derives from what we see, whereas only 11 percent derives from what we hear (Gatlin, 1988). Because we are good at acquiring information through sight, a document that includes a visual element beyond words on the page is more effective than one that doesn't. People studying a text with graphics learn about one-third more than people studying a text without graphics (Levie & Lentz, 1982). And people remember some 43 percent more when a document includes graphics (Morrison & Jimmerson, 1989). Readers like graphics. According to one survey, readers of computer documentation consistently want more graphics and fewer words (Brockmann, 1990, p. 203).

Graphics offer benefits that words alone cannot.

- *Graphics are almost indispensable in demonstrating logical and numerical relationships.* For example, an organization chart is an effective way to represent the lines of authority in the organization. If you want to communicate the number of nuclear power plants completed in each of the last 10 years, a line graph would be much easier to understand than a paragraph full of numbers.

- *Graphics can communicate spatial information more effectively than words alone.* If you want to show the details of the bicycle derailleur mechanism, a diagram of the bicycle with a close-up of the derailleur is more effective than a verbal description.

- *Graphics can communicate steps in a process more effectively than words alone.* A troubleshooter's guide, a common kind of table, explains what might be causing a problem in a process and how you might fix it. Or a diagram can explain clearly how acid rain forms.

- *Graphics can save space.* Consider the following paragraph:

    In the Wilmington area, some 90 percent of the population aged 18–34 watches movies on a VCR or a DVD player. They watch an average of 2.86 movies a week. Among 35- to 49-year-olds, the percentage is 82, and the average number of movies is 2.19. Among the 50–64 age group, the percentage is 67, and the number of movies watched averages 2.5. Finally, among those people 65 years old or older, the percentage is 48, and the average number of movies watched weekly is 2.71.

    Presented as a paragraph, this information is uneconomical and hard to remember. Presented as a table, however, the information is more concise and more memorable.

Age	Percentage Watching Tapes/Movies	Number of Tapes Watched per Week
18–34	90	2.86
35–49	82	2.19
50–64	67	2.50
65+	48	2.71

- *Graphics can reduce the cost of documents intended for international readers.* Translation costs can reach 60 cents per word; used effectively, graphics can reduce the number of words you have to translate (Horton, 1993).

As you plan and draft your document, look for opportunities to use graphics to clarify, emphasize, summarize, and organize information.

CHARACTERISTICS OF AN EFFECTIVE GRAPHIC

To be effective, a graphic must be clear, understandable, and meaningfully related to the larger discussion. Follow these six principles:

- *A graphic should have a purpose.* Don't include a graphic unless it will help your reader understand or remember the information. Avoid content-free clip art, such as drawings of businesspersons standing with clipboards or shaking hands.

- *A graphic should be honest.* Graphics can be dishonest, just as words can. You are responsible for making sure the graphic does not lie or mislead the reader. Following are some common ethical concerns to keep in mind:

  - If you did not create the graphic or generate the data, cite your source and, if you want to publish it, obtain permission. For more on citing graphics, see page 326.
  - Include all relevant data. For example, if you have a data point that you cannot explain, it is unethical to change the scale to eliminate it.
  - Begin the axes in your graphs at zero—or mark them clearly—so that quantities are represented honestly.
  - Do not use a table to hide a data point that would be obvious in a graph.
  - Show items as they really are. Do not manipulate a photograph of a computer monitor to make the screen look bigger than it is.
  - Do not use color or shading to misrepresent an item's importance. A light-shaded bar in a bar graph, for example, appears larger and nearer than a dark-shaded bar of the same size.

  Common problem areas are pointed out in the discussions of various kinds of graphics throughout this chapter.

- *A graphic should be simple and uncluttered.* Three-dimensional bar graphs are easy to make, but they are harder to understand than two-dimensional ones, as shown in Figure 14.1.

- *A graphic should present a manageable amount of information.* Presenting too much information can confuse readers. Consider audience and purpose: what kinds of graphics are readers familiar with, how much do they already know about the subject, and what do you want the document to do? Because readers learn best if you present information in small chunks, it is better to create several simple graphics rather than a single complicated one.

- *A graphic should meet the reader's format expectations.* Through experience, readers learn how to read different kinds of graphics. Follow the conventions—for instance, use diamonds to represent decision points in a flowchart—unless you have a good reason not to.

The two-dimensional bar graph is clean and uncluttered, whereas the three-dimensional graph is more difficult to understand because the additional dimension obscures the main data points. The number of uninsured emergency-room visits in February, for example, is very difficult to see in the three-dimensional graph.

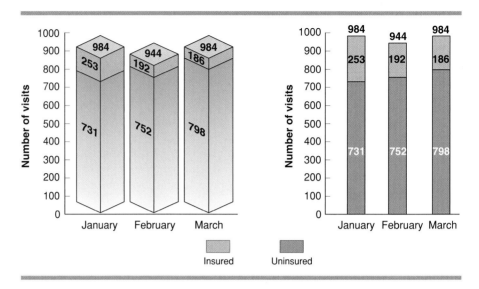

■ **Figure 14.1 Chartjunk and Clear Art**

Unnecessary 3-D is one example of chartjunk, a term used by Tufte (1983) to describe the ornamentation that clutters up a graphic, distracting readers from the message.

- *A graphic should be clearly labeled.* Every graphic (except a brief, informal one) should have a unique, clear, informative title. The columns of a table and the axes and lines of a graph should be labeled fully, including units of measurement. Readers should not have to guess whether you are using meters or yards, or whether you are also including statistics from the previous year.

GUIDELINES

Integrating Graphics and Text

▶ *Place the graphic in an appropriate location.* If readers need the information contained in a graphic to understand the discussion, put the graphic directly after the relevant point in the text—or as soon after it as possible. If the graphic merely supports or elaborates a point, include it as an appendix.

▶ *Introduce the graphic in the text.* Whenever possible, refer to a graphic before it appears (ideally, on the same page). Refer to the graphic by number (such as *Figure 7*). Do not refer to "the figure above" or "the figure below"; the graphic might be moved during the production process. If the graphic is in an appendix, tell your readers where to find it: "For complete details of the operating characteristics, see Appendix, Part B on page 19."

▶ *Explain the graphic in the text.* State what you want readers to learn from it. Sometimes a simple paraphrase of the title is enough: "Figure 2 is a comparison of the costs of the three major types of coal gasification plants." At other times, however, you might need to explain why the graphic is important or how to interpret it. If the graphic is intended to make a point, be explicit:

> As Figure 2 shows, a high-sulfur bituminous coal gasification plant is more expensive than either a low-sulfur bituminous or anthracite plant, but more than half of its cost is cleanup equipment. If these expenses could be eliminated, high-sulfur bituminous would be the least expensive of the three types of plants.

Graphics often are accompanied by captions, explanations ranging from a sentence to several paragraphs.

▶ *Make the graphic clearly visible.* Distinguish the graphic from the surrounding text by adding white space or rules (lines) or by enclosing it in a box.

▶ *Make the graphic accessible.* If the document is more than a few pages long and contains more than four or five graphics, consider including a list of illustrations so that readers can find them easily.

In This Book

For more on white space and rules, see Ch. 13, pp. 300 and 310.

For more on lists of illustrations, see Ch. 12.

UNDERSTANDING THE PROCESS OF CREATING GRAPHICS

Creating graphics involves planning, creating, revising, and citing.

Planning the Graphics

Whether you think first about the text or the graphics, you need to consider the following four aspects of the document as you plan.

- *Audience.* Will your readers understand the kinds of graphics you want to use? Are they familiar with the standard icons in your field? Are they already motivated to read your document, or do you need to enliven the text—by adding color for emphasis, for example—to hold their attention?

- *Purpose.* What point are you trying to make with the graphic? As Figure 14.2 shows, even a few simple facts can yield a number of different points. Your responsibility is to determine what you want to show and how best to show it. Don't rely on your software to do your thinking. It can't.

Rail Line	November		December		January	
	Disabled by electrical problems	Total disabled	Disabled by electrical problems	Total disabled	Disabled by electrical problems	Total disabled
Bryn Mawr	19	27	17	28	20	26
Swarthmore	12	16	9	17	13	16
Manayunk	22	34	26	31	24	33

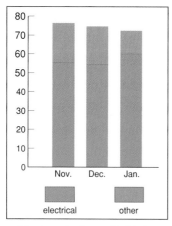

a. Number of rail cars disabled, November–January

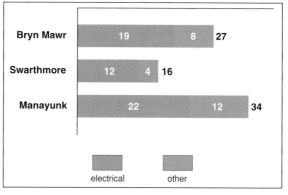

b. Number of rail cars disabled in November

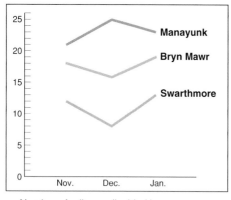

c. Number of rail cars disabled by electrical problems November–January

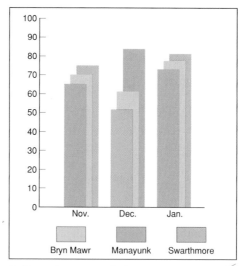

d. Range in percent of rail cars, by line, disabled by electrical problems, November–January

■ **Figure 14.2   Different Graphics Emphasizing Different Points**

Each of these four graphs emphasizes a different point. Graph (a) focuses on the total number of cars disabled each month, classified by cause; graph (b) focuses on the three rail lines during one month; and so forth. For information on bar graphs, see pp. 336–339; for information on line graphs, see pp. 341–342.

- *The kind of information you want to communicate.* Your subject will help you determine what type of graphic to include. For example, if you are writing about languages spoken by your state's citizens, you would probably use tables to present the statistical data, maps to show the patterns of language use, and graphs to show statistical trends over time.

- *Physical conditions.* The physical conditions in which a reader will use the document—amount of lighting, amount of surface space available, and so forth—will influence the type of graphic as well as its size and shape, the thickness of lines and size of type, and the color.

As you plan how you are going to create the graphics, consider four important factors:

- *Time.* Because making a complicated graphic can take a lot of time, you need to establish a schedule.

- *Money.* A high-quality graphic can be expensive. How big is the project budget? How can you use that money effectively?

- *Equipment.* Determine what tools and software you will require, such as spreadsheets for tables and graphs, and graphics software for diagrams.

- *Expertise.* How much do you know about creating graphics? Do you have access to the expertise of others?

In This Book

For more on planning and budgeting, see Ch. 3, p. 38.

Creating the Graphics

Except for special projects, you usually won't have all the resources you would like. You will probably have to choose one of the following four approaches:

- *Using existing graphics.* For a student paper that *will not be published*, some instructors allow the use of photocopies or scans of existing graphics; other instructors do not. For a document that *will be published*, whether written by a student or a professional, using an existing graphic is permissible if the graphic is the property of the writer's organization or if that organization has obtained permission to use it. For more on citing graphics, see page 326. Aside from the issue of copyright, think carefully before you use existing graphics. The style of the graphic might not match that of the others you want to use, and the graphic might lack some features you want or include some you don't. If you use an existing graphic, assign it your own number and title.

- *Modifying existing graphics.* You can redraw an existing graphic or use a scanner to digitize the graphic and then modify it electronically with graphics software.

- *Creating graphics on a computer.* Computer graphics offer two main advantages over hand-drawn graphics: variety and reusability. And because they are digital, computer graphics can be stored, copied, and revised. See the Selected Bibliography on page 676 for a list of books about

In This Book

For more on works-made-for-hire, see Ch. 2, p. 19.

computers and technical communication. But beware: any book about computer graphics is probably out of date as soon as it is published. For more information on computer graphics, see pages 355–357.

- *Having someone else create the graphics.* Professional-level software can cost hundreds of dollars, and you need considerable artistic ability to create professional-quality graphics. Even if you have the ability, attaining proficiency with a sophisticated graphics package can require hundreds of hours of practice. Some companies have technical-publications departments with graphics experts, but others subcontract this work. Many print shops and service bureaus have graphics experts on staff or can direct you to them.

Revising the Graphics

As with any other aspect of technical communication, build in enough time and money to revise the graphics. Create a checklist and evaluate each graphic for effectiveness. The Revision Checklist at the end of this chapter (p. 357) is a good starting point. Show the graphics to people whose backgrounds are similar to your intended readers' and ask them for suggestions. Revise the graphics and solicit more reactions.

Citing the Graphics

In most cases, you are ethically and legally obligated to cite graphics in documents. You *do not* need to cite graphics in the following cases:

In This Book

For more information on copyright, see Ch. 2.

- You created the graphic yourself, from scratch. (You do need to cite the graphic if you merely revised an existing graphic.)
- Your organization owns the copyright to the graphic.
- You are using the graphic in a document that is written for a course assignment and that will not be published.
- The graphic is in the public domain and therefore not covered by copyright laws. Very old graphics, and all graphics created by an agency or department of the United States government, are in the public domain.

In all other cases, you must include a citation. Be particularly careful about graphics you find on the Web. Many people mistakenly think that anything on the Web can be used without permission. The same copyright laws that apply to printed material apply to Web-based material, whether words or graphics.

In This Book

For information on style manuals, see Appendix, Part A, p. 592.

If you are following a style manual, such as the CBE style manual, check to see whether it presents a format for citing graphics. Most style manuals call for a source statement in the caption to the graphic:

Source: Anderson Machine Tools, 2003: "Reconfiguration Project: Progress Report"

If your graphic is based on an existing graphic, the source statement should indicate that your graphic is "based on" or "adapted from" your source.

USING COLOR EFFECTIVELY

Color draws attention to information you want to emphasize, establishes visual patterns to promote understanding, and adds interest. But it is also easy to misuse. The following discussion is based on Jan V. White's excellent text *Color for the Electronic Age* (1990).

In using color in graphics and page design, keep these seven principles in mind:

On TechComm Web

See Colorize.com for articles about color theory and about graphics software. Click on Links Library for Ch. 14 on <bedfordstmartins.com /techcomm>.

- *Don't overdo it.* Readers can interpret only two or three colors at a time. Use colors for small items, such as portions of graphics and important words. And don't use colors where black will work better.

- *Use color to emphasize particular items.* People interpret color before they interpret shape, size, or placement on the page. Color effectively draws a reader's attention to a particular item or group of items on a page. In Figure 14.3, for example, color adds emphasis to several different kinds of items.

- *Use color to create patterns.* The principle of repetition—readers learn to recognize patterns—applies in graphics and document design. In creating patterns, include shape. For instance, use red for safety comments but place them in octagons resembling a stop sign. This way, you give your

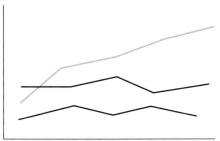

Color draws the reader's attention to the line.

The colored frame focuses the reader's attention on the information in the graph.

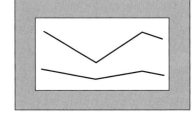

Color is useful for emphasizing short phrases. Used for longer passages, color loses its impact.

Pixel Driver Renders **600,000 Polygons** per Second

Here the color emphasizes a row; it could also be used to emphasize a column or a single data cell.

Table 2
Israeli Power Plant Sites

Site	Generating	Installed Capacity (MW)
Haifa	4	430
Hadera	4	1400
Tel Aviv	4	530
Ashdod	9	1210
Total		**3570**

Source: B. Golany, Y. Roll, & D. Rybak. (1994, August). ™Measuring efficiency of power plants in Israel by data envelopment analysis, *IEEE Transactions on Engineering Management 41*, 3, p. 292.

■ **Figure 14.3   Color Used for Emphasis**

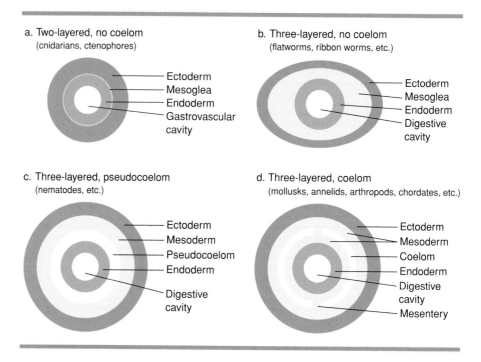

a. Two-layered, no coelom
(cnidarians, ctenophores)

- Ectoderm
- Mesoglea
- Endoderm
- Gastrovascular cavity

b. Three-layered, no coelom
(flatworms, ribbon worms, etc.)

- Ectoderm
- Mesoglea
- Endoderm
- Digestive cavity

c. Three-layered, pseudocoelom
(nematodes, etc.)

- Ectoderm
- Mesoderm
- Pseudocoelom
- Endoderm
- Digestive cavity

d. Three-layered, coelom
(mollusks, annelids, arthropods, chordates, etc.)

- Ectoderm
- Mesoderm
- Coelom
- Endoderm
- Digestive cavity
- Mesentery

■ **Figure 14.4   Color Used to Establish Patterns**

In This Book

For more on designing your document, see Ch.13.

readers two visual cues to help them recognize the pattern. Figure 14.4 (Curtis & Barnes, 1989, p. 532) shows a page in a biology textbook that uses color to establish patterns. Color is also an effective way to emphasize design features such as text boxes, rules, screens, and headers and footers.

- *Use contrast effectively.* The visibility of a color is a function of the background against which it appears, as shown below. The strongest contrasts are between black and white and between black and yellow.

Notice that a color washes out if the background color is too similar.

The need for effective contrast also applies to graphics used in presentations, as shown here.

In This Book

For more on presentation graphics, see Ch. 22, p. 573.

≡ *New Video Interfaces*
* Video Scope
* Video Space Icon
* Video Space Monitor
* Paper Video

≡ *New Video Interfaces*
* Video Scope
* Video Space Icon
* Video Space Monitor
* Paper Video

In graphic (a), the text is hard to read because of insufficient contrast. In graphic (b), the increased contrast makes the text easier to read.

a. Insufficient contrast   b. Effective contrast

* *Take advantage of any symbolic meanings colors may already have.* In American culture, for example, red signals danger, heat, or electricity; yellow signals caution; and orange signals warning. Using these warm colors in ways that depart from these familiar meanings could be confusing. The cooler colors—blues and greens—are more conservative and subtle. (Figure 14.5 illustrates these principles.) Keep in mind, however, that different cultures interpret colors differently.

In This Book

For more on cultural patterns, see Ch. 5, p. 87.

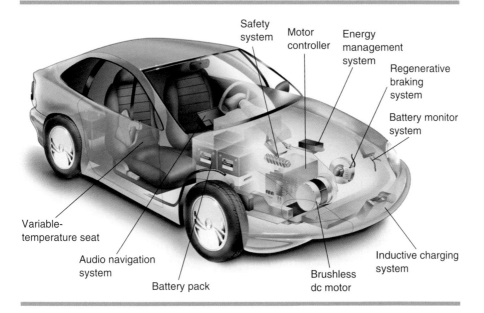

Safety system
Motor controller
Energy management system
Regenerative braking system
Battery monitor system
Variable-temperature seat
Audio navigation system
Battery pack
Brushless dc motor
Inductive charging system

The batteries are red. The warm red contrasts effectively with the cool green of the car body.

■ **Figure 14.5   Colors Already Have Clear Associations for Readers**

• *Be aware that color can obscure or swallow up text.*

If you are using print against a colored background, you might need to make the type a little bigger, because color makes text look smaller.

Text printed against a white background looks bigger than the same size text printed against a colored background. White letters counteract this effect.

| This text looks bigger because of the white background. | This text looks smaller, even though it is the same size, because of the colored background. |

This line of type appears to reach out to the reader.
This line of type appears to recede into the background.

• *Use light colors to make objects look bigger.*

The light orange box looks bigger than the blue box even though they are the same size.

Categories of technical information:

Numerical information

Logical relationships

Process descriptions and instructions

Visual and spatial characteristics

CHOOSING THE APPROPRIATE KIND OF GRAPHIC

Graphics used in technical documents fall into two categories: tables and figures. Tables are lists of data, usually numbers, arranged in columns. Figures are everything else: graphs, charts, diagrams, photographs, and the like. Generally, tables and figures are numbered separately: the first table in a document is Table 1; the first figure is Figure 1. In documents of more than one chapter (like this book), the graphics are usually numbered within each chapter. That is, Figure 3.2 is the second figure in Chapter 3.

There is no simple system for choosing a graphic, because in many situations several types would work. In general, however, graphics can be categorized according to the kind of information they contain. The discussion that follows is based on the classification system in William Horton's "Pictures Please—Presenting Information Visually," in *Techniques for Technical Communicators* (Barnum & Carliner, 1993).

Technical information can be classified into four categories. Figure 14.6 presents an overview of the following discussion.

Some kinds of graphics can convey several kinds of information. For instance, a table can include both numerical values and procedures.

Illustrating Numerical Information

The basic kinds of graphics used to display numerical values are tables, bar graphs, pictographs, line graphs, and pie charts.

■ **Figure 14.6   Choosing the Appropriate Kind of Graphic (Based on Horton [1993])**

Purpose	Type of Graphic		What the Graphic Does Best
Illustrating numerical information	Table		Shows large amounts of numerical data, especially when there are several variables for a number of items.
	Bar graph		Shows the relative values of two or more items.
	Pictograph		Enlivens statistical information for the general reader.
	Line graph		Shows how the quantity of an item changes over time. A line graph can accommodate much more data than a bar graph can.
	Pie chart		Shows the relative size of the parts of a whole. Pie charts are instantly familiar to most readers.
Illustrating logical relationships	Diagram		Represents items or properties of items.
	Organization chart		Shows the lines of authority and responsibility in an organization.
Illustrating instructions and process descriptions	Checklist		Lists or shows what equipment or materials to gather, or describes an action.
	Table		Shows numbers of items or indicates the state (on/off) of an item.

■ **Figure 14.6**   *(Continued)*

Purpose	Type of Graphic	What the Graphic Does Best
Illustrating instructions and process descriptions *(continued)*	Flowchart	Shows the stages of a procedure or a process.
	Logic box	Shows which of two or more paths to follow.
	Logic tree	Shows which of two or more paths to follow.
Illustrating visual and spatial characteristics	Drawing	Shows simplified representations of objects.
	Map	Shows geographical areas.
	Photograph	Shows precisely the external surface of objects.
	Screen shot	Shows what appears on a computer screen.

Tables   *Tables* convey large amounts of numerical data easily, and they are often the only way to present several variables for a number of items. For example, if you want to show how many people are employed in six industries in 10 states, a table would probably be most effective. Although tables lack the visual appeal of other kinds of graphics, they can handle much more information with complete precision.

Figure 14.7 illustrates the standard parts of a table. Tables are identified by number ("Table 1") and an informative title that includes the items being compared and the basis (or bases) of comparison:

Mallard Population in Rangeley, 1996–2002

The Growth of the Robotics Industry in Japan and the United States, 2003

Number —— **Table 6.   Test Results for Valves #1 and #2** —— *Title*

Valve Readings	Maximum Bypass Cv	Minimum Recirculation Flow (GPM)	Pilot Threads Exposed	Main ΔP at Rated Flow (psid)
Valve #1				
Initial	43.1	955	+3	4.4
Final	43.1	955	+3	. . .
Valve #2				
Initial	48.1	930	+3	4.5
Final	48.2	950	+2	. . .

Stub head — *Valve Readings*

Row head — *Valve #1*
Row subhead — *Initial* / *Final*

Column head

Source statement —— *Source:* "Third Progress Report: Anderson Machine Tools Reconfiguration Project."

■ **Figure 14.7   Parts of a Table**

Most tables are numbered and titled above the data. The number and title are left justified or centered horizontally.

GUIDELINES

Creating Effective Tables

▶ *Indicate the units of measure.* If all the data are expressed in the same unit, indicate that unit in the title:

Farm Size in the Midwestern States (in Hectares)

If the data in different columns are expressed in different units, indicate the units in the column headings:

Population (in millions)	Per Capita Income (in thousands of U.S. dollars)

If all the *data cells* in a column use the same unit, indicate that unit in the column head, not in each data cell:

Speed (knots)
15
18
14

You can express data in both real numbers and percentages. A column heading and the first data cell under it might read as follows:

Number of Students (Percentage)
53 (83)

▶ *In the stub—the left-hand column—list the items being compared.* Arrange the items in a logical order: big to small, important to unimportant, alphabetical, chronological, geographical, and so forth. If the items fall into several categories, include the names of the categories in the stub:

Snow Belt States . . . .
    Connecticut . . . .
    New York . . . .
    Vermont . . . .
Sun Belt States . . . .
    Arizona . . . .
    California . . . .
    New Mexico . . . .

In This Book

For more about screens, see Ch. 13, p. 310.

If the items in the stub are not grouped in logical categories, skip a line after every five rows to help the reader follow the rows across the table. Or use a screen or a colored background for every other set of five rows. Also useful are dot leaders: a row of dots that links the stub and the next column.

▶ *In the columns, arrange the data clearly and logically.* Use the decimal-tab feature to line up the decimal points:

  3,147.4
    365.7
46,803.5

In general, don't change units unless the quantities are so dissimilar that your readers would have a difficult time understanding them if expressed in the same units.

 3.4 hr
12.7 min
 4.3 sec

This list would probably be easier for most readers to understand than one in which all quantities were expressed in the same unit.

▶ *Do the math.* If your readers will need to know the totals for the columns or the rows, provide them. If your readers will need to know percentage changes from one column to the next, present them:

Number of Students (Percentage Change from Previous Year)

2000	2001	2002
619	644 (+4.0)	614 (−4.7)

▶ *Use dot leaders if a column contains a "blank" spot: a place where there are no appropriate data:*

3,147

. . .

46,803

But don't substitute dot leaders for a quantity of zero.

▶ *Don't make the table wider than it needs to be.* The reader should be able to scan across a row easily. As White (1984) points out, there is no reason to make the table as wide as the text column in the document. If a column heading is long—more than five or six words—stack the words:

Computers Sold
Without a CD-RW Drive

▶ *Minimize the use of rules.* Grimstead (1987) recommends using rules only when necessary: to separate the title and the headings, the headings and the body, and the body and the notes. When you use rules, make them thin rather than thick.

▶ *Provide footnotes where necessary.* All the information your readers need to understand the table should accompany the table.

▶ *If you did not generate the information yourself, indicate your source.* See the discussion of citing graphics on page 326.

COMPARE!	Pultruded Fiberglass Structural Shapes	Steel A-36 Carbon
CORROSION RESISTANCE	Pultrusions are available in either polyester or vinyl ester resin for resistance to a broad range of chemicals. Painting required only when exposed to direct sunlight.	Subject to oxidation and corrosion. Requires painting or galvanizing for many applications.
CONDUCTIVITY	Does not conduct electricity. Low Thermal Conductivity 4 (BTU/SF/HR/F°/IN).	Conducts electricity. Grounding potential. Thermal Conductivity 260–460 (BTU/SF/HR/F°/IN).
EASY FIELD FABRICATION	Pultruded fiberglass can be field fabricated using simple carpenter tools with carbon or diamond tip blades. Lightweight for easier erection and installation.	Often requires welding and cutting torches. Heavier material requires special handling equipment to erect and install.

■ **Figure 14.8 Text Table**

Source: Pultrusion Industry Council, 2001 <www.cfa-hq .org/pic/pultrusion/steel.htm>.

In addition to numerical information, tables can also effectively convey textual information, as shown in the excerpt presented in Figure 14.8.

Bar Graphs Like tables, *bar graphs* can communicate numerical values, but they are better at showing the relative values of two or more items. Figure 14.9 shows typical horizontal and vertical bar graphs.

Horizontal bars are best for showing quantities such as speed and distance. Vertical bars are best for showing quantities such as height, size, and amount. However, these distinctions are not ironclad; as long as the axes are clearly labeled, readers should have no trouble understanding the graph.

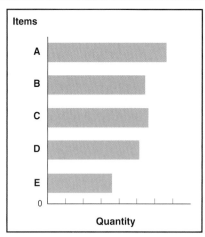

Figure 1. Horizontal graph

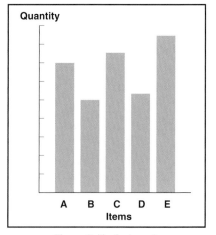

Figure 1. Vertical graph

■ **Figure 14.9 Structures of Horizontal and Vertical Bar Graphs**

Creating Effective Bar Graphs

▶ *Make the proportions fair.* Make your vertical axis about 25 percent shorter than your horizontal axis. An excessively long vertical axis exaggerates the difference in quantities; an excessively long horizontal axis minimizes the differences. Make all the bars the same width, and make the space between them about half as wide as a bar. Here are two poorly proportioned graphs.

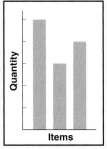
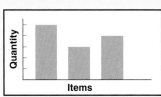

a. Excessively long vertical axis   b. Excessively long horizontal axis

▶ *If possible, begin the quantity scale at zero.* Doing so ensures that the bars accurately represent the quantities. Notice how misleading a graph can be if the scale doesn't begin at zero.

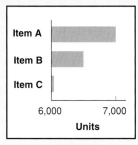
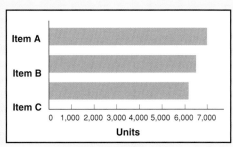

a. Misleading   b. Accurately representative

If it is not practical to start the quantity scale at zero, break the quantity axis clearly at a common point on all bars.

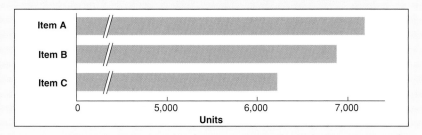

▶ *Use tick marks—marks along the axis—to signal the amounts.*

Use grid lines—tick marks that extend through the bars—if the table has several bars, some of which are too far away from tick marks to allow readers to gauge the quantity easily. (See Figure 14.12.)

▶ *Arrange the bars in a logical sequence.* For a vertical bar graph, use chronology if possible. For a horizontal bar graph, arrange the bars in order of descending size, beginning at the top of the graph, unless some other logical sequence seems more appropriate.

▶ *Place the title below the figure.* Unlike tables, which are usually read from top to bottom, figures are usually read from the bottom up.

▶ *Indicate the source of your information if you did not generate it yourself.*

Figure 14.10 shows an effective bar graph that uses grid lines.

The four variations on the basic bar graph shown in Table 14.1 can help you accommodate different communication needs.

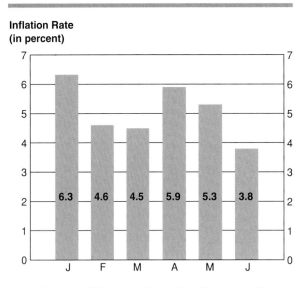

Figure 1. Tri-County Inflation Rate This Year to Date

■ **Figure 14.10**
Effective Bar Graph

■ **Table 14.1   Modifying the Basic Bar Graph**

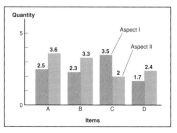

a. Grouped bar graph

The *grouped* bar graph lets you compare two or three quantities for each item. Grouped bar graphs would be useful, for example, for showing the numbers of full-time and part-time students at several universities. One bar could represent full-time students; the other, part-time students. To distinguish between the bars, use hatching (striping), shading, or color, and either label one set of bars or provide a key.

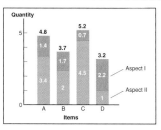

b. Subdivided bar graph

In the *subdivided* bar graph, Aspect I and Aspect II are stacked like wooden blocks placed on top of one another. Although totals are easy to compare in a subdivided bar graph, individual quantities are not.

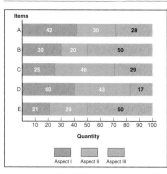

c. 100-percent bar graph

The *100-percent* bar graph, which shows the relative proportions of the elements that make up several items, is useful in portraying, for example, the proportion of full-scholarship, partial-scholarship, and no-scholarship students at a number of colleges.

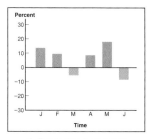

d. Deviation bar graph

The *deviation* bar graph shows how various quantities deviate from a norm. Deviation bar graphs are often used when the information contains both positive and negative values, such as profits and losses. Bars on the positive side of the norm line represent profits, bars on the negative side, losses.

Pictographs   Pictographs—bar graphs in which the bars are replaced by a series of symbols—are used primarily to present statistical information to the general reader. The quantity scale is usually replaced by a statement indicating the numerical value of each symbol. Thousands of clip-art symbols and pictures are available for use in pictographs. Figure 14.11 shows an example.

Represent quantities in a pictograph honestly. Figure 14.12 shows an inherent problem: a picture drawn to scale can appear many times larger than it should.

Clip-art pictures and symbols are available online for use in pictographs. Arrange pictographs horizontally rather than vertically. Pictures of computer monitors balanced on top of each other can look foolish.

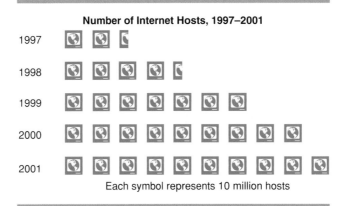

■ **Figure 14.11   Pictograph**

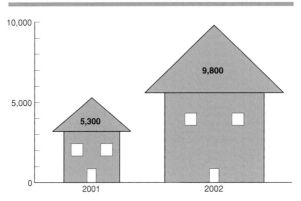

Figure 3. Housing Starts in the Tri-State Area, 2001– 2002

■ **Figure 14.12   Misleading Pictograph**

The reader sees the total area of the symbol rather than its height.

Interactive Sample Document:
Balancing Clarity and Drama in Graphics
The following graphic, a bar graph accompanied by a drawing, is included on a
Web site addressed to general readers. The questions in the margin ask you to think
about the principles of graphics (p. 321), color (p. 327), and bar graphs (p. 337). The
answers to these questions are available on TechComm Web.

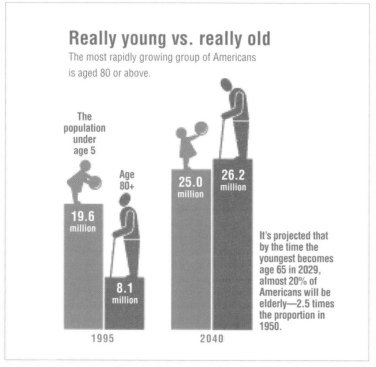

Source: Holmes & Bagby, 2002 <www.understandingusa.com/chaptercc=2&cs=18.html>.

1. How effectively has the
   designer used the two
   colors?

2. How do the drawings of
   the child and of the elderly man help communicate the point?

3. Create a rough sketch of
   a graph that communi-
   cates the text on the
   right. Should this information be communicated in
   words or in a graphic?
   Why?

On TechComm Web

To find the answers to these
questions, click on Interactive
Sample Documents for Ch. 14 on
<bedfordstmartins.com/techcomm>.

Line Graphs   *Line graphs* are used almost exclusively to show changes in
quantity over time, for example, the month-by-month production figures for
a product. A line graph focuses the reader's attention on the change in quantity, whereas a bar graph emphasizes the quantities themselves.

You can plot three or four lines on a line graph. If the lines intersect, use
different colors or patterns to distinguish them. If the lines intersect too often,
however, the graph will be unclear; in this case, draw separate graphs. Figure
14.13 shows a line graph.

Million Barrels per Day

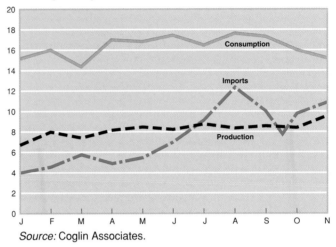

Source: Coglin Associates.

Figure 1. U.S. Petroleum Consumption, Production,
and Imports, January–November 2000

■ **Figure 14.13   Line Graph**

The writer has used different colors and patterns to distinguish the lines.

GUIDELINES

Creating Effective Line Graphs

▸ *If possible, begin the quantity scale at zero.* Doing so is the best way to portray the information honestly. If you cannot begin at zero, clearly indicate a break in the axis.

▸ *Use reasonable proportions for the vertical and horizontal axes.* As with bar graphs, try to make the vertical axis about 25 percent shorter than the horizontal axis.

▸ *Use grid lines—horizontal, vertical, or both—rather than tick marks when your readers need to read the quantities precisely.*

Pie Charts   The *pie chart* is a simple but limited design used for showing the relative size of the parts of a whole. Figure 14.14 (Mankiw, 1997, p. 37) shows a typical example.

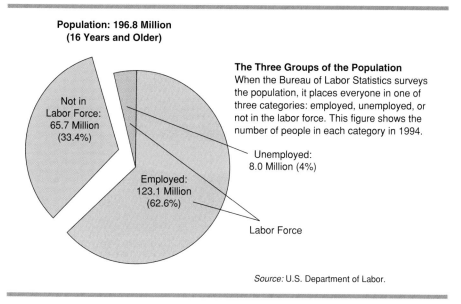

Population: 196.8 Million
(16 Years and Older)

Not in
Labor Force:
65.7 Million
(33.4%)

The Three Groups of the Population
When the Bureau of Labor Statistics surveys
the population, it places everyone in one of
three categories: employed, unemployed, or
not in the labor force. This figure shows the
number of people in each category in 1994.

Unemployed:
8.0 Million (4%)

Employed:
123.1 Million
(62.6%)

Labor Force

Source: U.S. Department of Labor.

■ **Figure 14.14   Pie Chart**

Creating Effective Pie Charts

▶ *Restrict the number of slices to six or seven.* As the slices get smaller, judging their relative sizes becomes more difficult.

▶ *Begin with the largest slice at the top and work clockwise in decreasing size order, unless you have a good reason to arrange them otherwise.*

▶ *Include a miscellaneous slice for very small quantities that would make the chart unclear.* Explain its contents in a footnote. This slice, sometimes called "other," follows the other sections.

▶ *Label the slices (horizontally, not radially) inside the slice, if space permits.* Include the percentage that each slice represents and, if appropriate, the raw numbers.

▶ *To emphasize one slice, use a bright, contrasting color or separate the slice from the pie.* Do this, for example, when you introduce a discussion of the item represented by that slice.

▶ *Check to see that your software follows the appropriate guidelines for pie charts.* Some software adds fancy visual effects that can hurt comprehension. For instance, many programs portray the pie in three dimensions, as shown here.

In this three-dimensional pie chart about the percentages of a college's student body, by year, the sophomore slice looks bigger than the freshman slice, even though it isn't, because it appears closer to the reader. To communicate clearly, make the pies two dimensional.

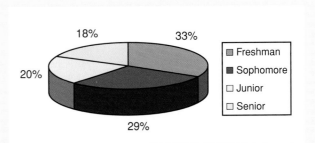

▶ *Don't overdo fill patterns.* Fill patterns are designs, shades, or colors that distinguish one slice from another. In general, use simple, understated patterns, or none.

▶ *Check that your percentages add up to 100.* If you are doing the calculations yourself, check your math.

Illustrating Logical Relationships

Graphics can help you present logical relationships among items. For instance, in describing a piece of hardware, you might want to show its major components. The two kinds of graphics most useful in showing logical relationships are diagrams and organization charts.

Diagrams   A *diagram* is a visual metaphor that uses symbols to represent items or their properties. In technical communication, common kinds of diagrams are blueprints, wiring diagrams, and schematics. Figure 14.15 is a schematic diagram.

A popular form of diagram is the block diagram, in which simple geometric shapes, usually rectangles, suggest logical relationships. In Figure 14.16, the block diagram is much clearer than the prose version of the same information.

Organization Charts   An *organization chart* is a block diagram that portrays the lines of authority and responsibility in an organization. In most cases, the positions are represented by rectangles. Figure 14.17 on page 346 is a typical organization chart.

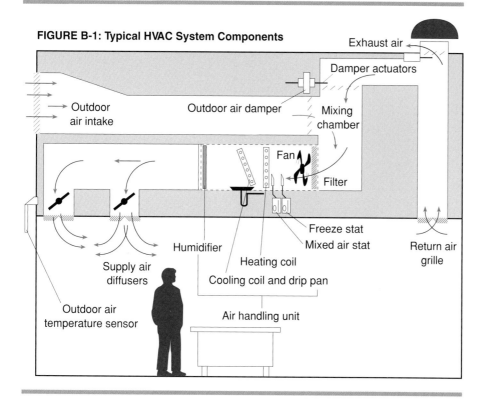

FIGURE B-1: Typical HVAC System Components

The artist has used visual symbols, such as the fan and the filter, to represent components working together.

The clip art of the person helps clarify the location and size of the HVAC equipment.

■ **Figure 14.15   Schematic Diagram**

Although the silhouette of the person looks realistic, the HVAC system itself is drawn to show its function, not its actual appearance.
Source: U.S. Environmental Protection Agency, 1991, p. 124.

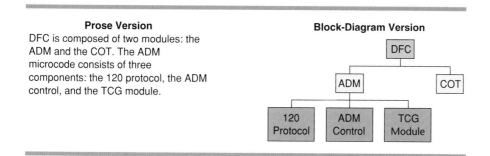

Prose Version

DFC is composed of two modules: the ADM and the COT. The ADM microcode consists of three components: the 120 protocol, the ADM control, and the TCG module.

Block-Diagram Version

■ **Figure 14.16   Block Diagram and Prose Description**

Unlike most other figures, the title of an organization chart generally appears above the chart because the chart is read from the top down.

In this organization chart, different levels are distinguished by color. Levels can also be distinguished by the size of the boxes, the width of the lines that form the boxes, or the typeface. If space permits, the boxes can contain brief descriptions of the positions, duties, or responsibilities.

■ **Figure 14.17 Organization Chart**

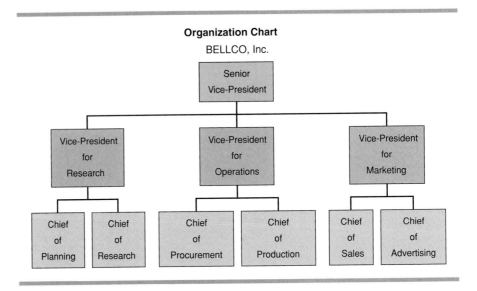

Illustrating Process Descriptions and Instructions

Graphics often accompany process descriptions (Chapter 9) and instructions (Chapter 20). The following discussion looks at some of the graphics used in writing about actions: checklists, tables, flowcharts, logic boxes, and logic trees.

Checklists In explaining how to carry out a task, you often need to show the reader what equipment or materials to gather, or describe an action or series of actions to take. A *checklist* is simply a list of items, each preceded by a check box. If readers might be unfamiliar with the items you are listing, include drawings of the items, as shown in Figure 14.18.

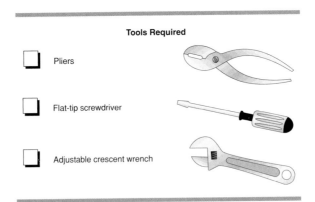

■ **Figure 14.18 Checklist**

SMART GUIDE

MAINTENANCE SCHEDULE INTERVALS				MAINTENANCE SCHEDULE SERVICES					
Months	Kilometers	Months	Kilometers	1	2	3	4	5	6
03	5,000	51	85,000						
06	10,000	54	90,000						
09	15,000	57	95,000						
12	20,000	60	100,000						
15	25,000	63	105,000						
18	30,000	66	110,000						
21	35,000	69	115,000						
24	40,000	72	120,000						
27	45,000	75	125,000						
30	50,000	78	130,000						
33	55,000	81	135,000						
36	60,000	84	140,000						
39	65,000	87	145,000						
42	70,000	90	150,000						
45	75,000	93	155,000						
48	80,000	96	160,000						

Maintenance Schedule Services box:
- Lube, Oil and Filter Service* with 15 point inspection
- Powertrain/Chassis Component Inspection (includes Goodwrench Tire Rotation and Goodwrench Brake Inspection)

This Web-based maintenance schedule uses colors and a table. To learn what services are required, the user holds the cursor over the appropriate colored tab. In this case, the user is finding out what services are needed at six months by holding the cursor over the blue tab.

■ **Figure 14.19   A Table Used to Illustrate a Maintenance Schedule**

Source: General Motors of Canada, 2002 <www.gmcanada.com/english/maintenance/goodwrench /gw_smartguide.html>.

Often you need to indicate that your reader is to carry out certain tasks at certain intervals. A table is a useful graphic for this kind of information, as illustrated in Figure 14.19.

Flowcharts   A *flowchart*, as the name suggests, shows the various stages of a process or a procedure. Flowcharts are useful, too, for summarizing instructions. On a basic flowchart, stages are represented by labeled geometric shapes. Flowcharts can portray open systems (those that have a "start" and a "finish") or closed systems (those that end where they began).

Figure 14.20 is an open-system flowchart that shows the stages of a procedure.

Figure 14.21 shows a closed-system flowchart used to portray a process.

Logic Boxes and Logic Trees   *Logic boxes* guide the reader along one of two or more decision paths. Figure 14.22 on page 349 shows a typical example.

Logic trees are like logic boxes but use a branching metaphor. The logic tree shown in Figure 14.23 on page 349 helps students think through the process of registering for a course.

On TechComm Web

To view Fig. 14.22 in context on the Web, click on Links Library for Ch. 14 on <bedfordstmartins.com /techcomm>.

Figure A. Can You Deduct Business Use of the Home Expenses?*

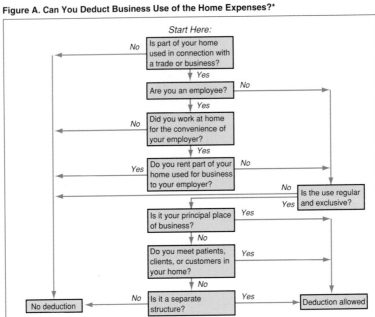

Start Here:

Is part of your home used in connection with a trade or business? — No / Yes

Are you an employee? — No / Yes

Did you work at home for the convenience of your employer? — No / Yes

Do you rent part of your home used for business to your employer? — Yes / No

Is the use regular and exclusive? — No / Yes

Is it your principal place of business? — Yes / No

Do you meet patients, clients, or customers in your home? — Yes / No

No deduction — No / Is it a separate structure? — Yes — Deduction allowed

* Do not use this chart if you use your home for the storage of inventory or product samples, or to operate a day-care facility. See *Exceptions to Exclusive Use,* earlier, and *Day-Care Facility,* later.

■ **Figure 14.20 An Open-System Flowchart Used to Portray a Procedure**

Source: U.S. Department of the Treasury, 1999 <http://ftp .fedworld.gov/pub/irs-pdf/p587 .pdf>.

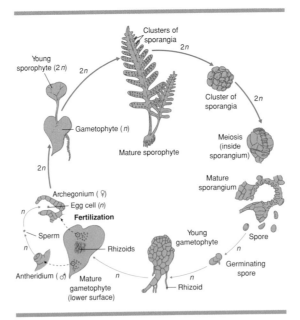

Clusters of sporangia

Young sporophyte (2n)

Gametophyte (n)

Mature sporophyte

Cluster of sporangia

Meiosis (inside sporangium)

Mature sporangium

Archegonium (♀)

Egg cell (n)

Fertilization

Sperm

Rhizoids

Antheridium (♂)

Mature gametophyte (lower surface)

Rhizoid

Young gametophyte

Germinating spore

Spore

■ **Figure 14.21 A Closed-System Flowchart Used to Portray a Process**

Source: Curtis & Barnes, 1989, p. 251.

Do you want to replace all occurrences of the first word with the second word?		
YES	NO	
Press Y. The computer replaces all occurrences of the first word with the second word.	Press N. The cursor moves to the next occurrence of the word.	
	Do you want to replace that occurrence of the word?	
	YES	NO
	Press SHIFT/F2.	Press F2.
	Press F4 to move the cursor to the next occurrence of the word. Then press SHIFT/F2 or F2, as you did above, to replace that occurrence of the word or to leave it as is.	
Do you want to use the search function again?		
YES	NO	
Press F8.	Press F10.	

■ **Figure 14.22**
Logic Boxes

Logic boxes can contain a lot of textual information. However, some readers might have trouble understanding how to read them.

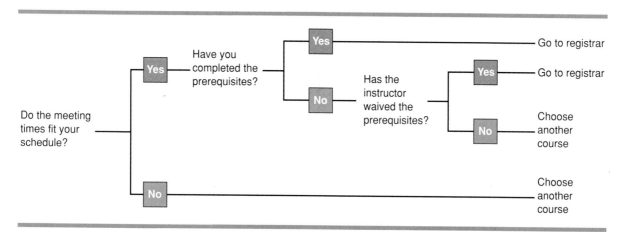

■ **Figure 14.23   Logic Trees**

Logic trees are probably somewhat easier to understand than logic boxes because the tree metaphor is visually more distinct than the box metaphor. However, logic trees cannot handle as much textual information as logic boxes can.

Illustrating Visual and Spatial Characteristics

To illustrate visual and spatial characteristics, use photographs, screen shots, line drawings, and maps.

Photographs   *Photographs* are unmatched for reproducing visual detail. Sometimes, however, a photograph can provide too much information. In an advertising brochure for an automobile, a glossy photograph of the dashboard might be very effective. But in an owner's manual, if you want to show how to use the trip odometer, a diagram will probably work better because it focuses on that one item.

Sometimes a photograph can provide too little information; the item you want to highlight might be located inside the mechanism or obscured by some other component.

GUIDELINES

Presenting Photographs Effectively

▶ *Eliminate extraneous background clutter that can distract your reader.* Crop the photograph or digitize it and delete unnecessary detail. Figure 14.24 shows examples of cropped and uncropped photographs.

▶ *Do not electronically manipulate the photograph.* There is nothing unethical about digitizing a photograph, removing blemishes, and cropping it. However, manipulating a photograph—for example, enlarging the size of the monitor that comes with a computer system—is unethical.

▶ *Help the reader understand the perspective.* Most objects in magazines and journals are photographed at an angle to show the object's depth as well as its height and width.

▶ *If appropriate, include some common object, such as a coin or a ruler, in the photograph to give readers a sense of scale.*

▶ *If appropriate, label components or important features.*

■ **Figure 14.24   Cropping a Photograph**

Cropping a photograph lets you direct the reader's attention to the important information. The image on the right is a cropped and enlarged version of the photo on the left.
Source: NASA, 1977 <http://images.jsc.nasa.gov/images/pao/ALT/10076588.jpg>.

Screen Shots *Screen shots*—images of what appears on the computer monitor—are often used in software manuals to show the reader what the screen looks like at various points during the use of a program. Figure 14.25 is an example of a screen shot.

Opening a
Workbook

602Tab can open many file types. It specializes in opening Excel files. To open a compatible file press the Open button or use the Open dialog in the File menu. If a file has been associated to 602Tab, you may double click on that file to open it in 602Tab.

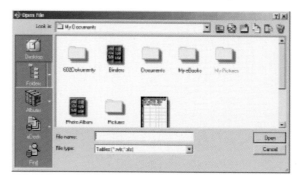

In this portion of a page from a user manual for a Software602 product, the writer uses a screen shot to help orient readers. The screen shot gives readers confidence that they are performing the task correctly.

Note that screen shots cannot explain conceptual information. In this example, explanatory text following the screen shot explains the five buttons to the left in the screen shot.

The five buttons in the left section of the dialogue allow you to choose the way files and folders are viewed and the source of the file in the Open dialogue:
* **Desktop**–displays the documents or folders that are on the Windows desktop. It also displays the **My Computer** icon and **Network neighborhood** icon from which you can access documents on a local drive or network folder.

■ **Figure 14.25 Screen Shot**

Source: Software602, Inc., 2002 <http://download.software602.com/pdf/pcs/2001/602tab_manual.pdf>.

Line Drawings *Line drawings* are simplified visual representations of objects. Line drawings can have three advantages over photographs:

* Line drawings can focus the reader's attention on desired information better than a photograph can.
* Line drawings can highlight information that might be obscured by bad lighting or a bad angle in a photograph.
* Line drawings are sometimes easier for readers to understand than photographs are.

Figure 14.26 shows the effectiveness of line drawings.

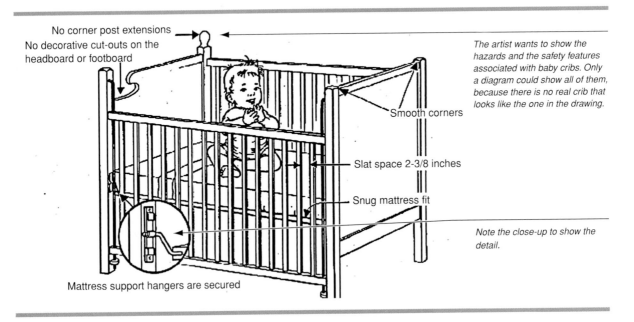

No corner post extensions
No decorative cut-outs on the
headboard or footboard

The artist wants to show the hazards and the safety features associated with baby cribs. Only a diagram could show all of them, because there is no real crib that looks like the one in the drawing.

Smooth corners

Slat space 2-3/8 inches

Snug mattress fit

Note the close-up to show the detail.

Mattress support hangers are secured

■ **Figure 14.26   Line Drawing**

Source: U.S. Consumer Product Safety Commission, 1999 <www.cpsc.gov/cpscpub/pubs/usedcrib.pdf>.

You have probably seen the three variations on the basic line drawing shown in Figure 14.27.

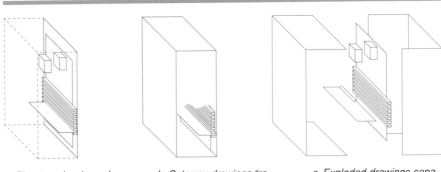

a. Phantom drawings show parts hidden from view by outlining external items that would ordinarily obscure them.

b. Cutaway drawings "remove" a part of the surface to expose what is underneath.

c. Exploded drawings separate components while maintaining their physical relationship.

■ **Figure 14.27   Phantom, Cutaway, and Exploded Views**

Maps   Maps are readily available as clip art that can be modified with a graphics program. Figure 14.28 shows a map derived from clip art.

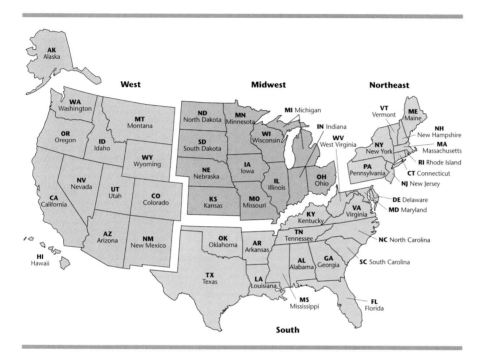

■ **Figure 14.28   Map**

Include a scale and a legend if the map is one that is not thoroughly familiar to your readers. Also, use conventional colors, such as blue for water.

Showing Motion in Your Graphics

In technical documents, you will often want to show motion. For instance, in an instruction manual for military-helicopter technicians, you might want to illustrate the process of removing an oil dipstick or tightening a bolt, or you might want to show a warning light flashing. Although document designers frequently use animation or video, printed graphics are still needed to communicate this kind of information.

If the reader is to perform the action, show the action from the reader's point of view, as in Figure 14.29.

Figure 14.30 illustrates four additional techniques for showing action. These symbols are conventional but not universal. If you are addressing readers from another culture, consult a qualified person from that culture to make sure your symbols are clear and inoffensive.

■ **Figure 14.29**
Showing the Action from the Reader's Perspective

In many cases, you need to show only the person's hands, not the whole body.

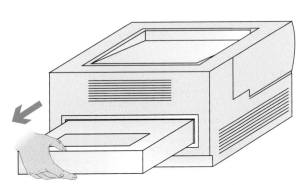

a. Use arrows or other symbols to suggest the direction in which something is moving or should be moved.

c. Shake lines suggest vibration.

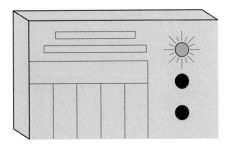

b. Starburst lines suggest a blinking light.

d. An image of an object both before and after the action suggests the action.

■ **Figure 14.30   Showing Motion**

In This Book

For more on multicultural audiences, see Ch. 5, p. 87, and Ch. 11, p. 259.

STRATEGIES FOR INTERCULTURAL COMMUNICATION

Creating Effective Graphics for Multicultural Readers

Whether you are writing for people within your organization or outside it, consider the needs of readers whose first language is different from your own. Like words, graphics have cultural meanings. If you are unaware of these meanings, you could communicate something very different from what you intend. The following guidelines are based on William Horton's (1993) article "The Almost Universal Language: Graphics for International Documents."

- *Be aware that reading patterns differ.* In some countries, people read from right to left or from top to bottom. In some cultures, direction signifies value: the right-hand side is superior to the left, or the reverse. You need to think about how to sequence graphics that show action, or where you put "before" and "after" graphics. If you want to show a direction, as in an informal flowchart, consider using arrows to indicate how to read the chart.

- *Be aware of varying cultural attitudes toward giving instruction.* Instructions for products made in Japan are highly polite and deferential: "Please attach the cable at this time." Some cultures favor spelling out general principles but leaving the reader to supply the details. For people in these cultures, instructions containing a detailed close-up of how to carry out a task might appear insulting. An instructional table with the headings "When You See This . . ." and "Do This . . ." might be inappropriate.

- *Deemphasize trivial details.* Because common objects, such as plugs on the ends of power cords, come in different shapes around the world, draw them to look generic rather than specific to one country.

- *Avoid culture-specific language, symbols, and references.* Don't use a picture of a mouse to symbolize a computer mouse, because the device is not known by that name everywhere. Avoid the casual use of national symbols (such as the maple leaf or national flags), because you might make an error in a detail that would insult your readers. Use colors carefully: red means danger to most people from Western cultures, but it is a celebratory color to the Chinese.

- *Portray people very carefully.* Every aspect of a person's appearance, from clothing to hairstyle to features, is culture- or race-specific. A photograph of a woman in casual Western attire seated at a workstation would not be effective in an Islamic culture, where only the hands and eyes of a woman may be shown. Horton (1993) recommends using stick figures or silhouettes that do not suggest any one culture, race, or gender.

- *Be particularly careful in portraying hand gestures.* Many Western hand gestures, such as the "okay" sign, are considered obscene in other cultures, and long red fingernails would also be inappropriate. Use hands in graphics only when necessary, for example, carrying out a task, and obscure the person's sex and race.

Cultural differences are many and subtle. Learn as much as possible about your readers and about their culture and outlook, and make sure to have the graphics reviewed by a native of the culture.

UNDERSTANDING GRAPHICS SOFTWARE

Graphics software available for the personal computer falls into two categories: spreadsheet business graphics, and paint programs and draw programs.

Spreadsheet Business Graphics

Spreadsheet programs—software designed for calculating budgets and evaluating hypothetical business scenarios—can be used to produce business graphics. Once you have typed in numerical data, such as the profits and losses of the divisions of your company, you can have the software display the data in various kinds of graphics and charts.

Spreadsheets generate different kinds of displays in both two-dimensional and three-dimensional formats. You then add labels and a title and customize the graphic to suit your needs. Figure 14.31 shows how data entered on a spreadsheet can be displayed as a table and then as a bar chart. Most spreadsheets can display the same numerical data in dozens of styles of graphics.

Keep in mind that the software doesn't provide advice on the kind of graphic to make or how to modify the basic presentation—it simply draws whatever you tell it to—and it often makes poor choices: unnecessary 3-D, useless clip art, and lurid color combinations. To use the graphics capabilities effectively, you need to understand the basics of the various kinds of graphics.

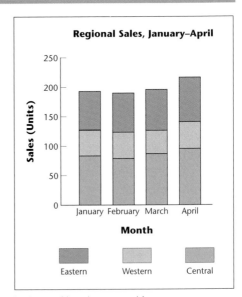

	A	B	C	D
1		Eastern	Western	Central
2	January	83.5	43.7	65.6
3	February	78.9	44.6	66.3
4	March	86.7	39.5	69.5
5	April	95.3	45.7	75.4

a. Spreadsheet data

b. Grouped bar chart created from the spreadsheet data

■ **Figure 14.31**
Creating a Graphic from a Spreadsheet

Paint Programs and Draw Programs

Paint programs and *draw programs* let you produce and then modify freehand drawings in a number of ways. For instance, you can

- modify the width of lines
- modify the size of shapes
- copy, rotate, and flip images
- fill in shapes with different colors and textures
- add text with a simple text editor

With both kinds of programs, you can begin in one of three ways:

- by drawing on a blank screen
- by importing an image from a clip-art library
- by scanning an image, which involves using a piece of hardware—a scanner—and a special software program that translates a graphic into a digital image

You probably already have a paint program in your computer operating system and a draw program in your word processor. These programs are not professional-level, but they are powerful enough to create many kinds of graphics.

Revision Checklist

This checklist focuses on the characteristics of an effective graphic.

❏ Does the graphic have a purpose? (p. 321)
❏ Is the graphic honest? (p. 321)
❏ Is the graphic simple and uncluttered? (p. 321)
❏ Does the graphic present a manageable amount of information? (p. 321)
❏ Does the graphic meet the reader's format expectations? (p. 321)
❏ Is the graphic clearly labeled? (p. 322)

❏ Does the graphic appear in a logical location in the document? (p. 322)
❏ Is the graphic introduced clearly in the text? (p. 322)
❏ Is the graphic explained in the text? (p. 323)
❏ Is the graphic clearly visible in the text? (p. 323)
❏ Is the graphic easily accessible to your readers? (p. 323)
❏ For an existing graphic, do you have the legal right to use it? (p. 325) If so, have you cited it appropriately? (p. 326)
❏ Is the graphic inoffensive to your readers? (p. 354)

Exercises

On TechComm Web

For more exercises, click on Additional Exercises, Projects, and Cases for Ch. 14 on <bedfordstmartins.com/techcomm>.

1. Find out from the admissions department at your college or university the number of students enrolled from the different states or from the different counties in your state. Present this information in four different kinds of graphics:

   a. a map
   b. a table
   c. a bar graph
   d. a pie chart

In three or four paragraphs, explain why each graphic is appropriate for a particular audience and purpose, and how each emphasizes different aspects of the information.

2. Design a flowchart for a process you are familiar with, such as applying for a summer job, studying for a test, preparing a paper, or performing some task at work. Your audience is someone who will be carrying out the process.

3. The following table (U.S. Bureau of the Census, 2002, p. 140) provides statistics on disabilities. Study the table, then perform the following tasks:

a. Create two different graphics, each of which communicates information about the cost of lost wages and productivity.

b. Create two different graphics, each of which compares wage and productivity losses to the total of other losses due to unintentional injuries.

No. 180. Costs of Unintentional Injuries: 1999

[469.0 represents $469,000,000,000. Covers costs of deaths or disabling injuries together with vehicle accidents and fires]

Cost	Amount (bil. dol.)					Percent distribution				
	Total[1]	Motor vehicle	Work	Home	Other	Total[1]	Motor vehicle	Work	Home	Other
Total..	469.0	181.5	122.6	101.7	78.4	100.0	100.0	100.0	100.0	100.0
Wage and productivity losses[2].........	245.6	66.1	63.9	66.7	52.5	52.4	36.4	52.1	65.6	67.0
Medical expense................................	77.4	20.1	19.9	21.8	16.7	16.5	11.1	16.2	21.4	21.3
Administrative expenses[3]................	77.6	53.3	23.5	4.6	4.3	16.5	29.4	19.2	4.5	5.5
Motor vehicle damage.....................	40.2	40.2	2.0	(NA)	(NA)	8.6	22.1	1.6	(NA)	(NA)
Employer cost[4]................................	20.0	1.8	11.0	4.2	3.4	4.3	1.0	9.0	4.1	4.3
Fire loss..	8.2	(NA)	2.3	4.4	1.5	1.7	(NA)	1.9	4.3	1.9

NA Not available.   [1] Excludes duplication between work and motor vehicle ($15.2 billion in 1999).   [2] Actual loss of wages and household production, and the present value of future earnings lost.   [3] Home and other costs may include costs of administering medical treatment claims for some motor-vehicle injuries filed through health insurance plans.   [4] Estimates of the uninsured costs incurred by employers, representing the money value of time lost by noninjured workers.

Source of Tables 179 and 180: National Safety Council, Itasca, IL, *Injury Facts, 2000 Edition* (copyright).

4. For each of the following four graphics, write a paragraph evaluating its effectiveness and describing how you would revise it.

a.

	2000	2001	2002
Civil Engineering	236	231	253
Chemical Engineering	126	134	142
Comparative Literature	97	86	74
Electrical Engineering	317	326	401
English	714	623	592
Fine Arts	112	96	72
Foreign Languages	608	584	566
Materials Engineering	213	227	241
Mechanical Engineering	196	203	201
Other	46	42	51
Philosophy	211	142	151
Religion	86	91	72

b.

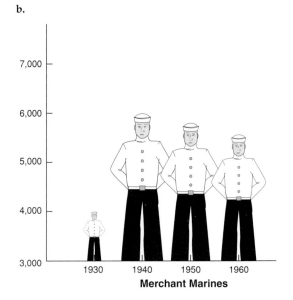

Merchant Marines

c.

Expenses at Hillway Corporation

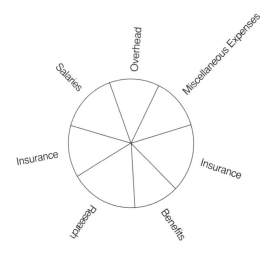

d.

Costs of the Components of a PC

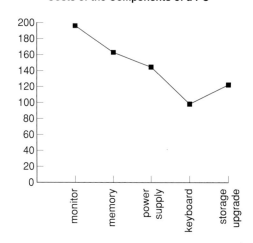

5. The following three graphs illustrate the sales of two products—Series 1 and Series 2—for each quarter of 2002. Which is the most effective in conveying the information? Which is the least effective? What additional information would make the best graph better?

a.

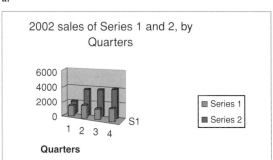

b.

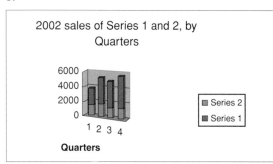

c.

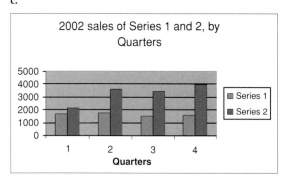

Projects

On TechComm Web

For more projects, click on Additional Exercises, Projects, and Cases for Ch. 14 on <bedfordstmartins.com/techcomm>.

6. **Group Activity** Form small groups. Go to one of the campus computer labs and study a popular piece of software, such as a spreadsheet or graphics package. Have each group member, working separately, print out three of the basic kinds of graphics, such as graphs, tables, and pie charts, and take notes on the process. Come together as a group and share your experiences in learning how to use the software. What techniques did you try: using a tutorial, reading a manual, trial-and-error, asking someone for help? If appropriate, have the group go back to the labs together and work through some of the questions that arose in the group meeting. Write a memo to your instructor describing how easy or how difficult it was to learn how to produce these graphics and evaluate their quality. How well do the graphics conform to the basic guidelines presented in this chapter? Would you recommend the software to other members of your class? Why or why not? (For more on memos, see Chapter 15, page 378.)

7. **Internet Activity** Locate a graphic on the Web that you consider inappropriate for an international audience because it might be offensive or unclear in some cultures. Imagine an intended audience for the graphic, such as people from the Middle East, and write a brief statement explaining the potential problem. Finally, revise the graphic so that it would be appropriate for its intended audience.

On TechComm Web

For more cases, click on Additional Exercises, Projects, and Cases for Ch. 14 on <bedfordstmartins.com /techcomm>.

C A S E
Evaluating Graphics on a Web Site

You are a student intern working for Marshall Brain at his Web site, How Stuff Works <www.howstuffworks.com>. He has asked you to evaluate the effectiveness of the graphics on the site. Select one of the topics, such as How Web Pages Work, then analyze Brain's use of graphics. Are there enough graphics to illustrate the topic? Are the graphics clear and informative? Are they well integrated with the text on the pages? What changes would you recommend? Write a memo to Marshall Brain presenting your conclusions and recommendations. If appropriate, attach copies of excerpts from the site. (For more on memos, see Chapter 15, page 378.)

PART FIVE

APPLICATIONS

Writing Letters, Memos, and E-mails 15

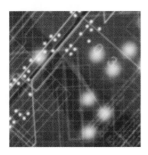

Joel Bowman (1999), a business-communication scholar, on persuasion in business correspondence:

Whenever you are writing to someone who has no compelling reason to do (or think) as you ask in your message—and perhaps even no reason to read or reply to it—you need to write a persuasive message. How persuasive you need to be depends on how obvious it is to your reader that he or she stands to benefit from acting (or thinking) in the manner you suggest.

On TechComm Web

For additional samples, activities, and links related to this chapter, see <bedfordstmartins.com/techcomm>.

This chapter focuses on the three formats used for correspondence in the working world:

- *Letters.* The oldest, most formal of the three formats, letters always conclude with a signature in ink. Letters are most often addressed to someone in another organization, not in the writer's own organization. Today, letters are often sent by fax.

- *Memos.* Because memos are less formal and shorter than letters, they are used most often for communication among those within one organization.

- *E-mails.* E-mail is replacing many memos because it offers all of the advantages of digital communication: the writer can send an e-mail to dozens, or even thousands, of readers instantly and effortlessly; and the recipient can store and revise an e-mail easily. Though e-mail is generally the least formal of the three, it still needs to be professional and free of errors.

WRITING LETTERS

On TechComm Web

For more about letter writing, search for "business letters" at Purdue University's OWL. Click on Links Library for Ch. 15 on <bedfordstmartins.com/techcomm>.

Letters are still a basic means of communication between organizations: millions are written each workday. Writing a letter is much like writing any other technical document. First you have to analyze your audience and determine your purpose. Then you have to gather your information, make an outline, write a draft, and revise it.

Projecting the "You Attitude"

A letter must convey a courteous, positive tone. The key to an effective letter is the *you attitude:* looking at the situation from your reader's point of view and adjusting the content, structure, and tone to meet the person's needs. If, for example, you are writing to a supplier who has failed to deliver some merchandise on the agreed-upon date, the you attitude dictates that you not discuss problems you are having with other suppliers—those problems don't concern your reader. Rather, you should concentrate on explaining clearly and politely that your reader has violated your agreement and that not having the merchandise is costing you money. Then you should propose ways to expedite the shipment.

Following are examples of thoughtless sentences, each followed by an improved version that exhibits the you attitude.

ACCUSING	You must have dropped the engine. The housing is badly cracked.
BETTER	The badly cracked housing suggests that your engine must have fallen onto a hard surface from some height.
SARCASTIC	You'll need two months to deliver these parts? Who do you think you are, the Post Office?
BETTER	Surely you would find a two-month delay for the delivery of parts unacceptable in your business. That's how I feel too.
BELLIGERENT	I'm sure you have a boss, and I doubt if he'd like to hear about how you've mishandled our account.
BETTER	I'm sure you would prefer to settle the account between us rather than have it brought to your supervisor's attention.

When you draft a letter, put yourself in your reader's place. A calm, respectful tone makes the best impression and increases the chances that you will achieve your goal.

Avoiding Letter Clichés

Over the decades, a set of words and phrases has come to be associated with business letters; one common example is *as per your request*. These phrases sound stilted and insincere. If you would feel awkward or uncomfortable saying these clichés to a friend, avoid them in your letters.

Figure 15.1 is a list of the common clichés and their more natural equivalents.

Figure 15.2 shows two versions of the same letter: one written in clichés, the other in plain language.

In This Book

For more on choosing the right words and phrases, see Ch. 11, p. 248.

Letter Clichés	Natural Equivalents
attached please find	attached is
enclosed please find	enclosed is
pursuant to our agreement	as we agreed
referring to your ("referring to your letter of March 19, the shipment of pianos . . . ")	"As you wrote in your letter of March 19, the . . ." (or subordinate the reference at the end of your sentence)
wish to advise ("We wish to advise that . . . ")	(The phrase doesn't say anything. Just say what you want to say.)
the writer ("The writer believes that . . . ")	"I believe . . . "

■ **Figure 15.1**
Letter Clichés and Natural Equivalents

Letter Containing Clichés	Letter in Natural Language
Dear Mr. Smith:	Dear Mr. Smith:
Referring to your letter regarding the problem encountered with your new Trailrider Snowmobile, our Customer Service Department has just submitted its report.	Thank you for writing to us about the problem with your new Trailrider Snowmobile.
It is their conclusion that the malfunction is caused by water being present in the fuel line. It is our conclusion that you must have purchased some bad gasoline. We trust you are cognizant of the fact that while we guarantee our snowmobiles for a period of not less than one year against defects in workmanship and materials, responsibility cannot be assumed for inadequate care. We wish to advise, for the reason mentioned hereinabove, that we cannot grant your request to repair the snowmobile free of charge.	Our Customer Service Department has found water in the fuel line. Apparently some of the gasoline was bad. While we guarantee our snowmobiles for one year against defects in workmanship and materials, we cannot assume responsibility for problems caused by bad gasoline. We cannot, therefore, grant your request to repair the snowmobile free of charge.
Permit me to say, however, that the writer would be pleased to see that the fuel line is flushed at cost, $30. Your Trailrider would then give you many years of trouble-free service.	However, no serious harm was done to the snowmobile. We would be happy to flush the fuel line at cost, $30. Your Trailrider would then give you many years of trouble-free service. If you will authorize us to do this work, we will have your snowmobile back to you within four working days. Just fill out the enclosed authorization card and drop it in the mail.
Enclosed please find an authorization card. Should we receive it, we shall perform the above-mentioned repair and deliver your snowmobile forthwith.	Sincerely yours,
Sincerely yours,	

■ **Figure 15.2**
Sample Letters with and Without Clichés

The letter on the right side avoids clichés and shows an understanding of the you attitude. Instead of focusing on the violation of the warranty, it presents the conclusion as good news: the snowmobile is not ruined, and it can be repaired and returned in less than a week for a small charge.

Understanding the Elements of the Letter

Almost every letter includes a heading, inside address, salutation, body, complimentary close, signature, and reference initials. Some letters also include one or more of the following: attention line, subject line, enclosure line, and copy line. Figure 15.3 shows the elements of a letter.

Learning the Format of the Letter

Three common formats are used for letters: modified block, modified block with paragraph indentations, and full block. Figure 15.4 on page 370 illustrates each of these three formats.

Understanding Common Types of Letters

Organizations send out many different kinds of letters. This section focuses on four types of letters written frequently in the technical workplace.

Inquiry Letter   Your purpose in writing an inquiry letter is to obtain information. If the recipient is expecting the letter, your task is simple. For example, if a company manufacturing institutional furniture has advertised that it will send its 48-page, full-color brochure to prospective clients, you need write merely a one-sentence letter: "Would you please send me the brochure advertised in *Higher Education Today*, May 13, 2003?" If you want to ask a technical question, or set of questions, about any product or service for sale, your inquiry letter might begin "We are considering purchasing your new X-15 workstations for an office staff of 35 and would like some further information. Would you please answer the following questions?"

If the recipient is not expecting the letter, however, your task is more difficult: you must ask a favor. Only careful, persuasive writing will make the recipient want to respond when no direct benefit or potential profit seems likely.

Figure 15.5 on page 371 shows an example of a letter of inquiry.

Common types of letters:

Inquiry

Response to an inquiry

Claim

Adjustment

In This Book

Two other types of letters are discussed in this book: the transmittal letter in Ch.12, p. 269, and the job-application letter in Ch. 16, p. 414.

In This Book

For more on persuasion, see Ch. 6.

GUIDELINES

Writing an Inquiry Letter

▶ *State why you are writing to the person or organization.* You might use subtle flattery—for example, "I was hoping that, as the leader in solid-state electronics, your company might be able to furnish some information about. . . ." Then explain why you want the information. You have to show that your interests are not commercial—for instance, "I will be using this information in a senior project in agronomy at Texas A&M. I am trying to devise a. . . ." If you need the information by a certain date, mention it: "The project is to be completed by April 15, 2003."

Heading. *Most organizations use letterhead stationery with their heading printed at the top. This preprinted information and the date the letter is sent make up the heading. If you are using blank paper rather than letterhead, your address [without your name] and the date form the heading. Use letterhead for the first page and do not number it. Use blank paper for the second and all subsequent pages.*

Inside Address. *If you are writing to an individual who has a professional title, such as Professor, Dr., or—for public officials—Honorable, use it. If not, use Mr. or Ms. (unless you know the recipient prefers Mrs. or Miss). If the reader's position fits on the same line as the name, add it after a comma; otherwise, drop it to the line below. Spell the name of the organization the way the organization itself does: for example, International Business Machines calls itself IBM. Include the complete mailing address: street number and name, city, state, and zip code.*

Attention Line. *Sometimes you will be unable to address a letter to a particular person because you don't know (and cannot easily find out) the name of the individual who holds that position in the company.*

Subject Line. *Use either a project number (for example, "Subject: Project 31402") or a brief phrase defining the subject (for example, "Subject: Price Quotation for the R13 Submersible Pump").*

Salutation. *The traditional salutation is* Dear, *followed by the reader's courtesy title and last name:* Dear Ms. Hawkins. *If you are unsure of the reader's name, you can write* Dear Sir or Madam. *If you are writing to a group, you can use* Ladies and Gentlemen. *Note that all salutations end with a colon, not a comma.*

DAVIS TREE CARE
1300 Lancaster Avenue
Berwyn, PA 19092
www.davisfortrees.com
(215) 555-9187

May 13, 2003

Fairlawn Industrial Park
1910 Ridgeway Drive
Rollins, PA 19063

Attention: Eric Smith, Director of Maintenance

Subject: Fall pruning

Dear Mr. Smith:

Do you know how much your trees are worth? That's right—your trees. As a maintenance director, you know how much of an investment your organization has in its physical plant. And the landscaping is a big part of your total investment.

Most people don't know that even the hardiest trees need periodic care. Like shrubs, trees should be fertilized and pruned. And they should be protected against the many kinds of diseases and pests that are common in this area.

At Davis Tree Care, we have the skills and experience to keep your trees healthy and beautiful. Our diagnostic staff is made up of graduates of major agricultural and forestry universities, and all of our crews attend special workshops to keep current with the latest information on tree maintenance. Add to this our proven record of 43 years of continuous service in the Berwyn area, and you have a company you can trust.

■ **Figure 15.3**
Elements of a Letter

Letter to Fairlawn Industrial Park
Page 2
May 13, 2003

May we stop by to give you an analysis of your trees—absolutely
without cost or obligation? A few minutes with one of our diagnos-
ticians could prove to be one of the wisest moves you've ever
made. Just give us a call at 555-9187 and we'll be happy to arrange
an appointment at your convenience.

Sincerely yours,

Jasmine Brown

Jasmine Brown
President

Enclosure: Davis Tree Care brochure

c: Darrell Davis, President

Header *for second page*

Body. *In most cases, the body contains at least three
paragraphs: an introductory paragraph, a concluding
paragraph, and one or more body paragraphs.*

Complimentary Close. *The conventional phrases*
Sincerely, Sincerely yours, Yours sincerely, Yours very
truly, *and* Very truly yours *are interchangeable.*

Signature. *Type your full name on the fourth line below
the complimentary close. Sign the letter, in ink, above
the typewritten name. Most organizations prefer that
you include your position under your typed name.*

Enclosure Line. *If the envelope contains documents
other than the letter, include an enclosure line that
indicates the number of enclosures. For more than one
enclosure, add the number: "Enclosures (2)." In
determining the number of enclosures, count only
separate items, not pages. A 3-page memo and a
10-page report constitute only two enclosures. Some
writers like to identify the enclosures:*

Enclosure: *2002 Placement Bulletin*
Enclosures (2):   *"This Year at Ammex"*
                    2002 Annual Report

Copy Line. *If you want the primary recipient to know
that other people are receiving a copy of the letter,
include a copy line. Use the symbol c (for "copy")
followed by the names of the other recipients (listed
either alphabetically or according to organizational
rank).*

■ **Figure 15.3**
(continued)

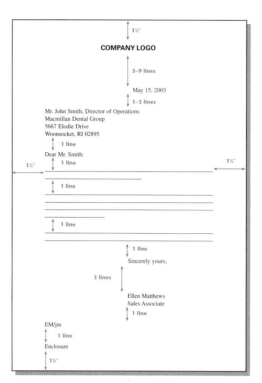

The dimensions and spacing shown here also apply to the other two formats.

a. Modified block format

Paragraphs are generally indented about one-half inch.

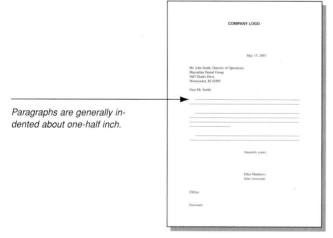

■ **Figure 15.4**
Common Letter Formats

b. Modified block with paragraph indentations

c. Full block style — everything aligned along the left margin

14 Hawthorne Ave.
Belleview, TX 75234
November 3, 2003

Dr. Andrew Shakir
Director of Technical Services
Orion Corporation
721 West Douglas Avenue
Maryville, TN 31409

Dear Dr. Shakir:

I am writing to you because of Orion's reputation as a leader in the manufacture of adjustable X-ray tables. I am a graduate student in biomedical engineering at the University of Texas, and I am working on an analysis of diagnostic equipment for a seminar paper. Would you be able to answer a few questions about your Microspot 311?

1. Can the Microspot 311 be used with lead oxide cassettes, or does it accept only lead-free cassettes?
2. Are standard generators compatible with the Microspot 311?
3. What would you say is the greatest advantage, for the operator, of using the Microspot 311? For the patient?

My project is due on January 15. I would greatly appreciate your assistance in answering these questions. Of course, I would be happy to send you a copy of my report when it is completed.

Yours very truly,

Albert K. Stern

Albert K. Stern

■ **Figure 15.5**
Inquiry Letter

▶ *Make your questions precise.* "Is your Model 311 compatible with Norwood's Model B12?" is better than "Would you please tell me about your Model 311?" If your questions can be answered briefly, leave space for a reply after each question or in the margin.

▶ *Offer something in return.* In many cases, all you can offer are the results of your research, but if so, say that you would be happy to send a copy of your final report. Express your appreciation: "I would greatly appreciate any help you could give me in answering these questions." Finally, if the answers will be brief, enclose a stamped self-addressed envelope to make it easy for the recipient to reply.

▶ *Always write a thank-you note to the person who has responded to your inquiry letter.*

Response to an Inquiry Letter   In responding to an inquiry letter, keep the following suggestions in mind. If the questions are numbered, number your responses to correspond. If you cannot answer the questions, either because you don't know the answers or because you cannot divulge proprietary information, explain the reasons and perhaps offer to assist with other requests. Figure 15.6 shows a response to the inquiry letter in Figure 15.5.

Claim Letter   A *claim letter* is a polite, reasonable complaint. If you purchase a defective or falsely advertised product, or receive inadequate service, you write a claim letter. Your purpose is to convince the recipient that you are a fair and honest customer who is justifiably dissatisfied. If the letter is convincing, your chances of receiving an equitable settlement are good because most organizations realize that unhappy customers are bad for business. In addition, claim letters help manufacturers identify weak points in their product or service.

GUIDELINES

Writing a Claim Letter

1. *Identify the product or service.* List model numbers, serial numbers, sizes, and any other pertinent data.

2. *Explain the problem.* State the symptoms clearly and specifically. What function does not work? What exactly is wrong with the service?

3. *Propose an adjustment.* Explain what you want the company to do: for example, refund the purchase price, replace or repair the item, improve the service.

4. *Conclude courteously.* You might suggest that you trust the company, in the interest of fairness, to agree to your proposed adjustment.

ORION

721 WEST DOUGLAS AVE.
MARYVILLE, TN 31409

(615) 619-8132
www.orioninstruments.com

November 7, 2003

Mr. Albert K. Stern
14 Hawthorne Ave.
Belleview, TX 75234

Dear Mr. Stern:

I would be pleased to answer your questions about the Microspot 311. We think it is the best unit of its type on the market today.

1. The 311 can handle lead oxide or lead-free cassettes.
2. At the moment, the 311 is fully compatible only with our Duramatic generator. However, special wiring kits are available to make the 311 compatible with our earlier generator models — the Olympus and the Saturn. We are currently working on other wiring kits.
3. For the operator, the 311 increases the effectiveness of the radiological procedure while at the same time cutting down the amount of film used. For the patient, it reduces the number of repeat exposures and therefore reduces the total dose.

I am enclosing a copy of our brochure on the Microspot 311. If you would like additional copies, please let me know. I would be happy to receive a copy of your analysis when it is complete. Good luck!

Sincerely yours,

Andrew Shakir, M.D.

Andrew Shakir, M.D.
Director of Technical Services

AS/le

Enclosure

c: Robert Anderson, Executive Vice-President

■ **Figure 15.6**
Response to an Inquiry
Letter

In a claim letter, you must project a calm, rational tone. "I'm sick and tired of being ripped off by companies like yours" is less effective than "I am very disappointed in the performance of the SureGrip masonry fasteners." There is no reason to show anger in a claim letter. Calmly explain what you plan to do, and why. The company will then be more likely to see the situation from your perspective. Figure 15.7 is an example of a claim letter that the writer faxed to the reader.

Adjustment Letter An *adjustment letter,* a response to a claim letter, tells the customer how you plan to handle the situation. Your purpose, whether you are granting the customer everything proposed in the claim letter, only part of it, or none of it, is to show that your organization is fair and reasonable, and that you value the customer's business.

If you can grant the request, the letter is easy to write. Express your regret about the situation, state the adjustment you are going to make, and end on a positive note by encouraging the customer to continue doing business with you.

If you cannot grant the request, salvage as much goodwill as you can by showing that you have acted reasonably. In denying a request, explain your side of the matter, thus educating the customer about how the problem occurred and how to prevent it in the future.

Figures 15.8 (page 376) and 15.9 (page 377) show examples of "good-news" and "bad-news" adjustment letters. The first is a reply to the claim letter shown in Figure 15.7.

On TechComm Web

For excellent advice on adjustment letters, see *Business Communication: Managing Information and Relationships.* Click on Links Library for Ch. 15 on <bedfordstmartins.com/techcomm>.

GUIDELINES

Writing a "Bad-News" Adjustment Letter

In this more difficult kind of adjustment letter, try to accomplish the following four tasks:

1. *Meet the customer on some neutral ground.* Express regret or even thank the customer for bringing the matter to your attention. But be careful about admitting that the customer is right. If you say "We are sorry that the engine you purchased from us is defective," it would bolster the customer's claim if the dispute ended up in court.

2. *Explain why your company is not at fault.* Most often, you explain to the customer the steps that led to the problem. Do not say "You caused this." Instead, use the more tactful passive voice: "Apparently, the air pressure was not monitored."

3. *State that your company is denying the request for the reasons you have noted.* If you begin with this statement, most readers will not finish reading, and you will not achieve your goals of education and goodwill.

4. *Create goodwill.* Close on a positive note. You might, for instance, offer a special discount on another, similar product.

ROBBINS CONSTRUCTION, INC.
255 Robbins Place, Centerville, MO 65101 (417) 555-1850
www.robbinsconstruction.com

August 19, 2003

Mr. David Larsyn
Larsyn Supply Company
311 Elmerine Avenue
Anderson, MO 63501

Dear Mr. Larsyn:

As steady customers of yours for over 15 years, we came to you first when we needed a quiet
pile driver for a job near a residential area. On your recommendation, we bought your Vista
500 Quiet Driver, at $14,900. We have since found, much to our embarrassment, that it is not
substantially quieter than a regular pile driver.

We received the contract to do the bridge repair here in Centerville after promising to keep
the noise to under 90 db during the day. The Vista 500 (see enclosed copy of bill of sale for
particulars) is rated at 85 db, maximum. We began our work and, although one of our workers
said the driver didn't seem sufficiently quiet to him, assured the people living near the job site
that we were well within the agreed sound limit. One of them, an acoustical engineer,
marched out the next day and demonstrated that we were putting out 104 db. Obviously,
something is wrong with the pile driver.

I think you will agree that we have a problem. We were able to secure other equipment, at
considerable inconvenience, to finish the job on schedule. When I telephoned your company
that humiliating day, however, a Mr. Meredith informed me that I should have done an
acoustical reading on the driver before I accepted delivery.

I would like you to send out a technician — as soon as possible — either to repair the driver so
that it performs according to specifications or to take it back for a full refund.

Yours truly,

Jack Robbins

Jack Robbins, President

Enclosure

■ **Figure 15.7**
Claim Letter

Larsyn Supply Company
311 Elmerine Avenue
Anderson, MO 63501
www.larsynsupply.com

August 21, 2003

Mr. Jack Robbins, President
Robbins Construction, Inc.
255 Robbins Place
Centerville, MO 65101

Dear Mr. Robbins:

I was very unhappy to read your letter of August 19 telling me about the failure of the Vista 500. I regretted most the treatment you received from one of my employees when you called us.

Harry Rivers, our best technician, has already been in touch with you to arrange a convenient time to come out to Centerville to talk with you about the driver. We will of course repair it, replace it, or refund the price. Just let us know your wish.

I realize that I cannot undo the damage that was done on the day that a piece of our equipment failed. To make up for some of the extra trouble and expense you incurred, let me offer you a 10 percent discount on your next purchase or service order with us, up to a $1,000 total discount.

You have indeed been a good customer for many years, and I would hate to have this unfortunate incident spoil that relationship. Won't you give us another chance? Just bring in this letter when you visit us next, and we'll give you that 10 percent discount.

Sincerely,

Dave Larsyn

Dave Larsyn, President

■ **Figure 15.8**
"Good-News" Adjustment
Letter

QUALITY STORAGE MEDIA
2077 Highland
Burley, ID 84765
www.qualstorage.com

February 3, 2003

Mr. Dale Devlin
1903 Highland Avenue
Glenn Mills, NE 69032

Dear Mr. Devlin:

Thank you for writing us about the portable disk you purchased on January 11, 2003. I know from personal experience how frustrating it is when a disk fails.

According to your letter, you used the disk to store the business plan for your new consulting business. When you attempted to copy that file to your hard drive, the portable disk failed, and the business plan was lost. You have no other copy of that file. You are asking us to reimburse you $1,500 for the cost of re-creating that business plan from notes and rough drafts.

As you know, our disks carry a lifetime guarantee covering parts and workmanship. We will gladly replace the defective portable disk. However, the guarantee states that the manufacturer and the retailer will not assume any incidental liability. Thus we are responsible only for the retail value of the blank disk, not for the cost of duplicating the work that went into making the files stored on the disk.

However, your file might still be recoverable. A reputable data-recovery firm might be able to restore the data from the file at a very reasonable cost. To prevent such problems in the future, we always recommend that you back up all valuable files periodically.

We have already sent out your new portable disk by overnight delivery. It should arrive within the next two days.

Please contact us if we can be of any further assistance.

Sincerely yours,

Paul R. Blackwood

Paul R. Blackwood, Manager
Customer Relations

Enclosure

■ **Figure 15.9**
"Bad-News" Adjustment
Letter

Writing effective memos:

Analyze your audience.

Include the identifying
information.

Clearly state your
purpose.

Use headings to help your
readers.

If appropriate, summarize
your message.

Provide adequate back-
ground for the discussion.

Organize the discussion.

Highlight action items.

WRITING MEMOS

The memo is a means of communication that is likely to survive even in the age of e-mail. The following discussion explains how to write effective memos.

Analyze Your Audience

Think about your readers—who they are and what they know and think about your subject—as you plan the content, organization, and style of the memo.

Include the Identifying Information

In almost all memos, five elements appear at the top:

- the organization's logo or an abbreviated letterhead
- the "to" line
- the "from" line
- the "subject" line
- the "date" line

Some organizations also have a "copies" or "c" (copy) heading. Figure 15.10 shows several styles for presenting identifying information.

When you write the subject heading—the title of the memo—be accurate, unique, and specific. Avoid naming only the subject, such as *Tower Load Test,* which does not indicate whether the memo is about the date, the location, the methods, the results, or any number of other factors related to the test. *Tower Load Test Results* or *Results of Tower Load Test* is more informative.

Print the second and all subsequent pages of memos on plain paper rather than on letterhead. Include three items in the upper right-hand corner of each page: the name of the recipient, the date of the memo, and the page number. See Figure 15.3 on page 368.

Clearly State Your Purpose

The first sentence of the body of a memo should explain its purpose:

> The purpose of this memo is to request authorization to travel to the Brownsville plant Monday to meet with the other quality inspectors.

> This memo presents the results of the internal audit of the Phoenix branch, an audit that you authorized March 13, 2003.

The best purpose statements are concise and direct. Use a form of the verb that clearly communicates what you want the memo to accomplish, such as *to request, to explain,* or *to authorize.*

In This Book

For more about titles, see Ch. 10,
p. 219.

In This Book

For more about analyzing your
purpose, see Ch. 5, p. 97.

AMRO   MEMO

To: B. Pabst
From: J. Alonso J. A.
Subject: MIXER RECOMMENDATION FOR PHILLIPS
Date: 11 June 2003

Write out the month instead of using the all-numeral format (6/11/03); multicultural readers might use a different notation for dates and could be confused.

INTEROFFICE

To: C. Cleveland   c: B. Aaron
From: H. Rainbow H. R.   K. Lau
Subject: Shipment Date of Blueprints   J. Manuputra
to Collier   W. Williams
Date: 2 October 2003

List the names of persons receiving photocopies of the memo, either alphabetically or in descending order of organizational rank.

**NORTHERN PETROLEUM COMPANY
INTERNAL CORRESPONDENCE**

Date: January 3, 2003
To: William Weeks, Director of Operations
From: Helen Cho, Chemical Engineering Dept. H. C.
Subject: Trip Report — Conference on Improved Procedures
for Chemical Analysis Laboratory

Most writers put their initials or signature next to their typed name (or at the end of the memo) to show that they have reviewed the memo and accept responsibility for it.

■ **Figure 15.10   Identifying Information in a Memo**

Some organizations prefer the full name of the writer and the reader; others want only the first initials and the last name. Some prefer job titles; others do not. If your organization does not object, include your job title and your reader's. The memo will then be informative for someone who refers to it after either of you has moved on to a new position, and for others in the organization who might not know you.

Use Headings to Help Your Readers

Use headings liberally in memos. Headings help your readers in two main ways:

- *Headings help your readers decide what to read.* If a section is labeled *What Is a Splash Page?* readers who already know can simply skip to the next section.

- *Headings help readers understand the information.* A heading such as *Summary* states the function of the section, helping readers concentrate on the information without wondering why it is included and how it relates to other information.

In This Book

For more about writing effective headings, see Ch. 10, p. 219.

If Appropriate, Summarize Your Message

In This Book

For more about writing effective summaries, see Ch. 12, p. 274.

Memos of one page or less do not generally contain summaries. But longer ones, particularly those addressed to multiple readers, can benefit from a summary at the beginning. A summary has three main goals:

- to help all readers understand the body of the memo
- to enable executive readers to skip the body if they so desire
- to remind readers of the main points

Here are some examples of summaries:

The annual ATC conference was of great value. The lectures on new coolants suggested techniques that might be useful in our Omega line, and I met three potential customers who have since gotten in touch with Marketing.

The analysis of the beam shows that lateral stress caused the failure. We are now trying to determine why the beam did not sustain a lateral stress weaker than that it was rated for.

The summary should reflect the length and complexity of the memo. It might range from one sentence to a long, technical paragraph. If possible, it should reflect the sequence of information in the body.

Provide Adequate Background for the Discussion

Explain the background: the events that led to the current situation. Although each background discussion is unique, some basic guidelines are useful. For example, if the memo defines a problem — a flaw detected in a product line — you might discuss how the problem was discovered or present the basic facts about the product line: what the product is, and how long it has been produced and in what quantities. If the memo reports the results of a field trip, you might discuss why the trip was undertaken, what its objectives were, who participated, and so on.

The following background paragraph is from a memo requesting authorization to have a piece of equipment retooled:

Background
The stamping machine, a Curtiss Model 6143, is used in the sheet-metal shop. We bought it in 1998, and it is in excellent condition. However, since we switched the size of the tin rolls last year, the stamping machine no longer performs to specifications.

Organize the Discussion

The discussion is the section in which you present your main arguments. You might divide a detailed discussion into the subsections typical of a more formal report: methods, results, conclusions, and recommendations. Or you might give it headings that relate specifically to the subject you are discussing. You might also include brief tables or figures but should attach more-extensive ones as appendices.

The discussion can be developed according to any of the basic organizational patterns, such as chronological, spatial, more important to less important, and cause and effect.

In This Book

For more about patterns of organization, see Ch. 8. For more about graphics, see Ch. 14.

Highlight Action Items

Some correspondence requires follow-up action, by either the writer or the reader. For example, a memo addressing a group of supervisors might explain a problem, then state what the writer is going to do about it. Or a supervisor might delegate tasks to other employees. In writing a memo, state clearly who is to do what and when. Here are two examples of ways to highlight action items:

Action Items:

I would appreciate it if you would work on the following tasks and have your results ready for the meeting on Monday, June 9.

1. Henderson: recalculate the flow rate.
2. Smith: set up meeting with the regional EPA representative for sometime during the week of February 13.
3. Falvey: ask Armitra in Houston for his advice.

Action Items:

As we discussed, I will finish these tasks this week:

1. Send the promotional package to the three companies.
2. Ask Customer Relations to work up a sample design to show the three companies.
3. Request interviews with the appropriate personnel at the three companies.

Notice that in the first example, although the writer is the supervisor of his readers, he uses a polite tone in the lead-in to the list of tasks.

Figure 15.11 shows a sample memo.

WRITING E-MAILS

E-mail offers four chief advantages over delivery of paper documents.

- *E-mail is fast.* Delivery usually takes only a few seconds.
- *E-mail is cheap.* Once the network is in place, it doesn't cost anything to send a message to one person or to thousands.
- *E-mail is easy to use.* Once you learn how to use your software, it is easy to send e-mail to one person or to an entire group. It is also simple to respond to or to forward an e-mail.
- *E-mail is digital.* Because e-mail can be stored like any other electronic file, it can be used in other documents. For this reason, e-mail is a convenient way for people in different places to collaborate.

The headings make the memo easier to read and easier to write, because they are prompts to provide the kind of information readers need.

Note that this writer has provided a summary, even though the memo is less than a page. The summary gives the writer an opportunity to convey his main request: he would like to meet with the reader.

The word *recommendation* will catch the reader's attention, increasing the chances that the reader will get in touch with the writer.

In This Book

For other sample memos, see Ch. 18.

Dynacol Corporation

INTEROFFICE COMMUNICATION

To: G. Granby, R&D
From: P. Rabin, Technical Services   *P.R.*
Subject: Trip Report—Computer Dynamics, Inc.
Date: September 22, 2003

The purpose of this memo is to present my impressions of the Computer Dynamics technical seminar of September 19. The goal of the seminar was to introduce their new PQ-500 line of high-capacity storage drives.

Summary
In general, I was impressed with the technical capabilities and interface of the drives. Of the two models in the 500 series, I think we ought to consider the external drives, not the internal ones. I'd like to talk to you about this issue when you have a chance.

Discussion
Computer Dynamics offers two models in its 500 series: an internal drive and an external drive. Each model has the same capacity (10 G of storage), and they both work the same way. They act just like any other kind of drive, preserving the user's directory structure.

Although the internal drive is convenient—it is already configured for the computer—I think we should consider only the external drive. Because so many of our employees do teleconferencing, the advantages of portability outweigh the disadvantage of inconvenience. The tech rep from Computer Dynamics walked me through the process of reconfiguring the drive for a second machine; the process will take most of our employees only a few minutes to learn. A second advantage of the external drive is that it can be salvaged easily when we take a computer out of service.

Recommendation
I'd like to talk to you, when you get a chance, about negotiating with Computer Dynamics for a quantity discount. I think we should ask McKinley and Rossiter to participate in the discussion. Give me a call (x3442) and we'll talk.

■ **Figure 15.11 Sample Memo**

This memo is a trip report, a record of a business trip written after the employee returns to the office. Readers are less interested in an hour-by-hour narrative of what happened than in a carefully structured discussion of what was important. Although writer and reader appear to be relatively equal in rank, the writer goes to the trouble of organizing the memo to make it easy to read and refer to later.

E-mail continues to grow in popularity. In 2001, some 1.4 trillion e-mails were sent from North American businesses (Flynn, 2002). The typical worker with e-mail access spends between 49 minutes and 4 hours per day writing and reading e-mail (Flynn, 2002). With this growth in the use of e-mail come other problems. Large attachments use up bandwidth, employees download viruses, and people inadvertently send confidential company information through e-mail.

In writing an e-mail, follow three principles:

On TechComm Web

For statistics on e-mail usage in business, see the ePolicy Institute. Click on Links Library for Ch. 15 on <bedfordstmartins.com/techcomm>.

- *Learn and abide by your organization's rules for using e-mail.* And understand that e-mail, like all traffic on a network, is usually archived, that is, backed up on some kind of tape or disk system, even if the recipient has deleted it. The organization has a legal right to look at all e-mails on its network (Crowe, 1994). Therefore, do not write anything that would embarrass you or your organization if the e-mail became public information.

- *Use an appropriate level of formality.* In some organizations, managers expect e-mail messages to be as formal as printed documents; in others they expect them or want them to be quite informal. Before you begin to send e-mail messages, read those written by fellow employees to learn your organization's approach.

- *Adhere to netiquette guidelines. Netiquette* refers to etiquette on a network.

GUIDELINES

Following Netiquette

▶ *Stick to business.* Don't send jokes or other nonbusiness messages.

▶ *Don't waste bandwidth.* Keep the message brief so that it doesn't clog up the network or the recipient's mailbox. When you reply to another e-mail, don't quote long passages from it. Instead, establish the context of the original e-mail by paraphrasing it briefly or by including a short quotation from it. (When you excerpt a small portion of an e-mail, add a phrase such as <*snip*> at the start and the end of the quotation, to indicate that you have omitted part of the original message.) When you quote, delete the routing information from the top as well as the signature block from the bottom. And make sure that everyone who is to receive a copy of your e-mail really needs to read it.

▶ *Take some care with your writing.* Although e-mail is informal, messages shouldn't be sloppy. Because text-editing functions on many e-mail systems are more limited than on a word processor, edit and proofread your e-mails before sending them.

▶ *Don't flame.* To *flame* is to scorch a reader with scathing criticism, usually in response to something that person wrote in a previous message. Flaming is rude. When you are really angry, keep your hands away from the keyboard.

On TechComm Web

See Albion.com's discussion of netiquette. Click on Links Library for Ch. 15 on <bedfordstmartins .com/techcomm>.

▶ *Use the subject line.* Readers like to be able to decide whether they want to read the message. Therefore, write specific, accurate, and informative subject lines, just as you would in a memo.

▶ *Make your message easy on the eyes.* Use uppercase and lowercase letters, and skip lines between paragraphs. Don't use italics, underlining, or boldface for emphasis, even if your e-mail software can accommodate them, because you can't be sure your reader's e-mail system can. Instead, use uppercase letters for emphasis. Keep the line length under 65 characters so that lines do not get broken up if the recipient's monitor has a smaller screen.

▶ *Don't forward a message to another person or to an online discussion forum without the writer's permission.* Doing so is unethical and it might be illegal (the courts haven't decided yet).

▶ *Don't send a message unless you have something to say.* Resist the temptation to write that you agree with another message. If you can add something new, fine, but don't send a message just to be part of the conversation.

Figure 15.12 shows an e-mail that violates some of these guidelines. The writer is a technical professional working for a microchip manufacturer. Figure 15.13 on page 386 shows a revised version of this e-mail message.

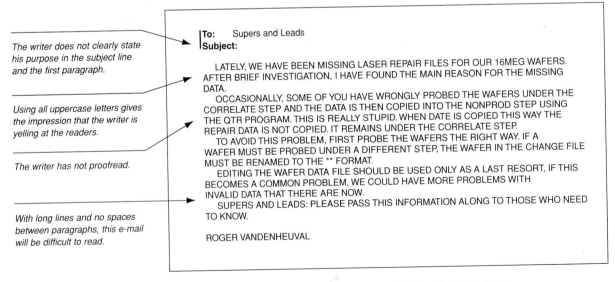

The writer does not clearly state his purpose in the subject line and the first paragraph.

Using all uppercase letters gives the impression that the writer is yelling at the readers.

The writer has not proofread.

With long lines and no spaces between paragraphs, this e-mail will be difficult to read.

To: Supers and Leads
Subject:

LATELY, WE HAVE BEEN MISSING LASER REPAIR FILES FOR OUR 16MEG WAFERS. AFTER BRIEF INVESTIGATION, I HAVE FOUND THE MAIN REASON FOR THE MISSING DATA.
OCCASIONALLY, SOME OF YOU HAVE WRONGLY PROBED THE WAFERS UNDER THE CORRELATE STEP AND THE DATA IS THEN COPIED INTO THE NONPROD STEP USING THE QTR PROGRAM. THIS IS REALLY STUPID. WHEN DATE IS COPIED THIS WAY THE REPAIR DATA IS NOT COPIED. IT REMAINS UNDER THE CORRELATE STEP.
TO AVOID THIS PROBLEM, FIRST PROBE THE WAFERS THE RIGHT WAY. IF A WAFER MUST BE PROBED UNDER A DIFFERENT STEP, THE WAFER IN THE CHANGE FILE MUST BE RENAMED TO THE ** FORMAT.
EDITING THE WAFER DATA FILE SHOULD BE USED ONLY AS A LAST RESORT, IF THIS BECOMES A COMMON PROBLEM, WE COULD HAVE MORE PROBLEMS WITH INVALID DATA THAT THERE ARE NOW.
SUPERS AND LEADS: PLEASE PASS THIS INFORMATION ALONG TO THOSE WHO NEED TO KNOW.

ROGER VANDENHEUVAL

■ **Figure 15.12   E-mail Message That Violates Netiquette Guidelines**

Interactive Sample Document:
Participating in an Online Discussion Group

This post to a discussion list, TECHWR-L, was written by Geoff Hart (2002) in response to a question posted to the group by Bruce Byfield. Postings to an online discussion group should adhere to the principles of effective e-mails and proper netiquette. The questions in the margin ask you to think about these principles (explained on pages 381–384). The answers to these questions are available on TechComm Web.

Bruce Byfield reports: <<This week, a PR person contacted me about "collaborating" with a company. At first, the comments suggested that the intent was to produce some marketing collateral. However, further e-mails made clear that the point was to cooperate in writing reviews about the company's products. I replied that any reviews would be completely independent, and would need to be based on personal testing. The reply suggests that this is fine. However, I'm still uneasy.>>

1. Byfield's original post was titled "An Ethical Question?" How effectively has Hart quoted Byfield before presenting his own comments?

The appearance of a conflict of interest can be as damaging as the reality of a conflict of interest, and that's why you're right to be cautious. But provided that the company isn't paying you to talk about their product, and has no right to edit what you say (other than to review technical details for you and correct any errors or misunderstandings on your part), there's no conflict of interest and no reason to be uneasy.

2. How professional is the tone of Hart's response to Byfield?

Every computer journalist receives tons of "free" products in exchange for writing reviews, and there are no explicit strings attached; the implicit strings, of course, are that you'll eventually stop receiving free products if you keep panning a company's product or write unfair, biased, error-filled reviews. The cynic might note that major industry periodicals tiptoe very delicately around reviews of products from their major advertisers; step too hard on the wrong toes and they might lose the advertiser to a rival magazine. This is one reason why you won't see reviews about new releases of Windows or MS Office that dwell on anything wrong with the product, apart from obvious glitches such as repeated crashes that they can't credibly gloss over.

3. How effectively has Hart taken care with the quality of his writing?

—Geoff Hart, geoff-h@mtl.feric.ca
Forest Engineering Research Institute of Canada
580 boul. St-Jean
Pointe-Claire, Que., H9R 3J9 Canada
"User's advocate" online monthly at
www.raycomm.com/techwhirl/usersadvocate.html

On TechComm Web

To find the answers to these questions, click on Interactive Sample Documents for Ch. 15 on <bedfordstmartins.com/techcomm>.

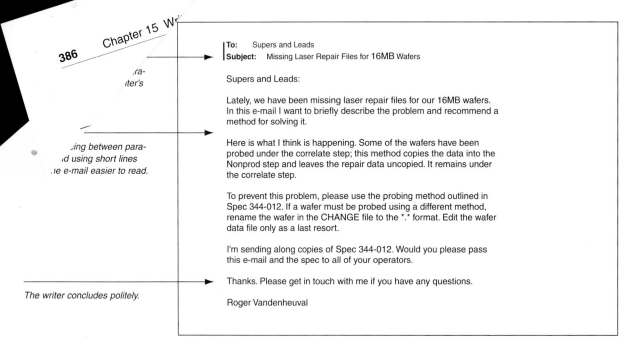

.ra-
iter's

..ing between para-
..d using short lines
..e e-mail easier to read.

The writer concludes politely.

To: Supers and Leads
Subject: Missing Laser Repair Files for 16MB Wafers

Supers and Leads:

Lately, we have been missing laser repair files for our 16MB wafers.
In this e-mail I want to briefly describe the problem and recommend a
method for solving it.

Here is what I think is happening. Some of the wafers have been
probed under the correlate step; this method copies the data into the
Nonprod step and leaves the repair data uncopied. It remains under
the correlate step.

To prevent this problem, please use the probing method outlined in
Spec 344-012. If a wafer must be probed using a different method,
rename the wafer in the CHANGE file to the *.* format. Edit the wafer
data file only as a last resort.

I'm sending along copies of Spec 344-012. Would you please pass
this e-mail and the spec to all of your operators.

Thanks. Please get in touch with me if you have any questions.

Roger Vandenheuval

■ **Figure 15.13   E-mail That Adheres to Netiquette Guidelines**

The writer diplomatically diagnoses the problem and clearly states the correct method for the
procedure. In addition, the writer has edited and proofread the e-mail.

STRATEGIES FOR INTERCULTURAL COMMUNICATION

Writing Culture-Specific Letters, Memos, and E-mails

Letters, memos, and e-mails differ from one culture to another. Here are
a few examples:

- *Letters.* The role, format, and tone of letters in the target culture might
  be different. In many high-context cultures, such as Japan, letters are
  expected to begin with a paragraph about the seasons and not to make
  explicit sales messages.

- *Memos.* In the United States, most memos are less formal in style and
  tone than letters. In cultures in which documents tend to be formal, letters might be preferred to memos, or memos might be more formal
  than in the United States. For instance, they might not use contractions,
  and they might not include a set of action steps directing the reader to
  carry out tasks.

In This Book

For more about cultural variables
in letter writing and about high-
context and low-context cultures,
see Ch. 5, p. 93.

- *E-mails.* In some cultures, e-mails are not as popular as they are in the United States. In Asia, for instance, face-to-face meetings are more common for short, informal communications, because they show more respect for the other person.

Try to study letters, memos, and e-mails written by people from the culture you will be addressing, and try to have important letters, memos, and e-mails reviewed by a person from that culture before you send them.

Reviewing the Process

Analyze your audience.

Consider the readers' characteristics and attitudes, and how they will use the document. Remember that the tone, content, and format of letters, memos, and e-mails differ from culture to culture.

Analyze your purpose.

After they read the document, what do you want your readers to know or do?

Gather information about your subject.

Use appropriate techniques of primary and secondary research. (See Chapter 7.)

Choose a type of document.

Letters are best for formal situations. Memos are less formal than letters. E-mails are the least formal, but they still require professionalism and accuracy.

Draft the document.

Clearly state your purpose, use headings to help your readers, summarize your message, provide adequate background, organize the discussion, and highlight action items.

Format the document.

Use a conventional format, but adapt it to meet the special needs of your audience, purpose, and subject.

Revise the document.

Let it sit as long as you can. Many careful writers draft e-mails in a text editor such as Notepad, then revise them later. For more-formal occasions, ask subject-matter experts to review your documents. See the Revision Checklist on page 388.

Revision Checklist

Letter Format

- ❏ Is the first page typed on letterhead stationery? (p. 368)
- ❏ Is the date included? (p. 368)
- ❏ Is the inside address complete and correct? (p. 368)
- ❏ Is the appropriate courtesy title used? (p. 368)
- ❏ If appropriate, is an attention line included? (p. 368)
- ❏ If appropriate, is a subject line included? (p. 368)
- ❏ Is the salutation appropriate? (p. 368)
- ❏ Is the complimentary close typed with only the first word capitalized? (p. 369) Is the complimentary close followed by a comma? (p. 369)
- ❏ Is the signature legible and is the writer's name typed beneath the signature? (p. 369)
- ❏ If appropriate, is an enclosure line included? (p. 369)
- ❏ If appropriate, is a copy line included? (p. 369)
- ❏ Is the letter typed in one of the standard formats? (p. 370)

Types of Letters

Does the inquiry letter
- ❏ explain why you chose the reader to receive the inquiry? (p. 367)
- ❏ explain why you are requesting the information and to what use you will put it? (p. 367)
- ❏ specify by what date you need the information? (p. 367)
- ❏ list the questions clearly and, if appropriate, provide room for the reader's responses? (p. 372)
- ❏ offer, if appropriate, the product of your research? (p. 372)
- ❏ Does the response to an inquiry letter answer the reader's questions or explain why they cannot be answered? (p. 372)

Does the claim letter
- ❏ identify specifically the unsatisfactory product or service? (p. 372)
- ❏ explain the problem(s) clearly? (p. 372)
- ❏ propose an adjustment? (p. 372)
- ❏ conclude courteously? (p. 372)

Does the "good-news" adjustment letter
- ❏ express your regret? (p. 376)
- ❏ explain the adjustment you will make? (p. 376)
- ❏ conclude on a positive note? (p. 376)

Does the "bad-news" adjustment letter
- ❏ meet the reader on neutral ground, expressing regret but not apologizing? (p. 374)
- ❏ explain why the company is not at fault? (p. 374)
- ❏ clearly deny the reader's request? (p. 374)
- ❏ attempt to create goodwill? (p. 374)

Memos

- ❏ Does the identifying information adhere to your organization's standards? (p. 378)
- ❏ Did you clearly state your purpose at the start of the memo? (p. 378)
- ❏ Did you use headings to help your readers? (p. 379)
- ❏ If appropriate, did you summarize your message? (p. 380)
- ❏ Did you provide appropriate background for the discussion? (p. 380)
- ❏ Did you organize the discussion clearly? (p. 380)
- ❏ Did you highlight items requiring action? (p. 381)

E-mail

- ❏ Is the tone appropriate? (p. 383)
- ❏ Did you write the message carefully and revise it? (p. 383)
- ❏ Did you avoid flaming? (p. 383)
- ❏ Did you write a specific, accurate subject line? (p. 384)
- ❏ Did you use uppercase and lowercase letters? (p. 384)
- ❏ Did you skip lines between paragraphs? (p. 384)
- ❏ Did you set the line length under 65 characters? (p. 384)
- ❏ Did you check with the writer before forwarding his or her message? (p. 384)

Exercises

On TechComm Web

For more exercises, click on Additional Exercises, Projects, and Cases for Ch. 15 on <bedfordstmartins.com/techcomm>.

1. A beverage container you recently purchased for $8.95 has a serious leak. The grape drink you put in it ruined a $35.00 white tablecloth. Inventing any reasonable details, write a claim letter to the manufacturer of the container.

2. As the recipient of the claim letter described in exercise 1, write an adjustment letter granting the customer's request.

3. You are the manager of a private swimming club. A member has written saying that she lost a contact lens (value $75) in your pool and she wants you to pay for a replacement. The contract that all members sign explicitly states that the management is not responsible for loss of personal possessions. Write an adjustment letter denying the request. Invent any reasonable details.

4. As manager of a stereo equipment retail store, you guarantee that you will not be undersold. If a customer who buys something from you can prove within one month that another retailer sells the same equipment at a lower price, you will refund the difference. A customer has written to you and enclosed an ad from another store showing that it is selling the CD-RW drive he purchased for $26.50 less than he paid at your store. The advertised price at the other store was a one-week sale that began five weeks after the date of his purchase. He wants a $26.50 refund. Inventing any reasonable details, write an adjustment letter denying his request. You are willing, however, to offer him a 10-pack of blank CR-R disks worth $7.95 for his equipment if he would like to come pick it up.

5. **Group Activity** Form small groups for this exercise on claim and adjustment letters. Have each member of your group study the following two letters. Meet and discuss your reactions to the two letters. How effectively does the writer of the claim letter present his case? How effective is the adjustment letter? Does its writer succeed in showing that the company's procedures for ensuring hygiene are effective? Does its writer succeed in projecting a professional tone? Write a memo to your instructor discussing the two letters. Attach a revision of the adjustment letter to the memo. (For more on memos, see page 378.)

Seth Reeves
19 Lowry's Lane
Morgan, TN 30610

April 13, 2003

Sea-Tasty Tuna
Route 113
Lynchburg, TN 30563

Gentlemen:

I've been buying your tuna fish for years, and up to now it's been OK.

But this morning I opened a can to make myself a sandwich. What do you think was staring me in the face? A fly. That's right, a housefly. That's him you see taped to the bottom of this letter.

What are you going to do about this?

Yours very truly,

SEA-TASTY TUNA
Route 113
Lynchburg, TN 30563
www.seatastytuna.com

April 21, 2003

Mr. Seth Reeves
19 Lowry's Lane
Morgan, TN 30610

Dear Mr. Reeves:

We were very sorry to learn that you found a fly in your tuna fish.

Here at Sea-Tasty we are very careful about the hygiene of our plant. The tuna are scrubbed thoroughly as soon as we receive them. After they are processed, they are inspected visually at three different points. Before we pack them, we rinse and sterilize the cans to ensure that no foreign material is sealed in them.

Because of these stringent controls, we really don't see how you could have found a fly in the can. Nevertheless, we are enclosing coupons good for two cans of Sea-Tasty tuna.

We hope this letter restores your confidence in us.

Truly yours,

6. Bill, the writer of the following e-mail, is the primary technical supervisor on the production line in a microchip manufacturing facility. He is responding to Larry, a supervisor who reports to him. Larry has sent him the following note: "Bill, I can't seem to find a spec that describes coat tracks. Some of the new hires don't know what they are. What should I tell them?" Bill's reply:

Larry—

Coat tracks are the machines used in the first step of the photo process. The wafers coem to coat to have a layer of a photosensitive resist applyed. This requires several operations to be done by the same machine. First the wafer is coated with a layer of primer or hmds. This ensures that the resist will adhere to the wager. The wafer is then caoted with resist. There are 5 different types of resist in use, each has its won characteristics, and all are used on different levels and part types. I dont really have time to go into all the details now. The photo resist must be applyed ina uniform layer as the unfioromity of the resist can effect several other steps to include exsposure on the stepper to the etch rate on a lam. To insure the proper unfiromity and resist volumes the tracks are inspected at 24 hour intervals, all the functions are checked and partical monitors are ran to ensure proper operation and cleanyness. After the wafer is coated it is soft baked, this rids the wafer of solvents in the primer and resist and also hardens the resist. The wafers are then ready to go to the next step at the p&e or the stepper.

If, in fact, there is no specification that Bill can give to Larry, what would be the best way to communicate the information to him? What impression will his e-mail make on Larry? Why?

7. Louise and Paul work for the same manufacturing company. Louise, a senior engineer, is chairing a committee to investigate ways to improve the hiring process at the company. Paul, a technical editor, also serves on the committee. The excerpts quoted in Louise's e-mail are from an e-mail written by Paul to all members of the committee in response to Louise's request that members describe their approach to evaluating job-application materials. How would you revise Louise's e-mail to make it more effective?

To: Paul

From: Louise

Sometimes I just have to wonder what you're thinking, Paul.

>Of course, it's not possible to expect perfect
>resumes. But I have to screen them, and last
>year I had to read over 200. I'm not looking for
>perfection, but as soon as I spot an error I make
>a mental note of it and, when I hit a second and
>then a third error I can't really concentrate on the
>writer's credentials.

Listen, Paul, you might be a sharp editor, but the rest of us have a different responsibility: to make the products and move them out as soon as possible. We don't have the luxury of studying documents to see if we can find errors. I suggest you concentrate on what you were hired to do, without imposing your "standards" on the rest of us.

>From my point of view, an error can include a
>misused tradmark.

Misusing a "tradmark," Paul? Is that Error Number 1?

Project

On TechComm Web

For more projects, click on Additional Exercises, Projects, and Cases for Ch. 15 on <bedfordstmartins.com/techcomm>.

8. **Internet Activity**   Because students use e-mail to communicate with other group members when they write collaboratively, your college or university would like to create a one-page handout on how to use e-mail responsibly. Using a search engine, find three or four netiquette guides on the Internet that focus on using e-mail. Study these guides and write a one-page student guide to using e-mail to communicate with other students. Somewhere in the guide, be sure to list the sites you studied, so that students can visit them for further information about netiquette.

On TechComm Web

For more cases, click on Additional Exercises, Projects, and Cases for Ch. 15 on <bedfordstmartins.com /techcomm>.

C A S E
Dangerous Wrenches

Your group works for the Customer Service Department at United Tools, a manufacturer of hand tools. Recently, you received the following letter from a hardware store that carries your products.

Handee Hardware, Inc.
Millersville, AL 61304
www.handeehardware.com

December 4, 2003

United Tools
20 Central Avenue
Dover, TX 76104

Gentlemen:

I have a problem I'd like to discuss with you. I've been carrying your line of hand tools for many years.

Your 9" pipe wrench has always been a big seller. But there seems to be something wrong with its design. I have had two complaints in the last few months about the handle snapping off when pressure is exerted on it. In one case, the user cut his hand seriously enough to require stitches.

Frankly, I'm hesitant to sell any more of the 9" pipe wrenches, but I still have more than two dozen in inventory.

Have you had any other complaints about this product?

Sincerely yours,

You decide to investigate the problem. You learn that in the last two quarters United Tools has sold more than 300 of these wrenches to retailers and received four complaints from retailers and retail customers about the handle snapping. No one reported injuries. You go to the company engineers and learn that two months ago they discovered a design flaw that accounts for the problem. At that time, the engineers redesigned the wrench, manufactured samples, tested them thoroughly, and found no problems. Like the old design, the new design exceeds ANSI standards for this type of tool. The old design is no longer sold; all new orders are being filled with the new design.

What additional steps should you take? Are there other people in the company with whom you should meet? Draft a letter, to be sent to the retailers and the retail customers who wrote claim letters to your company, offering an appropriate adjustment. Does the situation you have uncovered within your company merit further action? If so, write a memo or letter to an appropriate officer in the company. For a discussion of ethical and legal considerations, see Chapter 2.

16

Preparing Job-Application Materials

Yana Parker (1999), a
résumé consultant,
advises job applicants:

*Too many people forget that a résumé is a marketing
piece—not a career obituary! And it's not a confessional
either. Its purpose is to sell the writer's skills.*

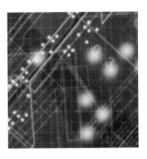

For most of you, the first nonacademic test of your technical-communication
skills comes when you prepare job-application materials. These materials tell
prospective employers about your academic and employment experience,
your personal characteristics, and your reasons for applying for a job with
their organization. But they also tell prospective employers how well you
communicate.

Some students think that once they get a satisfactory job, they will never
again have to worry about résumés and application letters. However, the typical professional changes jobs more than five times, and many organizations
require employees to maintain up-to-date résumés.

On TechComm Web

For additional samples, activities,
and links related to this chapter, see
<bedfordstmartins.com/techcomm>.

PLANNING THE JOB SEARCH

Planning a job search is a lot of work, stretching over weeks and months, not
days. You have three main tasks:

- *Do a self-inventory.* Before you can start thinking of where you want to
  work, you need to answer some questions about yourself:
  - *What are your strengths and weaknesses?* Are your skills primarily techni-
    cal? Do you work well with people? Do you work best with supervision
    or on your own?
  - *What subjects do you like?* Think about what you have liked or disliked
    about your jobs and college courses.
  - *What kind of organization would you like to work for?* Profit or nonprofit?
    Government or private industry? Small or large?
  - *What are your geographical preferences?* If you are free to relocate, where
    would you like to live? How do you feel about commuting?

On TechComm Web

To find the *Occupational Handbook*, click on Links Library for Ch. 16 on <bedfordstmartins .com/techcomm>.

In This Book

For more on online portfolios, see p. 425.

- *Learn about the employers.* Don't base your job search exclusively on the information in an ad. Learn about the organization through other means as well:
  - *Attend job fairs.* Your college and your community probably hold job fairs, where various employers provide information about their organizations. Sometimes, a single organization will hold a job fair to find qualified candidates for a wide variety of jobs.
  - *Find out about trends in your field.* Read the *Occupational Handbook*, published by the U.S. Department of Labor, for information about your field and related fields. Talk with professors and with the people at your job-placement office.
  - *Research the companies that interest you.* Visit their Web sites. Scan the index of the *Wall Street Journal* for articles about them. Study their annual reports, which are usually available on the organizations' Web sites.
- *Prepare your materials.* You know you will write application letters and résumés and go on interviews. Start planning early by obtaining materials from the career-placement office. Talk with friends who have gone through the process successfully; study their application materials. Read some of the books on different aspects of the job search.

  One more very important part of preparing your materials: make a *portfolio*, a collection of your best work. You'll want to give a prospective employer a copy of the portfolio to demonstrate the kind of work you can do. For a technical communicator, the portfolio will include a variety of documents you made in courses and in previous positions. For technical professionals, the portfolio might include proposals and reports as well as computer simulations, Web sites, or presentation graphics. A portfolio is often presented in a loose-leaf notebook, with each item preceded by a descriptive and evaluative statement. Frequently, a portfolio contains a table of contents and an introductory statement.

STRATEGIES FOR INTERCULTURAL COMMUNICATION

Applying for International Positions

When you apply for a position in another country, keep in mind that the conventions of the process vary—sometimes quite dramatically. You will need to adapt your résumé to the expectations of the country in which you would like to work. Consult one of the following sources for advice on drafting résumés for applying to international positions:

- Krannich, R. L., & Enelow, W. S. (2002). *Best resumes and CVs for international jobs.* Manassas Park, VA: Impact Publications.
- Krannich, R. L., & Krannich, C. (1993). *Complete guide to international jobs and careers.* Manassas Park, VA: Impact Publications.
- Goinglobal.com <www.goinglobal.com/topic/resumes.asp>
- Monster.com Work Abroad <http://international.monster.com>

UNDERSTANDING SEVEN WAYS TO LOOK FOR A POSITION

Search for a position through:

A college or university placement office

A professional placement bureau

A published job advertisement

An organization's Web site

A job board on the Internet

An unsolicited letter to an organization

Connections

Once you have done your planning, you can start to look for a position. There are seven major ways to find a job.

- *Through a college or university placement office.* Placement offices bring companies and students together. Generally, students submit a résumé — a brief list of credentials — to the placement office. The résumés are then made available to representatives of business, government, and industry, who arrange on-campus interviews with selected students. Students who do best in the campus interviews are then invited by the representatives to visit the organization for a tour and another interview. The advantages of this system are that it is free and it is easy. You merely deliver a résumé to the placement office and wait to be contacted.

- *Through a professional placement bureau.* A professional placement bureau offers essentially the same service as a college placement office but charges a fee. Sometimes the fee is paid by the employer, sometimes by the new employee. Placement bureaus cater primarily to more advanced professionals who are changing jobs.

- *Through a published job advertisement.* Organizations publish ads in three kinds of print publications: public-relations catalogs (such as *College Placement Annual*), technical journals, and newspapers. Check the major technical journals in your field and the large metropolitan newspapers. In responding to an ad, you most likely will include with the résumé a job-application letter that highlights the crucial information on the résumé.

- *Through an organization's Web site.* Many organizations list their job offerings on their Web sites and explain how to apply.

In This Book

For more on job-application letters, see p. 414. For more on electronic résumés, see p. 409.

- *Through a job board on the Internet.* Job boards are sites sponsored by federal agencies, Internet service providers, and private organizations to help introduce employers to prospective employees. Some sites merely list positions, to which you respond by regular mail or by e-mail; others let you submit your résumé electronically, so that employers can get in touch with you. Use a search engine to search for "employment," "careers," and "jobs." Or combine one of these terms with the name of your field, as in "careers and forestry." Among the biggest job boards are the following:

  - America's Job Bank (sponsored by the U.S. Department of Labor)
  - Monster®
  - CareerBuilder®
  - FlipDog
  - AfterCollege
  - Careermag

On TechComm Web

To find these sites and additional job-related resources on the Web, click on Links Library in Ch. 16 on <bedfordstmartins.com/techcomm>.

Many of these have links to articles about searching for jobs electronically, including how to research companies, how to write electronic résumés, and how to prepare for interviews.

One caution about using job boards: once you post something to an Internet site, you probably have lost control of it. Here are four questions to ask before you post to a job board:

– Who has access to your résumé? You might wish to remove your home address and phone number from it if anyone can view it.
– How will you know if an employer requests your résumé? Will you be notified by the job board?
– Can your current employer see your résumé? If your employer knows you are looking for a new job, your current position could be jeopardized.
– Can you update your résumé at no cost? Some job boards charge you each time you update it.

- *Through an unsolicited letter to an organization.* Instead of waiting for an ad or a notice on a Web site, consider sending unsolicited applications to organizations you would like to work for. The disadvantage is obvious: there might not be an opening. Yet many professionals favor this technique, because there are fewer competitors for those jobs that do exist, and organizations do not advertise all available positions. And sometimes an impressive unsolicited application can prompt an organization to create a position.

Before you write an unsolicited application, learn as much as you can about the organization: current and anticipated major projects, hiring plans, and so forth. The business librarian at your college or university will be able to point out additional sources of information, such as the Dun and Bradstreet guides, the *F&S Index of Corporations,* and indexed newspapers such as the *New York Times,* the *Washington Post,* and the *Wall Street Journal.* You should also study the organization's Web site.

- *Through connections.* A relative or an acquaintance who can exert influence, or at least point out a new position, can help you get a job. Other good contacts include past employers and professors. Also consider becoming active in the student chapter of your field's professional organization, through which you can meet professionals in your area.

WRITING RÉSUMÉS

This section discusses the fundamentals for preparing résumés — print and electronic. A section with more techniques specific to electronic résumés follows this one.

Many students wonder whether to write their résumé themselves or use a résumé-preparation agency. It is best to write your own résumé, for three reasons:

On TechComm Web

For an excellent article on researching organizations, see the Boston College Graduate School of Management. Click on Links Library for Ch. 16 on <bedfordstmartins.com/techcomm>.

- *You know yourself better than anyone else does.* No matter how thorough and professional the work of a résumé-preparation agency, you can do a better job communicating important information about yourself.

- *Employment officers know the style of the local agencies.* Readers who realize that you did not write your own résumé might wonder what kinds of deficiencies you are hiding.

- *If you write your own résumé, you will be more likely to adapt it to different situations.* You are not likely to return to a résumé-preparation agency and pay an additional fee to make a minor revision.

The résumé communicates in two ways: through its appearance and through its content.

Appearance of the Résumé

Because potential employers normally see your résumé before they see you, it has to make a good first impression. Employers believe that the résumé's appearance reflects the writer's professionalism. When employers look at a résumé, they see the documents they will be reading if they hire you.

Résumés should appear neat and professional. They should have

- *Generous margins.* Leave a one-inch margin on all four sides.
- *Clear type.* Use a good-quality laser printer.
- *Balance.* Arrange the information so that the page has a balanced appearance.
- *Clear organization.* Use adequate white space. The line spacing between items should be greater than the line spacing within an item. That is, there should be more space between your education section and your employment section than between items within either of those sections. You should be able to see the different sections clearly if you stand and look down at the résumé on the floor by your feet.

Use indentation clearly. When you arrange items in a vertical list, indent *turnovers*, the second and subsequent lines of any item, a few spaces. The following list, from the computer-skills section of a résumé, could be confusing:

Computer Experience

Systems: PC, Macintosh, UNIX, Andover AC-256, Prime 360
Software: Lotus 1-2-3, DBase V, PlanPerfect, Micrografx Designer, Adobe
PageMaker, Microsoft Word
Languages: Pascal, C++, HTML, XHTML

When the second line of the long entry is indented, the arrangement is much easier to understand:

In This Book

For more on page design, see
Ch. 13, p. 298.

Computer Experience

Systems: PC, Macintosh, UNIX, Andover AC-256, Prime 360
Software: Lotus 1-2-3, DBase V, PlanPerfect, Micrografx Designer, Adobe
    PageMaker, Microsoft Word
Languages: Pascal, C++, HTML, XHTML

Content of the Résumé

Although experts advocate different approaches to résumé writing, they all agree on three things:

- *The résumé must be honest.* One survey (JobWeb.com, 2002) found that of the top 10 qualities that employers look for in job applicants, number one is communication skills (both written and oral), and number two is honesty and integrity. Many employers today routinely check candidates' credentials.

- *The résumé must be completely free of errors.* Writing errors cast doubt on the accuracy of the information in the résumé. Ask for assistance after you have written the draft, and proofread the finished product at least twice. Then have someone else proofread it, too.

- *The résumé must provide clear, specific information, without generalizations or self-congratulation.* Your résumé is a sales document, but you are both the salesperson and the product. You cannot say "I am a terrific job candidate" as if you were a toaster or a car. Instead, you have to show the reader by providing the details that will lead the reader to conclude that you are a terrific job candidate. Telling the reader is graceless and unconvincing.

A résumé should be long enough to include all pertinent information but not so long that it bores or irritates the reader. In general, if you have less than 10 years' experience or are applying for an entry-level position, readers will expect a one-page résumé. If you have more than 10 years' experience or the job is more advanced than an entry-level position, readers will expect a two-page résumé (Isaacs, 2002). If the information comes to just over a page, either eliminate or condense some of the material to make it fit onto one page, or modify the layout so that it fills a substantial part of a second page.

Two common styles are the *chronological* résumé and the *analytical* résumé. In a chronological résumé, you use time as the organizing factor for each section, including education and experience. In the analytical résumé, you include a section called *skills*, which is organized according to your talents and achievements.

Recent graduates usually use the chronological résumé because in most cases, they haven't built up the record of skills and accomplishments they need for an analytical résumé. However, if you have professional work experience, you might consider the analytical style.

Elements of the Chronological Résumé

Most chronological résumés have six basic elements.

A chronological résumé contains:

Identifying information

Job objectives

Education

Employment history

Interests and activities

References

Identifying Information   Include your full name, address, phone number, and e-mail address. Generally, you should present your name in boldface letters at the top. Use your complete address, with the zip code. Use the two-letter state abbreviations used by the U.S. Postal Service.

If your address during the academic year differs from your home address, list both and identify them clearly. An employer might call during an academic holiday to arrange an interview.

Job Objectives   After the identifying information, add a statement of objectives, in the form of a brief phrase or sentence—for example, "Objective: Entry-level position as a hospital dietitian," or "A summer internship in manufacturing processes that could lead to a full-time position focusing on quality control." According to one study, 88.5 percent of managers making personnel decisions consider a statement of objectives important, because it gives the impression that the writer has a clear sense of direction and solid goals (Harcourt, Krizan, & Merrier, 1991). In drafting your statement of objectives, follow these two suggestions:

- *State only the goals or duties explicitly mentioned, or clearly implied, in the job advertisement.* If you unintentionally suggest that your goals are substantially different from the job responsibilities, the reader might infer that you would not be happy working there and not consider you further.

- *Avoid meaningless generalities.* You accomplish little by writing, "Position offering opportunities for advancement in the field of health science, where I can use my communication and analytical skills." What kind of position in health science: a nurse or physician, a hospital administrator, a pharmaceutical researcher? Be more specific.

Education   If you are a student or a recent graduate, place the education section next. If you have substantial professional experience, place the employment experience section before the education section.

Include at least the following information in the education section:

- *The degree.* After the degree abbreviation (such as B.S., B.A., A.A., or M.S.), list your academic major (and, if you have one, your minor)—for example, "B.S. in Materials Engineering, minor in General Business."

- *The institution.* Identify the institution by its full name: "Louisiana State University," not "LSU."

- *The location of the institution.* Include the city and state.

- *The date of graduation.* If your degree has not yet been granted, add "Anticipated date of graduation" or a similar phrase.

- *Information about other schools you attended.* List any other institutions you attended beyond high school, even those at which you did not earn a degree. The description for other institutions should include the same information as in the main listing. Arrange entries in reverse chronological order: that is, list first the school you attended most recently.

GUIDELINES

Elaborating on Your Education

The following guidelines can help you elaborate on your education in a résumé.

▶ *List your grade-point average.* If your average is significantly above the median for the graduating class, list it. Or list your average in the courses in your major, if that is more impressive.

▶ *Compile a list of courses.* Include courses that will be of particular interest to an employer, such as advanced courses in your major, or communications courses, such as technical communication, public speaking, and organizational communication. For example, a list of business courses on an engineer's résumé shows special knowledge and skills. But don't bother listing traditional required courses. Include the substantive titles of listed courses; employers won't know what "Chemistry 450" is. Call it by its official title: "Chemistry 450. Organic Chemistry."

▶ *Describe a special accomplishment.* For a special senior design or research project, for example, include the title and objective of the project, any special or advanced techniques or equipment you used, and—if you know them—the major results: "A Study of Shape Memory Alloys in Fabricating Actuators for Underwater Biomimetic Applications—a senior design project to simulate the swimming styles and anatomy of fish." A project discussion makes you seem more like a professional—someone who designs and carries out projects.

▶ *List honors and awards you received.* Scholarships, internships, and academic awards suggest exceptional ability. If you have received a number of such honors, or some that were not exclusively academic, you might list them separately (in a section called *Honors* or *Awards*) rather than in the education section. Decide where this information will make the best impression.

The education section is the easiest part of the résumé to adapt in applying for different positions. For example, a student majoring in electrical engineering who is applying for a position requiring strong communications skills can list communications courses in one version of the résumé and advanced electrical engineering courses in another version. As you compose the education section, emphasize those aspects of your background that meet the requirements for the particular job.

Employment History   Like the education section, the employment section should convey at least the basic information about each job you have held: the dates of employment, the organization's name and location, and your position or title. Then, add carefully selected details. Readers want to know what you actually did. Provide at least a two- to three-line description for each position. For particularly important or relevant jobs, give a more extensive description, focusing on one or more of the following factors:

- *Documents.* What kinds of documents did you write or assist in writing? List, especially, various governmental forms and any long reports, manuals, proposals, or Web sites.
- *Clients.* What kinds of, and how many, clients did you do business with in representing your organization?
- *Skills.* What technical skills did you use on the job?
- *Equipment.* What equipment did you operate or oversee? Mention, in particular, computer skills.
- *Money.* How much money were you responsible for? Even if you considered your bookkeeping position fairly easy, the fact that the organization grossed, say, $2 million a year shows that the position involved real responsibility.
- *Personnel.* How many people did you supervise?

Whenever possible, emphasize *results*. If you reorganized the shifts of the weekend employees you supervised, state the results:

> Reorganized the weekend shift, resulting in a cost savings of more than $3,000 per year.
>
> Wrote and produced (with Adobe® FrameMaker® software) a 56-page parts catalog that is still used by the company and that increased our phone inquiries by more than 25 percent.

When you describe positions, use the active voice — "supervised three workers" — rather than the passive voice — "three workers were supervised by me." The active voice emphasizes the action of the verb. In thinking about your functions and responsibilities, choose strong action verbs that clearly communicate your activities. Also note that résumés often omit the *I* at the start of sentences. Rather than write, "I prepared bids. . ." many would write, "Prepared bids." Whichever style you use, be consistent.

Figure 16.1 lists some strong verbs.

In This Book

For more on using strong verbs, see Ch. 11, p. 245.

administered	coordinated	evaluated	maintained	provided
advised	corresponded	examined	managed	purchased
analyzed	created	expanded	monitored	recorded
assembled	delivered	hired	obtained	reported
built	developed	identified	operated	researched
collected	devised	implemented	organized	solved
completed	directed	improved	performed	supervised
conducted	discovered	increased	prepared	trained
constructed	edited	instituted	produced	wrote

■ **Figure 16.1**
Strong Action Verbs Used in Résumés

Here is a sample listing:

June–September 2003: Student Dietitian

Millersville General Hospital, Millersville, TX.

> Gathered dietary histories and assisted in preparing menus for a 300-bed hospital. Received "excellent" on all items in evaluation by head dietitian.

In just a few lines, you can show that you sought and accepted responsibility and that you acted professionally. Do not write, "I accepted responsibility"; instead, present facts that lead the reader to that conclusion.

Naturally, not all jobs entail professional skills and responsibilities. Many students find summer work as laborers, sales clerks, short-order cooks, and so forth. If you have not held a professional position, list the jobs you have held, even if they were unrelated to your career plans. If the job title is self-explanatory—such as waitperson or service-station attendant—don't elaborate. If you can write that you contributed to your tuition or expenses—such as by earning 50 percent of your annual expenses through a job—employers will be impressed by your self-reliance.

One further suggestion: if you have held a number of nonprofessional as well as several professional positions, group the nonprofessional ones:

> Other Employment: cashier (summer, 1999), salesperson (part-time, 1999), clerk (summer, 1998)

This strategy prevents the nonprofessional positions from drawing the reader's attention away from the more important positions.

List jobs in reverse chronological order on the résumé to highlight the most recent employment.

Interests and Activities   Most résumés do not include such information as the writer's height, weight, date of birth, and marital status; federal legislation prohibits organizations from requiring this information. In addition, most people feel that such personal information is irrelevant to a person's ability.

However, the interests-and-activities section of the résumé is the appropriate place for several kinds of information about you:

- participation in community-service organizations—such as Big Brothers/Big Sisters—or volunteer work in a hospital
- hobbies related to your career—for example, electronics for an engineer
- sports, especially those that might be socially useful in your professional career, such as tennis, racquetball, and golf
- university-sanctioned activities, such as membership on a team, participation in the college newspaper, or election to a responsible position in an academic organization or a residence hall

Do not include activities that might create a negative impression, such as hunting, gambling, or performing in a rock band. And always omit such activities as meeting people and reading—everybody meets people and reads.

References   Potential employers will want to learn more about you from your professors and previous employers. In providing references, follow three steps:

- *Decide how you want to present the references.* On your résumé, you can list the names of three or four referees—people who have written letters of recommendation or who have agreed to speak on your behalf. Or you may say that you will furnish the names of the referees upon request. The length of your résumé sometimes dictates which approach to use. If the résumé is already long, the abbreviated form might be preferable. If it does not fill out the page, the longer form might be the better one. However, each style has advantages and disadvantages.

     Furnishing the referees' names and contact information appears open and forthright. It shows that you have already secured your referees, and the reader can easily phone them or write them a letter. Listing the referees makes it easy for the prospective employer to proceed with the hiring process. The only disadvantage is that it takes up space you might need for other information.

     Writing "References will be furnished upon request" requires only one line and it leaves you in a more flexible position. You can still secure referees after you have submitted the résumé. You can also send selected letters of reference to prospective employers according to your analysis of what they want. However, some readers will interpret the lack of names as evasive or perhaps assume that you have not yet asked prospective referees. A bigger disadvantage: if readers are impressed by your résumé and want to learn more about you, they cannot do so quickly and directly.

     What do personnel officers prefer? According to Bowman (2000), 70 percent of hiring officials want to see the full references, including the name, title, organization, mailing address, and phone number of each referee.

- *Choose your referees carefully.* Solicit references only from those who know your work best and for whom you have done your best work—for instance, a previous employer with whom you worked closely or a professor from whom you received A's. Don't ask prominent professors who do not know your work well; they will be unable to write informative letters.

- *Give the potential referee an opportunity to decline gracefully.* Sometimes the person has not been as impressed with your work as you think. If you simply ask "Would you please write a reference letter for me?" the potential referee might accept and then write a lukewarm letter. It is better to follow the first question with "Would you be able to write an enthusiastic letter for me?" or "Do you feel you know me well enough to write a strong recommendation?" If the person shows any signs of hesitation or reluctance, withdraw the request. The scene may be a little embarrassing, but it is better than receiving a weak recommendation.

Other Elements   The sections discussed so far appear on almost everyone's résumé. Other sections are either discretionary or appropriate for only some job seekers.

- *Computer skills.* Classify your skills in categories such as hardware, software, and operating systems. List any professional certifications you have been awarded.

- *Military experience.* If you are a veteran, include a military-service section. Describe your military service as if it were any other job, citing dates, locations, positions, ranks, and tasks. List positive job-performance evaluations.

- *Language ability.* If you have a working knowledge of another language, include a Language Skills section. Language skills are particularly relevant if the potential employer has international interests and you could be useful in translation or foreign service.

- *Willingness to relocate.* If you are willing to relocate, state that fact. Many organizations will find you a more attractive candidate if they know you are willing to move around as you learn the business.

Elements of the Analytical Résumé

The analytical résumé differs from the chronological one in that it includes a separate section, usually called *skills* or *skills and abilities,* to convey job skills and information.

In an analytical résumé, the employment section becomes a brief list of information about the candidate's employment history: name of the company, dates of employment, and name of the position. The skills section is usually placed prominently near the top of the résumé. Here is an example:

An analytical résumé contains:

Identifying information

Job objective

Skills and abilities

Education

Employment history

Interests and activities

References

Skills and Abilities

Management
   Served as weekend manager of six employees in the retail clothing business. Also trained three summer interns at a health-maintenance organization.

Writing and Editing
   Wrote status reports, edited performance appraisals, participated in assembling and producing an environmental impact statement using desktop publishing.

Teaching and Tutoring
   Tutored in the University Writing Center. Taught a two-week course in electronics for teenagers. Coach youth basketball.

In a skills section, you choose the headings, the arrangement, and the level of detail. Your goal, of course, is to highlight those skills the employer is seeking.

Figures 16.2, 16.3, and 16.4 show three examples of effective résumés.

For a nontraditional student, there are two strategies for presenting information. Alice Linder feels that her nontraditional status is an asset: her maturity and experience will make her a more effective employee than the traditional student. Therefore, she mentions her children and her self-financed tuition on the résumés in Figures 16.3 and 16.4. Others might omit this information because they feel it is irrelevant and draws attention away from important credentials. As a compromise between these two strategies, applicants could omit the nontraditional status from their résumés but mention it briefly in their job-application letters.

Using Tables in Formatting a Résumé

Students and professionals alike spend hours trying to format résumés. The goal is to present the headings in one typeface and size and the body content in another typeface and size. This goal can be hard to achieve when the heading is a long one, such as "Skills and Abilities," because the length cuts into the amount of space left for content. Here is an example of this problem:

Skills and Abilities: *Laboratory Skills*

   • Analyze molecular data on E & S PS300, Macintosh, and IBM PCs. Write programs in C++.

   • Have taken 12 credits in biology and chemistry labs.

Trying to format "Skills and Abilities" on two lines to leave a wider column for the content is a nuisance.

In This Book

Many of the job boards listed on p. 395 include samples of résumés.

CARLOS RODRIGUEZ

3109 Vista Street   Philadelphia, PA 19136   (215) 555-3880   crodrig@dragon.du.edu

Objective

Entry-level position in signal processing

Education

B.S. in Electrical Engineering
Drexel University, Philadelphia, PA
Anticipated June 2003
Grade-Point Average: 3.67 (on a scale of 4.0)
Senior Design Project: "Enhanced Path-Planning Software for Robotics"

Advanced Engineering Courses

Digital Signal Processing	Computer Hardware
Introduction to Operating Systems I, II	Systems Design
Digital Filters	Computer Logic Circuits I, II

Employment

6/2000–1/2001   Electrical Engineering Intern II
RCA Advanced Technology Laboratory, Moorestown, NJ
Designed ultra large-scale integrated circuits using VERILOG and VDHL hardware description languages. Assisted senior engineer in CMOS IC layout, modeling, parasitic capacitance extraction, and PSPICE simulation operations.

6/1998–1/1999   Electrical Engineering Intern I
RCA Advanced Technology Laboratory, Moorestown, NJ
Verified and documented several integrated circuit designs. Used CAD software and hardware to simulate, check, and evaluate these designs. Gained experience on the VAX and Applicon.

Honors and Organizations

Eta Kappa Nu (Electrical Engineering Honor Society)
Tau Beta Pi (General Engineering Honor Society)
Institute of Electrical and Electronics Engineers, Inc.

References

Ms. Anita Feller	Mr. Fred Borelli	Mr. Sam Shamir
Engineering Consultant	Unit Manager	Comptroller
700 Church Road	RCA Corporation	RCA Corporation
Cherry Hill, NJ 08002	Route 38	Route 38
(609) 555-7836	Moorestown, NJ 08057	Moorestown, NJ 08057
	(609) 555-2435	(609) 555-7849

■ **Figure 16.2**
Chronological Résumé of a Traditional Student

Carlos Rodriguez entered college right after high school and has proceeded on schedule. Because some of his referees are well known, he lists their names at the end of the résumé.

Alice P. Linder

1781 Weber Road
Warminster, PA 18974
(215) 555-3999
linderap423@aol.com

Objective

An internship in molecular research that uses my computer skills

Education

Harmon College, West Yardley, PA
B.S. in Bioscience and Biotechnology
Expected Graduation Date: June 2003

Related Course Work

General Chemistry I, II, III   Biology I, II, III
Organic Chemistry I, II   Statistical Methods for Research
Physics I, II   Technical Communication
Calculus I, II

Employment Experience

6/2000–present (20 hours per week): Laboratory Assistant Grade 3
GlaxoSmithKline, Upper Merion, PA
Analyze molecular data on E & S PS300, Macintosh, and IBM PCs.
Write programs in C++, and wrote a user's guide for an instructional
computing package. Train and consult with scientists and deliver in-
house briefings.

8/1997–present: Volunteer, Physical Therapy Unit
Children's Hospital of Philadelphia, Philadelphia, PA
Assist therapists and guide patients with their therapy. Use play therapy to
enhance strengthening progress.

6/1989–1/1993: Office Manager
Anchor Products, Inc., Ambler, PA
Managed 12-person office in a $1.2 million company. Also performed
general bookkeeping and payroll.

Honors

Awarded three $5,000 tuition scholarships (1996–1999) from the Gould
Foundation.

Additional Information

Member, Harmon Biology Club, Yearbook Staff
Raising three school-age children
Tuition 100% self-financed

References

Available upon request

■ **Figure 16.3**
Chronological Résumé of a Nontraditional Student

Alice Linder is a single mother returning to school. She is applying for an internship.

Alice P. Linder

1781 Weber Road	(215) 555-3999
Warminster, PA 18974	linderap423@aol.com

Objective

A position in molecular research that uses my computer skills

Skills and Abilities

Laboratory Skills
- Analyzed molecular data on E & S PS300, Macintosh, and IBM PCs. Wrote programs in C++.
- Have taken 12 credits in biology and chemistry labs.

Communication Skills
- Wrote a user's guide for an instructional computing package.
- Trained and consulted with scientists and delivered in-house briefings.

Management Skills
- Managed 12-person office in a $1.2 million company.

Education

Harmon College, West Yardley, PA
B.S. in Bioscience and Biotechnology
Expected Graduation Date: June 2003

Related Course Work

General Chemistry I, II, III	Biology I, II, III
Organic Chemistry I, II	Statistical Methods for Research
Physics I, II	Technical Communication
Calculus I, II	

Employment Experience

6/2000–present (20 hours per week)
GlaxoSmithKline, Upper Merion, PA
Laboratory Assistant Grade 3

8/1997–present
Children's Hospital of Philadelphia, Philadelphia, PA
Volunteer, Physical Therapy Unit

6/1989–1/1993
Anchor Products, Inc., Ambler, PA
Office Manager

Honors

Awarded three $5,000 tuition scholarships (1996–1999) from the Gould Foundation.

Additional Information

Member, Harmon Biology Club, Yearbook Staff
Raising three school-age children
Tuition 100 percent self-financed

References

Available upon request

■ **Figure 16.4**
Analytical Résumé of a Nontraditional Student

Another version of the résumé in the previous figure.

A good solution is to use a table format. First, create a table with the layout you want. Here is a format that might work for the basic layout:

Skills and Abilities	*Laboratory Skills* • Analyze molecular data on E & S PS300, Macintosh, and IBM PCs. Write programs in C++. • Have taken 12 credits in biology and chemistry labs.

Next, select a table format that hides the grid lines.

Skills and Abilities	*Laboratory Skills* • Analyze molecular data on E & S PS300, Macintosh, and IBM PCs. Write programs in C++. • Have taken 12 credits in biology and chemistry labs.

WRITING ELECTRONIC RÉSUMÉS

Most large and medium-sized organizations now use computerized *applicant-tracking systems* to evaluate the hundreds or even thousands of job applications they receive every day. Companies store the information from these applications in databases, which they search electronically to generate a pool of applicants for specific positions.

An electronic résumé can take several forms:

- *A formatted résumé attached to an e-mail message.* You attach the word-processing file to an e-mail message. Keep in mind, however, that some e-mail software is unable to read attached files. If the job notice requests "a plain text document sent in the body of the message," do not attach a file.

- *An ASCII résumé.* You can attach or send an ASCII résumé, one that uses the limited ASCII character set and saved as a .txt file, which can be entered directly into the organization's database.

- *A scannable résumé—one that will be scanned into an organization's database.* There are several popular database programs for this purpose, such as ResTrac or Resumix. This fact means that even when you submit a printed résumé to a company, you should consider how well the document will scan electronically.

- *A Web-based résumé.* You can put your résumé on your own Web site and hope that employers will come to you, or you can post it to a job board on the Web.

Ways of creating and sending résumés will undoubtedly change as the technology changes. For now, you need to know that the traditional printed résumé is only one of several ways to present your credentials, and you

Interactive Sample Document:
Modifying the Basic Résumé

The following résumé was written by a graduating college senior who wanted to work for Horizon Airlines Information Technology Customer Support. The questions in the margin ask you to think about the discussion of résumés (on pages 396–409). The answers to these questions are available on TechComm Web.

1. In the Objectives section, why does the writer specifically name the organization he wishes to work for?

2. What is the function of a summary section in this résumé?

3. The employment section precedes the education section. Why do you think the writer decided on this sequence?

4. Why does the writer use a first-level heading for the security clearance?

5. Why does the writer place the education section so low in the résumé?

On TechComm Web

To find the answers to these questions, click on Interactive Sample Documents for Ch. 16 on <bedfordstmartins.com/techcomm>.

| **Mel Larson** | 917 Fourth Avenue | Phone: 435 555-4389 |
| | Logan, UT 83712 | E-mail: mlarson465@aol.com |

Objective
Entry-level position in customer service with Horizon Airlines Information Technology Customer Support

Summary of Qualifications
Have a strong background in Office 2002 and its applications, Horizon Skies computer language, and World Share. Have had experience working in Horizon's IT Customer Support.

Employment
03/2001–present   **Horizon Airlines,** Salt Lake City, UT
Ramp Service Agent
• Loading and unloading of customer baggage and United States Postal Mail.
• Operation of belt loader as well as other duties.
• Temporary duties in Information Technology Customer Support.

02/2000–03/2001   **Touchdown Zone Bar and Grill,** Logan, UT
Assistant Manager
• Supervision of employees with a strong emphasis on customer satisfaction and cost control. Created inventory ordering forms and reports.

04/1996–02/2000   **Partners Bar,** Logan, UT
Lead Bartender/Manager
• Customer service and inventory maintenance.

Security Clearance
Have passed the FAA 10-year background screening for airport employees.

Education
1998–present **Utah State University,** Logan, UT
B.A. in History and English, Expected Graduation 2003
GPA: 3.1

1997–1998 **Southern Nevada Community College,** Las Vegas, NV

References
Dr. Karen Williams, Professor of History
Utah State University
1220 University Drive
Logan, UT 83713
435 555-3678

Mr. Jose Velasquez
Horizon Airlines Customer Support
1210 Geerson
Logan, UT 83713
435 555-9867

Mr. Stephen Urson, Owner
Touchdown Zone Bar and Grill
970 College Way
Logan, UT 83713
435 555-2396

should keep abreast of new techniques for applying for positions. Which form should your résumé take? Whichever form the organization prefers. If you learn of a position from an ad on the organization's own site, the ad will tell you how to apply.

Content of an Electronic Résumé

Most of the earlier discussion of the content of a printed résumé also applies to an electronic résumé. The résumé must be honest, it must be free of errors, and it must provide clear, specific information, without generalizations.

But if the résumé is to be entered into a database instead of read by a person, you need to include industry-specific jargon: all the keywords an employment officer might use in searching for qualified candidates. If an employment officer is looking for someone with experience writing Web pages, be sure you include the terms "Web page," "Internet," "HTML," "Java," and any other relevant keywords. If your current position requires an understanding of programming languages, name the languages you know. Also use keywords that refer to your communication skills, such as "public speaking," "oral communication," and "communication skills." In short, whereas a traditional printed résumé focuses on *verbs*—tasks you have done—an electronic résumé focuses on *nouns*.

The approach used by defense contractor Telos shows the importance of keywords in an electronic résumé (Vaas, 2002). Two days after the company posts a job opening on a job board, it receives about 100 résumés. The company performs a keyword search, reducing the stack to about 60 résumés, then reads them. What happens to the other 40? Nothing.

Format of an Electronic Résumé

Because electronic résumés must be easy to read and scan, they require a very simple design. Consequently, they are not as attractive as paper-based résumés, and they are longer, because they use only a single narrow column of text.

GUIDELINES

Preparing an ASCII Résumé

▶ *Use ASCII text only.* ASCII text includes the letters, numbers, and basic punctuation marks. Avoid boldface, italics, underlining, and special characters such as "smart quotation marks" or math symbols. Also avoid horizontal or vertical lines or graphics. To be sure you are using only ASCII characters, save your file as "text only." Then open it up using your software's text editor, such as Notepad, and check to be sure it contains only ASCII characters.

> *Left align the information.* Do not try to duplicate the formatting of a traditional paper résumé. It won't work. Instead, left align each new item. For example, here is a sample listing from the employment-experience section:

6/99–present
(20 hours per week)
GlaxoSmithKline
Upper Merion, PA
Analyst I

Analyze molecular data on E & S PS300, Macintosh, and IBM PCs. Write programs in C++, and wrote a user's guide for an instructional computing package. Train and consult with scientists and deliver in-house briefings.

> *Send yourself a test version of the résumé.* When you finish writing and formatting the résumé, send yourself a copy, then open it in your text editor and see if it looks professional.

Figure 16.5 is an example of a scannable résumé.

If you are mailing a paper résumé that will be scanned, follow these seven additional guidelines:

GUIDELINES

Preparing a Scannable Résumé

> *Use a good-quality laser printer.* The better the resolution, the better the scanner will work.

> *Use white paper.* Even a slight tint to the paper can increase the chances that the scanner will misinterpret a character.

> *Do not fold the résumé.* The fold line can confuse the scanner.

> *Use a simple sans-serif typeface.* Scanners can easily interpret large, open typefaces such as Arial.

> *Use a single-column format.* A double-column text will not scan accurately. Left align everything.

> *Use wide margins.* Instead of an 80-character width, set your software for 60 or 65; this way, regardless of the equipment the reader is using, the lines will break as you intend.

> *Use the space bar instead of the tab key.* Tabs will be displayed according to the settings on the reader's equipment, not the settings on yours. Therefore, use the space bar to move text horizontally.

Alice P. Linder
1781 Weber Road
Warminster, PA 18974
(215) 555-3999
linderap423@aol.com

Objective: A position in molecular research that uses my computer skills

Skills and Abilities:
Laboratory Skills. Analyze molecular data on E & S PS300, Macintosh, and IBM PCs.
Write programs in C++. Have taken 12 credits in biology and chemistry labs.

Communication Skills. Wrote a user's guide for an instructional computing package.
Train and consult with scientists and deliver in-house briefings.

Management Skills. Managed 12-person office in a $1.2 million company.

Education:
Harmon College, West Yardley, PA
B.S. in Bioscience and Biotechnology
Expected Graduation Date: June 2003

Related Course Work:
General Chemistry I, II, III
Organic Chemistry I, II
Physics I, II
Calculus I, II
Biology I, II, III
Statistical Methods for Research
Technical Communication

Employment Experience:
June 2000–present (20 hours per week)
GlaxoSmithKline, Upper Merion, PA
Laboratory Assistant Grade 3

August 1997–present
Children's Hospital of Philadelphia, Philadelphia, PA
Volunteer, Physical Therapy Unit

June 1989–January 1993
Anchor Products, Inc., Ambler, PA
Office Manager

■ **Figure 16.5**
Electronic Résumé

This is an electronic version of the résumé in Figure 16.4. Notice that the writer uses ASCII text and left justification.

Honors:
Awarded three $5,000 tuition scholarships (1996-1999) from the Gould Foundation.

Additional Information:
Member, Harmon Biology Club, Yearbook Staff
Raising three school-age children
Tuition 100% self-financed

Keywords:
C+, IBM, PC, Macintosh, molecular research, programming, presentations, management, laboratory assistant, volunteer, physical therapy

References:
Available upon request.

The writer has added a keywords list.

■ **Figure 16.5**
(Continued)

WRITING JOB-APPLICATION LETTERS

Most job applications call for a letter as well as a résumé. The letter is crucial because it is the first thing your reader sees. If the letter is ineffective, the reader probably will not bother to read the résumé. Unlike the résumé, which most applicants do not customize for each application, the letter is addressed to a particular individual at a specific address. Therefore, it makes sense to have the letter appeal as directly and specifically as possible to a particular person.

The Concept of Selectivity

Like the résumé, the letter is a sales document. Its purpose is to convince the reader that you are an outstanding candidate who should be invited for an interview.

The key to a good letter is selectivity. Don't try to cover every point on your résumé. Choose two or three points of greatest interest to the potential employer and develop them into paragraphs. Emphasize results, such as improved productivity or quality or decreased costs. If one of your previous part-time positions called for skills that the employer is looking for, write a substantial paragraph about that position, even though the résumé devotes only a few lines to it.

In most cases, a job-application letter should fill the better part of a page. Like all business letters, it should be single spaced, with an extra line between paragraphs. For more-experienced candidates, the letter may be longer, but most students find that they can adequately describe their credentials in one page. Again, selectivity is important. If you write at length on a minor point,

In This Book

For more about formatting letters, see Ch.15, p. 367.

you become boring and appear to have poor judgment. Employers seek candidates who can say a lot in a small space.

Elements of the Job-Application Letter

The inside address—the name, title, organization, and address of the recipient—is important because you want to be sure your materials get to the right person. And you don't want to offend that person with a misspelling or an incorrect title. If you are uncertain about any of the information—the reader's name, for example, might have an unusual spelling—verify it by phoning the organization.

When you do not know who should receive the letter, phone the company to find out who manages the department. If you are unsure of the appropriate department or division to write to, address the letter to a high-level executive, such as the president. The letter will be directed to the right person. Also, because the application includes both a letter and a résumé, use an enclosure notation.

The four-paragraph example that will be discussed here is only a basic model, consisting of an introductory paragraph, two body paragraphs, and a concluding paragraph. At a minimum, your letter should include these four paragraphs, but there is no reason it cannot have five or six.

Plan the letter carefully. Present information that best responds to the needs of the potential employer. Draft the letter and then revise it. Let it sit for a while, then revise it again. Spend as much time on it as you can. Make each paragraph a unified, functional part of the whole letter. Supply clear transitions from one paragraph to the next.

In This Book

For more about developing paragraphs, see Ch. 10, p. 224.

The Introductory Paragraph   The introductory paragraph establishes the tone of the letter and captures the reader's attention. It has four specific functions.

- *It identifies your source of information.* In an unsolicited application, all you can do is ask if a position is available. For a solicited application, however, name your source of information: the organization's Web site, a published ad, or a current employee. For an ad, identify the publication and its date of issue. If an employee told you about the position, identify that person by name and title.

- *It identifies the position you are interested in.* Often, the organization you are applying to has advertised many positions; if you omit the title of the position you are interested in, your reader might not know which one you seek.

- *It states that you wish to be considered for the position.* Although the context makes your wish obvious, you should mention it because the letter would be awkward without it.

- *It forecasts the rest of the letter.* Choose a few phrases that forecast the body of the letter, so that the letter flows smoothly. For example, if you use the phrase "retail experience" in the opening paragraph, you are preparing your reader for the discussion of your retail experience later in the letter.

These four points need not appear in any particular order, nor does each need to be covered in a single sentence. The following sample paragraphs demonstrate different ways of providing the necessary information:

Response to a job ad
I am writing in response to your notice in the May 13 *New York Times*. Please consider me for the position in system programming. I hope you find that my studies in computer science at Eastern University, along with my programming experience at Airborne Instruments, would qualify me for the position.

Unsolicited
My academic training in hotel management and my experience with Sheraton International have given me a solid background in the hotel industry. Would you please consider me for any management trainee position that might be available?

Unsolicited personal contact
Mr. Howard Alcott of your Research and Development Department suggested that I write to you. He thinks that my organic chemistry degree and my practical experience with Brown Laboratories might be of value to XYZ Corporation. Do you have an entry-level position in organic chemistry for which I might be considered?

The difficult part of the introductory paragraph—and of the whole letter—is to achieve the proper tone: quiet self-confidence. Your tone must be modest but not self-effacing or negative. Never say, for example, "I do not have a very good background in computers, but I'm willing to learn." The reader will take this kind of statement at face value and probably stop reading right there.

The Education Paragraph   For most students, the education paragraph should come before the employment paragraph because the education paragraph will be stronger. If, however, your employment experience is stronger, present it first.

In writing your education paragraph, take your cue from the job ad (if you are responding to one). What aspect of your education most directly fits the job requirements? If the ad stresses versatility, you might structure your paragraph around the range and diversity of your courses. Also, you might discuss course work in a subject related to your major, such as business or communication skills. Extracurricular activities are often very valuable; if you were an officer in a student organization, you could discuss the activities and programs that you coordinated. Perhaps the most popular strategy for developing the education paragraph is to discuss skills and knowledge gained from advanced course work in your major field.

Develop one unified idea. Do not present a series of unrelated facts. Notice how each of the following education paragraphs develops a unified idea.

EXAMPLE 1   At Eastern University, I have taken a wide range of science courses, but my most advanced work has been in chemistry. In one laboratory course, I developed a new aseptic brewing technique that lowered the risk of infection by more than 40 percent. This new technique was the subject of an article in the *Eastern Science Digest*. Representatives from three national breweries have visited our laboratory to discuss the technique with me.

EXAMPLE 2   To broaden my education at Southern University, I took eight business courses in addition to my requirements for the civil engineering degree. Because your ad mentions that the position will require substantial client contact, I believe that my work in marketing, in particular, would be of special value. In an advanced marketing seminar, I used FrameMaker® to produce a 20-page sales brochure describing the various kinds of building structures for sale by Oppenheimer Properties to industrial customers in our section of the city. That brochure is now being used at Oppenheimer, where I am an intern.

EXAMPLE 3   The most rewarding part of my education at Western University took place outside the classroom. My entry in a fashion-design competition sponsored by the university won second place. More important, through the competition I met the chief psychologist at Western Regional Hospital, who invited me to design clothing for people with disabilities. I have since completed six different outfits, which are now being tested at the hospital. I hope to be able to pursue this interest once I start work.

Each of these paragraphs begins with a topic sentence, then adds details to develop the main idea. An additional point: if you haven't already specified your major and your college or university in the introductory paragraph, be sure to do so here.

The Employment Paragraph   Like the education paragraph, the employment paragraph should begin with a topic sentence and develop a single idea. That idea might be that you have a broad background or that one job in particular has given you special skills that make you especially well suited for the available job. Here are several examples of effective experience paragraphs.

EXAMPLE 1   For the past three summers and part-time during the academic year, I have worked for Redego, Inc., a firm that specializes in designing and planning industrial complexes. I began as an assistant in the drafting room. By the second summer, I was accompanying a civil engineer on field inspections. Most recently, I have used AutoCAD to assist an engineer in designing and drafting the main structural supports for a 15-acre, $30 million chemical facility.

EXAMPLE **2**   Although I have worked every summer since I was 15, my most recent position, as a technical editor, has been the most rewarding. I was chosen by Digital Systems, Inc., from among 30 candidates because of my dual background in computer science and writing. My job was to coordinate the editing of computer manuals. Our copy editors, who are generally not trained in computer science, need someone to help verify the technical accuracy of their revisions. When I was unable to answer their questions, I was responsible for interviewing our systems analysts to find the correct answer and to make sure the computer novice could follow it. This position gave me a good understanding of the process by which operating manuals are created.

EXAMPLE **3**   I have worked in merchandising for three years as a part-time and summer salesperson in men's fashions and accessories. I have had experience running inventory-control software and helped one company switch from a manual to an online system. Most recently, I assisted in clearing $200,000 in out-of-date men's fashions: I coordinated a campaign to sell half of the merchandise at cost and was able to convince the manufacturer's representative to accept the other half for full credit. For this project, I received a certificate of appreciation from the company president.

The writers of these paragraphs carefully define their duties to explain the nature and extent of their responsibilities.

Although you will discuss your education and experience in separate paragraphs, try to link these two halves of your background. If an academic course led to an interest that you were able to pursue in a job, make that point in the transition from one paragraph to the other. Similarly, if a job experience helped shape your academic career, tell the reader about it.

The Concluding Paragraph   The purpose of the concluding paragraph is to stimulate action. You want the reader to invite you for an interview. In the preceding paragraphs, you provided the information that should have convinced the reader to give you another look. In the last paragraph, you want to make it easy for him or her to do so. The concluding paragraph contains three main elements:

- *A reference to your résumé.* If you have not yet referred to it, do so now.

- *A polite but confident request for an interview.* Use the phrase *at your convenience.* Don't make the request sound as if you're asking a personal favor.

- *Your phone number and e-mail address.* State the time of day you can be reached. Adding an e-mail address gives the employer one more way to get in touch with you.

Here are two examples of effective concluding paragraphs.

EXAMPLE **1**   The enclosed résumé provides more information about my education and experience. Could we meet at your convenience to discuss further the skills and experience I could bring to Pentamax? You can leave a message for me anytime at (303) 555-5957 or cfilli@claus.cmu.edu.

EXAMPLE **2**   More information about my education and experience is included on the enclosed résumé, but I would appreciate the opportunity to meet with you at your convenience to discuss my application. You can reach me after noon on Tuesdays and Thursdays at (212) 555-4527 or leave a message anytime.

The examples of effective job-application letters in Figures 16.6 and 16.7 correspond to the résumés in Figures 16.2 and 16.3.

PREPARING FOR JOB INTERVIEWS

If your job-application letter is successful, you will be invited to a job interview: a face-to-face meeting with one or more representatives from the organization. The purpose of a job interview is to help you and the organization determine whether you would be a good fit working there. Probably, you are thinking about how to impress the organization so that it proceeds to the next step: scheduling another interview or making an offer of employment. But don't forget your other purpose: to determine whether you would like to work there. You gain very little if you get a job that won't be satisfying.

GUIDELINES

Preparing for a Job Interview

For every hour you spend in a job interview, you need to do many hours of preparation.

▶ *Study job interviews.* There are dozens of books and Web sites devoted to job interviews. Many are quite comprehensive, covering everything from how to do your initial research to common interview questions to how to dress. You can't prepare for everything that will happen in a job interview, but you can prepare for a lot of things.

▶ *Study the organization to which you applied.* Perhaps your single most important task is to learn everything you can about the organization. If you inadvertently show that you haven't done your homework, the interviewer will assume that you're always unprepared. Learn what

On TechComm Web

For links to Web sites about employment, click on Links Library for Ch. 16 on <bedfordstmartins .com/techcomm>.

In This Book

Many of the job boards listed on p. 395 include samples of application letters.

3109 Vista Street
Philadelphia, PA 19136

January 20, 2003

Mr. Stephen Spencer, Director of Personnel
Department 411
Boeing Naval Systems
103 Industrial Drive
Wilmington, DE 20093

Dear Mr. Spencer:

I am writing in response to your advertisement in the January 16 *Philadelphia Inquirer*. Would you please consider me for the position in Signal Processing? I believe that my academic training in electrical engineering at Drexel University, along with my experience with RCA Advanced Technology Laboratory, would qualify me for the position.

My education at Drexel has given me a strong background in computer hardware and system design. I have concentrated on digital and computer applications, developing and designing computer and signal-processing hardware in two graduate-level engineering courses. For my senior-design project, I am working with four other undergraduates in using OO programming techniques to enhance the path-planning software for an infrared night-vision robotics application.

While working at the RCA Advanced Technology Laboratory, I was able to apply my computer experience to the field of the VLSI design. I designed ultra large-scale integrated circuits using VERILOG and VHDL hardware description languages. In addition, I assisted a senior engineer in CMOS IC layout, modeling, parasitic capacitance extraction, and PSPICE simulation operations.

The enclosed résumé provides an overview of my education and experience. Could I meet with you at your convenience to discuss my qualifications for this position? Please write to me at the above address or leave a message anytime at (215) 555-3880. My e-mail address is crodrig@dragon.du.edu.

Yours truly,

Carlos Rodriguez

Carlos Rodriguez

Enclosure (1)

An enclosure notation refers to the résumé.

■ **Figure 16.6**
Job-Application Letter

1781 Weber Road
Warminster, PA 18974

January 17, 2003

Mr. Harry Gail
Fox Run Medical Center
399 N. Abbey Road
Warminster, PA 18974

Dear Mr. Gail:

Last April I contacted your office regarding the possibility of an internship as a laboratory assistant at your center. Your assistant, Mary McGuire, told me then that you might consider such a position this year. With the experience I have gained since last year, I believe I would be a valuable addition to your center in many ways.

At Harmon College, I have earned a 3.7 GPA in 36 credits in chemistry and biology; all but two of these courses had laboratory components. One skill stressed at Harmon is the ability to communicate effectively, both in writing and orally. Our science courses have extensive writing and speaking requirements; my portfolio includes seven research papers and lab reports of more than 20 pages each, and I have delivered four oral presentations, one of 45 minutes, to classes.

At GlaxoSmithKline, where I currently work part-time, I analyze molecular data on an E & S PS300, a Macintosh, and an IBM PC. I have tried to remain current with the latest advances; my manager at GlaxoSmithKline has allowed me to attend two different two-day in-house seminars on computerized data analysis using SAS. My experience as the manager of a 12-person office for four years helped me acquire interpersonal skills that would benefit Fox Run.

More information about my education and experience is included on the enclosed résumé, but I would appreciate the opportunity to meet with you at your convenience to discuss my application. If you would like any additional information about me or Harmon's internship program, please write to me at the above address, call me at (215) 555-3999, or e-mail me at linderap423@aol.com.

Very truly yours,

Alice P. Linder

Alice P. Linder

Enclosure

The first two paragraphs of the body discuss the applicant's qualifications for the internship position.

Here the applicant explains how her additional experience as an office manager has enabled her to develop skills that would be of value to anyone in any field.

■ **Figure 16.7**
Job-Application Letter

The writer discusses her nontraditional background without overemphasizing it. She exploits her situation gracefully, always appealing to the reader's needs, without asking for special consideration.

In This Book

For more on research techniques, see Ch. 7.

products or services the organization provides, how well it has done in recent years, what its plans are, and so forth. Start with the organization's own Web site, then proceed to online and print resources. Search for the organization's name on the Internet.

▶ *Think about what you can offer the organization.* Although you want to discover whether you would like to join the organization, your goal during the interview is to make the case that you can help the organization accomplish its goals. Think about how your academic career, your work experience, and your personal characteristics and experiences have prepared you to solve problems and carry out projects to help the organization succeed. Jot down notes about projects you carried out in courses, experiences you have had on the job, and activities you pursue in your personal life that can serve as persuasive evidence to support claims about your qualifications.

In This Book

For more on communicating persuasively, see Ch. 6.

▶ *Study lists of common interview questions.* Interviewers study these lists; you should, too. You're probably familiar with some of the favorites:

–Where do you see yourself in five years?
–Why did you apply to our company?
–What do you see as your greatest strengths and weaknesses?
–Tell me about an incident that taught you something important about yourself.
–What was your best course in college? Why?

▶ *Compile a list of questions you wish to ask.* Near the end of the interview, the interviewer will probably ask if you have any questions. This is not mere politeness. The interviewer expects you to have compiled a brief list of questions about working for the organization. Do not focus on salary, vacation days, or sick leave. Instead, ask about ways you can continue to develop as a professional, improving your ability to contribute to the organization.

▶ *Rehearse the interview.* It's one thing to think about how you might answer an interview question. It's another to have to answer it. Rehearse the interview by asking friends or colleagues to play the role of the interviewers, making up questions that you haven't thought about. Then ask these people for constructive criticism.

In This Book

For a list of Internet job boards, see p. 395.

The job boards on the Internet do an excellent job in preparing candidates for the experience of a job interview. They discuss questions such as the following:

• When should you arrive for the interview?
• What should you wear?
• How do interviewers interpret your body language?

- What questions is the interviewer likely to ask?
- How long should your answers be?
- How do you know when the interviewer wishes to end the interview?
- How can you get the interviewer's contact information to write a follow-up letter?

WRITING FOLLOW-UP LETTERS

After an interview, you should write a thank-you letter and perhaps one of the others listed here:

- *The letter of appreciation after an interview.* Thank the representative for taking the time to see you, and emphasize your particular qualifications. You can also restate your interest in the position. The follow-up letter can do more good with less effort than any other step in the job-application procedure, because so few candidates take the time to write it. Here is an example:

In This Book

Many of the job boards listed on p. 395 include samples of follow-up letters.

Dear Mr. Weaver:

Thank you for taking the time yesterday to show me your facilities and to introduce me to your colleagues.

Your advances in piping design were particularly impressive. As a person with hands-on experience in piping design, I can appreciate the advantages your design will have.

The vitality of your projects and the good fellowship among your employees further confirm my initial belief that Cynergo would be a fine place to work. I would look forward to joining your staff.

Sincerely yours,

Harriet Bommarito

Harriet Bommarito

- *The letter accepting a job offer.* This one is easy: express appreciation, show enthusiasm, and repeat the major terms of your employment. Here is an example:

Dear Mr. Weaver:

Thank you very much for the offer to join your staff. I accept.

I look forward to joining your design team on Monday, July 19. The salary, as you indicate in your letter, is $38,250.

As you have recommended, I will get in touch with Mr. Matthews in Personnel to get a start on the paperwork.

I appreciate the trust you have placed in me, and I assure you that I will do what I can to be a productive team member at Cynergo.

Sincerely yours,

Mark Greenberg

Mark Greenberg

- *The letter of rejection in response to a job offer.* If you decide not to accept a job offer, express your appreciation and, if appropriate, explain why you are declining the offer. Remember, you might want to work for this company some time in the future. Here is an example:

Dear Mr. Weaver:

I appreciate very much the offer to join your staff.

Although I am certain that I would benefit greatly from working at Cynergo, I have decided to take a job with a firm in Pittsburgh, where I have been accepted at Carnegie-Mellon to pursue my master's degree at night.

Again, thank you for your generous offer.

Sincerely yours,

Cynthia O'Malley

Cynthia O'Malley

- *The letter acknowledging a rejection.* Why write back after you have been rejected? To maintain good relations. You might get a phone call the next week explaining that the person who accepted the job has had to change her plans and offering you the position. Here is an example of this kind of letter.

Dear Mr. Weaver:

I was disappointed to learn that I will not have a chance to join your staff, because I feel that I could make a substantial contribution. However, I appreciate that job decisions are complex, involving many candidates and many factors.

Thank you very much for the courtesy you have shown me. I have long believed — and I still believe — that Cynergo is a first-class organization.

Sincerely yours,

Paul Goicochea

Paul Goicochea

CREATING ELECTRONIC PORTFOLIOS

An increasingly popular way to search for a job is to create an *electronic portfolio,* an online collection of materials including the applicant's résumé and other samples of his or her work. Students and professionals alike display the electronic portfolio on the Internet or copy it to a disk and make it available to prospective employers.

Items typically presented in an electronic portfolio include the following:

- a résumé

- letters of recommendation

- transcripts and professional certifications

- reports, papers, Web sites, slides of oral presentations, and other documents the applicant has written or created as a student or an employee

Because the portfolio is electronic, it can include all kinds of media, from simple word-processed documents to HTML files, video, audio, and animation. And it's relatively easy to update an electronic portfolio: just add the new items as you create them. One important point that comes across clearly in a carefully prepared electronic portfolio: you know how to make a Web site.

Figure 16.8 shows an excerpt from the home page of a student's electronic portfolio.

On TechComm Web

For more on online portfolios, see "Developing Your Online Portfolio," by Kevin M. Barry & Jill C. Wesolowski. Click on Links Library for Ch. 16 on <bedfordstmartins.com/techcomm>.

In This Book

For information about making Web sites, see Ch. 21.

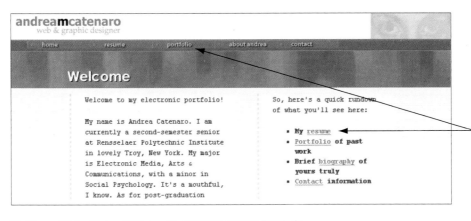

Andrea M. Catenaro has created an attractive and professional-looking portfolio.

She uses button links, as well as textual links, to the main items in the portfolio. See Ch. 21 for a discussion of the use of textual links.

■ **Figure 16.8   Excerpt from a Student Electronic Portfolio**

Source: Catenaro, 2002 <www.andreacatenaro.com/index.html>.

Creating an Electronic Portfolio

To create an electronic portfolio, follow these seven steps:

1. *Analyze your audience and purpose.* Are you writing to potential employers? To a supervisor at work? Consider your purpose. Are you trying to showcase your technical skill? Your ability to write different kinds of documents? Your analysis of audience and purpose will determine what items to include in the portfolio and how to present them.

2. *Gather your materials.* Always include your current résumé. Consider, too, evidence of your accomplishments, such as transcripts, licenses or certifications, and reference letters. Finally, gather your work samples from courses or the workplace. Think of reports and other kinds of documents you have written, Web sites you have created, and graphics from oral presentations.

3. *Organize your materials.* With all your materials before you, organize them to display your credentials effectively. If you wish to emphasize how your skills have developed over time, consider a chronological organization. Most readers, however, will probably expect a topical organization, with categories such as background, certifications and honors, course projects, and workplace samples. Some categories, such as workplace samples, might be subdivided into subcategories such as computer skills, oral presentations, and project reports.

4. *Write introductory statements for each major item in the portfolio and for the whole portfolio.* The statement about each portfolio item helps readers understand what the item is, when and why you created it, what tools you used, what skills you learned, and what you would do differently if you had other resources. The statement about the whole portfolio is your opportunity to explain how the different items fit together and how they demonstrate your professionalism.

In This Book

For more information on coding materials for on-screen display, see Ch. 21, p. 550.

5. *Prepare the materials for electronic display.* For print documents, use software such as Adobe® Acrobat® to create portable documents that can be stored and displayed online but that retain their print formatting. For online documents, such as Web pages, use a Web editor or work in a text editor such as Notepad to create hypertext. Use graphics software to code graphics to add to the site.

6. *Review and revise the portfolio draft.* Test the draft to make sure all the links work and that the material is well organized, attractive, and professional. Ask others to help you determine areas to improve.

7. *Assemble the portfolio.* After revising the portfolio, either upload it to a Web site or burn it to a CD.

Reviewing the Process

Plan the job search.

Do a self-inventory, learn as much as you can about the employers, and begin to plan your materials.

Decide how to look for a position.

Use as many techniques as you can: the college-placement office on campus, published ads, company Web sites, and so forth.

Learn as much as you can about the organizations to which you will apply.

Use appropriate techniques of primary and secondary research. See Chapter 7.

Draft the résumé and the application letter.

Decide whether to write a chronological or an analytical résumé. Include the traditional sections—identifying information, job objectives, education, employment history, personal information, and references—and other appropriate sections, such as military service, language skills, or computer skills. For an analytical résumé, include a skills section. Decide whether to write a scannable résumé.

Draft the letter to elaborate on several key points from the résumé. Include the traditional introductory and concluding paragraphs, as well as at least one paragraph on your job experience and one on your education.

Revise the résumé and letter. You want these documents to be perfect. Try to have several people help you revise and edit them. See the Revision Checklist on page 428.

Prepare for job interviews.

Study job interviews, research the organization you applied to, think about what you can offer the organization, study lists of common interview questions, compile a list of questions to ask, and rehearse the interview.

Write appropriate follow-up letters.

With any luck, you'll get to write a letter of appreciation after an interview, and then a letter accepting a job offer.

Revision Checklist

Printed Résumé

❏ Does the résumé have a professional appearance, with generous margins, a symmetrical layout, adequate white space, and effective indentation? (p. 397)

❏ Does the résumé respond to the needs of its readers? (p. 398)

❏ Is the résumé honest? (p. 398)

❏ Is the résumé free of errors? (p. 398)

❏ Does the identifying information section contain your name, address(es), phone number(s), and e-mail address(es)? (p. 399)

❏ Does the résumé include a clear statement of your job objectives? (p. 399)

❏ Does the education section include your degree, your institution and its location, and your anticipated date of graduation, as well as any other information that will help a reader appreciate your qualifications? (p. 399)

❏ Does the employment section include, for each job, the dates of employment, the organization's name and location, and (if you are writing a chronological résumé) your position or title, as well as a description of your duties and accomplishments? (p. 401)

❏ Does the interests and activities section include relevant hobbies or activities, including extracurricular interests? (p. 402) Have you omitted any personal information that might reflect poorly on you? (p. 403)

❏ Does the references section include the names, job titles, organizations, mailing addresses, and phone numbers of three or four referees? (p. 403) If you are not listing this information, does the strength of the rest of the résumé offset the omission? (p. 403)

❏ Does the résumé include any other appropriate sections, such as military service, language skills, or honors? (p. 404)

Electronic Résumé

In addition to the items mentioned in the checklist for the printed résumé, did you

❏ use ASCII text? (p. 411)

❏ use a simple sans-serif typeface? (p. 412)

❏ use a single-column format? (p. 412)

❏ use wide margins? (p. 412)

❏ use the space bar instead of the tab key? (p. 412)

Job-Application Letter

❏ Is the letter honest? (p. 398)

❏ Does the letter look professional? (p. 414)

❏ Does the letter respond to the needs of its readers? (p. 415)

❏ Does the introductory paragraph identify your source of information and the position you are applying for, state that you wish to be considered, and forecast the rest of the letter? (p. 415)

❏ Does the education paragraph respond to your reader's needs with a unified idea introduced by a topic sentence? (p. 416)

❏ Does the employment paragraph respond to your reader's needs with a unified idea introduced by a topic sentence? (p. 417)

❏ Does the concluding paragraph include a reference to your résumé, a request for an interview, your phone number, and your e-mail address? (p. 418)

❏ Does the letter include an enclosure notation? (p. 420)

Preparing for a Job Interview

Did you

❏ study job interviews? (p. 419)

❏ study the organization to which you applied? (p. 419)

❏ think about what you can offer the organization? (p. 422)

❏ study lists of common interview questions? (p. 422)

❏ compile a list of questions you wish to ask? (p. 422)

❏ rehearse the interview? (p. 422)

Follow-up Letters

❏ Does the letter of appreciation for a job interview thank the interviewer and briefly restate your qualifications? (p. 423)

❏ Does the letter accepting a job offer show enthusiasm and repeat the major terms of your employment? (p. 423)

❏ Does the letter of rejection in response to a job offer express your appreciation and, if appropriate, explain why you are declining the offer? (p. 424)

❏ Does the letter acknowledging a rejection maintain a positive tone that will help you maintain good relations? (p. 424)

Exercises

1. **Internet Activity** Using a job board on the Web, list and briefly describe five positions in your field in your state. What skills, experience, and background does each position require? What is the salary range for each position?

2. **Internet Activity** Locate and provide the URLs of three job boards that provide interactive forms for creating a résumé automatically. In a brief memo to your instructor, describe the strengths and weaknesses of each. Which appears to be the easiest to use? Why? (For more on memos, see Chapter 15, page 378.)

3. The following résumé was submitted in response to an ad describing the following duties: "Research and develop key technology and system concepts for spectrally efficient digital radio frequency data networks such as digital cellular mobile radio telephones, public safety trunked digital radio systems, and satellite communications." In a brief memo to your instructor, describe how effective the résumé is. What are some of its problems? (For more on memos, see Chapter 15, page 378.)

Rajiv Siharath
2319 Fifth Avenue
Waverly, CT 01603
Phone: 611-3356

Personal Data:	22 Years old Height 5'11" Weight 176 lbs.
Education:	B.S. in Electrical Engineering University of Connecticut, June, 2003
Experience:	6/01–9/01 Falcon Electronics Examined panels for good wiring. Also, I revised several schematics.
	6/00–9/00 MacDonalds Electrical Supply Co. Worked parts counter.
	6/99–9/99 Happy Burger Made hamburgers, fries, shakes, fish sandwiches, and fried chicken.
	6/98–9/98 Town of Waverly Outdoor maintenance. In charge of cleaning up McHenry Park and Municipal Pool picnic grounds. Did repairs on some electrical equipment.
Backround:	Born and raised in Waverly. Third baseman, Fisherman's Rest softball team.

Hobbies:	jogging, salvaging and repairing appliances, reading magazines, politics.
References:	Will be furnished upon request.

4. The following application letter responds to an ad describing the following duties: "Buyer for a high-fashion ladies' dress shop. Experience required." In a brief memo to your instructor, describe how effective the letter is, and how it could be improved.

April 13, 2003

Marilyn Grissert
Best Department Store
113 Hawthorn
Atlanta, Georgia

Dear Ms. Grissert:

As I was reading the *Sunday Examiner*, I came upon your ad for a buyer. I have always been interested in learning about the South, so would you consider my application?

I will receive my degree in fashion design in one month. I have taken many courses in fashion design, so I feel I have a strong background in the field.

Also, I have had extensive experience in retail work. For two summers I sold women's accessories at a local clothing store. In addition, I was a temporary department head for two weeks.

I have enclosed a résumé and would like to interview you at your convenience. I hope to see you in the near future. My phone number is 555-6103.

Sincerely,

Brenda Sisneros

5. How effective is the following letter of appreciation? How could it be improved? Present your findings in a brief memo to your instructor.

914 Imperial Boulevard
Durham, NC 27708

November 13, 2003

Mr. Ronald O'Shea
Division Engineering
Safeway Electronics, Inc.
Holland, MI 49423

Dear Mr. O'Shea:

Thanks very much for showing me around your plant. I hope I was able to convince you that I'm the best person for the job.

Sincerely yours,

Robert Harad

Project

6. **Internet Activity** In a newspaper or journal or on the Internet, find a job ad for a position in your field for which you might be qualified. Write a résumé and a job-application letter in response to the ad; include the job ad or a photocopy. You will be evaluated not only on the content and appearance of the materials, but also on how well you have targeted them to the job ad.

CASE
Updating Career-Center Materials

The members of your group are student interns in the Career Center at your school. The director of the center, William Karey, would like your group to assist him in updating the materials he distributes to students looking for work. "What I'd like you to do," he tells you, "is to take a look at what is out there on the Web and integrate it with what we already have on résumés and job letters." If possible, secure an electronic copy of available materials from your school's Career Center. Then search the Web for additional information about résumés and job letters. Is the information from the Web consistent with the information from the Career Center? Which sources on the Web seem to be of most use to students at your school? Decide whether you should integrate the new information with the material the Career Center already distributes, put part or all of the new information on the school's Web site, or both. Regardless of your ultimate decision, submit a copy of the existing materials as well as a copy of the new materials. Submit your findings in a memo to Mr. Karey. (For more on memos, see Chapter 15, page 378.)

Writing Proposals

17

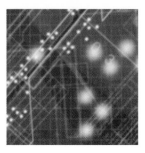

Alice Reid (2001), of Delaware Technical and Community College, Wilmington, Delaware, describes the criteria according to which proposals are evaluated:

Any proposal offers a plan to fill a need, and your reader will evaluate your plan according to how well your written presentation answers questions about WHAT you are proposing, HOW you plan to do it, WHEN you plan to do it, and HOW MUCH it is going to cost.

On TechComm Web

For additional samples, activities, and links related to this chapter, see <bedfordstmartins.com/techcomm>.

Most projects undertaken by organizations, and most major changes made within organizations, begin with a proposal. A proposal is an offer to carry out research or to provide a product or service.

THE LOGISTICS OF PROPOSALS

Proposals can be classified as either external or internal and as either solicited or unsolicited. Figure 17.1 shows the relationship among these four terms.

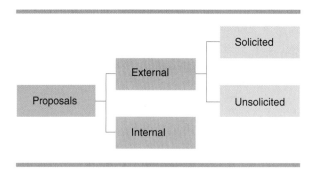

■ Figure 17.1   The Logistics of Proposals

External and Internal Proposals

Proposals are either external (if submitted to another organization) or internal (if submitted to the writer's own organization).

External Proposals   No organization produces all the products or provides all the services it needs. Office furniture and equipment has to be purchased, and offices must be cleaned and maintained. Sometimes projects require unusual expertise, such as sophisticated market analyses. Because many companies supply these products and services, most organizations require that a prospective supplier compete for the business by submitting a proposal, a document arguing that it deserves the business.

Internal Proposals   One day, while working on a project in the laboratory, you realize that if you had a new centrifuge you could do your job better and faster. The increased productivity would save your company the cost of the equipment in a few months. You call your supervisor, who tells you to send a memo describing what you want, why you want it, what you're going to do with it, and what it costs; if your request seems reasonable and the money is available, you'll likely get the new centrifuge.

Your memo is an *internal proposal*—a persuasive argument, submitted within an organization, for carrying out an activity that will benefit the organization. An internal proposal might recommend that the organization conduct research, purchase a product, or change some aspect of its policies or procedures. The scope of the proposal determines its format. A request for a small amount of money might be conveyed orally, either in person or on the phone, or by e-mail or a brief memo. A request for a large amount, however, is generally presented in a formal proposal.

Solicited and Unsolicited Proposals

External proposals are either solicited or unsolicited. A solicited proposal is submitted in response to a request from the customer. An unsolicited proposal is submitted by a prospective supplier who believes that the customer has a need for goods or services.

Solicited Proposals   When an organization wants to purchase a product or service, it publishes one of two basic kinds of statements:

- An IFB—*information for bid*—is used for standard products. When an agency of the federal government needs desktop computers, for instance, it informs computer manufacturers of the configuration it needs. All other things being equal, the supplier that offers the lowest bid wins the contract.

- An RFP—*request for proposal*—is issued for more-customized products or services. For example, if the Air Force needs a friend-or-foe radar device, the RFP it publishes might be a long and detailed set of technical specifications. The supplier that can design, produce, and deliver the device most closely resembling the specifications—at a reasonable price—will probably win the contract.

On TechComm Web

For links to these government journals, click on Links Library for Ch. 17 on <bedfordstmartins.com /techcomm>.

Most organizations issue RFPs and IFBs in newspapers or send them in the mail to past suppliers. Government RFPs and IFBs are published in the journals *Commerce Business Daily* (for contracts under $25,000) and *FedBizOps* (for contracts over $25,000), both of which are available online. Figure 17.2 shows a sample entry.

Unsolicited Proposals   An unsolicited proposal looks like a solicited proposal except that it does not refer to an RFP. Even though the potential customer never formally requested the proposal, in almost all cases the supplier

The reader clicks on this link to view the full description of the solicitation.

> *Attn: Department of Veterans Affairs, Acquisition Operations and Analysis Service, (049A3), 810 Vermont Avenue, N.W., Washington, District Of Columbia 20420*
> B3112 APR18 FOR MORTALITY STUDY OF THE VETERAN POPULATION (SRCSGT) SOL 101-05-02-RFI DUE 050302 POC
>
> Contracting Officer - Domenico M. Ventura, Senior Contracting Officer, (202) 273-8764 WEB: RFI 101-05-02-RFI
> http://www.bos.oamm.va.gov/solicitation?number=101-05-02-RFI
>
> E-MAIL: E-mail your questions to Domenico M. Ventura
> domenico.ventura@mail.va.gov
>
> REQUEST FOR INFORMATION Department of Veterans Affairs (VA) request your comments and recommendations on the attached draft statement of work (SOW) for Mortality Study of the Veteran Population. VA is in the process of identifying offerors capable of providing the subject services listed in the attached draft SOW for a future procurement. We would like interested parties to provide a rough order of magnitude estimate of the cost for the subject work and provide us with the qualifications and experience of your firm. Please provide your comments, recommendations, rough order estimate, and qualifications to Mr. Domenico M. Ventura via e-mail by 4:00 p.m., May 3, 2002, at Domenico.ventura@mail.va.gov indicating your interest in this program.
>
> Originally issued as a special notice Fed Biz Ops Number VA-SNOTE-020416-001 Posted 04/16/02 (fbodaily.com W-SN00060557). (0106)

■ **Figure 17.2   Extract from CBDNET**

Source: CBD/FBO Online, 2002 <www.cbdweb.com/cgi-bin/cbd>.

was invited to submit the proposal after people from the two organizations met and discussed the project. Because proposals are expensive to write, suppliers are reluctant to submit them without assurances that the potential customer will study them carefully. Thus, the word *unsolicited* is only partially accurate.

External proposals—both solicited and unsolicited—can culminate in contracts of several types: a flat fee for a product or a one-time service; a leasing agreement; or a "cost-plus" contract, under which the supplier is reimbursed for the actual cost plus a profit set at a fixed percentage of the costs.

THE "DELIVERABLES" OF PROPOSALS

A *deliverable* is what the supplier will deliver at the end of the project. Deliverables can be classified into two major categories, as shown in Figure 17.3.

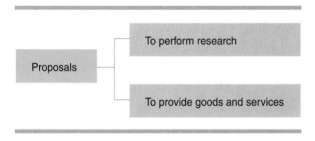

■ **Figure 17.3   "Deliverables" of a Proposal**

Research Proposals

In a research proposal, you are promising to provide a research report of some sort. Here are two examples:

A biologist for a state bureau of land management writes a proposal to the National Science Foundation asking for resources to build a window-lined tunnel in the forest to study tree and plant roots and the growth of fungi. The biologist also wishes to investigate the relationship between plant growth and the activity of insects and worms. The deliverable will be a report submitted to the National Science Foundation and, perhaps, an article published in a professional journal.

A manager of the technical-publications department at a manufacturing company writes a proposal to her supervisor asking for resources to study whether the company should adopt XML for writing its product documentation. The deliverable will be a report that contains her recommendations.

On TechComm Web

For sample proposals and writing checklists, see Writing Guidelines for Engineering and Science Students. Click on Links Library for Ch. 17 on <bedfordstmartins .com/techcomm>.

In This Book

For more about progress reports and completion reports, see Ch. 18, p. 466, and Ch. 19.

A research proposal often leads to two other kinds of documents: progress reports and completion reports.

After the proposal has been approved and the researchers have begun work, they often submit one or more *progress reports*. A progress report tells the sponsor of the project how the work is proceeding. Is it following the plan of work outlined in the proposal? Is it going according to schedule? Is it staying within budget?

At the end of the project, researchers prepare a *completion report*, often called a *final report*, a *project report*, or simply a *report*. A completion report tells the readers the whole story of the research project, beginning with the problem or opportunity that motivated it, the methods used in carrying it out, and the results, conclusions, and recommendations.

People undertake research projects to satisfy their curiosity and to advance professionally. Organizations often require that their professional employees carry out research and publish in appropriate reports, journals, or books. Government researchers and university professors, for instance, are expected to remain active in their fields. Writing proposals is one way to get the resources — time and money for travel, equipment, and assistants — to carry out the research.

Goods-and-Services Proposals

A *goods-and-services proposal* leads to a tangible product (a fleet of automobiles), a service (building maintenance), or some combination of the two (the construction of a building).

A vast network of goods-and-services contracts spans the working world. The U.S. government, the world's biggest customer, spent $48 billion in 2000 buying military equipment from organizations that submitted proposals (U.S. Department of Commerce, 2001, p. 360). But goods-and-services contracts are by no means limited to government contractors. One auto manufacturer buys engines from another; a company that makes spark plugs buys its steel from another company. The world of work depends on goods-and-services proposals.

PERSUASION AND PROPOSALS

Regardless of whether the deliverable is a research report or goods and services, the proposal will receive careful, skeptical analysis. The supervisor of an employee writing the internal proposal wants to be satisfied that the employee has isolated a real problem and devised a feasible strategy for solving it, and that the employee has a good record of carrying through on similar projects.

A proposal, then, is an argument. To be successful, it must be persuasive. You must convince readers that the future benefits will outweigh the immediate and projected costs. Basically, you must clearly show the following:

- that you understand the readers' needs
- that you have decided what you plan to do, and that you are able to do it
- that you are a professional, and that you are committed to fulfilling your promises

In This Book

For more on persuasion, see Ch. 6.

Understanding Readers' Needs

The most crucial element of the proposal is the definition of the problem or opportunity to which the proposed project responds. Although this point would seem to be obvious, people who evaluate proposals agree that an inadequate or inaccurate understanding of the problem or opportunity is the most common weakness of the proposals they see.

In This Book

For more on analyzing your audience, see Ch. 5, p. 74.

Readers' Needs in an External Proposal   Most often, the suppliers submitting the proposal fail to define the problem or opportunity clearly. For instance, they might not have read the RFP carefully and simply assumed that they understood the client's needs. Or perhaps, knowing they couldn't satisfy a client's needs, they prepared a proposal describing a project they *could* complete, hoping that company managers wouldn't notice or that no other supplier will come any closer.

But most readers will reject a proposal as soon as they realize that it doesn't address their needs. When you receive an RFP, study it thoroughly. If you don't understand something in it, contact the organization that issued it. They will be happy to clarify it, because a poor proposal wastes everyone's time.

When you write an unsolicited proposal, analyze your audience carefully. How can you define the problem or opportunity so that your readers will understand it? Keep in mind their needs (even if they are oblivious to them) and, if possible, their backgrounds. Concentrate on how the problem has decreased productivity or quality or on how your ideas would create new opportunities. When you submit an unsolicited proposal, your task in many cases is to convince readers that a need exists. Even when you have reached an understanding with some of your customer's representatives, your proposal still will have to persuade other officials in the company.

Readers' Needs in an Internal Proposal   An internal proposal also must respond to readers' needs. If you propose hiring a new person, you have to make the case that the person is needed and would save or bring in more money than he or she costs, and that there is a place for the new person in your current facilities.

Writing an internal proposal is both more simple and more complicated than writing an external proposal. It is simpler because you have more access to your readers than you would to external readers. And you can get more information more easily. However, it is more complicated because you might find it difficult to get a true sense of the situation in your organization. Some colleagues might not be willing to tell you directly if your proposal is a long shot, or if your ideas might threaten a person in your organization. Before you write an internal proposal, discuss your ideas thoroughly with as many potential readers as you can to learn what the organization really thinks of your idea.

STRATEGIES FOR INTERCULTURAL COMMUNICATION

Writing International Proposals

When you address a proposal to a reader from another culture, keep the following two suggestions in mind:

- *Be sure you have read and understood the proposal requirements.* The following proposal guidelines published by the National Research Foundation (2002) in South Africa describes the management plan that is required for one of its grants:

  This section requires detail on the time that will be spent by various resources on the following list of activities:

  - Project Co-ordination/Management
  - Research and Development
  - Financial Reporting
  - Project Reporting
  - Marketing/Commercialisation
  - Product Management
  - Other (please specify)

  An organogram illustrating which tasks will be completed by particular resources and the hierarchy of the project team would be useful.

  An *organogram* is a combination of *organizational* and *diagram*. In the United States, it's called an *organization chart*.

- *Understand that persuasive messages may require more than just attention to the bottom line.* In some cultures, paying attention to the welfare of the company or the community may be more persuasive. An American company was surprised to learn that the Venezuelan readers of its proposal had selected a French company that "had been making personal visits for years, bringing their families, and engaging in social activities long before there was any question of a contract" (Thrush, 2000).

Describing What You Plan to Do

Once you have shown that you understand what needs to be done and why, describe what you plan to do. Convince your readers that you can respond effectively to the situation you have just described. Discuss the procedures and equipment you would use. If appropriate, justify your choices. For example, if you say you want to do ultrasonic testing on a structure, explain why, unless the reason is obvious.

Present a complete picture of what you would do from the first day of the project to the last. You need more than enthusiasm and good faith; you need a detailed plan showing that you have already started to do the work. Although no proposal can anticipate every question about what you plan to do, the more planning you have done before you submit the proposal, the greater the chances you will be able to do the work successfully if it gets approved.

Demonstrating Your Professionalism

Once you have shown that you understand the readers' needs and can offer a well-conceived plan, demonstrate that you are the kind of person—or that yours is the kind of organization—that is committed to delivering what is promised. Convince readers that you have the pride, ingenuity, and perseverance to solve the problems that are likely to occur in any big undertaking. In short, you want to show that you are a professional.

GUIDELINES

Demonstrating Your Professionalism in a Proposal

In your proposal, you can demonstrate your ability to carry out a project by providing four kinds of information:

▶ *Credentials and work history.* Show that you know how to do this project because you have done similar projects. Who are the people in your organization with the qualifications and experience to carry out the project? What equipment and facilities do you have that will enable you to do the work? What management structure will you use to maintain coordination and keep different activities running smoothly?

▶ *Work schedule.* Sometimes called a *task schedule,* a work schedule is a graph or chart that shows when the various phases of the project will be carried out. The work schedule in fact reveals more about your attitudes toward your work than about what you will actually be doing on any given day. A detailed work schedule shows that you have done your homework, that you have attempted to foresee the kinds of problems that might threaten the project.

↓

> ▶ *Quality-control measures.* Describe how you would evaluate the effectiveness and efficiency of your work. Quality-control procedures might consist of technical evaluations carried out periodically by the project staff, or on-site evaluations by recognized authorities or by the potential client. Quality control is also measured by progress reports.
>
> ▶ *Budget.* Most proposals conclude with a detailed budget, a statement of how much the project will cost—and another way of showing that you have done your homework on a project.

WRITING A PROPOSAL

In writing a proposal, you use the same techniques of planning, drafting, and revising that you use in any other kind of writing. However, a proposal can be such a big project that two aspects of the writing process—resource planning and collaboration—are even more important than they are in smaller documents.

On TechComm Web

For a proposal-writing checklist, see Alice Reid's "A Practical Guide for Writing Proposals." Click on Links Library for Ch. 17 on <bedfordstmartins.com/techcomm>.

As discussed in Chapter 5, planning a project requires a lot of work. You need to see whether your organization can devote resources to writing the proposal and then to carrying out the project if the proposal is approved. Sometimes an organization writes a proposal, wins the contract, and then loses money because it doesn't have the resources to do the project and must subcontract major portions of it.

The resources you need fall into three basic categories:

- *Personnel.* Will you have the necessary technical personnel, managers, and support people?
- *Facilities.* Will you have the facilities, or can you lease them? Can you profitably subcontract parts of the job to companies that have the right facilities?
- *Equipment.* Do you have the right equipment? If not, can you buy it or lease it or subcontract the work? Some contracts provide for the purchase of equipment, but others don't.

Don't write the proposal unless you are confident that you can carry out the project if the proposal is successful.

In This Book

For more on collaboration, see Ch. 4.

Collaboration is critical in large proposals because no one person has the time and expertise to do all the work. Writing major proposals requires the expertise of technical personnel, writers, editors, graphic artists, managers, lawyers, and document-production specialists. Usually, a project manager coordinates the process.

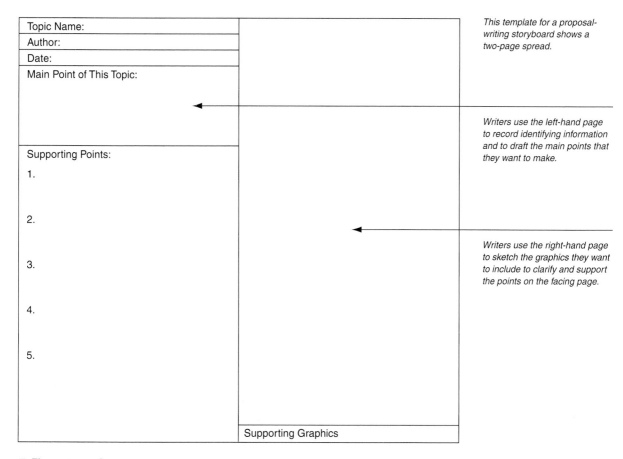

		This template for a proposal-writing storyboard shows a two-page spread.
Topic Name:		
Author:		
Date:		
Main Point of This Topic:		Writers use the left-hand page to record identifying information and to draft the main points that they want to make.
Supporting Points:		
1.		
2.		Writers use the right-hand page to sketch the graphics they want to include to clarify and support the points on the facing page.
3.		
4.		
5.		
	Supporting Graphics	

■ **Figure 17.4   Storyboard Template**

Many organizations present their proposals as a series of two-page spreads, each of which is called a topic. *This storyboard helps writers visualize the organization of each of the topics.*

Many organizations that write proposals use storyboards as they plan. A *storyboard* is an outline that describes the major points that the writers will make and sketches the important graphics they will include. Figure 17.4 shows a storyboard template.

THE STRUCTURE OF THE PROPOSAL

If the authorizing agency provides an IFB, an RFP, or a set of guidelines, follow it closely. If guidelines have not been supplied, or if you are writing an unsolicited proposal, use the structure shown here as a starting point. Then modify it according to your subject, your purpose, and the needs of your audience.

On TechComm Web

For more on storyboards, see Gerald H. Fisher's "Model-based Proposal Development." Click on Links Library for Ch. 11 on <bedfordstmartins.com/techcomm>.

On TechComm Web

To view the proposal guidelines of the Society for Human Resource Management, click on Links Library for Ch. 17 on <bedfordstmartins.com/techcomm>.

In This Book

For more about summaries, see Ch. 12, p. 274.

Summary

For a proposal of more than a few pages, provide a summary. Many organizations impose a length limit—for example, 250 words—and ask the writer to present the summary, single spaced, on the title page. The summary is crucial, because in many cases it will be the only item that readers study in their initial review of the proposal.

The summary covers the major elements of the proposal but devotes only a few sentences to each. Define the problem in a sentence or two. Next describe the proposed program, then provide a brief statement of your qualifications and experience. Some organizations wish to see the completion date and the final budget figure in the summary; others prefer that this information be presented separately on the title page along with other identifying information about the supplier and the proposed project.

Figure 17.5 shows an effective summary taken from a proposal submitted by a group of three students. (An additional example of a summary appears at the end of this chapter, page 453.)

---

page 2

Summary

This proposal recommends that we be authorized to use our time and the Student Special Service's resources to research the possibility of classifying Central State University's American Sign Language classes as a foreign language in the Area I core group. We would then write a recommendation on whether American Sign Language should be considered a foreign language and how we could incorporate it.

Despite the widespread use of sign language in America, Central State University does not give American Sign Language (ASL) any special place among its offered courses. Currently, the ASL courses are only elective credits. Almost half of the states have recognized ASL as a foreign language and grant academic credit for completion of these courses. Six states have universities that independently recognize ASL as a foreign language, while 18 more have passed legislation on the state level recognizing ASL. Central State University is one of 15 states that grant only elective credit to ASL courses.

ASL itself is gaining prominence in mainstream culture and is also being recognized as a foreign language in the educational arena. The CSU English Department, for example, does grant ASL foreign-language status for linguistics majors, but in other departments, ASL is excluded. We propose to research the standards held by Central State University in deeming a language foreign. Our purpose is to determine whether ASL fulfills those requirements. In addition, we propose to research the legislative measures passed in the state of Texas that give ASL statewide recognition as a foreign language. If ASL fulfills CSU's requirements, we will submit a recommendation explaining how it can be implemented. As a safeguard and in the interest of Oklahoma education in general, we propose to investigate the legislative measures needed to attain formal recognition in the same manner as was achieved by the state of Texas.

We have several contacts in the deaf and educational communities in Oklahoma and Texas. With their cooperation we can begin on April 25 and have our research completed and our recommendations prepared by May 12. At that time, we will submit a completion report for your review.

The background

The research the writer has already done

The proposal

The writers' credentials and the schedule

■ **Figure 17.5**
Summary of a Proposal

Note that proposals are often double spaced if they are presented as reports, not memos.
Source: Wells, Tommack, & Tuck, 1997.

Introduction

The purpose of the introduction is to help the reader understand the context, scope, and organization of the proposal.

GUIDELINES

Introducing a Proposal

The introduction to the proposal should answer the following seven questions:

▶ *What is the problem or opportunity?* Describe the problem or opportunity in specific monetary terms, because the proposal itself will include a budget of some sort and you want to convince your readers that spending money on what you propose is smart. Don't say that a design problem is slowing down production; say that it is costing $4,500 a day in lost productivity.

▶ *What is the purpose of the proposal?* The purpose of the proposal is to describe a problem or opportunity and propose a course of action that will culminate in a deliverable. Be specific in explaining what you want to do.

▶ *What is the background of the problem or opportunity?* Although you probably will not be telling your readers anything they don't already know, you want to show them that you understand the problem or opportunity: the circumstances that led to its discovery, the relationships or events that will affect the problem and its solution, and so on.

▶ *What are your sources of information?* Review the relevant literature, ranging from internal reports and memos to published articles or even books, so that readers will understand the context of your work.

▶ *What is the scope of the proposal?* If appropriate, indicate what you are—and are not—proposing to do.

▶ *What is the organization of the proposal?* Explain the organizational pattern you will use.

▶ *What are the key terms that will be used in the proposal?* If you will use any new, specialized, or unusual terms, define them in the introduction.

Figure 17.6 is the introduction to the proposal about American Sign Language.

Introduction

Sign language is the fourth most prominent language in the United States. In usage, it ranks below Spanish but above French, German, Russian, and Japanese, which together constitute all the foreign languages taught at CSU. But despite its prominence, Central State University offers few classes in ASL. With a student population of approximately 15,000, only 25 students per semester are given the opportunity to begin study in American Sign Language. These courses offered are not foreign-language credits. We want to research whether this course can or should be included.

Teresa O'Malley, Chair of the Modern Languages Department at CSU, said that her office receives several calls per semester regarding the inclusion of ASL in the core group of foreign languages. She is supportive of ASL's inclusion and cited other state-funded institutions that recognize ASL as a foreign language. The states have various approaches to ASL in the classroom, as shown in Figure 1. The University of Arizona and the University of Delaware, for example, are part of the 12% that have state-funded institutions that independently recognize ASL as a foreign language. An additional 36% of the states have passed legislative bills that formally recognize ASL as a foreign language, such as Texas. CSU is part of the 30% of states that recognize ASL as an elective credit but not a foreign language. Roughly one-half of the state-funded institutions in the United States recognize ASL as a foreign language. CSU does not.

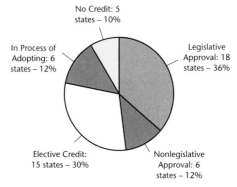

No Credit: 5 states – 10%

In Process of Adopting: 6 states – 12%

Legislative Approval: 18 states – 36%

Elective Credit: 15 states – 30%

Nonlegislative Approval: 6 states – 12%

Source: Rhonda Jacobs, *ASL as a Truly Foreign Language,* 1996.

Figure 1: Treatment of ASL in the 50 States

Current research strongly supports ASL's inclusion in the foreign-language category. Both Teresa O'Malley and Suzanne Christopher, the ASL instructor on campus, feel that ASL probably fits into the foreign-language category. Blaine Lee, the Student Special Services Coordinator, and June Yunker, the CSU Interpreter Coordinator, both feel that ASL deserves

The writers describe the problem they wish to study and note that it has both a local and a national dimension.

Some of the primary and secondary research the writers have already done

■ **Figure 17.6**
Introduction to a Proposal

Note that proposals are double spaced if they are presented as reports, not memos.
Source: Wells, Tommack, & Tuck, 1997.

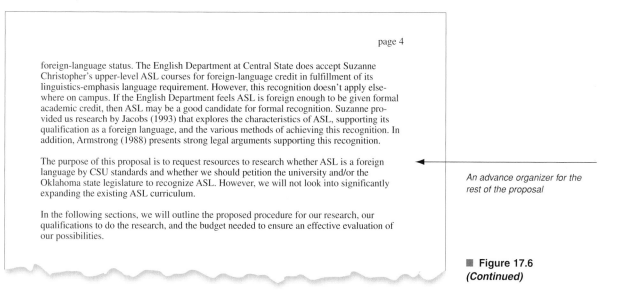

page 4

foreign-language status. The English Department at Central State does accept Suzanne Christopher's upper-level ASL courses for foreign-language credit in fulfillment of its linguistics-emphasis language requirement. However, this recognition doesn't apply elsewhere on campus. If the English Department feels ASL is foreign enough to be given formal academic credit, then ASL may be a good candidate for formal recognition. Suzanne provided us research by Jacobs (1993) that explores the characteristics of ASL, supporting its qualification as a foreign language, and the various methods of achieving this recognition. In addition, Armstrong (1988) presents strong legal arguments supporting this recognition.

The purpose of this proposal is to request resources to research whether ASL is a foreign language by CSU standards and whether we should petition the university and/or the Oklahoma state legislature to recognize ASL. However, we will not look into significantly expanding the existing ASL curriculum.

In the following sections, we will outline the proposed procedure for our research, our qualifications to do the research, and the budget needed to ensure an effective evaluation of our possibilities.

An advance organizer for the rest of the proposal

■ **Figure 17.6**
(Continued)

Proposed Program

In the proposed program, you explain what you want to do. Be specific. You won't persuade anyone by saying that you plan to "gather the data and analyze it." How will you gather and analyze the data? Justify your claims. Every word you say—or don't say—will give your readers evidence on which to base their decision. If you know your subject, the proposed program will show it. If you don't, you will probably slip into meaningless generalities or include erroneous information that undermines the whole proposal.

If your project concerns a subject written about in the professional literature, show your familiarity with the scholarship by referring to the pertinent studies. However, don't just string together a bunch of citations. For example, don't write, "Carruthers (2000), Harding (2001), and Vega (2000) have all researched the relationship between acid-rain levels and groundwater contamination." Rather, use the recent literature to sketch the necessary background and provide the justification for your proposed program. For instance:

> Carruthers (2000), Harding (2001), and Vega (2000) have demonstrated the relationship between acid-rain levels and groundwater contamination. None of these studies, however, included an analysis of the long-term contamination of the aquifer. The current study will consist of . . .

You might include only one reference to recent research. However, if you have researched your topic thoroughly, you might devote several paragraphs or even several pages to recent scholarship.

On TechComm Web

For a sample literature review, see Writing Guidelines for Engineering and Science Students. Click on Links Library for Ch. 17 on <bedfordstmartins.com/techcomm>.

In This Book

For more on researching a subject, see Ch. 7.

Whether your project calls for primary research, secondary research, or both, the proposal will be unpersuasive if you haven't already done a substantial amount of the research. For instance, say you are writing a proposal to do research on industrial-grade lawn mowers. You are not being persuasive if you write that you are going to visit Sears, Lowe's, and Home Depot to see what kinds of lawn mowers they carry. This statement is unpersuasive for two reasons:

- You need to justify why you are going to visit those three retailers rather than others. Anticipate your readers' questions: Why did you choose these three retailers? Why didn't you choose more-specialized dealers?

- You should already have visited the appropriate stores and completed any other preliminary research. If you haven't done the homework, readers have no assurance that you will in fact do it or that it will pay off. If your supervisor authorizes the project and then learns that none of the lawn mowers on the market meets your organization's needs, you will have to go back and submit a different proposal—an embarrassing move.

Unless you can show in your proposed program that you have done the research—and that the research indicates that the project is likely to succeed—the reader has no reason to authorize the project.

Figure 17.7 on pages 447–448 shows the proposed program for the American Sign Language project.

Qualifications and Experience

After you have described how you would carry out the project, show that you can do it. The more elaborate the proposal, the more substantial the discussion of your qualifications and experience has to be. For a small project, include a few paragraphs describing your technical credentials and those of your co-workers. For larger projects, include the résumés of the project leader—often called the *principal investigator*—and the other important participants.

External proposals should also discuss the qualifications of the supplier's organization, describing similar projects the supplier has completed successfully. For example, a company bidding on a contract to build a large suspension bridge should describe other suspension bridges it has built. It should also focus on the equipment and facilities the company already has and on the management structure that will ensure the project's successful completion.

Figure 17.8 on page 449 shows the qualifications-and-experience section of the ASL proposal.

Budget

Good ideas aren't good unless they're affordable. The budget section of a proposal specifies how much the proposed program will cost.

page 5

Proposed Procedure

We will perform the following tasks for your review in determining whether Central State University should recognize ASL as foreign language and how this recognition could be achieved at Central State University (by a university petition) and at all Oklahoma post-secondary institutions (by state legislation):

1. compile a summary of the criteria required by Central State University for a language to be considered foreign
2. research whether ASL fulfills the university-mandated requirements
3. investigate the broad approach of state legislative recognition as used in the state of Texas
4. provide a completion report detailing our findings and recommendations

Task 1. Compile a summary of the criteria required by Central State University for a language to be considered foreign

We interviewed Teresa O'Malley, Chair of the Modern Languages Department. She did not know the exact criteria for languages to be considered foreign at CSU, but she did know that only languages taught at the intermediate level counted as foreign-language credits. At present, CSU has two ASL courses that could qualify as intermediate courses: CM221: Intermediate American Sign Language, and CM321: Conversational American Sign Language. All beginner-level courses taught are counted as elective credits, including CM121: Beginning Sign Language. She can provide us the exact specifications for a class to count as a foreign-language credit at the end of this week. We request time on Friday morning, April 25, to visit with Teresa O'Malley to discuss the exact qualifications for a language to be considered foreign.

Task 2. Research whether ASL fulfills the university-mandated requirements

We have also met with Suzanne Christopher, the current ASL instructor at Central State. She has done considerable research in American Sign Language and has prepared various proposals to expand the ASL program at the university. Currently, we have several works by Armstrong (1988), Wilcox (1977), and Jacobs (1996) that will assist us in understanding the current status of ASL in university curricula and in making our recommendation. In addition, we have contacted the Oklahoma chapter of the Registry for Interpreters for the Deaf (ORID) and the Oklahoma Association for the Deaf (OAD). Kelly Eastwick, President of ORID, and Janis Seymour, committee member of OAD, are both interested and willing to assist us in our research and deliberations. After we learn the exact criteria for a language to be considered foreign, we request time to meet with Suzanne, Kelly, and Janis to compile our research concerning ASL's qualifications. We request a four-hour reservation of the Centennial Room in the Student Union Building on Monday morning, April 28, to meet with Suzanne Christopher, Kelly Eastwick, and Janis Seymour to prepare our recommendation. After our analysis of the university's requirements and ASL's qualifications, we will submit to you a progress report detailing whether an internal approach to approve ASL is viable.

An advance organizer for this section of the proposal

Describing the proposed program in terms of clear tasks makes the proposal look credible.

A further discussion of the research the writers will complete

■ **Figure 17.7**
Proposed Program of a Proposal

Source: Wells, Tommack, & Tuck, 1997.

page 6

Task 3. Investigate the broad approach of state legislative recognition as used in the state of Texas

Regardless of whether ASL as a foreign language is approved at Central State University, we would like to investigate the measures needed to have the state of Oklahoma extend legal recognition of the language. As employees of the state, we see CSU as only one of the several postsecondary institutions in Oklahoma. If ASL is deserving of this status, we wish to extend these benefits to other universities by investigating the feasibility of passing a bill recognizing ASL as a foreign language. If ASL as a foreign language is approved by CSU, it will strengthen our petition to the state. If internal approval is not feasible, petitioning the state will give us one more opportunity. We hope to work on the internal and external research simultaneously.

The alternative method of granting ASL foreign-language recognition is to have a bill passed in the state legislature. According to Figure 1 on page 3, 18 states have legislative approval for ASL to be considered a foreign language in postsecondary schools. Texas is one of these states. We have contacted Sha H. Cowan from the Texas Education Agency, Services for the Deaf Department. He referred us to three educators involved with the legislative measures passed in Texas: Dr. Jean Andrews, Communication Disorders, Lamar University in Beaumont, Texas, and Carol Seeger and Lisa Bissin, deaf ASL instructors at the University of Texas at Austin. We request Friday afternoon, April 25, and Monday afternoon, April 28, to communicate with these individuals and gather research. In addition we request Tuesday, April 29, to follow up with the legislative proposal plan, analyze a feasible Oklahoma legislature approach, contact Oklahoma state representatives, compile our research, and prepare a completion report.

Task 4. Provide a completion report detailing our findings and recommendations

Following the completion of our research, we will submit to you a report summarizing our findings and recommendations. We will explain the criteria required by CSU for a language to be considered foreign, whether ASL fulfills these requirements, and how we could implement a legislative approach to obtain formal recognition for ASL. In this last area, we will report on the strategies used in the state of Texas and provide a list of contact personnel in the Oklahoma state government with whom we will work. This completion report will be on your desk May 12 at 9 A.M.

Figure 2 is our estimated task schedule, beginning on April 25 and ending with our recommendation to you on May 12.

Because the report is the main deliverable, writing the report is one of the tasks.

The writers present their schedule as part of the proposed program. Such schedules are often presented as a separate element in the proposal. See p. 450 for more on task schedules.

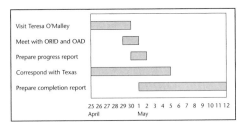

Figure 2: Task Schedule

■ **Figure 17.7**
(Continued)

page 7

Qualifications and Experience

We believe we have the skills and experience to conduct this research. Each of us brings to the team talents and strengths that, when combined, help us to work effectively and efficiently.

Danny Tommack, our team leader, has the skills to direct the team's efforts and to help us keep our goals in focus. He has developed strong management and communication skills while working at McU Sports. His professional approach in meetings and planning sessions will help us work closely with members of our community and our long-distance contacts in Texas.

Brandon Tuck has been an American Sign Language interpreter for three years. He works for the Department of Student Special Services at Central State University and is a freelance interpreter. He brings to the group a strong knowledge of deafness and sign language, and contacts in the deaf community.

Megan Wells has highly developed research skills she obtained while working for three years in a research laboratory. She has excellent communication and interviewing skills. Her experience at several universities will help us to investigate Central State University and other postsecondary institutions.

■ **Figure 17.8 Qualifications and Experience Section of a Proposal**

The writers describe the qualifications of each group member.
Source: Wells, Tommack, & Tuck, 1997.

Budgets vary greatly in scope and format. For simple internal proposals, add the budget request to the statement of the proposed program: "This study will take me two days, at a cost of about $400" or "The variable-speed recorder currently costs $225, with a 10 percent discount on orders of five or more." For more-complicated internal proposals and for all external proposals, include a more explicit and complete budget.

Most budgets are divided into two parts: direct costs and indirect costs.

- *Direct costs* include such expenses as salaries and fringe benefits of program personnel, travel costs, and necessary equipment, materials, and supplies.

- *Indirect costs* cover the intangible expenses that are sometimes called *overhead:* general secretarial and clerical expenses not devoted exclusively to any one project, as well as operating expenses such as utilities and maintenance. Indirect costs are usually expressed as a percentage—ranging from less than 20 percent to more than 100 percent—of the direct expenses.

Figure 17.9 shows the budget section from the ASL proposal.

Appendices

Many types of appendices might accompany a proposal. Most organizations have *boilerplate* descriptions (standard wording that can be modified or

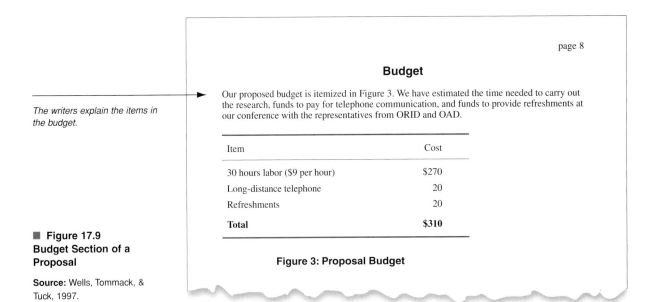

The writers explain the items in the budget.

■ **Figure 17.9**
Budget Section of a Proposal

Source: Wells, Tommack, & Tuck, 1997.

inserted directly into a document) of other projects they have performed. Another popular kind is the supporting letter—a testimonial to the supplier's skill and integrity written by a reputable and well-known person in the field. Two other kinds of appendices deserve special mention: the task schedule and the description of evaluation techniques.

Task Schedule The *task schedule* is almost always drawn in one of three graphical formats: a table, bar chart, or network diagram.

TABLES The simplest but least informative way to present a schedule is in a table, as shown in Figure 17.10. As with all graphics, you should provide a textual reference that introduces and, if necessary, explains it.

TASK SCHEDULE

Activity	Start Date	Finish Date
Design the security system	4 Oct. 02	19 Oct. 02
Research available systems	4 Oct. 02	3 Jan. 03
Etc.		

■ **Figure 17.10   Tabular Schedule**

Although displaying information in a table is better than writing it out in sentences, readers still cannot "see" the information. They have to read it to figure out how long each activity will last, and they cannot tell whether any of the activities are interdependent. They have no way of determining what would happen to the overall project schedule if one of the activities faced delays.

BAR CHARTS   Bar charts, also called *Gantt charts* after the early twentieth-century civil engineer who first used them, are a distinct improvement over tables. The basic bar chart shown in Figure 17.11 allows readers to see how long each activity will take and when different activities occur simultaneously. Like tables, however, bar charts do not indicate the interdependency of tasks.

NETWORK DIAGRAMS   Network diagrams show interdependence among various activities, clearly indicating which must be completed before others can begin. Even the relatively simple network diagram shown in Figure 17.12 can be difficult to read. You would probably not use this type of diagram in a document intended for general readers.

Description of Evaluation Techniques   The term *evaluation* can mean different things to different people, but in general an *evaluation technique* is any procedure used to determine whether the proposed program is both effective and efficient. Evaluation techniques can range from simple progress reports to sophisticated statistical analyses. Some proposals call for evaluation by an outside agent, such as a consultant, a testing laboratory, or a university. Other proposals describe evaluation techniques that the supplier itself will perform, such as cost/benefit analyses.

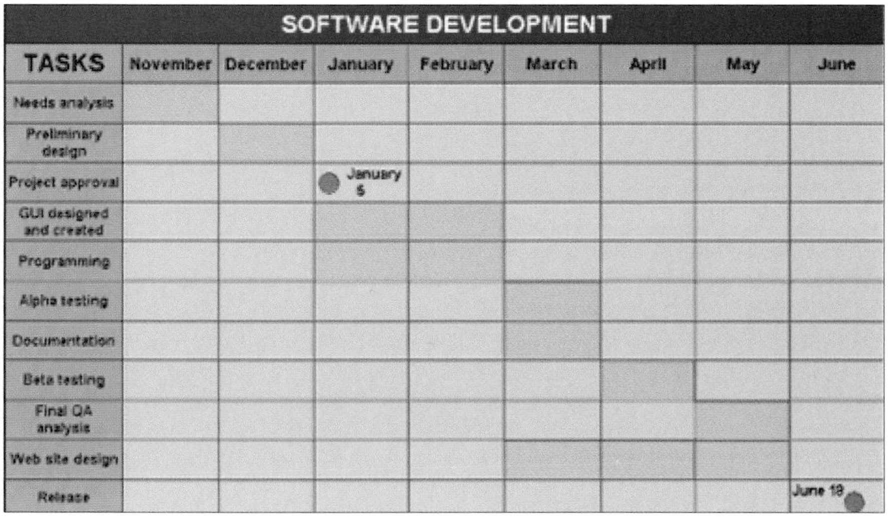

On TechComm Web

To see a tutorial on using Microsoft Excel to create a Gantt chart, click on Links Library for Ch. 17 on <bedfordstmartins.com/techcomm>.

On TechComm Web

To view Fig. 17.11 in context on the Web, click on Links Library in Ch. 17 on <bedfordstmartins.com /techcomm>.

■ **Figure 17.11**
Bar Chart

Source: SmartDraw.com, 2002 <www.smartdraw.com/resources /examples/business/gantt15.htm>.

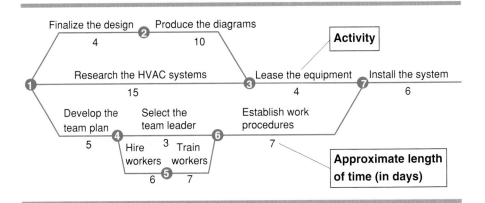

■ **Figure 17.12** **Network Diagram**

A network diagram provides more useful information than either a table or a bar chart.

The issue of evaluation techniques is complicated by the fact that some people think in terms of *quantitative evaluations*—tests of measurable quantities, such as production increases—whereas others think in terms of *qualitative evaluations*—tests of whether a proposed program is improving, say, the workmanship of a product. And some people include both qualitative and quantitative testing when they refer to evaluation. An additional complication is that projects can be tested while they are being carried out (*formative evaluations*) as well as after they have been completed (*summative evaluations*).

When an RFP calls for "evaluation," experienced proposal writers know that it's a good idea to contact the sponsoring agency's representatives to determine precisely what they mean.

SAMPLE INTERNAL PROPOSAL

The following example of an internal proposal (Ewing & Lipus, 2002) has been formatted as a memo rather than as a formal proposal. (See Chapter 18, page 471, for the progress report written after this project was under way and Chapter 19, page 504, for the completion report.)

Rydell & Associates

556 N. Orchard   **Telephone: (208) 555-2267**
Boise, ID 83705   **Fax:**   **(208) 555-8391**
www.rydellaccounting.com

Memo

Date: April 15, 2002

To: Joanna Rydell, President, Rydell & Associates

From: Marne Ewing, Technical-Communication Intern
           Teresa Lipus, Technical-Communication Intern

Subject: Proposal for Feasibility Study on Printer Capability

Purpose

The purpose of our proposal is to request authorization and funding to study whether replacing or augmenting our existing printers would increase employee productivity.

Summary

Rydell & Associates accountancy firm has a reputation for efficient, high-quality service to its customers. Because of this reputation, business volume has increased dramatically, resulting in the addition of four associate accountants in the past year. Our expanded staff and workload have increased demands on our current printers: two HP LaserJet 1200s and one Canon BJC-85 Inkjet. As a result, we are losing valuable employee time due to print-job delays.

Because of growing employee concerns over this loss of time, we propose to research options for improving our printing capabilities and therefore employee productivity. We will begin by evaluating our current printing capabilities and calculating the cost of the lost productivity as employees wait for their print jobs. Next, we will establish criteria for evaluating printers and compare new printers on the market according these criteria.

To perform this research and present a report on our findings, we estimate that we will require 20 hours over the next four weeks, for a total cost of $240. Our research team consists of Marne Ewing and Teresa Lipus, technical-communication interns with experience configuring computer and printer purchases.

If you accept this proposal, we will begin immediately, submitting to you a progress report on April 29, 2002, and a completion report on May 13, 2002. The completion report will include the details of our research and a recommendation for the best configuration of printers to maximize the resources of Rydell & Associates.

An effective subject line indicates the purpose ("proposal") and the subject of the memo ("feasibility study on printer capability").

Memos of more than one page should begin with a clear statement of purpose and a summary.

The background of the problem

A summary of the proposed program

A summary of the schedule, the budget, and the credentials of the writers

A summary of the other documents the writers will submit

Introduction

We are seeking approval for a project to research and evaluate options for improving the printing capability of Rydell & Associates accountancy firm. This proposal is based on growing concerns over the efficiency and productivity problems we have been experiencing with our current printers.

Here the writers present a more detailed explanation of the problem.

Because of the firm's reputation for high-quality work, Rydell & Associates has experienced a recent growth in business volume, resulting in the addition of four new associates in the past year. The expanded staff and workload have increased demands on our current printing equipment: two HP LaserJet 1200s and one Canon BJC-85 Inkjet. At the staff meeting on April 12, two of the associates brought up the issue of lost productivity due to the nature of our networked printers. Ms. Rydell responded that she knew that our two good printers were overused, and that other employees had also mentioned their frustration at having to wait while their print jobs were queued. Ms. Rydell asked us to look into the problem and see whether we could propose a solution that costs no more than $5,000 in initial capital outlay.

Referring to Ms. Rydell's comments about the printing problem adds credibility to the writers' argument that the proposal be approved.

Currently, we have three networked printers: two HP LaserJet 1200s and one Canon BJC-85 Inkjet. The laser printers are in good working order and can print 10 pages per minute (ppm), which is near the average of current models. The inkjet printer is trouble-prone and can print only 2 ppm.

The writers explain why the two laser printers are used more than the inkjet printer.

Most of our firm's employees prefer to use the laser printers because they want original, crisp, non-smearing copies of their documents. Due to high demands on the printers, the print jobs queue, costing employees valuable time because they must leave their desks to check on the status of their print jobs, and they often stand and wait for their documents. Sometimes, they need to separate their print jobs from those of other employees.

The writers conclude this paragraph with an advance organizer for the rest of the proposal.

We propose to study options for improving our printing capabilities. Our research will help Ms. Rydell determine whether we should purchase additional equipment to augment or replace our existing equipment. The following sections of this memo include the proposed procedure, the schedule, our qualifications, the proposed budget for the research, and the references.

By presenting the project as a set of tasks, the writers show that they are well organized. This organization by tasks will be used in the progress report (see p. 471) and the completion report (see p. 504).

Proposed Procedure

We will perform the following tasks to determine the best configuration of printing equipment for Rydell & Associates.

Task 1: Calculate the cost of the lost productivity incurred by using our current printers. We will interview all 10 appropriate employees of the firm to find an average of minutes per day spent waiting for print jobs, and calculate the cost of this lost productivity.

The writers will start with primary research to determine the cost of the problem.

page 3

Task 2: Establish printer-selection criteria by determining our needs.

We know that any solution we recommend will need to cost less than $5,000. We will need to determine whether our employees' needs will be best served by continuing our networked printing configuration, or whether we should move to a distributed configuration, in which each of the 10 appropriate employees has his or her own printer. The question we would need to answer is whether we can afford 10 printers that have the technical characteristics we require: speed, resolution, and expandability.

We have already begun to study the current array of small-business printers. We have secured the current reviews and benchmarks tests from three reputable organizations: *PC World* (Top Ten, 2002), *ZDNET.com* (Most Popular, 2002), and *CNET.com* (Top 5, 2002).

Task 3: Evaluate printers according to our criteria.

Once we have established our criteria, we will use the reviews and benchmark tests to determine which printers best meet our needs. Then, we will analyze the information and derive conclusions and recommendations.

Task 4: Prepare a completion report.

We will prepare a completion report that explains the problem, the methods, and our findings. We will include detailed information about our current printing situation, about how we established criteria, and about how we selected the printers to study. We will include the specifications from the benchmark tests and comparisons of selected printers that helped shape our conclusions and recommendations. We will submit the completion report by May 13, 2002.

Schedule

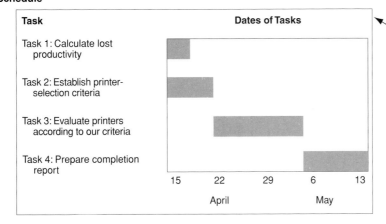

Task	Dates of Tasks
Task 1: Calculate lost productivity	
Task 2: Establish printer-selection criteria	
Task 3: Evaluate printers according to our criteria	
Task 4: Prepare completion report	15 22 29 6 13
	April May

In conducting a feasibility study, it is smart to determine your criteria first, before you study the options.

The writers begin with the most important criterion: cost.

Notice how effectively they describe the main question they seek to answer in the study.

Because the writers have begun their secondary research, they look like professionals. Managers are more likely to approve a proposal that shows that the authors have already done a lot of their research.

Preparing the completion report is part of the project.

Organizing the project by tasks makes it easy for the writers to present a Gantt chart.

Note that each task is presented with parallel grammar: each is a second-person imperative phrase.

This Gantt chart is a table. The bars are made by adding a gray background to certain cells, then hiding the grid lines of the table. You can also use a spreadsheet or project-management program to create a Gantt chart.

page 4

Qualifications and Experience

We bring to the project the following qualifications:

Marne Ewing, Technical-Communication Intern
- three years experience as manager of a small office
- author of a similar printer-configuration study for a previous employer
- experience interviewing subject-matter experts and writing technical reports for school projects and on the job
- senior in technical communication at Boise State University

Teresa Lipus, Technical-Communication Intern
- five years' experience in library reference and research
- experience interviewing subject-matter experts and writing technical reports for school projects and on the job
- senior in technical communication at Boise State University

The writers summarize their credentials to perform the study.

Budget

Following is an itemized budget for the proposed research.

Name	Hours	Rate	Cost
Teresa Lipus	10	12.00	120
Marne Ewing	10	12.00	120
		Total:	$240

A simple budget makes it easy for readers to understand the cost of carrying out the research study.

References

CNET editors' top 5 personal laser printers. (2002, March). Retrieved April 10, 2002, from the CNET Web site: http://computers.cnet.com/hardware/0-2645882-8-5700867-1.html

Most popular printers. (2002, March). Retrieved April 10, 2002, from the ZDNet Web site: http://zdnetshopper.cnet.com/shopping/0-8399-1410-0-0.html?tag=pop&cobrand=29

Ozer, J. (2002, January). Print more for less. *Computer Shopper, 22,* 126–130.

Top ten monochrome laser printers. (2002, March). Retrieved April 10, 2002, from the PC World Web site: www.pcworld.com/reviews/article/0,aid,92901,00.asp

References provide the bibliographic data for sources cited in the proposal.

Interactive Sample Document:
Analyzing an External Proposal
The author of the following sample proposal (Miner, 2002) works for a nonprofit organization that studies police-community relations. The proposal is addressed to a foundation that funds law-enforcement research and projects. The author is requesting $66,240 to carry out a research project. The questions in the margin ask you to think about some of the ways an external proposal differs from an internal proposal. The answers to these questions are available on TechComm Web.

February 3, 2002

Mr. Hubert Williams, President
Law Enforcement Foundation
1001 23rd Street, N.W., Suite 200
Washington, DC 20037

Dear Mr. Williams:

The Center for Urban Problems (CUP), as Washington's largest organization dealing with police-community relations, invites your investment in a $66,240 special project to improve community relations with minorities. We are encouraged that the Law Enforcement Foundation supports innovative projects that improve the delivery of police services. Over 85 percent of your grant dollars during the past three years have been invested at the local community level. Clearly, your support fills a valuable niche in light of the more conservative funding offered by the federal government. This strong commitment to unique projects is shared by the researchers and evaluation specialists at CUP.

The Problem: Spiraling Tensions. Despite proactive community relations programs, an unchecked tension exists between municipal police and minority community members. Relationships between law enforcement officers and minorities—Chicano, African American, Puerto Rican—are at a critical stage. One out of every three arrests in Washington, DC, currently involves a member of a minority community; the incidence is even higher in such cities as San Antonio, Kansas City, and Los Angeles.

Many factors contribute to the growing minority community-police tensions: increasing complexity of urban life, unemployment discrimination, and housing problems. Although these nationwide social problems were not created by the police, the police must cope with the consequences of these problems. This vast social dislocation spawns minority attitudes of prejudice and contempt. To counterbalance these problems, many police communities have adopted public relations programs to "sell" their departments to the minority communities without the concomitant need to be ready to work with those communities. As a result, there is an ever-widening gap between present and potential minority community acceptance of police behavior.

1. Beginning in the second sentence of this paragraph, the writer describes the reader's own organization. What is the function of this description?

2. The writer's description of the problem does not provide specific statistical evidence. Is this a weakness of the proposal, or is there a good reason for the lack of specifics?

3. At the end of the solutions section, the writer refers to Attachment A, a task schedule. What are the advantages and disadvantages of attaching an appendix, compared with incorporating this information into the body of the proposal?

4. Assuming that the reader is not familiar with CUP (the writer's organization), how effective is this description of CUP in establishing its credentials?

On TechComm Web

To find the answers to these questions, click on Interactive Sample Documents for Ch. 17 on <bedfordstmartins.com/techcomm>.

The Solution: Evaluating Police-Community Relations Bureaus. Successful claims regarding the effectiveness of police-community relations bureaus remain undocumented. Police departments are latching on to a new fad without understanding the key components of a police-community relations program. Some features of the bureau approach work; others don't. The goal of this project is to identify the successful features of existing bureaus, so that success can be delivered more quickly to police departments serving substantial numbers of minority citizens. The CUP research staff will follow standard social science research techniques as detailed in our time-and-task chart, Attachment A.

CUP Credentials: National Experience and Networks. CUP is uniquely suited to conduct this evaluation project on police-community relations bureaus. As a nonpolice-linked organization, it can objectively and independently assess current practices. This project represents a systematic continuation of prior CUP efforts in this area with state and municipal organizations as well as private police-related associations. Its staff has a cumulative 100 years of experience in evaluating police-related projects. Finally, local and national networking with 28 regional offices make it well postured to effectively conduct this assessment.

Budget Request: $66,240 Payable over Six Months. With the demonstrated concern that you've shown in the delivery of police services to minorities, I am requesting a grant of $66,240. Quite frankly, the project extends beyond the financial boundaries of CUP. Accordingly, we must now reach out to the community for assistance in what surely is a vital service to the police community. The outcome of this project will touch the operations of over 6,000 law enforcement groups nationwide, resulting in a $13 investment in each existing municipal and state police organization, or a cost of seven cents (7¢) per police official.

In making this investment, the Law Enforcement Foundation will be supporting a cost-effective approach to the delivery of police services for the minority communities where major problems exist. Mr. Lloyd Solomon, National Program Director for CUP, can be reached at (202) 123-4567 to answer questions or give further information.

Sincerely,

Carolyn Smith, President

P.S. Please come visit us and see this important project for yourself.

Enclosures:
Attachment A: Time-and-Task Chart
Attachment B: IRS Nonprofit Certification

Reviewing the Process

Analyze your audience.

In particular, consider the readers' knowledge about, and attitudes toward, what you are proposing.

Analyze your purpose.

Make clear exactly what you are requesting that the readers of your proposal do.

Gather information about your subject.

A successful proposal is based on solid research about the readers' needs and about the subject.

Choose the appropriate type of proposal.

Internal proposals are submitted to the writer's own organization; external proposals are directed to another organization.

Draft the proposal.

Follow the instructions in any RFP or IFB. If there is none, include an **introduction,** which shows specifically that you understand your reader's problem or opportunity; a **proposed program,** which describes what you would do if the proposal were accepted; a **qualifications and experience** section, including evidence of other successful projects; a **budget;** and **appendices,** such as a task schedule and a description of evaluation techniques.

Format the proposal.

For external proposals, study the RFP. For internal proposals, study other proposals submitted in your organization.

Revise and submit the proposal.

External proposals usually have a firm deadline. You need to build in time to revise the proposal thoroughly and still get it to readers in time. See the Revision Checklist that follows.

Revision Checklist

The following checklist covers the basic elements of a proposal. Guidelines established by the recipient of the proposal should take precedence over these general suggestions.

Does the summary provide an overview of
- ❏ the problem or the opportunity? (p. 442)
- ❏ the proposed program? (p. 442)
- ❏ your qualifications and experience? (p. 442)

Does the introduction indicate
- ❏ the problem or opportunity? (p. 443)
- ❏ the purpose of the proposal? (p. 443)
- ❏ the background of the problem or opportunity? (p. 443)
- ❏ your knowledge of the professional literature? (p. 443)
- ❏ the scope of the proposal? (p. 443)

❏ the organization of the proposal? (p. 443)
❏ the key terms that will be used in the proposal? (p. 443)

❏ Does the description of the proposed program provide a clear, specific plan of action and justify the tasks you propose performing? (p. 445)

Does the description of qualifications and experience clearly outline
❏ your relevant skills and past work? (p. 446)
❏ the skills and background of the other participants? (p. 446)

❏ your department's (or organization's) relevant equipment, facilities, and experience? (p. 446)

Is the budget
❏ complete? (p. 449)
❏ correct? (p. 449)
❏ accompanied by an in-text reference? (p. 450)

❏ Do the appendices include the relevant supporting materials, such as a task schedule, a description of evaluation techniques, and evidence of other successful projects? (p. 449)

Exercises

On TechComm Web

For more exercises, click on Additional Exercises, Projects, and Cases for Ch. 17 on <bedfordstmartins.com/techcomm>.

1. **Internet Activity** Study the National Science Foundation's Grant Proposal Guide (click on Links Library for Chapter 17 on TechComm Web <bedfordstmartins.com/techcomm>). What are the important ways in which the NSF's guide differs from the advice provided in this chapter? What accounts for these differences? Present your findings in a 500-word memo to your instructor. (For more on memos, see Chapter 15, page 378.)

2. **Group Activity** Form groups according to major. Using *Commerce Business Daily* or *FedBizOps,* find a request for proposals (RFP) for a project related to your academic field (click on Links Library for Chapter 17 on TechComm Web <bedfordstmartins.com/techcomm>). Study the RFP. What can you learn about the needs of the organization that issued it? How effectively does the RFP describe what the issuing organization expects to see in the proposal? Is the RFP relatively general or specific? What sorts of evaluation techniques does the RFP call for? In your response, include a list of questions that you would ask the issuing organization if you were considering responding to the RFP. Present your results in a memo to your instructor. (For more on memos, see Chapter 15, page 378.)

Project

On TechComm Web

For more projects, click on Additional Exercises, Projects, and Cases for Ch. 17 on <bedfordstmartins.com/techcomm>.

3. Write a proposal for a research project that will constitute a major assignment in this course. Your instructor will tell you whether the proposal is to be written individually or collaboratively. Start by defining a technical subject that interests you. (This subject could be one that you are involved with at work or in another course.) Using abstract services and other bibliographic tools, compile a bibliography of articles and books on the subject. (See Chapter 7 for a discussion of finding information.) Create a reasonable real-world context. Here are three common scenarios from the business world:

• Our company uses Technology X to perform Task A. Should we instead be using Technology Y to perform Task A? For instance, our company uses traditional surveying tools in its contracting business. Should we be using GPS surveying tools instead?

• Our company has decided to purchase a particular kind of tool to perform Task A. Which make and model of the tool should we purchase, and from which supplier should we buy or lease it? For instance, our company has decided to purchase 10 multimedia computers. Which brand and model should we buy, and from whom should we buy them?

- Our company does not currently perform Function X. Is it feasible to perform Function X? For instance, we do not currently offer day care for our employees. Should we? What are the advantages and disadvantages of doing so? What forms can day care take? How is it paid for?

Here are some additional ideas for topics.

- the need to provide high-speed Internet access to students
- the value of using the Internet to form ties with another technical-communication class on another campus
- the need for expanded opportunities for internships in your major
- the need to create an advisory board of people from industry to provide expertise about your major
- the need to raise money to keep the college's computer labs up-to-date
- the need to evaluate your major to ensure that it is responsive to students' needs

- the advisability of starting a campus branch of a professional organization in your field
- improving parking facilities on campus
- creating or improving organizations for minorities or for women on campus

These topics can be approached from different perspectives. For instance, the first one—on providing high-speed Internet access to students—could be approached in several ways:

- Our college currently purchases journals but does not provide high-speed Internet access for students. Should we consider reducing the library's journal budget to subsidize high-speed Internet access for students?
- Our college has decided to provide high-speed Internet access for its students. How should it do so? What vendors provide such services? What are the strengths and weaknesses of each vendor?
- Our college does not offer high-speed Internet access to students. Should we make it a goal to do so? What are the advantages of doing so? The disadvantages?

C A S E
Ethics and Proposals

You work for Devon Electronics, a company that does contract work for the federal government. Your department has submitted a proposal to build a friend-or-foe electronic device to be used in military aircraft. You have just learned that Martha Ruiz, the chief technical person for the project, has accepted a position with another company and will be leaving in two weeks. Your company has not yet decided who would replace her if the project is funded. Your Director of Operations favors delaying a decision until the company learns whether it has won the contract. The government agency is currently reviewing all the proposals and is not scheduled to announce the winner of the contract for three weeks. Should you notify them of Ruiz's impending resignation? If you think you should notify the government agency, draft the letter you would send. (See Chapter 15, page 364, for a discussion of letters.) If you think you should not notify the government agency, explain your reasoning in a memo to your instructor. (For more on memos, see Chapter 15, page 378.)

On TechComm Web

For more cases, click on Additional Exercises, Projects, and Cases for Ch. 17 on <bedfordstmartins.com /techcomm>.

18 Writing Informal Reports

Leo Finkelstein (2000, p. 85), technical-communication professor, on the role of progress reports:

Does the progress report requirement indicate that your client does not trust you? Maybe—but that is not the point. Normal business practice requires specific, written documentation, not abstract trust.

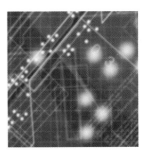

A report is a statement—oral or written—that helps listeners or readers understand, analyze, or take action on some situation, idea, or action. This book classifies reports into two categories: formal and informal. This chapter discusses informal reports; Chapter 19 discusses formal reports.

Here are a few examples of informal reports:

An e-mail describing a problem in the management of an office and recommending action to solve it

A presentation at a meeting, in which an employee analyzes a set of architectural plans for the company's new offices

A memo describing the projects undertaken in the quality-assurance department of a company over the last quarter

A memo recording what occurred at a recent meeting of a department

As this list indicates, informal reports cover many subjects, have many purposes, and take many forms. Although an informal report is a routine communication of information about an everyday matter, it can be very important. An incident report written by police officers at the scene of an automobile accident might have enormous implications for the people involved in the accident and for many others.

PLANNING, DRAFTING, AND REVISING INFORMAL REPORTS

Writing informal reports involves the same planning, drafting, and revising techniques used in most other kinds of technical communication.

- *Analyze your audience and purpose.* In some cases, it is easy to identify your audience and purpose. For instance, a set of meeting minutes is addressed to

On TechComm Web

For additional samples, activities, and links related to this chapter, see <bedfordstmartins.com/techcomm>.

In This Book

For more about analyzing audience and purpose, see Ch. 5.

all the members of the committee or department, and its purpose is to serve as the official record of a meeting. In other cases, the audience and purpose are not as obvious. For example, you might be reporting on an accident on the job. To whom should you address the report: your direct supervisor? Your direct supervisor and others? What is your purpose: to describe what happened? To recommend steps that might reduce the chance that such accidents recur? In this situation, you need to analyze the audience and purpose just as carefully as you would for any other kind of document.

- *Gather and compile your information.* Sometimes, assembling your information is as simple as printing a file. At other times, it requires sophisticated information-gathering techniques using primary and secondary research.

In This Book

For more about memos and front matter, see Chs. 15 and 12.

- *Choose an appropriate format.* The most common format for informal reports is the memo, but many organizations have preprinted forms or templates to follow. In some organizations, a title page, a cover, and other elements usually associated with more-formal reports are used for all reports. The choice of format is therefore often determined by your organization as well as by your audience and purpose.

In This Book

For more about drafting and revising, see Ch. 3.

- *Draft the report.* For routine reports, you sometimes can use sections of previous reports. In a status report, for instance, you can copy the description of your current project from the previous report and then update it as necessary. Some informal reports are drafted on site. For instance, a site study might be "drafted" using a handheld computer or a checklist on a clipboard as an engineer walks around a site.

- *Revise the report.* Informal reports must be revised like any other kind of technical document. *Informal* does not mean *careless*.

STRATEGIES FOR INTERCULTURAL COMMUNICATION

Considering Informal Reports for Multicultural Audiences

Before you draft an informal report for people from other cultures, consider the following:

- *How might your readers react to your informal report?* According to Walsham (2001, p. 30), a software company in India "resisted the introduction of monthly progress reports, a practice that was routine" for the North American company it was working with. The North American company was seen as attempting "to make the [Indian company] conform to a range of their standard practices."

- *Will your readers be comfortable with your choice of document?* For example, is an e-mail sufficiently formal for the occasion? (See the Strategies box in Chapter 15 on page 386.)

- *Do you need to adjust your writing style?* Should you include a glossary or add parenthetical definitions? Use shorter sentences? Use more headings?

FORMATS FOR INFORMAL REPORTS

Informal reports can be oral—live, on the phone, or in a teleconference—or presented in four basic kinds of documents:

In This Book

For more about memos, e-mails, and letters, see Ch. 15.

- *Memos.* A memo is a relatively informal medium used for communicating with another person in the same organization. It can range from less than a page to as long as 10 pages or more.

- *Forms.* Routine informal reports are often written or typed on preprinted forms or on templates used with a word processor.

- *E-mails.* E-mails are an increasingly popular format for transmitting informal reports because e-mails are easy to distribute and can be revised and pasted into another document.

- *Letters.* Letters, the most formal of the documents, are preferred when the writer and the reader work at different organizations.

  The following sections discuss five types of informal reports.

WRITING DIRECTIVES

In a *directive,* you report on a policy or a procedure you want your readers to follow. If possible, explain the reason for the directive; otherwise, it might seem like an arbitrary order. For brief directives, place the explanation before the directive itself, to prevent the appearance of bluntness.

Figure 18.1 shows an example of a directive.

Types of informal reports:

Directives

Field and lab reports

Progress and status reports

Incident reports

Meeting minutes

Quimby Interoffice

Date:	March 19, 2003
To:	All supervisors and sales personnel
From:	D. Bartown, Engineering
Subject:	Avoiding Customer Exposure to Sensitive Information Outside Conference Room B

Recently I have learned that customers meeting in Conference Room B have been allowed to use the secretary's phone directly outside the room. This practice presents a problem: the proposals that the secretary is working on are in full view of the customers. Proprietary information such as pricing can be jeopardized unintentionally.

In the future, would you please escort any customers or non-Quimby personnel needing to use a phone to the one outside the Estimating Department? Thanks very much.

The writer begins with a clear explanation of the problem that the directive will address.

The writer's polite but informal tone throughout the memo is likely to motivate readers to cooperate.

■ **Figure 18.1**
A Directive

WRITING FIELD AND LAB REPORTS

A common kind of informal report describes inspections, maintenance, and site studies. These reports, often known as *field reports* or *lab reports*, explain the problem, methods, results, and conclusions, but they deemphasize methods and can include recommendations.

GUIDELINES

Responding to Readers' Questions in a Field or Lab Report

Be sure to answer the following questions:

▶ What is the purpose of the report?

▶ What are the main points covered in the report?

▶ What were the problems leading to the decision to perform the procedure?

▶ What methods were used?

▶ What were the results?

▶ What do the results mean?

▶ What should be done next?

The report in Figure 18.2 illustrates possible variations on this standard report structure.

WRITING PROGRESS AND STATUS REPORTS

In This Book

For more on proposals, see Ch. 17; for completion reports, see Ch. 19.

A *progress report* describes an ongoing project. A *status report,* sometimes called an *activity report,* describes the entire range of operations of a department or division. For example, the director of marketing for a manufacturing company might submit a monthly status report.

A progress report is an intermediate communication between the proposal (the argument that a project be undertaken) and the completion report (the comprehensive record of a completed project). Progress reports let you check in with your audience. Supervisors are vitally interested in the status of their projects, because they have to integrate them with other present and future commitments and because they want the projects to be done right and on time.

Regardless of how well the project is proceeding, explain clearly and fully what has happened and how it will affect the overall project. Your tone should be objective, neither defensive nor casual. Unless ineptitude or negligence caused the problem, you're not to blame. Regardless of the news you are delivering—good, bad, or mixed—your job is the same: to provide a clear and complete account of your activities and to forecast the next stage of the project.

LOBATE CONSTRUCTION
3311 Industrial Parkway
Speonk, NY 13508

Quality Construction Since 1957

April 11, 2003

Ms. Christine Amalli, Head
Civil Engineering
New York Power
Smithtown, NY 13507

Dear Ms. Amalli:

We are pleased to report the results of our visual inspection of the Chemopump after Run #9, a 30-day trial on Kentucky #10 coal.

The word visual *describes the methods.*

The inspection was designed to determine if the new Chemopump is compatible with Kentucky #10, the lowest-grade coal that you anticipate using. In preparation for the 30-day test run, the following three modifications were made by your technicians:

The writer states the purpose of the inspection.

• New front-bearing housing buffer plates of tungsten carbide were installed.
• The pump-casting volute liner was coated with tungsten carbide.
• New bearings were installed.

Our summary is as follows. A number of small problems with the pump were observed, but nothing serious and nothing surprising. Normal break-in accounts for the wear. The pump accepted the Kentucky #10 well.

This writer has chosen to incorporate the words summary *and* conclusion *in the body of the letter rather than use headings as a method of organization.*

The following four minor problems were observed:

• The outer lip of the front-end bell was chipped along two-thirds of its circumference.
• Opposite the pump discharge, the volute liner received a slight wear groove along one-third of its circumference.
• The impeller was not free-rotating.
• The holes in the front-end bell were filled with insulating mud.

The following three components showed no wear:

• 5-1/2" impeller
• suction neck liner
• discharge neck liner

■ **Figure 18.2**
A Field Report

Because the writer and the reader work for different companies, the letter is the appropriate format for this brief informal report.

page 2

Our conclusion is that the problems can be attributed to normal break-in for a new Chemopump. The Kentucky #10 coal does not appear to have caused any extraordinary problems. In general, the new Chemopump seems to be operating well.

We would recommend, however, that the pump be modified as follows:

1. Replace the front-end bell with a tungsten carbide-coated front-end bell.
2. Replace the bearings on the impeller.
3. Install insulation plugs in the holes in the front-end bell.

Further, we recommend that the pump be reinspected after another 30-day run on Kentucky #10.

The writer concludes politely.

If you have any questions, or would like to authorize these modifications, please call me at 555-1241. As always, we appreciate the trust you have placed in us.

Sincerely,

Marvin Littridge

Marvin Littridge
Director of Testing and Evaluation

■ **Figure 18.2**
(Continued)

When things go wrong, you might be tempted to cover up problems and hope that you can solve them before the next progress report. This course of action is unwise and unethical. Chances are that problems will multiply, and you will have a harder time explaining why you didn't alert your readers earlier.

GUIDELINES

Reporting Your Progress Honestly

Withholding bad news is unethical because it can mislead readers. As sponsors or supervisors of the project, readers have a right to know how it is going. If you find yourself faced with any of the following three common problems, consider responding in these ways:

▶ *The deliverable—the document or product you will submit at the end of the project—won't be what you thought it would be.* The progress report is your opportunity to explain that even though you thought you would be able to recommend an action, you will not be able to do so. Then explain why. Or explain that the deliverable will not meet one of the specifications in the proposal.

▶ *You won't meet your schedule.* Explain why you are going to be late and state when the project will be complete.

▶ *You won't meet the budget.* Explain why you need more money, and state how much more you will need.

Interactive Sample Document:
Reporting Inconclusive Information

The following passage is from a progress report written by a state forestry worker who is researching laptop computers to be purchased and used by her colleagues. One of the criteria she is studying is ruggedness. The questions in the margin ask you to think about the discussion of progress reports (on pages 466–468). The answers to these questions are available on TechComm Web.

A small segment of the industry builds "ruggedized" laptops. Unfortunately, the term *ruggedized* is used differently by different manufacturers.

Some manufacturers use the Ingress Protection scale, but because the manufacturer is the only one who performs the test, there is no guarantee of accuracy. The National Electrical Manufacturers Association (NEMA) also has a rating system, but it is not widely used by computer makers.

The military standards (Milspec), perhaps the most widely cited scales, are difficult to interpret because there are hundreds of them, and they measure different things. None of them applies specifically to laptops or even to computers in general. Milspec 810E, which measures ability to withstand repeated drops onto concrete from 2 meters, is the one most often cited by computer manufacturers.

Given the lack of precise information on ruggedness, I conclude that we should use Milspec 810E in our analysis. Although Milspec 810E measures only one aspect of ruggedness, and cannot make precise distinctions among laptops, manufacturers who have met 810E have at least undergone monitored testing by the military.

1. What is the problem that the writer is confronting in this portion of her progress report?

2. How effective is the writer's tone?

3. How honest does the writer seem in reporting her progress?

On TechComm Web

For answers to these questions, click on Interactive Sample Documents for Ch. 18 on <bedfordstmartins.com/techcomm>.

Organizing Progress and Status Reports

The time pattern and the task pattern, two organizational patterns frequently used in progress or status reports, are illustrated in Figure 18.3.

In the time pattern, you describe the work completed during the reporting period; then you sketch in the work that remains. Some writers include a section on present work, which enables them to focus on a long or complex task still in progress.

The Time Pattern	The Task Pattern
Discussion	Discussion
A. Past Work	A. Task 1
B. Future Work	1. Past work
	2. Future work
	B. Task 2
	1. Past work
	2. Future work

The task pattern allows you to describe, in order, what has been accomplished on each task. Often, a task-oriented structure incorporates the chronological structure, shown here.

■ **Figure 18.3
Organizational Patterns in Progress and Status Reports**

A status report is usually organized according to task; by its nature, a status report covers a specified time period.

Concluding Progress and Status Reports

In the conclusion of a progress or status report, evaluate how the project is proceeding. In the broadest sense, there are two possible messages: things are going well, or things are not going as well as anticipated.

GUIDELINES

Projecting an Appropriate Tone in a Progress or Status Report

▶ *If the news is good, convey your optimism but avoid overstatement.*

OVERSTATED   We are sure the device will do all that we ask of it, and more.

REALISTIC   We expect that the device will perform well and that, in addition, it might offer some unanticipated advantages.

Beware of promising early completion. Such optimistic forecasts rarely prove accurate, and it is always embarrassing to have to report a failure to meet the promised deadline.

▶ *Don't panic if the preliminary results are not as promising as you had planned or if the project is behind schedule.* Even the best-prepared proposal writers cannot anticipate all problems. As long as the original proposal was well planned and contained no wildly inaccurate computations, don't feel responsible. Just do your best to explain unanticipated problems and the status of the project. If you suspect that the results will not match earlier predictions, say so, clearly. If your news is bad, at least give the reader as much time as possible to deal with it effectively.

On TechComm Web

To see another sample progress report, for a study on American Sign Language, click on Links Library for Ch. 18 on <bedfordstmartins.com/techcomm>.

Find other samples of progress reports at Writing Guidelines for Engineering and Science Students. Click on Links Library for Ch. 18 on <bedfordstmartins .com/techcomm>.

If appropriate, use appendices for supporting materials, such as computations, printouts, schematics, diagrams, charts, tables, or a revised task schedule. Be sure to cross-reference these appendices in the body of the report, so that the reader can consult them at the appropriate stage of the discussion.

Sample Progress Report

The following progress report (Ewing & Lipus, 2002) was written for the project proposed on page 453 in Chapter 17. (The completion report for this study is on page 504 in Chapter 19.)

Rydell & Associates

556 N. Orchard   **Telephone: (208) 555-2267**
Boise, ID 83705   **Fax: (208) 555-8391**
www.rydellaccounting.com

Memo

Date: April 29, 2002

To: Joanna Rydell, President, Rydell & Associates

From: Marne Ewing, Technical-Communication Intern
               Teresa Lipus, Technical-Communication Intern

Subject: Progress Report for Feasibility Study on Printer Capability

Purpose

This is a progress report on our feasibility study on printer capability for Rydell &
Associates.

Summary

We have been researching options for improving our printing capabilities and thereby increasing employee productivity. We have evaluated our current printing capabilities and
determined printer-selection criteria. We are currently reviewing specifications and benchmark performance tests on laser printers.

Our study is currently on budget and on schedule, and we expect to submit a completion
report by the May 13 deadline noted in the proposal.

Introduction

On April 22, we received approval of our proposal to research and evaluate options for improving the printing capabilities of Rydell & Associates accountancy firm. This proposal
was based on growing concerns over the productivity problems we have been experiencing
with our current system. The results of this research will be presented in the form of a
completion report delivered to Joanna Rydell, President, on May 13.

Because of the firm's reputation for high-quality work, Rydell & Associates has experienced a recent growth in business volume, resulting in the addition of four new associates
in the past year. The expanded staff and workload have increased demands on our networked printing equipment: two HP LaserJet 1200s and one Canon BJC-85 Inkjet. At the
staff meeting on April 12, two of the associates brought up the issue of lost productivity.
Ms. Rydell responded that she knew that our associates often have to wait for their print
jobs to queue. She asked us to study the problem and see whether we could propose a solution that costs no more than $5,000 in initial capital outlay.

*The subject line and the
purpose statement identify the
purpose of the document: to
report on progress.*

*The summary briefly explains
the purpose of the project and
answers the question, "How is
the project going, and will it be
completed on schedule and
under budget?"*

*Most of the information in the
introduction is taken directly
from the proposal.*

Currently, we have three networked printers: two HP LaserJet 1200s and one Canon BJC-85 Inkjet. The laser printers are in good working order and can print 10 pages per minute (ppm), which is near the average of current models. The inkjet printer is trouble-prone and can print only 2 ppm.

Results of Research

The writers begin by describing the organization of the results section.

First we discuss the completed work: Tasks 1 and 2. Then we discuss our future work: Tasks 3 and 4.

Completed Work

The writers organize their discussion by task, as they did in the proposal.

Task 1: Calculate the cost of the lost productivity incurred by using our current printers. We interviewed all appropriate employees of the firm to find an average of minutes per day spent waiting for print jobs, and calculated the cost of this lost productivity. Employees must leave their desks to go to pick up print jobs. Often, they find themselves waiting for other jobs in the print queue to finish before their documents can print. Employees also spend time separating out their print jobs from those of other employees.

These data will be presented again in the completion report.

For the week of April 15, we asked employees to estimate the amount of time they spent waiting for print jobs. The average wait per day was over 6 minutes, which we converted to hours per month. The total wait time for the 10 employees was 28 hours, which translates to approximately $570 per month.

Employee Name	Title	Hourly Salary	Hours per Month Waiting for Printer	Cost to Firm
Drew Collins	CPA	28	1.50	42.00
Roland Green	CPA	23	1.85	42.55
Penny Parkyn	CPA	23	2.30	52.90
Rajiv Gupta	Associate	22	2.60	57.20
Barry Gathers	Associate	22	3.25	71.50
Kay Merrill	Associate	21	3.25	68.25
Brian Woolley	Associate	21	2.75	57.75
Bill Menendez	Associate	19	3.00	57.00
Carly Matthews	Associate	18	3.75	67.50
Bill Fredericks	Manager	15	3.60	54.00
Monthly Total			27.85	$570.65

page 3

Currently, our three printers are networked. According to Bill Fredericks, our office manager, we use 15,000 sheets of paper per month. He estimated that approximately 95 percent of our printing (14,250 pages) is done on the two HP LaserJet printers and only 5 percent (750 pages) on the Canon Inkjet, because employees are dissatisfied with its print quality. For this reason, our associates often need to wait as their print jobs are queued on the two HP LaserJet printers.

(There is an additional problem with the networked-printing configuration. Experts recommend that a printer be used to print no more than one quarter the number of pages listed in its duty cycle [Ozer, 2002]. This means that each LaserJet, with a duty cycle of 3,500, should be printing no more than 875 pages per month for optimum equipment wear. Each of our LaserJets is printing approximately 7,000 pages per month, eight times the Ozer recommendation. We are not using our printers efficiently; in fact, we are in danger of significantly reducing their effective useful lifetimes through overuse.)

Although this point does not directly relate to the research study, the writers include it because they think the reader ought to know it.

Task 2: Establish printer-selection criteria by determining our needs.
We know that any solution we recommend will need to cost less than $5,000. We need to determine whether our employees' needs will be best served by continuing our networked printing configuration, or whether we should move to a distributed configuration, in which each employee has his or her own printer. The question we need to answer is whether we can purchase 10 printers that have the technical characteristics we need: speed, resolution, and expandability.

The results of our quantitative analysis of current costs suggest that the main weakness of our printing situation is that the printers are networked. Associates have to leave their desks, wait for print jobs, and sort out their documents from the others at the printer. Based on this information, we decided that rather than having centralized, networked laser printers, it would be more efficient for each appropriate employee to have his or her own small-office laser printer. Therefore, we eliminated large-business printers from our study.

The writers explain and justify their process of determining criteria. If they did not, the reader would have no confidence in their findings.

Following were the five main criteria we considered during our research:

Initial purchase price
Our main goal was to find the most cost-effective approach to increasing our printing capacity and efficiency. Therefore, purchase cost was the initial criterion for evaluating laser printers; because we were working with an equipment budget of $5,000, and we knew we wanted to buy 10 printers, we narrowed the field by evaluating only printers under $500.

Print resolution
Because our documents often have fine, small print, and require clear, crisp text, we selected high resolution (1200 × 1200 dpi) as an essential criterion.

RAM-expandability
Accounting documents can be very complex, often including data from Microsoft® Excel and Access. Available RAM affects a printer's efficiency and resolution, and the ability to expand and upgrade the printer makes it more adaptable to future printing demands.

Cost per page
Cost per page is based on the average number of pages that can be printed from one toner cartridge.

Printing speed
Printing speed is another factor that contributes to efficient printing capabilities. We evaluated the printers by the pages per minute (ppm) they can produce.

Future Work
We are now at work on Task 3, evaluating the printers according to our criteria.

Task 3: Evaluate printers according to our criteria.
To narrow the selection of printers, we chose 14 laser printers from reviews and benchmark tests of small-office laser printers in *PC World* (Top Ten, 2002), *ZDNET.com* (Most Popular, 2002), and *CNET.com* (Top 5, 2002):

Brother HL 1270N	Lexmark E320
Brother HL 1440	Lexmark Optra M412n
Brother HL 1650	Samsung ML 1210
Brother HL 1670N	Samsung ML 1250
HP LaserJet 1000	Samsung ML 1651N
HP LaserJet 1200se	Samsung ML 6060
Lexmark E 210	Samsung ML 1450

After eliminating printers with resolutions less than 1200×1200 dpi, we narrowed the scope of our research to the following 5 printers:

Printer	Price
Samsung ML 1450	$299.99
HP LaserJet 1200se	$399.00
Brother HL 1650	$600.00
Samsung ML 1651N	$650.00
Brother HL 1670N	$750.00

Only the first 2 on this list meet our purchase-price criterion. To be sure that we are not eliminating appropriate printers on the basis of price alone, we will study the other 3 as well.

Task 4: Prepare a completion report.
We will prepare a completion report that explains the problem, the methods, and our findings. We will include detailed information about our current printing situation,

page 5

about how we established criteria, and about how we selected the printers to study. We will include the specifications from the benchmark tests and comparisons of selected printers that helped define our recommendations. We will submit the completion report by May 13, 2002.

Updated Schedule

Black bars represent completed tasks; gray bars represent tasks yet to be completed.

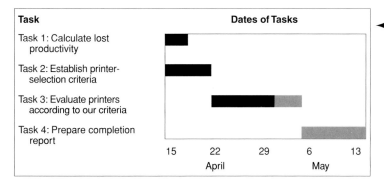

This Gantt chart shows the progress toward completing each of the project's tasks.

Conclusion

Our team has successfully completed Tasks 1 and 2 and begun Task 3. We are on schedule to complete Tasks 3 and 4 by the May 13 deadline. We have evaluated our current printing capabilities and determined essential printer-selection criteria. By applying these criteria, we have been able to narrow the field of suitable laser printers to 5, which we will evaluate in more detail. We are currently reviewing benchmark performance tests on these printers and comparing both purchase and projected maintenance costs. We will include our recommendations for replacing or augmenting our existing equipment in the May 13 completion report.

The conclusion summarizes the status of the project.

Please contact Marne Ewing at extension 2645 or Teresa Lipus at extension 3406 if you have questions or comments, or would like to discuss this project further.

The writers end with a polite offer to provide additional information.

References

CNET editors' top 5 personal laser printers. (2002, March). Retrieved April 10, 2002, from the CNET Web site: http://computers.cnet.com/hardware/0-2645882-8-5700867-1.html

Most popular printers. (2002, March). Retrieved April 10, 2002, from the ZDNet Web site: http://zdnetshopper.cnet.com/shopping/0-8399-1410-0-0.html?tag=pop&cobrand=29

Ozer, J. (2002, January). Print more for less. *Computer Shopper, 22,* 126–130.

Top ten monochrome laser printers. (2002, March). Retrieved April 10, 2002, from the PC World Web site: www.pcworld.com/reviews/article/0,aid,92901,00.asp

WRITING INCIDENT REPORTS

An incident report describes events such as workplace accidents, health or safety emergencies, and equipment problems. (Specialized kinds of incident reports go by other titles, such as *accident reports* or *trouble reports*.) The purpose of an incident report is to explain what happened, why it happened, and what the organization did — or is going to do — to follow up on the incident.

Figure 18.4 on page 478 is an incident report written after toxic fumes forced the evacuation of a building.

WRITING MEETING MINUTES

In This Book

For more about conducting meetings, see Ch. 4, p. 55.

Minutes, an organization's official record of a meeting, are distributed to all those who belong to the committee or any other unit represented at the meeting. Sometimes, minutes are written by administrative assistants; other times, they are written by technical professionals.

In writing a set of minutes, be clear, comprehensive, objective, and diplomatic. Do not interpret what happened; just report it. Because meetings rarely follow the agenda perfectly, you might find it challenging to provide an accurate record of the meeting. If necessary, interrupt the discussion to request a clarification.

Do not record emotional exchanges between participants. Because minutes are the official record of the meeting, you want them to reflect positively on the participants and the organization. Figure 18.5 on page 478 is an example of an effective set of minutes.

INCIDENT REPORT

Incident Title: Toxic Cloud Forces Evacuation of Montreal High-Rise

Location: Montreal, Quebec, Canada   **Date of Incident:** 10/29/2002

Incident Types: Release to Environment

Location Types: Fixed Facility

Evacuations: 250 (Estimate)   **Injuries:** 20 (Estimate)   **Fatalities:** None

Chemicals Involved: Solvents, plus additional chemicals not specified or identified

Description or Latest Development:
Chemicals used in cleaning and maintenance set off toxic fumes today (10/29/2002) that forced about 250 people from a high-rise office building and sent nine people to hospital. Fire crews evacuated the building and sent in a hazardous-materials response team to ventilate the building.

It was a combination of vapours from a solvent being used to clean the floor of the building's garage and fumes from a sealant used while the building was being painted, said fire and ambulance officials. The mix of chemicals sent a toxic odour through the building, affecting about 20 people, said the fire official. Nine people were sent to hospital complaining of headaches, nausea and shortness of breath. All were expected to be discharged later on Tuesday, said an ambulance-services spokesman.

Ian Harrison, who works on the seventh floor, said he and his colleagues had noticed a lingering smell since Monday. He blamed the building's ventilation system for the evacuation. "I've always thought the ventilation here was inferior," said Harrison.

Fire crews did not assess the building's ventilation system on Tuesday but workplace health and safety officials were on site, said fire department spokesman Robert Liebmann. "We managed to clear out all the air," Liebmann said in an interview.

"The building's been transferred back to the owner's responsibility. If they're going to continue the painting operations and it's going to continue to produce vapours, then they're going to have to keep people out for the next little while." Most of the 250 evacuees were told not to return to work on Tuesday and officials said it could be some time before the high-rise reopens. The 14-storey building houses a number of businesses, including a car dealership.

Here the writer begins to describe the incident. Provide as much detail as you can about the exact time and location of the incident.

The writer provides additional detail on the incident, reporting on the emergency workers' analysis of what caused the incident. Be honest in describing what caused the incident. If you are not sure of the cause, state that fact clearly.

The writer uses quotations but maintains an objective tone.

This quotation identifies what the organization should do to avoid evacuation and injuries in the future.

On TechComm Web

To see an online incident-report form, click on Links Library for Ch. 18 on <bedfordstmartins.com /techcomm>.

■ **Figure 18.4   Incident Report**

This incident report reads like a newspaper story. Other incident reports include headings in the body. Many organizations have incident-report forms—on paper or online—which call for the writer to respond to questions about the incident.
Source: United States Chemical Safety and Hazard Investigation Board, 2002 <www.chemsafety.gov/circ /post.cfm?incident_id=6092>.

In the title and the first paragraph, the writer records the logistical details of the meeting: date, name of the body that met, names of those attending, and so forth.

The writer records the reading, revision, and approval of the previous meeting's minutes.

The writer records the main topic of the meeting: the authorization of funding for a guest speaker.

The writer records the action taken at the meeting.

The writer downplays an emotional exchange. She briefly explains the arguments made in a discussion but doesn't comment on angry exchanges or quote people.

The writer records the logistical details about how the meeting concluded.

Robbins Junior High School
Weekly Planning Committee Minutes
Minutes of the February 14, 2003 Meeting

The meeting was called to order by Ms. De Grazia at 3:40 P.M. in the conference room. In attendance were Mr. Sipe, Ms. Leahy, Mr. Zaerr, Mr. Simon, and Principal Barson. Ms. Evett was absent.

The minutes of the February 7, 2003 meeting were read. The following correction was made: In paragraph 2, "800 hours" was replaced with "80 hours." The minutes were then unanimously approved.

There was one topic: authorization for the antidrug presentations by motivational speaker Alan Winston. Principal Barson reported on his discussion with Peggy Giles of the School District. She offered positive comments about Winston's presentations at other schools in the district last year. Principal Barson has also been in contact with the three other principals who invited Mr. Winston last year; they all spoke highly of his presentations.

Principal Barson moved that the committee authorize Winston's visit, to be scheduled in late May. The motion was seconded by Louis Simon.

Mr. Sipe asked whether the individual school or the district was to pay for the expenses (approximately $2,800) for the visit. Principal Barson replied that the school and the district would split the costs evenly, as had been done last year. The school has more than $4,000 surplus in operating expenses.

Mr. Zaerr expressed serious concerns about the effect of the visit on the teaching schedule. The visit would disrupt one whole day for all three grades in the school. Principal Barson acknowledged this but replied that in his weekly meeting with department chairs earlier in the week, they gave their approval to the idea. Since student participation would be voluntary, teachers were to offer review sessions to those students who elected not to attend Winston's presentation.

There being no more discussion, Ms. De Grazia called for a vote on the motion. The motion carried 4–0, with one abstention.

Principal Barson asked the committee if they would assist him in planning and publicizing Winston's visit. The committee agreed. Ms. De Grazia asked if there was any new business. There was none.

Ms. De Grazia adjourned the meeting at 4:20 P.M.

Zenda Hill
Recording Secretary

■ **Figure 18.5**
Set of Meeting Minutes

Reviewing the Process

Analyze your audience.

Consider the readers' knowledge about, and attitudes toward, your informal report. Determine whether readers are expecting a communication from you.

Analyze your purpose.

Determine whether you are informing or persuading, or both in your informal report.

Gather information about your subject.

Use appropriate secondary and primary research techniques. See Chapter 7.

Choose the appropriate format for the communication.

E-mails, memos, forms, and letters are the most common formats for informal reports.

Draft the report.

In a **directive,** you present a policy or procedure you want your readers to follow. In a **field or lab report,** you present the problem, methods, results, and conclusions. Sometimes, you also include recommendations. In a **progress report,** you communicate the status of an ongoing project. In a **status report,** you communicate on the entire range of operations of a department or division. In an **incident report,** you describe what happened, what caused the incident, and what you did or will do about the situation. In a set of **meeting minutes,** you record the logistical details of the meeting and provide an accurate record of the meeting.

Revise the report.

Even though the report is informal, it should be professional in all ways. Set aside time to revise it carefully to make sure it is clear and attractive. See the Revision Checklist that follows.

Revision Checklist

❏ Did you choose an appropriate format for the informal report? (p. 465)

Does the directive
❏ clearly and politely explain your message? (p. 465)
❏ explain your reasoning, if appropriate? (p. 465)

Does the field or lab report
❏ clearly explain the important information? (p. 466)
❏ use, if appropriate, a problem-methods-results-conclusion-recommendations organization? (p. 466)

Does the progress or status report
❏ clearly and honestly report on the subject and forecast the problems and possibilities of the future work? (p. 468)
❏ use an appropriate organization? (p. 469)
❏ append supporting materials that substantiate the discussion? (p. 470)
❏ clearly announce that it is a progress or status report? (p. 471)

Does the incident report
- ❏ explain what happened? (p. 476)
- ❏ explain why it happened? (p. 476)
- ❏ explain what the organization did about it, or will do about it? (p. 476)

Do the minutes
- ❏ provide the necessary logistical details about the meeting? (p. 476)
- ❏ explain the events of the meeting accurately? (p. 476)
- ❏ reflect positively on the participants and the organization? (p. 476)

Exercises

On TechComm Web

For more exercises, click on Additional Exercises, Projects, and Cases for Ch. 18 on <bedfordstmartins.com/techcomm>.

1. As the manager of Lewis Auto Parts Store, you have noticed that some of your salespeople smoke in the showroom. You have received several complaints from customers. Write a directive in the form of a memo defining a new policy: salespeople may smoke in the employees' lounge but not in the showroom. (For more on memos, see Chapter 15, page 378.)

2. The following report could be improved in tone, substance, and structure. Revise it to increase its effectiveness, adding any reasonable details.

   KLINE MEDICAL PRODUCTS

   Date: 1 September 2003
   To: Mike Framson
   From: Fran Sturdiven
   Subject: Device Master Records

   The safety and efficiency of a medical device depends on the adequacy of its design and the entire manufacturing process.

   To ensure that safety and effectiveness are manufactured into a device, all design and manufacturing requirements must be properly defined and documented. This documentation package is called by the FDA a "Device Master Record."

   The FDA's specific definition of a "Device Master Record" has already been distributed.

   Paragraph 3.2 of the definition requires that a company define the "compilation of records" that makes up a "Device Master Record." But we have no such index or reference for our records.

   Paragraph 6.4 says that any changes in the DMR must be authorized in writing by the signature of a designated individual. We have no such procedure.

   These problems are to be solved by 15 September 2003.

Projects

On TechComm Web

For more projects, click on Additional Exercises, Projects, and Cases for Ch. 18 on <bedfordstmartins.com/techcomm>.

3. Write a progress report about the research project you are working on in response to project 3 on page 460 in Chapter 17. If the proposal was a collaborative effort, collaborate with the same group members on the progress report.

4. **Group Activity** You are one of three members of the Administrative Council of your college's student association. Recently, the three of you have concluded that your

weekly meetings have become chaotic, largely because you do not use rules for parliamentary procedure and because controversial issues have arisen that have attracted numerous students (the meetings are open to all students). You have decided that it is time to consider adopting some parliamentary procedures to make the meetings more orderly and more effective. Look on the Web for models of parliamentary procedure. Is there one that you

can adopt? Could you combine elements of several to create an effective model? Find or put together a brief set of procedures, being sure to cite your sources. In a memo to your instructor, discuss the advantages and disadvantages of the model you propose and submit it along with the procedures. (For more on memos, see Chapter 15, page 378.)

On TechComm Web

For more cases, click on Additional Exercises, Projects, and Cases for Ch. 18 on <bedfordstmartins.com /techcomm>.

C A S E
Amending a Proposal

You are the chief technician for United Paper Company, an Oregon manufacturer of paper and paper products. The company has decided to replace two of its older rolling machines with newer models, each of which will cost more than $300,000. Last month, you formally proposed to your supervisor that you be permitted to visit two of the leading manufacturers of this equipment to study their products; your proposal was approved. You have carried out more research and are preparing your first progress report on this project. You have described the two competing machines and explained how each would fit in your company's manufacturing processes, and you have completed arrangements for visiting the two companies. With a budget of $6,000, next week you will visit American Equipment in Hawthorne, California, and Consolidated Industrial Equipment, in Newark, New Jersey. Your supervisor had balked a little at the cost of the two trips, but he agreed that they were necessary, given the importance of the new machines to the company.

Studying your papers in preparing your progress report, your heart sinks. You discover that you made a serious omission in your proposal: there is a third manufacturer, Southern Printing Equipment, in Atlanta, Georgia. You look back through your materials and discover that Southern's equipment is fully competitive with that of the other two manufacturers. You remember that when you wrote the proposal you were having some problems at home. Your spouse had been laid off, and with your oldest child beginning college next year, you had spent some sleepless nights.

You realize now that adding Southern to your itinerary would delay the completion date, and you would have to request an increased budget. What would be the costs and benefits to you and to the company of explaining the oversight to your supervisor? Of not explaining it? What should you do? If you think it is best to explain the oversight, write a memo to your supervisor. If you think it is best not to mention it, write a memo to your instructor, explaining your thinking. (For more on memos, see Chapter 15, page 378.)

19 Writing Formal Reports

Technical-writing instructors J. C. Mathes and Dwight W. Stevenson (1991, p. 87) on planning a report:

Your first concern is . . . providing information that readers need in order to respond or act so that the report accomplishes its purpose. The information that most readers need, however, is minimal—far less than the information you have available and indeed considerably less than you put into your report. Thus, you plan your basic structure according to reader needs rather than in terms of your investigation.

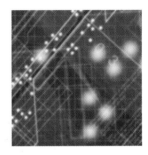

A formal report can be the final link in a chain of documents that begins with a proposal and continues with one or more progress reports. This last, formal report is often called a *final report, project report,* or *completion report.* The sample document beginning on page 504 is the final report in the series about selecting a printer presented in Chapters 17 and 18.

A formal report can also be a freestanding document, one that was not preceded by a proposal or by progress reports. For instance, your supervisor might ask you to find out employee attitudes toward comp pay: compensating employees who work overtime with time off rather than with overtime pay. Such a project would require that you research the subject and write a single complete report.

On TechComm Web

For additional samples, activities, and links related to this chapter, see <bedfordstmartins.com/techcomm>.

In This Book

For more about proposals and progress reports. see Ch. 17, p. 431, and Ch. 18, p. 466.

UNDERSTANDING THE TYPES OF FORMAL REPORTS

One of the challenges in talking about reports is that there is no standard terminology. Some terms refer to the topic of the report (*environmental-impact statements, lab reports*), some to the phase of the investigation (*progress reports, annual reports*), and some to the function or purpose of the report (*informational reports, analytical reports*). Some terms have special meanings in particular fields and in particular organizations. When you are asked to write a report, talk to more-experienced people first.

This section describes three kinds of reports, all classified according to their main purpose.

On TechComm Web

See Business Communication: Managing Information and Relationships. Click on Links Library for Ch. 19 on <bedfordstmartins.com/techcomm>.

Informational Report:	Presents results
Analytical Report:	Presents results + draws conclusions
Recommendation Report:	Presents results + draws conclusions + makes recommendations

Informational Reports

An informational report presents facts, often referred to as *results,* so that readers can understand a situation. For instance, the circulation department at a library might present an informational report to its planning board, communicating the number of patrons who visit the library, the kinds of items they borrow, the number and kinds of items the library purchases, the number and kinds of items stolen, and so forth.

In This Book

For more on status reports, see Ch. 18, p. 466.

If this report is routine and covers a particular period, such as the last quarter, then you would probably write an informal status report. However, if the report is nonroutine, requested by the planning board because it believes the library is not being run well or because the government body that funds the library requested it—you would probably write a formal informational report.

Here are examples of the kinds of questions an informational report addresses:

What is the status of Project X? What is the status of the project to reinforce the levees on the river? How many open-heart surgeries did the hospital perform last year, and what were the outcomes?

How do we do Function X? What procedures do we use to assess the performance of our clerical personnel? What quality-control procedures do we use for the laptops we manufacture?

What are the most popular ways of doing Function X? What are our major competitors' policies on returns? What is the ratio of surgical to laser operations for treating gallstones in the United States?

What do our people think of Situation X? How satisfied are our employees with our medical benefits? What do our production personnel think we could do to improve the quality of our products?

An informational report usually involves the primary- and secondary-research techniques discussed in Chapter 7, including using the library and the Internet, conducting interviews, and distributing questionnaires.

Analytical Reports

Like informational reports, analytical reports provide information, but then they analyze it and present *conclusions.* A conclusion is an interpretation of the results. For instance, in writing the report to the planning board of the library, the staff in the circulation department might present all the statistics but highlight the fact that thefts of CDs have increased substantially. With further analysis, the writers might conclude why some types of media are stolen more than others. An analytical report, therefore, tries to describe *why* something happens or *how* it happens or what it *means*.

Here are some examples of the kinds of questions an analytical report addresses:

What is the best way to do Function X? What is the most effective way to track manuscripts being edited by different people? Which therapy for people with spinal-cord injuries has the best outcome?

What causes Situation X? Why is there a high turnover in the Information Systems Department? Why is our competitor's new product doing so much better than ours?

What are the results of Situation X? If we create a Web site for our company, how much can we expect business to increase? If our accounting functions were performed by an outside firm, would we save money?

Could we do Function X? Do we have the infrastructure to compete with Company A in bidding on these government contracts? Can we afford to reimburse tuition for all college courses our employees wish to take?

Analytical reports usually include an informational element. For instance, if you work for a software manufacturer, you might write an analytical report to explain why your customer-support costs are high. In the informational section—the results—you describe your customer-support costs, focusing on which products (and which aspects of them) are causing your customers the most problems. In the analytical section—the conclusion—you use these data to explain why customers encounter these problems.

In This Book

For more on causal reasoning, see Ch. 8, p. 178.

Recommendation Reports

A recommendation report goes a step further than presenting information and analyzing it: it advocates a certain course of action. What is the difference between drawing conclusions and presenting recommendations? If your conclusion is that Product A meets our needs better than Product B or Product C, the recommendation would seem obvious: purchase Product A.

Maybe not. A report might recommend that, even though many CDs are being stolen, the library should take no action: we can't afford any of the available antitheft devices, none of the devices works well enough, all the devices create unacceptable problems, or next year there will be a better device available. A report can even recommend that, even though Product A is better for us than B or C, we should buy Product B, because B does 90 percent of what A does but costs only 50 percent as much.

Here are examples of the kinds of questions a recommendation report addresses:

What should we do about Problem X? What should we do about the fact that the number of calls to our Technical Support lines is very high? How should we celebrate our company's one-hundredth anniversary next year?

Should we do Function X? Although we could compete with Company A in bidding on these government contracts, is there a better way to increase our business? Although we cannot afford to reimburse tuition for all college courses our employees wish to take, can we reimburse them for classes directly related to their work?

Should we use Technology A or Technology B to do Function X? Should we buy copiers or lease them? Should we buy several high-output copiers or a larger number of low-output copiers?

We currently use Method A to do Function X. Should we be using Method B? Currently, we have a Technical Publications Department; should we instead subcontract that department's work? Currently, we sort our bar-coded mail by hand; should we buy an automatic sorter instead?

How reports are written is affected by organizational culture. In some organizations, only certain people are authorized to draw conclusions and make recommendations. For instance, bench chemists at a pharmaceuticals manufacturer might be permitted to present results but not to draw conclusions and make recommendations. Those tasks are left to more-senior people. In other organizations, managers like to segment the report-writing process so that different groups work on results, conclusions, and recommendations. One group writes the informational report, then hands the project over to a different group, which writes the analytical report. A third group writes the recommendation report. Each group, in effect, checks the work of the group or groups that preceded it. This method can reduce the chances that inaccurate or incomplete results are used to derive conclusions, and that nonvalid conclusions are used to formulate unwise recommendations.

A PROBLEM-SOLVING MODEL FOR PREPARING FORMAL REPORTS

Many writers find that a problem-solving approach helps them to put together an effective report. Figure 19.1 shows a basic problem-solving model and its relationship to the three types of reports.

Analyze Your Audience

Analyzing your audience is critical because it helps you determine how much information, and what kinds, you need to provide, and where to put it.

Before you start to write, think about these five audience-related questions:

- *How well do your readers know your field or the subject of your report?* The more they know, the less explanation you need to provide in the body. If some of them do not know the subject well, however, consider adding detailed explanations as appendices. Less knowledgeable readers can also benefit from glossaries.

On TechComm Web

See NASA's guide to report writing. Click on Links Library for Ch. 19 on <bedfordstmartins.com /techcomm>.

In This Book

For more on the writing process, see Ch. 3. For more on analyzing your audience, see Ch. 5.

In This Book

For more on appendices and glossaries, see Ch. 12, pp. 279 and 281. For more on patterns of organization, see Ch. 8.

- *Why are the readers reading the report?* If readers merely need to understand the subject, you can provide less information than if they plan to use your report as the basis for some further action. Again, it might be appropriate to put the complete description of the methods in an appendix.

- *Are your readers negative, neutral, or positive about the project?* The attitude of the readers might affect the organizational pattern, the amount of detail, and the vocabulary you choose.

- *What is your standing within the organization?* Writers with strong technical credentials and experience do not need to justify their assertions, conclusions, or recommendations as fully as writers who lack an extensive track record.

- *How routine is the project?* Some fields have accepted methods for carrying out certain tasks. For example, if you always perform a visual inspection first in assessing hurricane damage, there is no need to explain how or why you have done so. But if the project is unusual, readers will want to know why you used the approach you did.

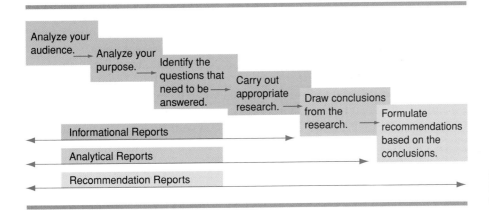

■ Figure 19.1
Problem-Solving Models
for Formal Reports

STRATEGIES FOR INTERCULTURAL COMMUNICATION

Writing Formal Reports for Readers from Another Culture

In the United States, formal reports are commonly organized from general information to specific information. The executive summary (which describes the big picture) and the introduction (which summarizes the major findings) are presented early in the report.

In many cultures, however, reports are organized from specific to general. Detailed discussions of methods and results precede discussions of the important findings.

When you write formal reports for people from other cultures, remember that the organization for formal reports as outlined in this chapter is culture-specific. If you can, study reports written by people from the culture you are addressing to see whether you can—and should—alter the organization of the report.

Analyze Your Purpose

In This Book

For more on determining your purpose, see Ch. 5.

In the broadest sense, you have one of three basic purposes:

- to present information
- to present information and analyze it
- to present and analyze information and make recommendations

However, you also have a purpose or set of purposes that relates more directly to your subject. Think about why you are doing the research, why your readers have requested it, and what they are going to do with it once they receive it. Is the report routine, or is there an unusual problem or opportunity that your readers need to examine? If, for instance, you work for a library and know that your research will help your readers understand the problem of theft of library materials, your purpose might be to help them understand how antitheft systems work and what they can be expected to do. Or your purpose might be to help the library trustees determine which of the systems (if any) would solve the library's problems. Of course, you can combine several purposes in one report.

In This Book

For more on writing this memo, see Ch. 3, p. 33.

Before you proceed too far in your planning, make sure your principal reader agrees with your understanding of your purpose. Writing a memo explaining to your supervisor the basic audience, purpose, and scope of the report can prevent you from going off in the wrong direction.

Identify Questions That Need to Be Answered

Think in detail about the subject of the investigation. What are the critical questions you will have to answer? Although sometimes it is your responsibility to determine these questions, often they are established before you begin.

Study your purpose statement carefully. If you are writing an informational report on library antitheft systems, here are some questions you might consider:

- What are antitheft systems, and what technologies do they use?
- How effective are they in reducing thefts?

- What kinds of library materials do they protect?
- What have been the experiences of libraries like ours that have used them?
- Are there reliable benchmark tests of the different systems?
- How easy is it to install and maintain the systems?
- How often do they break down?
- Do they pose any health risks to library workers or patrons?
- Is there some sort of financial support—grants, for instance—to help finance the purchase of the antitheft systems?

State these questions as precisely as you can.

VAGUE   How do library antitheft systems work?

SPECIFIC   What different technologies are used in the library antitheft systems currently available?

The vague question could refer to the different technologies or to the steps that library personnel have to follow to operate these devices.

VAGUE   What are some of the disadvantages of library antitheft systems?

SPECIFIC   Do any of the technologies pose any health risks to our workers or patrons?

Although the specific question doesn't address all the concerns suggested by "some of the disadvantages," it is a start. You could easily pose a half-dozen more questions about other disadvantages.

Carry Out Appropriate Research

The questions you need to answer will determine the kinds of research you should carry out. Often, you will consult company records, interview people, distribute questionnaires, perform experiments, make observations, and consult books, journals, and Internet sources. You should try to do as much research as time and other resources permit, and you should analyze the information to be sure it is valid and current.

In This Book

For more on conducting research, see Ch. 7.

Draw Conclusions from the Research

There is no foolproof way to draw valid conclusions from data. Some kinds of evidence are more valuable than others; benchmark tests conducted by independent groups are obviously more persuasive than claims from manufacturers about their own products. Look for a number of different kinds of evidence that all point to a causal relationship; one or two pieces of evidence are generally insufficient.

In This Book

For more about causal reasoning and avoiding logical fallacies, see Ch. 6, pp. 109 and 113.

Formulate Recommendations Based on Conclusions

In most cases, if you have carefully formulated the questions you need to answer, carried out appropriate research, and drawn valid conclusions, your recommendation will flow directly and inevitably from those conclusions.

But this is not necessarily the recommendation you will present. Perhaps your company does not have the funds to implement your recommendation or has changed its priorities. Or perhaps the problem has changed, making your recommendation irrelevant.

What should you do if you conclude that Plan A is best, but management favors Plan B and has no intention of implementing Plan A. Should you just tell them what they want to hear by recommending Plan B, adjusting your results and conclusions to lead to this recommendation? In most instances, the answer is simple. Recommending Plan B would be unethical, because it would entail lying or misleading. However, an appropriate course of action might be to recommend each plan equally, provided that the following conditions are present:

In This Book

For more on ethics, see Ch. 2.

- There is nothing unsafe or unethical about Plan B.
- Plan B is not clearly inferior to Plan A.
- You do not have to lie or mislead to recommend Plan B.

This recommendation would give you the opportunity to make the case for Plan A, while still making it easy for management to choose Plan B if they remain unconvinced of the superiority of Plan A.

UNDERSTANDING FEASIBILITY REPORTS

On TechComm Web

For sample reports, see Writing Guidelines for Engineering and Science Students. Click on Links Library for Ch. 19 on <bedfordstmartins.com/techcomm>.

One kind of recommendation report is written so often that it deserves special discussion. A *feasibility report* documents a study that evaluates at least two alternative courses of action. For example, should we expand our product line to include a new item, or should we make changes in an existing product?

A feasibility report is an argument that answers three kinds of questions:

- *Questions of possibility.* We would like to build a new rail line to link our warehouse and our retail outlet, but if we cannot raise the money, the project is not possible. Even if we have the money, do we have government authorization? If we do, are the soil conditions adequate for the rail link?

- *Questions of economic wisdom.* Even if we can afford to build the rail link, should we do so? If we use all our resources on this project, what other projects will have to be postponed or canceled? Is there a less expensive or a less financially risky way to achieve the same goals?

In This Book

For more about considering opposing viewpoints, see Ch. 6, p. 111.

- *Questions of perception.* If your company's workers have recently accepted a temporary wage freeze, they might view the rail link as unnecessary.

The truckers' union might see it as a threat to truckers' job security. Some members of the public might also be interested parties because any large-scale construction might affect the environment.

The following discussion explains the six steps that are particular to preparing feasibility reports.

Of course, you must begin by analyzing your audience and purpose, as you would for any technical document.

Identify the Problem or Opportunity

What is not working, or not working as well as it might? What situation presents an opportunity for us to decrease costs or improve the quality of our product or service? Without a clear statement of your problem or opportunity, you cannot plan your research.

For example, a number of employees at your company smoke, and these employees are absent and ill more often than nonsmoking employees. Your supervisor has asked you to investigate whether the company should offer a free smoking-cessation program. The company can offer the program only if the company's insurance carrier will pay for the program. The first thing you need to do is talk with the insurance agent; if the insurance carrier will pay for the program, then you can proceed with your investigation. If the agent says no, the problem shifts; now you have to determine whether another insurance carrier offers better coverage or whether there is some other way to encourage employees to stop smoking.

Establish Criteria for Responding to the Problem or Opportunity

Criteria are standards against which you measure your options. Criteria can take two forms: *minimum specifications* and *evaluative criteria*. Minimum specifications define what you *need*, while evaluative criteria define what you *want*. For example, in selecting photocopiers for your department, a minimum specification might be that each copy cost less than two cents to produce and that the photocopier be able to handle oversized documents. Evaluative criteria might include that the photocopier do double-sided copying and stapling. Evaluative criteria let you make distinctions among a variety of similar objects, objectives, actions, or effects.

Until you can establish your criteria, you don't know what your options are. Sometimes you inherit your criteria; your supervisor tells you how much money you can spend, for instance, and that figure becomes part of your minimum specifications. Sometimes you derive your criteria from your research; you study your photocopying needs and determine the minimum standards.

To prepare a feasibility report:

Identify the problem or opportunity.

Establish criteria for responding to the problem or opportunity.

Determine the options.

Study each option according to the criteria.

Draw conclusions about each option.

Formulate recommendations based on the conclusions.

In This Book

For more about establishing criteria, see Ch. 8, p. 169.

Determine the Options

After you establish your criteria, you determine your options. *Options* are potential solutions. For example, your options for the photocopier project are the different models on the market that meet your minimum specifications and evaluative criteria.

In This Book

For more on research techniques, see Ch. 7.

Determining your options is critically important because if you fail to identify all the appropriate options, the rest of the analysis will be flawed. For instance, if you fail to consider the photocopiers made by Xerox, the results, conclusions, and recommendations you present later, in your report, might well be invalid, because Xerox might manufacture the best copier for your needs. Therefore, you have to be especially careful that you carry out your research thoughtfully and thoroughly.

Study Each Option According to the Criteria

Once you have determined your options, study each option according to the criteria. For the photocopier project, secondary research would include studying articles about photocopiers in technical journals and specification sheets from the different manufacturers. Primary research might include observing product demonstrations as well as interviewing representatives from different manufacturers and managers who have purchased different brands.

To make the analysis of the options as objective as possible, investigators sometimes create a *matrix*, a method for systematically entering an evaluation for each option according to each criterion. A matrix is really just a table (or a spreadsheet), as shown in Figure 19.2.

Option	Criterion 1: Pages per Minute	Criterion 2: Ability to Duplex	Criterion 3: Extra Paper Bins	Criterion 4: Color Printing	Total Points
Option 1: Ricoh Model 311	9	8	7	9	33
Option 2: Xerox Model 4500	8	9	7	2	26
Option 3: Savin Model 12X	10	8	8	9	35
Option 4: Sharp Model S350	7	8	8	9	32

■ **Figure 19.2 A Matrix**

To use a matrix, you assign a value (0–10 is a common range) for each criterion for each option. Then you add up the values for each option and compare the totals. In this case, option 3 scores the highest, with 35 points; option 2 scores the lowest, with 26 points.

Does using a matrix ensure an objective analysis? No. Bias can creep in at three stages:

- *Determining which criteria to examine.* The Xerox Model 4500—Option 2— did very poorly on criterion 4; if criterion 4 were removed from the analysis, or if many other criteria were added, the Xerox might score much higher.

- *Deciding the range of values for each criterion.* If one of your criteria is whether the copier can staple, how do you decide to score a machine that does stapling? A machine that does not? If you give 10 points to a machine that does stapling and 0 points to a machine that doesn't, you have probably eliminated the nonstapling machine from contention. However, if the ability to staple is not very important, it might be more reasonable to assign a value of 8 points to nonstapling machines. To help readers understand your thinking, you should explain your ranking system. For instance, a note should accompany Figure 19.2 explaining that you give a copier 9 points if it can print duplex and 8 points if it cannot, because printing duplex is an unimportant criterion. However, you give a copier 9 points if it can print in color and 2 points if it cannot, because printing in color is a very important criterion.

- *Assigning values to criteria.* If, for example, one of your criteria is ease of operation, you might give one machine a 9, whereas someone else might give it a 3. Other criteria are equally difficult to assess objectively. For example, what value do you give to the cost criterion if one machine costs $12,500 per year to operate and another costs $14,300?

Evaluating options according to criteria is always subjective. Still, for you as the writer, the principal advantage of a matrix is that it helps you do a methodical analysis. For your readers, a matrix makes your analysis easier to follow by clearly presenting your methods and results.

Draw Conclusions about Each Option

Whether you use a matrix or some other, less-formal means of recording your evaluations, your next step is to draw conclusions about the options you have studied — by interpreting your results and writing evaluative statements about the options.

For the study of photocopiers, your conclusion might be that a particular model made by Ricoh is the best copier: it meets all your minimum specifications and the greatest number of your evaluative criteria, or it scores highest on your matrix. Depending on your readers' preferences, present your conclusions in any one of three ways.

- *Rank all the options*: the Ricoh copier is the best option, the Savin copier is second best, and so forth.

- *Classify all the options in two categories*: acceptable and unacceptable.

- *Present a compound conclusion*: the Ricoh offers the most technical capabilities; the Savin is the best value.

Formulate Recommendations Based on the Conclusions

The earlier discussion of recommendations (page 490) applies to feasibility reports, but with one additional note: don't be afraid to recommend that your organization take no action. Research projects can yield mixed or bad news: none of the options would be an unqualified success or none would work at all. A negative recommendation does not reflect negatively on you. Give the best advice you can, even if that advice is to do nothing.

GUIDELINES

Preparing Feasibility Reports

To prepare a feasibility report, follow these eight steps:

1. *Analyze your audience.* What do they need to know?
2. *Analyze your purpose.* What do you want to accomplish?
3. *Identify the problem or opportunity.* What is not working, or what improvements could we make?
4. *Establish criteria.* Decide on minimum specifications and evaluative criteria for responding to the problem or opportunity.
5. *Determine your options.* What are the available courses of action?
6. *Study each option according to your criteria.* Work out a systematic way to evaluate each option to reduce the subjectivity of the analysis.
7. *Draw conclusions about each option. Conclusions* are statements of what your data mean.
8. *Formulate recommendations based on your conclusions. Recommendations* are statements of what we ought to do next.

Elements of a typical report:

Front matter (see Ch. 12)

Introduction

Methods

Results

Conclusions

Recommendations

Back matter (see Ch. 12)

ORGANIZING THE BODY OF THE FORMAL REPORT

Every report should reflect the characteristics of its audience, purpose, and subject. One basic structure can serve as a good starting point for thinking about how to organize a report. A typical formal report contains many of the elements shown in Figure 19.3.

Most reports are read by multiple audiences: managers who need only an overview of the project; technical personnel who need detailed information; technical personnel in related fields; attorneys; or representatives of regulatory agencies. To accommodate all these audiences, a formal report generally consists of components that remain independent yet work together. For instance, in a typical formal report, an executive summary precedes the body of

Front Matter	Body	Back Matter
• title page	• introduction	• glossary
• abstract	• methods	• list of symbols
• table of contents	• results	• references
• list of illustrations	• conclusions	• appendices
• executive summary	• recommendations	

Front matter and back matter are discussed in Chapter 12.

The body of the report is discussed in this chapter.

■ **Figure 19.3   Elements of a Typical Report**

the document. Some readers will skip the executive summary; others will read nothing but the executive summary.

Introduction

The introduction enables readers to understand the technical discussion that follows. Start by analyzing who the readers are, then consider these standard questions:

- *What is the subject of the report?* If the report follows a proposal and progress report, you can probably copy this information from one of these documents and modify it as necessary.

- *What is the purpose of the report?* The purpose of the report is not the purpose of the project. The purpose of the report is to present information to enable readers to understand a subject, to affect readers' attitudes toward a subject, or to enable readers to carry out a task.

- *What is the background of the report?* Include this information, even if you have presented it before; some of your readers might not have read your previous documents, or might have forgotten them.

- *What are your sources of information?* Briefly describe your primary and secondary research, to prepare your readers for a more detailed discussion of your sources in subsequent sections of the report.

- *What is the scope of the report?* Indicate the topics you are including, as well as those you are not.

- *What are the most significant findings?* Summarize the most significant findings of the project.

- *What are your recommendations?* In a short report containing a few simple recommendations, include those recommendations in the introduction. In a lengthy report containing many complex recommendations, briefly summarize them in the introduction, then refer readers to the more detailed discussion in "Recommendations."

In This Book

For more about purpose statements, see Ch. 5, p. 97.

In This Book

For more on introductions, see Ch. 8, p. 179.

On TechComm Web

For examples of research reports, see OCLC. Click on Links Library for Ch. 19 on <bedfordstmartins .com/techcomm>.

- *What is the organization of the report?* Indicate the organizational pattern you will use, so readers can understand where you are going and why.
- *What key terms are you using in the report?* The introduction is an appropriate place to define new terms. If you need to define many terms, place the definitions in a glossary and refer readers to it in the introduction.

Figure 19.4 shows the introduction to the body of a formal report—in this case, a feasibility report. The subject of the report is an investigation to determine whether the writers' university should recognize American Sign Language as a foreign language and incorporate it into the foreign-language curriculum. The report is titled "Recognizing American Sign Language as a Foreign Language at Central State University: A Recommendation Report." Marginal notes have been added.

Methods

The methods section answers the question "What did you do?" In drafting the methods section, consider your readers' knowledge of the field, their perception of you, and the uniqueness of the project, as well as their reasons for reading the report and their attitudes toward the project. Provide enough information to enable readers to understand what you did and why you did it that way. If others will be using the report to duplicate your methods, include sufficient detail.

Figure 19.5 on page 498 shows the methods section from the report on American Sign Language.

Results

Results are the data you have discovered or compiled. Present the results objectively, without comment; save the interpretation of the results—your conclusions—for later. If you combine results and conclusions, your readers might be unable to follow your reasoning and might not be able to tell whether the evidence justifies your conclusions.

The methods section answers the question "What did you do?" The results section answers the question "What did you see?"

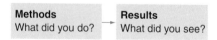

Methods
What did you do? → **Results**
What did you see?

Your audience's needs will help you decide how to structure the results. How much they know about the subject, what they plan to do with the report, what they expect your recommendation to be—these and many other factors will affect how you present the results.

For instance, suppose that your company is considering installing an intranet, a companywide computer network. In the introduction, you explained

2

INTRODUCTION

On April 24, we received approval to investigate whether Central State University (CSU) should formally recognize American Sign Language (ASL) as a foreign language and incorporate it into the foreign-language curriculum. We also received approval to investigate how this recognition could be achieved at CSU (through revision of university policy) and at all Oklahoma colleges and universities (by state legislation). Our goal in this project was to identify the criteria by which CSU defines a language as foreign, determine the extent to which ASL meets those criteria, and determine which of the two methods of granting recognition would be most appropriate for CSU.

The background and purpose of the report

Currently, Central State University (CSU) does not recognize American Sign Language (ASL) as a foreign language, meaning that students in CSU's three ASL courses may earn elective credits but not foreign-language credits. Dr. Teresa O'Malley, Chair of the Modern Languages Department, and Suzanne Christopher, CSU's ASL instructor, have noticed a growing demand for ASL courses at CSU, despite the fact that the students in the courses do not earn foreign-language credits. This growing interest in ASL is reflected throughout America, as more and more universities formally recognize ASL as a foreign language. In fact, almost half of the states in America recognize ASL as a foreign language and grant academic credit for these courses; these states have recognized ASL either through state legislation or revision of university policy. Oklahoma is one of 15 states in which colleges and universities grant only elective credit to students who complete ASL courses. Formally recognizing ASL as a foreign language, as this report recommends, would help CSU remain current with modern linguistic and educational trends.

The problem

In conducting our investigation, we drew upon the expertise of several individuals knowledgeable about ASL and its role in college and university curricula. For instance, Ceil Lucas' multivolume *Sociolinguistics in Deaf Communities* helped us analyze the non-English characteristics of ASL. We consulted interpreter/linguist Rhonda Jacobs' article "ASL as a Truly Foreign Language" (*Multicultural Aspects of Sociolinguistics in Deaf Communities*, C. Lucas, ed.) to determine how the Foreign Language Institute of the U.S. State Department classifies languages based on their differences from English. Finally, Sherman Wilcox, coauthor of *Learning to See: Teaching American Sign Language as a Second Language* and Associate Professor of Linguistics at the University of New Mexico, helped us evaluate the two methods by which CSU might recognize ASL as a foreign language.

The methods

We have focused our research on determining the linguistic characteristics that qualify ASL as a foreign language and on the methods by which CSU might recognize it as such. We have not looked into significantly expanding the current ASL program at CSU.

The scope

Our most significant findings are as follows:

- ASL meets the criterion by which CSU defines a language as foreign.
- Recognizing ASL through revision of university policy is preferable to recognizing it through state legislation.

The results

We therefore recommend that CSU revise university policy to formally recognize ASL as a foreign language and incorporate ASL into the foreign-language curriculum.

The recommendation

The following sections provide additional detail about the methods used in our research, the results we obtained, the conclusions we drew from those results, and our recommendations based on those conclusions.

An advance organizer

■ **Figure 19.4**
Introduction to the Body of a Formal Report

Note that reports are often double spaced.
Source: Wells, Tommack, & Tuck, 1997.

METHODS   3

In conducting our research, we completed the following tasks:

- We interviewed Dr. Teresa O'Malley, the acting Chair of the Modern Languages Department at CSU, to determine the criterion by which CSU defines a language as foreign.

- We studied the linguistic characteristics of ASL to determine if it met the criterion used at CSU. Suzanne Christopher, the current ASL instructor at CSU, assisted us with this portion of our project, primarily by directing us to sources of information and helping us to interpret that information. In addition, we consulted several books and periodicals to determine whether ASL meets the criterion by which CSU defines a language as foreign. These sources are listed in "References."

- We spoke with educators and specialists familiar with Texas legislation that recognizes ASL as a foreign language, to determine if CSU should grant recognition internally (through revision of university policy) or if recognition should be granted externally (through state legislation). Sha H. Cowan from the Texas Education Agency, Services for the Deaf Department, referred us to deaf educators in his area. We interviewed Marietta L. Yeates, Professor in the Deaf/Hard of Hearing Program at Stephen F. Austin State University, and Dr. Sherman Wilcox, Associate Professor of Linguistics at the University of New Mexico, to learn their views on the Texas legislation. Using the information supplied by Dr. Yeates and Dr. Wilcox, we analyzed the positive and negative aspects of internal recognition of ASL as a foreign language as compared to external recognition.

■ **Figure 19.5**
Methods Section of a Formal Report

Notice how specifically the methods are described.
Source: Wells, Tommack, & Tuck, 1997.

the disadvantages and limitations of the company's current system for internal communication. In the methods section, you described how you established the minimum specifications and evaluative criteria you applied to the available intranet systems, as well as your research procedures. In the results section, you provide the details of each intranet system you are considering, as well as the results of your evaluation of those systems.

Figure 19.6 is an excerpt from the results section of the American Sign Language report.

Conclusions

In This Book

For more on evaluating evidence and drawing conclusions, see Ch. 6, pp. 109 and 110.

Conclusions are the implications of the results. To draw conclusions, you need to think carefully about your results, weighing whether they point clearly to a single meaning. The conclusions answer the question "What does it mean?"

Methods	**Results**	**Conclusions**
What did you do?	What did you see?	What does it mean?

The conclusions section of the American Sign Language report is shown in Figure 19.7 on page 501.

4

RESULTS

Our research project investigated whether Central State University (CSU) should recognize American Sign Language (ASL) and incorporate it into the foreign-language curriculum. Specifically, we investigated the criterion by which CSU defines a language as foreign, the extent to which ASL meets this criterion, and the two methods by which CSU might recognize ASL as a foreign language (either internally, by revising university policy or externally, through state legislation). We obtained the following results:

An advance organizer for the results section

CSU's Requirement for a Language to Be Considered Foreign
According to Dr. Teresa O'Malley, Chair of the CSU Department of Modern Languages, the sole criterion for a language to be considered foreign at Central State University is that it be "non-English" in such matters as structure, grammar, syntax, and vocabulary. Dr. O'Malley also noted that any language that can be shown to be "non-English" could be incorporated as a foreign language.

Note that the three main parts of the results section match the tasks as defined in the methods section.

After reviewing the ASL courses offered at CSU, Dr. O'Malley said that two of them— CM221, Intermediate American Sign Language and CM321, Conversational American Sign Language—would be eligible for foreign-language credit if CSU recognized ASL and incorporated it into the foreign-language curriculum. Courses at the beginner level would be ineligible; such courses are considered equivalent to high-school courses, so students who complete them receive no credit.

ASL's Fulfillment of CSU's Requirement
Initially, we had planned to meet with Suzanne Christopher, the ASL instructor at CSU; Kelley Eastwick, the President of the Oklahoma Chapter of the Registry of Interpreters for the Deaf; and Janis Seymour, committee member of the Oklahoma Association of the Deaf. However, because of scheduling conflicts we were able to meet only with Suzanne Christopher. She assisted us in researching ASL's linguistic identity and determining the extent to which ASL meets the criterion by which CSU defines a language as foreign.

We found that ASL is a "highly elaborate and fully expressive language whose structure is determined in part by the articulating dynamics of the body" (Isenhath, 1990, p. 126); in this respect, ASL differs significantly from English. In conducting this portion of our research, we drew upon several linguistic manuals and other sociolinguistic resources to identify the "non-English" characteristics of ASL. This investigation of ASL's linguistic identity included research into grammatical structure, topicalization, spatial indexing, the use of multidirectional verbs, and rules governing questions and negations. (Appendix C, p. 11, contains summaries and examples of ASL's "non-English" characteristics in these five areas.)

We studied ASL's non-English characteristics in these five areas because they are linguistically simple yet illustrate profound differences between ASL and English. Three of these areas—topicalization, spatial indexing, and multidirectional verb usage—are key to ASL but are not found in English. Grammatical structure and rules governing questions and negation are key components of nearly all languages; however, ASL has a unique grammatical structure, as well as rules governing questions and negation that are quite different from those of English.

■ **Figure 19.6**
Results Section of a Formal Report

Source: Wells, Tommack, & Tuck, 1997.

5

Analysis of the Two Methods by Which ASL Could Be Formally Recognized

Two methods exist by which ASL could be formally recognized: internal recognition (through revision of university policy) and external revision (through state legislation).

Our research into these methods included communication with several members of the deaf-education community in Texas, which has recently recognized ASL as a foreign language at all Texas colleges and universities. We could have looked to Maryland, New York, or Washington D.C., where ASL recognition has been strongly advocated since the establishment of schools such as Gallaudet University and the National Technical Institute for the Deaf. But the per capita deaf population there far exceeds Oklahoma's.

Sha H. Cowan from the Texas Education Agency, Services for the Deaf Department, referred us to deaf educators in his area. Consequently, we interviewed Marietta L. Yeates, Professor in the Deaf/Hard of Hearing Program at Stephen F. Austin State University, and Dr. Sherman Wilcox, Associate Professor of Linguistics at the University of New Mexico.

Dr. Wilcox maintains a list of universities that recognize ASL as a foreign language. Dr. Wilcox's list (Appendix A, p. 9) shows that ASL is being recognized as a foreign language internally by colleges and universities more often than it is being recognized through state legislation. Moreover, his research was most recently updated on January 30, 1997, making it both more current and more inclusive than the original research we outlined in our proposal.

In our proposal, we referred to Rhonda Jacobs' research into the percentage of states that have passed legislation recognizing ASL as a foreign language. Though published in 1996, her article referred to raw data collected in 1993, making us question the relevance of her article. Also, she defined "legislative approval" (in our terms, "legislative recognition") as state-mandated recognition that was applicable to all state colleges and universities. However, we are interested only in approval legislatively granted to post-secondary institutions, though other relevant legislation would naturally give the petitioner greater weight. Dr. Wilcox's list, found in Appendix A on page 9, shows that more colleges are independently recognizing ASL as a foreign language.

Using the data from Dr. Yeates and Dr. Wilcox, we analyzed the positive and negative aspects of recognizing ASL internally (by revising university policy) and externally (through state legislation). Dr. Yeates explained that Stephen F. Austin State University recognized ASL as a foreign language *before* Texas state legislation recognized it for all Texas colleges and universities. Dr. Yeates encouraged us to seek state legislation that would recognize ASL at all Oklahoma colleges and universities.

However, Dr. Wilcox cautioned us about using this approach. Specifically, he said that conflict might arise if the legislature tried to mandate the university's curriculum; in his experience, the faculty and administration of colleges and universities often respond with distrust and resistance when legislation mandates changes to the curriculum. With this idea in mind, he suggested that the best course of action would be to recognize ASL as a foreign language internally, by revising university policy. In Dr. Wilcox's view, proponents of ASL as a foreign language could then use CSU's recognition to garner support for state legislation designating ASL as a foreign language at all Oklahoma colleges and universities.

Dr. Wilcox offered to assist CSU in formally recognizing ASL as a foreign language and incorporating it into the foreign-language curriculum. He is a strong advocate for the study of ASL and has experience in organizing presentations and petitions in support of ASL.

■ **Figure 19.6**
(Continued)

6

CONCLUSIONS

After carefully analyzing the non-English characteristics of American Sign Language (ASL) and the criterion by which Central State University (CSU) defines a language as foreign, we have concluded that ASL qualifies as a foreign language. CSU's criterion stipulates that a language must be "non-English" in such matters as grammar, syntax, and vocabulary; ASL clearly differs from English, particularly in such areas as grammatical structure, topicalization, spatial indexing, the use of multidirectional verbs, and rules governing questions and negations.

ASL's unique linguistic identity has been established in current literature and has been deemed sufficiently distinct for dozens of state universities to recognize ASL as a foreign language. Moreover, the complexity of ASL would make the intermediate ASL courses a challenging and rewarding addition to the foreign-language curriculum at CSU.

After reviewing the process by which the Texas state legislature officially recognized ASL as a foreign language, we have concluded that internal recognition would be in the best interests of CSU and would be the most effective method of officially recognizing ASL. Recognizing ASL internally would require revision of university policy, whereas external recognition would require passage of state legislation. Although state legislation would bring with it the benefit of statewide recognition, state legislation might also create political friction between the members of the legislature and the faculty and administration of Oklahoma colleges and universities. In short, representatives of Oklahoma colleges and universities may resent the idea of the state legislature mandating a change in curriculum and may work to defeat state legislation recognizing ASL as a foreign language, regardless of their feelings about the merits of ASL as a foreign language.

■ **Figure 19.7   Conclusions Section from a Formal Report**

Notice that the writers explain their reasoning carefully.
Source: Wells, Tommack, & Tuck, 1997.

Recommendations

Recommendations are suggestions to take particular actions. The recommendations section answers the question "What should we do now?" As discussed earlier in this chapter, recommendations do not always flow directly from conclusions. Always consider recommending that the organization take no action, or no action at this time.

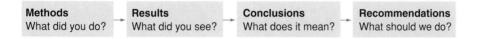

| **Methods** | **Results** | **Conclusions** | **Recommendations** |
| What did you do? | What did you see? | What does it mean? | What should we do? |

GUIDELINES

Writing Recommendations

As you draft your recommendations, consider the following four factors:

▶ *Content.* Be clear and specific. If the project has been unsuccessful, don't simply recommend that your readers "try some other alternatives." What alternatives do you recommend, and why?

▶ *Tone.* When you recommend a new course of action, you run the risk of offending whoever formulated the earlier course. Do not write that acting on your recommendations will "correct the mistakes" that have been made. Instead, write that acting on your recommendations "offers great promise for success." A restrained, understated tone is more persuasive: it shows that you are interested only in the good of your company, not personal rivalries.

▶ *Form.* If the report leads to only one recommendation, use traditional paragraphs. If the conclusion of the report leads to more than one recommendation, consider a numbered list.

▶ *Location.* Consider including a summary of the recommendations—or, if they are brief, the full list—after the executive summary or in the introduction as well as at the end of the body of the report.

Figure 19.8 shows the recommendations section of the American Sign Language report.

■ **Figure 19.8**
Recommendations
Section from a Formal
Report

Source: Wells, Tommack, & Tuck, 1997.

7

RECOMMENDATIONS

On the basis of our conclusions, we recommend the following:

1. Central State University (CSU) should recognize American Sign Language (ASL) as a foreign language and incorporate ASL into the foreign-language curriculum.

2. CSU should internally recognize ASL, through revision of university policy, rather than seek external recognition through state legislation.

3. CSU should seek the advice of Dr. Sherman Wilcox, of the University of New Mexico, in implementing the first two recommendations.

Interactive Sample Document:
Introducing a Report

The following passage introduces a formal report entitled "Assessing Health Risk Behaviors Among Young People: Youth Risk Behavior Surveillance System, At a Glance 2002" (Centers for Disease Control, 2002). The questions in the margin ask you to think about formal report introductions (as discussed on pages 495–496). The answers to these questions are available on TechComm Web.

Risk Behaviors Are Linked to the Leading Causes of Death

Today, the health of young people—and the adults they will become—is critically linked to the health-related behaviors they choose to adopt. A limited number of behaviors contribute markedly to today's major killers. These behaviors, often established during youth, include

- Tobacco use.

- Unhealthy dietary behaviors.

- Inadequate physical activity.

- Alcohol and other drug use.

- Sexual behaviors that may result in HIV infection, other sexually transmitted diseases, and unintended pregnancies.

- Behaviors that may result in violence and unintentional injuries (motor vehicle crashes).

Among both children and adults, the leading causes of death are closely linked to these behaviors. Among adults, chronic diseases—such as cardiovascular disease, cancer, and diabetes—are the nation's leading killers. Practicing healthy behaviors, such as eating low-fat, high-fruit-and-vegetable diets, getting regular physical activity, and refraining from tobacco use, would prevent many premature deaths. Because health-related behaviors are usually established in childhood, positive choices need to be promoted before damaging behaviors are initiated or become ingrained.

1. What is the subject of the report? How clearly is it stated in this introduction?

2. What recommendations is the writer making?

3. What questions has the writer neglected to answer in this introduction?

On TechComm Web

To find the answers to these questions, click on Interactive Sample Documents for Ch. 19 on <bedfordstmartins.com/techcomm>.

SAMPLE FORMAL REPORT

The following example (Ewing & Lipus, 2002) is the completion report on the project proposed in Chapter 17 on page 453. The progress report for the same project appears in Chapter 18 on page 471.

Transmittal "letters" can be presented as memos.

The purpose of the study

The methods

The major recommendation

A polite offer to provide more information

Rydell & Associates

556 N. Orchard   **Telephone: (208) 555-2267**
Boise, ID 83705   **Fax: (208) 555-8391**
www.rydellaccounting.com

Memo

Date: May 13, 2002

To: Joanna Rydell, President, Rydell & Associates

From: Marne Ewing, Technical-Communication Intern
Teresa Lipus, Technical-Communication Intern

Subject: Completion Report for the Feasibility Study on Printing Capability

Attached is a completion report on our feasibility study about improving our printing capability. We completed the tasks outlined in our proposal dated April 15, 2002: evaluating our current printing capabilities and researching various options for increasing our printing capability.

First, we calculated the lost productivity caused by associates' having to wait for their print jobs. Then we established printer-selection criteria and researched available laser printers according to the criteria.

Based on the information we gathered and reviewed, we recommend buying 10 small-business laser printers for our office. Because the HP LaserJet 1200se has proven reliability and Hewlett Packard has an excellent customer-service reputation, we recommend purchasing 10 HP LaserJet 1200se printers, for a total cost of $3,990. These printers will pay for themselves in less than one year.

Thank you for the opportunity to research options for enhancing printing capability at Rydell & Associates. We look forward to the possibility of working on future projects for the firm. Please contact Marne Ewing at extension 2645 or Teresa Lipus at extension 3406 if you have any questions or comments.

**FEASIBILITY STUDY ON PRINTER CAPABILITY:
A COMPLETION REPORT**

The title indicates the subject and purpose of the report.

Prepared for: **Joanna Rydell, President**
Rydell & Associates

Prepared by: Marne Ewing, Technical-Communication Intern
Teresa Lipus, Technical-Communication Intern

May 13, 2002

Abstract

"Feasibility Study on Printer Capability: A Completion Report"

Prepared by: Marne Ewing, Technical-Communication Intern
Teresa Lipus, Technical-Communication Intern

In April 2002, the president of Rydell & Associates authorized a feasibility study on improving the company's printing capability by replacing or augmenting current printing equipment. The president authorized a $5,000 budget for capital expenditures. The firm's three networked printers have not been able to meet the increased demands of the recently expanded staff and workload. As a result, the firm is losing valuable employee time (28 hours per month) as employees wait for the two reliable printers to complete 95 percent of the print jobs. We evaluated the cost of lost productivity as employees wait for print jobs, established essential printer-selection criteria, and evaluated available laser printers according to the criteria. Based on the information we gathered and reviewed, we recommend buying 10 HP LaserJet 1200se laser printers for our office printing needs. At a cost of $399 each, the 1200se prints at 1200×1200 dpi, comes with a standard 8 MB RAM (expandable), and has a 90MHz processor. It prints at 11.5 pages per minute, at a cost of 2 cents per page. By increasing printing capacity, Rydell & Associates can maintain its reputation for efficiency and high-quality work.

Keywords: printing, laser printers, HP LaserJet 1200se

The abstract briefly summarizes the purpose of the study and its methods, then focuses on the technical aspects of the subject: the specifications of the recommended printer.

A keywords list ensures that if the report is searched electronically, it will register "hits" for each of the terms listed.

ii

Contents

Note that the typeface and design of the headings in the contents page match the typeface and design of the headings in the report itself.

In This Book

For more about using styles to create a table of contents automatically, see Ch. 3, p. 40.

Executive Summary

Because of the reputation that Rydell & Associates has earned for efficiency and high-quality service, business volume has increased dramatically in the last five years, resulting in the addition of four associate accountants in the past year alone. Our expanded staff and workload have increased demands beyond our current printing capacity, and we are losing valuable employee time due to print-job delays.

Our team interviewed the office manager, Bill Fredericks, who reported that we use 15,000 sheets of paper per month, approximately 95 percent (14,250 sheets) of which are printed on our two HP LaserJet printers. Employees usually avoid our third printer, a Canon Inkjet, because of its poor output quality.

The heavy use of our two popular printers has resulted in lost time as employees wait at the printers to retrieve and sort out their print jobs. We surveyed employees and calculated the cost of this lost productivity. Our 10 employees average over 6 minutes per day waiting for print jobs, which translates to 28 hours ($570) per month of wasted employee time.

We were given a $5,000 budget for capital expenditures. With the objective of reducing this loss of employee productivity, we researched options for improving our printing capabilities. We established printer-selection criteria, reviewed performance tests on laser printers, and narrowed the field to two highly suitable models: the HP LaserJet 1200se and the Samsung ML 1450.

Based on the information we gathered and analyzed, we concluded that a purchase of 10 small-business laser printers would cut printer wait times by an estimated two-thirds, resulting in a savings of approximately $380 per month. That savings would pay for all 10 printers in less than one year. The HP LaserJet 1200se earns excellent reliability ratings, and Hewlett Packard has an outstanding reputation for customer service. For these reasons, we recommend purchasing 10 HP LaserJet 1200se printers, for a total cost of $3,990.

The executive summary describes the project with a focus on the managerial aspects, particularly the recommendation. Note the writers' emphasis on the problem at Rydell and their use of dollar figures.

Managers want the bottom line: how much would it cost to implement your recommendation, and how long is the payback period?

1

Introduction

On April 22, 2002, we received approval for our proposal to research and evaluate options for improving the printing capability of Rydell & Associates accountancy firm. This proposal was based on growing concerns over the efficiency and productivity problems we have been experiencing with our current printers.

This report presents the findings of our study. We calculated the cost of lost productivity, evaluated various options for improving our printing capabilities, and established printer-selection criteria. We researched specifications and performance data for available laser printers.

Because of the firm's reputation for high-quality work, Rydell & Associates has recently experienced a growth in business volume, resulting in the addition of four new associates in the past year. The expanded staff and workload have increased demands on our current printing equipment: two HP LaserJet 1200s and one Canon BJC-85 Inkjet. Consequently, employees are losing valuable time due to print-job delays. Our team interviewed the office manager, Bill Fredericks, who reported that we use 15,000 sheets of paper per month, approximately 95 percent (14,250 sheets) of which are printed on our two HP LaserJet printers. Employees avoid using our third printer, an inkjet, because of its low-quality output.

The inability of our current printers to keep pace with increased printing demand adversely affects our productivity: our employees average over 6 minutes per day (28 hours per month) of lost work time waiting at the printers to retrieve their print jobs and sort out their documents from those of other associates. This lost time translates to a loss of $570 per month in employee productivity. Continued loss of employee productivity could hurt the reputation that Rydell & Associates has earned for efficiency and high-quality service.

In view of these concerns, we recommend buying 10 small-business laser printers, at a total cost of $3,990. This reconfiguration would cut printer wait times by an estimated two-thirds, a savings of approximately $380 per month, and would pay for the 10 printers in less than one year. Although the Samsung ML 1450 is an excellent printer, we recommend purchasing 10 HP LaserJet 1200se printers because of their reliability and the company's excellent customer-service reputation.

In some organizations, all first-level headings begin a new page.

The background and purpose of the report

An overview of the methods

A more detailed statement of the background and problem

An introduction can present the basic findings of a report.

2

The writers use the same task organization that they used in the proposal and in the progress report.

Note the cross-reference in point 1 to the appendix, complete with a page number.

Research Methods

We performed the following research to determine the best option for our printing needs:

1. To calculate the cost of the lost productivity incurred by using our current printers, we interviewed all 10 appropriate employees of the firm to find the average time per day spent waiting for print jobs (Appendix, page 10).

2. To establish printer-selection criteria, we started with the assumption that any solution we recommend will need to cost less than $5,000. We needed to determine whether our associates' needs would be best served by continuing our networked printing configuration, or whether we should move to a distributed configuration, in which each employee has his or her own printer. The question we needed to answer is whether we can purchase 10 printers that have the technical characteristics we need: speed, resolution, and expandability.

3. To narrow the selection of printers, we chose 14 laser printers from reviews and benchmark tests of small-office laser printers in *PC World* (Top ten, 2002), *ZDNET.com* (Most popular, 2002), and *CNET.com* (Top 5, 2002). We eliminated printers with a resolution less than 1200 $\times$ 1200 dots per inch (dpi), the current standard for small-office printers, because of our associates' need to print documents containing small type sizes. To derive our conclusions and recommendations, we analyzed the five remaining printers again according to features, performance, and our particular needs. We created a comparison chart, drew a conclusion, and formulated the recommendation presented in this report.

3

Results

In this section, we present the findings of our research. We cover the costs of the lost productivity, the printer-selection criteria, and the technical comparisons of the printers.

An advance organizer for the results section

1. Costs of Lost Productivity

Currently, our three printers are networked. According to Bill Fredericks, our office manager, we use 15,000 sheets of paper per month. He estimated that approximately 95 percent of our printing (14,250 pages) is done on the two HP LaserJet printers and only 5 percent (750 pages) on the Canon Inkjet, because employees are dissatisfied with its print quality. This means that our employees often need to wait as their print jobs are queued on the two HP LaserJet printers.

(There is an additional problem with the networked-printing configuration. Experts recommend that a printer be used to print no more than one-quarter the number of pages listed in its duty cycle [Ozer, 2002]. This means that each LaserJet, with a duty cycle of 3,500, should be printing no more than 875 pages per month for optimum equipment wear. In fact, each LaserJet is printing approximately 7,000 pages per month, eight times the Ozer recommendation. We are not using our printers efficiently; in fact, we are in danger of significantly reducing their effective useful lifetimes through overuse.)

For the week of April 15, we asked all 10 appropriate employees to estimate the amount of time they spent waiting for print jobs. The average wait per day was over 6 minutes, which we converted to hours per month. The total wait time for 10 employees was 28 hours, which translates to approximately $570 per month (Appendix, page 10).

2. Printer-Selection Criteria

The results of our quantitative analysis of current costs suggest that the main weakness of our current networked printing configuration is that employees have to leave their desks, wait for print jobs, and sort out their documents from the others at the printer. Based on this information, we decided that rather than having centralized, networked large-business laser printers, it would be more efficient for each employee to have his or her own small-office laser printer. Therefore, we eliminated large-business printers from our study.

Following were the five main criteria we considered during our research:

Initial purchase price
Our main goal was to find the most cost-effective approach to increasing our printing capacity and efficiency. Therefore, purchase cost was the initial criterion for evaluating laser printers; because we were working with an equipment budget of $5,000, and we knew we wanted to buy 10 printers, we narrowed the field by evaluating only printers under $500.

Print resolution
Because our documents often have fine, small print, and require clear, crisp text, we selected high resolution (1200 $\times$ 1200 dpi) as an essential criterion.

4

RAM-expandability

Accounting documents can be very complex, often including data from Microsoft® Excel and Access. Available RAM affects a printer's efficiency and resolution, and the ability to expand and upgrade the printer makes it more adaptable to future printing demands.

Cost per page

Cost per page is based on the average number of pages that can be printed from one toner cartridge.

Printing speed

Printing speed is another factor that contributes to efficient printing capabilities. We evaluated the laser printers by the pages per minute (ppm) they can produce.

3. Evaluation of Qualified Printers

The reviews and benchmark tests we studied provided a set of 14 printers from which to choose:

Brother HL 1270N	Lexmark E320
Brother HL 1440	Lexmark Optra M412n
Brother HL 1650	Samsung ML 1210
Brother HL 1670N	Samsung ML 1250
HP LaserJet 1000	Samsung ML 1651N
HP LaserJet 1200se	Samsung ML 6060
Lexmark E 210	Samsung ML 1450

After eliminating printers with resolutions less than 1200×1200 dpi, we narrowed the scope of our research to the following five printers, listed here from least expensive to most expensive:

Printer	Price
Samsung ML 1450	$299.99
HP LaserJet 1200se	$399.00
Brother HL 1650	$600.00
Samsung ML 1651N	$650.00
Brother HL 1670N	$750.00

5

A strength of this report is that the writers explain their thinking clearly throughout.

Only the first two on this list meet our purchase-price criterion. To be sure that we were not eliminating appropriate printers on the basis of price alone, however, we studied the other three as well. The Brother HL 1670N and the Samsung ML1651N are high priced because they are designed to be network printers. The Brother HL 1650 is expensive because it offers a duplexer feature. Because neither networking nor duplexing is a feature that our office requires, we eliminated these printers from consideration.

Table 1 presents the technical comparison of the two printers that best met our needs.

Table 1. Final Feature Comparison of Two Selected Printers*

Criterion	HP LaserJet 1200se	Samsung ML 1450
Cost	$399	$299
Resolution	1200 × 1200 dpi	1200 × 1200 dpi
RAM/Processor	8MB 90MHz	4MB 66 MHz
ppm	11.5	10.3
Cost per page	2 cents	1.7 cents
Support	1-year warranty extended phone support	1-year warranty extended phone support
Expert overall ranking of top five	*PCWorld.com* and *CNET.com*: 3rd of 5	*CNET.com:* 5th of 5
Reviews and user comments	• holds 250 sheets • no on-off switch • some problems with paper curl • can buy copier/scanner attachment for $149	• holds 550 sheets • needs more memory to print at 1200 dpi
Price of additional memory	32MB: $29	8MB: $21 16MB: $29 32MB: $59
Size (inches)	approx. 16 × 19 × 10	approx. 16 × 14 × 12

*Sources: <http://www.satech.com/printermemory1.html> (memory prices)
     <http://CNET.com/hardware/0-1063.html?>
     <http://www.pcworld.com/reviews/article/0,aid,73855,pg,2,00.asp>
     <http://www.zdnet.com/products/filter/guide/0,7267,1500123,00.html>

6

The writers explain their conclusions carefully.

Conclusions

The HP LaserJet 1200se and the Samsung ML1450 both meet our needs. They produce excellent text quality at an average speed and received mostly good reviews by experts and users. The Samsung, a new model, is less expensive to purchase (even with a memory upgrade), the cost per page is very reasonable, and it holds an entire ream of paper. The HP LaserJet costs slightly more to purchase, the cost per page is a little higher, and it holds only 250 sheets of paper. However, the HP LaserJet comes with more RAM, and RAM upgrades are cheaper than for the Samsung. In addition, the HP LaserJet is slightly faster than the Samsung. Our existing HP LaserJet 1200s have proven to be very reliable performers in our office, even under very hard use, and the manufacturer's reputation for customer service is excellent.

7

Recommendation

We recommend buying 10 small-business laser printers for our office printing needs. We estimate that this reconfiguration of our workplace would cut printer wait times by an estimated two-thirds, a savings of approximately $380 per month. That savings of employee time would pay for the 10 printers in one year or less. Although the Samsung ML 1450 would be slightly cheaper, the technical merits of the HP LaserJet 1200se and HP's customer-service reputation make it an excellent choice. We recommend purchasing 10 HP LaserJet 1200se printers, for a total cost of $3,990.

This recommendation largely repeats the last paragraph in the introduction to the report. In technical communication, repetition can reinforce important information and increase your chances of reaching readers who read only selected portions of long documents.

References

CNET editors' top 5 personal laser printers. (2002, March). Retrieved April 10, 2002, from the CNET Web site: http://computers.cnet.com/hardware/0-2645882-8-5700867-1.html

Most popular printers. (2002, March). Retrieved April 10, 2002, from the ZDNet Web site: http://zdnetshopper.cnet.com/shopping/0-8399-1410-0-0.html?tag=pop&cobrand=29

Ozer, J. (2002, January). Print more for less. *Computer Shopper, 22,* 126–130.

Top ten monochrome laser printers. (2002, March). Retrieved April 10, 2002, from the PC World Web site: www.pcworld.com/reviews/article/0,aid,92901,00.asp

9

Appendix: Lost Productivity as Employees Wait for Print Jobs

For the week of April 15, we asked employees to estimate the amount of time they spent
waiting for print jobs. The average wait per day was over 6 minutes, which we converted to
hours per month.

Employee Name	Title	Hourly Salary	Hours per Month Waiting for Printer	Cost to Firm
Drew Collins	CPA	28	1.50	42.00
Roland Green	CPA	23	1.85	42.55
Penny Parkyn	CPA	23	2.30	52.90
Rajiv Gupta	Associate	22	2.60	57.20
Barry Gathers	Associate	22	3.25	71.50
Kay Merrill	Associate	21	3.25	68.25
Brian Woolley	Associate	21	2.75	57.75
Bill Menendez	Associate	19	3.00	57.00
Carly Matthews	Associate	18	3.75	67.50
Bill Fredericks	Manager	15	3.60	54.00
Monthly Total			27.85	$570.65

The writers present their primary-research results because they are critically important to the argument made in the report.

Reviewing the Process

Analyze your audience.

If the formal report is a follow-up to a previous proposal or report, determine whether the readers' responses to the previous document tells you anything new about your audience. Consider the five audience-related questions on pages 486–487.

Analyze your purpose.

Determine whether your readers are expecting an informational report, an analytical report, or a recommendation report.

Formulate questions you want to answer in your report.

If you have not already done this in a proposal, determine the questions that your readers want to see answered in the report.

Gather information about your subject.

Assemble any previous documents you have written, such as a proposal or progress reports. Also, carry out appropriate secondary and primary research. See Chapter 7.

Draft the report.

Draft the introduction, which describes the subject, purpose, and organization of the report; the methods section, which describes the research techniques—secondary and primary—that you used; the results, which present the data you created or found; the conclusions, which explain the meaning of the results; and the recommendations, which present your suggestions about what the organization ought to do next.

Format the report.

This is a good opportunity to make final decisions about what goes in the body (the most important information) and what goes in appendices (less important, supporting material). Also, make sure you have used styles correctly so that you can make a table of contents automatically. See Chapter 12 on front and back matter.

Revise the report.

For a document this big and this important, let it sit overnight before you revise, and try to get others to help you identify aspects that need more work. See the Revision Checklist on page 519.

Revision Checklist

In planning your informational, analytical, or recommendation report, did you
- ❏ analyze your audience? (p. 486)
- ❏ analyze your purpose? (p. 488)
- ❏ identify the questions that need to be answered? (p. 488)
- ❏ carry out appropriate research? (p. 489)
- ❏ draw valid conclusions about the results (if appropriate)? (p. 489)
- ❏ formulate recommendations based on the conclusions (if appropriate)? (p. 490)

Does the introduction
- ❏ explain the subject of the report? (p. 495)
- ❏ explain the purpose of the report? (p. 495)
- ❏ explain the background of the report? (p. 495)
- ❏ describe your sources of information? (p. 495)
- ❏ indicate the scope of the report? (p. 495)
- ❏ briefly summarize the most significant findings of the project? (p. 495)
- ❏ briefly summarize your recommendations? (p. 495)
- ❏ explain the organization of the report? (p. 496)
- ❏ define key terms used in the report? (p. 496)

- ❏ Does the methods section describe your methods in sufficient detail? (p. 496)

- ❏ Have you justified your methods where necessary, explaining, for instance, why you chose one method over another? (p. 496)

Are the results presented
- ❏ clearly? (p. 496)
- ❏ objectively? (p. 496)
- ❏ without interpretation? (p. 496)

Are the conclusions
- ❏ presented clearly? (p. 498)
- ❏ drawn logically from the results? (p. 498)

Are the recommendations
- ❏ clear? (p. 502)
- ❏ objective? (p. 502)
- ❏ polite? (p. 502)
- ❏ in an appropriate form (list or paragraph)? (p. 502)
- ❏ in an appropriate location? (p. 502)

Exercises

On TechComm Web

For more exercises, click on Additional Exercises, Projects, and Cases for Ch. 19 on <bedfordstmartins.com/techcomm>.

1. An important element in carrying out a feasibility study is determining the criteria by which to judge each option. For each of the following topics, list five minimum specifications and five evaluative criteria you might apply in assessing the options.

   a. buying a computer printer

   b. selecting a major

   c. choosing a company to work for

   d. buying a car

   e. choosing a place to live while you attend college

2. **Internet Activity** In Links Library for Chapter 7 on TechComm Web <bedfordstmartins.com/techcomm>, find a site that links to government agencies and departments. Find a government report on a subject that interests you. Determine whether it is an informative, an analytical, or a recommendation report. In what ways does the structure of the report differ from the structure described in this chapter? In other words, does it lack some of the elements described in this chapter, or does it have additional elements? Are the elements arranged in the same order in which they are described in this chapter? In what ways do the differences reflect the audience, purpose, and subject of the report?

Projects

On TechComm Web

For more projects, click on Additional Exercises, Projects, and Cases for Ch. 19 on <bedfordstmartins.com/techcomm>.

3. **Group Activity** Write the completion report for the research project you proposed in response to Project 3 on page 460 in Chapter 17. Your instructor will tell you whether the report is to be written individually or collaboratively, but work with a partner in reviewing and revising your report. You and your partner will work together closely at the end of the project as you revise your reports, but keep in mind that a partner can be very helpful during the planning phase, too, as you choose a topic, refine it, and plan your research.

4. **Internet Activity** Secure a completion report for a project subsidized by a city or federal agency, a private organization, or a university committee or task force. (Be sure to check your university's Web site; universities routinely publish strategic planning documents and other sorts of self-study reports. Also check <www.nas.edu>, which is the site for the National Academy of Sciences, the National Academy of Engineering, the Institute of Medicine, and the National Research Council, all of which publish reports on the Web.) In a memo to your instructor, analyze the report. Overall, how effective is the report? How could the writers have improved the report? If possible, submit a copy of the report along with your memo. (For more on memos, see Chapter 15, page 378.)

On TechComm Web

For more cases, click on Additional Exercises, Projects, and Cases for Ch. 19 on <bedfordstmartins.com /techcomm>.

CASE
Turning a Letter into a Report

Form small groups for this project. You and the members of your group are interns working for the Energy Information Administration, a branch of the Department of Energy. Your supervisor, Jill Schroeder, has asked you to help her with a project. Your department recently sent to the President a letter outlining the Department of Energy's recommendations on ways to improve and expand a voluntary reporting system that encourages companies to reduce greenhouse gas emission and to create a new, transferable credit system for those reductions (Abraham, Evans, Veneman, & Whitman, 2002). "We've got a copy of the official letter up on the Web, but I'd like to put up a version that looks more like what it is: a report." She asks you to download the letter <www.energy.gov/HQPress/releases02/julpr /GreenhouseGasRegistryLetter.pdf> and revise it so that it displays the traditional organization of a report, including headings. Download the report by using the copy function in Adobe Acrobat, then add appropriate headings that make the information easier to read and understand as a report. Present the report to your supervisor as a word-processing file.

Writing Instructions and Manuals

20

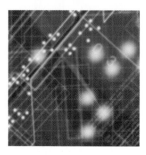

Elna Tynes, a technical communicator, on the role of instructions in selling the products they accompany:

When companies make products and sell them, they generally think that the product is what they're selling. Nope. The product is a symbol for all or part of the solution to their problem, and the information associated with the product is what actually sells the product and tells the user how to solve the problem. (qtd. in Mead, 1998, p. 375)

On TechComm Web

For additional samples, activities, and links related to this chapter, see <bedfordstmartins.com/techcomm>.

On TechComm Web

For examples of instructions, see Writing Guidelines for Engineering and Science Students. Click on Links Library for Ch. 20 on <bedfordstmartins.com/techcomm>.

In This Book

For more about ethical and legal considerations, see Ch. 2.

The customer-support staff at Dell Computer can tell you that no matter how hard their technical communicators try, their manuals never please everyone. A customer once called asking how to install batteries in her new laptop. When told that the instructions were on page 1 of the manual, she replied, "I just paid $2,000 for this [deleted] thing, and I'm not going to read a book" ("Befuddled," 1994). Because instructions and manuals have acquired a bad reputation over the years, many people don't even bother trying to read them. This situation is regrettable, because instructions and manuals are fundamentally important in carrying out procedures and using products safely and effectively.

Chapter 9 discussed process descriptions, which explain how a process occurs—for example, how a water heater burns natural gas to heat the water inside. This chapter discusses instructions, which are process descriptions written to help the reader perform a specific task—for instance, how to install a water heater in a house. This chapter also discusses manuals, which are larger documents consisting primarily of instructions.

UNDERSTANDING THE ROLE OF INSTRUCTIONS AND MANUALS

Instructions and manuals are central to technical communication. If you are a technical professional, such as an engineer, you will probably be asked to write or contribute to instructions and manuals often. If you are a technical communicator, you will write them more often than any other kind of major technical document. Organizations today see their instructions and manuals as critical in achieving the goal of making their products, procedures, and systems safe and "user-friendly."

ANALYZING YOUR AUDIENCE

When instructions and manuals are ineffective, chances are that the writer has inaccurately assessed the audience. Someone who doesn't know what a self-locking washer is might not be able to complete a process if it isn't explained.

Before you start to write a set of instructions or a manual, think carefully about the background and skill level of your audience. If you are writing to people who are experienced in the field, use technical vocabulary and concepts. But if you are addressing general readers, define technical terms and provide detailed directions. Don't be content to write "Make sure the tires are rotated properly." Instead, define proper rotation and explain how to achieve it. Consider, too, the language skills of your readers. If you are addressing multicultural readers, include instructions in their native languages or take other measures described later in this chapter.

The best way to make sure you have assessed your audience effectively is to find people whose backgrounds resemble those of your intended readers and test the effectiveness of the documentation. This process is called *usability testing*.

In This Book

For more about analyzing your audience, see Ch. 5, p. 74.

In This Book

For more about defining terms, see Ch. 9, p. 194.

In This Book

For more about usability testing, see Ch. 3, p. 46.

PLANNING FOR SAFETY

Your most important responsibility in writing documentation is to make sure you do everything you can to ensure the safety of your readers. Even though some kinds of tasks do not involve safety risks, many do.

Plan for safety by:

Writing clear safety information

Designing safety information

Placing safety information in the appropriate location

Writing Clear Safety Information

Be clear and concise. Avoid complicated sentences.

COMPLICATED	It is required that safety glasses be worn when inside this laboratory.
SIMPLE	You must wear safety glasses in this laboratory.
SIMPLE	Wear safety glasses in this laboratory.

Sometimes a phrase works better than a sentence: "Safety Glasses Required."

Because a typical set of instructions or manual can contain dozens of comments — both safety and nonsafety — experts have devised terms to indicate the seriousness of the advice. Unfortunately, the use of this terminology is not consistent.

For instance, the American National Standards Institute (ANSI) and the U.S. military's MILSPEC publish definitions that differ significantly, and many private companies have their own definitions. The following explanation of four common terms, presented here from most to least serious, points out the significant differences between ANSI and MILSPEC.

On TechComm Web

For advice on communicating safety information on Web pages, see Lisa A. Tallman's "Designing for the Web: Special Considerations for Safety Information." Click on Links Library for Ch. 20 on <bedfordstmartins.com/techcomm>.

- *Danger.* MILSPEC does not use this term, but for ANSI and many companies, *danger* alerts the reader to an immediate and serious hazard that will likely be fatal.

  DANGER. EXTREMELY HIGH VOLTAGE. STAND BACK.

- *Warning.* For MILSPEC, *warning* is the most serious level, indicating a risk of serious injury or death. For ANSI, it also suggests the potential for serious injury or death. Among different companies, however, the meaning of *warning* ranges from serious injury or death to serious damage to equipment.

  WARNING: TO PREVENT SERIOUS INJURY TO YOUR ARMS AND HANDS, MAKE SURE THE ARM RESTRAINTS ARE IN PLACE BEFORE YOU OPERATE THIS MACHINE.

- *Caution.* For MILSPEC, *caution* warns of the potential for both equipment damage and long-term health hazards. For ANSI, it indicates the risk of minor or moderate injury. Among companies, *caution* signals the potential for anything from moderate injury to serious equipment damage or destruction.

  Caution: Do not use nonrechargeable batteries in this charging unit; they could damage the charging unit.

- *Note.* A *note* is a tip or suggestion to help the readers carry out the procedure successfully.

  Note: Two kinds of washers are provided: regular washers and locking washers. Be sure to use the locking washers here.

If your organization does not already have guidelines for safety labeling, you might consider using the following definitions:

- *Danger.* Likelihood of serious injury, including death.
- *Warning.* Potential for minor, moderate, or serious injury.
- *Caution.* Potential for damage to equipment.
- *Note.* A suggestion on how to carry out a task.

Designing Safety Information

On TechComm Web

For information on designing safety labels, see MaverickLabel.com. Click on Links Library for Ch. 20 on <bedfordstmartins.com/techcomm>.

In This Book

For more about color, see Ch. 14, p. 327.

Whether printed in a document or on machinery or equipment, safety information should be prominent and easy to read. Many organizations use visual symbols to represent levels of danger, but these symbols are not standardized. If your organization doesn't have a set of symbols that you can use in your document, create a different design for each kind of comment.

Often, brief safety warnings are written in all-uppercase letters. The more critical the safety comment, the larger and more emphatic it should be. Safety information is often printed in color: text, for example, against a yellow, orange, or red background. Symbols are printed in color, too: flames, for example, in red.

Figure 20.1 shows common symbols for safety information. Figure 20.2 shows a safety label that would be affixed to a container used for a dangerous chemical.

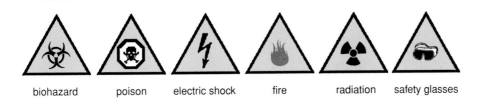

biohazard   poison   electric shock   fire   radiation   safety glasses

■ **Figure 20.1**
Common Symbols in
Safety Information

ACETONE
(CAS 67-64-1)

DANGER!   **FLAMMABLE**

Acute: **MAY CAUSE IRRITATION TO EYES, SKIN, NOSE, THROAT.**
EXPOSURE TO HIGH CONCENTRATIONS MAY CAUSE DIZZINESS,
UNCONSCIOUSNESS.
Chronic: **REPEATED OR PROLONGED EXPOSURE MAY CAUSE SKIN**
DRYING AND CRACKING. MAY CAUSE BRAIN OR NERVE DAMAGE.

Do not breathe mist or vapor.   Do not get in eyes, on skin, on clothing. Keep container tightly closed and away from heat, sparks, flames. Use only with adequate ventilation. Wash thoroughly after handling.   **FIRST AID:**

IF CONTACTED: Immediately flush eyes with plenty of water for at least 15 minutes while holding eyelids open. Wash skin with soap and water.   GET MEDICAL ATTENTION for eyes.   Remove contaminated clothing and wash before reuse.
IF INHALED: Remove to fresh air. If not breathing, give artificial respiration. If cough or difficulty in breathing develops GET MEDICAL ATTENTION.
IF SWALLOWED: Give water to dilute. DO NOT INDUCE VOMITING. CONTACT POISON CONTROL HOTLINE AT 1-800-222-1222. Never give anything by mouth to an unconscious or convulsive person.
HCL® 800/421-6710   WWW.HCLCO.COM   530-001-0203

On TechComm Web

To view Fig. 20.2 in context on the Web, click on Links Library for Ch. 20 on <bedfordstmartins.com /techcomm>.

■ **Figure 20.2**
Safety Label

Source: HCL, 2001 <www.hclco .com/labels/hazard/hazard/.htm>.

Placing Safety Information in the Appropriate Location

What is an appropriate location for safety information? This question has no easy answer because you cannot control how your audience reads your document. Be conservative: put safety information wherever you think the reader is likely to see it, and don't be afraid to repeat yourself. But don't repeat the same piece of advice in each of 20 steps, because readers will stop paying attention to it. But a reasonable amount of repetition — such as including the same safety comment at the top of each page — would be effective. If your

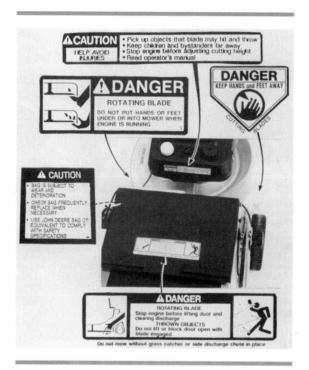

■ **Figure 20.3**
Safety Information on Machinery

Notice that the safety warnings are placed in locations where users will see them when performing certain tasks.
Source: Deere & Co., 1989.

company's procedure format calls for a safety section near the beginning of the document, place the information there and repeat it just before the appropriate step in the step-by-step section.

The Occupational Safety and Health Administration Guidelines (U.S. Department of Labor, 2000) describe proper standards for placing safety messages on products and manuals. These standards address the following questions:

- Is the message prominently displayed so that users see it?
- Is the message large enough and clearly legible under operating conditions?
- Are the graphics and the words of the message clear and informative?

Figure 20.3, from an operator's manual for a John Deere lawnmower, shows one company's approach to placing safety warnings on machinery.

DRAFTING EFFECTIVE INSTRUCTIONS

Instructions can be brief — a small sheet of paper — or extensive, up to 20 pages or more. Brief instructions might be produced by a writer, a graphic artist, and a subject-matter expert. Longer instructions might also call for other people, such as marketing and legal personnel.

Regardless of the size of the project, most instructions are organized like process descriptions. The main difference is that the conclusion of a set of instructions is not a summary but an explanation of how to make sure the reader has followed the instructions correctly. Most sets of instructions contain three elements.

Drafting General Introductions

The general introduction provides the preliminary information that readers will need to follow the instructions safely and easily.

In This Book

For more about process descriptions, see Ch. 9, p. 204.

Elements of a set of instructions:

General introduction

Step-by-step instructions

Conclusion

GUIDELINES

Drafting Introductions for Instructions

A general introduction answers these five questions:

▶ *Who should carry out the task?* Sometimes you need to describe or identify the person or persons who are to carry out a task. Some kinds of aircraft maintenance, for example, may be performed only by those certified to do it.

▶ *Why should the reader carry out this task?* Sometimes the reason is obvious: you don't need to explain why a backyard barbecue grill should be assembled. At other times, however, you do need to explain, as in the case of preventive-maintenance chores such as changing radiator antifreeze every two years.

▶ *When should the reader carry out this task?* Some tasks, such as rotating tires or planting crops, need to be performed at particular times or at particular intervals.

▶ *What safety measures or other concerns should the reader understand?* In addition to the safety measures that apply to the whole task, mention any tips that will make the job easier:

> NOTE: For ease of assembly, leave all nuts loose. Give only 3 or 4 complete turns on bolt threads.

▶ *What items will the reader need?* List necessary tools, materials, and equipment in the introduction so that readers will not have to interrupt their work to hunt for something. If you think readers might not be able to identify these items easily, include drawings next to the names.

In This Book

For more about graphics, see Ch. 14.

Following is a list of tools and materials from a set of instructions on replacing broken window glass:

Tools		Materials	
glass cutter	electric soldering iron	putty	work gloves
putty knife	razor blade	glass of proper size	linseed oil
window scraper	pliers	paint	glazier's points
chisel	paintbrush	hand cleaner	

Drafting Step-by-Step Instructions

The heart of a set of instructions is the step-by-step information.

GUIDELINES

Drafting Steps in Instructions

▶ *Number the instructions.* For long, complex instructions, use two-level numbering, such as a decimal system.

    1
        1.1
        1.2
    2
        2.1
        2.2
    etc.

On TechComm Web

For examples of instructions, see Learn2.com and Knowledge Hound. Click on Links Library for Ch. 20 on <bedfordstmartins.com /techcomm>.

If you need to present, say, 50 steps, group them logically into five sets of 10 steps, and begin each set with a clear heading.

▶ *Present the right amount of information in each step.* Each step should define a single task the reader can carry out easily, without having to refer to the instructions.

TOO MUCH INFORMATION

  1. Mix one part of the cement with one part water, using the trowel. When the mixture is a thick consistency without any lumps bigger than a marble, place a strip of the mixture about 1" high and 1" wide along the face of the brick.

TOO LITTLE INFORMATION

  1. Pick up the trowel.

RIGHT AMOUNT OF INFORMATION

  1. Mix one part of the cement with one part water, using the trowel, until the mixture is a thick consistency without any lumps bigger than a marble.

  2. Place a strip of the mixture about 1" high and 1" wide along the face of the brick.

▶ *Use the imperative mood.* For example, "Attach the red wire. . . ." The imperative is more direct and economical than the indicative mood ("You should attach the red wire . . ." or "The operator should attach the red wire . . ."). Avoid the passive voice ("The red wire is attached . . ."), because it can be ambiguous: Is the red wire already attached?

▶ *Don't confuse steps and feedback statements.* A *step* is an action to be performed by the reader. A *feedback statement* describes an event that occurs in response to a step. For instance, a step might read "Insert the disk in the drive." That step's feedback statement might read "The system will now update your user information." Do not make a feedback statement a numbered step. Present it as part of the step that it refers to. Some writers give all feedback statements their own design.

▶ *Include graphics.* When appropriate, add a photograph or a drawing to show the reader what to do. Some activities—such as adding two drops of a reagent to a mixture—do not need an illustration, but they might be clarified by charts or tables. Figure 20.4 (page 530) shows the extent to which a set of instructions can integrate words and graphics.

▶ *Do not omit the articles* (a, an, the) *to save space.* Omitting the articles can make the instructions unclear and hard to read. In the sentence "Locate midpoint and draw line," for example, the reader cannot tell if "draw line" is a noun (as in "locate the draw line") or a verb and its object (as in "draw the line").

In This Book

For more on the passive voice, see Ch. 11, p. 250. For more on the imperative mood, see Ch. 11, p. 248.

In This Book

For more about graphics, see Ch. 14.

Drafting Conclusions

Instructions often conclude with *maintenance tips.* Another popular conclusion is a *troubleshooter's guide,* usually in the form of a table, which identifies common problems and explains how to solve them.

Here is a portion of the troubleshooter's guide in the operating instructions for a lawnmower.

Problem	Cause	Correction
The mower does not start.	1. The mower is out of gas.	1. Fill the gas tank.
	2. The gas is stale.	2. Drain the tank and refill it with fresh gas.
	3. The spark plug wire is disconnected from the spark plug.	3. Connect the wire to the plug.
The mower loses power.	1. The grass is too high.	1. Set the mower to a "higher cut" position. See page 10.
	2. The air cleaner is dirty.	2. Replace the air cleaner. See page 11.
	3. There is a buildup of grass, leaves, or trash in the underside of the mower housing.	3. Disconnect the spark plug wire, attach it to the retainer post, and clean the underside of the mower housing. See page 8.

A LOOK AT SAMPLE INSTRUCTIONS

Figure 20.4 is a portion of the first screen of a Web-based set of instructions on how to build a CD holder. Figure 20.5 on page 531 shows an excerpt from the step-by-step section of a set of instructions. Figure 20.6 on page 532 shows the conclusion for a set of instructions.

The introduction begins with a brief description and photograph of the piece.

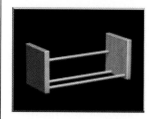

INTRODUCTION

The CD/videotape holder is a simple project. It is an attractive, adjustable stand that holds up to 23 compact discs or 10 videotapes. While making it, you'll practice how to square a board, machine parts, round an edge with a file, sand properly, and apply an oil stain.

The writers use a number of techniques to emphasize the safety information:

Important Safety Information

DANGER

HAZARDOUS CHEMICALS

- *color*

- *a warning label*

- *emphatic typography*

The stain used in this project is very dangerous:

- **THE STAIN IS HARMFUL OR FATAL IF SWALLOWED.**
- **THE STAIN IS A SKIN IRRITANT.**
- **THE STAIN IS COMBUSTIBLE.**
- **KEEP THE STAIN OUT OF REACH OF CHILDREN.**

- *mandatory language ("You must read . . .")*

You must read and follow these safety warnings:

DANGER: The stain contains mineral spirits. It is harmful or fatal if swallowed. Do not take it internally. It is a skin irritant. Avoid contact with skin and eyes. Wear rubber gloves and safety glasses when handling. It is combustible. Do not use or store it near heat, sparks, flame, or any other source of ignition. Close the container after each use. Avoid inhalation and use only with adequate ventilation. If using indoors, open all windows and doors to make sure there is fresh air movement. If you experience lightheadedness, dizziness, or headaches, increase fresh air movement or leave the area. Reports have associated repeated and prolonged occupational overexposure to solvents with permanent brain and nervous system damage. Intentional misuse by deliberately concentrating and inhaling the contents may be harmful or fatal.

FIRST AID: If swallowed, do not induce vomiting. Call a physician immediately.

FOR SKIN CONTACT: Wash the skin thoroughly with soap and water. If irritation persists, get medical attention.

FOR EYE CONTACT: IMMEDIATELY flush eyes thoroughly with water, then remove any contact lenses. Continue to flush eyes with water for at least 15 minutes. If irritation persists, get medical attention.

IF YOU ARE AFFECTED BY INHALATION: Immediately get into fresh air. If symptoms persist, call physician.

■ **Figure 20.4 Introduction to a Set of Instructions**

Source: Based on Minwax, 2002 <www.minwax.com /projects/cdhold/cdhold1.htm>.

Tools, Materials, and Finishes

Tools	Materials	Finishes
• Pencil • Tri square or combination square • Hand saw • $3/8$" forster bit, file • Clean cloths • High-quality brush • 120 and 150 grit sandpaper • Two-sided tape	• Two pieces of wood approximately $5/8$" × 6" × 6" each (oak, walnut, cherry or maple are preferred) • Three $11^3/4$" pieces of $3/8$" hardwood dowel rod (species should match the other pieces of wood) • Clean, lint-free rags • Paint thinner, if necessary • Tack cloths • Water-filled metal container with lid (if oil finishes used)	Choose one of the following: • Oil-based: Minwax® Wood Finish™ and Minwax® Fast-Drying Polyurethane • Water-based: Minwax Accents® and Minwax® Polycrylic® Protective Finish

The lists of tools and materials

■ **Figure 20.4**
(Continued)

---

3 Switch to the *Burst Usage* tab.

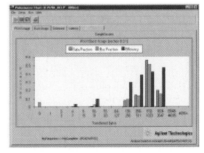

A screen shot helps readers visualize what they will see on their own screens.

This tab displays detailed information on the distribution of the data phases and the overhead over the different burst lengths in the traffic.

4 Switch through the different tabs to get an overview of the provided information.

Loading the Example Test Results   For convenience, the results of the example test also are included in the software package. To view these results, do the following steps:

1 In the Performance Charts window, select *Load* from the *File* menu.

A message box appears, informing you that the selected action might take a few minutes to complete.

2 Click the *Continue* button to open the file dialog box.

3 In the file dialog box, select the file *SampleSession.wfm* in the path *samples/demo/* and click the *Load* button.

After the loaded data is analyzed, the results are displayed in the Performance Charts window and the other windows of the Performance Optimizer.

NOTE   This example waveform file was produced on a 64-bit system using an Agilent E2929A/B_Deep PCI-X testcard. Thus, to successfully load it into the GUI, the bus width and the hardware need to be set up the same way.

If your software is set up differently, a message box informs you. Change the hardware settings and repeat the procedure above.

The steps are numbered and presented in the imperative mood. Notice that a feedback statement follows the step. The writer has presented the right amount of information in each step.

The note would be more effective if its typeface differed from that used in the steps.

■ **Figure 20.5**
Excerpt from Step-by-Step Instructions

Source: Agilent, 2001 <http://cp.literature.agilent.com /litweb/pdf/5988-4907EN.pdf>.

The instructions show the user how to download and install the program using three configurations: Minimum, Full, and Custom.

The conclusion explains that readers who downloaded the Minimum configuration should not worry if they later decide they want the Full configuration.

A final word:
Not to worry if you choose Minimum install and it later turns out that you need an additional software component; the installer downloads what's needed from the Apple QuickTime website—automatically, we might add—and even updates itself when new versions become available.

QuickTime's modular architecture is designed for efficiency; each QuickTime 4 component is loaded into memory only when it is needed. It's the kind of smart attribute that defines an industry standard (also known as the way things ought to be).

■ **Figure 20.6   Conclusion from a Set of Instructions**

This is the conclusion from the installation instructions for Apple QuickTime 4, a program that lets the user run videos and other kinds of files on an Apple computer.
Source: Apple Computer, Inc., 2002 <www.apple.com/quicktime/install/>.

In This Book

For more sources on manuals, see the Selected Bibliography, p. 676.

On TechComm Web

For ways of measuring the value of effective documentation, see Jay Mead's "Measuring the Value Added by Technical Documentation: A Review of Research and Practice." Click on Links Library for Ch. 20 on <bedfordstmartins .com/techcomm>.

DRAFTING EFFECTIVE MANUALS

A good manual reduces the possibility of injuries and liability, but it should also attract customers and reduce costs (because the organization needs fewer customer-support people). A poorly written manual is expensive to produce because it must be revised more often and because it alienates customers.

Most of the principles for effective instructions also apply to manuals. For example, when writing a manual, you have to analyze your audience, explain procedures clearly, and include graphics. However, manuals require more planning because a bigger investment is at stake.

Writing a manual is almost always a collaborative project. A full-size manual can require too many skills for one person to write: technical skills in the subject area, writing skills, graphics skills, production skills, even a knowledge of contracts and law to prevent lawsuits.

There are three stages to writing a manual.

- *Planning.* Start by analyzing your audience and purpose. The documentation for a sophisticated procedure or system usually addresses multiple audiences. You might decide to produce a set of manuals—one for the user, one for the manager, one for maintenance technicians, and so on. Or you might decide on a main manual combined with related documents, such as brochures, flyers, and workbooks.

    You also want to motivate your readers. You have to persuade people to read a manual. If your readers are uncomfortable with the product,

Interactive Sample Document:
Presenting Clear Instructions

The following page is from a set of instructions contained in a user manual. The questions in the margin ask you to think about the discussion of instructions (on pages 526–529). The answers to these questions are available on TechComm Web.

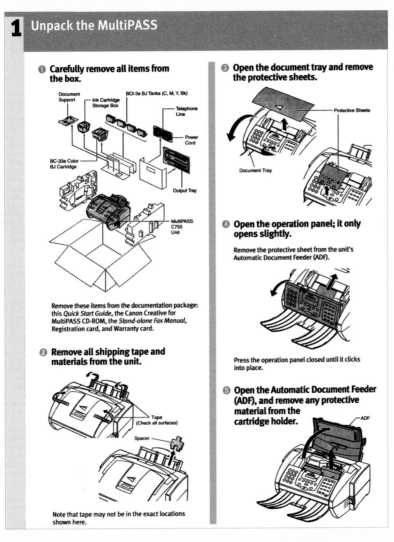

1. How has the designer tried to ensure that readers will follow the steps in the correct order?

2. Is the amount of information presented in each step appropriate?

3. What kind of information is presented in the imperative mood? What kind of information is not?

4. How effectively are graphics used to support the textual information on this page?

On TechComm Web

To find the answers to these questions, click on Interactive Sample Documents for Ch. 20 on <bedfordstmartins.com/techcomm>.

Source: Canon U.S.A, Inc., 2002 <www.usa.canon.com/cpr/pdf/Manuals/C755_Setup.pdf>.

procedure, or system, a well-designed manual, with plenty of white space and graphics, can help considerably.

- *Drafting.* Sometimes one person collects information from all the people on the documentation team and creates a draft based on that information. Sometimes various subject-matter experts write their own drafts, which a writer or a writing team then revises. In the drafting stage, you also need to create and integrate graphics and to design the whole manual as well as each page.

- *Revising.* Revision involves performing a series of checks on the accuracy of the technical information, structure, organization, emphasis, style, and correctness. Often, usability testing is performed at this stage.

Drafting Front Matter

In This Book

For more about revising, see Ch. 3, p. 42.

Front matter helps readers understand the content and the organization of the manual and the best ways to use it. Most manuals have a cover or title page, a table of contents, a preface, and a section about how to use the manual.

In This Book

For more about covers, see Ch. 12, p. 269.

To decide whether to use a cover or just a title page, consider the manual's size and intended use. Manuals that will receive some wear and tear, such as those used outside, need a hard cover, usually of a water-resistant material. Manuals used in an office usually don't need hard covers, unless they are large and require extra strength.

In This Book

For more about creating headings, see Ch. 10, p. 220, and Ch. 13, p. 309.

The title page contains the title of the manual, plus the company's name, address, and logo. An extensive table of contents is also important because people don't read a manual straight through but refer to it for specific information. To be effective, table of contents headings should focus on the tasks the readers want to accomplish.

Front matter might also include an "Introduction" or "Preface" or information presented in "about" phrases, as in "About Product X" or "About the Product X Documentation Set." This introductory information should answer five basic questions for your reader:

- Who should use this manual?
- What product, procedure, or system does the manual describe?
- What is the manual's purpose?
- What are the manual's major components?
- How should the manual be used?

Some manuals need to answer an additional question: what does the typography signify? If the typography signifies different kinds of information (10-point Courier typeface might represent the text the reader is supposed to type) and you want your readers to understand your conventions, define them in the front matter.

Figure 20.7 shows selected pages from the front matter of a manual. For more information on front matter, see Chapter 12, page 269.

Safety Instructions ◄────────────────

Dell Computer Corporation's manual for one of its products begins with safety information.

Use the following safety guidelines to help protect your computer system from potential damage and to ensure your own personal safety.

When Using Your Computer System

As you use your computer system, observe the following safety guidelines.

 CAUTION: Do not operate your computer system with any cover(s) (including computer covers, bezels, filler brackets, front-panel inserts, and so on) removed. ◄────────────────

Color is used to highlight cautions.

- To help avoid damaging your computer, be sure the voltage selection switch on the power supply is set to match the AC power available at your location.

  — 115 volts (V)/60 hertz (Hz) in most of North and South America and some Far Eastern countries such as South Korea and Taiwan

  — 100 V/50 Hz in eastern Japan and 100 V/60 Hz in western Japan

  — 230 V/50 Hz in most of Europe, the Middle East, and the Far East

  Also be sure your monitor and attached devices are electrically rated to operate with the AC power available in your location.

- Before working inside the computer, unplug the system to help prevent electric shock or system board damage. Certain system board components continue to receive power any time the computer is connected to AC power.

- To help avoid possible damage to the system board, wait 5 seconds after turning off the system before disconnecting a device from the computer.

- To help prevent electric shock, plug the computer and device power cables into properly grounded power sources. These cables are equipped with three-prong plugs to help ensure proper grounding. Do not use adapter plugs or remove the grounding prong from a cable. If you must use an extension cable, use a three-wire cable with properly grounded plugs.

- To help protect your computer system from sudden, transient increases and decreases in electrical power, use a surge suppressor, line conditioner, or uninterruptible power supply (UPS).

v

■ **Figure 20.7**
Pages from the Front Matter of a Manual

Source: Dell Computer Corporation, 2001, pp. v–vi, ix–xi.

Dell appropriately treats ergonomics as an aspect of safety. On this page and the two following pages (not shown here), the company discusses and shows the proper posture for using the computer. In addition, the front matter discusses how to remove the computer's cover and work on the machine safely.

- Be sure nothing rests on your computer system's cables and that the cables are not located where they can be stepped on or tripped over.
- Do not spill food or liquids on your computer. If the computer gets wet, refer to "If Your Computer Gets Wet" in Chapter 6.
- Do not push any objects into the openings of your computer. Doing so can cause fire or electric shock by shorting out interior components.
- Keep your computer away from radiators and heat sources. Also, do not block cooling vents. Avoid placing loose papers underneath your computer; do not place your computer in a closed-in wall unit or on a bed, sofa, or rug.

Ergonomic Computing Habits

CAUTION: Improper or prolonged keyboard use may result in injury.

CAUTION: Viewing the monitor screen for extended periods of time may result in eye strain.

For comfort and efficiency, observe the following ergonomic guidelines when setting up and using your computer system.

- Position your system so that the monitor and keyboard are directly in front of you as you work. Special shelves are available (from Dell and other sources) to help you correctly position your keyboard.
- Set the monitor at a comfortable viewing distance (usually 510 to 610 millimeters [20 to 24 inches] from your eyes).
- Make sure the monitor screen is at eye level or slightly lower when you are sitting in front of the monitor.
- Adjust the tilt of the monitor, its contrast and brightness settings, and the lighting around you (such as overhead lights, desk lamps, and the curtains or blinds on nearby windows) to minimize reflections and glare on the monitor screen.
- Use a chair that provides good lower back support.
- Keep your forearms horizontal with your wrists in a neutral, comfortable position while using the keyboard or mouse.
- Always leave space to rest your hands while using the keyboard or mouse.
- Let your upper arms hang naturally at your sides.
- Sit erect, with your feet resting on the floor and your thighs level.
- When sitting, make sure the weight of your legs is on your feet and not on the front of your chair seat. Adjust your chair's height or use a footrest, if necessary, to maintain proper posture.
- Vary your work activities. Try to organize your work so that you do not have to type for extended periods of time. When you stop typing, try to do things that use both hands.

vi

■ **Figure 20.7**
(Continued)

Preface

About This Guide

This guide is intended for anyone who uses a Dell Dimension L Series computer system. It can be used by both first-time and experienced computer users who want to learn about the features and operation of the systems or who want to upgrade their computers. The chapters and appendixes are summarized as follows:

- Chapter 1, "Introduction," provides an overview of the system features and information on preventitive maintenance to protect the computer.

- Chapter 2, "Installing Upgrades on the System Board," provides information on performing various upgrades, such as installing additional memory. The chapter includes a basic orientation to internal features of the computer.

- Chapter 3, "Installing Drives," provides instructions on how to install and remove drives.

- Chapter 4, "Basic Troubleshooting," contains checklists to use before calling Dell for technical assistance.

- Chapter 5, "Software Solutions," has information on using audio utilities and reinstalling software.

- Chapter 6, "Checking Inside Your Computer," presents troubleshooting procedures for system components such as expansion cards, memory, and drives.

- Chapter 7, "Getting Help," provides information on obtaining technical assistance. Users who have been unable to resolve problems using the troubleshooting information provided in this guide can refer to this chapter.

- Appendix A, "System Specifications," is supplemental reference material.

- Appendix B, "System Setup Program," describes the system setup program used for checking and changing system configuration data.

- Appendix C, "Diagnostic Codes, Beep Codes, and System Messages," documents status and error messages generated during system start-up. Included are possible causes and corrective actions.

- Appendix D, "Regulatory Notices," provides regulatory information on the system.

- Appendix E, "Limited Warranty and Return Policy," describes the warranty for your Dell system, the "Total Satisfaction" Return Policy.

ix

Front matter often provides an overview of the manual's contents.

This page begins with a statement of audience and purpose, followed by brief descriptions of the content of each chapter and appendix.

■ **Figure 20.7**
(Continued)

*Front matter often directs
readers to additional documents
and other resources.*

Warranty and Return Policy Information

Dell Computer Corporation ("Dell") manufactures its hardware products from parts and components that are new or equivalent to new in accordance with industry-standard practices. For information about the Dell warranty for your system, see Appendix E, "Warranty, Return Policy, and Year 2000 Statement of Compliance."

Other Documents You May Need

Besides this *Reference and Troubleshooting Guide,* the following documentation is included with your system:

* The *Getting Started* sheet provides step-by-step instructions for setting up your computer system.

* The *Dell Dimension Systems Setup Guide* describes how to properly set up your operating system and connect a printer.

* The *Dell Dimension L Series System Help* describes the features and operation of your computer. It includes tips on using your computer hardware and answers to commonly asked questions. To open the *Help,* click the **Start** button, point to **Programs –> User's Guides**, and then click **L Series System Help**.

* Online documentation is included for your computer devices (such as a video or modem card) and for any options you purchase separately from your system. To access this supplemental documentation, double-click the **Dell Documents** icon on the Windows desktop, click **System Information**, and then click **System Documentation**.

* Operating system documentation.

* Technical information files—sometimes called "readable" files—may be installed on your hard-disk drive to provide last-minute updates about technical changes to your system or reference material intended for experienced users.

*Here the writers explain their
use of three important terms:
notes, notices, and cautions.*

Notes, Notices, and Cautions

Throughout this guide, blocks of text may be accompanied by an icon and printed in bold type or in italic type. These blocks are notes, notices, and cautions, and they are used as follows:

NOTE: A NOTE indicates important information that helps you make better use of your computer system.

NOTICE: A NOTICE indicates either potential damage to hardware or loss of data and tells you how to avoid the problem.

CAUTION: A CAUTION indicates a potentially hazardous situation which, if not avoided, may result in minor or moderate injury.

x

■ **Figure 20.7**
(Continued)

Typographical Conventions

The following list defines (where appropriate) and illustrates typographical conventions used as visual cues for specific elements of text throughout this document:

*   *Interface components* are window titles, button and icon names, menu names and selections, and other options that appear on the monitor screen or display. They are presented in bold.

    Example: click **OK**.

*   *Keycaps* are labels that appear on the keys on a keyboard. They are enclosed in angle brackets.

    Example: <Enter>

*   *Key combinations* are series of keys to be pressed simultaneously (unless otherwise indicated) to perform a single function.

    Example: <Ctrl><Alt><Enter>

*   *Commands* presented in lowercase bold are for reference purposes only and are not intended to be typed when referenced.

    Example: "Use the **format** command to . . . . "

    In contrast, commands presented in the Courier New font are part of an instruction and intended to be typed.

    Example: "Type `format a:` to format the diskette in drive A."

*   *Filenames* and *directory* names are presented in lowercase bold.

    Examples: **autoexec.bat** and **c:\windows**

*   *Screen text* is a message or text that you are instructed to type as part of a command (referred to as a *command line*). Screen text is presented in the Courier New font.

    Example: The following message appears on your screen:

    `No boot device available`

    Example: "Type `md c:\programs` and press <Enter>."

*   *Variables* are placeholders for which you substitute a value. They are presented in italics.

    Example: DIMM_*x* [where *x* represents the DIMM socket designation)

xi

A conventions section helps readers understand the typographic styles that will be used in the manual.

This page would be easier to understand if the examples were indented. Using flush left alignment for everything within the bullet list can be confusing.

■ **Figure 20.7**
(Continued)

Drafting the Body

The structure, style, and graphics of the body of a manual will depend on its purpose and audience. For instance, the body of a manual might include summaries and diagnostic tests to help readers determine whether they have understood the discussion. A long manual might have more than one "body"; that is, each chapter might be a self-contained unit with its own introduction, body, and conclusion.

GUIDELINES

Drafting the Body of a Manual

▶ *Structure the body according to how the reader will use it.* If the reader is supposed to carry out a process, organize it chronologically, beginning with the first step in the process. If the reader needs to understand a concept, use a more-important-to-less-important organization. Consider the patterns discussed in Chapter 8, but be ready to combine or alter them to meet the needs of your audience.

▶ *Write clearly.* Simple, short sentences work best. Use the imperative mood to give instructions.

▶ *Be informal, if appropriate.* For some kinds of manuals, especially those intended for readers unfamiliar with the subject, an informal style that uses contractions and everyday vocabulary is effective. One caution: safety warnings and information about serious subjects, such as disease, usually require a formal style.

▶ *Use graphics.* Graphics break up the text and help readers understand the information. Whenever readers are to perform an action with their hands, include a drawing or photograph showing the action. Where appropriate, use tables and figures.

In This Book

For more on graphics, see Ch. 14.

Figure 20.8 shows a page from the body of a user manual for a data-projection unit. The task described here is adjusting the sound.

Drafting Back Matter

In This Book

For more about glossaries, see Ch. 12, p. 279.

Three items typically appear in the back matter: a glossary, an index, and appendices. A *glossary* is an alphabetized list of definitions of important terms in the document. An *index* is common for most manuals of 20 to 30 pages or more.

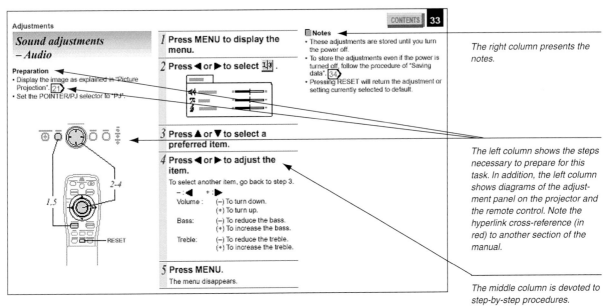

Figure 20.8   A Page from the Body of a Manual

*Note the generous use of white space and the use of colors to signal types of information:
green for the task being explained, red for hyperlinks, and blue for step-by-step instructions.*
Source: Toshiba, 2001 <www.mmgtechsupport.com/PDF/manual6.PDF>.

The word *appendices* refers to a range of elements. Appendices in procedures manuals often have flowcharts or other graphics that illustrate the processes described in the body. Appendices in user's guides often have diagnostic tests and reference materials, such as explanations of error messages or
troubleshooting guides.

Drafting Revisions of Manuals

In high-tech industries, a new generation of a product might come along as
often as every 18 months. As products evolve, technical communicators need
to revise the manuals that go with them. When a new version of the product
is released, you can take one of two approaches to revising.

- *Publish a "new" manual.* Although a new manual will most likely contain
  elements from the old manual, it might never mention the old manual.
  Although a new manual can reflect the look of the new product, people
  who are switching from the old product to the new one might have to
  spend time finding the information that applies specifically to the new
  product.

- *Publish a "revised" manual.* Revised manuals contain a lot of information from the old version, but the new information is flagged so that users can find it easily. The new information is usually marked with an icon in the margin or with a change bar: a vertical rule in the margin. Sometimes a section in the front matter describes the changes to this version of the product. Although a revised manual is easier for previous users to use, it can look like a patch job.

STRATEGIES FOR INTERCULTURAL COMMUNICATION

Writing Instructions and Manuals for Multicultural Audiences

Organizations work hard to ensure that their instructions and manuals are appropriate for their multicultural readers. Because important instructions and manuals can be addressed to readers representing several or even dozens of cultures, you need to answer three important questions as you plan the documents:

In This Book

For more about Simplified English, see Ch. 11, p. 259.

- *In what language should the information be written?* You can either translate the document into the reader's native language or try to make the English easy to understand. Although translation is sometimes the best or only alternative, companies often use Simplified English or some other form of English with a limited vocabulary and sentence structure and short sentences.

On TechComm Web

Read Michelle Delio's article about cultural factors and manuals in *Wired News.* Click on Links Library for Ch. 20 on <bedfordstmartins .com/techcomm>.

- *Do the text or graphics need to be modified?* As discussed in Chapter 5, communicators need to be aware of cultural differences. For example, a printer manual translated for an Italian audience presented nude models with strategically placed rectangles showing the various colors the machine could reproduce. But the manual carefully avoided explicit advice about how to use the printer, because Italian readers prefer suggestions (Delio, 2002).

- *What is your readers' technological infrastructure?* If your readers don't have Internet access, there is no point in making a Web version of the information. If your readers pay by the minute for Internet access, you want to create Web-based information that downloads quickly.

Reviewing the Process

Analyze your audience.

Determine the background and skill level of your readers. Also, determine their language skills in general and their knowledge of English.

Plan for safety.

Write clear safety information, design it appropriately, and plan where you will put it in the document and, if appropriate, on the equipment.

Draft the instructions or the manual.

For instructions, draft the introduction, the step-by-step instructions, and the conclusion. For manuals, draft the body, then draft the appropriate front matter and back matter.

Revise the instructions or manual.

Use subject-matter experts to review the instructions or manual. If possible, carry out usability testing. See the Revision Checklist that follows.

Deliver the instructions or manual.

If you discover important safety information that was omitted, get it to users as quickly as possible. Collect information to use in the next version of the document.

Revision Checklist

Instructions

Does the introduction to the set of instructions
- ❏ state the purpose of the task? (p. 527)
- ❏ describe safety measures or other concerns that readers should understand? (p. 527)
- ❏ list necessary tools and materials? (p. 527)

Are the step-by-step instructions
- ❏ numbered? (p. 528)
- ❏ expressed in the imperative mood? (p. 529)
- ❏ simple and direct? (p. 529)

- ❏ Are appropriate graphics included? (p. 529)

Does the conclusion
- ❏ include any necessary follow-up advice? (p. 529)
- ❏ include, if appropriate, a troubleshooter's guide? (p. 529)

Manuals

- ❏ Does the manual include, if appropriate, a cover? (p. 534)

- ❏ Does the title page provide all the necessary information to help readers determine whether they are reading the appropriate manual? (p. 534)
- ❏ Is the table of contents clear and explicit? (p. 534) Are the items phrased clearly to indicate the task readers are to carry out? (p. 534)

Does the other front matter clearly indicate
- ❏ the product, procedure, or system the manual describes? (p. 534)
- ❏ the purpose of the manual? (p. 534)
- ❏ the major components of the manual? (p. 534)
- ❏ the best way to use the manual? (p. 534)

- ❏ Is the body of the manual organized clearly? (p. 540)
- ❏ Are appropriate graphics included? (p. 540)
- ❏ Is a glossary included, if appropriate? (p. 540)
- ❏ Is an index included, if appropriate? (p. 540)
- ❏ Is the writing style clear and simple throughout? (p. 540)
- ❏ Are all other appropriate appendix items included? (p. 541)

Exercises

On TechComm Web

For more exercises, click on Additional Exercises, Projects, and Cases for Ch. 20 on <bedfordstmartins.com/techcomm>.

1. **Internet Activity** Study a set of instructions from Learn2.com <www.learn2.com> or Knowledge Hound <www.knowledgehound.com>. Write a memo to your instructor evaluating the quality of the instructions. Attach a print-out of representative pages from the instructions. (For more on memos, see Chapter 15, page 378.)

2. You work in the customer-relations department of a company that makes plumbing supplies. The head of product development has just handed you this draft of installation instructions for a sliding tub door. She has asked you to comment on their effectiveness. Write a memo to her, evaluating the instructions and suggesting improvements. (For more on memos, see Chapter 15, page 378.)

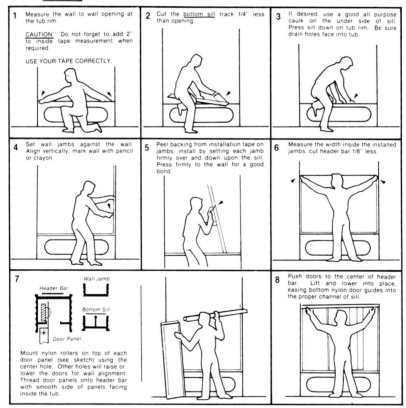

INSTALLATION INSTRUCTIONS

CAUTION: SEE BOX NO. 1 BEFORE CUTTING ALUMINUM HEADER OR SILL

1. Measure the wall to wall opening at the tub rim.

   CAUTION: Do not forget to add 2" to inside tape measurement when required.

   USE YOUR TAPE CORRECTLY.

2. Cut the bottom sill track 1/4" less than opening.

3. If desired, use a good all purpose caulk on the under side of sill. Press sill down on tub rim. Be sure drain holes face into tub.

4. Set wall jambs against the wall. Align vertically, mark wall with pencil or crayon.

5. Peel backing from installation tape on jambs, install by setting each jamb firmly over and down upon the sill. Press firmly to the wall for a good bond.

6. Measure the width inside the installed jambs, cut header bar 1/8" less.

7. Wall Jamb / Header Bar / Bottom Sill / Door Panel

   Mount nylon rollers on top of each door panel (see sketch) using the center hole. Other holes will raise or lower the doors for wall alignment. Thread door panels onto header bar with smooth side of panels facing inside the tub.

8. Push doors to the center of header bar. Lift and lower into place, easing bottom nylon door guides into the proper channel of sill.

TRIDOR MODEL ONLY:

To reverse direction of panels, raise panels out of bottom track and slide catches past each other thereby reversing direction so that shower head does not throw water between the panels.

HARDWARE KIT CONTENTS
TUDOR MODEL
4 nylon bearings
4 ball bearing screws # 8-32 × 3/8"
TRIDOR MODEL
6 nylon bearings
6 ball bearing screws # 8-32 × 3/8"

Projects

On TechComm Web

For more projects, click on Additional Exercises, Projects, and Cases for Ch. 20 on <bedfordstmartins.com/techcomm>.

3. Write a brief manual for a process familiar to you. Consider writing a procedures manual for a school activity or a part-time job, such as your work as the business manager of the school newspaper or as a tutor in the Writing Center.

4. **Group Activity**   Write instructions for one of the following activities or for a process used in your field. Include appropriate graphics. In a brief note preceding the instructions, indicate your audience and purpose. Exchange these materials with a partner. Observe your partner and take notes as he or she attempts to carry out the instructions. Then revise your instructions and share them with your partner; discuss whether the revised instructions are easier to understand and apply, and in what ways they are easier to understand and apply. Submit your instructions to your instructor.

a. how to change a bicycle tire

b. how to delete the contents of the cache in your browser

c. how to light a fire in a fireplace

d. how to copy a compact disc to a blank disc

e. how to find an online discussion group and subscribe to it

f. how to locate, download, and install a file from CNET shareware.com (shareware.cnet.com), FileDudes! (filedudes.com), or a similar download site

CASE
Writing a Set of Instructions

The instructor in your technical-communication class would like your help in familiarizing students with the process of downloading software from the Internet. She has asked you to write a set of instructions that students in the class can use to download an updated version of an Internet browser from Microsoft or Netscape. Visit one of these sites, download the software, install it, and configure it either for a home computer or a computer in one of your labs. Then write a clear set of instructions for someone who knows how to operate a computer but has not downloaded and installed software. Include instructions on how to modify the size of the cache.

On TechComm Web

For more cases, click on Additional Exercises, Projects, and Cases for Ch. 20 on <bedfordstmartins.com /techcomm>.

21

Creating Web Sites

Amy Gahran (2001), the editor of *Contentious*, a Web magazine for writers and editors who create content for online media, on one big difference between the way people read print and online documents:

Most Internet users are on information overload. Don't overwhelm your online audience. It's best to focus on providing small amounts of high-quality content. Don't pump out lots of lower-quality content—nobody's going to read it all, anyway. Reward your readers for every small investment of their precious attention.

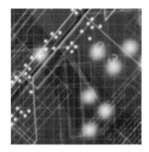

The Web is a gigantic publishing medium, made up of millions of Web pages and sites. Nobody has precise figures about Web usage because it changes too quickly and because there is no Internet headquarters. According to the Computer Industry Almanac (2002), by the year 2005, more than a billion people will be using the Internet. Because the Web is such an important publishing medium for organizations, professionals should understand the basics of creating a Web site.

On TechComm Web

For additional samples, activities, and links related to this chapter, see <bedfordstmartins.com/techcomm>.

UNDERSTANDING THE PROCESS OF CREATING WEB SITES

The process of building and maintaining a Web site is nonlinear. You will find yourself going forward, then doubling back and rewriting. In fact, a Web site is never finished, for you will add, delete, and revise information as long as the site exists.

The following sections discuss the process of creating Web sites.

Analyzing Your Audience and Purpose

Your first goal is to understand who will be viewing the site and why you are creating it. Who are your readers? Why would they visit the site? What kinds of information do they seek? How much do they already know about your subject? Are they looking mainly for links to other sites? Do they need to download information to their own computers? What are your specific goals in launching the site: to project a positive image for your organization? to publicize your products or services? to sell?

To create a Web site:

Analyze your audience and purpose.

Design the site and its pages.

Create and code the content.

Revise and test the site.

Launch the site.

Register the site with search engines.

Maintain the site.

In This Book

For more about audience and purpose, see Ch. 5.

You also need to think about four additional questions that can affect the design of your site:

- *What kind of equipment do your readers have?* If they have fast Internet connections, you can use more and bigger graphics without causing annoying delays as the information downloads. If they have slow connections, use only a few graphics and keep them small, and create a number of small pages rather than few large ones, because small pages load more quickly.
- *Do your readers want to print out the information on your site?* If so, create a version that prints as a single, unified document, not as a lot of small pages.
- *Do your readers have any disabilities?* If many of your readers are elderly, design the site to accommodate vision impairment and perhaps motion impairment. For more about designing sites for people with disabilities, see page 561.
- *Are your readers native speakers of English?* If not, consider creating the site in other languages. For more about designing sites for multicultural audiences, see page 562.

Depending on your answers to these questions, you may need to include extra time in your schedule and extra labor in your budget.

Designing the Site and Its Pages

On TechComm Web

For more help with designing for the Web, click on Tutorials on <bedfordstmartins.com/techcomm>.

Figure 21.1 shows the basic structure of a simple Web site. Almost all sites consist of a home page—the main page of the site—and other pages that are linked to it. A page refers to a file; the content for one file might fit on one screen, or you might have to scroll through several screens to see it all.

On a well-designed site, readers can easily find the information they need. Your job is to figure out the kinds of information they will need and how they will look for it. Consider your audience and purpose. For example, if you are creating a site for a small insurance agency, you might conclude that your readers will want to visit your site for five reasons:

- to understand the types of insurance offered
- to find out rates
- to follow links to other sources of information about insurance
- to e-mail questions
- to make appointments

Your site should be designed so that readers can figure out how to fulfill each of these purposes from the home page.

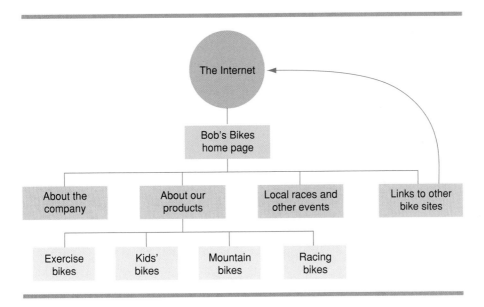

■ **Figure 21.1**
**Structure of a Basic
Web Site**

*Each box in the diagram
represents a page on the
Web site for Bob's Bikes.
The pages in the bottom
row are linked only to the
"About our products" page.*

For simple sites such as this one, a shallow design, like the one shown in
Figure 21.2, might work best. Larger sites often call for a deeper design, as
shown in Figure 21.3.

In designing the site as a whole, try to give all pages a consistent appearance. Although the content and function of different pages might vary greatly,
the typography, types of graphics, and colors should be consistent from page
to page. The site's navigation elements should also appear in the same place
on each page, creating a pattern that will help readers find the information
they seek.

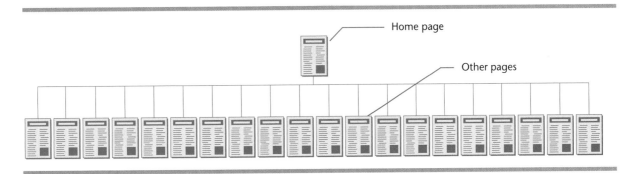

■ **Figure 21.2   A Shallow Site Design**

*If the home page clearly displays links to the second-level pages, a reader can easily navigate the site. Electronic phone books
and bibliographies are often presented using a shallow design.*

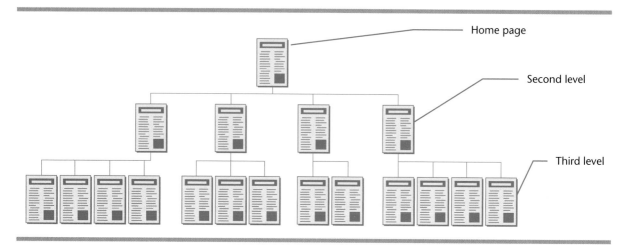

■ **Figure 21.3   A Deeper Site Design**

A deeper site lets you classify and subclassify information so that readers are not overwhelmed with links on a home page. Unfortunately, readers might overlook information on lower-level pages. Many site designers try to structure their sites so that a reader does not have to click more than twice to get from any one place on the site to any other.

On TechComm Web

For more links to online tutorials on making Web pages, click on Links Library for Ch. 21 on <bedfordstmartins.com/techcomm>.

For more specific advice about designing the site and its pages, see page 548, or consult one of the many excellent online tutorials on designing Web sites. Four well-known ones are the following:

- *Getting Started with HTML,* by Dave Raggett
- *W3Schools.com*
- *Webmonkey*
- *Web Style Guide*

Creating and Coding the Content

Once you have created a design for your site, you need to create or gather your content—both text and graphics—and code it so that it can be published on the Web.

Gathering your content can be a bigger job than you think. If you simply code print documents and put them on the Web, your site will be ineffective. Readers on the Web tend to jump from place to place rather than read consecutively. To make paper documents effective on the Web, you need to revise or even rewrite them.

In addition, you need to collect or make the graphics for the site. A graphic the size of a standard sheet of paper would work poorly on a Web site, because readers with slower modems or phone lines would have to wait several minutes for it to download.

The next step is to code your information into a digital format that can be transmitted on the Web. For text, the current standard is HTML (hypertext markup language), which is now evolving into XHTML (extensible hypertext markup language). Other new standards, such as WML (wireless markup language), will make Web pages more compatible with evolving technologies, such as PDAs and cell phones. Figure 21.4 shows a simple Web page; Figure 21.5 shows the HTML code that produced it.

How do you code material for use on the Web? To add HTML tags to text, use one of three techniques:

- *Save your word-processed files as Web code.* Unfortunately, most word processors add erroneous code. If you use word-processed code, open the file in a text editor and remove the faulty code.

- *Use a Web-editor program.* Sometimes called a *Web-authoring program,* a Web editor automates most of the coding. For example, instead of typing the tags for italics, you simply select the text you want to italicize, then click a button. Sophisticated Web editors, such as GoLive® or FrontPage®, contain numerous other features, including design templates, for creating complex sites and pages. Like word processors, however, Web editors often introduce unnecessary or erroneous code.

- *Enter the tags by hand in a text editor such as Notepad.* For simple sites, use the text editor that comes with your computer operating system. Creating the tags shown in Figure 21.5, for example, required only a few minutes in Notepad. Learning basic HTML tags will allow you to make changes to a file yourself.

Formatting graphics for use on the Web is a little trickier, because you sometimes have to open your graphics file in a graphics program, such as Photoshop®, then save it in one of the correct formats. Currently, .jpeg and .gif are the two most common formats used on the Web. In addition, graphics often have to be sized and compressed to decrease the file size so they will download rapidly.

The online tutorials listed on page 550 provide instruction on coding information for the Web.

Revising and Testing the Site

Test the site as you would a print document to make sure it accomplishes your purposes. Can readers understand the main point? Can they understand how the pages of the site work together? Are the hyperlinks clear and informative?

In This Book

For more about purpose, see Ch. 5, p. 97.

In addition, determine whether the technical aspects of the site work correctly. For instance, does the home page load correctly when you enter the URL on your browser? Do all the links work? Does the e-mail form for contacting you work?

On TechComm Web

To view XHTML versions of Figs. 21.4 and 21.5, click on Links Library for Ch. 21 on <bedfordstmartins.com/techcomm>.

Some Basic HTML Codes

HTML can be a complicated markup language, but most of the *tags* you will need for a simple page are easy to understand.

The default typeface on the Web is Times Roman. You can use tags to change the color, the size, or the typeface. The title of this page is formatted as H1, the largest of six heading sizes.

You can use most of the design features that you use all the time on your word processor. For instance, you can easily make a bulleted list, called an *unordered list:*

- first bulleted item
- second bulleted item

Or a numbered list, called an *ordered list:*

1. first numbered item
2. second numbered item

You can insert a graphic:

You can add a hyperlink to another file, such as the Web site of this textbook.

You can make a table:

Column head	Column head
data	data

Tables are useful in HTML because they let you create columns of text:

Here you place the text and graphics for the left-hand column of the screen. If you eliminate the grid lines, your reader sees only the text and graphics.

Here you place the text and graphics for the right-hand column of the screen.

To help chunk information, use a *horizontal rule,* which you see here.

◼ Figure 21.4
A Simple Web Page

Test the site with different kinds of computers, monitors, and browsers. If you find, for example, that one browser displays your tables as masses of meaningless, unformatted numbers, you will have to figure out a different way to display that information.

Launching the Site

Ordinarily, you create your Web site on your own computer. After you have tested it, you transfer the files to an Internet server, a computer that is connected to the Internet and has special software. If you are using an Internet

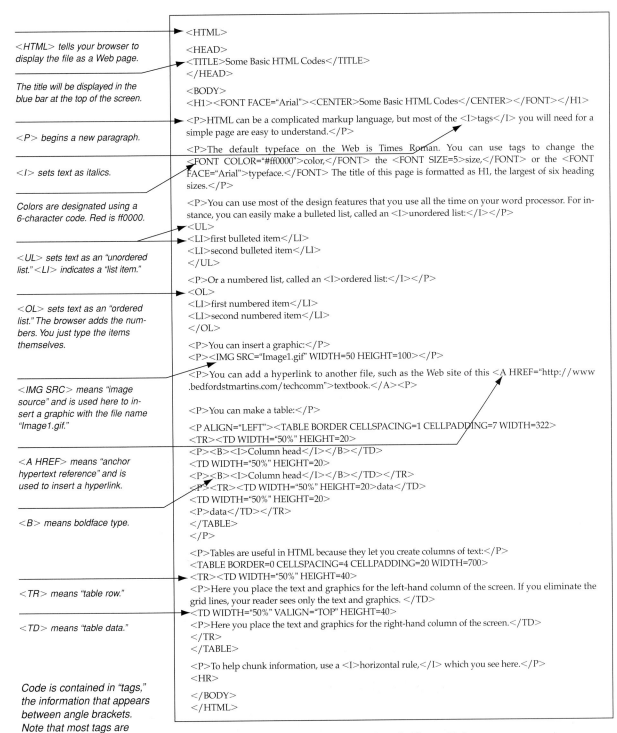

<HTML> tells your browser to display the file as a Web page.

The title will be displayed in the blue bar at the top of the screen.

<P> begins a new paragraph.

<I> sets text as italics.

Colors are designated using a 6-character code. Red is ff0000.

<UL> sets text as an "unordered list." <LI> indicates a "list item."

<OL> sets text as an "ordered list." The browser adds the numbers. You just type the items themselves.

<IMG SRC> means "image source" and is used here to insert a graphic with the file name "Image1.gif."

<A HREF> means "anchor hypertext reference" and is used to insert a hyperlink.

<B> means boldface type.

<TR> means "table row."

<TD> means "table data."

Code is contained in "tags," the information that appears between angle brackets. Note that most tags are used in pairs.

```
<HTML>

<HEAD>
<TITLE>Some Basic HTML Codes</TITLE>
</HEAD>

<BODY>
<H1><FONT FACE="Arial"><CENTER>Some Basic HTML Codes</CENTER></FONT></H1>

<P>HTML can be a complicated markup language, but most of the <I>tags</I> you will need for a
simple page are easy to understand.</P>

<P>The default typeface on the Web is Times Roman. You can use tags to change the
<FONT COLOR="#ff0000">color,</FONT> the <FONT SIZE=5>size,</FONT> or the <FONT
FACE="Arial">typeface.</FONT> The title of this page is formatted as H1, the largest of six heading
sizes.</P>

<P>You can use most of the design features that you use all the time on your word processor. For in-
stance, you can easily make a bulleted list, called an <I>unordered list:</I></P>
<UL>
<LI>first bulleted item</LI>
<LI>second bulleted item</LI>
</UL>

<P>Or a numbered list, called an <I>ordered list:</I></P>
<OL>
<LI>first numbered item</LI>
<LI>second numbered item</LI>
</OL>

<P>You can insert a graphic:</P>
<P><IMG SRC="Image1.gif" WIDTH=50 HEIGHT=100></P>

<P>You can add a hyperlink to another file, such as the Web site of this <A HREF="http://www
.bedfordstmartins.com/techcomm">textbook.</A><P>

<P>You can make a table:</P>

<P ALIGN="LEFT"><TABLE BORDER CELLSPACING=1 CELLPADDING=7 WIDTH=322>
<TR><TD WIDTH="50%" HEIGHT=20>
<P><B><I>Column head</I></B></TD>
<TD WIDTH="50%" HEIGHT=20>
<P><B><I>Column head</I></B></TD></TR>
<P><TR><TD WIDTH="50%" HEIGHT=20>data</TD>
<TD WIDTH="50%" HEIGHT=20>
<P>data</TD></TR>
</TABLE>
</P>

<P>Tables are useful in HTML because they let you create columns of text:</P>
<TABLE BORDER=0 CELLSPACING=4 CELLPADDING=20 WIDTH=700>
<TR><TD WIDTH="50%" HEIGHT=40>
<P>Here you place the text and graphics for the left-hand column of the screen. If you eliminate the
grid lines, your reader sees only the text and graphics. </TD>
<TD WIDTH="50%" VALIGN="TOP" HEIGHT=40>
<P>Here you place the text and graphics for the right-hand column of the screen.</TD>
</TR>
</TABLE>

<P>To help chunk information, use a <I>horizontal rule,</I> which you see here.</P>
<HR>

</BODY>
</HTML>
```

■ **Figure 21.5   The HTML Code for the Page in Figure 21.4**

service provider (an ISP), that provider will show you how to use File Transfer Protocol (FTP) to transport your files. If the Internet server is within your own organization, you might use FTP or even carry a disk down the hall.

Once you get the site up on the Web, test it again to make sure it is professional and attractive and that its technical features work.

Registering the Site with Search Engines

On TechComm Web

Some sites register your site with many search engines at the same time. Click on Links Library for Ch. 21 on <bedfordstmartins.com /techcomm>.

You should publicize your site in the traditional way: add the URL to all your product information and advertising. However, you should also make it easy for people to find the site through search engines on the Web. Although some search engines automatically add addresses of new sites to their databases, you should formally notify search engines that you have launched a site. Go to the most popular search engines and look for a link to a page where you can register your site by listing its keywords, describing its subject matter, and entering its URL. For sites that help you register your site with search engines, search for "site registration."

Maintaining the Site

Your goal in creating a Web site is to have people visit it frequently. To encourage visits, you need to actively maintain the site.

GUIDELINES

Keeping Your Site Current

▶ *Add new information.* Many sites have a "what's new" box on the home page that directs readers to new information.

▶ *Delete old information.* Few mistakes undercut your credibility more than a page describing an upcoming event from last year.

▶ *Test for link rot.* When you link to a site that no longer exists or that has moved to a new address, you have *link rot*. Web-editor programs and a number of sites on the Web help you test your links. But you can check yourself by visiting your own site and trying out the links.

In This Book

For more about designing documents, see Ch. 13.

▶ *Solicit comments from users.* Ask readers to e-mail you about any features that are not working and with suggestions for adding content to your site. When readers send you such e-mail, be sure to reply with a thank-you note.

DESIGNING EFFECTIVE SITES AND PAGES

Most of the principles of good Web page design are similar to the principles of good page design for printed documents. For instance, start with a page grid, use white space liberally, and use typography effectively. However, you need to apply these principles a little differently in designing your site.

This section covers seven design principles.

Aim for Simplicity

When you create a site, it doesn't cost anything to use all the colors in the rainbow, to add sound effects and animation, to make text blink on and off. Although these effects can sometimes help you communicate information, most of the time all they do is slow the download and annoy the reader. If a special effect serves no useful function, avoid it.

To design effective sites and pages:

Aim for simplicity.

Make the text easy to read and understand.

Create informative headers and footers.

Help readers navigate the site.

Create clear, informative links.

Avoid Web clichés.

Include extra features your readers might need.

GUIDELINES

Designing a Simple Site

▶ *Use simple backgrounds.* If you think a plain white background is ineffective, use a pale pastel or, at most, a muted background pattern. Avoid loud patterns that distract the reader from the words and graphics of the text. You don't want readers to "see" the background. Here is an example of what can go wrong:

▶ *Use conservative color combinations to increase text legibility.* The greater the contrast between the text color and the background color, the more legible the text. The most legible color combination is black text against a white background (see Figure 21.4). Bad idea: black on purple.

Some Basic HTML Codes

HTML can be a complicated markup language, but most of the *tags* you will need for a simple page are easy to understand. Note that each paragraph has a *paragraph tag* before it and after it.

The default typeface on the Web is Time Roman. You can use tags to change the color, the size, or the typeface. Note that the title of this page is tagged as H1, the largest of six heading sizes.

You can use most of the design features that you use all the time on your word processor. For instance, you can easily make a bulleted list, called an *unordered list*.

▶ *Avoid decorative graphics.* Don't waste space using graphics that convey no useful information. Hesitate before you use clip art.

▶ *Use thumbnail graphics.* Instead of a large graphic, which takes a long time to download, use a thumbnail so that readers can click on it to open a larger version of the image.

Make the Text Easy to Read and Understand

Web pages are harder to read than paper documents because screen resolution is much less sharp: usually, 72 dots per inch (dpi) versus 1200 dpi on a basic laser printer and 2400 dpi in some books.

On TechComm Web

For more on writing for the Web, see John Morkes and Jakob Nielsen's "Concise, SCANNABLE, and Objective: How to Write for the Web." Click on Links Library for Ch. 21 on <bedfordstmartins.com /techcomm>.

GUIDELINES

Designing Easy-to-Read Text

▶ *Keep the text short.* Poor screen resolution makes reading long stretches of text difficult. In general, pages should contain no more than two or three screens of information.

▶ *Chunk information.* When you write for the screen, chunk information to make it easier to understand. Use frequent headings, brief paragraphs, and lists.

▶ *Make the text as simple as possible.* Use common words and short sentences to make the information as simple as the subject allows.

Create Informative Headers and Footers

Headers and footers help readers understand and navigate your site, and they help establish your credibility. You want your readers know they are visiting the official site of your organization, and that it was created by professionals.

Figure 21.6 shows a typical Web site header. Figure 21.7 shows a typical Web site footer.

■ **Figure 21.6   Header**

This is the header on the Corel home page. Notice that the date is displayed, along with links to the major contents of the site. Notice, too, in the upper right corner, links to versions of the site for international visitors. Headers should always contain a link to the home page; on this page, the logo and the word Corel *in the upper left link to the home page.*
Source: Corel, 2002 <www3.corel.com/cgi-bin/gx.cgi/AppLogic+FTContentServer?pagename=Corel /Product/WordPerfect>.

■ **Figure 21.7   Footer**

A footer usually includes a copyright notice. This footer also includes links to legal information, accessibility information, the privacy policy, the Webmaster's e-mail, and several other areas of the site. Note that because the links in the footer are presented as text, they will be visible to visitors with handicaps and to those who have turned off the graphics.
Source: Corel, 2002 <www3.corel.com/cgi-bin/gx.cgi/AppLogic+FTContentServer?pagename=Corel/ Product/WordPerfect>.

Help Readers Navigate the Site

Readers of a Web site cannot hold the Web page in their hands. All they can see is the page on the screen. Therefore, each page should help readers see where they are in the site and get where they want to go.

One important way to help readers navigate is to create and sustain a consistent visual design on every page. Make the header, footer, background color or pattern, typography (typeface, size, and color), and placement of the navigational links the same on every page.

GUIDELINES

Making Your Site Easy to Navigate

▶ *Include a site map or index.* A site map, which lists the pages on the site, can be a graphic or a textual list of the pages, classified according to logical categories. An index is an alphabetized list of the pages. Figure 21.8 is a section of the Google site map.

On TechComm Web

To view Fig. 21.8 in context on the Web, click on Links Library for Ch. 21 on <bedfordstmartins.com /techcomm>.

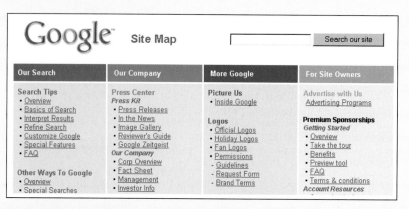

■ **Figure 21.8   Site Map**

Source: Google, 2002 <www.google.com/sitemap.html>.

▶ *Use a table of contents at the top of long pages.* If your page extends over more than a couple of screens, include a table of contents—a set of links to the items on that page—so that your readers do not have to scroll down to find the topic they want. Tables of contents can link one page to information further down on the same page or on separate pages. Figure 21.9 shows a table of contents at the top of an FAQ page.

On TechComm Web

To view Fig. 21.9 in context on the Web, click on Links Library for Ch. 21 on <bedfordstmartins.com /techcomm>.

Frequently Asked Questions (FAQ)

- What is GovBenefits?
- What benefits will GovBenefits screen for?
- How much time will it take to answer all the questions?
- What types of questions will GovBenefits ask?
- Do I have to answer all the questions?
- What if I am looking for a specific benefits program?
- What if I am helping someone else?
- What if I want to apply for a benefits program?
- How often should I use GovBenefits?
- How does the search work?
- What Federal agencies are participating in GovBenefits?

What is GovBenefits?

GovBenefits is a screening tool to help you find government benefits that you may be eligible to receive.

GovBenefits does NOT offer application services for benefits and cannot guarantee eligibility for specific programs. In addition, GovBenefits is not designed to be a comprehensive listing of all assistance programs for which someone is eligible. Its purpose is to give you a list of benefits

■ **Figure 21.9   Table of Contents**

In this excerpt from an FAQ, the questions are presented as links in a table of contents at the top of the page.
Source: GovBenefits, 2002 <www.govbenefits.gov/GovBenefits/jsp/FAQ.jsp>.

▶ *Help readers get back to the top of long pages.* If a page is long enough to justify a table of contents, include a "Back to top" link (a textual link or a button or icon) before the start of each new chunk of information.

▶ *Include a link to the home page on every page.* This link can be a simple "Back to home page" textual link, a button, or an icon.

▶ *Include textual navigational links at the bottom of the page.* If you are using a button or an icon for navigational links on your pages, include textual versions of those links at the bottom of the page. Readers who have turned off the images to speed up the download won't be able to understand the graphical link (unless you have added an alt tag—a tag that instructs the browser to display a word or phrase defining the graphic). In addition, readers with vision impairment might be using special software that reads the information on the screen. This software interprets text only, not graphics. Figure 21.7 on page 557 shows textual links in a footer.

Create Clear, Informative Links

Well-phrased links are easy to read and understand. By clearly telling the reader what kind of information the linked site provides, they help the reader decide whether to follow the link. The following guidelines are based on Sun Microsystems' "Guide to Web Style" (Sun, 1999).

GUIDELINES

Writing Clear, Informative Links

▶ *Structure your sentences as if there were no links in your text.*

AWKWARD   Click here to go to the Rehabilitation Center page, which includes numerous links to research centers across the nation.

SMOOTH   The Rehabilitation Center page includes numerous links to research centers across the nation.

▶ *Indicate what information the linked page contains.* Readers get frustrated if they wait for a file to download and then discover that it doesn't contain the information they expected.

UNINFORMATIVE   See the Rehabilitation Center.

INFORMATIVE   See the Rehabilitation Center for hours of operation.

▶ *Don't change the colors of the text links.* Readers are used to two common colors: blue for links that have not yet been clicked, and purple for links that have already been clicked.

Avoid Web Clichés

The Web has already developed its share of clichés. Tired, empty words or phrases can obscure the site's purpose and make readers suspect that they are wasting their time. The following Web clichés are particularly annoying because they insult visitors' intelligence by stating the obvious.

- *"Check out" your site.* If the information looks interesting and useful, they will.
- *"Under construction."* If the site is a mess, don't launch it. If you want to tell visitors that you update the contents periodically, state when the site was last revised.
- *"Cool."* Very uncool.
- *"Come back often."* If their visit was worth it, they will. If it wasn't, they won't.

Include Extra Features Your Readers Might Need

Because readers with a range of interests and needs will visit your site, consider adding several or all of the following five features:

- *An FAQ page.* A list of frequently asked questions helps new visitors by providing basic information, explaining how to use the site, and directing them to more-detailed discussions. Figure 21.10 is an excerpt from an FAQ page.
- *A search page or engine.* A search page or search engine lets readers enter a keyword or phrase and find all the pages on the site that contain it.

On TechComm Web

To view Fig. 21.10 in context on the Web, click on Links Library for Ch. 21 on <bedfordstmartins.com /techcomm>.

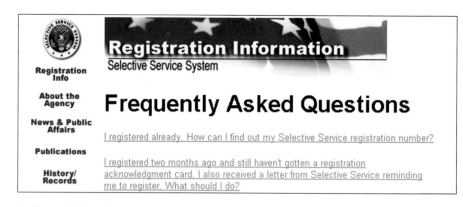

■ **Figure 21.10 Excerpt from an FAQ Page**

Each question here links to a separate page containing the answer. On other sites, the questions and answers are presented on the same page.
Source: Selective Service System, 2002 <www.sss.gov/qa.htm>.

- *Resource links.* If the main purpose of your site is to educate readers, you should provide links to other sites.

- *A printable version of your site.* A Web site is designed for a screen, not a page. Consider making a printable version of your site, with black text on a white background, and all the text and graphics consolidated into one big file.

- *A text-only version of your site.* Many readers with slow Internet connections set their browsers to view text only. In addition, as is discussed more fully in the next section, many readers with impaired vision rely on text because their specialized software cannot interpret graphics. Therefore, consider creating a text-only version of your site and include a link to it on your home page.

DESIGNING SITES FOR READERS WITH DISABILITIES

The Internet has proved to be a terrific technology for people with disabilities because it brings a world of information to their desktops, allowing them to work from home and participate in virtual communities. However, as sites have become more sophisticated over the last few years, many people with disabilities have found the Internet harder to use. In 1996, a court ruled that the Americans with Disabilities Act covered commercial Web sites, which must now be accessible to people with disabilities. Over the next few years, more effort will go into making hardware and software to help people with disabilities use the Internet.

The following discussion highlights several ways to make your site easier to use for people with disabilities. Consider three main types of disabilities as you design your site:

- *Vision impairment.* People who cannot see, or cannot see well, rely on text-to-speech conversion programs. Provide either a text-only version of the site or textual equivalents of all your graphics. Use the alt (alternate) tag to create a textual label that pops up when the reader holds the mouse over the graphic.

    Do not rely on color or graphics alone to communicate information. For example, if you use a red icon to signal a warning, also use the word *warning*. If you use tables to create columns on the screen, label each column clearly using a text label rather than just an image.

    Use 12-point type or larger on your site, and provide audio feedback — for example, having a button beep when the reader presses it.

- *Hearing impairment.* If you use video, provide captions and, if the video includes sound, a volume control. Also use visual feedback techniques; for example, make a button flash when the reader presses it.

On TechComm Web

See the Web Content Accessibility Guidelines, from the World Wide Web Consortium, for a detailed look at accessibility.

A site called Bobby will check your site, for free, to evaluate its adherence to accessibility options. Click on Links Library for Ch. 21 on <bedfordstmartins.com/techcomm>.

- *Mobility impairment.* Some people with mobility impairments find it easier to use the keyboard than a mouse. Therefore, build in keyboard shortcuts wherever possible. If readers have to click on an area of the screen using a pointing device, make the area large so that it is easy to see and click.

DESIGNING SITES FOR MULTICULTURAL AUDIENCES

More than 60 percent of the world's Web users are nonnative speakers of English (Global Reach, 2002). Therefore, it makes sense to plan your site as if many of your visitors will not be proficient in English.

On TechComm Web

See the World Wide Web Consortium's internationalization page for more about the challenges of creating markup languages that meet the needs of international users.

Also see "Guidelines for Accessible Web Sites: Technology & Users," by Michele Ward, Philip Rubens, and Sherry Southard. Click on Links Library for Ch. 21 on <bedfordstmartins.com/techcomm>.

STRATEGIES FOR INTERCULTURAL COMMUNICATION

Communicating Across Cultures Online

Planning for a multicultural Web site is similar to planning for a multicultural paper document.

- *Use short sentences and paragraphs, as well as common words.*
- *Avoid idioms, both verbal and visual, that might be confusing.* For instance, don't use sports metaphors, such as "full-court press," or a graphic of an American-style mailbox to suggest an e-mail link.
- *If a large percentage of your readers speak a language other than English, consider creating a version of your site in that language.* The expense can be considerable, but so can the benefits.

ETHICS, COPYRIGHT LAW, AND THE WEB

On TechComm Web

See Stan Morris's essay, "The Importance of International Laws for Web Publishers." Click on Links Library for Ch. 21 on <bedfordstmartins.com/techcomm>.

In This Book

For more about copyright law, see Ch. 2, p. 18.

Information on the Internet is easy to steal. Users can download and manipulate digital versions of the text and graphics, or claim credit for materials that they did not create. These practices are unethical and illegal: digital material is covered by the same copyright laws that apply to printed material, regardless of whether they include a copyright symbol. Unless the copyright owner specifically says that you may use the material, you must receive written permission, just as you would for printed material.

Benedict O'Mahoney (2002) has written a thoughtful essay on some of the complicated issues involved in interpreting copyright law. Here are just three of the puzzles he addresses:

- *Is the design of a Web page protected by copyright law?* Some would say no, because what readers see is a function of their hardware and software, and readers can customize the image. However, the design of a Web page is an original work and thus should be protected, regardless of how readers might change it after it is transmitted.

- *Are lists of links protected?* Is each link protected by copyright? No. Is the whole list of links protected? Probably, if the person showed some originality in creating the list. For example, a set of links to resources for agriculture students would be protected if the author did some original thinking in creating categories for the individual links.

- *May you link to anyone else's Web site? May anyone link to yours?* Although the Web was originally envisioned as an open environment, in which anyone can link to anyone else, a site owner might not want the extra traffic on its server or might not want to be associated with the linking site. Are you responsible for finding out who has linked to you, or should the linking site have to get permission to link to you?

As this discussion suggests, questions of digital ethics and legality are likely to remain unresolved for years. Over the next decade, the courts will be hearing many cases in which copyright law has to be reinterpreted in light of the unique technical, economic, and social implications of electronic media.

GUIDELINES

Creating an Ethical Site

▶ *Don't plagiarize.* If you want to publish material you found on the Internet, secure written permission from the copyright owner.

▶ *Ask permission to link.* Notify an organization if you wish to link to its site, then abide by its wishes. And ask before *deep linking*—linking to a page other than the home page.

▶ *Don't misuse meta tags.* If you look at the source code of a typical Web page, you will see a meta tag near the top. This is the place where you put keywords that describe the contents of your site. If you are a Ford dealer, you list "Ford," "dealer," and the names of Ford models. It is unethical and, according to some intellectual-property attorneys, illegal to list "Chevrolet" to get potential Chevrolet customers to come to your site.

A LOOK AT SAMPLE WEB PAGES

On TechComm Web

To view Figs. 21.11 and 21.12 in context on the Web, click on Links Library for Ch. 21 on <bedfordstmartins.com/techcomm>.

The best way to learn about designing Web sites and their pages is to study them. Figures 21.11 and 21.12 offer examples of good Web page design.

The name of the organization

The name of the page

Large, clear type

Frames are used effectively here. Users can scroll down to read additional information, but the header, the photograph, and the footer remain visible.

Large, easy-to-read textual links.

■ **Figure 21.11   The Silver Council Home Page**

This page is simple and attractive, with a clear purpose and effective organization.
Source: Silver Council, 2002 <www.silvercouncil.org/html/default.htm>.

The navigation links are clear. You always know where you are.

The content area has three clearly designated sections.

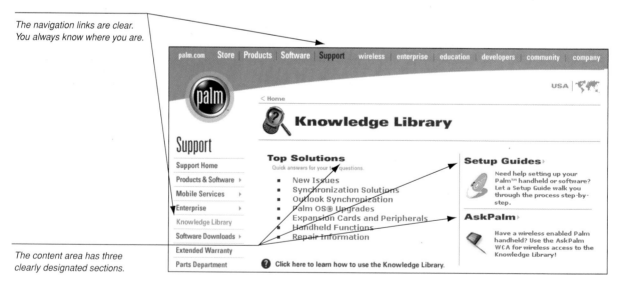

■ **Figure 21.12   Palm's Knowledge Library Page**

This is the Knowledge Library page, part of the Support section of the Palm Web site.
Source: Palm, Inc., 2002 <http://205.141.210.149/SRVS/CGI-BIN/WEBCGI.EXE?>.

Interactive Sample Document:
Making an Impression

The following home page was created by Ari Feldman, a Web designer. The questions in the margin ask you to think about creating and designing effective sites and pages. The answers to these questions are available on TechComm Web.

Source: Feldman, 2002 <www.arifeldman.com/index.html>.

1. What is the audience for this site? Which elements of this page indicate its audience?

2. What is the purpose of this site? Which elements of this page indicate its purpose?

3. Evaluate the ease of navigation. How easy do you think it would be to find what you needed on this site?

4. Evaluate the integration of the links in the text window. How smoothly has the author integrated the links with the text?

On TechComm Web

To find the answers to these questions, click on Interactive Sample Documents for Ch. 21 on <bedfordstmartins.com/techcomm>.

Reviewing the Process

Analyze your audience and purpose.

Consider their equipment and their needs. Do they have disabilities? Do they speak English fluently? Determine your purpose: to inform or persuade, or both.

Design the site.

In light of the information you want to communicate and the needs of your readers, create a design that makes it easy for readers to find the information they need. Create a clear and consistent design for the pages.

Create and code the content.

Aim for simplicity. Make the text easy to read and understand. Create informative headers and footers to help readers know where they are. Help readers navigate the site. Create clear, informative links. Avoid Web clichés. Include extra features your readers might need. Be sure the information on your site adheres to copyright law.

Revise and test the site.

Test the site using different browsers and computer equipment. Revise the site to make it as effective as it can be. See the Revision Checklist that follows.

Launch the site.

Get the files to the server that will host your site.

Register the site with search engines.

Search for sites that automatically register your site with many search engines.

Maintain the site.

Keep the information up to date, add new information, test for link rot, and solicit comments from users.

Revision Checklist

In designing the site, did you
- ❏ analyze your audience and purpose before planning your site? (p. 547)
- ❏ revise and test the information? (p. 551)
- ❏ get the files to an Internet server? (p. 552)
- ❏ register the site with search engines? (p. 554)
- ❏ use a plain, simple background? (p. 555)
- ❏ allow for effective contrast between the background color and the text color? (p. 555)
- ❏ avoid decorative graphics? (p. 556)
- ❏ use thumbnail graphics rather than large ones? (p. 556)
- ❏ make the text easy to read by using brief chunks of text? (p. 556)
- ❏ use simple language and short sentences? (p. 556)
- ❏ create informative headers and footers? (p. 556)
- ❏ include a site map or index? (p. 557)
- ❏ use a table of contents at the top of long pages? (p. 558)
- ❏ link to the home page on every page? (p. 559)
- ❏ include textual navigational links at the bottom of the page? (p. 559)
- ❏ link to the top of long pages? (p. 559)
- ❏ create clear and informative links? (p. 559)
- ❏ avoid Web clichés? (p. 560)
- ❏ include extra features your readers might need, such as an FAQ page, a list of links, a printable version of the site, and a text-only version of the site? (p. 560)
- ❏ design the site so that it is easy for people with vision, hearing, and movement disabilities to use? (p. 561)
- ❏ design the site to accommodate the needs of multicultural readers? (p. 562)
- ❏ get permission to publish any information that you did not generate? (p. 562)
- ❏ ask permission to link? (p. 563)
- ❏ link to another site's home page rather than a secondary page? (p. 563)
- ❏ avoid including misleading information in the meta tags? (p. 563)

Exercises

On TechComm Web

For more exercises, click on Additional Exercises, Projects, and Cases for Ch. 21 on <bedfordstmartins.com/techcomm>.

1. **Internet Activity** Find the sites of three manufacturers within a single industry, such as personal watercraft, cars, computers, or medical equipment. Study the three sites, focusing on one of these aspects of site design:

   - use of color
   - effectiveness of the graphics in communicating information
   - quality of the writing
   - quality of the site map or index
   - navigation, including the clarity and placement of links to other pages in the site
   - use of Web clichés
   - accommodation of multicultural readers
   - accommodation of people with disabilities
   - phrasing of the links

   Which of the three sites is most effective? Which is least effective? Why? Compare and contrast the three sites in terms of their effectiveness.

2. Using a search engine, find a site that serves the needs of people with a physical disability: for example, the Glaucoma Foundation <www.glaucoma-foundation.org /info/>. What attempts have the designers made to accommodate the needs of people with that disability? How effective are those attempts?

Projects

On TechComm Web

For more projects, click on Additional Exercises, Projects, and Cases for Ch. 21 on <bedfordstmartins.com/techcomm>.

3. **Internet Activity** Using a search engine, find five tutorials on making Web pages. For each site, determine the level of expertise of the intended audience and analyze the strengths and weaknesses of the site. Present your results in a memo to your instructor. (For more on memos, see Chapter 15, page 378.)

4. **Group Activity** Form small groups and describe and evaluate your college's or university's Web site. A different member of the group might carry out each of the following tasks:

   - E-mail the site's Webmaster to ask about the process of creating the site. For example, how involved with the content and design of the site was the Webmaster? What is the Webmaster's role in maintaining the site?
   - Analyze the kinds of information the site contains and determine whether the site is intended primarily for faculty, students, alumni, or prospective students.
   - Determine the overlap between the information on the site and the information in printed documents published by the school. In those cases in which they overlap, is the information on the site merely a duplication of the printed information, or has it been revised to take advantage of the unique capabilities of the Web?

   In a memo to your instructor, present your conclusions and recommendations for improving the site. (For more on memos, see Chapter 15, page 378.)

On TechComm Web

For more cases, click on Additional
Exercises, Projects, and Cases for
Ch. 21 on <bedfordstmartins.com
/techcomm>.

C A S E
Creating a Web Site

This case is best for small groups. You and the other members of your
group have learned that a student organization to which you belong (or your
academic major or a community group) is making space available on its
server for a Web site. Create a site. (For this case, you do not actually have
to put the site on the Web; you can create it and test it on a computer that
has a browser installed on it.) Follow these steps:

1. Analyze your audience and purpose. Who would view the site, and
   what would you hope to achieve with the site?

2. Gather or generate your text and other information. If you do not
   have a sufficient amount of information available in digital format,
   you can still proceed with building the site.

3. Design the site. What sort of design is appropriate for the information you wish to communicate and the needs of your audience?

4. Convert the text and graphics. What sorts of tools are most useful
   for the conversion process?

5. Revise and test the information. Other students in the class might
   help you in testing the site.

Keep a log of the activities each group member has carried out. Be prepared to describe your experiences in an oral presentation to the class. (For
advice about preparing oral presentations, see Chapter 22.) Which tasks
were easy to accomplish? Which were difficult? What surprised you about
the process? How satisfied are you with the finished product?

Making Oral Presentations 22

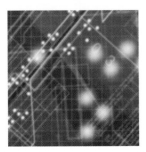

Vincent Kuraitis, health-care consultant, on how to take advantage of nervousness:

I look at nervousness as an opportunity to try to channel that adrenaline, to use it as something that will help me do my best rather than detract from my ability to be persuasive. I can get a little bit more alert, a little bit more in touch with my audience. And I look at the adrenaline rush that comes with speaking in front of an audience as something to look forward to because it makes me do my best.

On TechComm Web

For additional samples, activities, and links related to this chapter, see <bedfordstmartins.com/techcomm>.

The techniques for preparing written documents and oral presentations are quite similar: analyze your audience and purpose, gather information, organize it, and create graphics. The big difference, of course, is the form of delivery.

There are four basic types of presentations:

- *Impromptu presentations.* You deliver an impromptu presentation without advance notice. For instance, at a meeting, your supervisor calls on you to speak for a few minutes about a project you are working on.

- *Extemporaneous presentations.* In an extemporaneous presentation, you might refer to notes or an outline, but you actually make up the sentences as you go along. Regardless of how much you have planned and rehearsed the presentation, you create it as you speak. At its best, an extemporaneous presentation is clear and sounds spontaneous.

- *Scripted presentations.* In a scripted presentation, you read a text written out completely in advance (by you or someone else). You sacrifice naturalness for increased clarity and precision.

- *Memorized presentations.* In a memorized presentation, you speak without notes or script. Memorized presentations are not appropriate for most technical subjects because most people cannot memorize presentations of more than a few minutes.

This chapter discusses extemporaneous and scripted presentations.

UNDERSTANDING THE ROLE OF ORAL PRESENTATIONS

An oral presentation has one big advantage over a written one: it permits a dialogue between the speaker and the audience. Listeners can make comments or simply ask questions. And the speaker and listeners can talk before and after the presentation. Oral presentations are therefore common in technical communication. You can expect to give oral presentations to four types of audiences:

- *Clients and customers.* You present your product's features and its advantages over the competition. After the sale, you might provide oral operating instructions and maintenance tips to users.

- *Colleagues in your organization.* You might instruct fellow workers on a subject you know well. After you return from an important conference or an out-of-town project, your supervisors want a briefing—an oral report. If you have an idea for improving operations at your organization, you write an informal proposal and then present it orally to a small group of managers. Your presentation will help them determine whether to study the idea.

- *Fellow professionals at technical conferences.* You might speak about your own research project or about a team project. You might be addressing other professionals in your field or professionals in other fields.

- *The public.* As you assume greater prominence in your field, you will receive more invitations to speak to civic organizations and governmental bodies.

You might not have had much experience in public speaking, and perhaps your few attempts have been difficult. Gifted speakers who can talk off the cuff are rare. For most of us, an oral presentation requires deliberate and careful preparation.

PREPARING AN ORAL PRESENTATION

When you see an excellent 20-minute presentation, you are seeing only the last 20 minutes of a process that took many hours. How much time should you devote to preparing an oral presentation? Experts recommend devoting 20 to 60 minutes for each minute of the presentation (Smith, 1991, p. 6). At an average of 40 minutes preparation time, you would need more than 13 hours to prepare a 20-minute presentation. Obviously there are many variables, including your knowledge of the subject and your experience creating presentation graphics and giving presentations on that subject. But the point is that good presentations don't just happen.

Preparing an oral presentation requires five steps.

On TechComm Web

The Virtual Presentation Assistant gives advice and links to text and videos of speeches. Click on Links Library for Ch. 22 on <bedfordstmartins.com/techcomm>.

Assessing the Speaking Situation

First, analyze your audience and purpose and then determine how much information you can deliver in the allotted time.

To prepare an oral presentation:

Assess the speaking situation.

Prepare an outline or note cards.

Prepare presentation graphics.

Choose effective language.

Rehearse the presentation.

On TechComm Web

See Dave Zielinski's essay on addressing multicultural audiences. Click on Links Library for Ch. 22 on <bedfordstmartins.com/techcomm>.

Analyzing Your Audience and Purpose   In planning an oral presentation, consider audience and purpose, just as you would in writing a document.

- *Audience.* How much does the audience know about your subject? Your answer helps you determine the level of technical vocabulary and concepts you will use, as well as the types of graphics. Why are audience members listening to your presentation? Are they likely to be hostile, enthusiastic, or neutral? A presentation on the virtues of free trade, for instance, will be received one way by conservative economists and another way by U.S. steelworkers. Are they nonnative speakers of English? If so, prepare to slow down the pace of the delivery and use a simple vocabulary.

- *Purpose.* Are you attempting to inform, or to inform and persuade? If you are explaining how windmills can be used to generate power, you might describe the process. If you are explaining why your windmills are an economical way to generate power, you might compare their results with those of other power sources.

Your analysis of your audience and purpose will affect the content and the form of your presentation. For example, you might have to emphasize some aspects of your subject and ignore others altogether. Or you might have to arrange topics to accommodate a particular audience's needs.

Budgeting Your Time   At most professional meetings, each speaker is given a maximum time, such as 20 minutes. If the question-and-answer period is part of your allotted time, plan accordingly. Even at an informal presentation, you will probably have to work within an unstated time limit that you must determine from the speaking situation. If you take more than your time, eventually your listeners will resent you or simply stop paying attention.

For a 20-minute presentation, the time allotment shown in Table 22.1 is typical. For scripted presentations, most speakers need a little over a minute to deliver a double-spaced page of text effectively.

■ **Table 22.1 Time Allotment in a Presentation**

Task	Time (minutes)
• Introduction	2
• Body	
– First Major Point	4
– Second Major Point	4
– Third Major Point	4
• Conclusion	2
• Questions	4

Preparing an Outline or Note Cards

Some speakers prepare both an outline and a set of note cards. They prepare the outline when they are planning the presentation, just as they would if they were writing a document. Then, when they are ready to begin rehearsing, they prepare the note cards they will use in making the presentation. During rehearsals, they revise the notes cards as they consider how to present their information more effectively. Figure 22.1 shows an outline for a presentation.

In preparing note cards to bring to the presentation, your command of the facts—and your ability to remember them under stress—will determine how specific and detailed your make them. Figure 22.2 on page 575 shows one such note card.

You can also make notes using presentation-graphics software. One advantage of software is that revising is easy. As you prepare the notes, you also see the graphics, just as your audience will, and might think of ways to improve the organization and development of your presentation.

Preparing Presentation Graphics

Graphics clarify or highlight important ideas or facts. Statistical data, in particular, lend themselves to graphical presentation, as do descriptions of equipment or processes. Research reported by Smith (1991) indicates that presentations that include transparencies are judged more professional, persuasive, and credible than those that do not, and that audiences remember information better if presentations are accompanied by graphics. Smith (1991, p. 58) offers these figures:

	Retention after	
	3 hours	3 days
Without graphics	70%	10%
With graphics	85%	65%

One other advantage of using presentation graphics: the audience is not always looking at you. Giving the audience another visual focus can reduce your nervousness.

Characteristics of an Effective Graphic   Effective graphics have five characteristics:

- *Visibility.* The most common problem with presentation graphics is that they are too small. Don't transfer information from an 8.5 × 11-inch page to a slide or transparency. In general, text has to be in 24-point type or larger to be visible on the screen. To save space, compress sentences into brief phrases:

> **On TechComm Web**
>
> Writing Guidelines for Engineering and Science Students includes advice and sample presentation graphics. Click on Links Library for Ch. 22 on <bedfordstmartins.com/techcomm>.

> **In This Book**
>
> For more about creating graphics, see Ch. 14.

The speaker is a specialist in waste-treatment facilities. The audience is a group of civil engineers interested in understanding new developments in industrial-waste disposal. The speaker's purpose is to provide this information and to suggest that his company is a leader in the field.

This speaker uses a problem-methods-solution pattern in developing the presentation. The introduction describes the problem: new environmental regulations will mean cities have to develop new methods of waste treatment and disposal. The following sections present different methods of solving urban waste-management problems.

In This Book

For a discussion of organizational patterns, see Ch. 8.

OUTLINE: PRESENTATION TO CE MEETING

Purpose: to describe, to a group of civil engineers, a new method of treatment and disposal of industrial waste.

1. Introduction
   1.1 The recent Resource Conservation Recovery Act places stringent restrictions on plant engineers.
   1.2 With neutralization, precipitation, and filtration no longer available, plant engineers will have to turn to more sophisticated treatment and disposal techniques.

2. The Principle Behind the New Techniques
   2.1 Waste has to be converted into a cementitious load-supporting material with a low permeability coefficient.
   2.2 Conversion Dynamics, Inc., has devised a new technique to accomplish this.
   2.3 The technique is to combine pozzolan stabilization technology with the traditional treatment and disposal techniques.

3. The Applications of the New Technique
   3.1 For new low-volume-generators, there are two options.
       3.1.1 Discussion of the San Diego plant.
       3.1.2 Discussion of the Boston plant.
   3.2 For existing low-volume generators, Conversion Dynamics offers a range of portable disposal facilities.
       3.2.1 Discussion of the Montreal plant.
       3.2.2 Discussion of the Albany plant.
   3.3 For new high-volume generators, Conversion Dynamics designs, constructs, and operates complete waste-disposal management facilities.
       3.3.1 The Chicago plant now processes up to 1.5 million tons per year.
       3.3.2 The Atlanta plant now processes up to 1.75 million tons per year.
   3.4 For existing high-volume generators, Conversion Dynamics offers add-on facilities.
       3.4.1 The Roanoke plant already complies with the new RCRA requirements.
       3.4.2 The Houston plant will be in compliance within six months.

4. Conclusion
   The Resource Conservation Recovery Act will necessitate substantial capital expenditures over the next decade.

■ **Figure 22.1**
Outline Used to Organize an Oral Presentation

Principle Behind New Technique
— reduce permeability of waste
— use pozzolan stabilization
   technology

■ **Figure 22.2**
Note Card for an Oral
Presentation

If you are concerned that you will forget important facts or concepts during the presentation, include more of them on the note cards.

TEXT IN A
DOCUMENT

The current system has three problems:
- It is expensive to maintain.
- It requires nonstandard components.
- It is not compliant with the new MILSPEC.

SAME TEXT
ON A SCREEN

Three Problems:
- Expensive Maintenance
- Nonstandard Components
- Noncompliance with MILSPEC

- *Legibility.* Use clear, legible lines for drawings and diagrams: black on white works best. Use legible typefaces for text; a boldfaced sans-serif typeface such as Arial or Helvetica is effective because it reproduces clearly on a screen. Avoid shadowed and outlined letters.

- *Simplicity.* Text and drawings must be simple. Each graphic should present only one idea. Your listeners have not seen the graphic before and will not be able to linger over it.

- *Clarity.* In cutting words and simplifying concepts and visual representations, make sure the point of the graphic remains clear.

- *Correctness.* Everyone makes mistakes, but mistakes are particularly embarrassing when they are 10 inches tall on a screen.

Two points from Chapter 14 are important here: when you use graphics templates in your software, remember that some of them violate basic principles of design. And don't use clip art just to fill blank space on a transparency or slide.

One more point: you cannot use copyrighted material—images, text, music, video, or other material—in your presentation without written permission to do so.

Graphics and the Speaking Situation   To plan your graphics, analyze four aspects of the speaking situation:

In This Book

For more about typefaces, see Ch. 13, p. 303. For more about using color in graphics, see Ch. 14, p. 327.

On TechComm Web

See Dave Zielinski's essay on how copyright law applies to presentations. Click on Links Library for Ch. 22 on <bedfordstmartins.com /techcomm>.

- *Length of the presentation.* How many graphics should you have? As a guideline, try to have a different graphic for every 30 seconds of the presentation. It is far better to have a series of simple graphics than to have one complicated one that stays on the screen for 10 minutes.

- *Audience aptitude and experience.* What kinds of graphics can your audience understand easily? You don't want to present scatter graphs, for example, if your listeners do not know how to interpret them.

- *Size and layout of the room.* Graphics to be used in a small meeting room differ from those to be used in a 500-seat auditorium. Think first about the size of the images, then about the layout of the room. For instance, will a window create glare that you will have to consider as you plan the type or placement of the graphics?

- *Equipment.* Find out what kind of equipment will be available in the presentation room. Ask about backups in case of equipment failure. If possible, bring your own equipment. That way, you know it works and you know how to use it. Some speakers bring graphics in two media just in case; that is, they have slides but they also have transparencies of the same graphics.

Using Graphics to Signal the Organization of the Presentation

Used effectively, graphics can help you communicate how your presentation is organized. For example, you can use the transition from one graphic to the next to indicate the transition from one point to the next. Figure 22.3 shows the slides for a presentation that accompanied the report in Chapter 19 on selecting a printer (see page 504). Notice that the outline in Slide 2 is used in Slides 5, 7, and 16 to signal the transition to the next major section of the presentation.

On TechComm Web

To view Fig. 22.3 as slides, click on Links Library for Ch. 22 on <bedfordstmartins.com/techcomm>.

For your last graphic, consider a summary of your main points or a brief set of questions that restate your main points and prompt the audience to synthesize the information you have presented.

With presentation software, it is easy to create two other kinds of documents: *speaking notes* and *handouts.*

Figure 22.4 (page 579) shows a page of speaking notes. Figure 22.5 (page 579) shows a handouts page.

Different Media Used for Graphics

Table 22.2 on page 579 describes the basic media for graphics.

If you are using presentation-graphics software, keep in mind that many of the templates provided with the software are unnecessarily ornate, full of fancy shading and designs and colors. Choose a simple template, then modify it for your situation. You want the audience to focus on your delivery of the information, not on the complex design of the graphic.

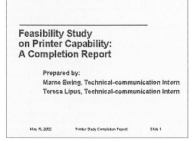

The first slide—the title slide—shows the title of the presentation and the name and affiliation of each speaker.

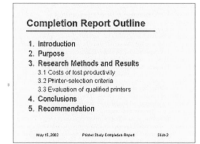

Next, the speakers present an overview, which outlines the presentation. Notice that, at the bottom of each slide, is a footer with the date, the name of the presentation, and the number of the slide.

Notice that the title of the third slide is numbered according to the list introduced in the previous slide. Such cues help readers understand the structure of your presentation.

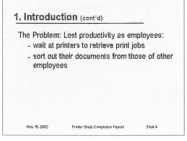

If a topic extends onto a second slide, as you see here, use a "cont'd" notation. Don't try to squeeze all the information onto one slide.

This slide is identical to Slide 2, except for the red arrow. The speakers use this slide—and Slides 7 and 16—to help orient the listener. The speakers are now beginning point 2, the statement of the purpose of the presentation.

2. Purpose

- Evaluate our current printing capabilities and costs
- Research various options for increasing our printing capacity
- Present our conclusions and recommendation

Notice that the bullet list on this slide uses parallel structure: all the phrases begin with the present tense of the verb.

Completion Report Outline

1. Introduction
2. Purpose
→ 3. Research Methods and Results
  3.1 Costs of lost productivity
  3.2 Printer-selection criteria
  3.3 Evaluation of qualified printers
4. Conclusions
5. Recommendation

If you are projecting your presentation graphics from a computer, you can set the software so that each item appears only after you click the mouse. This way, the audience will not read ahead; you control when the next item appears on the screen.

3.1 Costs of lost productivity

12 employees each wait 6 minutes/day =

28 hours/month =

$570/month

In this presentation, the speakers use color —sparingly—for emphasis.

3.2 Printer-selection criteria

- Category: Small-office laser printers <$500
- Most-important features:
  - Print resolution
  - RAM expandability
  - Cost per page
  - Printing speed

Try to keep the amount of text on a slide small. Some commentators recommend no more than 7 words per line, and no more than 7 lines.

■ **Figure 22.3   Slides for a Brief Presentation**

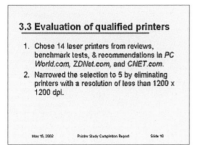

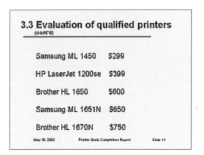

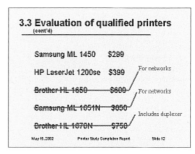

The speakers uses the red "strike-through" symbol to suggest that they eliminated three of the printers during their analysis.

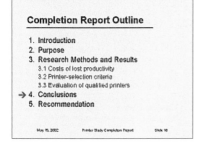

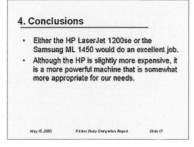

The red check marks here and in the next slide show which printer is superior according to a particular criterion.

As discussed in Ch. 19, conclusions are the inferences you draw from results.

The speakers use color to emphasize key information in their recommendation.

■ **Figure 22.3** *(Continued)*

On TechComm Web

For more help with preparing presentation slides, click on Tutorials on <bedfordstmartins.com/techcomm>.

In addition, set the software so that you use the mouse to control the rate of advance from one graphic to the next. Do not set it so that it advances automatically at a specified interval, such as 60 seconds. You will only be distracted by having to speed up or slow down your presentation to keep up with the graphics.

To create speaking notes for each slide, type the notes in the empty box under the picture of the slide, then print the notes pages.

You can choose to print the slides on your notes page either in color or in black and white.

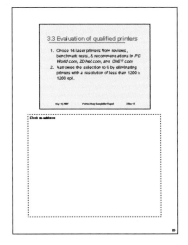

You can print multiple slides on a page, in color or in black and white. Here the software is set to print six on a page.

The advantage of using handouts is that if you announce at the start of the presentation that you will make them available at the end, your audience will concentrate on what you are saying and not be distracted by trying to take notes.

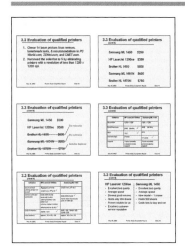

■ **Figure 22.4   Speaking Notes**

■ **Figure 22.5   Handouts Page**

■ **Table 22.2   Basic Media for Oral Presentations**

Medium	Advantages	Disadvantages
Computer presentations: images are projected from a computer to a screen.	• Very professional appearance. • You can produce any combination of static or dynamic images, from simple graphs to sophisticated, three-dimensional animations, as well as sound and video.	• The equipment is expensive and not available everywhere. • Preparing the graphics can be time consuming. • Presentations prepared using one piece of software might not run on all systems.
Slide projector: projects previously prepared slides onto a screen.	• Very professional appearance. • Versatile—can handle photographs or artwork, color or black-and-white. • With a second projector, you can eliminate the pause between slides. • During the presentation, you can easily advance and reverse the slides. • Graphics software lets you create small paper copies of your slides to distribute to the audience after the presentation.	• Slides can be expensive to produce. • Room has to be kept relatively dark during the slide presentation.
Overhead projector: projects transparencies onto a screen.	• Transparencies are inexpensive and easy to create. • You can draw transparencies "live." • You can create overlays by placing one transparency over another. • Lights can remain on during the presentation.	• Not as professional looking as slides. • Each transparency must be loaded separately by hand.

■ **Table 22.2** *(Continued)*

Medium	Advantages	Disadvantages
Chalkboard or other hard writing surface.	• Almost universally available. • You have complete control—can add, delete, or modify the graphic easily.	• Complicated or extensive graphics are difficult to create. • Ineffective in large rooms. • Very informal appearance.
Objects: models or samples of material that can be held up or passed around through the audience.	• Interesting for the audience. • Provide a close look at the object.	• Audience members might not be listening while they are looking at the object. • It can take a long while to pass an object around a large room. • The object might not survive intact.
Handouts: photocopies of written material given to each audience member.	• Much material can fit on the page. • Audience members can write on their copies and keep them.	• Audience members might read the handout rather than listen to the speaker.

Interactive Sample Document:
Designing a Presentation Slide

The following slide is part of a presentation about style manuals. The questions in the margin ask you to think about the discussion of preparing presentation graphics (on pages 573–579). The answers to these questions are available on TechComm Web.

Comment on the information included on this slide.

1. How effective is the contrast between the color of the text and the color of the background?

2. What is the function of the graphic of the key?

3. What information would you add to the footer?

4. What other changes would you make to the design of this slide?

On TechComm Web

To find the answers to these questions, click on Interactive Sample Documents for Ch. 22 on <bedfordstmartins.com/techcomm>.

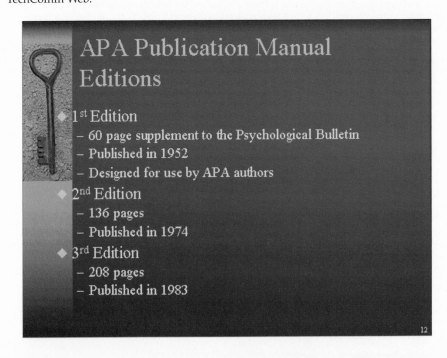

Choosing Effective Language

Delivering an oral presentation is more challenging than writing a document for two reasons:

- Listeners can't go back to listen again to something they didn't understand.

- Because you are speaking live, you must maintain your listeners' attention, even if they are hungry or tired or the room is too hot.

Using language effectively helps you meet these two challenges.

Using Language to Signal Advance Organizers, Summaries, and Transitions   Even if you use graphics effectively, listeners cannot "see" the organization of a presentation as well as readers can. For this reason, use language to alert your listeners to advance organizers, summaries, and transitions.

- *Advance organizers.* An advance organizer is a statement that tells the listener what you are about to say. Use an advance organizer in the introduction to tell your audience your purpose, scope, main points, and organization. In addition, use advance organizers when you introduce main ideas in the body of the presentation. Advance organizers have to be explicit:

  In the next 20 minutes, I'd like to discuss the implications of the new RCRA regulations on the long-range waste-management strategy for Radnor Township. I want to make three major points. First, that . . . Second, that . . . And third, that . . . After the presentation, I'll be happy to answer your questions.

  Notice that the speaker numbers his points. He can use this numbering system throughout the presentation to help listeners follow him.

- *Summaries.* The major summary is in the conclusion, but you might also summarize at strategic points in the body of the presentation. For instance, after a three- to four-minute discussion of a major point, you might summarize it in one sentence before going on to the next major point. Here is a sample summary from a conclusion:

  Let me conclude by summarizing my three main points about the implications of the new RCRA regulations on the long-range waste-management strategy for Radnor Township. The first point: . . . The second point: . . . The third point: . . . I hope this presentation will give you some ideas as you think about the RCRA. If you have any questions, I'd be happy to try to answer them at this time.

- *Transitions.* As you move from one point to the next, signal the transition clearly. Summarize the previous point, then announce that you are moving to the next point:

  It is clear, then, that the federal government has issued regulations without indicating how it expects county governments to comply with them. I'd like to turn now to my second main point: . . .

Using Memorable Language   Effective presentations require memorable language.

Using Memorable Language in Oral Presentations

Draw on these three techniques to help make a lasting impression on your audience.

▶ *Involve the audience.* People are more interested in their own concerns than in yours. Talk to the audience about their problems and their solutions. In the introduction, establish a link between your topic and the audience's interests. For instance, the presentation to the Radnor Township Council about waste management might begin like this:

> Picture yourself on the Radnor Township Council two years from now. After exhaustive hearings, proposals, and feasibility studies, you still don't have a waste-management plan that meets federal regulations. What you do have is a mounting debt: the township is being fined $1,000 per day until you implement an acceptable plan.

▶ *Refer to people, not to abstractions.* People remember specifics; they forget abstractions. To make a point memorable, describe it in human terms:

> What could you do with that $365,000 every year? You could buy more than 200 personal computers; that's a computer for almost every classroom in every elementary school in Radnor Township. You could expand your school-lunch program to feed every needy child in the township. You could extend your after-school programs to cover an additional 3,000 students.

▶ *Use interesting facts, figures, and quotations.* Do your research and find interesting information about your subject. For instance, you might find a brief quotation from an authoritative figure in the field or a famous person not generally associated with the field (for example, Theodore Roosevelt on waste management and the environment).

A note about humor: only a few hundred people in the United States make a good living being funny. Don't plan to tell a joke. If something happens during the presentation that provides an opening for a witty remark, and you are good at making witty remarks, fine. But don't *prepare* to be funny.

Rehearsing the Presentation

Even the most gifted speakers need to rehearse. It is a good idea to set aside enough time to rehearse your speech thoroughly.

Rehearsing an Extemporaneous Presentation   Rehearse your extemporaneous presentation at least three times.

- *First rehearsal.* Don't worry about posture or voice projection. Just compose your presentation aloud with your outline or notes before you. Your goal is to see if the speech makes sense—if you can explain all the points and create effective transitions. If you have trouble, stop and try to figure out the problem. If you need more information, get it. If you need a better transition, create one. You are likely to find that you need to revise the order of your outline or notes. Pick up where you left off and continue the rehearsal, stopping again where necessary to revise. When you have finished, put the outline or notes away and do something else.

- *Second rehearsal.* This time, the presentation should flow more easily. Make any necessary changes to the outline or notes. When you have complete control over the organization and flow, check to see if you are within the time limits.

- *Third rehearsal.* After a satisfactory second rehearsal, try the presentation under more realistic circumstances—if possible, in front of people. The listeners might offer questions or constructive advice about your speaking style. If people aren't available, tape-record or videotape the presentation and then evaluate your own delivery. If you can visit the site of the presentation to get the feel of the room and rehearse there, you will find giving the actual speech a little easier.

Rehearse again until you are satisfied with your presentation; don't try to memorize it.

Rehearsing a Scripted Presentation   Rehearsing a scripted presentation is a combination of revising the text and rehearsing it. As you revise, read the script aloud to hear how it sounds. Once you think the presentation says what you want to say, try reading it into a tape recorder. Revise it until you are satisfied, and then rehearse in front of real people. Do not memorize the presentation. There is no need to: you will have your script in front of you on the podium.

GIVING THE ORAL PRESENTATION

In giving the presentation, you will concentrate on what you have to say. However, you will have three additional concerns.

Calming Your Nerves

Most professional actors admit to being nervous before a performance, so it is no wonder that most technical speakers are nervous. You might well fear that you will forget everything or that no one will be able to hear you. These fears are common. But keep in mind three facts nervousness:

In giving the oral presentation:

Calm your nerves.

Use your voice effectively.

Use your body effectively.

- *You are much more aware of your nervousness than the audience is.* They are farther away from your trembling hands.
- *Nervousness gives you energy and enthusiasm.* Without energy and enthusiasm, your presentation will be flat. If you seem bored and listless, your audience will become bored and listless.
- *After a few minutes, your nervousness will pass.* You will be able to relax and concentrate on the subject.

This advice, however, is unlikely to make you feel much better if you are distracted by nerves as you wait to give your presentation. Experienced speakers suggest a few points to keep in mind when you find yourself getting nervous before a presentation:

- *Realize that you are prepared.* If you have done your homework, prepared speaking notes, and rehearsed the presentation, you'll be fine.
- *Realize that the audience is there to hear you, not to judge you.* Your listeners want to hear what you have to say. They are much less interested in your nervousness than you are.
- *Realize that your audience is made up of individual people who happen to be sitting in the same room.* You'll feel better if you realize that audience members also get nervous before making presentations.

GUIDELINES

Releasing Nervous Energy

Experienced speakers suggest the following strategies for dealing with nervousness before a presentation.

▶ *Walk around.* A brisk walk of a minute or two can calm you by dissipating some of your nervous energy.

▶ *Go off by yourself for a few minutes.* Getting away can help you compose your thoughts and realize that you can handle the nervousness.

▶ *Talk with someone for a few minutes.* For some speakers, distraction works best. Find someone to talk to.

▶ *Take several deep breaths, exhaling slowly.* Doing so will help you control your nerves.

When it is time to begin, don't jump up to the lectern and start speaking quickly. Walk up slowly and arrange your text, outline, or note cards before you. If water is available, take a sip. Look out at the audience for a few seconds before you begin. Begin with "Good morning" (or "Good afternoon," or "Good evening"), and refer to the officers and dignitaries present. If you have not been introduced, introduce yourself. In less formal contexts, just begin your presentation.

So that the audience will listen to you and have confidence in what you say, use your voice and your body to project an attitude of restrained self-confidence. Show interest in your topic and knowledge about your subject.

Using Your Voice Effectively

Inexperienced speakers often have problems with five aspects of vocalizing.

- *Volume.* Because acoustics vary greatly from room to room, you won't know how well your voice will carry until you have heard someone speaking there. In some auditoriums, speakers can use a conversational volume. Other rooms require greater voice projection. These circumstances aside, more people speak too softly. After your first few sentences, ask if the people in the back of the room can hear you. When people speak into microphones, they tend to speak too loudly. Glance at your audience to see if you are having volume problems. The body language of audience members will be clear.

- *Speed.* Nervousness makes people speak quickly. Even if you think you are speaking at the right rate, you might be going a little too fast for some listeners. Although you know your subject well, your listeners are trying to understand new information. For particularly difficult points, slow down for emphasis. After finishing one major point, pause before introducing the next one.

- *Pitch.* In an effort to control their voices, many speakers end up flattening their pitch. The resulting monotone is boring and, for some listeners, distracting. Try to let the pitch of your voice go up or down as it would in a normal conversation.

- *Articulation.* Nervousness can accentuate sloppy pronunciation. If you want to say *environment*, don't say *envirament*. A related problem involves technical words and phrases, especially the important ones. When a speaker uses a phrase over and over, it tends to get clipped and becomes difficult to understand. Unless you articulate carefully, *Scanlon Plan* will end up as *Scanluhplah.*

- *Nonfluencies.* Avoid such meaningless fillers as *you know, like, okay, right, uh,* and *um.* These phrases do not hide the fact that you aren't saying anything. A thoughtful pause is better than an annoying verbal tic.

Using Your Body Effectively

Besides listening to you, the audience will be looking at you. Effective speakers use their body language to help listeners follow the presentation.

GUIDELINES

Facing an Audience

As you give a presentation, keep in mind four guidelines about physical movement.

↓

▶ *Maintain eye contact.* Eye contact helps you see how the audience is receiving the presentation. You will see, for instance, if listeners in the back are having trouble hearing you. For small groups, look at each listener randomly; for larger groups, look at each segment of the audience frequently during your speech. Do not stare at your notes, at the floor, or out the window.

▶ *Use natural gestures.* When people talk, they often gesture with their hands. Most of the time, gestures make the presentation look natural and improve listeners' comprehension. You can supplement your natural gestures by using your arms and hands to signal pauses and to emphasize important points. When referring to graphics, walk to the screen and point to direct the audience's attention. Avoid mannerisms—physical gestures that serve no useful purpose, such as jiggling the coins in your pocket or pacing back and forth. They can quickly distract an audience from your message. Like verbal mannerisms, physical mannerisms are often unconscious. Constructive criticism from friends can help you pinpoint them.

▶ *Don't block the audience's view of the screen.* Stand off to the side of the screen. Use a pointer to indicate key words or images on the screen.

▶ *Control the audience's attention.* People will listen to and look at anything that is interesting. If you hand out photocopies at the start of the presentation, some people will start to read them and stop listening to you. If you leave an image on the screen after you finish talking about it, some people will keep looking at it instead of listening to you. When you want the audience to look at you and listen to you, remove the graphics or turn off the projector.

STRATEGIES FOR INTERCULTURAL COMMUNICATION

Making Oral Presentations to Multicultural Audiences

If your audience includes people of different cultures and native languages, keep the following suggestions in mind:

• *Use graphics effectively to reinforce your points for nonnative speakers.* Try to devise ways to present information using graphics—flowcharts, diagrams, and so forth—to help your listeners understand you. Putting more textual information on graphics will allow your listeners to hear you explain your points and see the accompanying text.

• *Be aware that gestures can have cultural meanings.* As discussed in Chapter 14, hand gestures (such as the thumbs-up or the "okay" gesture) have different—and sometimes insulting—meanings in other cultures. Therefore, it's a good idea to limit the use of these gestures. You can't go wrong with an arms-out, palms-up gesture that projects openness and inclusiveness.

ANSWERING QUESTIONS AFTER
THE PRESENTATION

When you finish a presentation, thank the audience simply and directly: "Thank-you for your attention." Then invite questions. Don't abruptly say "Any questions?" This phrasing suggests that you don't really want any questions. Instead, say something like this: "If you have any questions, I'll be happy to try to answer them now." If invited politely, people will be much more likely to ask; in that way, you will be more likely to communicate your information effectively.

When you respond to questions, you might encounter any of these five situations:

- *You're not sure everyone heard the question.* Ask if people have heard it. If they haven't, repeat or paraphrase it, perhaps as an introduction to your response: "Your question is about the efficiency of these three techniques. . . ." Some speakers always repeat the question, which also gives them an extra moment to think about their answer.

- *You don't understand the question.* Ask for a clarification. After responding, ask if you have answered the question adequately.

- *You don't know the answer to the question.* Tell the truth. No one knows all the answers. If you have some ideas about how to find out the answer—by checking a certain reference source, for example—share them. If the question is obviously important to the person who asked it, you might offer to meet with him or her to discuss ways for you to give a more complete response, perhaps by e-mail.

- *You get a question that you have already answered in the presentation.* Restate the answer politely. Begin your answer with a phrase such as the following: "I'm sorry I didn't make that point clear in my talk. I wanted to explain how. . . ." Never insult the person by pointing out that you already answered it.

- *A belligerent member of the audience rejects your response and insists on restating his or her original point.* Politely offer to discuss the matter further after the session. This way, the person won't bore or annoy the rest of the audience.

If it is appropriate to stay after the session to talk individually with members of the audience, offer to do so. Remember to thank them for their courtesy in listening to you.

ORAL-PRESENTATION EVALUATION FORM

Figure 22.6 is a list of questions that can help you focus your thoughts as you watch and listen to a presentation.

ORAL-PRESENTATION EVALUATION FORM

Speaker:
Topic:
Date:

In the parentheses to the left of each of the following statements, write a number from 1 to 5, with 5 signifying strong agreement and 1 signifying strong disagreement.

Organization and Development

( ) 1. In the introduction, the speaker tried to relate the topic to the audience's concerns.
( ) 2. In the introduction, the speaker explained the main points he or she wanted to make in the presentation.
( ) 3. In the introduction, the speaker explained the organization of the presentation.
( ) 4. Throughout the presentation, I found it easy to understand the organization of the presentation.
( ) 5. Throughout the presentation, the speaker used appropriate and sufficient evidence to clarify the subject.
( ) 6. In the conclusion, the speaker summarized the main points effectively.
( ) 7. In the conclusion, the speaker invited questions politely.
( ) 8. In the conclusion, the speaker answered questions effectively.

Verbal and Physical Presence

( ) 9. The speaker used interesting, clear language to get the points across.
( ) 10. The speaker used clear and distinct enunciation.
( ) 11. The speaker seemed relaxed and poised.
( ) 12. The speaker exhibited no distracting vocal mannerisms.
( ) 13. The speaker exhibited no distracting physical mannerisms.
( ) 14. The speaker made eye contact throughout the presentation.
( ) 15. The speaker seemed to be enthusiastic throughout the presentation.

Use of Graphics

( ) 16. The speaker used graphics in the right places to reinforce and explain the main points.
( ) 17. The speaker used appropriate kinds of graphics.
( ) 18. The speaker used graphics effectively to highlight the organization of the presentation.
( ) 19. The graphics were easy to see.
( ) 20. The graphics were easy to understand.
( ) 21. The graphics looked correct and professional.
( ) 22. The graphics helped me understand the organization of the presentation.
( ) 23. The speaker used the allotted time effectively.

For Group Presentations

( ) 24. The group seemed well rehearsed.
( ) 25. The graphics were edited so that they looked consistent from one group member to the next.
( ) 26. The transitions from one group member to the next were smooth.
( ) 27. Each group member seemed to have done an equal amount of work in preparing and delivering the presentation.

On the other side of this sheet, answer the following two questions.
28. What did you particularly like about this presentation?
29. What would you have done differently if you had been the speaker?

On TechComm Web

To download this form in an electronic format, see Forms for Technical Communication on <bedfordstmartins.com/techcomm>.

■ **Figure 22.6**
Oral-Presentation
Evaluation Form

Reviewing the Process

Analyze the speaking situation.

How much does your audience know about the subject? What are their goals? What is your purpose: to inform or persuade, or both? Budget your time for the presentation.

Prepare an outline or note cards.

As in writing, you need to plan the organization and development of the presentation.

Prepare the presentation graphics.

Effective graphics are visible, legible, simple, clear, and correct. Choose the appropriate technology based on the speaking situation and the resources available to you.

Choose effective language.

Use language to signal advance organizers, summaries, and transitions. Choose memorable language by involving the audience, referring to people, and using interesting facts, figures, and quotations.

Rehearse the presentation.

Rehearse at least three times to make sure you are comfortable with the information. Use the Speaker's Preparation Checklist that follows.

Deliver the presentation.

First, calm your nerves. In the presentation, use your voice effectively. Maintain eye contact and use natural gestures. Don't block the audience's view of the screen. At the end, politely solicit questions and answer them effectively.

Speaker's Preparation Checklist

❏ Did you assess the speaking situation—the audience and purpose of the presentation? (p. 572)

❏ Did you determine how much information you can communicate in your allotted time? (p. 572)

❏ Did you outline your information? (p. 573)

Did you prepare graphics that are

❏ visible? (p. 573)

❏ legible? (p. 575)

❏ simple? (p. 575)

❏ clear? (p. 575)

❏ correct? (p. 575)

❏ In planning your graphics, did you consider your audience's aptitude and experience, the size and layout of the room, and the equipment? (p. 576)

❏ Did you plan your graphics to help the audience understand the organization of your presentation? (p. 576)

❏ Did you choose appropriate media for your graphics? (p. 576)

❏ Did you make sure that the presentation room will have the necessary equipment for the graphics? (p. 576)

❏ Did you choose language to signal advance organizers, summaries, and transitions? (p. 581)

❏ Did you choose language that is vivid and memorable? (p. 582)

❏ Did you rehearse your presentation several times with a tape recorder or a live audience? (p. 583)

Exercises

On TechComm Web

For more exercises, click on Additional Exercises, Projects, and Cases for Ch. 22 on <bedfordstmartins.com/techcomm>.

1. Learn some of the basic functions of a presentation-graphics software program. For instance, modify a template, create your own original design, add footer information to a master slide, insert a graphic onto a slide, and set the animation feature to make each bullet item appear only after a mouse click.

2. Using presentation-graphics software, create a design to be used for the master slide of a computer presentation. Then, for the same information, create a design to be used in a transparency made on a black-and-white photocopier.

Projects

On TechComm Web

For more projects, click on Additional Exercises, Projects, and Cases for Ch. 22 on <bedfordstmartins.com/techcomm>.

3. Prepare a five-minute presentation, including graphics, on one of the topics listed here. For each presentation, your audience consists of the other students in your class, and your purpose is to introduce them to an aspect of your academic field.

   a. Define a key term or concept in your field.

   b. Describe how a particular piece of equipment is used in your field.

   c. Describe how to carry out a procedure common in your field.

   The instructor and the other students will evaluate the presentation by filling out the form in Figure 22.6.

4. **Group Activity**   Prepare a five-minute presentation based either on your proposal for a research-report topic or on your completion report. Your audience consists of the other students in your class, and your purpose is to introduce them to your topic. The instructor and the other students will evaluate the presentation by filling out the form in Figure 22.6. If your instructor wishes, this assignment can be done collaboratively.

On TechComm Web

For more cases, click on Additional Exercises, Projects, and Cases for Ch. 22 on <bedfordstmartins.com /techcomm>.

C A S E
Identifying Resources for Students in Your Major

The career-development office at your college or university is adding a new event to its monthly informational meetings: "Five Best Resources" presentations by students. The purpose of the presentations is to help students learn the best resources to use when preparing for a career in a particular field. For example, a chemical-engineering student will make a presentation on resources for students who are preparing to become chemical engineers. Your technical-communication instructor has agreed to do a 10-minute rehearsal of the presentation in class. Prepare a 10-minute presentation, complete with appropriate graphics, describing the five best resources for students preparing for a career in your field. These resources can include books, journals, organizations, and Web sites.

Appendix: Reference Handbook

PART A: DOCUMENTING SOURCES

On TechComm Web

For more help with evaluating online sources, click on Tutorials on <bedfordstmartins.com/techcomm>.

Documentation identifies the sources of the ideas and the quotations in your document. Integrated throughout your document, documentation consists of citations in the text and a reference list (or list of works cited) at the back of your document. Documentation serves three basic functions:

- *To help you acknowledge your debt to your sources.* Complete and accurate documentation is a professional obligation, a matter of ethics. Failure to document a source, whether intentional or unintentional, is plagiarism. At most colleges and universities, plagiarism means automatic failure of the course and, in some instances, suspension or expulsion. In many companies, it is grounds for immediate dismissal.
- *To help you establish credibility.* Effective documentation helps you place your document within the general context of continuing research and to define it as a responsible contribution to knowledge in the field. Knowing how to use existing research is one mark of a professional.
- *To help your readers find your source in case they want to read more about a particular subject.*

In This Book

For more about quoting and paraphrasing sources, see Ch. 7, pp. 139 and 141.

Three kinds of material should always be documented:

- *Any quotation from a written source or an interview, even if it is only a few words.*
- *A paraphrased idea, concept, or opinion gathered from your reading.* There is one exception. An idea or concept so well known that it has become general knowledge, such as Einstein's theory of relativity, needs no citation. If you are unsure about whether an item is general knowledge, document it, just to be safe.

In This Book

For more about using graphics from other sources, see Ch. 14, p. 325.

- *Any graphic from a written or electronic source.* Cite the source for a graphic next to the graphic or in the reference list. For an online source, be sure to include a retrieval statement in the bibliographic entry. If you are publishing your work, you must also request permission to use any graphic protected by copyright.

Just as organizations have their own preferences for formatting and punctuation, many organizations also have their own documentation style. The documentation systems included in this section of the appendix are based on the following style manuals:

- *Publication Manual of the American Psychological Association*, 5th ed. (Washington, DC: APA, 2001). This system, often referred to as APA, is used widely in the social sciences.
- *Scientific Style and Format: The CBE Manual for Authors, Editors, and Publishers*, 6th ed. (New York: Cambridge University Press, 1994). This sys-

tem, known as CBE, is from the Council of Science Editors (formerly the Council of Biology Editors) and is widely used in the natural sciences.

- *MLA Handbook for Writers of Research Papers*, 6th ed. (New York: MLA, 2003). This system, from the Modern Language Association, is used widely in the humanities.

Other organizations use other published style guides, such as the *U.S. Government Printing Office Style Manual*, the *American Chemical Society's Handbook for Authors*, or the *Chicago Manual of Style*. Find out what your organization's style is and abide by it. And check with your instructor to see which documentation system to use in the documents you write for class.

On TechComm Web

For advice about documentation styles, click on the link to Diana Hacker's Research and Documentation Online on <bedfordstmartins .com/techcomm>.

APA STYLE

APA style consists of two elements: the citation in the text and the references at the end of the document.

APA Textual Citations

In APA style, a textual citation typically includes the name of the source's author and the date of its publication. Textual citations will vary depending on the type of information cited, the number of authors, and the context of the citation. The following models illustrate a variety of common textual citations; for additional examples, consult the *Publication Manual of the American Psychological Association*.

APA Style for Textual Citations

1. Summarized or Paraphrased Material
2. Quoted Material or Specific Fact
3. Source with Multiple Authors
4. Source Issued by an Organization
5. Source with an Unknown Author

6. Multiple Sources in One Citation
7. Multiple Authors with the Same Last Name
8. Personal Communication
9. Electronic Document

---

1. Summarized or Paraphrased Material   For material or ideas that you have summarized or paraphrased, include the author's name and publication date in parentheses immediately following the borrowed information.

> This phenomenon was identified more than fifty years ago (Wilkinson, 1948).

If your sentence already includes the source's name, do not repeat it in the parenthetical notation.

> Wilkinson (1948) identified this phenomenon more than fifty years ago.

2. Quoted Material or Specific Fact   If the reference is to a specific fact, idea, or quotation, add the page number(s) of the source to your citation.

> This phenomenon was identified more than fifty years ago (Wilkinson, 1948, p. 36).

> Wilkinson (1948) identified this phenomenon more than fifty years ago (p. 36).

3. Source with Multiple Authors   For a source written by two authors, cite both names. Use an ampersand (&) in the citation itself, but use the word "and" in regular text.

> (Allman & Jones, 2002)

> As Allman and Jones (2002) suggested, . . .

For a source written by three, four, or five authors, include all the names the first time you cite the reference; after that, include only the last name of the first author followed by "et al."

> FOR THE FIRST REFERENCE:
>
> Bradley, Edmunds, and Soto (2001) argued . . .

> FOR SUBSEQUENT REFERENCES:
>
> Bradley et al. (2001) found . . .

For a source written by six or more authors, use only the first author's name followed by "et al."

> (Smith et al., 1997)

4. Source Issued by an Organization   If the author is an organization rather than a person, use the name of the organization.

> The causes of narcolepsy are discussed in a recent booklet (Association of Sleep Disorders, 2001).

> In a recent booklet, the Association of Sleep Disorders (2001) discusses the causes of narcolepsy.

If the organization name has a common abbreviation, you may include it in the first citation and use it in any subsequent citations.

> (International Business Machines [IBM], 2002)

5. Source with an Unknown Author   If the source does not identify an author, use a shortened version of the title in your parenthetical citation.

> This trend has been evident in American society since the beginning of the twentieth century ("Modernism," 2002).

If the author is identified as anonymous—a rare occurrence—treat "Anonymous" as a real name.

> (Anonymous, 2003)

6. Multiple Sources in One Citation   When you refer to two sources or more in one citation, present the sources in alphabetical order, separated by a semicolon.

> This phenomenon was identified more than fifty years ago (Betts, 1949; Wilkinson, 1948).

7. Multiple Authors with the Same Last Name   Use first initials if two or more sources have authors with the same last name.

> This phenomenon was identified more than fifty years ago (B. Wilkinson, 1948).

8. Personal Communication   Include the words "personal communication" and the date of the communication when citing personal interviews, phone calls, and e-mail.

> C. Coggins (personal communication, June 6, 2003) argued that . . .

9. Electronic Document   Cite the author and date of the source as you would for other kinds of documents. If the author is unknown, give a shortened version of the title of the document in your parenthetical citation. If the date is unknown, use "n.d." for "no date."

> Resnick (2000) discusses usability testing and the Palm Beach County election ballots.

If the document is posted as a PDF file, include a page number in the citation. If page numbers are not available, but the source contains paragraph numbers, give the paragraph number: (Tong, 2001, ¶ 4) or (Tong, 2001, para. 4). If no paragraph or page numbers are available and the source has headings, cite the appropriate heading and paragraph.

> Vidoli (2000) warns against using "jargon because it may be misinterpreted" (Writing Naturally section, para. 2).

The APA Reference List

A reference list provides the information your readers will need in order to find each source you have cited in the text. Note that the reference list includes only those sources that you actually used in researching and preparing your document; it should not include background reading. Following are some guidelines for an APA-style reference list.

On TechComm Web

For help with formatting an APA reference list, click on the link to Diana Hacker's Research and Documentation Online on <bedfordstmartins.com/techcomm>.

- *Arranging Entries.* The individual entries in the reference list are arranged alphabetically by author's last name. Two or more works by the same author are arranged by date, earliest to latest; two or more works by the same author in the same year should be listed alphabetically by title, and should also include a lowercase letter after the date: Smith 1999a, Smith

1999b, etc. Works by an organization are alphabetized by the first significant word in the name of the organization.

- *Book Titles.* Titles of books should be italicized. The first word of the book's title and subtitle are capitalized, but all other words (except for proper nouns) should be lowercase.

- *Publication Information.* Give the publisher's full name or consult your style guide for the preferred abbreviation. Include both the publisher's city and state or country, unless the city is well known (such as New York, Boston, or London).

- *Periodical Titles.* Titles of periodicals should be italicized, and all major words should be capitalized.

- *Article Titles.* Titles of articles should not be italicized or placed in quotation marks. The first word of the article's title and subtitle are capitalized, but all other words (except for proper nouns) should be lowercase.

- *Electronic Sources.* Include as much information as you can about electronic sources, such as date of publication, identifying numbers, and retrieval information. Also, be sure to record the date you retrieved the information, because electronic information changes frequently.

- *Indenting.* APA style recommends using a hanging indent, with the second and subsequent lines of each entry indented 5 to 7 spaces:

Chapman, D. L. (1995, June 12). Detroit makes a big comeback. *Motorist's*
    Metronome, 12, 17–26.`

Paragraph indents, in which the first line of each entry is indented 5 to 7 spaces, may be preferred by your instructor:

    Chapman, D. L. (1995, June 12). Detroit makes a big comeback. *Motorist's*
Metronome, 12, 17–26.

- *Spacing.* Double space the entire reference list; do not add extra spacing between entries.

- *Page Numbers.* When citing a range of page numbers for articles, always give the complete numbers (for example, 121–124, not 121–24). If an article continues on subsequent pages interrupted by other articles or advertisements, use a comma to separate the page numbers. Use the abbreviation "p." or "pp." only with articles in newspapers, chapters in edited books, and articles from proceedings.

- *Dates.* For a reference list, follow this format: year, month, day (2003, October 31).

The following are models of reference list entries for a variety of sources. For further examples of APA-style citations, consult the *Publication Manual of the American Psychological Association.*

On TechComm Web

For more information on electronic reference formats recommended by the American Psychological Association, click on the Links Library for the Appendix on <bedfordstmartins.com/techcomm>.

APA Style for Reference List Entries

BOOKS

1. Book by One Author
2. Book by Multiple Authors
3. Multiple Books by Same Author
4. Book Issued by an Organization
5. Book by an Unknown Author
6. Edited Book
7. Book in Edition Other Than First
8. Work in an Anthology
9. Multivolume Work
10. Encyclopedia or Dictionary Entry

PERIODICALS

11. Journal Article
12. Magazine Article
13. Newspaper Article
14. Unsigned Article
15. Review

ELECTRONIC SOURCES

16. Nonperiodical Web Document
17. Chapter or Section of a Nonperiodical Web Document
18. Article in an Online Periodical
19. Article from a Database
20. Software or Software Manual
21. E-mail Message
22. Online Posting

OTHER SOURCES

23. Government Document
24. Article from Conference Proceedings
25. Dissertation Abstract
26. Brochure or Pamphlet
27. Report
28. Personal Interview
29. Television Program
30. Film or Video
31. Unpublished Data

1. Book by One Author   Begin with the author's last name, followed by the first initial or initials. If the author has two first initials, include a space between the initials. Place the year of publication in parentheses, followed by a period. Give the title of the book, followed by the location and name of the publisher; end the citation with a period.

> Cunningham, W. S. (1980). *Crisis at Three Mile Island: The aftermath of a near melt-down.* New York: Madison.

2. Book by Multiple Authors   To cite two or more authors, use the ampersand (&) instead of "and" between their names. Use a comma to separate the authors' names.

> Bingham, C., & Withers, S. (1999). *Neural networks and fuzzy logic.* New York: IEEE.

To cite more than six authors, list only the first six followed by "et al."

3. Multiple Books by Same Author List the entries by the author's name, and then by date, the earliest date first.

> Brown, J. (1991). *Modern manufacturing processes.* New York: Industrial Press.
>
> Brown, J. (1998). *Advanced machining technology handbook.* New York: McGraw-Hill Professional.

If you use multiple works by the same author written in the same year, list the books alphabetically by title and include "a," "b," and so forth after the year—both in your reference list and in your parenthetical citations.

> Hacker, D. (2000a). *A pocket style manual* (3rd ed.). Boston: Bedford/St. Martin's.
>
> Hacker, D. (2000b). *Rules for writers* (4th ed.). Boston: Bedford/St. Martin's.

4. Book Issued by an Organization Use the full name of the organization in place of an author's name. If the organization is also the publisher, use the word "Author" in place of the publisher's name.

> American Psychological Association. (2001). *Publication manual of the American Psychological Association* (5th ed.). Washington, DC: Author.

5. Book by an Unknown Author If the author of the book is unknown, begin with the title in italics.

> *Reflections on the future of marketing: Practice and education.* (1997). Cambridge, MA: Marketing Science Institute.

6. Edited Book Place the abbreviation "Ed." in parentheses after the name. For sources with more than one editor, use the abbreviation "Eds."

> McDonald, R. (Ed.). (2002). *Disasters and their effects on buildings: Recovery and prevention.* Burlington, MA: Architectural Press.

7. Book in Edition Other Than First Include the edition number in parentheses following the title.

> Schonberg, N. (1997). *Solid state physics* (3rd ed.). London: Paragon.

8. Work in an Anthology Present the book editor's initials and name—unlike those of the article authors—in normal order. The pages on which the article appears are given after the book title.

> Falletta, S. V., & Combs, W. (2001). Surveys as a tool for organization development and change. In J. Waclawski & A. H. Church (Eds.), *Organization development: A data-driven approach to organizational change* (pp. 78–102). San Francisco: Jossey-Bass.

9. Multivolume Work   Include the number of volumes after the title.

> Carmichael, D. R., Persohn, C. A., & Reed, M. L. (1998). *Guide to audits of employee bene-*
> *fit plans* (Vols. 1–3). Fort Worth, TX: Practitioners Publishing Company.

10. Encyclopedia or Dictionary Entry   Begin with the title of the entry if it has no author.

> Machine model organization. (2000). In *Dictionary of international business terms* (2nd ed.).
> Hauppauge, NY: Barron's.

11. Journal Article   Follow the author's name and date with the article title; then give the journal title. If the journal issue is identified by a word such as "Spring," include that word in the date. Include the volume number, set off by commas, after the journal name. Volume numbers should be italicized, but issue and page numbers should not.

> Yaworski, J. (2002, Spring). How to build a web site in six easy steps. *Journal of*
> *College Reading and Learning, 32*, 148–153.

In citing an article from a journal paginated by issue, follow the volume number immediately with the issue number (not italicized) in parentheses.

> Tran, X. (1999). Report: Breeding pandas in captivity. *Nature, 14*(4), 10–17.

12. Magazine Article   Include the month and the volume number, if there is one, after the magazine title.

> Garfinkel, S. (2002, September). One face in 6 billion. *Discover, 23*, 17–18.

13. Newspaper Article   Include the specific publication date following the year.

> Eberstadt, A. (1995, July 31). Carpal tunnel syndrome. *Morristown Mirror and Telegraph*, p. B3.

14. Unsigned Article   If the author of a periodical article is not indicated, begin with the title. In the reference list, alphabetize the work by title, ignoring the initial articles "the," "a," and "an."

> The state of the art in microcomputers. (2000, Fall). *Newscene, 56*, 406–421.

15. Review   Cite a review in a periodical the same as an article in a periodical. After the title of the review, include in brackets the type of medium and the title of the item being reviewed.

> Morrow, L. (2002, April 29). Part devil, part angel [Review of the book *Master of the*
> *Senate: The years of Lyndon Johnson*]. *Time, 159*, 70–71.

16. Nonperiodical Web Document To cite a nonperiodical Web document, provide as much of the following information as possible: author's name, date of publication (use "n.d." if there is no date), title of the document (in italics), retrieval date, and URL for the document.

> Bly, R. W. (n.d.). *The fundamentals of persuasive writing*. Retrieved December 17, 2002, from http://bly.com/Pages/documents/TFOPW.html

If the author of a document is not identified, begin the reference with the title of the document.

> *Judgment against spammer*. (1997, November 11). Retrieved November 6, 2001, from http://www.matrix.net/company/news/19971111_spam.html

If the document is from a university program's Web site, identify the host institution and program or department, followed by a colon and the URL for the document.

> Hooser, S. (1997, October 2). *Tips for speakers*. Retrieved September 12, 2001, from New Mexico State University, Techprof Web site: http://www.nmsu.edu/techprof/ backgrnd/sueback.html

17. Chapter or Section of a Nonperiodical Web Document For a chapter or section of a Web document, give the author, year of publication, and chapter or section title, followed by "In" and the document title. Identify the chapter or section, instead of page numbers, in parentheses, followed by a retrieval date and URL for the chapter or section.

> Ware, W. H. (1998). Key elements of a solution approach. In *The cyber-posture of the national information infrastructure* (chap. 4). Retrieved August 27, 2001, from http://www.rand.org/publications/MR/MR976/mr976.html#chap4

18. Article in an Online Periodical To cite online articles, provide the same information you would for print articles. (See items 11–15 on page 599.) If an identical version of the article also appears in print, do not include a URL; instead, follow the title of the article with the words "Electronic version" in brackets.

> Quesenbery, W. (2001, May). On beyond help: Meeting user needs for useful online information [Electronic version]. *Technical Communication, 48*(2), 182–188.

If there is no print version, or if you are citing an online article that is different from the print version (for example, the format is different or the online version contains additional materials, such as animations), include the date you retrieved the article and its URL.

> Miller, D. (2001, February). Moving from documentation to usability: The Dangerfield effect. *The Willamett Galley, 4*(1). Retrieved August 28, 2001, from http://www .stcwvc.org/galley/jan01_newsletter/Moving.htm

If you are citing an article you retrieved from a searchable Web site, such as a newspaper's site, give the URL for the site rather than for the specific source.

> Bredemeier, K. (2001, June 18). Ethical dilemmas call for careful approaches. *The Washington Post.* Retrieved November 7, 2001, from http://www .washingtonpost.com

19. Article from a Database   To cite an article from an electronic database, provide the publication information followed by the access date, the name of the database, and the item number, if any.

> Johanek, J. (2000, January). Readability: Rule one in magazine design. *Folio: The Magazine for Magazine Management, 29*(1), 154. Retrieved August 28, 2001, from Business Index ASAP database (A58836541).

20. Software or Software Manual   Include the words "Computer software" in brackets after the title.

> Block, K. (1999). Planner (Release 3.1) [Computer software]. New York: Global Software.

If the software has no author, begin the entry with the name of the program. Use standard capitalization; do not italicize or underline the program title.

> Tools for Drafting (Version 2.3) [Computer software]. (1999). San Jose, CA: Software International.

If you are citing the manual, include the words "Software manual" in the brackets.

21. E-mail Message   E-mail messages are not cited in the reference list. Instead they should be cited in the text as personal communications. (See item 8 on page 595.)

22. Online Posting   If an online posting is not archived and therefore is not retrievable, cite it as a personal communication and do not include it in the reference list. If the posting can be retrieved from an archive, provide the author's name or screen name, the exact date of the posting, the title or subject line, and any identifier in brackets; finish with "Message posted to," followed by the address.

> Graham, T. (2001, August 27). Simple font size question [Msg 7815]. Message posted to http://groups.yahoo.com/group/wwp-users/message/7815

23. Government Document   For most government agencies, use the abbreviation "U.S." instead of spelling out "United States." Include identifying document numbers after the publication title.

U.S. Department of Energy. (2002, May 1). *Wind power today: Wind energy program highlights 2001* (Technical Publication 102002-1556). Washington, DC: U.S. Government Printing Office.

24. Article from Conference Proceedings After the proceedings title, give the page numbers on which the article appears.

Carlson, C. T. (1995). Advanced organizers in manuals. In K. Rainey (Ed.), *Proceedings of the 45th International Technical Communication Conference* (pp. RT56–58). Fairfax, VA: Society for Technical Communication.

25. Dissertation Abstract If you use *Dissertation Abstracts International* (*DAI*), include the *DAI* volume, issue, and page number. If you use UMI's digital dissertation services, include the UMI number in parentheses at the end.

Knievel, M. S. (2002). Rethinking the "humanistic": Technical communication and computers and writing as sites of change in English studies. (Doctoral dissertation, Texas Tech University, 2002). *Dissertation Abstracts International, 63* (06), 2229. (UMI No. 3056071)

26. Brochure or Pamphlet After the title of the document, include the word "brochure" or "pamphlet" in brackets.

U.S. Environmental Protection Agency. (1998). *Small engine standards: Answers to commonly asked questions from dealer and distributors* [Brochure]. Washington, DC: National Center for Environmental Publications and Information.

27. Report Include identifying numbers after the name of the technical report. After the location and name of the publisher, write the name of the service used to locate the item.

Birnest, A. J., & Hill, G. (1996). *Early identification of children with ATD* (Report No. 43-8759). State College, PA: Pennsylvania State University College of Education. (ERIC Document No. ED186389)

28. Personal Interview Interviews you conduct, whether in person or over the telephone, are considered personal communications and therefore are not included in the reference list. You should cite them in your parenthetical references in the text. (See item 8 on page 595.)

29. Television Program Start with the executive producer and the program aired. Include the words "Television broadcast" or "Television series" in brackets after the program title.

Hewitt, D. (Executive Producer). (2002, November 10). *60 minutes* [Television broadcast]. New York: CBS News.

For a single episode in a series, start with the writer and director of the episode. Include the words "Television series episode" in brackets followed by information about the series.

> Cort, J. (Writer), & Pannone, G., & Visalberghi, M. (Directors). (2002). Sinking city of
> Venice [Television series episode]. In P. S. Aspell (Executive Producer), *Nova.*
> Boston: WGBH.

30. Film or Video   Give the names of the primary contributors, such as the producer and director, and follow the film's title with the words "Motion picture" in brackets. List the country in which the film was produced and the studio's name. If the film was not widely distributed, give the distributor's address in parentheses.

> Cataldo, M. (Producer), & Massingham, G. (Director). (2000). *Technical rescue: Aware-*
> *ness* [Motion picture]. United States: Emergency Film Group. (Available from
> Emergency Film Group, 140 Cooke Street, Edgartown, MA 02539)

31. Unpublished Data   Include a description of the data in brackets.

> Dailey, J. A. (2003). [Operational statistics for Hornell Municipal Airport]. Unpublished
> raw data.

Sample APA Reference List

The following is a sample reference list using the APA citation system.

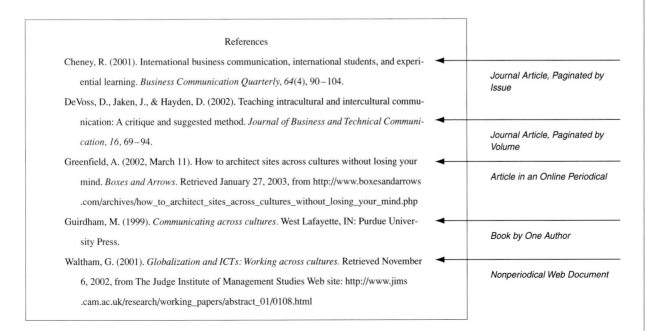

References

Cheney, R. (2001). International business communication, international students, and experi-
    ential learning. *Business Communication Quarterly, 64*(4), 90–104.   *Journal Article, Paginated by Issue*

DeVoss, D., Jaken, J., & Hayden, D. (2002). Teaching intracultural and intercultural commu-
    nication: A critique and suggested method. *Journal of Business and Technical Communi-*
    cation, 16, 69–94.   *Journal Article, Paginated by Volume*

Greenfield, A. (2002, March 11). How to architect sites across cultures without losing your
    mind. *Boxes and Arrows.* Retrieved January 27, 2003, from http://www.boxesandarrows
    .com/archives/how_to_architect_sites_across_cultures_without_losing_your_mind.php   *Article in an Online Periodical*

Guirdham, M. (1999). *Communicating across cultures.* West Lafayette, IN: Purdue Univer-
    sity Press.   *Book by One Author*

Waltham, G. (2001). *Globalization and ICTs: Working across cultures.* Retrieved November
    6, 2002, from The Judge Institute of Management Studies Web site: http://www.jims
    .cam.ac.uk/research/working_papers/abstract_01/0108.html   *Nonperiodical Web Document*

CBE STYLE

CBE style consists of two elements: the citation in the text and the list of references at the end of the document.

CBE Textual Citations

For CBE-style textual citations, you may use either the *citation-sequence system* or the *name-year system*. Find out which method your instructor or organization prefers.

- *The Citation-Sequence System.* In this method, superscript or parenthetical numbers are inserted into the text to indicate borrowed material.

  . . . travels at the speed of light[1], but still others contend that gravity is responsible for the phenomenon[2–4].

  or

  . . . travels at the speed of light (1), but still others contend that gravity is responsible for the phenomenon (2–4).

  Later textual references to the same sources repeat the numbers already used.

  . . . as experiments have shown[23]. If the velocity theory[1,6] is to be taken . . .

  The list of references at the end of the document includes each of the cited sources in numerical order.

- *The Name-Year System.* In this method, the author's last name(s) and year of publication are mentioned either in the text or in a parenthetical citation immediately following the borrowed material.

  . . . travels at the speed of light (Posdevna 1999), but still others contend that gravity is responsible for the phenomenon (Walters 1984; Chang 1999; Rivera 2000).

  . . . as experiments have shown (Rao and Leschley 1998). If Posdevna's velocity theory (1999) is to be taken . . .

  . . . the most recent study on this topic was inconclusive (Matthews and others 2000).

  The list of references at the end of the document lists each of the cited sources alphabetically by author's last name.

The CBE Reference List

On TechComm Web

For help with formatting a CBE reference list, click on the link to Diana Hacker's Research and Documentation Online on <bedfordstmartins.com/techcomm>.

Whether you use the citation-sequence system or the number-year system in the body of your paper, you will also need to prepare a list of references at the end. The following guidelines will help you prepare a CBE-style reference list.

- *Arranging Entries: Citation-Sequence System.* The entries are arranged in numerical order, each entry having a number that corresponds to a number in the text of the paper. Sources are not repeated in the list of references, even if one is referred to many times in the text.

- *Arranging Entries: The Name-Year System.* The individual entries in the reference list are arranged alphabetically by the author's last name. Two or more works by the same author are arranged by date, earliest to latest; two or more works by the same author in the same year have lowercase letters added: Smith 1999a, Smith 1999b, etc. Works by an organization are alphabetized by the first significant word in the name of the organization.

- *Book Titles.* Book titles should not be underlined, italicized, or placed in quotation marks. The first word of the book's title is capitalized, but all other words (except proper nouns) should be lowercase.

- *Publication Information.* Give the publisher's full name or consult your style guide for the preferred abbreviation. Give the publisher's city, and include the state or country in parentheses, unless the city is well known (such as New York, Boston, or London).

- *Periodical Titles.* Titles of periodicals should be abbreviated according to CBE style. The abbreviated titles should be capitalized, but not underlined, italicized, or placed in quotations.

- *Article Titles.* Titles of articles should not be underlined, italicized, or placed in quotations. The first word of the article title is capitalized, but all other words (except proper nouns) should be lowercase.

- *Electronic Sources.* Include as much information about electronic sources as you can, such as date of publication, identification numbers, and retrieval information. Also, be sure to record the date you retrieved the information, because electronic information changes frequently.

- *Spacing.* Double space the entire reference list and leave no extra spacing between entries.

- *Page Numbers.* Give the total number of pages for a book entry, followed by the abbreviation "p" with no period (for example, 298 p). If you are giving a range of pages for specific articles in books and periodicals, use the abbreviation "p" and the last digit of the second number, but only if the previous digits are identical (for example, p 151–3, not 151–153).

- *Dates.* Follow this format: year, month, day, with no periods or commas (2000 Oct 31). Use only the first three letters of each month.

- *Additional References.* A reference list includes only the sources you actually cite in your document. You may include other sources you used in researching and preparing your document (but didn't cite) in a separate alphabetical list entitled "Additional References."

The models in this section show CBE's citation-sequence system. In the name-year system, the reference list would be alphabetized rather than numbered, and the publication year would immediately follow the name of the author(s). In addition, the list would follow the hanging indent style, as shown here.

> Cunningham WS. 1980. Crisis at Three Mile Island: the aftermath of a near meltdown. New York: Madison; 342 p.

For further examples of both the citation-sequence system and the number-year system, consult the CBE style manual, *Scientific Style and Format*. The documentation models for online sources in this section are based on recommendations in *Online!* (Harnack & Kleppinger, 2000).

CBE Style for Reference List Entries

1. Book by One Author	10. Unsigned Article
2. Book by Multiple Authors	11. Web Site
3. Book Issued by an Organization	12. Online Book
4. Book in Edition Other Than First	13. Online Article
5. Journal Article	14. Online Abstract
6. Magazine Article	15. E-mail Message
7. Newspaper Article	16. Online Posting
8. Article Included in a Book	17. Synchronous Communication
9. Article from a Volume of Proceedings	

---

1. Book by One Author   Include the author's last name and initials (not separated by a comma), followed by the book title, the location and name of the publisher, the year of publication, and the number of pages in the book.

> [1]Cunningham WS. Crisis at Three Mile Island: the aftermath of a near meltdown. New York: Madison; 1980. 342 p.

2. Book by Multiple Authors   List all names in reverse order. Do not use the word "and" between names.

> [2]Bingham C, Withers S. Neural networks and fuzzy logic. New York: IEEE; 1999. 276 p.

3. Book Issued by an Organization   The organization takes the position of the author.

> [3]National Commission on Corrections. The future of incarceration. Publication 11346-53. St. Louis (MO): Liberty; 1998. 112 p.

In the name-year system, an abbreviated form of the organization name may be used in both the text and the reference list. The entry should be alphabetized according to the abbreviation, not the full name of the organization.

> [NCC] National Commission on Corrections. 1998. The future of incarceration. Publication 11346-53. St. Louis (MO): Liberty; 112 p.

4. Book in Edition Other Than First   The edition number follows the title of the book.

> [4]Schonberg N. Solid state physics. 3rd ed. London: Paragon; 1997. 354 p.

5. Journal Article   List the author's name, the article title, and the abbreviated journal title followed by the year, month, volume number, and page number(s). If the journal is paginated continuously by volume, include only the volume number after the year.

> [6]Hastings W. The space shuttle debate. Mod Inq 2003;13:311–8.

If the journal paginates each issue separately, include the issue number in parentheses after the volume number.

> [7]Juneja G. Asynchronous transmission techniques. Video Q 1994;6(2):11–9.

6. Magazine Article   List the author's name, the article title, and the abbreviated magazine title, followed by the issue date and page number(s).

> [8]Schwartz El. How you'll pay. Technology Rev 2002 Dec;105(10):50–7.

7. Newspaper Article   List the author's name, the article title, and the newspaper name, followed by the issue date and section, page, and column number(s). If the newspaper does not use section numbers, use a colon between the date and the page number.

> [9]Felder M. Smokeless tobacco: new danger signs. New York Post 1995 May 4; Sect A:13(col 2).

8. Article Included in a Book   Give the author and title of the article first, followed by the word "In" with a colon and the book editor and title. Then give the publication information for the book and the page numbers on which the article appears.

> [10]Hubbell JA. Matrix effects. In: Lanza RP, Langer R, Vacanti JP, editors. Principles of tissue engineering. 2nd ed. San Diego: Academic Pr; 2000. p 237–50.

9. Article from a Volume of Proceedings   List the author's name, the article title, and the word "In" followed by the proceedings editor(s) and title, the date and place of the conference, and publication information, including any identifying numbers. Because conference titles are proper nouns, they should be capitalized.

> [11]Carlson CT. Advanced organizers in manuals. In: Rainey K, editor. Proceedings of the 45th International Technical Communication Conference; 1995 Sep 23–26; Boston. Fairfax (VA): Society for Technical Communication; 1995. p RT56–8.

10. Unsigned Article   If the author of an article is not indicated, insert the word "Anonymous" in brackets.

> [12][Anonymous]. The state of the art in microcomputers. Newscene 2003;56:406–21.

11. Web Site   Begin with the author's name and date of publication. Next give the title of the document (if applicable) and the name of the site. Also provide the URL in angle brackets and your access date.

> [13]Hendl KB. 2000 Jan 1. Internet resources for nursing students. The nursing home page. <http://www.carney.edu/nursing/index.html>. Accessed 2002 May 10.

12. Online Book   Begin by giving the author's name and original publication year, followed by the book's title. Also provide the URL in angle brackets. End with the date of access.

> [14]Rawlins, GJE. 1997. Moths to the flame. <http://mitpress.mit.edu/e-books/Moths/>. Accessed 2002 Feb 10.

13. Online Article   Begin by giving the author's name, date of publication, article title, and abbreviated title of the periodical. Then give any volume, issue, and page numbers. Include the URL in angle brackets and end with the date of access.

> [15]Webster L. 1999. New hope for Alzheimer's sufferers. Ann Neur Online 13(2). <http://www.annals.com/neurology/issues.99spr>. Accessed 2002 May 27.

14. Online Abstract   Include "abstract" in square brackets following the title.

> [16]Kaufman L, Kaufman JH. 2000 Jan 4. Explaining the moon illusion [abstract]. In Proc Natl Acad Sci 97(1):500–5. <http://www.pnas.org/cgi/content/abstract/97/1/500>. Accessed 2002 Feb 8.

15. E-mail Message   List the author's name and the date of the message, the subject line (if any), the type of communication, and the date the e-mail was accessed.

> [17]Nelworth KC. 2002 May 7. Flat-panel displays. [Personal e-mail]. Accessed 2002
> May 8.

16. Online Posting   Give the author's name, date of message, subject line (if any), discussion group or newsgroup address, and date of access.

> [18]Rajiv CV. 1998 May 25. Portable document formats. <techwr-l@listserv
> .okstate.edu>. Accessed 1998 Jun 10.

17. Synchronous Communication   To cite a synchronous discussion from a MOO, a MUD, or an IRC, give the name of the speaker (if known) or the name of the site. Then provide the date and title of the discussion, the type of communication, the URL (in angle brackets) or command line instructions, and the date of access.

> [19]Prisley L. 1997 Oct 5. Seminar discussion on FTP. [Group discussion]. telnet
> moo.ku.edu/port=9999. Accessed 1997 Nov 19.

Sample CBE Reference List

Following is a sample list of references using the CBE citation-sequence system.

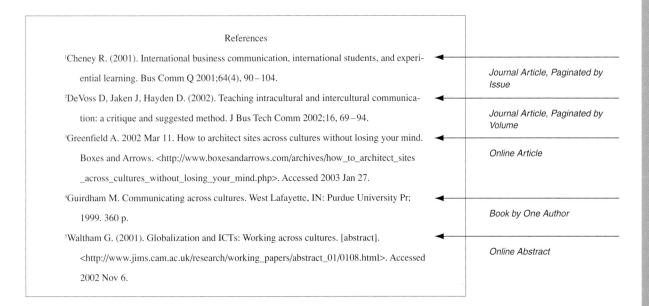

References

[1]Cheney R. (2001). International business communication, international students, and experiential learning. Bus Comm Q 2001;64(4), 90–104.

[2]DeVoss D, Jaken J, Hayden D. (2002). Teaching intracultural and intercultural communication: a critique and suggested method. J Bus Tech Comm 2002;16, 69–94.

[3]Greenfield A. 2002 Mar 11. How to architect sites across cultures without losing your mind.
Boxes and Arrows. <http://www.boxesandarrows.com/archives/how_to_architect_sites
_across_cultures_without_losing_your_mind.php>. Accessed 2003 Jan 27.

[4]Guirdham M. Communicating across cultures. West Lafayette, IN: Purdue University Pr;
1999. 360 p.

[5]Waltham G. (2001). Globalization and ICTs: Working across cultures. [abstract].
<http://www.jims.cam.ac.uk/research/working_papers/abstract_01/0108.html>. Accessed
2002 Nov 6.

Journal Article, Paginated by Issue

Journal Article, Paginated by Volume

Online Article

Book by One Author

Online Abstract

MLA STYLE

MLA style consists of two elements: the citation in the text and the list of works cited at the end of the document.

MLA Textual Citations

In MLA style, the textual citation typically includes the name of the source's author and the number of the page being referred to. Textual citations will vary according to the type of information cited, the authors' names, and the context of the citation. The following models illustrate a variety of common textual citations; for additional examples, consult the *MLA Handbook for Writers of Research Papers*.

MLA Style for Textual Citations

1. Citing Specific Pages
2. Citing Entire Works
3. Multiple Sources by Same Author
4. Source with Multiple Authors
5. Source Quoted Within Another Source
6. Source Issued by an Organization
7. Source with Unknown Author
8. Multiple Sources in One Citation
9. Multiple Authors with Same Last Name
10. Multivolume Work
11. Encyclopedia or Dictionary Entry
12. Electronic Sources

---

1. Citing Specific Pages Immediately following the borrowed material, include a parenthetical reference with the author's name and the page number(s) being referred to. Do not use a comma between the name and the page number, and do not use the abbreviation "p." or "pp."

> This phenomenon was identified more than fifty years ago (Wilkinson 134).

If your sentence already includes the author's name, include only the page number in the parenthetical notation.

> Wilkinson identified this phenomenon more than fifty years ago (134).

2. Citing Entire Works If you are referring to the whole source, not to a particular page or pages, use only the author's name.

> This phenomenon was identified more than fifty years ago (Wilkinson).
> Wilkinson identified this phenomenon more than fifty years ago.

3. Multiple Sources by Same Author   If you cite two or more sources by the same author, either include the full source title in the text or add a shortened title after the author's name in the parenthetical citation to prevent confusion.

> Wilkinson identified this phenomenon more than fifty years ago in his book *Particle Physics* (36–37).

> Later technologies were able to further prove the early genetic theories (Wilkinson, "Ascent" 11).

4. Source with Multiple Authors   For a source written by two or three authors, cite all names.

> . . . as early as 1974 (Allman and Jones 15–34).

> Finn, Crenshaw, and Zander contend that . . .

For a source written by four or more authors, list only the first author followed by "and coauthors" or "and others."

> Bradley and coauthors argued . . .

5. Source Quoted Within Another Source   Give the name of the author of the quotation in the text. In the parenthetical citation, give the author and page number of the source in which you found the quotation.

> According to Hanson, multimedia will be the dominant mode of instruction in colleges by 2007 (qtd. in Ortiz 211).

Note that only the source by Ortiz will appear in the list of works cited.

6. Source Issued by an Organization   If the author is an organization rather than a person, use the name of the organization.

> The causes of narcolepsy are discussed in a recent booklet (Association of Sleep Disorders 2–3).

> In a recent booklet, the Association of Sleep Disorders (2–3) discusses the causes of narcolepsy.

7. Source with Unknown Author   If the source does not identify an author, use a shortened form of the title in your parenthetical citation.

> This trend has been evident in American society since the beginning of the twentieth century ("Modernism" 179).

In a Web document, the author's name is often at the end of the document or in small print on the home page. Do some research before assuming a Web site does not have an author. (See also Source Issued by an Organization, above.)

8. Multiple Sources in One Citation   To refer to two sources at the same point, separate the sources in parentheses with a semicolon.

> This phenomenon was identified more than fifty years ago (Betts 29; Wilkinson 134).

9. Multiple Authors with Same Last Name   If two or more sources have authors with the same last name, spell out the first names of those authors in the text and use the authors' first initials in the parenthetical citation.

> This phenomenon was identified more than fifty years ago (B. Wilkinson 134).
>
> Renee Wilkinson has suggested two possible explanations for the digression (81).

10. Multivolume Work   If you use only one volume of a multivolume work, list the volume number in the works cited list only. If you cite more than one volume of a multivolume work, indicate the specific volume you are referring to, followed by a colon and the page number, in your parenthetical citation.

> "The Internet had Cold War roots, originating in a 1969 effort by the Pentagon to create a communication network that could survive a nuclear war" (Henretta et al. 2: 1027).

11. Encyclopedia or Dictionary Entry   If the entry does not have an author, alphabetize it by the word or term you referenced. You do not need to cite a page number for encyclopedias and dictionaries since they are arranged alphabetically.

> The term *groupism* is important to understand when preparing to communicate with Japanese business counterparts ("Groupism").

12. Electronic Sources   Follow the same rules as for print sources when citing electronic sources in your document, providing author names and page numbers if available. If an author's name is not given, use either the full title of the source in the text or a shortened version of the title in the parenthetical citation. If no page numbers are used, include any given identifying numbers, such as paragraph or section numbers, abbreviated "par." or "sec." Otherwise, use no number at all. Include URLs in the works cited list but not in the text.

> Twenty million books were in print by the early sixteenth century (Rawlins, ch. 3, sec. 2).

The MLA List of Works Cited

A list of works cited provides the information your readers will need to find each source you used. Note that the list includes only those items that you cite in your document; it should not include your background reading materials. Following are some guidelines for creating an MLA-style list of works cited.

On TechComm Web

For help with formatting an MLA list of works cited, click on the link to Diana Hacker's Research and Documentation Online on <bedfordstmartins.com/techcomm>.

- *Arranging Entries.* The individual entries in the works cited list are arranged alphabetically by the author's last name. Two or more works by the same author are arranged alphabetically by title. Works by an organization are alphabetized by the first significant word in the name of the organization.

- *Book Titles.* Titles of books should follow standard capitalization rules and should be either underlined or italicized; use a consistent method throughout your document.

- *Publication Information.* Give the publisher's full name or consult your style guide for the preferred abbreviations. Include both the publisher's city and state or country, unless the city is well known (such as New York, Boston, or London).

- *Periodical Titles.* Titles of periodicals should be either underlined or italicized (consistently), and they should be capitalized according to standard capitalization rules (all major words should be capitalized).

- *Article Titles.* Titles of articles and other short works should be placed in quotation marks and should follow standard capitalization rules.

- *Electronic Sources.* Include as much information as you can about electronic sources, such as author, date of publication, identifying numbers, and the URL or other electronic address. Also be sure to record the date you retrieved the information, because electronic information changes frequently. Titles of entire Web sites should be either underlined or italicized (consistently); titles of works within Web sites, such as articles and video clips, should be treated as in print sources.

On TechComm Web

For more information, see the MLA style site. Click on the Links Library for the Appendix on <bedfordstmartins.com/techcomm>.

- *Indenting.* Use a hanging indent, with second and subsequent lines of each entry indented one-half inch.

- *Spacing.* Double space the entire works cited list, with no extra spacing between entries.

- *Page Numbers.* Do not use the abbreviation "p." or "pp." when giving page numbers. For a range of pages, give only the last two digits of the second number if the previous digits are identical (for example, 243–47, not 243–247). Use a plus sign (+) to indicate that an article continues on subsequent pages interrupted by other articles or advertisements.

- *Dates.* Follow this format: day, month, year, with no commas (20 Feb. 1999). Spell out "May," "June," and "July"; abbreviate all other months by using the first three letters, with the exception of "Sept."

The following models of reference list entries include a variety of sources. For further examples of MLA-style citations, consult the *MLA Handbook for Writers of Research Papers.*

MLA Style for Works Cited Entries

BOOKS

1. Book by One Author
2. Book by Multiple Authors
3. Multiple Books by Same Author
4. Book Issued by an Organization
5. Book by an Unknown Author
6. Edited Book
7. Book in Edition Other Than First
8. Work in an Anthology
9. Multivolume Work
10. Encyclopedia or Dictionary Entry

PERIODICALS

11. Journal Article
12. Magazine Article
13. Newspaper Article
14. Unsigned Article
15. Review

ELECTRONIC SOURCES

16. Entire Web Site
17. Short Work from a Web Site

18. Online Book
19. Article in an Online Periodical
20. Online Sound Clip or Recording
21. Document from an Online Subscription Service
22. CD-ROM
23. E-mail Communication
24. Online Posting
25. Real-time Communication

OTHER SOURCES

26. Government Document
27. Article from Conference Proceedings
28. Dissertation Abstract
29. Pamphlet
30. Report
31. Personal Interview
32. Published Interview
33. Radio or Television Interview
34. Radio or Television Program
35. Lecture or Speech
36. Map or Chart

1. Book by One Author   Include the author's full name, in reverse order, followed by the book title. Next give the location and name of the publisher, followed by the year of publication.

> Cunningham, Walter S. *Crisis at Three Mile Island: The Aftermath of a Near Meltdown.* New York: Madison, 1980.

2. Book by Multiple Authors   For a book by two or three authors, present the names in the sequence in which they appear on the title page. Only the name of the first author is presented in reverse order. A comma separates the names of the authors.

> Bingham, Christine, and Stephen Withers. *Neural Networks and Fuzzy Logic.* New York: IEEE, 1999.

For a book by four or more authors, you may use the abbreviation "et al." ("and others") after the first author's name.

> Foster, Glenn, et al. *The American Renaissance.* Binghamton, NY: Archive, 1995.

3. Multiple Books by the Same Author
For second and subsequent entries by the same author, use three hyphens followed by a period. Arrange the entries alphabetically by title.

> Smith, Louis. *International Standards.* New York: IEEE, 1995.
>
> - - -. *Wave-Propagation Technologies.* Berkeley, CA: Stallings, 1994.

4. Book Issued by an Organization
The organization takes the position of the author.

> National Commission on Corrections. *The Future of Incarceration.* Publication 11346-53. St. Louis: Liberty, 1998.

5. Book by an Unknown Author
If the author of the book is unknown, begin with the title.

> *Reliability and Maintainability Guideline for Manufacturing Machinery and Equipment.* Warrendale, NY: Society of Automotive Engineers, 1999.

6. Edited Book
The book editor's name(s) followed by "ed." or "eds." is used in place of an author's name.

> Morgan, Donald E., ed. *Readings in Alternative Energies.* Boston: Smith-Howell, 1995.

7. Book in Edition Other Than First
The edition number follows the title of the book.

> Schonberg, Nathan. *Solid State Physics.* 3rd ed. London: Paragon, 1997.

8. Work in an Anthology
Give the author and title of the article first, followed by the book title and editor. Present the editor's name in normal order, preceded by "Ed." (for "Edited by"). After the publication information, give the pages on which the article appears.

> Njie, Ndey-Isatou. "Environmental Information Systems." *Africa's Valuable Assets: A Reader in Natural Resource Management.* Ed. Peter Veit. Washington: World Resources Inst., 1998. 365–72.

9. Multivolume Work
If you use two or more of the volumes, give the total number of volumes before the place of publication ("4 vols."). If you use only one volume, give that volume number before the place of publication, and give the total number of volumes after the publication date.

> Henretta, James A., et al. *America's History.* 4th ed. Vol. 2. Boston: Bedford, 2000. 2 vols.

10. Encyclopedia or Dictionary Entry   If the encyclopedia or dictionary is well known, you do not need to include the publisher or place of publication.

"Groupism." *Dictionary of International Business Terms.* 2nd ed. Hauppauge: Barron's, 2000.

11. Journal Article   List the author's name, the article title (in quotation marks), and the journal title (in italics), followed by the volume number, year, and page number(s). If the journal is paginated continuously throughout a volume, include only the volume number after the journal title.

Hastings, Wendy. "The Space Shuttle Debate." *Modern Inquirer* 13 (2003): 311–18.

If the journal paginates each issue separately, include the issue number after the volume number, and separate the two with a period.

Juneja, Gupta. "Asynchronous Transmission Techniques." *Video Quarterly* 6.2 (1994): 11–19.

12. Magazine Article   List the author's name, the article title (in quotation marks), and the magazine title (in italics), followed by the issue date and page number(s).

Newman, Daniel. "Passive Restraint Systems." *Car Lore* 12 Dec. 1995: 41+.

If the article has no author listed, begin with the title.

13. Newspaper Article   List the author's name, the article title (in quotation marks), and the newspaper name (in italics), followed by the issue date and page number(s). If the newspaper appears in more than one edition, cite the edition.

Felder, Melissa. "Smokeless Tobacco: New Danger Signs." *New York Post* 4 May 1995, morning ed.: 13.

14. Unsigned Article   If the author of an article is not indicated, begin with the title. In your list, alphabetize the work by title, ignoring the articles "the," "a," and "an."

"Gemstar May Unload E-Book Assets." *Publishers Weekly* 25 Nov. 2002: 18.

15. Review   For a book or film review, give the author of the review and the title of the review (in quotation marks), followed by the words "Rev. of" and the title of the work reviewed (in italics). End with the publication information for the periodical in which the review was published.

Menand, Louis. "What Comes Naturally." Rev. of *The Blank Slate,* by Steven Pinker. *New Yorker* 25 Nov. 2002: 96–101.

16. *Entire Web Site* If you are citing an entire Web site, begin with the author, the title or a description of the site, and the date of publication or most recent update. Then give the name of the sponsoring institution or organization (if any), your access date, and the URL in angle brackets.

> *The User-Friendly Manuals' Website.* 21 May 2002. Peter Ring Consultants. 18 Dec. 2002 <http://www.prc.dk/user-friendly-manuals/ufm/home.html>.

17. *Short Work from a Web Site* If you are citing a portion of a Web site, begin with the author, the title of the short work (in quotation marks), and the title of the site (in italics). Then include the date of publication and the site's sponsor before your retrieval information.

> Yamamura, Motoaki. "Wobbler Hoax." *Security Response.* 2002. Symantec. 18 Dec. 2002 <http://www.symantec.com/avcenter/venc/data/wobbler-hoax.html>.

If the URL is very long or complex, you may give the URL for the home page, followed by the word "Path" and the sequence of links you followed to find the document.

> Yamamura, Motoaki. "Wobbler Hoax." *Security Response.* 2002. Symantec. 18 Dec. 2002 <http://www.symantec.com/>. Path: Security Response; Hoaxes; Wobbler Virus.

18. *Online Book* Begin with the author's name and the title of the work, along with any available information about the print source. If the book has not been published before, include the online publication date and publisher. End with your access date, followed by the URL in angle brackets.

> Rawlins, Gregory J. E. *Moths to the Flame.* Cambridge: MIT P, 1997. 10 Feb. 2000 <http://mitpress.mit.edu/e-books/Moths/>.

19. *Article in an Online Periodical* Begin with the author's name and include both the title of the document and the name of the periodical, along with the date of publication. If the periodical is a scholarly journal, include relevant identifying numbers, such as volume, issue, and page numbers. For abstracts of articles, include the word "Abstract," followed by a period. End with your access date, followed by the URL in angle brackets.

> Carnevale, Dan. "University Uses New Format to Send Televised Courses by Computer." *The Chronicle of Higher Education* 11 Feb. 2000: A45. 16 Feb. 2000 <http://chronicle.com/weekly/v46/i23/23a04502.htm>.

20. *Online Sound Clip or Recording* Before the title, include the name of the writer, speaker, or director.

> Condee, Nancy. "Why Cultural Studies Matters." 24 Oct. 1998. *The English Server.* U of Washington. 20 Feb. 2003 <http://eserver.org/>. Path: Audio and Video.

21. Document from an Online Subscription Service If you are citing a document retrieved from an online subscription service, give the name of the service, the library where you retrieved the article, and your access date. End with the URL of the service in angle brackets.

> Siegfried, Tom. "A Way to Get the Message without Using Up Energy." *Dallas Morning News* 1 July 1996: 7D. Electric Lib. O'Neill Lib., Boston Coll., Chestnut Hill, MA. 8 Feb. 2000 <http://www.elibrary.com>.

22. CD-ROM Include "CD-ROM" before the place of publication.

> Hirshon, Arnold, and Barbara Winters. *Outsourcing Technical Services Ready to Import RFP Specifications.* CD-ROM. New York: Neal-Schuman, 1999.

23. E-mail Communication List the author's name, the subject line (if any), the word "E-mail," and the date the e-mail was sent.

> DeWitt, Caryn K. "Flat-panel Displays." E-mail to the author. 7 May 2003.

24. Online Posting List the author's name, the subject line (if any), the posting date, the words "Online posting," the name of the discussion group or newsgroup, any identifying number of the posting, the date you accessed the post, and the URL of the discussion group or newsgroup.

> Rajiv, Chris V. "Portable Document Formats." Online posting. 25 May 1998. TECHWR-L. 10 June 1998 <techwr-l@listserv.okstate.edu>.

25. Real-time Communication To cite a synchronous discussion from a MOO or a MUD, give the name of the speaker, the name and date of the discussion, the forum title (if any), the date you accessed the information, and the URL in angle brackets. If an archival version of the communication is unavailable, include the telnet address.

> Prisley, Lauren. "Seminar Discussion on FTP." 5 Oct. 1997. Tech MOOspace. 19 Nov. 1997 <telnet://moo.ku.edu/port=999>.

26. Government Document Give the government name and agency as the author, followed by the publication title, the edition or identifying number (if any), the place, and the date.

> United States. Dept. of Energy. *Wind Power Today: Wind Energy Program Highlights 2001.* Technical Pub. 102002-1556. Washington: GPO, 2002.

For an online government publication, begin with the name of the country and the government agency. Next give the title of the document and relevant publication information: author (if known) and the date of publication. End with your access date, followed by the URL in angle brackets.

United States. Federal Communications Commission. *FCC Consumer Alert on Internet Modem Switch Scam.* 25 Mar. 2002. 28 Jan. 2003 <http://www.fcc.gov/cgb/consumerfacts/ModemScam.html>.

27. Article from Conference Proceedings   List the author's name, the article title, and the proceedings title and editor's name, followed by the publication information.

Carlson, Carl T. "Advanced Organizers in Manuals." *Proceedings of the 45th International Technical Communication Conference.* Ed. Ken Rainey. Fairfax, VA: Soc. for Technical Communication, 1995. RT 56–58.

28. Dissertation Abstract   Include the abbreviation for *Dissertation Abstracts International, DAI,* followed by the *DAI* volume, date, and page number.

Cooke, Lynne Marie. "Remediation and the Visual Evolution of Design." Diss. Rensselaer Polytechnic Inst., 2001. *DAI* 62 (2001): 1973.

29. Pamphlet   Cite a pamphlet or brochure as you would a book.

How to Fit a Bicycle Helmet. Arlington, VA: Bicycle Helmet Safety Inst., 2002.

30. Report   Cite a report as you would a book.

Najork, Mark, and Allan Heydon. *Systems Research Center Report: High-Performance Web Crawling.* Palo Alto, CA: Compaq, 2001.

31. Personal Interview   List the interviewee's name, the words "Personal interview," and the date.

Gangloff, Richard. Personal interview. 24 Jan. 2003.

32. Published Interview   Begin with the name of the person interviewed. If the interview has a title, enclose it in quotation marks; otherwise use the word "Interview" followed by a period and the bibliographic information for the work in which it was published.

Pennebaker, D. A., and Chris Hegedus. "Piercing the Dot-Com Bubble." *Yahoo! Internet Life* 7.6 (2001): 70–72.

33. Radio or Television Interview   Begin with the name of the person interviewed. If the interview has a title, enclose it in quotation marks; otherwise use the word "Interview" followed by a period and the appropriate bibliographic information for the program on which it aired.

Mineta, Norman. Interview. *Larry King Live.* CNN. Los Angeles. 16 Jan. 2002.

34. Radio or Television Program Begin with the title of the episode or segment, if there is one (in quotation marks), followed by the names of performers, directors, or narrators, if relevant. Next cite the title of the program (in italics) and the title of the series (if any). Conclude with the name of the network, call letters and city of the station, and the air date.

> "Enron Hearings." Narr. Emily Harris. *All Things Considered*. Natl. Public Radio. WPLN, Nashville. 22 Feb. 2002.

35. Lecture or Speech Give the speaker's name and the title of the lecture or speech, followed by the place and date that the lecture or speech was given.

> Robbins, Bruce. "Trends in Secondary Education." Lecture. Boise State U. 2 May 1999.

36. Map or Chart Cite a map or chart as you would a book. Follow the title with the word "Map" or "Chart."

> *Central Orange County*. Map. Mill Creek, CA: King of the Road, 1999.

Sample MLA List of Works Cited

The following sample list of works cited illustrates the MLA citation system.

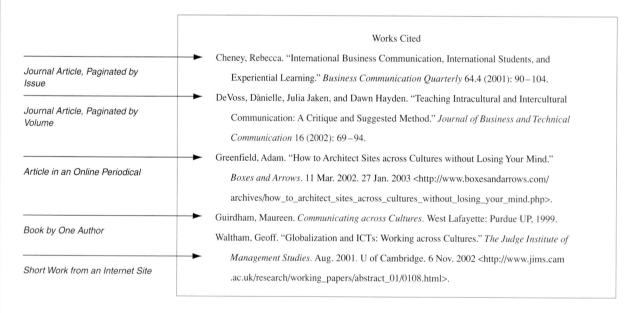

Journal Article, Paginated by Issue

Journal Article, Paginated by Volume

Article in an Online Periodical

Book by One Author

Short Work from an Internet Site

Works Cited

Cheney, Rebecca. "International Business Communication, International Students, and Experiential Learning." *Business Communication Quarterly* 64.4 (2001): 90–104.

DeVoss, Dànielle, Julia Jaken, and Dawn Hayden. "Teaching Intracultural and Intercultural Communication: A Critique and Suggested Method." *Journal of Business and Technical Communication* 16 (2002): 69–94.

Greenfield, Adam. "How to Architect Sites across Cultures without Losing Your Mind." *Boxes and Arrows*. 11 Mar. 2002. 27 Jan. 2003 <http://www.boxesandarrows.com/archives/how_to_architect_sites_across_cultures_without_losing_your_mind.php>.

Guirdham, Maureen. *Communicating across Cultures*. West Lafayette: Purdue UP, 1999.

Waltham, Geoff. "Globalization and ICTs: Working across Cultures." *The Judge Institute of Management Studies*. Aug. 2001. U of Cambridge. 6 Nov. 2002 <http://www.jims.cam.ac.uk/research/working_papers/abstract_01/0108.html>.

Mark In Margin	Instructions	Mark on Manuscript	Corrected Type
_e_	Delete	$10 billion ~~dollars~~	$10 billion
∧	Insert	envir∧ment	environment
(stet)	Let stand	let it stand	let it stand
(cap)	Capitalize	the english language	the English language
(lc)	Make lowercase	the English /anguage	the English language
—	Italicize	Technical Communication	*Technical Communication*
(tr)	Transpose	recieve	receive
◠	Close up space	electric lawn⌒mower	electric lawnmower
(sp)	Spell out	(Pres) Smithers	President Smithers
#	Insert space	3|amp light	3 amp light
¶	Start paragraph	. . . the results. These results	. . . the results. These results
run in	No paragraph	. . . the results.⌐ ⌐For this reason,	. . . the results. For this reason,
(sc)	Set in small capitals	Needle-nosed pliers	NEEDLE-NOSED PLIERS
(bf)	Set in boldface	Needle-nosed pliers	**Needle-nosed pliers**
⊙	Insert period	Fig⊙21	Fig. 21
⌄	Insert comma	the plant⌄which was built	the plant, which was built
=	Insert hyphen	menu=driven software	menu-driven software
⊙	Insert colon	Add the following ⊙	Add the following:
⌄;	Insert semicolon	. . . the plan⌄however the committee	. . . the plan; however the committee
⌄v	Insert apostrophe	the users preference	the user's preference
⌄/⌄	Insert quotation marks	⌄Furthermore,⌄she said . . .	"Furthermore," she said . . .
(/)	Insert parentheses	Write to us (at the Newark office)	Write to us (at the Newark office)
[/]	Insert brackets	President [John] Smithers	President [John] Smithers
⊣N⊢	Insert en dash	1984⊣N⊢2001	1984–2001
⊣M⊢	Insert em dash	Our goal⊣M⊢victory	Our goal—victory
v	Insert superscript	4,000 ft2	4,000 ft^2
∧	Insert subscript	H2O	H$_2$O
//	Align	$123.05// $86.95 //	$123.05 $86.95
[	Move to the left	[PVC piping	PVC piping
]	Move to the right	PVC piping]	PVC piping
⌐	Move up	⌐PVC piping⌐	PVC piping
⌊⌋	Move down	⌊PVC piping⌋	PVC piping

This part of the handbook contains advice on editing your documents for grammar, punctuation, and mechanics. The final section provides a concise guide to some of the most challenging aspects of English for nonnative speakers.

If your organization or professional field has a style guide with different recommendations about grammar and usage, you should of course follow those guidelines.

Your instructor might use the following abbreviations to refer you to specific topics in this section.

Abbreviation	Topic	Page Number	Abbreviation	Topic	Page Number
abbr	abbreviation	646	ref	ambiguous pronoun reference	625
adj	adjective (ESL)	627, 656	rep	repeated word (ESL)	658
adv	adverb (ESL)	657	run	run-on sentence	625
agr p/a	pronoun/antecedent agreement	629	sent	sentence part (ESL)	648
agr s/v	subject/verb agreement (ESL)	628, 654	sub	subordinating clause (ESL)	650
art	article (*a, an, the*) (ESL)	656	t	verb tense	629
cap	capitalization	647	vb	verb tense (ESL)	651
comp	comparison of items	627	.	period	635
cond	conditional sentence (ESL)	655	!	exclamation point	636
coor	coordinating clause (ESL)	649	?	question mark	636
cs	comma splice	624	,	comma	630
frag	sentence fragment	623	;	semicolon	634
help	helping verb and main verb (ESL)	653	:	colon	634
inf	infinitive form of the verb (ESL)	652	—	dash	636
-ing	*-ing* form of the verb (ESL)	652	( )	parentheses	637
ital	italics (underlining)	642	-	hyphen	643
num	number	644	,	apostrophe	638
omit	omitted word or words (ESL)	658	" "	quotation marks	639
			...	ellipses	641
			< >	angle brackets	643
			[ ]	square brackets	641

GRAMMATICAL SENTENCES

Avoid Sentence Fragments

frag

A sentence fragment is an incomplete sentence, an error that occurs when a sentence is missing either a verb or an independent clause. To correct a sentence fragment, use one of the following two strategies:

On TechComm Web

For online exercises covering these grammar skills, click on the link to Exercise Central on <bedfordstmartins.com/techcomm>.

1. **Introduce a verb.**

   FRAGMENT   The pressure loss caused by a worn gasket.

   This example is a fragment because it lacks a verb. (The word caused *does not function as a verb here; rather, it introduces a phrase that describes the pressure loss.)*

   COMPLETE   The pressure loss was caused by a worn gasket.

   Pressure loss *has a verb:* was caused.

   COMPLETE   We identified the pressure loss caused by a worn gasket.

   Pressure loss *becomes the object in a new main clause:* We identified the pressure loss.

   FRAGMENT   A plotting program with clipboard plotting, 3D animation, and FFTs.

   COMPLETE   It is a plotting program with clipboard plotting, 3D animation, and FFTs.

   COMPLETE   A plotting program with clipboard plotting, 3D animation, and FFTs will be released today.

2. **Link the fragment (a dependent element) to an independent clause.**

   FRAGMENT   The article was rejected for publication. Because the data could not be verified.

   Because the data could not be verified *is a fragment because it lacks an independent clause: a clause that has a subject and a verb and could stand alone as a sentence. To be complete, it needs more information.*

   COMPLETE   The article was rejected for publication because the data could not be verified.

   The dependent element is joined to the independent clause that precedes it.

   COMPLETE   Because the data could not be verified, the article was rejected for publication.

   The dependent element is followed by the independent clause.

FRAGMENT   Delivering over 150 horsepower. The two-passenger coupe will cost over $32,000.

COMPLETE   Delivering over 150 horsepower, the two-passenger coupe will cost over $32,000.

COMPLETE   The two-passenger coupe will deliver over 150 horsepower and cost over $32,000.

Avoid Comma Splices

CS

A comma splice is an error that occurs when two independent clauses are joined, or spliced together, by a comma. Independent clauses in a comma splice can be linked correctly in three ways:

1. **Use a comma and a coordinating conjunction (*and, or, nor, but, for, so,* and *yet*).**

    SPLICE   The 909 printer is our most popular model, it offers an unequaled blend of power and versatility.

    CORRECT   The 909 printer is our most popular model, for it offers an unequaled blend of power and versatility.

    The coordinating conjunction for *explicitly states the relationship between the two clauses.*

2. **Use a semicolon.**

    SPLICE   The 909 printer is our most popular model, it offers an unequaled blend of power and versatility.

    CORRECT   The 909 printer is our most popular model; it offers an unequaled blend of power and versatility.

    The semicolon creates a somewhat more distant relationship between the two clauses than the comma-and-coordinating-conjunction link; the link remains implicit.

3. **Use a period or another form of terminal punctuation.**

    SPLICE   The 909 printer is our most popular model, it offers an unequaled blend of power and versatility.

    CORRECT   The 909 printer is our most popular model. It offers an unequaled blend of power and versatility.

The two independent clauses are separate sentences. Of the three ways to punctuate the two clauses correctly, this punctuation suggests the most distant relationship between them.

Avoid Run-On Sentences

> **run**

In a run-on sentence (sometimes called a *fused sentence*), two independent clauses appear together with no punctuation between them. A run-on sentence can be corrected in the same three ways as a comma splice:

1. Use a comma and a coordinating conjunction (*and, or, nor, but, for, so,* and *yet*).

RUN-ON   The 909 printer is our most popular model it offers an unequaled blend of power and versatility.

CORRECT   The 909 printer is our most popular model, for it offers an unequaled blend of power and versatility.

2. Use a semicolon.

RUN-ON   The 909 printer is our most popular model it offers an unequaled blend of power and versatility.

CORRECT   The 909 printer is our most popular model; it offers an unequaled blend of power and versatility.

3. Use a period or another form of terminal punctuation.

RUN-ON   The 909 printer is our most popular model it offers an unequaled blend of power and versatility.

CORRECT   The 909 printer is our most popular model. It offers an unequaled blend of power and versatility.

Avoid Ambiguous Pronoun References

> **ref**

Pronouns must refer clearly to their antecedents—the words or phrases they replace. To correct ambiguous pronoun references, try one of these four strategies:

1. Clarify the pronoun's antecedent.

UNCLEAR   Remove the cell cluster from the medium and analyze it.

Analyze what: the cell cluster or the medium?

CLEAR	Analyze the cell cluster after removing it from the medium.
CLEAR	Analyze the medium after removing the cell cluster from it.
CLEAR	Remove the cell cluster from the medium. Then analyze the cell cluster.
CLEAR	Remove the cell cluster from the medium. Then analyze the medium.

2. **Clarify the relative pronoun, such as *which*, introducing a dependent clause.**

UNCLEAR	She decided to evaluate the program, which would take five months.
	What would take five months: the program or the evaluation?
CLEAR	She decided to evaluate the program, a process that would take five months.
	By replacing which *with* a process that, *the writer clearly indicates that it is the evaluation that will take five months.*
CLEAR	She decided to evaluate the five-month program.
	By using the adjective five-month, *the writer clearly indicates that it is the program that will take five months.*

3. **Clarify the subordinating conjunction, such as *where*, introducing a dependent clause.**

UNCLEAR	This procedure will increase the handling of toxic materials outside the plant, where adequate safety measures can be taken.
	Where can adequate safety measures be taken: inside the plant or outside?
CLEAR	This procedure will increase the handling of toxic materials outside the plant. Because adequate safety measures can be taken only in the plant, the procedure poses risks.
CLEAR	This procedure will increase the handling of toxic materials outside the plant. Because adequate safety measures can be taken only outside the plant, the procedure will decrease safety risks.
	Sometimes the best way to clarify an unclear reference is to split the sentence in two, drop the subordinating conjunction, and add clarifying information.

4. **Clarify the ambiguous pronoun that begins a sentence.**

UNCLEAR	Allophanate linkages are among the most important structural components of polyurethane elastomers. They act as cross-linking sites.
	What act as cross-linking sites: allophanate linkages or polyurethane elastomers?
CLEAR	Allophanate linkages, which are among the most important structural components of polyurethane elastomers, act as cross-linking sites.
	The writer has rewritten part of the first sentence to add a clear nonrestrictive modifier and combined it with the second sentence.

If you begin a sentence with a demonstrative pronoun that might be unclear to the reader, be sure to follow it immediately with a noun that clarifies the reference.

UNCLEAR   The new parking regulations require that all employees pay for parking permits. These are on the agenda for the next senate meeting.

What are on the agenda: the regulations or the permits?

CLEAR   The new parking regulations require that all employees pay for parking permits. These regulations are on the agenda for the next senate meeting.

Compare Items Clearly

comp

When comparing or contrasting items, make sure your sentence communicates their relationship clearly. A simple comparison between two items often causes no problems: "The X3000 has more storage than the X2500." Simple comparisons, however, can sometimes result in ambiguous statements:

AMBIGUOUS   Trout eat more than minnows.

Do trout eat minnows in addition to other food, or do trout eat more than minnows eat?

CLEAR   Trout eat more than minnows do.

If you are introducing three items, make sure the reader can tell which two are being compared:

AMBIGUOUS   Trout eat more algae than minnows.

CLEAR   Trout eat more algae than they do minnows.

CLEAR   Trout eat more algae than minnows do.

Beware of comparisons in which different aspects of the two items are compared:

ILLOGICAL   The resistance of the copper wiring is lower than the tin wiring.

LOGICAL   The resistance of the copper wiring is lower than that of the tin wiring.

Resistance cannot be logically compared with tin wiring. In the revision, the pronoun that *substitutes for* resistance *in the second part of the comparison.*

Use Adjectives Clearly

adj

In general, adjectives are placed before the nouns that they modify: *the plastic washer*. In technical communication, however, writers often need to use clusters of adjectives. To prevent confusion in technical communication, follow two guidelines.

1. **Use commas to separate coordinate adjectives.**

   Adjectives that describe different aspects of the same noun are known as coordinate adjectives.

   portable, programmable CD player

   adjustable, removable housings

   The comma is used instead of the word and.

   Sometimes an adjective is considered part of the noun it describes: *electric drill*. When one adjective modifies *electric drill*, no comma is required: *a reversible electric drill*. The addition of two or more adjectives, however, creates the traditional coordinate construction: *a two-speed, reversible electric drill*.

2. **Use hyphens to link compound adjectives.**

   A compound adjective is made up of two or more words. Use hyphens to link these elements when compound adjectives precede nouns.

   a *variable-angle* accessory

   increased *cost-of-living* raises

   The hyphens prevent increased *from being read as an adjective modifying* cost.

   A long string of compound adjectives can be confusing even if you use hyphens appropriately. To ensure clarity, turn the adjectives into a clause or a phrase following the noun.

UNCLEAR	an *operator-initiated default-prevention* technique
CLEAR	a technique *initiated by the operator to prevent default*

Maintain Subject-Verb Agreement

agr s/v

The subject and verb of a sentence must agree in number, even when a prepositional phrase comes between them. The object of the preposition may be plural in a singular sentence.

INCORRECT	The *result* of the tests *are* promising.
CORRECT	The *result* of the tests *is* promising.

The object of the preposition may be singular in a plural sentence.

INCORRECT	The *results* of the test *is* promising.
CORRECT	The *results* of the test *are* promising.

Don't be misled by the fact that the object of the preposition and the verb don't sound natural together, as in *tests is* or *test are*. Here, the noun *test(s)* precedes the verb, but it is not the subject of the verb. As long as the subject and verb agree, the sentence is correct.

Maintain Pronoun-Antecedent Agreement

agr p/a

A pronoun and its antecedent (the word or phrase being replaced by the pronoun) must agree in number. Often an error occurs when the antecedent is a collective noun—one that can be interpreted as either singular or plural, depending on its usage.

> INCORRECT   The *company* is proud to announce a new stock option plan for *their* employees.
>
> CORRECT   The *company* is proud to announce a new stock option plan for *its* employees.
>
> *Company acts as a single unit; therefore, the singular pronoun is appropriate.*

When the individual members of a collective noun are emphasized, however, plural pronouns are appropriate.

> CORRECT   The inspection team have prepared their reports.
>
> *The use of their emphasizes that the team members have prepared their own reports.*

Use Tenses Correctly

t

Two verb tenses are commonly used in technical communication: the present tense and the past perfect tense. It is important to understand the specific purpose of each.

1. The **present tense** is used to describe scientific principles and recurring events.

> INCORRECT   In 1992, McKay and his coauthors argued that the atmosphere of Mars *was* salmon pink.
>
> CORRECT   In 1992, McKay and his coauthors argued that the atmosphere of Mars *is* salmon pink.
>
> *Although the argument was made in the historical past—1992—the point is expressed in the present tense, because the atmosphere of Mars continues to be salmon pink.*

When the date of the argument is omitted, some writers express the entire sentence in the present tense.

> CORRECT   McKay and his coauthors *argue* that the atmosphere of Mars *is* salmon pink.

2. The **past perfect tense** is used to describe the earlier of two events that occurred in the past.

CORRECT   We *had begun* excavation when the foreman *discovered* the burial remains.

Had begun is the past perfect tense. The excavation began before the burial remains were discovered.

CORRECT   The seminar *had concluded* before I *got* a chance to talk with Dr. Tran.

PUNCTUATION

Commas

On TechComm Web

For online exercises covering punctuation, click on the link to Exercise Central on <bedfordstmartins.com /techcomm>.

The comma is the most frequently used punctuation mark, as well as the one about whose usage writers most often disagree. Examples of common misuses of the comma are noted within the following guidelines. This section concludes with advice about editing for unnecessary commas.

1. Use a comma in a compound sentence, to separate two independent clauses linked by a coordinating conjunction (*and, or, nor, but, so, for, yet*).

INCORRECT   The mixture was prepared from the two premixes and the remaining ingredients were then combined.

CORRECT   The mixture was prepared from the two premixes, and the remaining ingredients were then combined.

2. Use a comma to separate items in a series composed of three or more elements:

The manager of spare parts is responsible for ordering, stocking, and disbursing all spare parts for the entire plant.

Despite the presence of the conjunction *and*, most technical-communication style manuals require a comma after the second-to-last item. The comma clarifies the separation and prevents misreading.

CONFUSING   The report will be distributed to Operations, Research and Development and Accounting.

CLEAR   The report will be distributed to Operations, Research and Development, and Accounting.

3. Use a comma to separate introductory words, phrases, and clauses from the main clause of the sentence:

However, we will have to calculate the effect of the wind.

To facilitate trade, the government holds a yearly international conference.

In the following example, the comma actually prevents misreading:

Just as we finished eating, the rats discovered the treadmill.

NOTE: Writers sometimes make errors by omitting commas following introductory words, phrases, or clauses. A comma is optional only if the introductory text is brief and cannot be misread.

CORRECT	First, let's take care of the introductions.
CORRECT	First let's take care of the introductions.

INCORRECT	As the researchers sat down to eat the laboratory rats awakened.
CORRECT	As the researchers sat down to eat, the laboratory rats awakened.

4. Use a comma to separate a dependent clause from the main clause:

Although most of the executive council saw nothing wrong with it, the advertising campaign was canceled.

Most PCs use green technology, even though it is relatively expensive.

5. Use commas to separate nonrestrictive modifiers (parenthetical clarifications) from the rest of the sentence:

Jones, the temporary chairman, called the meeting to order.

NOTE: Writers sometimes introduce an error by dropping one of the commas around a nonrestrictive modifier.

INCORRECT	The phone line, which was installed two weeks ago had to be disconnected.
CORRECT	The phone line, which was installed two weeks ago, had to be disconnected.

In This Book

For more about restrictive and nonrestrictive modifiers, see Ch. 11, p. 346.

6. Use a comma to separate interjections and transitional elements from the rest of the sentence:

Yes, I admit that your findings are correct.

Their plans, however, have great potential.

NOTE: Writers sometimes introduce an error by dropping one of the commas around an interjection or a transitional element.

INCORRECT	Our new statistician, however used to work for Konaire, Inc.
CORRECT	Our new statistician, however, used to work for Konaire, Inc.

7. Use a comma to separate coordinate adjectives:

The finished product was a sleek, comfortable cruiser.

The heavy, awkward trains are still being used.

The comma here takes the place of the conjunction and.

If the adjectives are not coordinate—that is, if one of the adjectives modifies the combined adjective and noun—do not use a comma:

They decided to go to the first general meeting.

For more about coordinate adjectives, see page 628.

8. **Use a comma to signal that a word or phrase has been omitted from a sentence because it is implied:**

Smithers is in charge of the accounting; Harlen, the data management; Demarest, the publicity.

The commas after Harlen *and* Demarest *show that the phrase* is in charge *has not been repeated.*

9. **Use a comma to separate a proper noun from the rest of the sentence in direct address:**

John, have you seen the purchase order from United?

What I'd like to know, Betty, is why we didn't see this problem coming.

10. **Use a comma to introduce most quotations:**

He asked, "What time were they expected?"

11. **Use a comma to separate towns, states, and countries:**

Bethlehem, Pennsylvania, is the home of Lehigh University.

He attended Lehigh University in Bethlehem, Pennsylvania, and the University of California at Berkeley.

Note that a comma precedes and follows Pennsylvania.

12. **Use a comma to set off the year in a date:**

August 1, 2004, is the anticipated completion date.

If the month separates the date and the year, you do not need to use commas because the numbers are not next to each other:

The anticipated completion date is 1 August 2004.

13. **Use a comma to clarify numbers:**

12,013,104

NOTE: European practice is to reverse the use of commas and periods in writing numbers: periods signify thousands, and commas signify decimals.

14. **Use a comma to separate names from professional or academic titles:**

Harold Clayton, Ph.D.
Marion Fewick, CLU
Joyce Carnone, P.E.

NOTE: The comma also follows the title in a sentence:

Harold Clayton, Ph.D., is the featured speaker.

UNNECESSARY COMMAS

Writers often introduce errors by using unnecessary commas. Do not insert commas in the following situations:

- Commas are not used to link two independent clauses without a coordinating conjunction (known as a "comma splice"):

INCORRECT	All the motors were cleaned and dried after the water had entered, had they not been, additional damage would have occurred.
CORRECT	All the motors were cleaned and dried after the water had entered; had they not been, additional damage would have occurred.
CORRECT	All the motors were cleaned and dried after the water had entered. Had they not been, additional damage would have occurred.

  For more about comma splices, see page 624.

- Commas are not used to separate the subject from the verb in a sentence:

INCORRECT	Another of the many possibilities, is to use a "first in, first out" sequence.
CORRECT	Another of the many possibilities is to use a "first in, first out" sequence.

- Commas are not used to separate the verb from its complement:

INCORRECT	The schedules that have to be updated every month are, numbers 14, 16, 21, 22, 27, and 31.
CORRECT	The schedules that have to be updated every month are numbers 14, 16, 21, 22, 27, and 31.

- Commas are not used with a restrictive modifier:

INCORRECT	New and old employees who use the processed order form, do not completely understand the basis of the system.
	The phrase who use the processed order form *is a restrictive modifier necessary to the meaning: it defines which employees do not understand the system.*

CORRECT	New and old employees who use the processed order form do not completely understand the basis of the system.
INCORRECT	A company, that has grown so big, no longer finds an informal evaluation procedure effective.
	The clause that has grown so big *is a restrictive modifier.*
CORRECT	A company that has grown so big no longer finds an informal evaluation procedure effective.

- Commas are not used to separate two elements in a compound subject:

INCORRECT	Recent studies, and reports by other firms confirm our experience.
CORRECT	Recent studies and reports by other firms confirm our experience.

Semicolons

Semicolons are used in the following instances.

1. Use a semicolon to separate independent clauses not linked by a coordinating conjunction:

The second edition of the handbook is more up-to-date; however, it is also more expensive.

2. Use a semicolon to separate items in a series that already contains commas:

The members elected three officers: Jack Resnick, president; Carol Wayshum, vice president; Ahmed Jamoogian, recording secretary.

Here the semicolon acts as a "supercomma," grouping each name with the correct title.

MISUSE OF SEMICOLONS

Sometimes writers incorrectly use a semicolon when a colon is called for:

INCORRECT	We still need one ingredient; luck.
CORRECT	We still need one ingredient: luck.

Colons

Colons are used in the following instances.

1. Use a colon to introduce a word, phrase, or clause that amplifies, illustrates, or explains a general statement:

The project team lacked one crucial member: a project leader.

Here is the client's request: we are to provide the preliminary proposal by November 13.

We found three substances in excessive quantities: potassium, cyanide, and asbestos.

The week was productive: 14 projects were completed and another dozen were initiated.

NOTE: The text preceding a colon should be able to stand on its own as a sentence:

INCORRECT	We found: potassium, cyanide, and asbestos.
CORRECT	We found the following: potassium, cyanide, and asbestos.
CORRECT	We found potassium, cyanide, and asbestos.

2. **Use a colon to introduce items in a vertical list if the sense of the introductory text would be incomplete without the list:**

In This Book

For more on constructing lists, see Ch. 11, p. 238.

We found the following:

potassium

cyanide

asbestos

3. **Use a colon to introduce long or formal quotations:**

The president began: "In the last year . . ."

MISUSE OF COLONS

Writers sometimes incorrectly use a colon to separate a verb from its complement:

INCORRECT	The tools we need are: a plane, a level, and a T-square.
CORRECT	The tools we need are a plane, a level, and a T-square.
CORRECT	We need three tools: a plane, a level, and a T-square.

Periods

■

Periods are used in the following instances.

1. **Use a period at the end of sentences that do not ask questions or express strong emotion:**

The lateral stress still needs to be calculated.

2. **Use a period after some abbreviations:**

M.D.

U.S.A.

etc.

For more about abbreviations, see page 646.

3. **Use a period with decimal fractions:**

4.056

$6.75

75.6 percent

Exclamation Points

The exclamation point is used at the end of a sentence that expresses strong emotion, such as surprise or doubt.

> The nuclear plant, which was originally expected to cost $1.6 billion, eventually cost more than $8 billion!

In technical documents, which require objectivity and a calm, understated tone, exclamation points are rarely used.

Question Marks

The question mark is used at the end of a sentence that asks a direct question.

> What did the commission say about effluents?

NOTE: When a question mark is used within quotation marks, no other end punctuation is required.

> She asked, "What did the commission say about effluents?"

MISUSE OF QUESTION MARKS

Do not use a question mark at the end of a sentence that asks an indirect question.

> He wanted to know whether the procedure had been approved for use.

Dashes

To make a dash, use two uninterrupted hyphens (—). Do not add spaces before or after the dash. Some word-processing programs turn two hyphens into a dash, but with most, you have to use a special character to make a dash; there is no dash key on the keyboard.

Dashes are used in the following instances.

1. **Use a dash to set off a sudden change in thought or tone:**

   The committee found—can you believe this?—that the company bore full responsibility for the accident.

   That's what she said—if I remember correctly.

2. **Use a dash to emphasize a parenthetical element:**

   The managers' reports—all 10 of them—recommend production cutbacks for the coming year.

   Arlene Kregman—the first woman elected to the board of directors—is the next scheduled speaker.

3. **Use a dash to set off an introductory series from its explanation:**

   Wetsuits, weight belts, tanks—everything will have to be shipped in.

   NOTE: When a series follows the general statement, a colon replaces the dash.

   Everything will have to be shipped in: wetsuits, weight belts, and tanks.

MISUSES OF DASHES

Sometimes writers incorrectly use a dash as a substitute for other punctuation marks:

INCORRECT	The regulations—which were issued yesterday—had been anticipated for months.
CORRECT	The regulations, which were issued yesterday, had been anticipated for months.
INCORRECT	Many candidates applied—however, only one was chosen.
CORRECT	Many candidates applied; however, only one was chosen.

Parentheses

Parentheses are used in the following instances.

1. **Use parentheses to set off incidental information:**

   Please call me (x3104) when you get the information.

   Galileo (1546–1642) is often considered the father of modern astronomy.

   The cure rate for lung cancer has almost doubled in the last thirty years (Capron 1999).

2. Use parentheses to enclose numbers and letters that label items listed in a sentence:

To transfer a call within the office, (1) place the party on HOLD, (2) press TRANSFER, (3) press the extension number, and (4) hang up.

Use both a left and a right parenthesis—not just a right parenthesis—in this situation.

MISUSE OF PARENTHESES

Sometimes writers incorrectly use parentheses instead of brackets to enclose their insertion within a quotation.

INCORRECT	He said, "The new manager (Farnham) is due in next week."
CORRECT	He said, "The new manager [Farnham] is due in next week."

For more about square brackets, see page 642.

Apostrophes

Apostrophes are used in the following instances.

1. Use an apostrophe to indicate possession:

the manager's goals	the employee's credit union
the workers' lounge	Charles's T-square

For joint possession, add an apostrophe and an *s* only to the last noun or proper noun:

Watson and Crick's discovery

For separate possession, add an apostrophe and an *s* to each of the nouns or pronouns:

Newton's and Galileo's theories

NOTE: Do not add an apostrophe or an *s* to possessive pronouns: *his, hers, its, ours, yours, theirs.*

2. Use an apostrophe to indicate possession when a noun modifies a gerund:

We were all looking forward to Bill's joining the company.

The gerund joining *is modified by the proper noun* Bill.

3. **Use an apostrophe to form contractions:**

I've   shouldn't

can't   it's

The apostrophe usually indicates an omitted letter or letters:

can(no)t = can't

it (i)s = it's

NOTE: Some organizations discourage the use of contractions; others have no preference. Find out the policy your organization follows.

4. **Use an apostrophe to indicate special plurals:**

three 9's

two different JCL's

the why's and how's of the problem

NOTE: For plurals of numbers and abbreviations, some style guides omit the apostrophe: *9s, JCLs*. Because usage varies considerably, check with your organization.

MISUSE OF APOSTROPHES

Writers sometimes incorrectly use the contraction *it's* in place of the possessive pronoun *its*.

INCORRECT   The company does not feel that the problem is it's responsibility.

CORRECT   The company does not feel that the problem is its responsibility.

Quotation Marks

Quotation marks are used in the following instances.

1. **Use quotation marks to indicate titles of short works, such as articles, essays, or chapters:**

Smith's essay "Solar Heating Alternatives" was short but informative.

2. **Use quotation marks to call attention to a word or phrase used in an unusual way or in an unusual context:**

A proposal is "wired" if the sponsoring agency has already decided who will be granted the contract.

Do not use quotation marks to excuse poor word choice:

The new director has been a real "pain."

In This Book

For more about quoting sources, see Ch. 7, p. 141.

3. Use quotation marks to indicate a direct quotation.

"In the future," he said, "check with me before authorizing any large purchases."

As Breyer wrote, "Morale *is* productivity."

NOTE: Quotation marks are not used with indirect quotations.

INCORRECT	He said that "third-quarter profits will be up."
CORRECT	He said that third-quarter profits will be up.
CORRECT	He said, "Third-quarter profits will be up."

Also note that quotation marks are not used with quotations that are longer than four lines; instead, set the quotation in block format. In a word-processed manuscript, a block quotation is usually

- indented one-half inch from the left-hand margin
- typed without quotation marks
- introduced by a complete sentence followed by a colon

Different style manuals recommend variations on these basic rules; the following example illustrates APA style.

McFarland (1997) writes:

> The extent to which organisms adapt to their environment is still being charted. Many animals, we have recently learned, respond to a dry winter with an automatic birth control chemical that limits the number of young to be born that spring. This prevents mass starvation among the species in that locale. (p. 49)

Hollins (1999) concurs. She writes, "Biological adaptation will be a major research area during the next decade" (p. 2).

USING QUOTATION MARKS WITH OTHER PUNCTUATION

- If the sentence contains a *tag*—a phrase identifying the speaker or writer—a comma separates it from the quotation:

Wilson replied, "I'll try to fly out there tomorrow."

"I'll try to fly out there tomorrow," Wilson replied.

Informal and brief quotations require no punctuation before a quotation mark:

She asked herself "Why?" several times a day.

- In the United States (unlike most other English-speaking nations), commas and periods at the end of quotations are placed within the quotation marks:

The project engineer reported, "A new factor has been added."

"A new factor has been added," the project engineer reported.

- Question marks, dashes, and exclamation points are placed inside quotation marks when they are part of the quoted material:

He asked, "Did the shipment come in yet?"

When question marks, dashes, and exclamation points apply to the whole sentence, they are placed outside the quotation marks:

Did he say, "This is the limit"?

- When a punctuation mark appears inside a quotation mark at the end of a sentence, do not add another punctuation mark.

INCORRECT   Did she say, "What time is it?"?

CORRECT   Did she say, "What time is it?"

Ellipses

Ellipses (three spaced periods) indicate the omission of material from a direct quotation.

SOURCE   My team will need three extra months for market research and quality assurance testing to successfully complete the job.

QUOTE   She responded, "My team will need three extra months . . . to successfully complete the job."

Insert an ellipsis after a period if you are omitting entire sentences that follow:

Larkin refers to the project as "an attempt . . . to clarify the issue of compulsory arbition. . . . We do not foresee an end to the legal wrangling . . . but perhaps the report can serve as a definition of the areas of contention."

The writer has omitted words from the source after attempt *and after* wrangling. *After* arbitration, *the writer has inserted an ellipsis after a period to indicate that a sentence has been omitted.*

NOTE: MLA style recommends that writers insert brackets around an ellipsis that is introduced in a quotation.

Larkin refers to the project as "an attempt [. . .] to clarify the issue of compulsory arbitration."

Square Brackets

[ ]

Square brackets are used in the following instances.

1. **Use square brackets around words added to a quotation:**

   As noted in the minutes of the meeting, "He [Pearson] spoke out against the proposal."

   A better approach would be to shorten the quotation:

   The minutes of the meeting note that Pearson "spoke out against the proposal."

2. **Use square brackets to indicate parenthetical information within parentheses:**

   (For further information, see Charles Houghton's *Civil Engineering Today* [1997].)

MECHANICS

Italics

ital

On TechComm Web

For online exercises covering mechanics, click on the link to Exercise Central on <bedfordstmartins .com/techcomm>.

Although italics are generally preferred, you may use underlining in place of italics. Whichever method you choose, be consistent throughout your document. Italics (or underlining) are used in the following instances.

1. **Use italics for words used as words:**

   In this report, the word *operator* will refer to any individual who is actually in charge of the equipment, regardless of that individual's certification.

2. **Use italics to indicate titles of long works (books, manuals, and so on), periodicals and newspapers, long films, long plays, and long musical works:**

   See Houghton's *Civil Engineering Today.*

   We subscribe to the *Wall Street Journal.*

   Note that the is not italicized or capitalized when the title is used in a sentence.

   NOTE: The MLA style guide recommends that the names of Web sites be italicized.

   The Library of Congress maintains *Thomas*, an excellent site for legislative information.

3. **Use italics to indicate the names of ships, trains, and airplanes:**

   The shipment is expected to arrive next week on the *Penguin.*

4. **Use italics to set off foreign expressions that have not become fully assimilated into English:**

   The speaker was guilty of *ad hominem* arguments.

   Check a dictionary to determine whether a foreign expression has become assimilated.

5. **Use italics to emphasize words or phrases:**

   Do not press the red button.

Angle Brackets

Many style guides now advocate using angle brackets around URLs in print documents to set them off from the text.

> Our survey included a close look at three online news sites: the *New York Times* <http://www.nytimes.com>, the *Washington Post* <http://www.washingtonpost.com>, and *CNN* <http://www.cnn.com>.

You may want to check with your instructor or organization before following this recommendation.

Hyphens

Hyphens are used in the following instances.

1. **Use hyphens to form compound adjectives that precede nouns:**

   general-purpose register

   meat-eating dinosaur

   chain-driven saw

   NOTE: Hyphens are not used after adverbs that end in *-ly.*

   newly acquired terminal

   Also note that hyphens are not used when the compound adjective follows the noun:

   The Woodchuck saw is chain driven.

   Many organizations have their own preferences about hyphenating compound adjectives. Check to see if your organization has a preference.

   For more about compound adjectives, see page 628.

2. **Use hyphens to form some compound nouns:**

   once-over

   go-between

   NOTE: There is a trend away from hyphenating compound nouns (*vice president, photomicroscope, drawbridge*); check your dictionary for proper spelling.

3. **Use hyphens to form fractions and compound numbers:**

one-half

fifty-six

4. **Use hyphens to attach some prefixes and suffixes:**

post-1945

president-elect

5. **Use hyphens to divide a word at the end of a line:**

We will meet in the pavil-
ion in one hour.

Whenever possible, however, avoid such line breaks; they slow the reader down. When you do use them, check the dictionary to make sure you have divided the word between syllables. If you need to break a URL at the end of a line, do not add a hyphen. Instead, break it before a slash or a period:

http://www.stc.org
/ethical.asp

Numbers

num

Ways of handling numbers vary considerably. Therefore, in choosing between words and numerals, consult your organization's style guide. Many organizations observe the following guidelines.

1. **Technical quantities of any amount are expressed in numerals, especially if a unit of measurement is included:**

3 feet	43,219 square miles
12 grams	36 hectares

2. **Nontechnical quantities of fewer than 10 are expressed in words:**

three persons

six whales

3. **Nontechnical quantities of 10 or more are expressed in numerals:**

300 persons

12 whales

35 percent increase

4. **Approximations are written out:**

   approximately ten thousand people

   about two million trees

5. **Round numbers over nine million are expressed in both words and numerals:**

   14 million light-years

   $64 billion

6. **Decimals are expressed in numerals:**

   3.14

   1,013.065

   Decimals of less than one should be preceded by a zero:

   0.146

   0.006

7. **Fractions are written out, unless they are linked to technical units:**

   two-thirds of the members

   3½ hp

8. **Time of day is expressed in numerals if A.M. or P.M. is used; otherwise, it is written out:**

   6:10 A.M.

   six o'clock

   the nine-thirty train

9. **Page numbers and titles of figures and tables are expressed in numerals:**

   Figure 1

   Table 13

   page 261

10. **Back-to-back numbers are written using both words and numerals:**

    six 3-inch screws

    fourteen 12-foot ladders

    3,012 five-piece starter units

    In general, the technical unit should be expressed with the numeral. If the nontechnical quantity would be cumbersome in words, use the numeral for it instead.

11. **Numbers in legal contracts or in documents intended for international readers should be represented in both words and numerals:**

thirty-seven thousand dollars ($37,000)

five (5) relays

12. **Street addresses may require both words and numerals:**

3801 Fifteenth Street

SPECIAL CASES

- A number at the beginning of a sentence should be spelled out:

Thirty-seven acres was the size of the lot.

Many writers would revise the sentence to avoid this problem:

The lot was 37 acres.

- Within a sentence, the same unit of measurement should be expressed consistently in either numerals or words:

INCORRECT   On Tuesday the attendance was 13; on Wednesday, eight.

CORRECT   On Tuesday the attendance was 13; on Wednesday, 8.

CORRECT   On Tuesday the attendance was thirteen; on Wednesday, eight.

- In general, months should not be expressed as numbers. In the United States, 3/7/03 means March 7, 2003; in many other countries, it means July 3, 2003. The following forms, in which the months are written out, are preferable:

March 7, 2003

7 March 2003

Abbreviations

abbr

Abbreviations save time and space, but you should use them carefully because your readers may not understand them. Many companies and professional organizations provide lists of approved abbreviations.

Analyze your audience to determine whether and how to abbreviate. If your readers include a general audience unfamiliar with your field, either write out the technical terms or attach a list of abbreviations. If you are new to an organization or are publishing in a field for the first time, find out which abbreviations are commonly used. If for any reason you are unsure about a term, write it out.

The following are general guidelines about abbreviations:

1. **When an unfamiliar abbreviation is introduced for the first time, the full term should be given, followed by the abbreviation in parentheses. In subsequent references, the abbreviation may be used alone. For long works, the full term and its abbreviation may be written out at the start of major units, such as chapters.**

    The heart of the new system is the self-loading cartridge (slc).

    The cathode-ray tube (CRT) is your control center.

2. **To form the plural of an abbreviation, an *s* is added, either with or without an apostrophe, depending on the style of your organization:**

    GNPs

    PhD's

    Most unit-of-measurement abbreviations do not take plurals:

    10 in

    3 qt

3. **Most abbreviations in scientific writing are not followed by periods:**

    lb

    cos

    dc

    If the abbreviation can be confused with another word, however, a period should be used:

    in.

    Fig.

4. **If no number is used with a measurement, an abbreviation should not be used.**

    INCORRECT   How many sq meters is the site?

    CORRECT   How many square meters is the site?

Capitalization

cap

For the most part, the conventions of capitalization in general writing apply in technical communication.

1. **Proper nouns, titles, trade names, places, languages, religions, and organizations should be capitalized:**

   William Rusham

   Director of Personnel

   Quick-Fix Erasers

   Bethesda, Maryland

   Italian

   Methodism

   Society for Technical Communication

   In some organizations, job titles are not capitalized unless they refer to specific persons.

   Alfred Loggins, Director of Personnel, is interested in being considered for vice president of marketing.

2. **Headings and labels should be capitalized:**

   A Proposal to Implement the Wilkins Conversion System

   Mitosis

   Table 3

   Section One

   The Problem

   Rate of Inflation, 1995–2005

   Figure 6

GUIDELINES FOR SPEAKERS OF ENGLISH AS A SECOND LANGUAGE

Basic Characteristics of a Sentence

sent

A sentence has five characteristics.

1. **It starts with an uppercase letter and ends with a period, a question mark, or (rarely) an exclamation point.**

2. **It has a subject, usually a noun. The subject is what the sentence is about.**

3. **It has a verb, which tells the reader what happens to the subject or what the subject does.**

4. **It has a standard word order.**

   The most common sequence in English is subject-verb-object:

   subject   verb   object

   We hired a consulting firm.

   You can add information to the start of the sentence:

   Yesterday we hired a consulting firm.

   or to the end of the sentence:

   Yesterday we hired a consulting firm: *Sanderson & Associates*.

   or in the middle:

   Yesterday we signed a *nontransferable contract* with a consulting firm: Sanderson & Associates.

   In fact, any element of a sentence can be expanded.

5. **It has an independent clause (a subject and verb that can stand alone).**

   The following is a sentence because it can stand alone:

   The pump failed because of improper maintenance.

   The following is also a sentence:

   The pump failed.

   But the following is a phrase, not a sentence, because the thought is incomplete:

   Because of improper maintenance.

   An independent clause is required to complete this sentence:

   Because of improper maintenance, the pump failed.

Linking Ideas by Coordination

coor

One way to connect ideas in a sentence is by coordination. Coordination means that ideas in the sentence are roughly equal in importance. There are three main ways to coordinate ideas.

1. **Use a semicolon (;) to coordinate ideas that are independent clauses:**

   The information for bid was published last week; the proposal is due in less than a month.

2. **Use a comma and a coordinating conjunction (*and, but, or, nor, so, for,* and *yet*) to coordinate two independent clauses:**

The information for bid was published last week, but the proposal is due in less than a month.

In this example, but *clarifies the relationship between the two clauses: the writer hasn't been given enough time to write the proposal.*

3. **Use transitional words and phrases to coordinate two independent clauses:**

The Pentium III chip has already been replaced; *as a result*, it is hard to find a Pentium III in a new computer.

The Pentium III chip has already been replaced. *As a result*, it is hard to find a Pentium III in a new computer.

In This Book

For more about transitional words and phrases, see Ch. 10, p. 228.

Linking Ideas by Subordination

sub

Two ideas can also be linked by subordination, that is, by deemphasizing one of them. There are two basic ways to use subordination.

1. **Use a subordinating word or phrase to turn one idea into a subordinate clause.**

Subordinating words and phrases:

after	because	since	until	while
although	before	so that	when	who
as	even though	that	where	whom
as if	if	unless	which	whose

Start with two independent clauses:

The bridge was completed last year. The bridge already needs repairs.

Then choose a subordinating word and combine the clauses:

Although the bridge was completed last year, it already needs repairs.

Although *subordinates the first clause, leaving* it already needs repairs *as the independent clause.*

Note that the order of the ideas could be reversed:

The bridge already needs repairs *even though* it was completed last year.

Another way to subordinate one idea is to turn it into a nonrestrictive clause using the subordinating word *which*:

The bridge, which was completed last year, already needs repairs.

This version deemphasizes was completed last year *by turning it into a nonrestrictive clause and emphasizes* already needs repairs *by leaving it as the independent clause.*

In This Book

For more about restrictive and nonrestrictive modifiers, see Ch. 11, p. 246.

2. **Turn one of the ideas into a phrase modifying the other.**

   Completed last year, the bridge already needs repairs.

   Completed last year *was turned into a phrase by dropping the subject and verb from the independent clause. Here the phrase is used to modify* the bridge.

Verb Tenses

vb

Verb tenses in English can be complicated, but in general there are four kinds of time relationships that you need to understand.

1. **Simple past, present, and future**

   PAST   Yesterday we *subscribed* to a new ecology journal.

   PRESENT   We *subscribe* to three ecology journals every year.

          Meaning: We regularly subscribe to the three journals.

   FUTURE   We *will subscribe* to the new ecology journal next year.

          Or: We *are going to subscribe* to the new ecology journal next year.

2. **An action in progress at a known time (progressive)**

   PAST PROGRESSIVE

   We *were updating* our directory when the power failure occurred.

   PRESENT PROGRESSIVE

   We *are updating* our directory now.

   FUTURE PROGRESSIVE

   We *will be updating* our directory tomorrow when you arrive.

3. **An action completed before a known time (perfect)**

   PAST PERFECT   We *had* already *started* to write the proposal when we got your call.

          The writing began before the call.

   PRESENT PERFECT   We *have started* to write the proposal.

   FUTURE PERFECT   We *will have started* to write the proposal by the time you arrive.

          Both events are in the future, but in both cases, the writing begins before the arrival.

4. An action in progress until a known time (perfect progressive)

PAST PERFECT PROGRESSIVE

We *had been working* on the reorganization when the news of the merger was publicized.

The work was in progress when the news of the merger was publicized.

PRESENT PERFECT PROGRESSIVE

We *have been working* on the reorganization for over a year.

The work will continue into the future.

FUTURE PERFECT PROGRESSIVE

We *will have been working* on the reorganization for two years by the time it occurs.

Forming Verbs with *-ing*

-ing

English uses the *-ing* form of verbs in three major ways.

1. As part of a progressive or perfect progressive verb (see numbers 2 and 4 above):

We are *shipping* the materials by UPS.

We have been *waiting* for approval since January.

2. As a present participle, which functions as an adjective either by itself:

the *leaking* pipe

or as part of a participial phrase:

Analyzing the sample, we discovered two anomalies.

The sample *containing* the anomalies appears on Slide 14.

3. As a gerund, which functions as a noun either by itself:

Writing is the best way to learn to write.

or as part of a gerund phrase:

The designer tried *inserting* the graphics by hand.

Infinitives

inf

Infinitives consist of the word *to* plus the base form of the verb (*to write, to understand*). An infinitive can be used in three main ways.

1. **As a noun:**

   The editor's goal for the next year is *to publish* the journal on schedule.

2. **As an adjective:**

   The company requested the right *to subcontract* the project.

3. **As an adverb:**

   We established the schedule ahead of time *to prevent* the kind of mistake we made last time.

Helping Verbs and Main Verbs

help

There are a number of helping verbs in English. The following discussion explains four categories of helping verbs.

1. **Modals**

   There are nine modal verbs: *can, could, may, might, must, shall, should, will,* and *would*. After a modal verb, use the base form of the verb (the form of the verb used after *to* in the infinitive).

   base form

   The system *must meet* all applicable codes.

2. **Forms of *do***

   After a helping verb that is a form of *do*—*do, does,* and *did*—use the base form of the verb.

   base form

   Do we *need* to include the figures for the recovery rate?

3. **Forms of *have* plus the past participle**

   To form one of the perfect tenses (past, present, or future), use a form of *have* plus the past participle of the verb (usually the *-ed* or *-en* form of the verb).

   PAST PERFECT

   We *had written* the proposal before learning of the new RFP.

   PRESENT PERFECT

   We *have written* the proposal according to the instructions in the RFP.

   FUTURE PERFECT

   We *will have written* the proposal by the end of the week.

In This Book

For more about active and passive voice, see Ch. 11, p. 250.

4. Forms of *be*

To describe an action in progress, use a form of *be* (*be, am, is, are, was, were, being, been*) and the present participle (the *-ing* form of the verb).

We *are testing* the new graphics tablet.

The company *is considering* flextime.

To create the passive voice, use a form of *be* and the past participle.

The piping *was installed* by the plumbing contractor.

Agreement of Subject and Verb

agr s/v

The subject and the verb in a clause or sentence must agree in number:

The new *valve is* installed according to the manufacturer's specifications.

The new *valves are* installed according to the manufacturer's specifications.

When you edit your document for subject-verb agreement, keep in mind the following guidelines.

1. **Make sure the subject and verb agree when information comes between the subject and the verb.**

   The *result* of the tests *is* included in Appendix C.

   The *results* of the test *are* included in Appendix C.

2. **Certain pronouns and quantifiers always require singular verbs. Pronouns that end in *-body* or *-one* — such as *everyone, everybody, someone, somebody, anyone, anybody, no one,* and *nobody* — are singular. In addition, quantifiers such as *something, each,* and *every* are singular.**

   SINGULAR   *Everybody is* invited to the preproposal meeting.

   SINGULAR   *Each* of the members *is* asked to submit billable hours by the end of the month.

3. **When the clause or sentence contains a compound subject, the verb must be plural.**

   COMPOUND
   SUBJECT   *The contractor and the subcontractor want* to meet to resolve the difficulties.

4. **When a relative pronoun such as *who, that,* or *which* begins a clause, make sure the verb agrees in number with the noun that the relative pronoun refers to.**

The *numbers* that *are* used in the formula do not agree with the ones we were given at the site.

Numbers *is plural, so the verb in the* that *clause* (are) *is also plural.*

The *number* that *is* used in the formula does not agree with the one we were given at the site.

Number *is singular, so the verb in the* that *clause* (is) *is also singular.*

Conditions

cond

Four main types of condition are used with the word *if* in English.

1. **Conditions of fact**

   For conditions of fact, use the same verb tense in both clauses. In most cases, use a form of the present tense:

   If you *see* "Unrecoverable Application Error," the program *has crashed.*

   If rats *are* allowed to eat as much as they want, they *become* obese.

2. **Future prediction**

   For prediction, use the present tense in the *if* clause. Use a modal (*can, could, may, might, must, shall, should, will,* or *would*) plus the base form of the verb in the independent clause.

   If we *win* this contract, we *will have* to add three more engineers.

   If this weather *keeps* up, we *may need* to postpone the launch.

3. **Present-future speculation**

   The present-future speculation usage suggests a condition contrary to fact. Use *were* in the *if* clause. Use a modal plus the base form of the verb in the independent clause.

   If I *were* president of the company, I *would be* much more aggressive.

   This sentence implies that you are not president of the company.

4. **Past speculation**

   Use *had* plus the past participle in the *if* clause. Use a modal plus *have* in the independent clause.

   If we *had won* this contract, we *would have* had to add three engineers.

   This sentence implies that the condition is contrary to fact: the contract wasn't won, so the engineers were not added.

Articles

art

Few aspects of English can be as frustrating to the nonnative speaker of English as the correct usage of the simple words *a, an*, and *the*. Although there are a few rules that you should try to learn, remember that there are many exceptions and special cases. Here are three general guidelines.

1. **Singular proper nouns—those that name specific persons, places, and things—do not usually take an article:**

   Taiwan

   James Allenby

   But plural proper nouns often do take the article *the:*

   the United States

   the Allenbys

2. **Countable common nouns (persons, places, or things that can be counted) take an article:**

   the microscope

   a desk

   an electron

   Uncountable common nouns generally do not take an article:

   | overtime | integrity | information |
   | equipment | research | machinery |

3. **Common nouns can be referred to as either specific or nonspecific. The specific form takes *the*; the nonspecific form takes either *a* or *an*.**

   Our department received funding for *an experiment*. The experiment will take six months to complete.

   In the first sentence in this example, experiment *is a nonspecific noun; in the second sentence,* experiment *is a specific noun because it has been identified in the previous sentence.*

Adjectives

adj

Keep in mind three main points about adjectives in English.

1. **Adjectives do not take a plural form.**

   a complex project

   three complex projects

2. **Adjectives can be placed either before the nouns they modify or later in the sentence.**

The *critical* need is to reduce the drag coefficient.

The need to reduce the drag coefficient is *critical*.

3. **Adjectives of one or two syllables take special endings to create the comparative and superlative forms.**

Positive	*Comparative*	*Superlative*
big	bigger	biggest
heavy	heavier	heaviest

Adjectives of three or more syllables take the word *more* for the comparative form and the words *the most* for the superlative form.

Positive	*Comparative*	*Superlative*
qualified	more qualified	the most qualified
feasible	more feasible	the most feasible

Adverbs

adv

Like adjectives, adverbs are modifiers, but their placement in the sentence is somewhat more complex. Remember five points about adverbs.

1. **Adverbs can modify verbs.**

Management terminated the project *reluctantly*.

2. **Adverbs can modify adjectives.**

The executive summary was *conspicuously* absent.

3. **Adverbs can modify other adverbs.**

The project is going *very* well.

4. **Adverbs that describe how an action takes place can appear in different locations in the sentence.**

Carefully the inspector examined the welds.

The inspector *carefully* examined the welds.

The inspector examined the welds *carefully*.

NOTE: The adverb should not be placed between the verb and the direct object.

INCORRECT   The inspector examined *carefully* the welds.

5. **Adverbs that describe the whole sentence can also be placed in different locations in the sentence.**

Apparently, the inspection was successful.

The inspection was *apparently* successful.

The inspection was successful, *apparently*.

Omitted Words

omit

Except for imperative sentences, in which the subject *you* is understood (*Get the correct figures*), all sentences in English require a subject.

The company has a policy on conflict of interest.

In This Book

For more about expletives, see Ch. 11, p. 244.

Do not omit the expletives *there* or *it*.

| INCORRECT | Are three reasons for us to pursue this issue. |
| CORRECT | *There* are three reasons for us to pursue this issue. |

| INCORRECT | Is important that we seek his advice. |
| CORRECT | *It* is important that we seek his advice. |

Repeated Words

rep

1. **Do not repeat the subject of a sentence.**

| INCORRECT | The company we are buying from *it* does not permit us to change our order. |
| CORRECT | The company we are buying from does not permit us to change our order. |

2. **In an adjective clause, do not repeat an object.**

| INCORRECT | The technical communicator does not use the same software that we were writing in *it*. |
| CORRECT | The technical communicator does not use the same software that we were writing in. |

3. **In an adjective clause, do not use a second adverb.**

| INCORRECT | The lab where we did the testing *there* is an excellent facility. |
| CORRECT | The lab where we did the testing is an excellent facility. |

PART D: COMMONLY MISUSED WORDS

The list below explains the correct usage of words commonly confused and misused. Most examples include a sentence showing the words being defined in italics.

accept, except   *Accept* means to receive, while *except* means excluding or to exclude. "We will not *accept* delivery of any items *except* those we have ordered."

adapt, adopt   *Adapt* means to adjust or to modify; *adopt* means to accept. "Management decided to *adapt* the quality-circle plan rather than *adopt* it as is."

affect, effect   *Affect* is a verb: "How will the news *affect* him?" *Effect* is most commonly a noun: "What will be the *effect* of the increase in allowable limits?" *Effect* is also (rarely) a verb meaning to bring about or cause to happen: "The new plant is expected to *effect* a change in our marketing strategy."

already, all ready   "The report had *already* been sent to the printer when the writer discovered that it was not *all ready*."

alright, all right   *Alright* is a misspelling of *all right* and should not be used.

among, between   In general, *among* is used for relationships of more than two items, *between* for only two items. "The collaboration *among* the writer, the illustrator, and the printer," but "the agreement *between* the two companies."

amount, number   *Amount* is used for noncounting items; *number* refers to counting items: "the *amount* of concrete," but "the *number* of bags of concrete."

assure, ensure, insure   To *assure* means to put someone's mind at ease: "let me *assure* you." To *ensure* and to *insure* both mean to make sure: "the new plan will *ensure* [or *insure*] good results." Some writers prefer to use *insure* only when referring to insurance: "to *insure* against fire loss."

can, may, might   *Can* refers to ability: "We *can* produce 300 chips per hour." *May* refers to permission: "*May* I telephone your references?" *Might* refers to possibility: "We *might* see declines in prices this year."

compliment, complement   A *compliment* is a statement of praise: "The owner offered a gracious *compliment* to the architect on his design." *Compliment* is also a verb: "The owner graciously *complimented* the architect." A *complement* is something that fills something up or makes it complete, or something that is an appropriate counterpart: "The design is a perfect *complement* to the landscape." *Complement* is also a verb: "The design *complements* the landscape perfectly."

could of   This is not a correct phrase; it is a corruption of *could've*, the contraction of *could have:* "She *could have* mentioned the abrasion problem in the report."

criteria, criterion   *Criteria*, meaning standards against which something will be measured, is plural; *criterion* is singular.

data, datum   *Data* is plural; *datum* is singular. This distinction is fading in popular usage, although not in some scientific and engineering applications. Check to see how it is spelled in your company or field.

discreet, discrete   *Discreet* means careful and prudent: "She is a very *discreet* manager; you can confide in her." *Discrete* means separate or distinct: "The company will soon split into three *discrete* divisions."

effective, efficient   *Effective* means that the item does what it is meant to do; *efficient* also carries the sense of accomplishing the goal without using more resources than necessary. "Air Force One is an *effective* way to transport the president, but it is not *efficient*; it costs some $40,000 per hour to fly."

farther, further   *Farther* refers to distance: "one mile *farther* down the road." *Further* means greater in quantity, time, or extent: "Are there any *further* questions?"

feedback   Many writers will not use *feedback* to refer to a response by a person: "Let me have your *feedback* by Friday." They limit the term to its original meaning, dealing with electricity, because a human response involves thinking (or should, anyway).

fewer, less   *Fewer* is used for counting items: "*fewer* bags of cement"; *less* is used for noncounting items: "*less* cement." It's the same distinction as between *number* and *amount*.

foreword, forward   A *foreword* is a preface, usually written by someone other than the author, introducing a book. *Forward* refers to being in advance: "The company decided to move *forward* with the project."

i.e., e.g.   *I.e.*, Latin for *id est*, means *that is*. *E.g.*, Latin for *exempli gratia*, means *for example*. Writers often confuse them. That's why I recommend using the English versions. Also, add commas around them: "Use the main entrance, *that is*, the one on Broadway."

imply, infer   The writer or speaker *implies*; the reader or listener *infers*.

input   People who don't like to give their *feedback* also don't like to offer their *input*.

its, it's   *Its* is the possessive pronoun: "The lab rat can't make up *its* mind." *It's* is the contraction of *it is*: "*It's* too late to apply for this year's grant." Why do people mix up these two words? Because they remember learning that possessives take apostrophes — "*Bob's* computer" — when they use the possessive form of *it*, they add the apostrophe. But *its* is a possessive pronoun — like *his, hers, theirs, ours,* and *yours* — a word specifically created to indicate possession; it does not take an apostrophe.

-ize   Many legitimate words end in *-ize*, such as *harmonize* and *sterilize,* but many writers and readers can't stand new ones (such as *prioritize*) when there are perfectly fine words already (such as *rank*).

lay, lie   *Lay* is a transitive verb meaning *to place*: "*Lay* the equipment on the table." *Lie* is an intransitive verb meaning *to recline*: "*Lie* down on the couch." The complete conjugation of *lay* is *lay, laid, laid, laying*; of *lie*, it is *lie, lay, lain, lying.*

lead, led   *Lead* is the infinitive verb: "We want to *lead* the industry." *Led* is the past tense: "Last year we *led* the industry."

parameter This is a mathematical term referring to a constant whose value can vary according to its application. Many writers object to the nonmathematical uses of the term, including such concepts as *perimeter, scope, outline,* and *limit.* (You guessed it: the same people who don't provide *input* or *feedback* don't use *parameter* very much either.)

phenomena, phenomenon *Phenomena* is plural; *phenomenon* is singular.

plain, plane *Plain* means simple and unadorned: "The new company created a very *plain* logo." *Plane* has several meanings: an airplane, the act of smoothing a surface, the tool used to smooth a surface, and the flat surface itself.

precede, proceed *Precede* means to come before: "Should Figure 1 *precede* Figure 2?" *Proceed* means to move forward: "We decided to *proceed* with the project despite the setback."

shall, will *Shall* suggests a legal obligation, particularly in a formal specification or contract: "The contractor *shall* remove all existing debris." *Will* suggests intent; it does not suggest a legal obligation: "We *will* get in touch with you as soon as possible to schedule the job."

sight, site, cite *Sight* refers to vision; *site* is a place; *cite* is a verb meaning to document a reference.

than, then *Than* is a conjunction used in comparisons: "Plan A works better *than* Plan B." *Then* is an adverb referring to time: "First we went to the warehouse. *Then* we went to the plant."

their, there, they're *Their* is the possessive pronoun: "They brought *their* equipment with them." *There* refers to a place—"We went *there* yesterday"—and is used in expletive expressions—"*There* are three problems we have to solve." *They're* is the contraction of *they are.*

to, too, two *To* is used in infinitive verbs ("*to* buy a new microscope") and in expressions referring to direction ("go *to* Detroit"). *Too* means excessively: "The refrigerator is *too* big for the lab." *Two* is the number 2.

viable This is a fine Latin word meaning able to sustain life: "*viable* cell culture" and "*viable* fetus." Many writers avoid such clichés as *viable alternative* (while they're avoiding *input* and *feedback*).

weather, whether *Weather* refers to sunshine and temperature. *Whether* refers to alternatives. "The demonstration will be held outdoors *whether* or not the *weather* cooperates."

who's, whose *Who's* is the contraction of *who is. Whose* is the possessive case of *who:* "*Whose* printer are we using?"

-wise Don't say, "*RAMwise,* the computer has 512 MB." Instead, say "The computer has 512 MB of RAM."

Xerox The people at Xerox become unhappy when writers ask for a *xerox* copy. The correct word is *photocopy; Xerox* is a copyrighted term.

your, you're *Your* is the possessive pronoun: "Bring *your* calculator to the meeting." *You're* is the contraction of *you are.*

REFERENCES

Chapter 1   Introduction to Technical Communication

Canon Corporation. (2002). Canon Mexicana. Retrieved January 11, 2002, from http://www.canon.com/gateway/region/americas.html

Galvin, T. (2001). 2001 Industry report. Retrieved February 22, 2002, from *Trainingmag.com* Web site: http://www.trainingmag.com/training/images/pdf/2001_industry_report.pdf

March of Dimes. (2002). March of Dimes Walk America home page. Retrieved February 22, 2002, from the March of Dimes Web site: http://www.modimes.org/WalkAmerica/Default.htm

Mead, J. (1998, August). Measuring the value added by technical documentation: A review of research and practice. *Technical Communication Online.* Retrieved June 18, 2002, from http://www.techcomm-online.com/issues/v45n3/full/0285.html

Plain English Network. (2002). Writing and oral communication skills: Career-boosting assets. Retrieved August 5, 2002, from the Plain English Network Web site: http://www.plainlanguage.gov/Summit/writing.htm

Technical Communication. (1990). *37*(4), 385.

Xerox Corporation. (2000). *The document centre at a glance.* Webster, NY: Xerox Corporation.

Chapter 2   Understanding Ethical and Legal Considerations

Donaldson, T. (1989). *The ethics of international business.* New York: Oxford University Press.

Helyar, P. S. (1992). Products liability: Meeting legal standards for adequate instructions. *Journal of Technical Writing and Communication, 22*(2), 125–147.

Murphy, P. (1995). Corporate ethics statements: Current status and future prospects. *Journal of Business Ethics, 14,* 727–740.

Texas Instruments. (2002). TI ethics quick test. Retrieved June 19, 2002, from the Texas Instruments Web site: http://www.ti.com/corp/docs/company/citizen/ethics/quicktest.shtml

Valasquez, M. G. (1998). *Business ethics: Concepts and cases* (4th ed.). Upper Saddle River, NJ: Prentice-Hall.

Chapter 3   Understanding the Writing Process

Cormier, R. A. (1997). One last look: The final quality control review. *The Editorial Eye.* Retrieved July 21, 1997, from http://www.eeicom.com/eye/qc-lead.html

Dumas, J. S., & Redish, J. C. (1993). *A practical guide to usability testing.* Norwood, NJ: Ablex.

Kantner, L. (1994). The art of managing usability tests. *IEEE Transactions on Professional Communication, 37*, 143–148.

National Cancer Institute. (2002). Lessons learned. Retrieved August 7, 2002, from the Usability.gov Web site: http://www.usability.gov/lessons/IM_learned.html

Rubin, J. (1994). *Handbook of usability testing: How to plan, design, and conduct effective tests.* New York: Wiley.

Chapter 4 Writing Collaboratively

Borisoff, D., & Merrill, L. (1987). Teaching the college course in gender differences as barriers to conflict resolution. In L. B. Nadler, M. K. Nadler, & W. R. Todd-Mancillas (Eds.), *Advances in gender and communication research* (pp. 351–361). Lanham, MD: University Press of America.

Chodorow, N. (1978). *The reproduction of mothering: Psychoanalysis and the sociology of gender.* Berkeley: University of California Press.

Couture, B., & Rymer, J. (1989). Interactive writing on the job: Definitions and implications of collaboration. In M. Kogen (Ed.), *Writing in the business professions* (pp. 73–93). Urbana, IL: National Council of Teachers of English.

Duin, A. H., Jorn, L. A., & DeBower, M. S. (1991). Collaborative writing—Courseware and telecommunications. In M. M. Lay & W. M. Karis (Eds.), *Collaborative writing in industry: Investigations in theory and practice* (pp. 146–169). Amityville, NY: Baywood.

Ede, L., & Lunsford, A. (1990). *Singular texts/plural authors: Perspectives on collaborative writing.* Carbondale: Southern Illinois University Press.

Lustig, M. W., & Koester, J. (1993). *Intercultural competence.* New York: HarperCollins.

Matson R. (1996, April). The seven sins of deadly meetings. *Fast Company.* Retrieved July 22, 1999, from http://www.fastcompany.com/online/02/meetings.html

McMillan, J. R., Clifton, A. K., McGrath, D., & Gale, W. S. (1977). Women's language: Uncertainty or interpersonal sensitivity and emotionality? *Sex Roles, 3*, 545–549.

Polycom, Inc. (2002). The Polycom office (Catalog 2002). Retrieved August 8, 2002, from the Polycom, Inc. Web site: http://www.polycom.com/common/pw_item_show_doc/0,1449,1111,00.pdf

ʾen, D. (1990). *You just don't understand.* New York: Morrow.

E. (1999). *The fast forward MBA in project management.* New York: Wiley.

Understanding Your Audience and Purpose

ʾl, UCLA. (2002). Japanese communication styles. Retrieved January the Anderson School, UCLA Web site: http://www.anderson.ucla
ʾpan/mainfrm.htm

Eat the way your mama taught you. *Intercom, 46*(5), 22–24.

ʾomunication: Toward 2000. Cincinnati: South-Western.

ʾal elements in cross-cultural technical communication: Recognition as a function of cultural conventions. In C. R. Lovitt & ʾ (Eds.), *Exploring the rhetoric of international professional communication: ʾa for teachers and researchers* (pp. 253–276). Amityville, NY: Baywood.

Enäjärvi, M. (2002). The Director General's report. *National Board of Patents and Registration of Finland Annual Report 2000.* Retrieved February 4, 2002, from http://www.prh.fi/pdfdoc/vuosiker/year2000.pdf

Heilemann, J. (2001, December 2). Reinventing the wheel. *Time.* Retrieved January 22, 2002, from *Time Online Edition.* http://www.time.com/time/business/article/0,8599,186660,00.html

Hoft, N. L. (1995). *International technical communication: How to export information about high technology.* New York: Wiley.

Jain, S. J. S. (2002). Disaster management during super cyclone 1999 in Orissa—A case study of railways. Retrieved January 22, 2002, from South Eastern Railway (India) Web site: http://ce_ser.tripod.com/orissa.html

Kamen, D., Ambrogi, R. R., Duggan, R. J., Heinzmann, R. K., Key, B. R., Skoskiewicz, A., et al. (1999). *United States Patent 5,971,091.* Retrieved January 22, 2002, from http://www.uspto.gov

Lovitt, C. R. (1999). Introduction: Rethinking the role of culture in international professional communication. In C. R. Lovitt & D. Goswami (Eds.), *Exploring the rhetoric of international professional communication: An agenda for teachers and researchers* (pp. 1–13). Amityville, NY: Baywood.

Lustig, M. W., & Koester, J. (1999). *Intercultural competence.* New York: HarperCollins.

Norton, J. (2002, January 14). Tampa Post Office to test Segway™ Human Transporter. Retrieved January 22, 2002, from the Segway Web site: http://www.segway.com/consumer/team/press_releases/pr_011402.html

Schriver, K. A. (1997). *Dynamics in document design: Creating text for readers.* New York: Wiley.

Suzuki, N. (2002). Message from the president. Retrieved February 4, 2002, from the FDK Corporation Web site: http://www.fdk.co.jp/company_e/message-e.html

Tebeaux, E., & Driskill, L. (1999). Culture and the shape of rhetoric: Protocols of international document design. In C. R. Lovitt & D. Goswami (Eds.), *Exploring the rhetoric of international professional communication: An agenda for teachers and researchers* (pp. 211–251). Amityville, NY: Baywood.

U.S. Census Bureau. (2002). *Statistical abstract of the United States: 2000.* Washington, DC: U.S. Government Printing Office.

Chapter 6 Communicating Persuasively

AT&T Foundation. (2002). AT&T Foundation programs. Retrieved February 11, 2002, from the AT&T Foundation Web site: http://www.att.com/foundation/programs/community.html

Hewlett Packard Corporation. (2002). HP Omnibook 6100 product benefits. Retrieved August 15, 2002, from the Hewlett Packard Web site: http://www.hp.com/notebooks/us/eng/products/omnibook_6100/omnibook_6100_benefits.htm

Lucent Technologies. (2002). Privacy statement. Retrieved February 12, 2002, from the Lucent Technologies Web site: http://www.lucent.com/privacy.html

Mayberry, K. J. (2002). *For argument's sake: A guide to writing effective arguents* (4th ed.). New York: Longman.

Microsoft Corporation. (2002). Patrick Blackburn. Retrieved February 6, 2002, from the Microsoft Corporation Web site: http://www.microsoft.com/jobs/people/patrick.htm

Princess Cruises. (2001). Princes Cruises home page. Retrieved September 20, 2001, from http://www.princess.com/home.jsp

University of Michigan. (2001). Q&A re University of Michigan admissions policies. Retrieved February 7, 2002, from the University of Michigan Web site: http://www.umich.edu/%7Eurel/admissions/faqs/q&a.html

Chapter 7   Researching Your Subject

Bowman, J. P. (1999). Human relations: Conversations and interviews. *Business communication: Managing information and relationships.* Retrieved July 22, 1999, from http://spider.hcob.wmich.edu/bis/faculty/bowman/dyads.html

Chemical Abstracts Service. (2002). CA on CD quick start tips. Retrieved February 18, 2002, from the Chemical Abstracts Web site: http://www.cas.org/ONLINE/CD/CACD/QUICKSTART/author.html

Cohen, L. (2002). Conducting research on the Internet. Retrieved February 13, 2002, from the University at Albany Libraries Web site: http://library.albany.edu/internet/research.html

Lovgren, J. (2002). Achieving performance-centered design. Retrieved February 21, 2002, from the Reisman Consulting Group, Inc. Web site: http://www.reisman-consulting.com/pages/a-Perform.html

McComb, G. (1991). *Troubleshooting and repairing VCRs* (2nd ed.). Blue Ridge Summit, PA: TAB/McGraw-Hill.

Michael J. Fox Foundation for Parkinson's Research. (2002). Scientific advisory board. Retrieved August 16, 2002, from the Michael J. Fox Foundation for Parkinson's Research Web site: http://www.michaeljfox.com/foundation/sab.html

Zakon, R. H. (2002). Hobbes' Internet Timeline 5.5. Retrieved February 18, 2002, from http://www.zakon.org/robert/internet/timeline/

Chapter 8   Organizing Your Information

Andrews, T. (2000). Linux vs. Windows 2000. Retrieved March 5, 2002, from the ZDNet.com Web site: http://www.zdnet.com/devhead/stories/articles/0,4413,2163578,00.html

Bernard, B. P. (Ed.). (1997). Neck musculoskeletal disorders: Evidence for work-relatedness. In *Musculoskeletal disorders (MSDs) and workplace factors: A critical review of epidemiologic evidence for work-related musculoskeletal disorders of the neck, upper extremity, and low back.* (chap. 2). Retrieved July 5, 2002, from the U.S. Department of Health and Human Services Web site: http://www.cdc.gov/niosh/ergtxt2.html

Brusaw, C. T., Alred, G. J., & Oliu, W. E. (2000). *Handbook of technical writing.* (6th ed.). Boston: Bedford/St. Martin's.

Canon U.S.A., Inc. (2002). PowerShot S330 kit contents. Retrieved August 23, 2002, from the Canon U.S.A., Inc. Web site: http://www.powershot.com/powershot2/s330/kit.html

Jones International. (1999). Computers: History and development. In *Jones Tele-communications & Multimedia Encyclopedia*. Retrieved March 5, 2002, from http://www.digitalcentury.com/encyclo/update/comp_hd.html

National Transportation Safety Board. (2000). Putting children first. Retrieved June 25, 2001, from http://www.ntsb.gov/Publictn/2000/SR0002.pdf

University of Texas at Austin. (2000). Campus overview map. Retrieved March 5, 2002, from http://www.utexas.edu/maps/main/overview

U.S. Department of Energy. (2001). *Report to Congress on small modular nuclear reactors*. Retrieved March 7, 2002, from the U.S. Department of Energy Web site: http://nuclear.gov/reports/Cong-Rpt-may01.pdf

U.S. Department of Labor. (1997). Methylene chloride. OSHA 3144. Retrieved July 8, 1999, from http://www.oshaslc.gov/Publications/Osha3144.pdf

U.S. Environmental Protection Agency. (2000). Air quality criteria for carbon monoxide. Retrieved August 23, 2002, from the U.S. Environmental Protection Agency Web site: http://www.epa.gov/ncea/pdfs/coaqcd.pdf

Xerox Corporation. (2001). It's a colorful world. Retrieved June 18, 2001, from the Xerox Corporation Web site: http://www.xerox.com/go/xrx/template/009.jsp?view=Feature&Xcntry=USA&Xlang=en_US&Xseg=home&ed_name=Colorful_World_2

Chapter 9   Drafting and Revising Definitions and Descriptions

Eisenberg, A. (1992). *Effective technical communication* (2nd ed.). New York: McGraw-Hill.

Fraternity Insurance and Purchasing Group. (1997). Risk management policy. Retrieved March 8, 2002, from the Fraternity Insurance and Purchasing Group Web site: http://www.fipg.org/media/risk_man.pdf

Hewlett Packard Company. (2002). *HP digital projectors xb31 & sb21*. Page 9. Retrieved September 3, 2002, from the Hewlett Packard Web site: http://h200004.www2.hp.com/bc/docs/support/SupportManual/bpia6001/bpia6001.pdf

Masterson, U. O. (2001, November 20). Biometrics and the new security age. Retrieved March 11, 2002, from the MSNBC.com Web site: http://www.msnbc.com/news/654788.asp?cp1=1

National Telecommunications and Information Administration. (2000). The economic impact of third-generation wireless technology. Retrieved March 11, 2002, from the National Telecommunications and Information Administration Web site: http://www.ntia.doc.gov/ntiahome/threeg/ceareportoct2000.pdf

Praxis, Inc. (1999). SSULI brochure. Retrieved July 12, 1999, from http://www.pxi.com/public/brochures/ssuli/index.html

Roblee, C. L., & McKechnie, A. J. (1981). *The investigation of fires*. Englewood Cliffs, NJ: Prentice Hall.

Sweetman, B. (2002, March). Spy in the sky. *Popular Science*. Retrieved March 12, 2002, from the *Popular Science* Web site: http://www.popsci.com/popsci/aviation/article/0,12543,194509-4,00.html

U.S. Congress, Office of Technology Assessment. (1995a). *Bringing health care online: The role of information technologies* (OTA-ITC-624). Washington, DC: U.S. Government Printing Office.

U.S. Congress, Office of Technology Assessment. (1995b). *Renewing our energy future.* (OTA-ETI-614). Washington, DC: U.S. Government Printing Office.

U.S. Department of Agriculture. (2000). Irradiation of raw meat and poultry: Questions & answers. Retrieved September 3, 2002, from the U.S. Department of Agriculture Web site: http://www.fsis.usda.gov/oa/pubs/qa_irrad.htm

U.S. Department of Energy. (2001). The Nevada 1-MW Solar Dish-Engine Project. Retrieved March 8, 2002, from the U.S. Department of Energy Web site: http://www.energylan.sandia.gov/sunlab/PDFs/nevada.pdf

U.S. Environmental Protection Agency. (2001). Global warming. Retrieved June 25, 2001, from the Environmental Protection Agency Web site: http://www.epa.gov/globalwarming/climate/index.html

Chapter 10   Drafting and Revising Coherent Text

Benson, P. (1985). Writing visually: Design considerations in technical publications. *Technical Communication, 32,* 35–39.

Cohen, S., & Grace, D. (1994). Engineers and social responsibility: An obligation to do good. *IEEE Technology and Society, 13,* 12–19.

Darling, C. (2002). Coherence: Transitions between ideas. *Guide to grammar and writing.* Retrieved March 12, 2002, from http://ccc.commnet.edu/grammar/transitions.htm

Snyder, J. D. (1993). Off-the-shelf bugs hungrily gobble our nastiest pollutants. *Smithsonian, 24,* 66+.

U.S. Department of Health and Human Services. (1998). HIV cost and services utilization study. *Agency for Health Care Policy and Research.* Retrieved March 14, 2002, from http://www.ahcpr.gov/data/hcsus.htm

Chapter 11   Drafting and Revising Effective Sentences

Fuchsberg, G. (1990, December 7). Well, at least "terminated with extreme prejudice" wasn't cited. *Wall Street Journal,* p. B1.

Fujiura, G. T. (2001). Emerging trends in disabilities. Retrieved March 19, 2002, from the Population Reference Bureau Web site: http://www.prb.org/Content/NavigationMenu/PT_articles/Jul-Sep01/Emerging_Trends_in_Disability.htm

National Science Foundation. (2002). Announcement of Fall 2002 target date for proposal submissions, Division of Physics. Retrieved July 8, 2002, from the National Science Foundation Web site: http://www.nsf.gov/pubs/2002/nsf02139/nsf02139.txt

Peterson, D. A. T. (1990). Developing a Simplified English vocabulary. *Technical Communication, 37,* 130–133.

Snow, K. (2001). People First language. Retrieved March 19, 2002, from the Disability Is Natural Web site: http://www.disabilityisnatural.com/peoplefirstlanguage.htm

Strunk, W. (1918). *The elements of style* [Electronic version]. Ithaca, NY: Privately printed (Geneva, NY: Press of W.P. Humphrey). Retrieved November 1, 1999, from http://www.bartleby.com/141/strunk.html#13

Williams, J. (1997). *Style: Ten lessons in clarity & grace* (5th ed.). New York: Harper-Collins.

Chapter 12 Drafting and Revising the Front and Back Matter

Crowe, B. (1985). Design of a radio-based system for distribution automation. Unpublished manuscript, Drexel University.

Federal Emergency Management Agency. (2002). Glossary. Public assistance infrastructure recovery programs. Retrieved March 29, 2002, from the Federal Emergency Management Agency Web site: http://www.fema.gov/r-n-r/pa/glossary.htm

Honold, P. (1999). Learning how to use a cellular phone: Comparison between German and Chinese users. *Technical Communication 46*, 2. Retrieved September 11, 2002, from http://www.techcomm-online.org/issues/v46n2/full/0331.html

Vacca, R., in Rubens, P. (Ed.). (1992). *Science and technical writing: A manual of style.* New York: Henry Holt.

Chapter 13 Designing the Document and the Page

Agilent Technologies. (2002, March). *Agilent Telecommunications News 9*(1), 11. Retrieved April 5, 2002, from the Agilent Technologies Web site: http://literature.agilent.com/litweb/pdf/5988-4859ENUS.pdf

Biggs, J. R. (1980). *Basic typography.* New York: Watson-Guptill.

Bonneville Power Administration. (1993). *Resource programs: Final environmental impact statement, volume 1: Environmental analysis.* Washington, DC: U.S. Department of Energy.

CrystalGraphics, Inc. (2002). CrystalGraphics Web site. Retrieved April 2, 2002, from http://www.crystalgraphics.com

Felker, D. B., Pickering, F., Charrow, V. R., Holland, V. M., & Redish, J. C. (1981). *Guidelines for document designers.* Washington, DC: American Institutes for Research.

General Electric Company. (2001). GE Annual Report 2000. Retrieved April 2, 2002, from the General Electric Company Web site: http://www.ge.com/annual00/download/images/GEannual00.pdf

General Motors Corp. (2002). Corvette for 2002. Retrieved April 2, 2002, from the Chevy.com Web site: http://www.chevrolet.com/gmnav/brochure/pdf/cor_catalog.pdf

Haley, A. (1991). All caps: A typographic oxymoron. *U&lc, 18*(3), 14–15.

Hewlett Packard Company. (2000). HP WebQoS Priority for the Windows NT® Operating System installation and configuration guide, Edition 3. Retrieved April 5, 2002, from the Hewlett Packard Web site: http://ovweb.external.hp.com/lpe/doc_serv/

Hewlett Packard Company. (2002). HPDigital Entertainment Centerde100c Owner's Guide. Retrieved April 4, 2002, from the Hewlett Packard Web site: http://www.hp.com/cposupport/manual_set/lpg40530.pdf

Horton, W. (1993). The almost universal language: Graphics for international documents. *Technical Communication, 40,* 682–693.

Ichimura, M. (2001). Intercultural research in page design and layout for Asian/Pacific audiences. *Proceedings of the STC's 48th Annual Conference.* Retrieved April 9, 2002, from http://www.stc.org/proceedings/ConfProceed/2001/PDFs/STC48-000122.pdf

Keyes, E. (1993). Typography, color, and information structure. *Technical Communication, 40,* 638–654.

Kostelnick, C. & Roberts, D. D. (1998). *Designing visual language: Strategies for professional communicators.* Needham Heights, MA: Allyn & Bacon.

Poulton, E. (1968). Rate of comprehension of an existing teleprinter output and of possible alternatives. *Journal of Applied Psychology, 52,* 16–21.

Texas Instruments. (2001). SM320C6201B, SMJ320C6201B Digital Signal Processor. Retrieved April 5, 2002, from the Texas Instruments Web site: http://www-s.ti.com/sc/ds/sm320c6201b.pdf

U.S. Department of Agriculture. (2002, March 5). Thermometer usage messages and delivery mechanisms for parents of young children. Retrieved April 4, 2002, from the Food Safety and Inspection Service Web site: http://www.fsis.usda.gov/oa/research/rti_thermy.pdf

U.S. Federal Reserve Board. (2002). Industrial production and capacity utilization: The 2001 annual revision. Retrieved April 4, 2002, from the U.S. Federal Reserve Web site: http://www.federalreserve.gov/pubs/bulletin/2002/0302_2nd.pdf

White, J. V. (1990). *Great pages: A common-sense approach to effective desktop design.* El Segundo, CA: Serif.

Williams, T., & Spyridakis, J. (1992). Visual discriminability of headings in text. *IEEE Transactions on Professional Communication, 35,* 64–70.

Chapter 14   Creating Graphics

Barnum, C. M., & Carliner, S. (1993). *Techniques for technical communicators.* New York: Macmillan.

Brockmann, R. J. (1990). *Writing better computer user documentation: From paper to hypertext.* New York: Wiley.

Curtis, H., & Barnes, N. S. (1989). *Biology* (5th ed.). New York: Worth.

Dean, R. S., & Kulhavy, R. W. (1981). Influence of spatial organization in prose learning. *Journal of Educational Psychology, 73,* 57–64.

Gatlin, P. L. (1988). Visuals and prose in manuals: The effective combination. In *Proceedings of the 35th International Technical Communication Conference* (pp. RET 113–115). Arlington, VA: Society for Technical Communication.

General Motors of Canada. (2002). Smart guide. Retrieved April 12, 2002, from the General Motors of Canada Web site: http://www.gmcanada.com/english/maintenance/goodwrench/gw_smartguide.html

Grimstead, D. (1987). Quality graphics: Writers draw the line. *Proceedings of the 34th International Technical Communication Conference* (pp. VC 66–69). Arlington, VA: Society for Technical Communication.

Holmes, N., & Bagby, M. (2002). USA: An annual report. Retrieved July 11, 2002, from Richard Paul Wurman's Understanding Web site: http://www.understandingusa.com/chaptercc=2&cs=18.html

Horton, W. (1991). *Illustrating computer documentation: The art of presenting information graphically on paper and online.* New York: Wiley.

Horton, W. (1993). The almost universal language: Graphics for international documents. *Technical Communication, 40,* 682–693.

Levie, W. H., & Lentz, R. (1982). Effects of text illustrations: A review of research. *Journal of Educational Psychology, 73,* 195–232.

Mankiw, N. G. (1997). *Macroeconomics* (3rd ed.). New York: Worth.

Morrison, C., & Jimmerson, W. (1989, July). Business presentations for the 1990s. *Video Manager, 4,* 18.

Pultrusion Industry Council. (2001). Pultrusion vs. steel. Retrieved April 11, 2002, from the Pultrusion Industry Council Web site: http://www.cfa-hq.org/pic/pultrusion/steel.htm

Software602, Inc. (2002). 602Tab Manual. Retrieved April 12, 2002, from the Software602, Inc. Web site: http://download.software602.com/pdf/pcs/2001/602tab_manual.pdf

Tufte, E. R. (1983). *The visual display of quantitative information.* Cheshire, CT: Graphics Press.

Tufte, E. R. (1999). The visual display of quantitative information. Adapted by Saul Greenberg. Retrieved August 2, 1999, from http://www.cpsc.ucalgary.ca/projects/grouplab/699/vis_display.html

U.S. Census Bureau. (2002). *Statistical abstract of the United States: 2001* (p. 118). Retrieved July 10, 2002, from http://www.census.gov/prod/2002pubs/01statab/health.pdf

U.S. Consumer Product Safety Commission. (1999). Your used crib could be deadly. Retrieved August 3, 1999, from the Consumer Product Safety Commission Web site: http://www.cpsc.gov/cpscpub/pubs/usedcrib.pdf

U.S. Department of the Treasury. (1999). *Business use of your home* (IRS Publication No. 587, p. 4). Retrieved August 3, 1999, from http://ftp.fedworld.gov/pub/irs-pdf/p587.pdf

U.S. Environmental Protection Agency. (1991). *Building air quality: A guide for building owners and facility managers* (Publication No. 402-F-91-102). Washington, DC: U.S. Government Printing Office.

White, J. V. (1984). *Using charts and graphs: 1000 ideas for visual persuasion.* New York: R. R. Bowker.

White, J. V. (1990). *Color for the electronic age.* New York: Watson-Guptill.

Chapter 15   Writing Letters, Memos, and E-mails

Bowman, J. P. (1999). Writing persuasive messages. Business communication: Managing information and relationships. Retrieved September 21, 1999, from http://spider.hcob.wmich.edu/bis/faculty/bowman/persuade2.html

Crowe, E. P. (1994). *The electronic traveller: Exploring alternative online systems.* New York: Windcrest/McGraw-Hill.

Flynn, N. (2002). E-mail policy guide: A formula for safe and secure e-mail usage. Retrieved July 11, 2002, from the ePolicy Web site: http://www.elronsoftware.com /pdf/emailpolicy.pdf

Hart, G. (2002, July 12). Re: An Ethical Question? Message posted to TECHWR-L discussion group, archived at http://techwr-l@lists.raycomm.com

Chapter 16   Preparing Job-Application Materials

Bowman, J. P. (2000). Selling yourself. *Business communication: Managing information and relationships.* Retrieved April 17, 2002, from http://spider.hcob.wmich.edu/bis /faculty/bowman/job2.html

Catenaro, A. (2002). Andrea M. Catenaro, Web & graphic designer. Retrieved April 26, 2002, from the Andreacatenaro.com Web site: http://www.andreacatenaro.com /index.html

Harcourt, J., Krizan, A. C., & Merrier, P. (1991). Teaching résumé content: Hiring officials' preferences versus college recruiters' preferences. *Business Education Forum* 45(7), 13–17.

Isaacs, K. (2002). How to decide on résumé length. Retrieved April 25, 2002, from the Monster.com Web site: http://resume.monster.com/components/length/

JobWeb.com (2002). Your guide to resume writing. Retrieved April 25, 2002, from the JobWeb.com Web site: http://www.jobweb.com/Resumes_Interviews /resume_guide/comp.html

Parker, Y. (1999). Hot tips for résumé-writing from expert Yana Parker. *Mary Ellen Guffey's communication @ work.* Retrieved September 18, 1999, from http://www .westwords.com/GUFFEY/parker.html

Thompson, M. A. (2002). Writing your international résumé. Retrieved July 24, 2002, from the JobWeb.com Web site: http://www.jobweb.com/Resources/Library /International/Writing_Your_185_01.htm

Vaas, L. (2002, April 29). It pays to be outstanding. Retrieved May 3, 2002, from the eWEEK Web site: http://www.eweek.com/article/0,3658,s=25210&a=26116,00.asp

Chapter 17   Writing Proposals

CBD/FBO Online. (2002). Commerce Business Daily Online. Retrieved April 29, 2002, from http://www.cbdweb.com/cgi-bin/cbd

Ewing, M., & Lipus, T. (2002). Proposal for feasibility study on printer capability. Unpublished document.

Miner, L. E. (2002). A guide to proposal planning and writing. Retrieved July 24, 2002, from the University of Vermont Office of Sponsored Projects Web site: http: //www.oryxpress.com/miner.htm

National Research Foundation. (2002). Innovation Fund Trust call for pre-proposals: Round 6. Retrieved July 24, 2002, from the National Research Foundation Web site: http://www.nrf.ac.za/innovationfund/

Reid, A. N. T. (2001). A practical guide for writing proposals. Retrieved April 29, 2002, from http://members.dca.net/areid/proposal.htm

SmartDraw.com. (2002). SmartDraw cool examples. Retrieved April 30, 2002, from the SmartDraw.com Web site: http://www.smartdraw.com/resources/examples/business/gantt15.htm

Thrush, E. (2000, January 20). Writing for an international audience, Part I. *Communication Skills*. Retrieved November 5, 2002, from the Suite 101.com Web site: http://www.suite.101.com/article.cfm/5381/32233

U.S. Census Bureau. (2002). *Statistical abstract of the United States, 2001.* Retrieved July 10, 2002, from http://www.census.gov/prod/2002pubs/statab/sec11.pdf

Wells, M. Tommack, D., & Tuck, B. (1997). Proposal to research whether Central State University should recognize American Sign Language as a foreign language. Unpublished document.

Chapter 18   Writing Informal Reports

Ewing, M., & Lipus, T. (2002). Progress report for feasibility study on printer capability. Unpublished document.

Finkelstein, L., Jr. (2000). *Pocket book of technical writing for engineers and scientists.* New York: McGraw-Hill.

United States Chemical Safety and Hazard Investigation Board. (2002). Toxic cloud forces evacuation of Montreal high-rise. Retrieved November 6, 2002, from the United States Chemical Safety and Hazard Investigation Board Web site: http://www.chemsafety.gov/circ/post.cfm?incident_id=6092

Waltham, G. (2001). Globalization and ICTs: Working across cultures. Judge Institute of Management Studies Research Papers in Management Studies. Retrieved November 6, 2002, from the Judge Institute of Management Studies Web site: http://www.jims.cam.ac.uk/research/working_papers/abstract_01/0108.html

Chapter 19   Writing Formal Reports

Abraham, S., Evans, D. L. Veneman, A. L., & Whitman, C. T. (2002, July 8). Letter to George W. Bush, President of the United States. Retrieved August 1, 2002, from the Department of Energy Web site: http://www.energy.gov/HQPress/releases02/julpr/GreenhouseGasRegistryLetter.pdf

Centers for Disease Control. (2002). Assessing health risk behaviors among young people: Youth risk behavior surveillance system, at a glance 2002. Retrieved August 1, 2002, from the Centers for Disease Control Web site: http://www.cdc.gov/nccdphp/dash/yrbs/yrbsaag.htm

Ewing, M., & Lipus, T. (2002). Feasibility study on printer capability: A completion report. Unpublished document.

Mathes, J. C., & Stevenson, D. W. (1991). *Designing technical reports: Writing for audiences in organizations* (2nd ed.). New York: Macmillan.

Wells, M., Tommack, D., & Tuck, B. (1997). American Sign Language: A recommendation for foreign language recognition at Central State University. Unpublished document.

Chapter 20   Writing Instructions and Manuals

Agilent Technologies. (2001). *Agilent E2929A Opt. 200 PCI-X Performance Optimizer user's guide.* Retrieved July 3, 2001, from the Agilent Technologies Web site: http://www.tm.agilent.com/data/downloads/eng/tmo/EPSG083647.pdf

Apple Computer, Inc. (2002). Apple Quicktime. Retrieved September 30, 2002, from the Apple Computer, Inc. Web site: http://www.apple.com/quicktime/install/

Befuddled PC users flood help lines, and no question seems to be too basic. (1994, March 1). *Wall Street Journal,* p. B1.

Canon U.S.A., Inc. (2002). *MultiPASS C755 quick start guide.* Retrieved May 15, 2002, from the Canon U.S.A., Inc. Web site: http://209.85.7.18/techsupport/quickstart /mpc755/mpc755_quickstart.pdf

Deere & Co. (1989). *21-Inch walk behind rotary mowers* (p. 7). Moline, IL: Deere & Co.

Delio, M. (2002, June 4). Read The F***ing Story, Then RTFM. *Wired News.* Retrieved June 6, 2002, from http://www.wired.com/news/culture/0,1284,52901,00.html

Dell Computer Corporation. (2001). *Dell™ Dimension™ L Series Systems reference and troubleshooting guide.* Round Rock, TX: Dell Computer Corporation.

HCL, Inc. (2001). Hazard communication labels. Retrieved May 10, 2002, from the HCL, Inc. Web site: http://www.hclco.com/labels/hazard/hazard1.htm

Mead, J. (1998). Measuring the value added by technical documentation: A review of research and practice. *Technical Communication, 45,* 353–379.

Minwax Company. (2002). CD holder. Minwax Company Web page. Retrieved May 10, 2002, from http://www.minwax.com/projects/cdhold/cdhold1.htm

Toshiba America, Inc. (2001). *Toshiba 3LCD Data Projector owner's manual.* Retrieved May 15, 2002, from the Toshiba America, Inc. Web site: http://www.mmgtechsupport .com/PDF/manual6.PDF

U.S. Department of Labor, Occupational Safety and Health Administration. (2000). OSHA regulations (Standards - 29 CFR). Retrieved February 20, 2000, from http://www.osha-slc.gov/OshStd_toc/OSHA_Std_toc.html

Chapter 21   Creating Web Sites

Computer Industry Almanac, Inc. (2002). Internet users will top 1 billion in 2005. Wireless Internet users will reach 48% in 2005. Retrieved May 16, 2002, from the Computer Industry Almanac, Inc. Web site: http://www.c-i-a.com/pr032102.htm

Corel (2002). Corel WordPerfect Web page. Retrieved May 29, 2002, from http://www3 .corel.com/cgi-bin/gx.cgi/AppLogic+FTContentServer?pagename=Corel /Product/WordPerfect

Feldman, A. (2002). Retrieved May 31, 2002, from the Ari Feldman Web site: http://www.arifeldman.com/index.html

Gahran, A. (2001, February 20). Tips for online content businesses in 2001. *Contentious.* Retrieved August 2, 2002, from http://www.contentious.com/articles/010220-2 .htm

Global Reach. (2002). Global Internet statistics (by language). Retrieved May 31, 2002, from the Global Reach Web site: http://www.glreach.com/globstats/index.php3

Google Search Services. (2002). Google site map. Retrieved November 18, 2002, from the Google Search Services home page: http://www.google.com/sitemap.html

GovBenefits. (2002). Frequently asked questions (FAQ). Retrieved May 29, 2002, from the GovBenefits Web site: http://www.govbenefits.gov/GovBenefits/jsp/FAQ.jsp

O'Mahoney, B. (2002). Cyberspace issues—Web update. Retrieved July 12, 2001, from The copyright website: http://www.copyrightwebsite.com/digital/webIssues /webIssues.asp

Palm, Inc. (2002). Palm.com support: Knowledge library. Retrieved May 31, 2002, from the Palm, Inc. Web site: http://205.141.210.149/SRVS/CGI-BIN/WEBCGI.EXE?

Selective Service System. (2002). Registration information. FAQs. Retrieved September 12, 2002, from the Selective Service System Web site: http://www.sss.gov/qa.htm

Silver Council. (2002). About us. Retrieved May 31, 2002, from the Silver Council Web site: http://www.silvercouncil.org/html/default.htm

Sun Microsystems, Inc. (1999). Guide to Web style. Retrieved September 10, 1999, from the Sun Microsystems Web site: http://www.sun.com/styleguide/

Zakon, R. (2000). Hobbes' Internet timeline v. 5.0. Retrieved February 20, 2000, from http://info.isoc.org/guest/zakon/Internet/History/HIT.html

Chapter 22   Making Oral Presentations

Smith, T. C. (1991). *Making successful presentations: A self-teaching guide.* New York: Wiley.

SELECTED BIBLIOGRAPHY

Technical Communication

Allen, O. J., & Deming, L. H. (1994). *Publications management: Essays for professional communicators.* Amityville, NY: Baywood.

Beer, D. F. (1992). *Writing and speaking in the technology professions: A practical guide.* New York: IEEE.

Blicq, R. S., & Moretto, L. A. (2001). *Writing reports to get results: Quick, effective results using the pyramid method* (3rd ed.). Piscataway, NJ: IEEE.

Boiarsky, C. R., & Soven, M. K. (1995). *Writings from the workplace: Documents, models, cases.* Needham Heights, MA: Allyn & Bacon.

Brusaw, C. T., Alred, G. J., & Oliu, W. E. (2003). *Handbook of technical writing* (7th ed.). New York: St. Martin's.

Day, R. A. (1995). *Scientific English: A guide for scientists and other professionals* (2nd ed.). Phoenix, AZ: Oryx.

Dombrowski, P. M. (Ed.). (1994). *Humanistic aspects of technical communication.* Amityville, NY: Baywood.

Gurak, L., & Lay, M. M. (2002). *Research in technical communication.* Westport, CT: Greenwood.

Hoft, N. L. (1995). *International technical communication: How to export information about high technology.* New York: Wiley.

Pickett, N. A., Laster, A. A. (2000). *Technical English: Writing, reading, and speaking* (8th ed.). New York: Longman.

Sides, C. H. (1999). *How to write and present technical information* (3rd ed.). Phoenix, AZ: Oryx.

Also see the following journals:
IEEE Transactions on Professional Communication
Journal of Business and Technical Communication
Journal of Technical Writing and Communication
Technical Communication
Technical Communication Quarterly

Ethics

Beauchamp, T. L., & Bowie, N. E. (2000). *Ethical theory and business* (6th ed.). Upper Saddle River, NJ: Prentice-Hall.

Markel, M. (2000). *Ethics and technical communication: A synthesis and critique.* Stamford, CT: Greenwood.

Velasquez, M. G. (2001). *Business ethics: Concepts and cases* (5th ed.). Upper Saddle River, NJ: Prentice-Hall.

Collaborative Writing

Blyler, N. R., & Thralls, C. (Eds.). (1993). *Professional communication: The social perspective.* Newbury Park, CA: Sage.

Cross, G. A. (1993). *Collaboration and conflict: A contextual exploration of group writing and positive emphasis.* Cresskill, NJ: Hampton.

Ede, L., & Lunsford, A. (1990). *Singular texts/plural authors: Perspectives on collaborative writing.* Carbondale: Southern Illinois University Press.

Forman, J. (Ed.). (1992). *New visions of collaborative writing.* Portsmouth, NH: Boynton/ Cook.

Lay, M. M., and Karis, W. M. (1991). *Collaborative writing in industry: Investigations in theory and practice.* Amityville, NY: Baywood.

Research Techniques

Berkman, R. I. (2000). *Find it fast: How to uncover expert information on any subject* (5th ed.). New York: HarperInformation.

Harnack, A., & Kleppinger, E. (2000). *Online!: A reference guide to using Internet sources* (3rd ed.). Boston: Bedford/St. Martin's.

Levin, J. (1995). *The federal Internet source* (2nd ed.). Washington, DC: National Journal Inc. and NetWeek L.L.C.

Mount, E., & Kovacs, B. (1991). *Using science and technology information sources.* Phoenix, AZ: Oryx.

Schlein, A. M. (2002). *Find it online: The complete guide to online research* (3rd ed.). Tempe, AZ: Facts on Demand Press.

Also see the following journal:
How to Access the Federal Government on the Internet. Washington, DC: Congressional Quarterly.

Usage and General Writing

Burchfield, R. W., & Fowler, H. W. (Eds.). (1996). *The new Fowler's dictionary of modern English usage* (3rd ed.). New York: Oxford University Press.

Corbett, E. P. J. (1999). *Classical rhetoric for the modern student* (4th ed.). New York: Oxford University Press.

Maggio, R. (1997). *Talking about people: A guide to fair and accurate language.* Phoenix, AZ: Oryx.

Partridge, E. (1997). *Usage and abusage: A guide to good English.* New York: W. W. Norton.

Strunk, W., & White, E. B. (1999). *The elements of style* (4th ed.). Boston: Allyn & Bacon.

Williams, J. (2002). *Style: Ten lessons in clarity and grace* (7th ed.). New York: Longman.

Handbooks for Grammar and Style

Hacker, D. (2002). *The Bedford handbook* (6th ed.). Boston: Bedford/St. Martin's.

Lunsford, A. (2003). *The St. Martin's handbook* (5th ed.). Boston: Bedford/St. Martin's.

Style Manuals

American National Standards, Inc. (1979). *American National Standard for the preparation of scientific papers for written or oral presentation.* ANSI Z39.16–1972. New York: American National Standards Institute.

The Chicago manual of style. (1993). (14th ed.). Chicago: University of Chicago Press, 1993.

Dodd, J. S. (Ed.). (1997). *The ACS style guide: A manual for authors and editors* (2nd ed.). Washington, DC: American Chemical Society.

Nagle, J. (1995). *Handbook for preparing engineering documents: From concept to completion.* New York: IEEE.

Publication manual of the American Psychological Association. (2001). (5th ed.). Washington, DC: American Psychological Association.

Rubens, P. (2000). *Science and technical writing: A manual of style* (2nd ed.). New York: Routledge.

Style Manual Committee, Council of Biology Editors. (1994). *Scientific style and format: The CBE manual for authors, editors, and publishers* (6th ed.). Chicago: Cambridge University Press.

U.S. Government Printing Office style manual 2000. (2000). Washington, DC: United States Government Printing Office. http://www.access.gpo.gov/styleman/2000/browse-sm-00.html

Also, many private corporations, such as John Deere, DuPont, Ford Motor Company, General Electric, Microsoft, and Westinghouse, have their own style manuals.

Graphics, Design, and Web Pages

Campbell, K. S. (1995). *Coherence, continuity, and cohesion: Theoretical foundations for document design.* Hillsdale, NJ: Erlbaum.

Dillon, P. M., & Leonard, D. C. (1998). *Multimedia and the Web from a to z* (2nd ed.). Phoenix, AZ: Oryx.

Eccher, C. (2002). *Professional Web design: Techniques and templates.* Hingham, MA: Charles River Media.

Farkas, D. K., & Farkas, J. (2001). *Principles of Web design.* New York: Longman.

Fleishman, G., Molina, T., & Carlson, J. (2002). *Web design basics: Ideas and inspiration for working with type, color and navigation on the Web.* Gloucester, MA: Rockport.

Harris, R. L. (1999). *Information graphics: A comprehensive illustrated reference* (2nd ed.). Atlanta, GA: Management Graphics.

Horton, W. (1991). *The icon book: Visual symbols for computer systems and documentation.* New York: Wiley.

Horton, W., Taylor, L., Ignacio, A., & Hoft, N. L. (1996). *The Web page design cookbook.* New York: Wiley.

Johnson, S. (1996). *Electronic publishing construction kit.* New York: Wiley.

Jones, G. E. (1995). *How to lie with charts.* Alameda, CA: Sybex.

Kelvin, G. V. (1992). *Illustrating for science.* New York: Watson-Guptill.

Kosslyn, S. M. (1994). *Elements of graph design.* New York: W. H. Freeman.

Kostelnick, C., & Roberts, D. D. (1998). *Designing visual language: Strategies for professional communicators.* Boston: Allyn & Bacon.

Nielsen, J. (1999). *Designing Web usability: The practice of simplicity.* Indianapolis, IN: New Riders.

Parker, R. C., & Berry, P. (2000). *Looking good in print* (5th ed.). Albany, NY: Coriolis Group.

Tufte, E. R. (1983). *The visual display of quantitative information.* Cheshire, CT: Graphics Press.

Tufte, E. R. (1990). *Envisioning information.* Cheshire, CT: Graphics Press.

Tufte, E. R. (1997). *Visualizing explanations.* Cheshire, CT: Graphics Press.

Vaughan, T. (1998). *Multimedia: Making it work* (4th ed.). Berkeley, CA: Osborne Mc-Graw-Hill.

Wheildon, C. (1995). *Type & layout: How typography and design can get your message across—or get in the way.* Berkeley, CA: Strathmoor.

White, J. V. (1990). *Color for the electronic age.* New York: Watson-Guptill.

Williams, R., & Tollett, J. (2000). *The non-designer's Web book: An easy guide to creating, designing, and posting your own Web site* (2nd ed.). Berkeley, CA: Peachpit.

Also see the following journals:
Graphic Arts Monthly
Graphics: USA
InfoWorld
Internet Week
Internet World
Web Week
Wired

Technical Manuals

Barnum, C. (2001). *Usability testing and research.* Boston: Allyn & Bacon.

Barker, T. (1998). *Writing software documentation: A task-oriented approach.* Boston: Allyn & Bacon.

Dumas, J. S., & Redish, J. C. (1993). *A practical guide to usability testing.* Norwood, NJ: Ablex.

Hackos, J. T. (1994). *Managing your documentation projects.* New York: Wiley.

Haydon, L. M. (1995). *The complete guide to writing and producing technical manuals.* New York: Wiley.

Horton, W. (1994). *Designing and writing online documentation: Hypermedia for self-supporting products* (2nd ed.). New York: Wiley.

Lanyi, G. (1994). *Managing documentation projects in an imperfect world.* Columbus, OH: Battelle.

Nielsen, J., & Mack, R. L. (Eds.). (1994). *Usability inspection methods.* New York: Wiley.

Price, J., & Korman, H. (1993). *How to communicate technical information: A handbook of software and hardware documentation.* Redwood City, CA: Benjamin/Cummings.

Rubin, J. (1994). *Handbook of usability testing: How to plan, design, and conduct effective tests.* New York: Wiley.

Steehouder, M., Jansen, C., van der Poort, P., and Verheijen, R. (Eds.). (1994). *Quality of technical documentation.* Amsterdam: Editions Rodopi B. V.

Velotta, C. (1995). *Practical approaches to usability testing for technical documentation.* Arlington, VA: Society for Technical Communication.

Whitaker, K. (1995). *A guide to publishing user manuals.* New York: Wiley.

Wieringa, D., Moore, C., & Barnes, V. (1998). *Procedure writing: Principles and practices* (2nd ed.). Columbus, OH: Battelle.

Woolever, K. R., & Loeb, H. M. (1998). *Writing for the computer industry.* Upper Saddle River, NJ: Prentice-Hall.

Oral Presentations

Anholt, R. H. (1994). *Dazzle 'em with style: The art of oral scientific presentation*. New York: W. H. Freeman.

D'Arcy, J. (1998). *Technically speaking: A guide for communicating complex information*. Columbus, OH: Battelle.

Gurak, L. J. (2000). *Oral presentations for technical communication*. Boston: Allyn & Bacon.

Smith, T. C. (1991). *Making successful presentations: A self-teaching guide* (2nd ed.). New York: Wiley.

Proposals

Bowman, J. P., & Branchaw, B. P. (1992). *How to write proposals that produce*. Phoenix, AZ: Oryx.

Freed, R. C., Freed, S., & Romano, J. (2003). *Writing winning business proposals: Your guide to landing the client, making the sale, persuading the boss*. New York: McGraw-Hill.

Hill, J. W. and T. Whalen. (1993). *How to create and present successful government proposals*. New York: IEEE.

Johnson-Sheehan, R. (2001). *Writing proposals: Rhetoric for managing change*. New York: Longman.

Miner, L. E., Miner, J. T., & Griffith, J. (1998). *Proposal planning and writing* (2nd ed.). Phoenix, AZ: Oryx.

Acknowledgments (continued from p. iv)

Figure 2.1: Texas Instruments Ethics Quick Test from <http://www.ti.com/corp/docs/company/citizen/ethics/quicktest.shtml>. Courtesy Texas Instruments Company.

Figure 4.7: "A Videoconference" from <http://www.polycom.com/common/pw_item_show_doc/0,1449,1111,00.pdf>, page 6. Reprinted with the permission of Polycom, Inc.

Figure 5.4: Excerpt from John Heilemann, "Reinventing the Wheel" (December 2, 2001), <www.time.com/time/business/article/0,8599,186660,00.html>. Copyright © 2001 by Time, Inc. Reprinted by permission.

Figure 5.7: Nobuji Suzuki, "Message from the President," <www.fdk.co.jp/company_e/message-e.html>. Reprinted by permission.

Figure 5.7: Excerpt from Web site of the National Board of Patents and Registration of Finland Annual Report 2000, <www.prh.fi>. Reprinted by permission.

Figure 6.2: Product benefits page for the Omnibook 6100 from Hewlett Packard Web site, <www.hp.com/notebooks/us/eng/products/omnibook_6100/omnibook_6100_benefits.htm>. Reprinted with the permission of the Hewlett-Packard Company.

Figure 6.3: Princess Cruises home page from <www.princess.com/home.jsp>. Reprinted by permission.

Figure 6.5: "Lending a Helping Hand" from AT&T Web site, <www.att.com/foundation/programs/community.html>. Reprinted with the permission of the AT&T Foundation.

Lucent Technologies, Inc., "Privacy Statement" from Lucent Web site, <lucent.com/privacy.html>. Courtesy Lucent Technologies, Inc. Copyright © 2002 by Lucent Technologies, Inc. All rights reserved.

Figures 7.1, 7.2, and 7.3: Google Web Search screen, Google Advanced Search screen from <www.google.com/advanced_search?hl=en>, and Google Web Directory. Science screen from <http://directory.google.com/Top/Science/>. Copyright © 2002 Google. Reprinted by permission.

Figure 7.4: ProFusion Web Search Engines screen from <www.profusion.com/CatNav.asp?ID=1&AGTID=1&queryterm=>. Reprinted by permission.

Figure 7.6: Motorola Web page from <www.motorola.com/content/0,1037,12,00.html>. Reprinted by permission.

Figures 7.5 and 7.6: Microsoft Internet Explorer screen with "File Not Found" message and Microsoft Internet Explorer toolbar and "File" pull-down menu. Reprinted by permission of Microsoft Corporation.

Figures 7.7, 7.8, and 7.9: Boise State University Advanced Keyword Search screen from <http://catalyst.boisestate.edu/CHOOSE:next=html/!DBNAME!_> Result List screen from <http://catalyst.boisestate.edu/CHOOSE:next=html/!DBNAME!_> and detailed record screen from <http://catalyst.boisestate.edu/CHOOSE:next=html/!DBNAME!_>. Reprinted by permission.

Figure 7.10: Illustration of *CA on CD 1998* Record Window, displaying "Synchrotron studies of in situ deformation of rubber toughened . . ." screen from Chemical Abstracts Service Web site, <www.cas.org/ONLINE/CD/CACD/QUICKSTART/author.html>. Reprinted by permission.

Figure 7.11: "Inappropriate and Appropriate Paraphrased Notes" adapted from John Lovgren, "Achieving Performance-Centered Design" (2000), <www.reisman-consulting.com/pages/a-Perform.html>. Reprinted with the permission of John Lovgren.

Box, p. 148: Insurance Institute for Highway Safety, excerpt from "Fatality Facts: Teenagers" (as of October 2001), <www.highwaysafety.org/safety_facts/fatality_facts/teens.htm>. Reprinted with the permission of the Insurance Institute for Highway Safety.

Figure 8.2: Map, "University of Texas at Austin, Main Campus" from <www.utexas.edu/maps/main/overview>. Reprinted by permission.

Figure 8.7: Information Organized by Partition from Canon, 2002, <www.powershot.com/powershot2/s330/kit.html>. Copyright © 2003 Canon U.S.A., Inc. All rights reserved.

Figure 8.9: Discussion Organized by the Cause-and-Effect Pattern from <www.xerox.com/go/xrx/template/009.jsp?view=Featue&Xcntry=USA&Xlang=en_US&Xseg=home&ed_name=Colorful_World_2>. Courtesy Xerox Corporation.

Figure 9.2: Graphic of Hewlett-Packard remote control (Hewlett-Packard, 2002), <http://h200004.www2.hp.com/bc/docs/support/SupportManual/bpia6001/bpia6001.pdf>. Reprinted by permission.

Figure 9.4: "Biometrics 101: How It Works, Introduction" and "Biometrics 101: How It Works, Retinal Scanning" graphics/text boxes from Ursula Owre Masterson, "Biometrics and the New Security Age" from *MSNBC News* (November 20, 2001), <www.msnbc.com/news/654788.asp?cp1=1>. Copyright © Microsoft Corporation.

From John Brogan and S. Venkateswaran, "Diverse Choices for Hybrid and Electric Motor Vehicles," *Proceedings of the International Conference on Urban EVs* (Stockholm, Organization for Economic Cooperation and Development, May 1992). Copyright © 1992 by the Organization for Economic Cooperation and Development. Reprinted by permission.

Figures 9.5 and 9.6: Praxis, Inc., excerpt from SSULI brochure (1999), <www.pxi.com/public/brochures/ssuli/index.html>. Reprinted with the permission of Praxis, Inc.

Figure 10.1: Text based on S. Cohen and D. Grace, "Engineers and social responsibility: An obligation to do good" from *IEEE Technology and Society* 13 (1994): 12–19. Copyright © 1994 by the Institute of Electrical and Electronics Engineers, Inc. Reprinted with the permission of the IEEE.

Figure 13.1: Photograph of General Motors cars from <www.chevrolet.com/gmnav/brochure/pdf/cor_catalog.pdf>. Reprinted by permission.

Figure 13.2: Excerpt from CrystalGraphics, Inc. Web site, <www.crystalgraphics.com> (2002). Reprinted by permission.

Figure 13.3: Excerpt from Hewlett Packard Web site, <www.hp.com/cposupport/manual_set/lpg40530.pdf> (2002). Reprinted by permission.

Figure 13.4: Excerpt from General Electric Web site, <www.ge.com/annual00/download/images/GEannual00.pdf> (2002). Reprinted by permission.

Figure 13.19: Excerpt from Hewlett Packard manual, <http://ovweb.external.hp.com/lpe/doc_serv>. Reprinted by permission.

Box, p. 314: Excerpt from *Agilent Telecommunications News* 9, 1 (Agilent Technologies, 2002), page 11, <http://literature.agilent.com/liweb/pdf/5988-4859ENUS.pdf>. Copyright © 2002 Agilent Technologies, Inc. Reproduced with Permission, Courtesy Agilent Technologies, Inc.

Figure, p. 317: Texas Instruments, "CPU description" from Digital Signal Processor data sheet. Courtesy Texas Instruments.

Figure 14.3: Table, "Israeli Power Plant Sites" From B. Golany, Y. Roll, and D. Rybak, "Measuring efficiency of power plants in Israel by data envelopment analysis" from *IEEE Transactions on Engineering Management* 41, 3 (August 1994): 292. Copyright © 1994 by the Institute of Electrical and Electronics Engineers, Inc.. Reprinted with the permission of the IEEE.

Figure 14.6: "Choosing the Appropriate Kind of Graphic" based on W. Horton, "The Almost Universal Language: Graphics for International Documentation," *Technical Communication* 40 (1993): 682–693. Reprinted with the permission of the Society for Technical Communication.

Figure 14.8: Text Table, "Pultruded Fiberglass Structural Shapes/Steel A-35 Carbon" from Composite Fabricators Association Web site, <www.cfa-hq.org/pic/pultrusion/steel.htm>. Reprinted with the permission of the Composite Fabricators Association, <www.cfa-hq.org>.

Figure, p. 341: Graph, "Really young vs. really old" from Nigel Holmes & Meredith Bagby, "USA: An Annual Report" in Richard Saul Wurman, *Understanding USA* (Woodside, Calif.: TED Conferences, 2002). As found at <www.understandingusa.com/chaptercc=2&cs=20.html>. Copyright © 2002. Reprinted with permission.

Figure 14.21: Closed-system flowchart from H. Curtis and N.S. Barnes, *Biology, Fifth Edition*. Copyright © 1969, 1975, 1983, 1989 by Worth Publishers. Reprinted with the permission of W. H. Freeman and Company/Worth Publishers.

Figure 14.25: Screen shot from <http://download.software602.com/pdf/PCS/2001/602tab_manual.pdf>. Reprinted with the permission of Software602, Inc., <www.software602.com>.

Box, p. 354: "Strategies for Intercultural Communication" based on W. Horton, "The Almost Universal Language: Graphics for International Documentation," *Technical Communication* 40 (November 1993): 682–693. Copyright © 1993. Reprinted with the permission of the Society for Technical Communication.

Table, p. 358: "Costs of Unintentional Injuries: 1999" from National Safety Council, *Injury Facts, 2000 Edition* (Itasca, Ill.: NSC, 2000). Copyright © 2000 by the National Safety Council. Reprinted with the permission of the National Safety Council, Research and Statistical Services Group.

Geoff Hart, p. 385, response to Bruce Byfield post on TECHWR-L discussion board (2002) ["User's advocate" column, <www.raycomm.com/techwhirl/usersadvocate.html>]. Copyright © 2002 by RayComm, Inc. Reprinted with the permission of Bruce Byfield and Geoff Hart.

Figure 17.11: Bar chart from SmartDraw, <www.smartdraw.com/resources/exampls/business/gantt15.html> (2002). Created using SmartDraw software, <www.SmartDraw.com>. Used by permission.

Figure 20.2: Safety Label for Acetone (HCL, 2002), <www.hclco.com/labels/hazard/hazard1.htm>. Reprinted by permission of HCL, Inc.

Figure 20.3: "Safety information on machinery." Reprinted with the permission of John Deere & Company.

Figure 20.4: "Introduction to a Set of Instructions" from Minwax (2002), <www.minwax.com/projects/cdhold/cdhold1.htm>. Reprinted with the permission of The Sherwin-Williams Company.

Figure 20.5: "Excerpt from Step-by-Step Instructions" from Agilent Technologies (2002), <http://cp.literature.agilent.com/litweb/pdf/5988-4907EN.pdf>. Copyright © 2002 Agilent Technologies, Inc. Reproduced with Permission, Courtesy Agilent Technologies, Inc.

Figure 20.6: "Conclusion from a Set of Instructions" (Apple Computer, Inc., 2002), <www.apple.com/quicktime/install>. Reprinted with the permission of Apple Computer, Inc.

Box, p. 533: Sample instructions, "Unpack the MultiPASS" (Canon, 2002), <www.usa.canon.com/cpr/pdf/Manuals/C755_Setup.pdf>. Reprinted by permission.

Figure 20.7: Excerpt from manual for Dell Dimension L Series computer (Dell Computer Corporation, 2001), pp. v-vi, ix-xi. Reprinted by permission.

Figure 20.8: Excerpt from Toshiba manual (Toshiba, 2001), <www.mmgtechsupport.com/PDF/manual6.PDF>. Reprinted by permission.

Figure 21.6 and 21.7: Corel home page header (Corel, 2002), <www3.corel.com/sgi-bin/gx.cgi/AppLogic+FTCContentServer?pagename=Corel/Product/WordPerfect> and Corel home page footer (Corel, 2002), <www3.corel.com/sgi-bin/gx.cgi/AppLogic+FTCContentServer?pagename=Corel/Product/WordPerfect>. Copyright © 2002 Corel Corporation. All rights reserved. Reprinted by permission.

Figure 21.8: Google Site Map (Google, 2002), <www.google.com/sitemap.html>. Copyright © 2002 Google. Reprinted by permission.

Figure 21.11: Silver Council Home Page (Silver Council, 2002), <www.silvercouncil.org/html/default.htm>. Reprinted by permission.

Figure 21.12: Palm Knowledge Library page (Palm, Inc., 2002), <http://205.141.210.149/SRVS/CGI-BIN/WEBCGI.EXE?>. Reprinted by permission of Palm, Inc.

Box, p. 565: Ari Feldman home page (Feldman, 2002), <www.arifeldman.com/index.html>. Reprinted by permission.

INDEX

INDEX OF GUIDELINES AND CHECKLISTS

GUIDELINES

Preparing Feasibilit...

To prepare a feas...

4. *Establish criteria. Decide on minimum specifications and evaluative criteria for responding to the problem or opportunity.*
5. *Determine your options. What are the available courses of action?*
6. *Study each option according to your criteria. Work out a systematic way to evaluate each option to reduce the subjectivity of the analysis.*
7. *Draw conclusions about each option. Conclusions are statements of what your data mean.*
8. *Formulate recommendations based on your conclusions. Recommendations are statements of what we ought to do next.*

Guidelines (arranged by topic)